The Soviet Union

The International Library of Essays on Political History
Series Editor: Jeremy Black

Titles in the Series:

The Soviet Union

Edited by

Peter Waldron

University of East Anglia, UK

Routledge
Taylor & Francis Group

LONDON AND NEW YORK

First published 2007 by Ashgate Publishing

Reissued 2018 by Routledge
2 Park Square, Milton Park, Abingdon, Oxon OX14 4RN
711 Third Avenue, New York, NY 10017, USA

Routledge is an imprint of the Taylor & Francis Group, an informa business

First issued in paperback 2018

A Library of Congress record exists under LC control number: 2007011456

Notice:
Product or corporate names may be trademarks or registered trademarks, and are used only for identification and explanation without intent to infringe.

Publisher's Note
The publisher has gone to great lengths to ensure the quality of this reprint but points out that some imperfections in the original copies may be apparent.

Disclaimer
The publisher has made every effort to trace copyright holders and welcomes correspondence from those they have been unable to contact.

ISBN 13: 978-0-815-39827-1 (hbk)
ISBN 13: 978-1-138-62284-5 (pbk)
ISBN 13: 978-1-351-14520-6 (ebk)

Contents

PART IV STAGNATION: KHRUSHCHEV AND BREZHNEV

PART V GORBACHEV AND THE COLLAPSE OF THE SOVIET UNION

Acknowledgements

The editor and publishers wish to thank the following for permission to use copyright material.

Blackwell Publishing for the essays: Sheila Fitzpatrick (1986), 'New Perspectives on Stalinism', *Russian Review*, **45**, pp. 357–73; Lynne Viola (1986), '"Bab'i bunty" and Peasant Women's Protest during Collectivization', *Russian Review*, **45**, pp. 23–42; Sheila Fitzpatrick (1993), 'How the Mice Buried the Cat: Scenes from the Great Purges of 1937 in the Russian Provinces', *Russian Review*, **52**, pp. 299–320; Sarah Davies (1997), '"Us against Them": Social Identity in Soviet Russia, 1934–41', *Russian Review*, **56**, pp. 70–89; Blair A. Ruble (1990), 'The Leningrad Affair and the Provincialization of Leningrad', *Russian Review*, **42**, pp. 301–20; David Nordlander (1993), 'Khrushchev's Image in the Light of Glasnost and Perestroika', *Russian Review*, **52**, pp. 248–64; John Gooding (1992), 'Perestroika as Revolution from Within: An Interpretation', *Russian Review*, **51**, pp. 36–57; Vladimir N. Brovkin (1990), 'The Making of Elections to the Congress of People's Deputies (CPD) in March 1989', *Russian Review*, **49**, pp. 417–42; Thomas Remington (1989), 'A Socialist Pluralism of Opinions: *Glasnost* and Policy-Making under Gorbachev', *Russian Review*, **48**, pp. 271–304.

John Channon for the essay: John Channon (1988), 'The Bolsheviks and the Peasantry: The Land Question during the First Eight Months of Soviet Rule', *Slavonic and East European Review*, **66**, pp. 593–624.

J. Arch Getty, Gábor Rittersporn and Victor N. Zemskov for the essay: J. Arch Getty, Gábor Rittersporn and Victor N. Zemskov (1993), 'Victims of the Soviet Penal System in the Pre-war Years: A First Approach on the Basis of Archival Evidence', *American Historical Review*, **98**, pp. 1017–49.

Israel Getzler for the essay: Israel Getzler (1996), 'Lenin's Conception of Revolution as Civil War', *Slavonic and East European Review*, **74**, pp. 464–72.

Taylor & Francis Group for the essays: J. Erickson (1992), 'The Soviet Response to Surprise Attack: Three Directives, 22 June 1941', *Soviet Studies*, **23**, pp. 519–53; Yoram Gorlizki (2001), 'Stalin's Cabinet: The Politburo and Decision Making in the Post-war Years', *Europe-Asia Studies*, **53**, pp. 291–312; Donald Filtzer (1999), 'The Standard of Living of Soviet Industrial Workers in the Immediate Postwar Period, 1945–48', *Europe-Asia Studies*, **51**, pp. 1013–38; William J. Tompson (1991), 'The Fall of Nikita Khrushchev', *Soviet Studies*, **43**, pp. 1101–21; John P. Willerton, Jr (1987), 'Patronage Networks and Coalition Building in the Brezhnev Era', *Soviet Studies*, **39**, pp. 175–20; Linda J. Cook, (1992), 'Brezhnev's "Social Contract" and Gorbachev's Reforms', *Soviet Studies*, **44**, pp. 37–56. http://www.tandf.co.uk/journals

University of Chicago Press for the essay: Diane Koenker (1985), 'Urbanization and Deurbanization in the Russian Revolution and Civil War', *Journal of Modern History*, **57**, pp. 424–50.

Series Preface

This series focuses on key episodes and issues in political history and does so by bringing together essays selected from journals that exhibit careful analysis of political history. The volumes, each of which is edited by an expert in the field, cover crucial time periods and geographical areas, particularly Europe and the USA. Each volume represents the editor's selection of seminal essays on political history in his particular area of expertise, while an introduction presents an overview of the issues in the area, together with comments on the background and significance of the essays chosen.

The strength and nature of political beliefs reflect, to a great extent, the degree to which ideologies provide a sense of identity, value and purpose to both individuals and the community. Like all important questions about recent and modern society, this is one that can be answered in a different way by commentators and by readers. Secular ideologies over the last 250 years tended to rely on the notion of progress and the desire of humans to improve their condition, and thus rejected the Christian lapsardian view of human existence with its emphasis on sin and humankind's fallible nature. Although they varied in the political, economic, social and cultural analyses and prescriptions, such ideologies shared a belief that it is possible, and necessary, to improve the human condition and that such a goal gives meaning to politics and society. In short, reform was seen as an end in itself and progress as something attainable.

There was only limited support for continuity and stability, as opposed to reform, as public goals. For an institution or government to pledge itself to inaction would have been extraordinary. Instead, as with Islamic and Christian fundamentalism, conservative politics were propounded primarily in terms of a return to an earlier situation (true or mythical), and thus as reform through reaction, against a perception of the present, rather than as a static maintenance of the present. Commitment to change rested on prudential considerations, especially the need to modernize in order to compete successfully on the international scene, but also on powerful ideological currents. Reform, as a means and goal, was the foremost secular ideology and one that was shared by governments with very different political outlooks. There is no sign that this will change. However, across the world, reform meant very different attitudes and policies and focused on both improving and abandoning the past. This was true not only of domestic policies but also of those abroad, both foreign and colonial policy. Thus, reform could entail the development of empires and also their dissolution. Like 'freedom', 'liberty' and 'justice', 'reform' was a value-laden term. It could mean both more and less government intervention and this helped to contribute to controversy.

Politics was not only a matter of ideologies and government initiatives. As volumes in this series indicate, it is also important to consider the extent and consequences of popular participation in politics, the nature of accountability and the conception of the public: from corporatism to individualism.

Any selection of what to include is difficult. The editors in this series have done an excellent job and it has been a great pleasure working with them.

JEREMY BLACK
Series Editor
University of Exeter

Introduction

On 25 October 1917, the Bolshevik party staged a *coup d'état* in Petrograd and overthrew the Provisional Government that had ruled Russia since the abdication of Tsar Nicholas II less than eight months earlier.[1] Almost nobody expected that the Bolshevik revolution would be anything more than a 'nine days wonder', but the regime that Lenin established lasted for nearly three quarters of a century and came to bestride the globe as one of the world's two superpowers. Bolshevism was unique: it came to power proclaiming explicit ideological goals, while none of its leaders had any experience of government before 1917. Lenin's party was committed to establishing socialism, even though Russia was an unpromising arena for the world's first Marxist regime. The European Left had expected that a successful socialist revolution would first take place in a highly industrialised state, and Germany appeared to be the most likely country where the Left could take power. Russia was the most rural of all the Great Powers and its industrial working class comprised less than 10 per cent of the population. Russia did not appear to have an adequate social base on which the Bolsheviks could build their power, and in the first heady days of revolution, most of Russia's new rulers believed that their regime could only survive if socialist revolution broke out elsewhere in Europe, enabling their fledgling government to gain support from elsewhere. Trotsky, the first Bolshevik Commissar for Foreign Affairs, said that he expected to be able 'to publish a few revolutionary proclamations and then shut up shop' (Deutscher, 1970).

The Bolshevik Consolidation of Power

The Bolsheviks faced formidable obstacles in establishing themselves as the rulers of Russia. The Provisional Government had set in train the process of national elections to a Constituent Assembly that would then determine the final form of post-revolutionary government for Russia, and voting took place at the end of November 1917. The Bolsheviks gained only 24 per cent of the votes, and held fewer than half the number of seats of the largest party, the Socialist Revolutionaries (Radkey, 1989). Lenin argued that the assembly was an irrelevance in Russia, since its 'bourgeois' character had now been overtaken by the Soviets that the Bolsheviks instituted.[2] These councils of workers, peasants and soldiers provided a legitimacy to the Bolshevik regime, but their importance was swiftly reduced as the Bolshevik party apparatus became institutionalised as the main policy-making apparatus of Russia. The Constituent Assembly met in January 1918, but the Bolsheviks allowed it to sit only for a single day before forcibly dissolving it. The new regime was also quick to stamp its authority on Russia by establishing and making wide use of a political police force, the Cheka (See Leggett, 1981). Terror rapidly became an essential weapon in the Bolshevik armoury: the former Tsar, Nicholas II, and his family were shot in Ekaterinburg in July 1918 and arbitrary violence was

---

1 The best analysis of the Bolshevik revolution is Rabinowitch, 1976.
2 Service, 2000, is a comprehensive assessment of Lenin's life.

used right across Russian society to sustain the Bolsheviks' hold on power. Emboldened by their success at gaining power, Lenin and his party took steps to neutralise political opposition by condemning the Kadets, the chief pre-revolutionary liberal party, as 'enemies of the people' and proscribing them. The Socialist Revolutionaries split into two, and the Left SRs opted to join the Bolshevik government, a short-lived move that lasted for only three months, but which fractured the anti-Bolshevik forces and gave Lenin's government a breathing space in which it could establish itself and retitle itself as explicitly communist. The Orthodox Church was a particular target for the new regime: the Bolsheviks were very conscious of the part that religion traditionally played in the consciousness of the rural population. Church lands and property were seized, and in January 1918, the Orthodox Patriarch called on his flock to engage in active opposition to the Bolshevik regime. The new government had less success in dealing with some of the non-Russian nationalities that had been part of the Tsarist empire. The Finns declared independence six weeks after the October revolution, and they were followed by the Poles, Ukrainians and the nationalities of the Caucasus in seeking to shake off Russian rule. Ukraine and the Caucasus were brought back under Russian control, but the Poles were able to inflict a military defeat on Russia, as the communists tried to recapture Poland in 1920, and an attempted socialist revolution in Finland was defeated in a bloody civil war.[3]

By early 1918, Russia itself was engulfed in civil war. Led by officers from the former Tsarist army and navy, opposition to the revolutionary regime sprang up on all sides. The communists, however, controlled the Russian heartland and were able to use the railway network to good advantage to move their troops to face the threats from the White armies. The Whites never formed a united front against the communists: their commanders distrusted each other and they were unable to launch a concerted set of attacks on the Red forces. There was only limited popular support for the Whites. They were seen as standing for the restoration of the old order, and there was very little enthusiasm for a return to the social and political structures of Tsarism. Foreign governments were almost universal in their desire to dislodge the communists from power and the British, French, American and Japanese governments all despatched troops to aid the Whites in their struggle. This foreign intervention was, however, only half-hearted as governments understood the popularity of the communist state among working people in their own countries, while the presence of foreign troops fighting on Russian soil provided the communists with a powerful nationalist weapon that they could use to motivate the Russian people in their own support. As Figes shows in Chapter 2, the communists were able to mobilize the population into a very effective fighting force. The Red forces were highly motivated: the communists were fighting in defence of an ideal and were determined to defend their nascent socialist state against the forces of reaction. The Red Army was moulded into an effective fighting force by Trotsky, who displayed exceptional and unexpected talent as a military leader, and it was able to inflict significant defeats on the Whites in both Siberia and the south. The crux of the civil war came late in 1919, as White troops approached both Moscow and Petrograd, but the Whites were unable to press home their advantage and the Red Army was successful in bitter struggles to keep the enemy away from the gates of Russia's twin capitals.[4] After these defeats, the White armies began to disintegrate and many of their commanders, along with a significant number of the former

---

3   Davies, 1972 is the best account of the conflict with Poland.
4   Mawdsley, 1987 is the standard work on the Civil War.

social elite of the Tsarist state, recognised that communist victory was now assured and made the decision to emigrate. More than 1 million officers, nobles and civil servants left Russia as the communists cemented their victory.

By the end of the civil war, Russia had been torn apart by war and revolution for nearly seven years in what has been termed a 'continuum of crisis'.[5] The stresses of the First World War placed the Russian economy under great strain and German troops continued to occupy large tracts of western Russian and Ukraine until late 1918. The encroachment of White troops exacerbated the strains: food supply fell sharply and industrial production collapsed. But, the new communist regime was keen to put its principles into practice and to transform Russia into a socialist economy. It took the initial steps in this direction on its first day in power, issuing a Land Decree that abolished private landed property and nationalised land. This measure recognised the realities of the situation in the countryside where the peasantry had taken advantage of the disintegration of authority during 1917 to seize as much land as they could. But the peasants' liking for the communists swiftly dissipated as inflation continued to roar ahead and output of manufactured goods declined. The peasantry thus had no incentive to produce agricultural surpluses and, as Lih demonstrates in Chapter 3, the communists rapidly resorted to the forcible seizure of grain and livestock in order to be able to feed the urban population and the Red Army. The communist policy of War Communism was implemented right across the economy as industry was nationalised and private trade prohibited. This attempt at central control of the economy failed dismally, as industrial production continued to decline and, as Koenker makes plain in Chapter 5, the urban population deserted Russia's towns and cities in search of a reliable supply of food. Economic collapse was accompanied by popular discontent: a major peasant uprising in Tambov in 1920 could only be put down by the use of the Red Army. Most worrying for the communists, however, was the March 1921 rebellion by the sailors of the Baltic fleet at Kronstadt, the great naval base close to Petrograd itself. This showed the depths of disillusionment with the communist regime and prompted a fundamental change in economic policy. War Communism was abandoned and replaced by the New Economic Policy: most of Russian industry was returned to its former owners, with the state retaining control of only the 'commanding heights' of Russian industry. The peasantry were to receive a proper price for their produce and private trade was legalised (See Siegelbaum, 1992). The Russian economy gradually recovered, but the communists did not forget how their ideals had been frustrated by the power that the peasant could exert.

Stalin and Stalinism

Lenin's health deteriorated sharply after he suffered a stroke in May 1922 and he died in January 1924, having ruled Soviet Russia for less than seven years. The struggle to succeed him was bitter and prolonged, but by 1927 Stalin had emerged as the clear leader of the Soviet Union.[6] His success was unexpected, as other leading figures in the communist party appeared to have a much better claim on power. Stalin gave the main oration at Lenin's funeral, identifying himself as committed to carrying on Lenin's work, and he proved to be a skilled political operator, able to outmanoeuvre his opponents and to portray them as lacking

5 The phrase is that of Holquist, 2002.
6 McDermott, 2006 is a good biography.

real commitment to the ideals of the revolution. Stalin had gained a deep knowledge of the workings of the communist party through his position as General Secretary and this provided him with unrivalled insight into the views of party officials across the Soviet Union (Harris, 2005). The other contenders for the post were disunited and did not recognise the lengths to which Stalin would go to achieve power. Zinoviev and Kamenev, characterised as the Left Opposition, both suffered demotion in 1925 and 1926 before their final defeat in 1927, but it was the defeat of Trotsky that most clearly demonstrated Stalin's power. Dismissed as Commissar of War in 1925, Trotsky condemned Stalin as 'the grave-digger of the revolution', and was then removed from the central decision-making bodies of the communist party. He was exiled to Soviet Central Asia in 1927 and expelled from the USSR in 1929, never to return. Stalin then turned his attention to the Right of the party, condemning Bukharin – described by Lenin as the 'darling of the party' – as lacking commitment to the revolution. Removed from the Politburo, the heart of the party, in 1929, Bukharin lived in a limbo until the mid-1930s, unable to offer any real challenge to Stalin's supremacy.[7] Stalin was hugely pragmatic in the policies that he espoused, seeking political advantage as he grasped for power, but by 1928 he had formulated a set of policies that gave him both a weapon with which he could attack opposition and that allowed him to gain wider popular support.

By the mid-1920s, it was evident that the October revolution had failed to bring about substantive economic and social change in Russia. Stalin was determined to bring real socialism to the Soviet Union, even though revolution had failed elsewhere in Europe. He argued that Russia did not need support from outside and that 'Socialism in one country' was wholly feasible. This appeal to Russian patriotism gave Stalin significant popular support, but it also allowed him to pursue the ideals that had driven the communists to seize power. Stalin was determined to transform the Soviet Union into a great industrial power: he was concerned that Russia's international isolation and economic weakness made it vulnerable to attack from abroad. The memory of foreign intervention in the civil war was still fresh and the Russian communists genuinely believed that the outside world was still determined to destroy their revolution. Stalin enunciated this fear very clearly in 1931 when he declared that 'we are 50 or 100 years behind the advanced countries. Either we make good this lag in 10 years or we will go under'. Rapid industrialization was therefore essential, and it would also advance socialism by increasing the strength of the proletariat. Stalin intended that his industrial revolution would transform Soviet society by changing the outlook of the population and inculcating them with communist ideals and values. He wanted to create 'new Soviet man' and finally to destroy the remnants of Tsarist society. In 1928, the first Five Year Plan was promulgated, setting what appeared to be impossibly high targets for industrial output. Coal production, for example, was planned to increase by 115 per cent and steel output by 250 per cent. Even though these targets were not met, the progress of Soviet industry was startling: by 1937 gross industrial production had increased more than five-fold, electricity output had grown by more than 700 per cent and oil production had doubled (Nove, 1969). This huge growth in Russia's industrial output was accompanied by an equivalent expansion in the industrial labour force and in the urban population. New cities sprang up: the city of Magnitogorsk was founded on virgin territory in 1929, but had more than 200,000 inhabitants by 1932 (Kotkin, 1995). This

---

7 Larina, 1991 gives a gripping account of Bukharin's final years.

presented the Soviet state with a considerable challenge: how to guarantee food supply for the industrial working class?

During the mid-1920s, the Soviet leadership was consumed by debates about how to achieve socialism. Industrialisation demanded investment capital and the only realistic source for this was the Soviet peasantry. Agricultural output had to be increased to provide enhanced income that could then be invested in industry. But Stalin was all too aware of the reaction of the peasantry to the intervention of the state during War Communism and was determined that his industrial revolution would not be frustrated by peasant resistance. He therefore set in train the greatest transformation ever experienced by the Russian countryside: the collectivisation of agriculture. The process began in 1928 and within twelve months, more than 55 per cent of peasant households had been collectivised. The peasantry opposed collectivisation with great vigour and Viola's essay (Chapter 8) analyzes one important aspect of this resistance. The disruption being caused to Soviet agriculture worried Stalin so much that he called a temporary halt to the process in March 1930, fearful lest the spring sowing be thrown into chaos. By the autumn of 1930, collectivization was under way again and by 1936 some 90 per cent of Russian peasant households and cultivated land had been collectivised. Great brutality was used in the countryside to subdue the peasantry. Peasants who opposed the process were condemned as kulaks – wealthy peasants – and deported, sent to labour camps or else simply killed (Viola, 1996). 'Dekulakization' was intended both to remove opposition from the countryside and also to destroy an influential segment of rural society that could encourage resistance to Stalin's plans. The peasants who remained in the countryside did not give up their independence willingly: rather than see their produce and livestock seized by the new collectives, many embarked on an orgy of destruction, slaughtering their animals and devouring as much produce as they could (Fitzpatrick, 1994). This had drastic consequences in 1932 and 1933 when poor harvests combined with the state taking produce from collective farms to feed the urban workforce and for export. Famine struck the Soviet countryside as the peasantry were left with insufficient to eat. Between 4 and 5 million people perished in the countryside as a result of collectivization, but for Stalin the policy had proved its worth. He had broken the power of the peasantry once and for all and, even though the rural population still dominated the Soviet Union numerically, the centre of power had shifted irreversibly to the Soviet Union's cities.

The process of political manoeuvring that brought Stalin to power left him conscious of the frailty of his own position. He was determined to use great force to deal with any source of opposition – whether real or imagined – and to protect his own position and that of the communist regime. Terror had been a part of communist policy since the first weeks of the revolution as the instinct for survival pushed the new regime into taking drastic measures. Stalin, however, took the use of terror to new heights. He used it as a deliberate element of policy to impose the social ideals of the communist party on the Soviet people and to deter them from opposing his regime. The great industrial revolution of the early 1930s brought with it many examples of machine failures; the regime labelled this as deliberate sabotage and those held to be responsible were sent to labour camps. The communist party itself was purged of members judged to be unreliable, and Stalin also used this process to rid the party of most of its veteran members. More than half of the delegates to the party's 1934 congress were purged in the following five years. The assassination of Kirov, the Leningrad party chief, in December 1934 sparked off a wave of arrests: Kamenev and Zinoviev were put on trial in

1935 and executed the following year. During 1937 and 1938 terror ruled over Soviet society: central and local government were particularly ravaged as their members were arrested and shot. Fitzpatrick (Chapter 9) illuminates some of the issues in the purges in the provinces. The military was not immune from terror, as more than 10,000 Red Army officers were arrested and eight of its most senior generals shot. The secret police was not immune from the process and Ezhov, its head between 1936 and 1938, was himself executed in 1940. Nearly 700,000 people were shot in the Great Terror of 1937/8 and over a million sent to labour camps.[8] Terror had a dramatic and long-lasting impact on Soviet society: it removed much of the social elite that had come to prominence during the 1920s and early 1930s, allowing men to come to power who owed their career to Stalin and who were imbued with the values of post-revolutionary Russia. The technical intelligentsia whom Stalin promoted were able to remain in power for decades after the 1930s and their values and experiences dominated the post-Stalinist Soviet Union.

War and Post-War Recovery

The Soviet state was still internationally isolated when Stalin came to power. There was substantial mistrust of Soviet international ambition: the Comintern had been established in 1919 with the explicit aim of promoting revolution abroad, and its activities helped persuade the international community of the subversive nature of the Moscow regime. Nevertheless, Russia could not be completely excluded from trade and diplomacy, and by the middle of the 1920s the Soviet Union had received diplomatic recognition from the major European powers, although not from the USA. The emergence of fascism in Italy and Germany made the position of the USSR more precarious, since the Nazi regime proclaimed its absolute hostility to the principles of communism. Stalin understood the weakness of the Soviet Union's position as it underwent industrial revolution and as society was being ravaged by terror and, while he recognised that war was likely in Europe, he wanted to postpone Soviet involvement for as long as possible. A Soviet attempt to pursue a policy of collective security failed finally in 1938 as the extent of the British and French policy of appeasement became clear, and Stalin began to consider how to protect the USSR's security in the face of an increasingly powerful Germany (Haslam, 1984). Negotiations with Britain stalled and in the summer of 1939, the Soviet Union signed a pact with Nazi Germany. This treaty promised non-aggression between the two, while a secret protocol defined the boundary between German and Soviet spheres of influence, allowing the USSR to dominate Finland, Estonia, Latvia and the eastern part of Poland. After the German invasion of Poland in September 1939, Soviet troops moved into Poland and in mid-1940 the Baltic states lost their independence to the USSR. Finland proved to be much more resistant to Soviet influence; the Finns initially repulsed a Soviet attack in the Winter War of 1939/40 and even when Soviet troops prevailed, Finnish independence was preserved. Stalin was fully aware that the Nazi-Soviet pact was a purely pragmatic move by both states and that war between the USSR and Germany was highly likely. But, as Erickson shows in Chapter 11, Stalin was taken by surprise when the Nazis launched their attack on the Soviet Union in June 1941, believing that a German attack was unlikely while Britain remained undefeated.

---

8   The best history of the terror is Getty and Naumov, 1999.

The Great Patriotic War of 1941–45 was the defining event in Soviet history. German armies advanced to within 20km of the centre of Moscow in the autumn of 1941 and Leningrad endured a siege of more than 900 days that left its population decimated and the city scarred. But, German defeat at Stalingrad in 1943 marked the turning point of both the war with the USSR and the Second World War overall, and it was Soviet troops that eventually seized Berlin in May 1945.[9] By the end of the war more than 25 million Soviet citizens were dead, and both industry and agriculture across the west of the USSR had suffered wholesale destruction. Soviet victory in the war demonstrated the power of the communist regime: it was able to mobilize the population of the USSR to fight, despite the huge upheavals in both city and countryside and the terror that Stalin had unleashed. Stalin's industrial revolution gave the Soviet Union the economic strength to manufacture weaponry and equipment to defeat the Germans. The communist regime was also able to create a mood of patriotism among the population that sustained it through a deeply destructive war, persuading people to fight in the armed forces and to suffer huge depredations at home. Stalin appealed directly to Russian nationalism and, despite the communist contempt for religion, he enlisted the help of the Orthodox Church in moulding the Soviet people into a united force that was able to resist the Germans. The experience of war gave a unity to the Soviet Union that transcended the bitter and divisive history of revolution and its consequences that had dominated Soviet life since 1917. Victory in war gave the Soviet state a legitimacy that had hitherto eluded it and demonstrated that the USSR had reached a position of power unequalled for Russia since the defeat of Napoleon. The experience of war was both so traumatic and so triumphant that it provided Soviet society with a narrative that justified the privations that it had endured and provided a memory of heroism that sustained the state and its population through the difficult times that followed (Tumarkin, 1994). The annual celebration of the victory over Germany gave a regular reminder of the power that the Soviet state had been able to accumulate and of the transformation of the USSR into a superpower to rank alongside the United States.

War also allowed the Soviet Union to acquire an empire in eastern Europe. Soviet troops occupied most of the region as they defeated the Nazis and this gave them the opportunity to extend their influence. There was significant popular support for communism in the wake of Nazi occupation and the Soviet Union found fertile soil for its ideas in eastern Europe. For Stalin, the creation of Soviet satellite states in eastern Europe provided a buffer against the possibility of western attack and he was particularly insistent on the need to ensure that a united Germany could not again threaten the USSR. The Soviet-occupied zone in eastern Germany became a separate state, the German Democratic Republic, in 1949 and the USSR attempted to take control of West Berlin by cutting off land access to the city from the west. Soviet-inspired governments were also established in Poland, Czechoslovakia, Hungary, Romania, Bulgaria, Yugoslavia and Albania, although the last two states retained their independence from Moscow. The USSR's power extended well beyond its traditional confines in the aftermath of the war. In 1949 it exploded its first atomic weapon, vividly demonstrating how far the Soviet Union had progressed (See Holloway, 1994). Stalin remained convinced that the West was determined to undermine the Soviet position in eastern Europe and that the USSR itself was under threat. He provided military assistance to North Korea when it invaded South Korea in

---

9   The standard works on the military aspects of the war are Erickson, 1975 and 1983; See also Overy, 1997 for a general account of the war.

1950 in a war that became a proxy struggle between the Soviet Union and the USA. Stalin was determined that the newly-powerful Soviet Union would not be humiliated and he reacted to every attempt by the western powers to reinforce their position with a show of strength. The Cold War became institutionalized with the establishment of NATO in 1949, followed by the creation of the Warsaw Pact in the east in 1955, turning Europe in to two armed camps.

The ravages of war on the Soviet people were dramatic. Almost 15 per cent of the population had perished during the conflict and the most productive areas of the country – both industrially and agriculturally – had been fought over as armies moved across them. The process of reconstruction was skewed by the continuing emphasis on military expenditure after 1945: although Soviet industrial production had returned to its pre-war level by 1949, the proportion of output devoted to consumer goods remained low. Agricultural output was much slower to recover, and it took a full decade before grain production returned to its pre-1941 level, with livestock production needing more than 15 years to recover. Housing remained a particular problem as the urban population continued to grow, but without a corresponding increase in the provision of living space. Filtzer (Chapter 14) discusses the standard of living after 1945 when many Soviet citizens lived in cramped shared apartments, eating a meagre and limited diet and working long hours. The regime needed to maintain its control over the population to maximize output and allow the Soviet Union to retain its hard-won status as a superpower. Stalin sought to demonstrate his continued control over every section of Soviet society: after 1945 he orchestrated attacks on prominent intellectuals, purged the leadership of Leningrad – the USSR's second city – and began to implement openly anti-Semitic policies. Stalin was seen in public only rarely after the war, but his close associates could see that he was ageing rapidly: the renewal of repression after 1945 was the work of an old man conscious of his declining powers but still insistent that he held absolute power and intent, as Gorlizki shows (Chapter 12), on keeping his subordinates in check. At the end of 1952, Stalin instituted a purge of doctors who had treated the Soviet elite, alleging that they had poisoned their patients, but the dictator himself died from natural causes in March 1953 before the full force of this onslaught on the medical profession could be put into effect (See Gorlizki and Khlevniuk, 2004).

Stagnation: Khrushchev and Brezhnev

The stresses that Stalinism imposed on the USSR were so severe that they were unsustainable without the apparatus of coercion and terror of Stalin's dictatorship. None of Stalin's successors was prepared to use his level of brutality and Khrushchev, who emerged as leader of the USSR by 1956, adopted a deliberate policy of 'de-Stalinization'.[10] Speaking at the 20th congress of the Communist Party in 1956, he condemned Stalin for his arbitrary violence and for the way in which he had distorted the course of the revolution. Khrushchev was faced with two difficult issues: he himself had been an integral part of Stalin's inner circle since the mid-1930s and any criticism of Stalin would, implicitly, reflect on Khrushchev himself. Admitting that Stalin had perverted the revolution begged the question of how the structure of the communist regime had allowed him to gain power in the first place. De-Stalinisation had therefore to be approached with great caution by Stalin's successors. The 1962 publication

---

10 The definitive biography of Khrushchev is Taubman, 2003.

of Solzhenitsyn's story, 'One day in the life of Ivan Denisovich' marked the high-point of the process, but his gripping description of life in a labour camp was too much for the Soviet leadership and it threatened to open the floodgates to general criticism of the Soviet system. The limits of de-Stalinisation were made even clearer by events in eastern Europe: in 1956 there were uprisings against communist regimes in both Poland and Hungary. Hungarian demonstrators called for the withdrawal of Soviet troops and demolished the statue of Stalin that stood in Budapest. The USSR responded by sending in troops to quell the revolution, killing some 3,000 people and installing a new government that was completely loyal to Moscow. In Poland, national and social tensions combined to produce potent anti-communist sentiment, and Moscow intervened here too to ensure that the Warsaw regime remained completely true to the principles that the Soviet Union espoused. Khrushchev attempted to contain his criticism of Stalinism to the person of the dictator himself, suggesting that the 'cult of personality' that Stalin had created around him was responsible for the repression of the 1930s and that it had come to an end with Stalin's death. The apparatus of a single-party state remained firmly in place with, as Willerton demonstrates in Chapter 17, a tightly-knit system of patronage and buttressed by an immensely powerful secret police that suppressed dissent. Khrushchev's successors retreated from even his limited liberalization of Soviet society: under Brezhnev's leadership in the late 1960s and 1970s, dissident intellectuals were put on trial, imprisoned, or exiled from the chief cities of the Soviet Union. The regime refrained from the savage terror of Stalin's era but nevertheless imposed a dull uniformity upon the Soviet Union, restricting free expression and stamping hard upon any hint of political dissent.

The Soviet economy stagnated in the decades after Stalin's death. The system of collective farming produced low yields, and the peasants' private plots that had been permitted since the early 1950s produced an ever-increasing proportion of the USSR's agricultural output. The state-controlled system of agriculture became steadily less efficient during the 1960s and 1970s: by 1977 the 3 per cent of farmland that was occupied by private plots produced more than a quarter of the USSR's entire agricultural output. Grain production was under particular pressure, but private plots could make little contribution towards Soviet grain output: by the end of the Brezhnev era, the USSR had to import more than 35 million tonnes of grain annually to feed its population (See Keep, 1996). Khrushchev was unable to formulate a consistent agricultural policy and failed to recognise the need for farming production to keep pace with the growing urbanization of the Soviet Union (McCauley, 1976). The Soviet population grew increasingly frustrated with food shortages and could only be kept placated by low prices in the shops. Industrial performance was equally disappointing, as the needs of the military took an increasing priority. The maintenance of the Soviet Union's superpower status demanded significant expenditure on sophisticated technological equipment, while the system of central economic planning grew evermore cumbersome and inefficient. The availability of consumer goods was a particular problem, as heavy industry and the military dominated Soviet industry and the USSR's scarce foreign currency resources were used to import grain and other basic materials. The rate of Soviet industrial growth steadily reduced from the 1950s, and by the time of Brezhnev's death in 1982, it had halted completely. Economic decline had a serious impact on living standards, and housing, food supply and consumer goods were all deteriorating during the 1970s. Even though everyday existence was difficult for the Soviet people, there were very few overt demonstrations of discontent (Andrle, 1994). As Cook argues in Chapter 18, a type of social contract existed between state and society, by which the state provided social benefits and the population did not mount any challenge to the party's authority. The apparatus of coercion was powerful enough to act as a deterrent, while the Soviet people resorted to an enormous black market to try to obtain goods and services that were in short supply. The Soviet leadership was not prepared to make economic reforms that would address the structural problems that lay at the heart of declining output, since the system of central planning and the dominance of the military sector were integral elements of the overall policy of the Soviet state and any attempt to reform them would, as Gorbachev discovered in the late 1980s, have dramatic implications for the stability of the USSR.

Khrushchev's approach to politics was confused but, as Nordlander argues in Chapter 15, highly significant. He recognised the dreadful effects of Stalin's dictatorship on Soviet society and his reassessment of Stalin's policies resulted in the rehabilitation of millions of Soviet citizens – many of them posthumously. In the months after Stalin's death, his successors vowed that they would not allow a single leader again to achieve absolute power and committed themselves to a collective leadership. But Khrushchev and his fellow Politburo members proved unable to restrain their individual ambitions after 1953 and they fought vigorously to establish their own primacy. Beria, the head of the secret police, was unceremoniously arrested, subjected to a secret trial and executed less than twelve months after Stalin's death. Khrushchev proved able to outmanoeuvre his rivals and to emerge as the clear leader of the USSR by 1955, but he was not able to instil sufficient fear or respect into his vanquished colleagues to dissuade them from conspiring against him. In 1964, irritated by Khrushchev's bombast, and concerned at the failure of his attempts to reform the Soviet economy, the Politburo deposed him, as Tompson describes in Chapter 16. This was the only occasion in the history of the Soviet Union in which a leader did not die in office and Khrushchev lived out the remaining seven years of his life in complete obscurity, out of the public gaze. There was a further attempt at installing a collective leadership after Khrushchev's removal and while this proved more successful than in the wake of Stalin's death, by 1970 Brezhnev had emerged as the central figure in the Soviet leadership. Brezhnev ruled the USSR until his death in 1982, and he showed himself to be averse to taking any risks that might jeopardise the stability of his regime.

The main concern of the Soviet leadership during the 1960s and 1970s was to preserve its international status. In the wake of victory in 1945, the USSR extended its influence across the world and the Cold War required the Soviet Union to develop its presence in parts of the globe that had never previously been the object of Russian attention: as west European states withdrew from empire the USSR gave its support to national liberation movements in the Third World. Marxist governments came to power in parts of Africa, while the regime established by the 1959 revolution in Cuba helped to spread the communist ideal as a proxy for the Soviet Union. It supplied aid of all kinds to its followers, hoping to attract adherents to the communist cause and to provoke anti-Western sentiment. This worldwide role prompted a huge expansion in the Soviet navy: dozens of new submarines were launched and new capital ships constructed during the 1960s under the leadership of Admiral Gorshkov. The Soviet nuclear arsenal was also hugely expanded as the Cold War reached its height, and Khrushchev's attempt to station Soviet nuclear weapons in Cuba in 1962 provoked the greatest crisis of the Cold War when the USA demanded the immediate withdrawal of the missiles. Soviet land forces also played a role in buttressing the USSR's international position and huge armies were garrisoned in eastern Europe after 1945 both to buttress the power of its satellite regimes and to deter attack from the west (Holloway, 1983). This rapid and dramatic expansion in military power proved to be a huge drain on the economic resources of the Soviet state. At the same time as the USSR was trying to recover from the devastation of the war, it was faced with the need to expend an increasing proportion of its budget on sustaining its position as a superpower. By the end of the 1960s it was clear that this situation could not continue and the Soviet Union began to explore ways of decreasing its military expenditure. Negotiations with the USA resulted in a series of treaties to limit the numbers of nuclear weapons on each side as a process of détente between east and west began. But, the Soviet leadership remained extremely wary of taking any action that might suggest weakness, while their resistance to any relaxation in domestic policies made the USA less willing to engage in the process of arms reduction. The Soviet invasion of Afghanistan in 1979 brought an end to the process of détente: Soviet foreign policy had failed in its aim of allowing the USSR to rein in its military spending. The consequences of this inability to retrench were to be dramatic.

Gorbachev and the Collapse of the USSR

After Brezhnev's death in 1982, the USSR was led by two old and ill men. Andropov died after less than 18 months in power and his successor, Chernenko, survived for only a year before his own death in 1985. The new – and as it turned out, the final – leader of the Soviet Union was Mikhail Gorbachev, the most radical politician to rise to power in the USSR since the 1920s. Gorbachev had a clear grasp of the problems that faced the Soviet Union: he understood that economic and political stagnation was crippling the USSR, and he also appreciated the way in which the Soviet leadership had lost its radicalism and had become deeply conservative. Gorbachev focussed on shrinking the USSR's international commitments since this would permit substantial reductions in expenditure and allow the state to concentrate on more productive areas (Gorbachev, 1996). He embarked on negotiations with the USA to reduce the numbers of nuclear weapons, withdrew Soviet troops from the disastrous war in Afghanistan and, most dramatically, indicated that the USSR would no longer intervene to keep communist regimes in power in eastern Europe. In 1989, the Soviet empire in Europe dissolved in a matter of months, and the 1990 treaty to reunite the two German states marked the formal end of the Cold War. Gorbachev's foreign policy diminished the importance of the USSR in international affairs and, while it freed resources that could be utilized for domestic purposes, it was deeply unpopular with the Soviet military establishment who saw their importance shrink. While Gorbachev's emphasis on bringing about a fundamental shift in international affairs was welcomed in the West, his apparent willingness to surrender the Soviet Union's superpower status did not enhance his reputation at home.

Gorbachev understood that the Soviet economy needed radical reform to restore its efficiency and productiveness, but he was less sure at actually implementing effective change. Central control of the economy was reduced by allowing farm and factory managers much greater autonomy and by permitting the establishment of small business co-operatives that were entirely independent of the state. These measures had only limited impact, since local party authorities were jealous of their own power and were extremely reluctant to relax their control over economic affairs. Agricultural reform posed a particular difficulty, since Gorbachev could not risk selling off land to farmers for fear of the conservative reaction and the most he could propose was to lease land. But this too ran into difficulties, with local communist party officials seeing the prospect of their influence declining, while farmers were mistrustful of the state's intentions and were reluctant to take the risk of moving from their secure, albeit unrewarding, collective farms. Gorbachev believed that one of the main brakes on Soviet economic performance was the population's dependence on alcohol. Vodka was easily and cheaply available and one of Gorbachev's first actions was to restrict its availability. But his approach failed completely: people turned to distilling their own vodka which both caused severe shortages of sugar in the shops and, more significantly for the state, resulted in a dramatic drop in revenue from taxes on alcohol. The relaxation of central control over the Soviet economy contributed to price rises, but the state was still subsidising the costs of basic goods. Gorbachev's economic reforms were the worst of all worlds: he was constrained by the traditional conservatism that had been institutionalized under Brezhnev, but the problems that faced the Soviet economy were so substantial that small-scale change was inadequate to deal with them. Radical reform was needed, but the vested interests of the communist party obstructed change.

By 1988, Gorbachev recognised that political reform was essential if he was to be able to make any real reforms. He followed a twin track: he embarked on *perestroika*, the reconstruction of the politics of the Soviet Union and alongside this, he embraced *glasnost*, opening up the workings of the Soviet state and society to public discussion. In 1989, as Brovkin discusses in Chapter 20, elections were held to the Soviet parliament that introduced an element of real democracy into the process for the first time since 1917. At the same time, censorship was relaxed and the Soviet people became able to discuss issues with a degree of freedom that they had not experienced since the 1920s; this included contemporary political and social questions, as well as allowing the discussion of topics from the Soviet past. The brittleness of the Soviet regime was revealed by the explosion at the Chernobyl nuclear power station in 1986, when Gorbachev's regime had initially tried to keep the incident secret, but was quickly forced to reveal the details. This incident showed the level of mistrust that existed between state and society, a mistrust that was accentuated in the non-Russian parts of the Soviet Union. National sentiment came quickly to the surface as *glasnost* advanced, and the peoples of the three Baltic nations – Estonia, Latvia and Lithuania – were especially vocal in calling for independence from the Soviet Union (Lieven, 1993). In the Caucasus, violence erupted and even the use of troops could not restore Moscow's control. The development of a more democratic politics in the USSR lifted the lid off a Pandora's box of discontent which the regime was entirely unable to cope with. People raised issues reaching back to Stalin's terror of the 1930s, along with the day to day problems they were experiencing as Gorbachev's reforms were introduced, but by the late 1980s the Soviet state was too enfeebled to be able to cope with popular discontent.

The conservative Soviet establishment was deeply suspicious of Gorbachev's intentions. As Gooding suggests in Chapter 19, they were horrified at the prospect of the communist party losing its dominant position in Soviet society, and were very uncomfortable with the reduction in the USSR's international status. By 1990, the Russian Republic was flexing its muscles with the election of Yeltsin as Russian President and the authority of the Soviet Union itself was being challenged. Gorbachev attempted to stem calls for autonomy from the USSR's component republics by proposing a new union treaty to give them much greater power. This was the final straw for the USSR's conservatives and they attempted to depose Gorbachev in August 1991 in a coup. Yeltsin was instrumental in bringing the coup to an end and, although Gorbachev was restored to power, his authority had been fatally undermined. Yeltsin and other republican leaders agreed that they would declare their independence from the Soviet Union, destroying it as a state. On 25 December 1991, Gorbachev accepted the inevitable and the USSR passed into history.

Conclusion

During the 74 years of the Soviet state, society was transformed. The communists succeeded in reshaping a rural-dominated country into a great industrial power that proved capable of winning the most devastating war in Russia's history. The Soviet Union became a highly-educated society that proved able to launch the first man into space in 1961, and to guarantee at least a basic level of social provision for its people. But, the communists were never able to shake off the authoritarianism and violence of the 1920s and 1930s, and after Stalin's death the USSR's political structures ossified and failed to confront global processes of social and economic change. The speed of communism's collapse showed very clearly the lack of social support for the Soviet regime and how far the state had become distanced from the interests of its citizens. The rejection of democracy that had been symbolized by the dissolution of the Constituent Assembly in 1918 came home to haunt Lenin's successors in the 1980s when the voice of the Soviet people could no longer be silenced.[11]

References

Andrle, V. (1994), *A Social History of Twentieth Century Russia*, London: Edward Arnold, pp. 253–68.
Davies, I. (1972), *White Eagle, Red Star. The Polish-Soviet War, 1919–1920*, London: Macmillan.
Deutscher, I. (1970), *The Prophet Armed. Trotsky: 1879–1921*, Oxford: Oxford University Press, p. 327.
Erickson, J. (1975), *The Road to Stalingrad: Stalin's War with Germany*, New York: Harper and Row.
Erickson, J. (1983), *The Road to Berlin: Stalin's War with Germany*, New York: Harper and Row.
Fitzpatrick, S. (1994), *Stalin's Peasants: Resistance and Survival in the Russian Village after Collectivization*, New York: Oxford University Press, pp. 48–79.
Getty, J.A. and Naumov, O.V. (1999), *The Road to Terror: Stalin and the Self-Destruction of the Bolsheviks, 1932–1939*, New Haven, CT: Yale University Press.
Gorbachev, M. (1996), *Memoirs*, London: Doubleday, pp. 171–200.
Gorlizki, Y. and Khlevniuk, O. (2004), *Cold Peace: Stalin and the Soviet Ruling Circle, 1945–1953*, Oxford: Oxford University Press.
Harris, J. (2005), 'Stalin as General Secretary: the appointments process and the nature of Stalin's power', in S. Davies and J. Harris (eds), *Stalin. A New History*, Cambridge: Cambridge University Press, pp. 63–82.
Haslam, J. (1984), *The Soviet Union and the Struggle for Collective Security in Europe, 1933-39*, London: Macmillan.
Holloway, D. (1983), *The Soviet Union and the Arms Race*, New Haven, CT: Yale University Press.
Holloway, D. (1994), *Stalin and the Bomb: the Soviet Union and Atomic Energy, 1939-1956*, New Haven, CT: Yale University Press.

11 Good general accounts of Soviet history are Hosking, 1992; Service, 1997, and Suny, 1998.

Holquist, P. (2002), *Making War, Forging Revolution. Russia's Continuum of Crisis, 1914–1921*, Cambridge, MA: Harvard University Press.

Hosking, G. (1992), *A History of the Soviet Union*, London: Fontana.

Keep, J. (1996), *Last of the Empires: A History of the Soviet Union 1945–1991*, Oxford: Oxford University Press, pp. 244–62.

Kotkin, S. (1995), *Magnetic Mountain: Stalinism as a Civilization*, Berkeley, CA: University of California Press, pp. 37–71.

Larina, A. (1991), *This I Cannot Forget: The Memoirs of Nikolai Bukharin's Widow*, New York: Norton.

Leggett, G. (1981), *The Cheka: Lenin's Political Police, the All-Russian Extraordinary Commission for Combating Counter-revolution and Sabotage (December 1917 to February 1922)*, Oxford: Oxford University Press.

Lieven, A. (1993), *The Baltic Revolution: Estonia, Latvia, Lithuania and the Path to Independence*, New Haven, CT: Yale University Press, pp. 214–315.

Mawdsley, E. (1987), *The Russian Civil War*, London: Unwin.

McCauley, M. (1976), *Khrushchev and the Development of Soviet Agriculture*, London: Macmillan.

McDermott, K. (2006), *Stalin*, London: Palgrave Macmillan.

Nove, A. (1969), *An Economic History of the USSR*, London: Allen Lane, pp. 191; 225.

Overy, R. (1997), *Russia's War*, London: Allen Lane.

Rabinowitch, A. (1976), *The Bolsheviks Come to Power*, New York: Norton.

Radkey, O.H. (1989), *Russia Goes to the Polls: The Elections to the All-Russian Constituent Assembly, 1917*, Ithaca: Cornell University Press.

Service, R (1997), *A History of Modern Russia from Nicholas II to Putin*, London: Penguin.

Service, R. (2000), *Lenin: A Biography*, London: Macmillan.

Siegelbaum, L.H. (1992), *Soviet State and Society between Revolutions, 1918–1929*, Cambridge: Cambridge University Press.

Suny, R.G. (1998), *The Soviet Experiment: Russia, the USSR and the Successor States*, New York: Oxford University Press.

Taubman, W. (2003), *Khrushchev: The Man and his Era*, New York: Norton.

Tumarkin, N. (1994), *The Living and the Dead: The Rise and Fall of the Cult of World War II in Russia*, New York: Basic Books.

Viola, L. (1996), *Peasant Rebels under Stalin: Collectivization and the Culture of Peasant Resistance*, New York: Oxford University Press, pp. 67–99.

Part I
The Bolshevik Seizure
and Consolidation of Power

Part I

[1]

Lenin's Conception of Revolution As Civil War

ISRAEL GETZLER

CHARACTERIZATIONS of Lenin as 'power-crazed' and 'a fanatical believer in a Communist utopia',[1] do not quite convince me. In an attempt to find a further key to an understanding of Lenin's historical role, I have had a closer look at some of his private drafts and jottings, particularly those of 1905–06 and 1919. These were not intended for publication and seem to me to be more revealing than his largely polemical writings, especially when interpreted in the light of evidence newly available with the opening up of the Russian archives.

That evidence, already absorbed into a number of works on the Russian revolution and on Lenin,[2] suggests that Lenin was both much more of an internationalist à la Trotskii than had been assumed and even more of a ruthless state terrorist than had been believed — his bite was often as bad as his bark. The new evidence, if further evidence were needed, also confirms that he was a 'revolutionary of genius'.[3]

My findings suggest that what distinguished Lenin from other revolutionaries (for example Martov — his 'repressed alter ego') was not so much his intense revolutionism or his absolute conviction that a European socialist revolution was within reach, but rather his simplistic, narrow and brutal understanding of revolution as civil war *tout court*. It was that understanding, and the corresponding strategy and tactics, mentality and *modus operandi*, which he injected into his 'belligerent party' of Bolsheviks.[4] With that credo of civil war he marched the Bolsheviks into the October revolution and the construction of the Soviet state. And it was that revolutionary Soviet state power, which he defined as merely 'a <u>tool</u> of the proletariat in its class struggle, a special <u>bludgeon</u>, *rien de plus* !',[5] that he bequeathed to his Bolshevik heirs.

Israel Getzler is Emeritus Professor of European History and Russian Studies at the Hebrew University of Jerusalem.

[1] Peter Scheibert, *Lenin an der Macht*, Weinheim, 1984, p. 479; Dmitrii Volkogonov, *Lenin*, vol. I, Moscow, 1994, pp. 17–18; Richard Pipes, *Russia under the Bolshevik Regime*, New York, 1994, pp. 501–02; the notable exeption is Robert Service, *Lenin, A Political Life: the Iron Ring*, London, 1995, pp. 8 and 323.

[2] As above, with the exception of Scheibert.

[3] Leonard Schapiro, 'Lenin After Fifty Years' in *Lenin, the Man, the Theorist, the Leader: A Reappraisal*, London, 1967, p. 8.

[4] Lenin, *Polnoe sobranie sochinenii* (hereafter *PSS*), Moscow, 1960, vol. 14, p. 8.

[5] *PSS*, vol. 39, p. 261.

Civil war is what Lenin wanted and civil war is what he got, as he boasted on 11 January 1918 at the third Congress of Soviets:

> In answer to all reproaches and accusations of terror, dictatorship and civil war, we say: yes, we have openly proclaimed what no other government would ever proclaim: we are the first government in the world which openly speaks of civil war; yes, we started and continue to wage war against the exploiters.[6]

And more than two years later, when the Civil War was at its height, he reaffirmed Bolshevik responsibility:

> We brought the Civil War upon ourselves: we have never concealed from the people that we were taking that risk.[7]

And again, even as late as December 1922, he was still applauding civil war, as he jotted down for a speech to the Tenth Congress of Soviets:

> The Civil War has welded together the working class and the peasantry and this is the guarantee of our invincible strength. The Civil War has taught and tempered us (Denikin etc. were good teachers, good ones, they taught seriously).[8]

Lenin began to develop his understanding of revolution in 1905–06 when all revolutionary parties were busy formulating their revolutionary strategies. Lenin set this down in two private drafts — 'Scenario of the Provisional Revolutionary Government'[9] of June 1905 and 'Phases, Direction and Perspectives of the Revolution'[10] of December 1905 (both were published only twenty years later).

He expected the 'final destruction of tsardom' to take the form and be the final outcome of 'full-scale civil war'. Similarly, he envisaged a second even fiercer civil war between the bourgeoisie — 'strengthened by the gigantic development of capitalist progress' — on the one hand, and the 'revolutionary dictatorship of the proletariat and the peasantry' which would result from elections to the Constituent Assembly on the other. In that contest, the 'fortress' (state) was likely to change hands and the bourgeoisie might well overthrow the revolutionary government unless the latter 'sets Europe on fire'; and 'what then?' he asks. The answer came half a year later when he urged that in the second civil war, when the liberal bourgeoisie, the well-off peasantry and a fair section of the middling peasantry would join to do battle against the revolutionary democratic dictatorship, then

[6] *PSS*, vol. 35, p. 268.
[7] *PSS*, vol. 38, p. 339.
[8] *PSS*, vol. 45, p. 440.
[9] *PSS*, vol. 10, pp. 359–60.
[10] *PSS*, vol. 12, p. 157.

466 ISRAEL GETZLER

the proletariat, left on its own would prove almost hopeless in such a contest and would inevitably be defeated (like the German revolutionary party in 1848/50, or the French proletariat in 1871) <u>if the European socialist proletariat does not come to the assistance of the Russian proletariat</u>.[11]

If these were his private drafts, he gave public expression to the last point in May 1906 at the Fourth Congress of the RSDRP in London when he countered Plekhanov's argument that Lenin's project of land nationalization would strengthen a despotic state if ever there were to be a restoration. Whether the land was 'municipalized' or nationalized would make no difference, Lenin told Plekhanov: 'the only guarantee against restoration is a socialist revolution in the West.'[12]

Predictably, the chief lesson that Lenin drew in 1908 from the Paris Commune of 1871 was that 'it demonstrated the power of civil war', while one of its major mistakes was 'its uncalled-for magnanimity': 'it ought to have annihilated its enemies rather than attempt to influence them morally [. . .] it underestimated the importance of purely military operations in civil war':[13]

> For the proletariat must never forget that in certain conditions the class struggle turns into armed struggle and civil war and that there are times when the interests of the proletariat demand the merciless annihilation of the enemy in open military engagements.[14]

And, turning against the Menshevik denunciation of Bolshevik 'partisan warfare' and bank 'expropriations', he wrote:

> Any moral condemnation of [civil war] is absolutely impermissible from the point of view of Marxism [. . .] For us, the sole acceptable critique of the various forms of civil war is that advanced from the point of view of military expediency. In an epoch of civil war, the ideal of the party of the proletariat must be that of a *belligerent party*.[15]

It was at the same time that Lenin (who as early as 1902 had managed to saddle the RSDRP with a programmatic commitment to the 'dictatorship of the proletariat') spelled out clearly and precisely what he understood by dictatorship. 'An unlimited state power based on force in the most literal sense of the word, and not on law.'[16] This he linked to his understanding of civil war and revolution: 'In times of civil war any victorious state power can be nothing but a dictatorship.'[17]

[11] Ibid.
[12] *PSS*, vol. 12, pp. 362–63.
[13] *PSS*, vol. 16, pp. 451–54.
[14] Ibid.
[15] *PSS*, vol. 14, pp. 8, 11.
[16] *PSS*, vol. 12, pp. 318, 320.
[17] Ibid., p. 288.

It was to this intimate connection between class struggle, civil war, revolution, dictatorship and European socialist revolution as an indispensable part of a victorious Russian revolution that Lenin was committed right to the end of his life.

With the coming of World War I, Lenin turned his civil war conception of revolution into an appeal to 'transform' the imperialist war into civil war: 'Let us hoist the banner of civil war!'[18] was his answer to Martov's call for 'Peace and peace at any price!'[19] He also insisted later that there was no longer any validity whatever to exceptions that Marx, Engels and their disciples may have envisaged as providing a parliamentary non-violent road from bourgeois capitalism to proletarian socialism in some Western countries. All states were now tarred with the same imperialist, militarist brush.[20]

Stranded in Switzerland in February 1917, Lenin enjoined on Bolsheviks a party-minded 'separateness'. His sharp letter to Anatolii Lunacharskii of 14 March is telling:

> The independence and separateness of our party — no rapprochement whatever with other parties — these are, as I see it, ultimative demands. Without them it will be impossible to take the proletariat through the democratic revolution to the commune, and I am prepared to serve no other aims.[21]

(And, as evidenced by Lenin's copious notes of January/February 1917 'Marxism on the State',[22] following Marx and Engels, for him, too, commune equalled dictatorship of the proletariat.)

Upon his arrival in Petrograd, he told his Bolsheviks that although 'the first civil war has already ended in Russia, and we are now proceeding to the second — that between imperialism and the armed people' — they must in the first place engage 'in peaceful, sustained and patient class propaganda': 'We stand for civil war, but only when it is waged by a politically conscious class.'[23] In his private notes, he spelt out his programme for the transition:

> To be rock-hard in the proletarian line against petty-bourgeois waverings. To prepare for a *Krach* and a revolution a thousand times more powerful than February.[24]

In August and September, preparing for the plunge into the October revolution, Lenin again raised the banner of civil war. Taking

[18] *PSS*, vol. 26, p. 41.
[19] Martov, 'Nash lozung — mir!', *Novyi mir*, New York, no. 219, 17 November 1914.
[20] *PSS*, vol. 33, p. 38.
[21] *PSS*, vol. 49, pp. 410–11.
[22] *PSS*, vol. 33, pp. 212, 222, 244, 246; vol. 35, p. 192.
[23] *PSS*, vol. 31, p. 351.
[24] *PSS*, vol. 32, p. 441.

ISRAEL GETZLER

advantage of Martov's warning against civil war, he told him that such a self-denying ordinance would be tantamount to

> a manifest rejection of any form of class struggle, of any revolution [. . .] who does not know that the world history of all revolutions shows that class struggle turns inevitably and not just by accident to civil war.[25]

Almost at the same time, he repeated that point in 'The Russian Revolution and Civil War', where he extolled the blessings of civil war:

> Gentlemen, do not frighten us with civil war [. . .] it is inevitable [. . .] it gives victory over the exploiters, land to the peasants, peace to the nations, it opens up the road that leads to the victorious revolution of the international socialist proletariat.[26]

It was with that credo of civil war and revolutionary dictatorship that Lenin took his Bolsheviks into the October revolution and into a 'homogeneous', that is, a one-party Bolshevik government. He overcame the resistance of the Bolshevik moderates in the night session of the Central Committee on 2 November which, from the outset, he dubbed 'a session of historic importance' — the moderates, he urged, were sabotaging 'the dictatorship of the proletariat and of the poorest peasantry' with their hankering after a broadly-based. multi-party, socialist government.[27] In December, he dismissed the Bolshevik members of the commission of the Constituent Assembly who, 'oblivious to the real conditions of class struggle and civil war', took the Constituent Assembly seriously.[28] In January 1918, he dispersed the Constituent Assembly and in July anchored his understanding of class struggle, civil war and dictatorship in the Soviet constitution.[29]

I know of no other document which so faithfully reflects and embodies Lenin's understanding of revolution as class war, and of the revolutionary state which he founded and bequeathed to his Bolshevik heirs as the particular instrument of that class war.

Lenin took an active part in the drafting of the Soviet constitution. He wrote the 'Declaration of the Rights of the Toiling and Exploited People', which formed its first section and ideological preamble.[30] He

[25] *PSS*, vol. 34, p. 80.

[26] Ibid., p. 228.

[27] *Protokoly Tsentral'nogo Komiteta RSDRP(b) Avgust 1917 — Fevral' 1918*, Moscow, 1958, pp. 131–32.

[28] Ibid., pp. 160, 279–80.

[29] 'Konstitutsiia (Osnovnoi zakon) Rossiiskoi Sotsialisticheskoi Federativnoi Sovetskoi Respubliki' was adopted on 10 July 1918 at the Fifth All-Russian Congress of Soviets and is reprinted in full in O. I. Chistiakov, *Konstitutsiia RSFSR 1918 goda*, Moscow, 1984, pp. 190–204.

[30] For Lenin's active part in the drafting and final phrasing of the constitution, see *V. I. Lenin, Biograficheskaia khronika*, vol. 5, Moscow, 1974, pp. 374, 571, 582, 595, 599, 603; *PSS*, vol. 35, pp. 221–23.

LENIN'S CONCEPTION OF REVOLUTION   469

took a special interest in such matters as the class composition of the soviets and the form of the dictatorship of the proletariat.

The 'Declaration' itself already shows the heavy imprint of Lenin the class warrior: a 'fundamental task' of the constitution is 'the merciless crushing of the exploiters', their exclusion from 'all organs of power', 'the arming of toilers and the complete disarming of the propertied classes', and 'universal labour conscription of the parasitical elements of society'. It is followed by Lenin's beloved Paragraph 9 which proclaims as 'the fundamental task of the constitution' (to be fair, 'for the present transitional period') 'the establishment of the dictatorship of the urban and rural proletariat and of the poorest peasantry in the form of the mighty All-Russian soviet state power for the purpose of the complete crushing of the bourgeoisie'. And, for Lenin, dictatorship meant simply and crudely a system of government resting on force or violence unfettered by law. In fact, there is no section on law in Lenin's constitution, nor is there any mention of the Bolshevik party. Of particular interest to Lenin was the punitive Paragraph 23 which deprived 'individuals and separate groups of any rights which may be used by them to the detriment of the socialist revolution'.

The financial policy of the 'dictatorship of the toilers' has as its fundamental objective 'the expropriation of the bourgeoisie [...] the smashing of the economic and political power of the propertied classes'. The following social categories are disfranchised: 'employers of labour for profit, rentiers living on the interest from capital or on incomes from enterprises and property, private commercial agents, monks, priests and former police officers, gendarmes, secret police agents and the tsarist family'.

Turning outwards, the constitution amounts to little less than a declaration of war on the bourgeois capitalist world. The abrogation of the tsarist debts is merely 'the first blow against international banking and finance capital'. It is followed by 'Soviet state power marching firmly towards the complete victory of the insurrection of the workers of the world against the yoke of capital'. It declares 'an unbending determination to tear mankind out of the clutches of finance capitalism and imperialism' and promises 'revolutionary means' to achieve a democratic peace.

How important the constitution was to Lenin, notably Paragraphs 9 and 23, can be gauged from his furious reaction to Martov, who, on 6 December 1919, at the Seventh Congress of Soviets, had accused the Bolsheviks of violating, if not in fact abolishing, their own constitution.

Lenin's reply to Martov would have done a Stalin proud:

I maintain that we do keep to our constitution and in the strictest possible manner. Paragraph 23 reads: 'guided by the interests of the working class as a whole, the All-Russian Socialist Federative Soviet Republic deprives

470   ISRAEL GETZLER

individuals and separate groups of rights which are used by them to the
detriment of the socialist revolution.[31]

And for good measure he quoted Paragraph 9 and its reference to
'the dictatorship of the proletariat and of the poorest peasantry [. . .]
for the purpose of the complete crushing of the bourgeoisie'. In the
notes for the speech, next to Paragraph 23, there appear the words
'terror and *Cheka*' contained in a box and heavily underscored.[32]
That this was no mere strident rhetoric to intimidate the Menshevik
remnants and reassure his own Bolsheviks can be gauged from four sets
of notes on the dictatorship of the proletariat which Lenin jotted down
in preparation for a brochure in September/October 1919, but which
were published only in 1925.[33] These notes spell out unequivocally his
socio-political scenario of soviet state power: the dictatorship of the
proletariat 'is the <u>continuation</u> in new forms of the class struggle of the
proletariat, that is the *crux* which people do not comprehend.' 'The
state is merely — the <u>tool</u> of the proletariat in its class struggle [it is] a
special <u>bludgeon</u>, *rien de plus*.' [For] there are 'new forms of resistance
(conspiracies, sabotage, influence on petty-bourgeoisie) which are
fiercer after the exploiters have been overthrown'.[34] As for 'the class of
exploiters, one can and must destroy it — it can be written off'. But
one must not write off the non-exploiting or not directly exploiting
classes (bourgeois intelligentsia, the petty-bourgeoisie) which as *Eigen-
tümerin der Produktionsmittel* is <u>in so far</u> an 'exploiter *in potentia et partialiter
in praxi*'.[35]
Lenin postulates two lines of class struggle taking place during the
dictatorship of the proletariat:

A) The crushing of exploiters as task (and content) of epoch — this war is
more merciless than other wars; B) The neutralization of middle element,
petty-bourgeoisie, peasantry — by persuasion, example, learning from
experience, repression of deviations by violence *etcetera*.[36] The proletariat
[as a ruling class] not in general, *in abstracto*, but after the imperialist war in
the 20th century a split with the upper strata of the proletariat inevitable.
[Therefore] the dictatorship of the proletariat is a dictatorship of the
revolutionary elements of the exploited class (there is a break with the
opportunist upper strata of the proletariat).[37]

Lenin would not allow even the slightest tampering with the
constitution which to him was synonymous with Soviet state power:

---

[31] *PSS*, vol. 39, pp. 422–24.
[32] Ibid., p. 466.
[33] Ibid., pp. 261–68, 453–61.
[34] Ibid., pp. 261–62.
[35] Ibid., p. 455.
[36] Ibid., p. 456.
[37] Ibid., pp. 457, 459.

LENIN'S CONCEPTION OF REVOLUTION 471

when, in January 1919, the revolutionary committee of Ufa, while negotiating an agreement with the SRs in the fight against Admiral Kolchak, enquired whether some changes could not be made in the Soviet constitution, Lenin cabled:

> The SRs must be told unequivocally that there can be no talk of changes in the Soviet constitution. The Soviet state power of the exploited classes for the crushing of the exploiters has thoroughly proven its indispensability in attaining victory over the bourgeoisie; the soviet movement is already spreading all over the countries of the world.[38]

Similarly, when late in January 1922 Grigorii Chicherin, People's Commissar for External Affairs, in preparation for the Genoa conference, inquired: 'Should the Americans strongly press for "representative institutions" don't you think we could, in return for some decent compensation, make some minor changes in our constitution?' Lenin wrote 'madness' on the letter and sent it to Molotov 'for all members of the politburo: This and the following letter show clearly that Chicherin is sick, very sick. We would be fools not to pack him off straight away into a sanatorium.'[39]

To sum up: while one can only agree with Leonard Schapiro that Lenin was 'a revolutionary of genius', certainly in 1917, when it mattered, he was, as I have been trying to suggest, a revolutionary with a difference.

He understood revolution solely in the narrow terms of civil war where there are no compromises, no neutrals, where his favourite question was 'who devours whom?' And when laying the foundations of the Soviet state, it was Lenin the <u>revolutionary</u> who made it into an instrument of class struggle, civil war and dictatorship, embodying in its constitution as its fundamental aim 'the complete crushing of the bourgeoisie' and the disfranchisement of entire categories of citizens as well as the partial disfranchisement of the peasantry.

True, the saving clause of the constitution was that it was designed for the 'present transition period', but Lenin himself expected that transition period to last throughout 'an entire epoch of fiercest civil war'.[40] It was that repressive Soviet state power, with its <u>Cheka</u> and the terror, a <u>bludgeon</u> and *'rien de plus*, which he bequeathed to his Bolsheviks in 1924.

Not satisfied with saddling Russia with a Bolshevik Soviet state and with a civil war, Lenin and his Bolsheviks were determined to commit socialist parties abroad to 'the Russian model which shows all countries something highly essential to their own inevitable, and none too distant

[38] *PSS*, vol. 50, p. 239.
[39] *PSS*, vol. 54, pp. 136–37.
[40] *PSS*, vol. 36, p. 405; vol. 35, p. 192; vol. 42, pp. 306–07.

future'.[41] This they did by imposing on parties seeking admission to the Comintern the notorious Twenty-One Points on the grounds that the 'present epoch is one of sharpening civil war'.[42]

Yet hardly any of the revolutions that shook Europe during and in the wake of World War I conformed to Lenin's understanding that revolution equals civil war.

The 1917 February revolution which, as Lenin put it in May, 'gave the Russian people an unprecedented freedom not enjoyed at present by any other nation', was almost bloodless and quite charitable. Such civil war violence as occurred was mainly confined to Kronstadt and Helsingfors where irate sailors squared accounts with their officers. And even the October revolution need not have resulted in civil war had not Lenin and Trotskii pre-empted it. Indeed a relatively peaceful ousting of the discredited and isolated Kerenskii government was on the cards and could have been realized either by the Left Bloc in the Pre-parliament, or by the formation of a broadly-based socialist coalition government, or as a result of the elections to the Constituent Assembly when 85–87 per cent voted for socialist parties.

Nor were the October and November 1918 revolutions in Austria, Germany and Hungary civil war revolutions in the Leninist sense. Indeed, all later attempts to emulate the Leninist model in Germany, Bavaria and Hungary proved disastrous failures.

As for the time-hallowed question of the Marxist credentials of his conception of revolution, Lenin may have found some support in the revolutionary writings of Marx and Engels of the 1848–50 period. But while he insisted on their centrality, claiming them to be 'the most inseparable constituent part of their entire revolutionary world view!'[43] many would dispute that view.

---

[41] *PSS*, vol. 41, p. 4.
[42] For 'The Twenty-One Points', i.e. 'The Conditions of Acceptance into the Communist International', see V. I. Lenin, *Sochineniia* (2nd edition), vol. 25, Moscow, 1935, pp. 575–85.
[43] *PSS*, vol. 16, p. 24.

[2]

THE RED ARMY AND MASS MOBILIZATION DURING THE RUSSIAN CIVIL WAR 1918-1920

Orlando Figes

The Red Army began life in 1918 as a small volunteer force of proletarians from the major urban citadels of Bolshevik power in northern and central Russia. By the end of the civil war against the Whites and the various armies of foreign intervention, in the autumn of 1920, it had grown into a mass conscript army of five million soldiers, 75 per cent of them peasants[1] by birth — a figure roughly proportionate to the size of the peasant population in Russia.[2]

For the Bolsheviks, this represented a tremendous social change. In October 1917 their support had been confined to the working-class districts of the big industrial cities, the Baltic Fleet, and the (soon to be demobilized) garrisons and armies of northern and western Russia. Without support in the countryside, where the vast majority of the population lived, no one had expected the Bolsheviks to hold on to power for more than a few weeks. The peasants, it was widely assumed, would rise up against them, joining the various armies of counter-revolution. Yet, contrary to expectations, the Red Army won the civil war, and it did so precisely because of its superior success, compared with the Whites, in mobilizing millions of peasants for military service. "In this social fact", concluded Trotsky, was "rooted the final cause of our victories".[3]

The mass conscription of the peasantry gave rise to a number of major debates within the Bolshevik party. Most Bolsheviks viewed the peasantry as an alien force, hostile to the socialist revolution

[1] "Peasants" are defined here (and throughout) as household members of small-scale family farms.

[2] N. Gorlov, "O sotsial'noi strukture krasnoi armii" [On the Social Structure of the Red Army], *Politrabotnika* (1922), no. 2, p. 55. The 1920 census of the Red Army and Navy gave the slightly higher figure of 77 per cent: see V. Efremov, "Profes-sional'nyi sostav krasnoi armii i flota po perepisi 1920 g." [The Professional Composition of the Red Army and Fleet According to the Census of 1920], *Biulleten' TsSU* (1922), no. 66, p. 2. According to the Red Army census, only 66 per cent of soldiers registered farming as their main occupation: *Biulleten' TsSU* (1922), no. 59, p. 41. Peasants counting domestic industry as their main occupation represented a significant component of the Red Army. Military service was also a popular means of social mobility from the peasantry to other social groups, especially the bureaucracy.

[3] L. Trotsky, *How the Revolution Armed*, trans. B. Pearce, in *The Military Writings and Speeches of Leon Trotsky*, 5 vols. (London, 1979), i, p. 15.

THE RED ARMY AND MASS MOBILIZATION 1918-1920   **169**

because of its "petty-bourgeois" nature (its social inclination towards small-scale property rights and market relations). The Bolshevik party had always supported the ideal of a "class" army — one dominated by the proletariat, as opposed to an army based upon universal military service.[4] Although the rapid escalation of the civil war in the summer of 1918 had forced the Bolsheviks to adopt the latter principle, many in the party continued to express their belief that a small but "pure" proletarian army, like the Red Guards or factory militia of 1917, would prove more reliable and effective than a mass conscript army infiltrated and weakened by non-proletarian elements. This was one of the central arguments of the Military Opposition in the Bolshevik party to Trotsky's policy of constructing a regular conscript army commanded by "bourgeois" military specialists under the political supervision of Bolshevik commissars.[5] The need to preserve the hegemony of the industrial worker over the peasant was also an important consideration for those (including Trotsky himself) who stressed the desirability of moving — as soon as the military situation permitted — away from the mass conscript army towards a militia system.[6]

These issues went far beyond the question of military organization. The principles upon which the Red Army was built served as a model for the rest of the Soviet system. The centralization of the Bolshevik state apparatus ran parallel to similar changes in the Red Army's political and command structure. Trotsky compared the transition from workers' control to one-man management in industry with the transfer of military authority in the Red Army from elected officers to military specialists, appointed by the Revolutionary Military Council of the Republic (RVSR).[7] The experience of mass mobilization gained by the Bolsheviks through the Red Army fundamentally shaped their governmental attitudes not only during the period of War Communism (1918-21), when the whole of Soviet society was militarized, but also during the Stalinist period. Even the language of the Bolsheviks — with its continual references to "campaigns", "combats", "fronts" and "brigades" — had military overtones.

The problems of military organization associated with the mass

---

[4] *Ibid.*, i, pp. 134, 420-1, iii, pp. 4, 8, *passim.*
[5] F. Benvenuti, *The Bolsheviks and the Red Army, 1918-1922* (Cambridge, 1988), p. 66.
[6] J. Erickson, "Some Military and Political Aspects of the 'Militia Army' Controversy, 1919-1920", in C. Abramsky and B. Williams (eds.), *Essays in Honour of E. H. Carr* (London, 1974), p. 217.
[7] Trotsky, *How the Revolution Armed*, ii, p. 105.

conscription of the peasantry had particular relevance to these broader issues of government. The difficulties of registering the rural population eligible for military service and of enforcing the Red Army conscriptions in the countryside pointed towards the general problems of administration which the Bolsheviks were bound to confront outside their strongholds in the major industrial cities. The tasks of training and disciplining the unruly peasant recruits served as an important lesson in the methods of rule for those (mostly Bolshevik and working-class) officers who were to enter the provincial organs of Soviet government in their thousands after the end of the civil war. The contempt and hatred felt by many of the proletarian officers for the peasantry was expressed in such brutal punishments (sanctioned by the disciplinary code of the Red Army) as hitting soldiers in the teeth with the butt of a rifle. Beneath this naked violence lay a deeper political struggle, as D. D. F. White put it, "between the anarchistic, anti-centralist tendencies of the village and the centralist, dictatorial trends of the Communist party. It was not merely a conflict between groups with different economic and political interests. It was a deep-rooted antagonism between two ways of living, two different cultural practices and concepts".[8]

Isaac Babel symbolized this conflict in his brilliant story, *Konnaia armiia* (Red Cavalry), in the episode when one of Budenny's élite cavalry brigades charges on a group of their own peasant infantrymen, thrashing them with whips to assert their superiority over them.

Of all the problems of military organization associated with the mass conscription of the peasantry, none was as serious, or had as many consequences for the civilian sector, as the difficulties of military supply. The decision to maintain a Red Army of five million soldiers, rather than one or two million, necessitated the militarization of the Soviet economy (War Communism) to supply it with food, uniforms, boots, weapons, transport and medical services. But the Red Army grew much faster than the productive capacity of the economy. Material shortages in the army increased. Living conditions deteriorated. Diseases spread. Discipline broke down. And desertion accelerated out of control, so that hastily mobilized — and often untrained — reinforcements had increasingly to be sent to the front-line units, although these were precisely those most likely to desert. The problem was made more acute by the fact that the army became dependent on peasant recruits, whose technical incompetence and

[8] D. D. F. White, *The Growth of the Red Army* (Princeton, 1944), p. 121.

THE RED ARMY AND MASS MOBILIZATION 1918-1920   171

natural homing instincts during the agricultural season made them
harder to train and discipline than skilled industrial workers.[9] It was
this consideration that had largely determined the decision of the
Bolsheviks to go for a pattern of "extensive recruitment" — to
mobilize all the possible age groups of the rural population in the
hope of finding among them a sufficient number of reliable recruits.
Yet opting for quantity rather than quality only exacerbated the
problems of supply and desertion. In short, the Red Army became
inextricably locked into a vicious circle, in which its fighting capacity
was largely dependent upon the efficiency of its own social and
economic organization. (See Diagram.)

DIAGRAM
THE VICIOUS CIRCLE OF MASS CONSCRIPTION

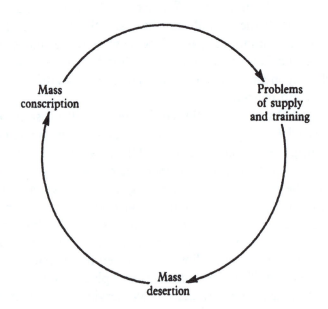

The White armies suffered similar problems of organization as they
attempted to expand from their social base of 1918 (small but well-
disciplined volunteer forces, mainly consisting of Cossacks and officers) into the mass peasant-conscript armies which were ultimately

[9] Many sources noted that the best-disciplined Red Army units tended to have a
higher proportion of workers in them: see *ibid.*, p. 105. The Bolsheviks pursued a
conscious policy of reinforcing as many military units as possible — especially
those on the important fronts — with workers and party members. See Efremov,
"Professional'nyi sostav", p. 4; M. A. Molodtsygin, *Raboche-krest'ianskii soiuz, 1918-
1920* [The Workers' and Peasants' Union, 1918-1920] (Moscow, 1987), pp. 149-54.

to decide the military struggles of 1919-20. The more peasants the White armies recruited, the weaker they became, as the familiar problems of military supply, training and indiscipline increased.[10] In the summer of 1919, Lenin predicted that mass conscription would destabilize Denikin's army, as it had already weakened Kolchak's army during the previous spring:

> universal mobilization will be the ruin of Denikin as it was of Kolchak; as long as he had a class army of volunteers who hated socialism it was strong and sound, but when he began universal recruitment he did, of course, get an army together more quickly, but the army became the weaker, and its class character less pronounced. Peasants recruited into Denikin's army will do the same in that army as the Siberian peasants did in Kolchak's army — they brought complete disintegration into the army.[11]

The importance of the civil war armies' social and economic organization can only be understood if we bear in mind two specific features of the Russian civil war. First, there was the sheer speed with which the two armies were forced to mobilize the peasants, an alien social element to both. Neither had the time or the infrastructure to establish a solid territorial-military base among the peasantry, as the Red Army was able to do in China between 1927 and 1940. Secondly, the rapidly shifting fronts of the Russian civil war disrupted regular supply lines and local state structures, so that the two armies were frequently forced to mobilize reinforcements and military supplies from areas close to the fighting.

The effect of these two factors was to militarize vast civilian areas, so that terror and coercion by the military against the population — as well as popular rebellions against the military authorities — became an integral element of the civil war. Civilian dead and wounded accounted for 91 per cent of all losses in the Russian civil war, compared with 63 per cent during the First World War.[12] The ability of the armies to mobilize the peasantry and their economic resources depended almost entirely upon their relations with the rural population at large. Indiscriminate looting and confiscation of peasant property by military units was invariably followed by peasant upris-

---

[10] See, for example, *Poslednie dni kolchakovshchiny* [The Last Days of the Kolchak Regime], ed. M. M. Konstantinov (Moscow and Leningrad, 1926), pp. 9-10; facsimile repr. in *Kolchak i Sibir': Dokumenty i issledovaniia, 1919-1926* [Kolchak and Siberia: Documents and Research, 1919-1926], ed. D. Collins and J. Smerle, 2 vols. (Pubns. of the Study Group on the Russian Revolution, xi, New York, 1988); E. Wollenberg, *The Red Army*, trans. C. Sykes (London, 1978), pp. 97-8; Trotsky, *How the Revolution Armed*, iii, pp. 6-7.

[11] V. I. Lenin, *Collected Works*, 4th edn., 47 vols. (London, 1960-80), xxix, p. 460.

[12] A. Bubnov, *Grazhdanskaia voina, partiia i voennoe delo* [The Civil War, the Party and Military Science] (Moscow, 1928), p. 29.

THE RED ARMY AND MASS MOBILIZATION 1918-1920   173

ings against conscription and the requisitionings of food and other
supplies, as well as an increase in peasant desertion from the army
itself.

It is rather surprising, in view of all this, that Western historians
have chosen to write about the Russian civil war almost exclusively
from the perspective of traditional military history.[13] True, its outcome, like any war, was decided by force of arms. Military organization, strategy and performance on the battlefield were, in the end,
decisive. But the civil war was also an exercise in mass mobilization
and state-building. It was a test of how far the two military regimes,
the Reds and the Whites, were able to enlist the support of the
population which they aspired to rule. Teodor Shanin explains:

> Much has been argued about the reasons why the "White Cause" (*Beloe
> delo*) was defeated by the Reds, who lacked, at least initially, the state-
> administrative know-how, the organized military forces, foreign support,
> basic equipment and international legitimation . . . The reasons since
> offered for the Bolsheviks' victory ranged from the stupidity of their foes
> and the marvels of Lenin's party organization, to geography (the centrality
> of Moscow and the country's size) and the mistaken military tactics adopted
> by the White Generals. All this, relevant as it may have been, disregards
> the fact that the civil war was fought not between Bolshevik party members
> and monarchist officers, but between armies in which both these groups
> were in a minority. In the conditions of civil war those armies' loyalties
> could not be taken for granted, and they thereby became a decisive element
> in defining the outcome of the battles. The ability to mobilise resources
> necessary for army operations was equally important . . . the recruits and
> the resources were not volunteered, but the question continually was how
> much would be volunteered, how much effort would be spent taking
> the rest, and how much was eventually at the disposal of the armies'
> command.[14]

This shortcoming in the Western literature is particularly surprising in the case of the Whites, given the abundant archival materials
available on this subject in the West. We still lack a detailed social
history of the counter-revolution and its armies. But the shortcoming
is especially apparent in the case of the Reds, where access to archival
materials has hitherto been very limited for Western historians.
Consequently, there has been a marked reliance in the West on the

[13] Typical of this approach are D. Footman, *Civil War in Russia* (London, 1961);
R. Luckett, *The White Generals* (London, 1971); J. Bradley, *Civil War in Russia, 1917-
1920* (London, 1975); P. Kenez, *Civil War in South Russia, 1918: The First Year of the
Volunteer Army* (Berkeley, 1971); P. Kenez, *Civil War in South Russia, 1919-1920: The
Defeat of the Whites* (Berkeley, 1977); E. Mawdsley, *The Russian Civil War* (London,
1987).
[14] T. Shanin, *The Roots of Otherness: Russia's Turn of Century*, ii, *Russia, 1905-07:
Revolution as a Moment of Truth* (London, 1986), pp. 200-1 (grammatical corrections
made to published source).

works of Soviet historians for information about the organization of the Red Army. Yet the latter have tended to underestimate and simplify the particular problems faced by the Bolsheviks in the mass mobilization of the peasants. It is to this subject, in the hope of redressing some of the imbalance in the literature, that the following pages are devoted.

I

THE RED ARMY IN 1918

The disintegration of the imperial army during the autumn and winter of 1917, and the absence of an adequate administrative apparatus in the countryside to enforce the conscription of the war-weary peasants, necessitated the foundation of the Red Army on volunteer principles during the early months of 1918. For those Bolsheviks who put a premium on the Red Guards, formed by the factory workers in 1917, as the proletarian nucleus of the revolutionary army, the volunteer principle had virtues in itself.[15] But, by and large, the first volunteer brigades of the Red Army came into being as a pragmatic and hasty response by local revolutionaries to the threat of Cossack or other counter-revolutionary forces. Most were formed by their local town soviet or trade unions to defend the railways and roads, although rural brigades were also common. They were small, irregular infantry brigades, numbering anything between 25 and 1,200 partisans, under the loose command of elected "officers". The majority functioned in a disorganized and eccentric manner. It was not uncommon for operative plans — which usually consisted of driving the enemy out of the immediate locality and then abandoning the military struggle — to be decided collectively by a show of soldiers' hands. Attacks were launched without adequate scouting of the enemy terrain, sometimes using no more than a school geography map. The soldiers fought in a fierce but undisciplined manner, too frequently succumbing to panic firing and breaking up ranks on first sight of the enemy. The military defeats of May and June at the hands of well-disciplined Cossack and Czech units made it clear to the majority of the Bolshevik leaders that there was an urgent need to reorganize the Red Army into an equally disciplined force, with regular regiments and divisions, and a centralized chain of command.[16]

[15] See J. Erickson, "The Origins of the Red Army", in R. Pipes (ed.), *Revolutionary Russia* (Harvard, 1968), pp. 233, 242; Benvenuti, *Bolsheviks*, p. 20.

[16] O. Figes, *Peasant Russia, Civil War: The Volga Countryside in Revolution (1917-1921)* (Oxford, 1989), p. 308; Tsentral'nyi gosudarstvennyi arkhiv oktiabr'skoi revoliutsii, Moscow (hereafter TsGAOR), f. 130, op. 2, d. 120, l. 27.

THE RED ARMY AND MASS MOBILIZATION 1918-1920   175

The majority of the earliest volunteers for the Red Army were either urban workers, or "vagabond, unstable elements that" — in Trotsky's words — "were so numerous at that time".[17] The former were probably in the minority. Of the 306,000 Red Army volunteers registered on 10 May 1918, only 34,000 were from the Red Guards, while 24,000 were from various other brigades (for example, party formations and food-requisitioning detachments).[18] Whereas N. I. Podvoiskii, the first People's Commissar of Military Affairs, had expected 300,000 urban workers from Moscow to join the Red Army during February 1918, the actual number amounted to no more than 20,000 (in Petrograd the figure was 6,000), and even these few had to be recruited "with the party's military organization working flat out".[19] Many of the volunteers — 70 per cent according to a survey by the Supreme Military Inspectorate in the autumn of 1918 — had previously been soldiers in the imperial army.[20] They had grown used to military life, or simply found it preferable to the harsh conditions and difficult adjustments of post-war civilian life (armed robbery was the easiest way for many of them to feed themselves in the semi-anarchic and hungry conditions of early 1918).[21] The urban unemployed, migrants, "hooligans" and criminal elements also made up a large contingent of the first Red Army volunteer units — as, indeed, they are almost bound to in any *armée revolutionnaire*.[22]

Partly because of their social origins, the volunteer brigades proved a highly unstable form of military organization. Too many signed up just to get a gun and some uniform before running off home, or deserting to sell their booty and start the process over again. Consequently the turnover of volunteers was very high. Many recruiting stations were even left without supplies for the new volunteers.[23] Too

[17] Trotsky, *How the Revolution Armed*, i, p. 5.

[18] N. Movchin, *Komplektovanie krasnoi armii* [The Recruitment of the Red Army] (Moscow, 1926), p. 36.

[19] *Ibid.*, p. 26.

[20] *Izvestiia Narodnogo Komissariata po Voennym Delam* [News of the People's Commissariat for Military Affairs], no. 10, 16 Jan. 1919, p. 3. See also V. D. Polikarpov, "Dobrovol'tsy 1918 goda" [The Volunteers of 1918], *Voprosy istorii* (1983), no. 2.

[21] The first Red Army detachments were known to rob and loot villages in many localities, especiallywhere they were responsible for food requisitioning. See, for example, TsGAOR, f. 130, op. 2, d. 443, ll. 38, 112; f. 393, op. 3, d. 327, ll. 278-9, 282; d. 334, l. 105; d. 337, l. 64; Figes, *Peasant Russia*, p. 101; I. N. Shteinberg, *In the Workshop of the Revolution* (London, 1953), pp. 153-5.

[22] Movchin, *Komplektovanie*, p. 85; Trotsky, *How the Revolution Armed*, i, p. 165. On the Jacobin armies, which suffered from similar problems, see R. Cobb, *The People's Armies*, trans. M. Elliot (New Haven and London, 1987), pp. 150-5.

[23] Movchin, *Komplektovanie*, p. 26; Trotsky, *How the Revolution Armed*, i, pp. 138-9; White, *Growth of the Red Army*, p. 31.

many brigades were formed in response to the immediate military threat, only to be disbanded once that threat had died away. The Supreme Military Inspectorate found that during the summer of 1918 the proportion of adult men volunteering for the Red Army from regions close to the civil war front was four times as high as in regions further away from the fighting. Above all, too few volunteers came from the stable farming peasantry, the majority of the toiling population. Even in the predominantly agricultural provinces of Voronezh and Kursk, only 49 per cent of the Red Army volunteers were registered as peasants, whereas industrial and unskilled workers comprised 43 per cent. In the semi-industrial provinces of Tver and Moscow, the latter provided as many as 62 per cent of the recruits. A similar proportion were bachelors (68 per cent were younger than thirty-one) — in other words, young men without a peasant family farm.[24] Most of those who had their own farm were more concerned to work on it and restore it to order after four years of war than to volunteer for military service in the Red Army.[25]

Given the inadequacies of the volunteer system, the Bolsheviks had little choice but to opt for a system of compulsory universal mobilization at the end of May, when the revolt of the Czech Legion and the establishment of the Samara government initiated a new period of full-scale civil war. In view of the weakness of the Soviet apparatus, and the impossibility of carrying out a nationwide mobilization, it was decided to call up only the most reliable recruits: the 21 to 22-year-old workers (born 1897-1896) of Moscow and Petrograd; and the 21 to 25-year-olds (1897-1893) in those military districts (Volga, Urals, Western Siberia) closest to the military front against the Samara regime. Similar mobilizations were called during the summer on a local basis, mainly in the northern and central regions of Russia (for example, in Vladimir, Perm and Viatka). Finally, the local party cells and the *kombedy* (Committees of Poor Peasants) each mobilized, in addition, approximately forty thousand Red Army recruits.[26]

The results of the mobilization reflected a wide discrepancy be-

[24] *Izvestiia Narodnogo Komissariata po Voennym Delam*, no. 10, p. 3. See further, Figes, *Peasant Russia*, p. 310.
[25] This may help to explain why the survey by the Supreme Military Inspectorate noted a general increase in the number of volunteers in September and October, after the end of the agricultural peak season. The establishment of volunteer brigades by the *kombedy* (Committees of Poor Peasants) and local party cells also accounts for the increase during these months.
[26] Movchin, *Komplektovanie*, pp. 42-50; Figes, *Peasant Russia*, p. 311.

THE RED ARMY AND MASS MOBILIZATION 1918-1920   177

tween the ability of the Bolsheviks to mobilize workers and their ability to mobilize peasants. Of the fifteen compulsory mobilizations between 12 June and 29 August, no less than eleven applied exclusively to urban workers. The mobilization of Moscow and Petrograd workers born between 1897-1896 went "without a hitch", according to Trotsky.[27] Of the ten to twelve thousand recruits anticipated from Moscow, nine thousand actually appeared.[28] Overall, as many as 200,000 workers were mobilized from Moscow and Petrograd during the summer and autumn of 1918.[29] Since it was well known that the authorities lacked the means, even in the biggest cities, to enforce the conscriptions (which should thus be seen as semi-voluntary), these figures should be seen as a reflection of the willingness of large numbers of workers to sign up for military service, given growing unemployment and food shortages in the cities. The urban population of Russia was at least halved during the civil war, as workers flooded into the Red Army and the countryside.[30]

The mobilization of the peasants, by contrast, produced disappointing results. Of the 275,000 recruits anticipated from the call-up of 1897-1893 in the civil war areas, only 40,000 actually appeared during the first two months (June and July).[31] Later mobilizations were more successful (overall, 890,000 recruits were registered between June 1918 and February 1919),[32] especially those called after the agricultural season. Peasants were reluctant to leave their farms before the harvest; most of those conscripted from the rural areas during the summer came from the mobile and proletarian margins of peasant society.[33] Also, by the autumn many peasants had suffered under White rule in the Volga and the Urals, and were consequently more likely to support the Red Army, at least on conditional terms.[34]

[27] Trotsky, *How the Revolution Armed*, i, p. 300.

[28] Movchin, *Komplektovanie*, p. 44.

[29] *Sovetskie vooruzhenye sily: istoriia stroitel'stva* [The Soviet Armed Forces: A History of their Development] (Moscow, 1978), p. 49.

[30] See generally D. Koenker, "Urbanization and Deurbanization in the Russian Revolution and Civil War", *Jl. Mod. Hist.*, lvii (1985).

[31] Molodtsygin, *Raboche-krest'ianksii soiuz*, p. 57.

[32] *Velikii oktiabr' i zashchita ego zavoevanii* [Great October and the Defence of its Conquests] (Moscow, 1987), pp. 41-2.

[33] Figes, *Peasant Russia*, pp. 310-11. Trotsky cited the devastating effect on army morale of a telegram from Volokolamsk *uezd* (district) in Moscow province, threatening to deprive of their "peasant status" (i.e. their rights in the peasant commune) all those soldiers who failed to return to their villages by 30 June, the beginning of the harvest season: see Trotsky, *How the Revolution Armed*, i, p. 429.

[34] On the relationship between the peasants' experience of White rule and their readiness to serve in the Red Army, see Figes, *Peasant Russia*, pp. 177-83, 314.

However, throughout 1918 the Red Army continued to experience difficulties in mobilizing the peasantry.

There were three main difficulties, according to a secret memorandum to Trotsky written in mid-May by M. D. Bonch-Bruevich, head of the Supreme Military Council: the lack of adequate food supplies, uniforms, boots, weapons, barracks accommodation and cash to provide for the new recruits; the shortage of officers to train and organize the recruits into proper military units; and the almost complete absence of a military apparatus in the localities.[35] The first was a problem for the Red Army throughout the civil war.[36] The shortage of officers (put at 55,000 in the early summer of 1918) was partially overcome during the summer by the call-up of N.C.O.s from the imperial army. It was later eradicated by the mobilization of "military specialists" (officers) from the same source.[37] But the last of the three problems — the weakness of the military apparatus in the localities — was probably the most serious difficulty facing the Bolsheviks in 1918. All the military authorities reporting on the progress of the mobilization campaign in the provinces during that summer and autumn stressed as their main problem the absence of experienced administrators, agitators and instructors.[38] Few *volosti* (rural townships) had their own military committee (Voenkom) integrated into the national structure of military command. One survey found that only 28 per cent of the *volosti* in European Russia had established a Voenkom as late as 1919.[39]

Refusing to set up a Voenkom in their locality proved a highly effective means for the peasants to sabotage the Red Army mobilization, since that organ was exclusively responsible for making an account of the population eligible for military service, enforcing the recruitment, arming and training the recruits, and sending them on to the higher authorities. Where a Voenkom was established at the *volost'* level, its work could easily be slowed down — and even brought to a halt — by the non-co-operation of the mir (village commune), since the register of those eligible for the military call-up

---

[35] TsGAOR, f. 130, op. 2, d. 120, ll. 67-8.

[36] See below, section III, pp. 190-8.

[37] *Velikii oktiabr'*, p. 48. On the Red Army's mobilization of N.C.O.s, see White, *Growth of the Red Army*, pp. 52-5. On the mobilization of "Tsarist officers" and other personnel from the imperial army, see A. G. Kavtaradze, *Voennye spetsialisty na sluzhbe respubliki sovetov, 1917-1920 gg.* [Military Specialists in the Service of the Soviet Republic, 1917-1920] (Moscow, 1988).

[38] TsGAOR, f. 130, op. 2, d. 120, l. 41.

[39] A. I. Lepeshkin, *Mestnye organy vlasti sovetskogo gosudarstva (1917-1920 gg.)* [Local Organs of the Soviet State (1917-1920)] (Moscow, 1957), p. 257.

THE RED ARMY AND MASS MOBILIZATION 1918-1920   179

required up to fifty different categories of information, most of which were available only from the mir. Throughout the early phases of the civil war, the Red Army suffered from grossly inaccurate methods of accounting. People were often called up who had died, disappeared or emigrated (migration, and employment on the railways, were two common ways to avoid military service). Sometimes more recruits turned up at the mobilization point than had been anticipated. The first full register of the population eligible for military service was not completed until the beginning of 1919, and it was only later that year, with the introduction of roll-call meetings (*poverochnye sbory*) at places of work, that it became remotely systematic. Until then the compulsory mobilizations were in effect semi-voluntary for, without reliable registers or a military infrastructure in the rural localities, the Red Army could not compel anyone to join it.[40]

Peasant resistance to the mobilization was widespread — and highly effective — in 1918. Many village communes and soviets passed resolutions condemning the civil war as an unnecessary "war between brothers" (*bratoubiistvennaia voina*) and calling on both sides to end it through negotiations.[41] Some even declared themselves "neutral zones" or "neutral republics" and formed their own brigades to keep the civil war armies out of their territory.[42] Others refused to implement the compulsory mobilization, but allowed volunteers to join up.[43] Where the military authorities sent recruiting brigades to enforce the conscription order, the latter were likely to meet open, and armed, peasant opposition. In Pskov province, peasant uprisings — many of them led by bands of deserters — were noted in dozens of *volosti* during the autumn of 1918 in protest against the Red Army mobilization.[44] Similar uprisings were noted during November and December in Moscow, Tula, Kaluga, Riazan', Tambov, Smolensk, Vitebsk, Mogilev and Samara provinces. Some involved peasants refusing to be conscripted or trained. Others consisted of newly mobilized recruits protesting against the requisitioning of their family's livestock (the households of Red Army soldiers were legally

[40] Movchin, *Komplektovanie*, pp. 43, 61, 154-7, 162-7.

[41] TsGAOR, f. 130, op. 2, d. 120, l. 54; Figes, *Peasant Russia*, pp. 312-13; M. Gavrilova, "Moe uchastie v grazhdanskoi voine" [My Part in the Civil War], *Krest'ianka* (1925), no. 5, p. 5.

[42] N. Rabichev, "Krasnaia armiia i rabota na sele" [The Red Army and Work in the Village], *Proletarskaia mysl'* (1923), no. 2, p. 41.

[43] Movchin, *Komplektovanie*, p. 49.

[44] "Iz istorii organizatsii krasnoi armii v Pskovskoi gubernii v 1918-19 gg." [From the History of the Organization of the Red Army in Pskov Province in 1918-19], *Krasnaia letopis'* (1930), no. 34 (1), pp. 73-5, 79.

exempt from taxes), the short supply of uniforms and food rations, or simply the lack of heating in army barracks.[45] A report by the chairman of the Military Revolutionary Tribunal, P. G. Smidovich, to the All-Russian Central Executive Committee (VTsIK) on the big peasant risings in Tula and Riazan' provinces during November concluded that one of their primary causes was the poor organization of the Red Army mobilization. Hundreds of horses requisitioned from the peasants had died for lack of feed. Some of the peasant recruits, having been forcibly conscripted, had been sent back home for want of a gun. Many others, fed up with conditions in the barracks, had deserted, taking with them their guns and forming armed detachments. These "Greens" (so called because they made the woods their strongholds) played a leading role in the peasant uprisings. Not surprisingly, the destruction of all local military records was one of their major objectives. "Where we went wrong", concluded Smidovich,

> was to declare the mobilization simultaneously throughout the region, since this enabled the peasants to unite against the central authorities, while making it difficult for the latter to concentrate their military forces and intervene effectively to enforce the recruitment. In future, the mobilizations should be spread out over time, and the conscripts taken out of the region in which they signed up as quickly as possible.[46]

II

MASS CONSCRIPTION

The Red Army's capture of Kazan' on 10 September proved a major turning-point in the history of the civil war. Until then, the Red Army had been in constant retreat on the crucial eastern front, surrendering town after town to the small but well-disciplined Czech and volunteer forces of the Samara government. The fall of Kazan', on 6 August, marked the high point of the anti-Bolsheviks' fortunes in the summer of 1918, bringing them within striking distance of Moscow itself. "For the first time", recalled Trotsky, "everyone realised that the country was facing mortal danger", and that Soviet power might fall.[47] It was this realization, argued Trotsky, that brought discipline back into Red Army ranks, and made possible the organization of a mass conscript army based on regular units with a centralized chain of command.[48]

[45] TsGAOR, f. 130, op. 2, d. 120, l. 45; Figes, *Peasant Russia*, p. 313.
[46] TsGAOR, f. 130, op. 2, d. 277, l. 183.
[47] Trotsky, *How the Revolution Armed*, i, p. 454.
[48] *Ibid.*, pp. 5-6.

THE RED ARMY AND MASS MOBILIZATION 1918-1920   181

Trotsky's was a romantic view, but not without an element of truth. The Kazan' campaign did indeed mark the beginning of the Red Army's growth on a mass scale. The experience — or fear — of White rule galvanized thousands of peasants into joining the Red Army. It is not coincidental that after 1918 more peasants were mobilized from the Volga military district than from any other in the Soviet Republic, since it was here that the peasantry had gained most from the redivision of gentry land during the revolution, and it was here that the threat of the White counter-revolution was greatest, with all the losses of land this would entail for the peasantry.[49] The Kazan' campaign also marked the start of the Red Army's reorganization on more disciplined and centralized lines. At the beginning of September the Soviet Republic was declared by the VTsIK to be a single military camp, headed by the RVSR under the chairmanship of Trotsky. On 11 September, the day after the capture of Kazan', the RVSR put forward its plan to reorganize the Red Army into five army groups, with eleven divisions, each consisting of six to nine regiments plus reserve units, on three properly structured fronts (eastern, northern and southern) and a fortified western area.[50] During the following three months, as Kolchak's White forces in western Siberia and Denikin's in the Don and the Kuban built up, the Bolsheviks were primarily concerned to work out how the fragile economic structure of the Soviet Republic could support the maximum number of soldiers. On 3 October Lenin declared at an enlarged meeting of the VTsIK that it had been "decided to have an army of one million men by the spring; now we need an army of three million. We can have it. *And we shall have it*".[51] Lenin's own Defence Council (*Sovet oborony*) was forced to conclude on 18 December that the Soviet economy could actually support an army of only 1.5 million, and 300,000 horses.[52] However, plans were simultaneously laid to conscript and train another million reserves through the Voenkoms of the military districts (*Voennye okruga*).[53] Although these reserve units developed slowly at first, we shall see that they were to become — in terms of numbers alone — the most important component of the Red Army in 1919-20.

The Red Army still experienced difficulties in mobilizing the

---

[49] See Figes, *Peasant Russia*, pp. 126-8, 314.
[50] Movchin, *Komplektovanie*, pp. 52-3.
[51] Lenin, *Collected Works*, xxviii, p. 102.
[52] *Velikii oktiabr'*, p. 42.
[53] TsGAOR, f. 130, op. 2, d. 120, ll. 50-1, 79.

peasantry during 1919. The disorganization of the military apparatus continued to present problems, especially in the far western areas, only recently liberated from German occupation,[54] and the Ukraine, where guerrilla methods continued to be effective.[55] Most recruitment stations experienced shortages of uniforms, boots, weapons and food; some even had to send conscripts home when the problem became too acute.[56] In parts of the north and west, such as Novgorod and Gomel', it was reported that famine conditions had made the conscription of the peasants impossible.[57] Even more so than in 1918, peasant uprisings against the mobilization were commonplace, many of them organized by the "Green" bands of deserters. At the height of the agricultural season, in June (when the rate of desertion reached its seasonal peak), the whole of the Red Army rear was engulfed by peasant uprisings. In Voronezh, Tambov and Saratov provinces the "Greens" numbered several thousand, and were well armed in organized bands that at times posed a serious threat to the Red Army rear on the southern front. The presence of "Green" bands several thousand strong, and a wave of peasant uprisings against the mobilization in Gomel', Vitebsk, Minsk and Smolensk provinces, were said to have presented a major threat to the Red Army on the western front during the summer, when it was pushed back towards the Dnepr by Polish forces. In Pskov, Novgorod, Tver, Yaroslavl', Kostroma, Vologda, Cherepovets, Moscow and Riazan' provinces, peasant uprisings were said to have combined in a highly effective manner with the deserters' bands to disrupt the mobilization, destroy the railways and lines of communication, and terrorize the local officials of Soviet power: "suppressed in one region, they soon broke out again in another as large-scale rebellions, sometimes with well-armed bands of up to several thousand men".[58]

Despite these problems, the Red Army grew rapidly in size during 1919. (See Table 1.) Two million recruits were enlisted in 1919 and a further two million by the end of 1920, when the overall size of the Red Army was estimated at over five million. Over 80 per cent of the

[54] See the reports from Vilna and Smolensk at the beginning of February 1919, in TsGAOR, f. 130, op. 3, d. 529, ll. 2-3, 6.

[55] Trotsky, *How the Revolution Armed*, i, pp. 457-9.

[56] TsGAOR, f. 130, op. 3, d. 449, ll. 1-2; d. 529, l. 12; Molodtsygin, *Raboche-krest'ianskii soiuz*, p. 63.

[57] TsGAOR, f. 130, op. 3, d. 422, l. 244; d. 529, l. 55.

[58] TsGAOR, f. 130, op. 3, d. 198, l. 14. See also S. Olikov, *Dezertirstvo v krasnoi armii i bor'ba s nim* [Desertion in the Red Army and the Struggle against it] (Leningrad, 1926), p. 27; Movchin, *Komplektovanie*, p. 138. For similar reports from 1920, see TsGAOR, f. 130, op. 4, d. 281.

THE RED ARMY AND MASS MOBILIZATION 1918-1920   **183**

TABLE 1
THE GROWTH OF THE RED ARMY IN 1919*

	Total size of the army at beginning of month	Recruits joining the army during month
January	800,000	65,000
February	1,000,000	240,000
March	1,400,000	345,000
April	1,500,000	110,000
May	1,700,000	155,000
June	1,900,000	200,000
July	2,100,000	200,000
August	2,300,000	110,000
September	2,400,000	95,000
October	2,500,000	70,000
November	2,600,000	225,000
December	2,800,000	160,000
January 1920	3,000,000	

* Source: N. Movchin, *Komplektovanie krasnoi armii* [The Recruitment of the Red Army] (Moscow, 1926), pp. 100-1.

recruits mobilized in 1919 were registered as peasants, a disproportionate number of them from central Russia itself.[59] Given the limitations of Bolshevik power in the countryside, how can we explain this rapid numerical growth?

First, a note of caution has to be added to the figures themselves. The number of registered Red Army men at any one moment included not only the active fighters, but also the wounded and sick, reserves, trainees, those on labour duty and in transit to the front. It also included those — a number running into tens of thousands — who had disappeared, or deserted from their unit and had not yet surrendered or been caught. Most of the apprehended deserters from the units — a number running into hundreds of thousands — were sent back to the reserves, where they were registered as Red Army men for a second time. Since the Bolsheviks had no effective means of checking, man by man, the deserters who left from one unit against those who returned to another, many Red Army men must have been counted more than once (and some even more than twice). Indeed, since the individual units were in fierce competition with each other over scarce supplies, they had a vested interest in concealing their losses through desertion in order to keep the number of men on Red Army rations artificially high. Thus the Red Army's real strength

[59] Thus the Red Army in the Ukraine was more Russian than Ukrainian: Gorlov, "O sotsial'noi strukture krasnoi armii", p. 57.

was a good deal smaller — and more variable — than suggested by the grandiloquent statistic of five million men so often cited in both Soviet and Western history books. It really only approximated to that number for the last three months of 1920, after which the Red Army was rapidly demobilized (only 1,428,000 soldiers were left by January 1922).[60] At the height of the civil war in the spring of 1919, there were 383,000 active fighters on the various fronts out of a total Red Army force of 1.8 million men — a ratio of fighters to eaters of 1:4.7.[61] That ratio varied during the civil war as a whole from about 1:3 in the units in the field to about 1:10 in the entire Red Army. It fluctuated seasonally in line with the rates of desertion and the general

TABLE 2

"EATERS" AND FIGHTERS IN THE RED ARMY 1920*

	Number on rations	Number of fighters	Ratio of fighters to eaters
Troops in the field			
1 June 1920	873,829	294,349	1: 3
1 August 1920	948,728	393,683	1: 2.4
Red Army in general			
1 June 1920	4,587,061	337,620	1: 13.6
1 August 1920	4,876,110	494,572	1: 9.9

* Source: Movchin, *Komplektovanie*, p. 229.

supply of foodstuffs. (See Table 2.) Even at the height of its strength, in October 1920, when the Red Army amounted to nearly 5.5 million men, there were 2,250,000 recruits undergoing training who had still not been formed into military units; 391,000 in reserve units; 159,000 in labour armies; and only 2,250,000 in the armies at the front, of whom no more than 700,000 would have been active fighters (and no more than 500,000 of these properly armed).[62] Given its enormous social and political significance, the Russian civil war was actually fought between miniscule armies (the forces deployed by either side on a given front rarely exceeded 100,000). Proportionate to the civilian population, this was no more than the number of fighters in the English civil wars of the 1640s.[63]

[60] Movchin, *Komplektovanie*, pp. 237-9, 259.
[61] *Velikii oktiabr'*, pp. 112-13.
[62] Movchin, *Komplektovanie*, pp. 228-9. John Maynard was not far off the mark when he wrote: "Though the Red Army in the Civil War ultimately totalled over five million men, it never had more than half a million rifles, and the maximum number of combatants in it never exceeded 600,000, with 700 guns and 2,800 machine-guns": H. J. Maynard, *The Russian Peasant: And Other Studies* (London, 1942), p. 116.
[63] During the English civil wars about 140,000 men were under arms out of a total population of about five million (2.8 per cent). During the Russian civil war perhaps four million men were armed and put into active units out of a total population of about 160 million (2.5 per cent).

THE RED ARMY AND MASS MOBILIZATION 1918-1920   185

The growth of the Red Army during 1919-20 was facilitated by several political factors. The completion of the military register allowed the Red Army to abandon the semi-voluntary "*volost'* mobilization" called at the end of April (whereby each *volost'* was to enlist and equip between ten and twenty recruits) and to concentrate instead on the universal mobilization of particular age groups. The results of the former had proved disappointing: of the 118,000 recruits anticipated (on the basis of twenty per *volost'*) from twenty-seven provinces in European Russia, only 13,633 (11.5 per cent) had actually appeared by the middle of June.[64] Part of the problem was that the *volost'* mobilization represented an unfairly heavy burden for the smaller *volosti*, whose authorities thus felt justified in ignoring it.[65] The conscription of all the males born in one year, to which the peasants had grown accustomed during the First World War, was seen to be fairer since it affected everyone equally (sometimes the peasants cast lots to see who should go to the army from the age groups called up).[66] It also created fewer administrative problems — the main one now being the tendency of the peasant communes to send to the army only those enlisted from the biggest household farms, on the grounds that the loss of an adult male worker was more likely to harm the smaller family farms.[67] This was said to have resulted in "kulak" elements joining the Red Army, which some commanders used to explain the poor military discipline and performance of their units.[68]

The enforcement of the universal mobilization was facilitated by a second political factor: the general strengthening of the Soviet apparatus in rural areas.[69] During 1919-20 the *volost'* soviets became more reliable, centralized and bureaucratized organs, under the domination

---

[64] Molodtsygin, *Raboche-krest'ianskii soiuz*, pp. 135, 254.

[65] For this reason, the instructions on the *volost'* mobilization were revised on 20 May to allow the smaller *volosti* to lower their recruitment quotas: *ibid.*, p. 134.

[66] TsGAOR, f. 130, op. 3, d. 529, l. 61; Movchin, *Komplektovanie*, pp. 72-3; Figes, *Peasant Russia*, p. 314.

[67] TsGAOR, f. 130, op. 3, d. 529, ll. 68, 70, 107. The result of this selection bias was that the larger peasant households tended to lose a higher proportion of their adult males to the army, which left them with a much less favourable ratio of consumers to workers compared with the smaller households, since they contained a relatively larger number of dependants. Thus the military conscription was likely to have encouraged the bigger households to partition — itself already a mass phenomenon during this period because of the threat of revolutionary expropriation: Figes, *Peasant Russia*, pp. 315-16.

[68] Figes, *Peasant Russia*, p. 314.

[69] On this subject generally, see *ibid.*, ch. 5.

of local Bolshevik party cadres. The whole apparatus of the *volost'* soviet was supposed to be subordinated to the immediate tasks of recruitment during the call-up period. The head of the Voenkom was to become the chairman of the soviet. The Voenkoms themselves were increasingly appointed by the higher military authorities rather than elected by the peasants, so that urban workers and party members tended to become a dominant element within them.[70] A final political factor behind the growth of the Red Army during 1919-20 was the tremendous effect of Bolshevik propaganda — a subject discussed elsewhere.[71]

The Red Army grew on an extensive rather than an intensive basis. In other words it called up more and more age groups rather than trying to increase the rate of recruitment from targetted groups or reducing the rate of desertion (this only became a priority after all the eligible age groups had been called up). The extensive system of mobilization inevitably developed into a vicious and recurrent cycle: as the number of recruits grew, so too did the pressure on military supplies; the number of deserters increased as a consequence, so that more and more reinforcements were required. As the chairman of the Military Inspectorate put it to Trotsky: "each new mobilization produces a diminishing percentage increase in the size of our armed forces".[72]

By June 1919, all the eligible age groups — bar the very youngest (1901) — had been mobilized. The call-up of 1901 was held back for as long as possible (and was only implemented during the war with Poland in 1920).[73] This was probably because of the burden which the call-up of this age group was likely to place on military supplies. For the younger age groups tended (with the exception of 1898-1897) to produce a higher rate of recruitment. (See Table 3.) When the Revolutionary Military Council of the Southern Front found itself in desperate need of reinforcements towards the end of June 1919, it called on Lenin and Trotsky to call up the youngest possible age groups, since "experience shows that the older the age group, the smaller tends to be the percentage of those called up actually being recruited. The shortfall ranges from 34 per cent in the youngest years to 90 per cent in the oldest".[74] This was no doubt partly because

[70] *Ibid.*, pp. 312-13.
[71] For an introduction to this subject, see P. Kenez, *The Birth of the Propaganda State: Soviet Methods of Mass Mobilization, 1917-1929* (Cambridge, 1985).
[72] Movchin, *Komplektovanie*, p. 131.
[73] Molodtsygin, *Raboche-krest'ianskii soiuz*, pp. 204-5.
[74] TsGAOR, f. 130, op. 3, d. 529, l. 89.

THE RED ARMY AND MASS MOBILIZATION 1918-1920   **187**

TABLE 3
MOBILIZATION OF VARIOUS AGE GROUPS 1918-1919*

Year of birth	Number turning up for recruitment
1901	550,000 (approx.)
1900	228,546
1899	292,139
1898	341,780
1898-1897	1,056,809
1896-1892	232,848
1892-1891	120,000
1890-1899	130,238
1890-1886	80,666

* Source: Movchin, *Komplektovanie*, pp. 57, 268-9.

younger men tended to be more healthy: 70 per cent of the 1900 cohort passed their army medical, compared with only 56 per cent of the 1890-1889 cohort.[75] It was also because a higher proportion of the older age groups comprised family men, with farms of their own. They had already fought in the 1914-17 war, and were now understandably reluctant to join any army. A final explanation of this phenomenon may be found in the greater revolutionary enthusiasm of the young, a factor constantly stressed by Trotsky himself: "We must draw into the work of creating the army the younger generations, the youth who have not yet experienced war, and who are always distinguished by the *élan* of their revolutionary spirit and their display of enthusiasm".[76]

There is another sense in which the growth of the Red Army could be characterized as "extensive". From the early summer of 1919, the Red Army pushed eastwards into the Urals and Siberia, forcing into headlong retreat both Kolchak's White army and the Allied interventionary forces. During the following autumn and winter, the Reds pushed southwards, forcing the Whites back into the Don, and then through the Kuban to the coast. The expansion of territory under Red occupation during the latter half of 1919 enabled the Bolsheviks to carry out mobilizations in the areas recently liberated from the Whites. This marked a shift in the conscription policies of the Red Army away from the principle of raising troops in the rear, and towards the practice of both mobilizing conscripts and forming military units directly behind the front. In fact mobilizations at the

[75] Movchin, *Komplektovanie*, p. 169.
[76] Trotsky, *How the Revolution Armed*, i, p. 166.

front had long since become a practical necessity for both civil war armies, since the to-and-fro movements of the front disrupted transport and supply lines from the rear, making the question of raising adequate reinforcements a constant headache for the military authorities. Less than 30 per cent of the Red Army's demand for reinforcements on the eastern, southern and northern fronts was satisfied from its rear army reserves during the winter of 1918-19.[77] On the eastern and southern fronts during the early months of 1919 the soldiers in the front-line units were deserting and falling sick or wounded much faster than reinforcements could be trained, equipped or despatched. To make matters worse, a large proportion of the reinforcements deserted *en route* to the front, or arrived there unfit to do any fighting because of illness, or lack of equipment or training. Trotsky called the Red Army reversals on the eastern front during the spring of 1919, which brought Kolchak's army to within a few days' march of the River Volga, a "crisis of reinforcements". Much the same verdict could be applied to virtually all the Red Army's major defeats.[78]

Trotsky, as head of the RVSR, was reluctant to allow front mobilizations to become a general practice given all the obvious military considerations: the importance of not antagonizing the civilian population behind the front through rapidly improvised mobilizations that were likely to break down into coercive methods; the poor discipline — and questionable motives — of so many of those recruited at the front; and (for Trotsky this was the key) the decentralization of the Red Army's military organization entailed by the front mobilizations (that is adopting the "guerrilla" or "partisan" methods advocated by the Military Opposition).[79] During the winter of 1918-19 the RVSR had sanctioned front mobilizations strictly in cases where the supply of trained reinforcements from the rear had completely broken down. But as this became the norm in 1919, it was forced to endorse the stop-gap measure of despatching untrained reinforcements to the front. This effectively gave the front armies the right to form their own military units, while turning the rear reserve armies, which had previously done this for them, into no more than temporary holding-stations for the mass of raw recruits awaiting

[77] P. Dmitrev, "Sozdanie strategicheskikh rezervov krasnoi armii v gody grazhdanskoi voiny" [The Creation of Strategic Reserves of the Red Army in the Civil War], *Voenno-istoricheskii zhurnal* (1974), no. 6, pp. 67-8.

[78] Movchin, *Komplektovanie*, pp. 79, 109-10, 272.

[79] Trotsky, *How the Revolution Armed*, ii, pp. 353, 377.

THE RED ARMY AND MASS MOBILIZATION 1918-1920   189

transfer to the front. According to one recent Soviet source, "the vast majority of military formations and units during the civil war . . . were formed not in the rear, but directly at the fronts, in the course of the fighting itself".[80] From forming their own units, it was but a short step for the front armies to carry out their own mobilizations as well. Indeed, during the course of 1919, they did this with increasing frequency, often with official approval from the central military authorities.[81]

In all, probably something in the region of half a million soldiers were mobilized on the Red Army fronts, usually when and where the civil war was at its fiercest. Some front mobilizations were carried out over a wide area prior to a major retreat so as not to leave potential recruits to the enemy. The entire male population between the ages of eighteen and forty was usually conscripted in these circumstances.[82] A more common type of front mobilization was that carried out by individual units in urgent need of reinforcements. Where there was enough time for the army to establish political structures and carry out agitation, such mobilizations could prove moderately effective, since many peasants were afraid of the Whites, and could be persuaded to join the Red Army if it was seen to refrain from violence and looting.[83] A typical example was the mobilization carried out by the 1st Brigade of the 41st Division during the struggle against the Poles and Petliura's Ukrainian forces near Odessa in May 1920. First, it mobilized the Odessa party organization, whose members were assigned to the political departments of the various regiments. Over the next two weeks, it raised six hundred volunteers through agitation, and organized them into recruitment brigades, along with pro-Communist soldiers selected from the regular units by their political departments. The recruitment brigades then went around the villages, agitating, shooting "traitors to the revolution" and mobilizing — by force if necessary — the able-bodied peasants. In the course of three and a half months, three thousand recruits were raised, along with a heavy-artillery division and a 645-man battalion. Two light-artillery

[80] Dmitrev, "Sozdanie", p. 66. S. I. Gusev, one of the Red Army's top commanders, put the proportion of units formed at the fronts at about two-thirds: S. I. Gusev, *Grazhdanskaia voina i krasnaia armiia* [The Civil War and the Red Army] (Moscow, 1958), p. 81.

[81] Movchin, *Komplektovanie*, pp. 89, 111-15.

[82] *Ibid.*, pp. 90-2.

[83] On the relationship between the peasants' fear of the Whites and their willingness to join the Red Army, see the military reports in TsGAOR, f. 130, op. 3, d. 449, l. 24. See also Olikov, *Dezertirstvo*, pp. 28-9; Trotsky, *How the Revolution Armed*, ii, p. 275; Figes, *Peasant Russia*, pp. 176-83, 314.

divisions were also reinforced.[84] Of course, it was common for mobilizations at the front to be done in a hurry, with the use of coercion. During May 1919 units of the 8th and 13th Armies in the Donbass region carried out forcible mobilizations at the Bakhmut coal-mines by occupying the pits and simply rounding up at gunpoint all the miners under the age of forty. When the Bakhmut authorities complained to the Defence Council in Moscow that this would bring coal production to a halt, Lenin wrote back defending the actions of the army as a necessary evil in time of civil war.[85]

III
PROBLEMS OF SUPPLY AND DISCIPLINE

A bad-tempered Trotsky told a conference of Red Army political workers in December 1919:

> We have mobilized millions, but our bayonets are numbered in hundreds of thousands. Somehow, an enormous number of soldiers have slipped through our fingers! . . . the expenditure of material that takes place in the army goes beyond our resources. The figures of the indents made by the Central Supply Administration or the Central Army Procurement Department are fantastic: tens of millions of pairs of underwear, many millions of overcoats, boots — for example, three or four pairs of boots per year per man! . . . Comrades, I don't want to frighten you, but I do want to say that, although we have not been brought down by Denikin or Kolchak, we may yet be brought down by overcoats or boots.[86]

The problem underlying Trotsky's observation was quite simple. The Red Army was growing too quickly — and losing too many deserters — for the Soviet economic system to support it. The problem went back to the winter of 1918-19, when the proliferation of the civil war on a national scale and the move towards mass conscription had coincided with — and directly contributed to — the almost complete collapse of the Soviet economy. The occupation at that time of the Ukraine, the Caucasus and the Urals by anti-Bolshevik forces, together with the blockade of the Baltic, the Black and the Caspian Seas by Allied and White naval forces, deprived the Soviet Republic of vital food and fuel supplies. Industrial discipline and production fell sharply in the hungry north, as workers flooded into the countryside in search of food, and factories closed down for want

[84] *Sbornik vospominanii neposredstvennykh uchastnikov grazhdanskoi voiny* [A Collection of Reminiscences by Direct Participants in the Civil War], ii (Moscow, 1922), pp. 129-33.

[85] TsGAOR, f. 130, op. 3, d. 529, ll. 33-4, 50. See similarly f. 130, op. 3, d. 422, l. 183.

[86] Trotsky, *How the Revolution Armed*, ii, pp. 108-9.

THE RED ARMY AND MASS MOBILIZATION 1918-1920   191

of fuel and raw materials. The transport system came to a virtual halt — or rather ceased to work for the state, becoming instead the main artery of the black-market network through which most Russians supported themselves during the civil war. Without the industrial base, the distribution system or indeed the political infrastructure to organize a stable market-based system of state relations with the peasantry, the Bolsheviks used increasing levels of coercion in order to obtain the peasant foodstuffs and recruits necessary for their civil war campaign. Yet, even by making production for the Red Army a top priority, they were unable to supply the millions of conscripts with adequate foodstuffs, uniforms, boots, weapons, transport, medical services and all the other paraphernalia of war. Supply and distribution — rather than production itself — lay at the heart of the problem. The devaluation of money and the rampant inflation of industrial prices resulted in the peasants reducing their food sales to the state and entering the black market, where exchange and barter with the townsmen proved more profitable. Thus the Bolsheviks were constantly faced with the problem of getting adequate stocks of food not only to the Red Army, but also to those workers in munitions and other state industries essential for the supply of basic military goods. The difficulties of transport in fuel-deprived Soviet Russia, especially during the winter and spring, when the climate became an added factor, exacerbated the distribution problem, as did the disorganization and voracious corruption of Soviet supply officials. Given these obstacles it was, as Trotsky detected, becoming an almost Sisyphean task to supply an army in which for every active fighter there were ten inactive men, and perhaps another five or so who had already deserted (taking with them, of course, their gun and their army coat).

The military reports on the supply situation received by the Defence Council during 1919-20 showed that virtually every division in the Red Army had at least some units with shortages of food, fodder, uniforms, footwear, weapons and bedding, or other goods of lesser importance, such as soap, tobacco, sugar and salt. It was not long before the Red Army ration set in February 1919 (0.4 kg. of bread per day) was recalled by the average soldier as only a distant fantasy.[87] Some unfortunate units, having advanced too far and been cut off

---

[87] The Red Army ration is detailed in *Izvestiia Narodnogo Kommissariata po Voennym Delam*, no. 36, 20 Feb. 1919, p. 4. The ration in the imperial army during the First World War was lowered to this level only at the end of 1916; it contributed to the mutiny of the Petrograd garrison during the February revolution of 1917.

from their supply stations, were forced to go several days, and sometimes even weeks, without food, during which time some men inevitably starved.[88] Horses died or simply fell from exhaustion in all parts of the army throughout the civil war, partly because of disease, but much more often because of simple shortages of fodder.[89] The supply of uniforms was so bad — with 60 per cent, and even up to 90 per cent, of the men in some units going without one — that fights often broke out between the soldiers, especially during the winter, when the possession of a warm army coat could make the difference between life and death. Thousands of Red Army men fell ill, or died from the cold, during the harsh winter of 1919-20.[90] The supply of shoes was not such a serious problem, if only because most infantry-men wore bast shoes, which were easily fabricated by local peasant craftsmen.[91] But lack of adequate footwear was sometimes known to prevent whole units leaving the confines of their barracks.[92]

By all accounts, the outward appearance of the Red Army units was ragged.[93] Even Lenin was taken aback by the model troops taking part in the Red Square parade on the first anniversary of the October revolution. "Look at them, how they march", he was heard to say, "like bags of sand".[94] As for the supply of weapons, once Tsarist stocks ran out in 1919, Soviet production — especially of rifle ammunition — fell increasingly behind demand.[95] In May 1919, as his eastern and southern fronts collapsed, I. I. Vatsetis, Main Commander-in-Chief, reported to the Defence Council that the sup-ply of ammunition was heading for "catastrophe". While the army was firing between seventy and ninety million rounds a month, the main arsenal at Tula was producing only twenty million. Moreover important armaments factories on the eastern front (for example, Votkinsk, Izhevsk and Lugansk) had recently been captured by the Whites.[96] Trotsky was to look back on this period as a critical crisis,

[88] TsGAOR, f. 130, op. 3, d. 192, l. 30; d. 414, ll. 109-13; d. 422, ll. 184, 202; d. 443, l. 4; Tsentral'nyi gosudarstvennyi arkhiv narodnogo khoziaistva, Moscow (hereafter TsGANKh), f. 3429, op. 1, d. 1487, ll. 33, 121. For a general report on food supply conditions in the Red Army at the end of 1920, see TsGANKh, f. 3429, op. 1, d. 1586, ll. 8 ff.

[89] TsGAOR, f. 130, op. 3, d. 414, ll. 109-13.

[90] TsGAOR, f. 130, op. 3, d. 414, ll. 109-13; d. 436, l. 9.

[91] On the supply of bast shoes and other products to the Red Army by peasant craftsmen, see Figes, *Peasant Russia*, p. 293.

[92] TsGANKh, f. 3429, op. 1, d. 1487, l. 88.

[93] White, *Growth of the Red Army*, pp. 115-17.

[94] *Ibid.*, p. 118.

[95] Mawdsley, *Russian Civil War*, pp. 183-4.

[96] *Direktivy glavnogo komandovaniia krasnoi armii (1917-1920): sbornik dokumentov* [Directives of the High Command of the Red Army (1917-1920): A Collection of Documents] (Moscow, 1969), p. 320; *Velikii oktiabr'*, p. 136.

THE RED ARMY AND MASS MOBILIZATION 1918-1920   193

when "every one of a soldier's stock of cartridges counted . . . and when a delay in the arrival of a special train bringing ammunition resulted in whole divisions retreating".[97]

Another major problem for the Red Army was the spread of epidemics. More people died in the civil war from disease than from battle.[98] Typhus, influenza, smallpox, cholera, typhoid and venereal diseases were the main killers, but many more men suffered from various skin rashes, stomach bugs, dysentery and toothache. On average, perhaps about 10-15 per cent of the men in a given unit would be ill on any one day. But it was not unusual for a unit to be taken out of operation by rates of illness of up to 80 per cent.[99] The inadequacy of medical checks on new recruits meant that many brought illnesses with them into the army.[100] But the real cause of the problem lay elsewhere: first, in the unhygienic conditions of an army where soap was a rarity, and the men were known to be on the move without washing for several weeks on end; and secondly, in the chronic shortages of doctors, nurses, hospital space, transport facilities for the sick and wounded, medicines, alcohol, bandages, antiseptic, food and so on.[101] Part of the problem was that the rapid to-and-fro movements of the civil war fronts made it impossible to set up proper field hospitals and dressing stations with good transport connections to the rear. In these circumstances — which were all too common (especially in the Ukraine) — the sick and wounded could neither be swiftly evacuated, nor properly cared for at the front.[102] Trotsky complained bitterly in June 1919 about the poor treatment received by wounded Red Army men on the southern front:

> Transports arrived by rail at Liski station containing wounded men who were in a frightful condition. The trucks were without bedding. Many of the men lay, wounded and sick, without clothes, dressed only in their underwear, which had long remained unchanged: many of them were

[97] Trotsky, *How the Revolution Armed*, i, p. 13.

[98] For a brief survey of the published figures, see Mawdsley, *Russian Civil War*, pp. 285-6.

[99] TsGAOR, f. 130, op. 3, d. 192, ll. 3, 5; d. 347, ll. 47, 122, 149, 209, 253, 332; d. 414, l. 114; d. 105, l. 21; d. 436, l. 15; TsGANKh, f. 3429, op. 1, d. 1487, l. 151; *Izvestiia Narodnogo Kommissariata po Voennym Delam*, no. 8, 14 Jan. 1919, p. 4.

[100] Movchin, *Komplektovanie*, p. 167.

[101] On such matters, see particularly TsGAOR, f. 130, op. 3, d. 414, l. 114; d. 192, l. 5; d. 436, l. 8; f. 5451, op. 3, d. 78, l. 7; G. S. Pukhov, "Stroitel'stvo krasnoi armii v Petrograde i okruge" [The Development of the Red Army in Petrograd and its District], *Krasnaia letopis'* (1929), no. 6 (33), p. 95.

[102] *Izvestiia Narodnogo Kommissariata po Voennym Delam*, no. 175, 12 Aug. 1919, p. 1; *ibid.*, no. 192, 3 Sept. 1919, p. 1.

infectious. There were no medical personnel, no nurses and nobody in charge of the trains. One of the trains, containing over 400 wounded and sick Red Army men, stood in the station from early morning until evening, without the men being given anything to eat. It is hard to imagine anything more criminal and shameful![103]

Trotsky blamed bad management and red tape for the problem. But there was in fact a policy, at least from November 1919, of deliberately *not* evacuating those with infectious diseases, and of forbidding passenger transport into the infected front-line zones, for fear of spreading the diseases to the civilian rear.[104] It was this policy, above all, that was to blame for the overcrowding in hospitals near the civil war fronts, and the truly horrific scenes of sick and wounded men sitting for days on end, without food or attention, in unheated third-class carriages at God-forsaken railway stations.

The problems of supplying the army from stores in the rear encouraged many units to supply themselves from local army depots, civilian institutions and, indeed, the population itself. Virtually every army unit was forced to practise "self-feeding" at some point in its life, especially when it was cut off from the main supply base because it had advanced into enemy — or inaccessible — terrain. The Caucasus Army Group, for example, having advanced deep into the northern Caucasus (hundreds of miles from its supply base at Tsaritsyn) during the winter of 1919-20, had little choice but to feed itself from the local population; between 71 per cent (in the case of millet) and 97 per cent (vegetables) of its food was supplied in this fashion between October 1919 and March 1920.[105] In parts of the Ukraine, where much of the Red Army's fighting was done by peasant-guerrilla units (such as Makhno's) without a supply base at all, self-feeding remained the norm throughout the civil war.[106] Elsewhere, it was often no more than the sheer incompetence and corruption of the Soviet officials running the army supply system that forced the units to feed themselves from local resources. Trotsky, whose impatience with the "criminal red-tape-ism of the army supply organs" was notorious, advocated legalizing independent procurements by the local Red Army units — and even private trade! — in the struggle to overcome

[103] Trotsky, *How the Revolution Armed*, ii, p. 298.
[104] TsGAOR, f. 130, op. 3, d. 347, ll. 35, 84, 110. It was the Main Military-Sanitary Administration that, in November 1919, passed the resolution "categorically forbidding the evacuation from the front to the rear of anyone infected with contagious diseases, with the exception of the Turkestan front". Those from the latter were to be evacuated only as far west as Syzran', Simbirsk or Kazan'.
[105] Bubnov, *Grazhdanskaia voina, partiia i voennoe delo*, p. 44.
[106] M. Malet, *Nestor Makhno in the Russian Civil War* (London, 1982), p. 99.

THE RED ARMY AND MASS MOBILIZATION 1918-1920   195

shortages. This was a far cry from his views on strict centralization, which he applied in all other areas of military organization.[107]

As in the White Army (and no doubt every army since time began), the practice of independent procurements often broke down into looting, uncontrolled requisitioning, and conflict between Red Army units. It was not uncommon for the latter to carry around with them their own supplies (and sometimes their families too) in long lines of carts, for fear of being left without them. Sometimes the units occupied local factories and farms in order to control the production of basic goods.[108] This inevitably antagonized the local Soviet organs of power, as did the Red Army's seizure of foodstuffs from railway stations, government granaries and food collection points under the control of Narkomprod (the People's Commissariat of Food Supply). Hundreds of local provisions committees complained to the central authorities during the autumn and winter of 1918-19 that Red Army units interfered in their work, redirecting foodstuffs from the civilian sector to the military.[109] Even greater friction was caused when the Red Army resorted to requisitioning directly from the civilian population itself, as they all too frequently did, for this often broke down into violence and robbery. Although the Red Army probably managed to maintain a better record on this issue than the Whites,[110] its rank-and-file soldiers frequently became involved in violent looting, especially when passing through non-Russian (particularly Jewish) areas. The Red Army, it is important to bear in mind, was predominantly Russian in its ethnic composition. Even units conscripted in the Ukraine and other non-Russian regions (for example, the Tatar Republic) were largely made up of Russians.[111] Anti-Semitism was a powerful and growing force in the Red Army during the civil war, despite the fact that a Jew, Lev Davidovich Trotsky

[107] Trotsky, *How the Revolution Armed*, ii, pp. 72-4 (July 1919).

[108] TsGAOR, f. 130, op. 2, d. 743, l. 118; op. 3, d. 192, l. 34; TsGANKh, f. 3429, op. 1, d. 857, ll. 63-4; d. 1245, l. 27; d. 1485, l. 450; Trotsky, *How the Revolution Armed*, i, p. 13. It may be that such practices owed something to the traditions of the imperial army before 1914, when the soldiers were made largely responsible for their own upkeep. Sometimes organized into regimental artels, they spent much of their time in economic activities: J. Bushnell, *Mutiny and Repression: Russian Soldiers in the Revolution of 1905-06* (Indiana, 1985), pp. 11-15. During the civil war, Red Army units were deployed for specific economic tasks, such as harvest work, timber-felling or road-repairs.

[109] See, for example, TsGANKh, f. 1943, op. 1, d. 448, l. 87; d. 223, ll. 113, 223, 224, 273, 351; d. 513, ll. 99, 242; op. 4, d. 116, l. 82.

[110] See D. V. Lehovich, *White against Red: The Life of General Anton Denikin* (New York, 1974), pp. 325-7.

[111] Gorlov, "O sotsial'noi strukture krasnoi armii", p. 57.

(Bronstein), stood at its political head. Trotsky received hundreds of reports about his own soldiers' violence and looting in Jewish-Ukrainian settlements, some of which he must have known from his youth.[112] Mass murders and robberies of the civilian population were also carried out by the Red Army in Bashkir regions during March 1919, partly as a result of antagonisms between the Russian regulars and Bashkir volunteer units allied to the Reds.[113]

Within the Red Army itself, the poor and irregular supply of foodstuffs and goods resulted in the frequent breakdown of discipline. Drunkenness was perhaps the most common — one might say universal — form of indiscipline, along with card-playing and generally rowdy behaviour. As the Red Army pushed southwards into the Ukraine during the autumn and winter of 1919, one of Trotsky's main anxieties was that this was a region "well-stocked with alcohol in all its forms, and we may take a heavy fall as a result of that".[114] Soldiers found drinking were ordered to be shot in a number of Red Army units on the southern front during this campaign.[115] The other really major problem — the refusal of units to carry out orders, or to recognize the authority of officers appointed by Moscow — was also broadly associated with the Red Army's advance into the Ukraine, where the authority of the Soviet regime (or any state authority) was almost non-existent, and guerrilla-style warfare by partisan brigades still predominated. Several top commanders blamed the reverses suffered by the Red Army in the Ukraine during the spring and early summer of 1919 on the influence of anarchist elements (for example Makhno), whose agitation among the rank-and-file soldiers, calling on them to obey only their elected officers and to return to the principles of army democracy embodied in the soldiers' committees of 1917, was said to have undermined all military discipline. Daily reports were received about soldiers demanding leave and better provisions; refusing to take up positions; lapsing into banditry and looting; killing army officers, Jews and Communists; and deserting in whole units to the rear. Some units were also said to have called for Ukrainian independence.[116]

[112] TsGAOR, f. 130, op. 3, d. 192, ll. 26-35; d. 422, ll. 256, 267; d. 436, l. 12; d. 449, ll. 118-19, 142, 143, 180.

[113] TsGAOR, f. 130, op. 3, d. 184, ll. 37-8, 72, 76. On the alliance between the Bashkir forces and the Red Army, see further R. Pipes, *The Formation of the Soviet Union: Communism and Nationalism, 1917-1923* (Cambridge, Mass., 1964), pp. 162-3.

[114] Trotsky, *How the Revolution Armed*, ii, p. 113. In so far as the Whites occupied the alcohol-rich regions for most of the civil war, it is logical to assume that they suffered more than the Reds from this problem.

[115] TsGAOR, f. 130, op. 3, d. 414, l. 117; d. 422, l. 267.

[116] TsGAOR, f. 130, op. 3, d. 192, ll. 27-30; d. 422, ll. 164, 267; d. 449, l. 139.

(cont. on p. 197)

But such indiscipline was not limited to the Ukraine. Virtually every Red Army division had units to report where the men had refused to carry out orders, or had threatened not to fight until promised leave or better conditions. Some reported cases where the men had protested against taking in new recruits and prisoners, because of the added burden on food supplies that this would entail.[117] It was commonplace for officers and administrative staff to receive threats — and become the victims — of physical violence from the rank-and-file soldiers, especially if they were suspected (often with justification) of corruption in handling army supplies and wages; or if they were simply seen to be too well dressed, fed and supplied with vodka and women; or if — indeed, worst of all — they were accused of restoring the disciplinarianism of the old imperial army, authorizing capital and other physical punishments for soldiers failing to carry out orders. It was often said — though not proved — that the "Tsarist officers" appointed by Trotsky from the imperial staff were particularly mistrusted by the soldiers because of their upper-class origins and alleged record of treason.[118]

Soldiers' uprisings were also widespread, most of them sparked by material shortages, official corruption or some punishment popularly deemed by the soldiers as unjust. These uprisings usually culminated in the occupation of the military headquarters, the arrest or murder of the officers and commissars, and the election of new commanders. But some spread into the civilian sector, often on account of rumours — many of them no doubt true — that the Soviet organs had held up military supplies or provisions for soldiers' families. Army

(n. 116 cont.)
Trotsky agreed that "guerrilla-ism" had been largely to blame for the collapse of the Ukrainian front, perhaps because it suited his arguments for strict military centralization against the demands of the Military Opposition for looser partisan units: Trotsky, *How the Revolution Armed*, ii, pp. 109-10, 308, 323.

[117] TsGAOR, f. 130, op. 3, d. 105, ll. 207-8; d. 422, ll. 34, 43, 59, 61, 208; d. 449, l. 97; d. 192, ll. 26-7, 34.

[118] TsGAOR, f. 130, op. 3, d. 414, ll. 17-21, 105-6; d. 422, ll. 11, 20, 31, 43, 191; d. 525, l. 27; f. 4085, op. 1, d. 14, ll. 25-6, 63-4; TsGANKh, f. 3429, op. 1, d. 857, ll. 57-8. See also Trotsky, *How the Revolution Armed*, ii, pp. 113, 116. On the soldiers' attitudes towards "Tsarist officers", see *ibid.*, p. 140; Benvenuti, *Bolsheviks*, pp. 37, 66-70; White, *Growth of the Red Army*, pp. 50-3, 60-1. In fact there is evidence to suggest that the "Tsarist officers" were less likely than "Red officers" or others (e.g. former N.C.O.s and untrained officers) to desert to the enemy or commit a criminal offence (such as theft of military stores). Between 3 August and 12 November 1919 there were sixty reported cases of desertion to the enemy and sixty reported cases of flight from battle by former ("Tsarist") officers, compared with 373 reported cases of desertion to the enemy and 416 reported cases of flight from battle by "Red" or other officers: TsGAOR, f. 130, op. 3, d. 453, ll. 2-46.

depots were seized and ransacked, or the local town occupied, where shops and stores were usually looted and Communist officials arrested or shot. In some towns, especially where a garrison was situated, the soldiers installed in power a new soviet dominated by soldiers' delegates.[119]

Even where the officers retained enough authority to march their men into battle, they could do little to prevent them from running away as soon as the first shots were fired. The Red Army, in more or less any battle, was likely to lose more soldiers through panic desertions than actual fighting: of the 294,000 "lost" by the Reds between February and April 1920, for example, only 20,000 were killed or wounded.[120] On several occasions during 1918-19, Trotsky had cause to complain about the ways in which Red Army operational reports were written to "conceal and cover up one's failures and exaggerate one's successes":

> When our units capture some locality, this never happens, if the reports are to be believed, otherwise than after a fierce battle. Yet this "battle" is, more often than not, an affair of aimless and fruitless shooting, that is, of squandering of cartridges and shells . . . When our units retreat, this happens, if one is to believe these same reports, only as a result of the onslaught of superior enemy forces and, again, never without a battle. Yet what is often hidden under these phrases is the sad reality of a panicky abandonment of their positions by large units at the sight of isolated mounted patrols, or even just under the influence of panic and provocational rumours about the enemy's approach.[121]

All this is reminiscent of Jaroslav Hasek's Schweikian hero, Gashek, the *Red Commissar* in the Bugulma stories. When the Whites break through his unit's lines on the River Ik and attack from the right, he orders his troops to retreat to the left, and sends a telegram to military headquarters: "Great victory. Positions on the river Ik broken through. We are attacking from all directions. Cavalry in enemy's rear. Heaps of prisoners".[122]

IV

DESERTION

The problems of supply and discipline were largely to blame for the astronomical rates of desertion from the Red Army during 1919-20.

[119] TsGAOR, f. 130, op. 3, d. 184, l. 4; d. 422, ll. 4, 31, 107, 247; d. 414, l. 25; op. 2, d. 631, ll. 4, 6, 8, 13-14, 32, 38, 42-3; d. 648, ll. 1, 7, 8, 12; d. 751, l. 99.
[120] Movchin, *Komplektovanie*, p. 225.
[121] Trotsky, *How the Revolution Armed*, ii, pp. 287, 288; see also *ibid.*, i, p. 483.
[122] J. Hasek, *The Red Commissar*, trans. C. Parrott (London, 1983), p. 23.

THE RED ARMY AND MASS MOBILIZATION 1918-1920   **199**

Table 4 shows that from June 1919 to June 1920 as many as 2,638,000 deserters were registered by the Central Committee for Struggle against Desertion (*Ts.K. po bor'be s dezertirstvom*) and its local organs, upon whose figures the table is based. (See Table 4.) During the same period, the overall size of the Red Army grew from about 1,900,000 to 4,600,000 — an increase of 2,700,000.[123] In other words, the Red Army was losing through desertion as many men as it was successfully recruiting. If we add the best available estimates for the number of deserters from the summer of 1918 to the summer of 1919 (576,000), and for the latter half of 1920 (500,000), then we arrive at a rough figure for the whole of the civil war period of 3,714,000.[124] The number of unregistered deserters is anyone's guess — perhaps something in the region of one million.

Most of the deserters in Table 4 were registered as "weak-willed" (*po slabosti voli*), meaning they had gone missing for less than fourteen days, or had turned up after fourteen days with a "reasonable excuse". "Malicious" (*zlostnye*) deserters were deemed to be those who had gone for more than fourteen days; run away with Red Army property; deliberately concealed themselves at the time of the call-up; resisted arrest; or deserted more than once.[125]

A common form of "hidden desertion" by the "weak-willed" in the rear was to find a job in a Soviet institution, or in some essential sector of the economy (such as the railways or timber-felling) where, on account of the shortage of manpower, it was in the interests of their employer to apply on their behalf to the relevant authorities for an exemption from military service.[126] However, the majority in this category were registered as "deserters" simply because they had failed to turn up on time at the recruiting station. Sometimes this was for no other reason than the late arrival of the army's conscription apparatus (that is agitators, copies of instructions and decrees, and so on). S. Olikov, the major authority on desertion from the Red Army, who had first-hand experience of dealing with it, knew of whole districts during the civil war where even the representatives of the Soviet regime knew nothing of the mobilization orders.[127] Many of these "deserters" did eventually appear at the recruiting station,

---

[123] Movchin, *Komplektovanie*, pp. 101, 229.
[124] *Ibid.*, p. 130; Olikov, *Dezertirstvo*, p. 33.
[125] Olikov, *Dezertirstvo*, p. 27; Molodtsygin, *Raboche-krest'ianskii soiuz*, p. 138.
[126] TsGANKh, f. 3429, op. 1, d. 529, l. 10; Olikov, *Dezertirstvo*, p. 76; Trotsky, *How the Revolution Armed*, ii, pp. 127, 199; Figes, *Peasant Russia*, p. 311.
[127] Olikov, *Dezertirstvo*, pp. 38, 82.

TABLE 4
DESERTION FROM THE RED ARMY 1919-1920*

	Total	Registered deserters (in thousands)				Caught in raids	Caught on railways	Caught elsewhere
		Malicious	Weak-willed	From units in military districts[a]	Surrendered voluntarily			
1919								
June	200	8	192	—	156	31	3	10
July	266	4	262	17[c]	205	54	2	5
August	284	14	270	40	188	78	6	12
September	262	18	244	13[c]	155	90	10	7
October	191	13	178	14[c]	91	78	7	15
November	170	8	162	30	93	64	6	7
December	172	30	142	12[b]	87	61	6	8
1920								
January	175	25	150	35	101	60	6	8
February	137	21	116	19[b]	62	54	4	17
March	188	30	158	22[b]	88	70	9	21
April	129	22	107	48	42	61	8	18
May	214	35	179	33[b]	108	78	11	17
June	250	30	220	28[b]	155	58	11	26
Total (13 months)	2,638	258	2,380	—	1,531	837	89	181

* Notes and source: Tsentral'nyi gosudarstvennyi arkhiv oktiabr'skoi revoliutsii, Moscow, f. 130, op. 3, d. 198, ll. 17-18, 26, 33, 36, 42, 60, 63, 70, 72, 100-1, 105-6, 115, 125-6; op. 4, d. 281, ll. 5, 10, 16-17, 21-2, 24, 26, 30, 32, 42-3, 50-1, 56-7; Movchin, *Komplektovanie*, p. 133.
[a] Figures incomplete
[b] Figures for first half of month only
[c] Figures for second half of month only

THE RED ARMY AND MASS MOBILIZATION 1918-1920　　201

some of them calling themselves "volunteers".[128] This explains the large number of deserters registered in Table 4 as having surrendered voluntarily to the authorities.

The primary motivation of these deserters was economic. Some just wanted a temporary escape from the appalling conditions of army life. Others went off for a few days to provide for their families, most of whom had never received the welfare benefits (state pensions, food and clothing rations, and agricultural assistance) promised to them by the government during the recruitment campaigns.[129] But there were probably just as many cases of soldiers running away to get food from the local villages, especially when their army rations failed to come through. A good pair of army boots and a rifle, or a winter coat, could usually buy enough bread for a dozen or so hungry men.[130] In the autumn, large numbers of Red Army men without a warm coat ran off to get one for the winter campaign.[131] But the level of temporary desertions reached its peak in the summer, when the peasant soldiers returned to their farms for the agricultural season.[132] (See Table 4.) This seasonal variation was obviously most pronounced in the central agricultural region (mainly contained in the military district of Orel), where the weekly number of registered deserters from July to September (between twenty thousand and forty thousand) was up to ten times higher than the corresponding figures for October to December (two thousand to seven thousand). In the semi-industrial military district of Moscow, by contrast, the weekly summer figures (five thousand to twenty-four thousand) were only slightly higher, overall, than the weekly figures for October to December (nine thousand to twelve thousand).[133]

The tendency of soldiers to desert during the harvest season posed one of the major problems of constructing a national army out of peasant conscripts. During the early phases of the civil war, when most of the fighting was done on a local basis, the Red Army partisan brigades had managed to retain close ties with the villages: the latter fed and equipped their own soldiers, who returned home between

[128] TsGAOR, f. 5451, op. 3, d. 113, l. 8; Olikov, *Dezertirstvo*, p. 84.
[129] Figes, *Peasant Russia*, pp. 318-19.
[130] TsGAOR, f. 130, op. 3, d. 198, l. 113; Trotsky, *How the Revolution Armed*, iii, p. 18. In the cities deserters from the Red Army were known to sell forged ration cards: TsGAOR, f. 130, op. 4, d. 281, l. 12.
[131] Olikov, *Dezertirstvo*, p. 29.
[132] TsGAOR, f. 130, op. 3, d. 422, ll. 22, 59; op. 3, d. 198, l. 35; Olikov, *Dezertirstvo*, p. 51.
[133] TsGAOR, f. 130, op. 3, d. 198, ll. 18, 26, 33, 36, 42, 72, 101, 106, 115, 126.

military campaigns. The spread of the civil war, and consequently the reorganization of the Red Army on a national scale, threatened these ties, since the peasant conscript was likely to be sent off to fight a long way from his village. Indeed it became a matter of deliberate policy, as part of the struggle against desertion, to send recruits as far away as possible from their native region.[134] Hence many desertions took place from the military units in transit from their place of formation in the rear to the armies at the front (one source estimated that the figure accounted for 18 to 20 per cent of all desertions).[135] According to a survey by the Moscow military authorities in 1919, 23 per cent of deserters questioned had run away because their unit was due to go to the front, while 44 per cent had deserted because their unit was close to — or passing by — their home village.[136] The number of soldiers lost from any one echelon *en route* to the front varied, on average, between 10 and 20 per cent, but at times the figure crept up to 50 per cent, 70 per cent and sometimes even higher, if the men were badly fed and supervised during the journey.[137]

Fewer soldiers deserted from the front-line units — a number, in all, representing perhaps 5 to 7 per cent of the total number of desertions from the Red Army.[138] Some came under the category of "malicious" deserters, since they would not return voluntarily to the ranks, and if arrested, were likely to run off again, perhaps joining one of the many "Green" bands which roamed the woods, living from banditry.[139] Panic flight from the battlefield to the rear or (less likely) to the enemy probably accounted for the majority of those deserting from the front-line units, especially during a general retreat. "The natives of districts being abandoned", explained one of the Red Army's top commanders, "desert in order to remain near their homes. Thus, during an offensive the advancing party is continuously strengthened, while the retreating party is continuously weakened".[140]

[134] For figures on the location of army recruits relative to their place of birth, see Movchin, *Komplektovanie*, p. 246.

[135] *Ibid.*, p. 124.

[136] Molodtsygin, *Raboche-krest'ianskii soiuz*, p. 141.

[137] TsGAOR, f. 130, op. 3, d. 184, l. 34; d. 198, ll. 16, 22, 24, 38, 103-4; 124; d. 199, ll. 28-9; d. 422, l. 21; op. 4, d. 281, ll. 29, 65; d. 282, ll. 19-21; Olikov, *Dezertirstvo*, pp. 30-1; White, *Growth of the Red Army*, p. 102; Movchin, *Komplektovanie*, p. 117.

[138] Movchin, *Komplektovanie*, p. 124.

[139] In all, fifty thousand Red Army deserters were said to have deserted more than once between June 1919 and June 1920: *ibid.*, p. 137.

[140] M. N. Tukhachevskii, *Izbrannye proizvedeniia* [Collected Works], i (Moscow, 1964), pp. 41-2.

THE RED ARMY AND MASS MOBILIZATION 1918-1920   203

One of the main causes of desertion from the front-line units — in the White as well as the Red Army — was the poor training and preparation given to reinforcements before being despatched to the front.[141] The lack of facilities and personnel to organize military training in the rear, and the constant demand for reinforcements, meant that units were sent to the front often with no more than a few days training (and increasingly without any training at all).[142] By the summer of 1919, only 800,000 recruits had been trained out of a total Red Army force of 2,177,000 (37 per cent). Thereafter spiralling desertion and demands for reinforcements dashed all hopes of a fully trained army.[143]

In political terms, most of the reinforcements were also poorly equipped. Few had anything but the dimmest notion of why — and whom — they were fighting. There was little party agitation in the units according to most reports, and what took place was all too quickly broken down into free-for-all meetings (*mitingovanie*), at which it was common to hear soldiers reject outright the authority of officers and political commissars, in the revolutionary spirit of the early partisan detachments.[144] Not surprisingly, the front-line units could be severely weakened by such reinforcements, especially if the latter were taken from regions close to the front, where the peasantry was hostile to the military authorities. A good example was the 202nd Artillery Brigade of the 23rd Division (9th Army), at the core of which stood a Communist brigade and a number of volunteer workers. Having suffered heavy losses in August 1919, it was reinforced by local peasant conscripts from Saratov province, "most of whom were infected by Green elements [deserters]". During a subsequent attack, two hundred of the peasant conscripts broke off from the main force, killed the political commissar of the brigade, and deserted to the enemy. The result was further losses, and a collapse in the morale of the rest of the troops, necessitating the break-up and reformation of the whole brigade.[145]

Mass desertion from the Red Army was a direct expression of general peasant protest against the Bolsheviks. The struggle against desertion was the struggle to win the active support of the peasantry,

[141] On the Whites, see Lehovich, *White against Red*, p. 358.
[142] TsGAOR, f. 130, op. 3, d. 184, ll. 4, 8-9; Trotsky, *How the Revolution Armed*, i, p. 482, ii, p. 66; Movchin, *Komplektovanie*, pp. 65, 111-15; White, *Growth of the Red Army*, p. 118.
[143] Movchin, *Komplektovanie*, pp. 64-5, 202.
[144] TsGAOR, f. 130, op. 3, d. 184, ll. 3, 6-7, 34.
[145] TsGAOR, f. 130, op. 3, d. 449, l. 68.

the silent majority of the Russian population. To wage that struggle by administrative means alone was obviously futile. Only a very small number of deserters — no doubt the most hardened, anti-Soviet types — were shot. (See Table 5.) Trotsky's infamous order of November 1918 to execute all deserters on the spot was a propaganda exercise at a time when there was no real apparatus to deal with the problem, and it was not — and never could have been — carried out: there were simply too many deserters to shoot.[146] By the same token, only the most dangerous from the category of "malicious" deserters were brought before the courts, sent into penal units (*shtraf- nye chasti*) or imprisoned (the prospect of imprisonment, safe from the dangers of war, would have encouraged many more to desert!). The great majority of deserters (those registered as "weak-willed") were handed back to the military authorities, and formed into units for transfer to one of the rear armies or directly to the front. Even those registered as "malicious" deserters were returned to the ranks when the demand for reinforcements became desperate. On 20 Au- gust 1920 the general staff (*Vseroglavshtab*) ordered that only "the very worst of the malicious" deserters should be formally punished, while "as many as possible who could feasibly return to the army" should be put into reserve units.[147] The practice of returning deserters to their original unit — usually with a black arm-band sewn on to their uniforms to set them apart from the other soldiers — had been popular in 1919, but it was phased out at the beginning of 1920, since it antagonized the rest of the soldiers, who were known to beat up or even kill former deserters.[148]

Equally unsuccessful were the purely punitive measures increas- ingly adopted by the military authorities, especially in areas close to the front: confiscating property and land allotments from anyone suspected of concealing deserters; taking as hostages the relatives or fellow-villagers of deserters; occupying the villages thought to be strongholds of deserters; imposing fines on them; shooting the village leaders; or even setting fire to the villages. Such measures rarely had the intended effect, since they were bound to strengthen the opposition of not only the deserters, but also the whole of the rural population. Wherever these measures were adopted, the "Greens" invariably grew in strength. They often united with the peasants, embittered by the grain requisitionings and other Bolshevik policies,

[146] Trotsky, *How the Revolution Armed*, i, pp. 487-8.
[147] TsGAOR, f. 130, op. 4, d. 282, l. 10.
[148] TsGAOR, f. 130, op. 3, d. 449, l. 68.

TABLE 5
MEASURES TAKEN AGAINST DESERTION FROM THE RED ARMY*

1919	Rejected deserters sent to					Rejected deserters sentenced by court			
	Own unit	Reserve unit	Voenkom	Unit assigned to front	Court	To penal unit	To prison	To be shot	Conditionally
June	38,000	65,000	52,000	18,000	7,000	12,000	1,300	70	760
July	1,000	159,000	38,000	32,000	6,000	8,000	900	75	550
August	4,000	177,000	17,000	118,000	6,000	4,000	354	53	521
September	6,000	190,000	24,000	75,000	7,000	6,000	950	100	320
October	6,000	131,000	29,000	29,000	5,000	8,000	1,302	188	911
November	7,000	137,000	13,000	4,000	3,000	4,000	378	38	162
December	4,000	123,000	19,000	10,000	6,000	13,000	750	88	888
Total	66,000	982,000	192,000	286,000	40,000	55,000	5,934	612	4,112

* Source: Movchin, *Komplektovanie*, pp. 140, 146.

to turn their localities into "no-go" areas. Railways and lines of communication were destroyed, local Communists and Soviet officials were terrorized, and guerrilla attacks were launched on passing units of the Red Army.[149]   Much more effective in the struggle against desertion was the introduction of a whole series of political and agitational measures. The establishment of Committees for the Struggle against Desertion at the *volost'* level — and their merger at all levels with the Voenkoms — brought the punitive power of the state closer to the rural strongholds of desertion.[150] Raids on Soviet institutions, railway stations, factories, timber-felling teams and other economic organs in competition with the army for manpower produced much the same effect, and flushed out thousands of hidden deserters.[151] As the number of deserters surrendering voluntarily declined during 1919-20, the importance of such raids increased. (See Table 4.) Propaganda and other means of moral persuasion were also known to be effective, particularly the show-trials of captured deserters, and the encouragement of loyal Red Army soldiers to write home appealing to their fellow-villagers not to help deserters.[152] But the most successful means of combatting desertion were the amnesty weeks, the biggest of which was called on 3-9 June 1919. As many as 98,000 deserters returned voluntarily to the Red Army during that week in the knowledge that no punitive measures would be taken against them. During the next week, while the amnesty was extended, the figure rose to 132,000.[153] It is from this moment that deserters began to return to the Red Army in massive waves. (See Table 4.)

The sharp increase in the number of deserters returning to the Red Army during the summer of 1919 was also explained by another factor — one which says a great deal about the nature of the civil war and why the Bolsheviks won it.

In May and June 1919 on the southern front the Red Army had been desperately short of recruits: the numbers lost daily through desertion, disease and battle far outstripped the number of reinforcements arriving at the front. On 6 July the Command of the Southern Front sent the last of a long series of urgent telegrams to Trotsky and

[149] Figes, *Peasant Russia*, pp. 319-20; Olikov, *Dezertirstvo*, pp. 53, 61-2; Movchin, *Komplektovanie*, p. 142. Detailed accounts of the property and fines exacted from villages are in TsGAOR, f. 130, op. 3, d. 198; op. 4, dd. 281, 282.

[150] Olikov, *Dezertirstvo*, pp. 17-24.

[151] TsGAOR, f. 130, op. 3, d. 580, l. 21; op. 4, d. 281, ll. 12, 15, 57, 66-7; d. 282, l. 9; Movchin, *Komplektovanie*, pp. 142-4.

[152] Olikov, *Dezertirstvo*, p. 59; TsGAOR, f. 130, op. 3, d. 199, l. 12.

[153] Olikov, *Dezertirstvo*, pp. 27, 42.

THE RED ARMY AND MASS MOBILIZATION 1918-1920   207

Lenin demanding the immediate mobilization of several age groups (including 1901) in the military districts of Kharkov and Orel, situated immediately on the front. It was claimed that "four of our divisions are missing 80 per cent to 90 per cent of their men, horses and carts".[154] These shortages were largely to blame for the White advance towards Moscow during June and July — prompting Lenin's famous circular of 9 July, "All Out for the Fight against Denikin!", in which he called for the Soviet Republic to be turned into a "single military camp".[155] Yet it was precisely this threat of a White victory that galvanized thousands of peasants, previously registered as deserters, to return to the Red Army between July and September 1919. (See Table 4.) In fact, so many deserters returned during these months that a serious shortage of rifles and uniforms resulted.[156] The Command of the Southern Front dropped its demand for the mobilization of more recruits, and began to complain instead about chronic material shortages. A telegram to Lenin sent from Orel on 22 July complained that: "because of the enormous numbers of deserters returning to our ranks, all the reserve units of Orel province are completely overfilled . . . New recruits are arriving every day. The supply situation is critical. Bread shortages in Mtsensk have resulted in rebellions, with the soldiers breaking into private houses".[157] Despite such problems, the massive influx of these former deserters gave the Red Army the numerical strength to launch a successful counter-offensive during the autumn and winter of 1919. Pushed south by the Reds, and constantly attacked in the rear by Makhno's Ukrainian peasant guerrillas, Denikin's army retreated deep into the Kuban, and finally fled for the Crimea, where in 1920 the Whites made their last stand under Wrangel.[158]

Many of the deserters who returned to the Red Army during these months called themselves "volunteers", ready to fight against the

[154] TsGAOR, f. 130, op. 3, d. 529, ll. 82, 89-90. Similar estimates of the situation on the southern front by the military command may be found in TsGAOR, f. 130, op. 3, d. 525, ll. 118-19.

[155] Lenin, *Collected Works*, xxix, pp. 436-55. The importance of the Red Army's "crisis of reinforcements" has been neglected by Western historians seeking to explain the Whites' advance on the southern front during this period. See, for example, Mawdsley, *Russian Civil War*, pp. 166-77.

[156] Trotsky, *How the Revolution Armed*, ii, pp. 315, 361; Movchin, *Komplektovanie*, pp. 111, 122.

[157] TsGAOR, f. 130, op. 3, d. 529, l. 111.

[158] Again, the influx of former deserters into the Red Army during the summer of 1919 has been overlooked by Western historians seeking to explain the Bolshevik victory against Denikin. See, for example, Mawdsley, *Russian Civil War*, pp. 202-15; Kenez, *Civil War in South Russia*.

Whites in defence of the land gained from the gentry in 1917-18. This explains why so many of them came from the military districts of Orel and Moscow, the central agricultural regions of Russia, where the Whites had directed the brunt of their attack during the summer of 1919. No less than 230,000 deserters from these two districts alone returned to the Red Army during July and August — more than 40 per cent of the total for the whole of the Soviet Republic.[159] These were regions in which the peasantry had made substantial land gains from the gentry during the revolution. In Orel province, for example, the amount of land in peasant use had increased by 28 per cent between 1917-19, mainly as a result of the seizure of the private estates, which before the revolution had occupied 23.5 per cent of all the agricultural land in the province. In the five provinces of Moscow military district (Kaluga, Tula, Riazan', Tambov and Moscow) the amount of land in peasant use had increased by as much as 35 per cent since 1917. Before the revolution, private landowners had owned 28 per cent of all the agricultural land in these provinces.[160] The threat of a White victory signalled to the peasants of these regions the prospect of losing their newly acquired land to the gentry squires, whose sons dominated the officer corps of Denikin's army. Such fears were played on by the Bolsheviks, whose propaganda in the countryside presented the Red Army as the sole protector of the peasantry's land gains against the White gentry counter-revolution. The fact that so many peasants of central Russia rallied to the Red Army on the two occasions when the Whites really threatened Moscow — first on the Volga in 1918; and then in the Orel region in 1919 — suggests that such propaganda was not without effect. The defeat of the Whites was determined, above all, by their failure to win over the peasantry of central Russia, because of their opposition to the land redistribution of 1917-18. The victory of the Bolsheviks was assured by their ability to call on the peasants of these same regions whenever the Whites threatened to break through from their bases in the periphery. The central Russian peasants were bitterly opposed to the Bolshevik policies of War Communism, but the fact that they would take up arms in defence of Soviet power, when —

[159] TsGAOR, f. 130, op. 3, d. 198, ll. 18, 26, 33, 36.
[160] V. P. Danilov, "Pereraspredelenie zemel'nogo fonda Rossii v rezul'tate velikoi oktiabr'skoi revoliutsii" [The Redistribution of Russia's Land Fund as a Result of the October Revolution], in *Leninskii dekret o zemle v deistvii: sbornik statei* [The Application of Lenin's Decree on the Land: A Collection of Articles] (Moscow, 1979), pp. 284-7.

THE RED ARMY AND MASS MOBILIZATION 1918-1920   **209**

and only when — it was threatened by the Whites, proved decisive in determining the outcome of the civil war.

*   *   *

Of all the problems confronting the two civil war armies, the mass mobilization of the Russian peasantry proved the most difficult, and the most decisive in military terms. The support of the peasantry was essential to the conduct of all military campaigns in Russia. Any mass army would have to be made up largely of peasants. It would have to be fed and even transported by them. Yet the vast majority of the Russian peasantry, having consolidated its hold on the land and village affairs during 1917-18, proved reluctant to become involved in fighting a civil war, a "war between brothers". Neither the Whites nor the Reds had any real political authority in the countryside to secure the mass mobilization of the peasantry. The White leaders were too closely associated with the old landowning class to have any lasting influence over the peasantry. The Tsarist epaulettes worn by the White officers were associated by the peasants with the old regime and the discipline of the imperial army, both of which they had rejected in 1917. The Reds, on the other hand, lacked a reliable political or military infrastructure in the countryside. They also lacked the active support of the rural population, although, as we have seen, when the peasants sensed the imminent threat of a White victory, they would rally behind the Reds. The peasants' mistrust of the Bolsheviks, it would seem, was not as powerful, and certainly not as ingrained, as their hatred and fear of the old landed order.

The Red Army, with its hold over the densely populated agricultural regions of central Russia, succeeded in mobilizing more peasants than the Whites. In this fact, as Trotsky acknowledged, was rooted the cause of its victory during the civil war. Yet because the Red Army consisted mainly of peasants, it was more susceptible to the seasonal fluctuations of peasant life when compared with the White armies, which remained largely non-peasant in their composition. In the summer peak season of the agricultural year the Red Army suffered from high rates of desertion, as food stocks ran down and the peasant recruits ran off to their farms in preparation for the harvest. After the harvest, the Red Army suffered less from either problem. The food-supply situation improved and desertion declined. Indeed many peasants, having deserted from the Red Army before the harvest, voluntarily returned to it for the winter low season of the agricultural year. Perhaps it is not coincidental that the Red Army tended to suffer its worst setbacks in the spring and early summer, but usually made advances in the period immediately following the harvest.

At the centre of the Red Army's "peasant problem" lay the issues of mass conscription, supply and desertion. The Bolsheviks' decision at the end of 1918 to go for an extensive system of mass mobilization created enormous problems of supply and training within the Red Army. Material conditions deteriorated, discipline broke down and desertion increased, so that untrained reinforcements had increasingly to be sent into the front-line units. The military system, in short, was being overloaded. Mass desertion was the inevitable outcome of an army growing too fast for the economy to supply it with all the necessary means. The large size of the army in turn dictated the need to maintain the system of War Communism. Large sectors of the economy had to be militarized in order to keep afloat an army full of holes.

The policy of mass mobilization was decided in the autumn of 1918. Lenin's call at that time for an army of three million men was a panic response to the threat of Allied intervention, a threat he almost certainly overestimated. But does this mean that the Red Army was larger than necessary, or that a smaller army would have been more effective as a fighting force? There is no doubt that the reliance of the Red Army on large numbers of peasant recruits, and the consequent problems of supply and training, made it much less effective than the White armies. To overcome the latter, the Red Army had to outnumber them in soldiers by at least four to one, and sometimes by as many as ten or even fifteen to one. It is logical to suppose that after the defeat of Kolchak, Iudenich and Denikin, at the beginning of 1920, the Red Army could have been reduced in size without posing a danger to defence interests. Such reductions might even have increased the Red Army's effectiveness. As A. Potiaev, a member of the Military Revolutionary Council of the Western Front, recommended to Lenin in a memo written on 18 December 1919: "In the interests of increasing the might and combat-fitness of the Red Army it is a thousand times more expedient to have no more than a million Red Army men in all, but well-fed, clothed and shod ones, rather than three million half-starved, half-naked, half-shod ones".[161] In the autumn of 1918, however, when the White

---

[161] *The Trotsky Papers*, ed. J. M. Meijer, 2 vols. (The Hague, 1964-71), i, p. 797

THE RED ARMY AND MASS MOBILIZATION 1918-1920   211

armies were growing in strength, and the threat of large-scale foreign intervention appeared imminent, the Bolsheviks probably had no real alternative to the mass mobilization of the peasantry, in spite of the far-reaching political and economic consequences which this policy was to have for the Red Army and the Soviet system.

Trinity College, Cambridge   *Orlando Figes*

[3]

Bolshevik *Razverstka* and War Communism

LARS T. LIH

Few would dispute the claim that the *razverstka*, the Bolshevik method of grain procurement, was a centerpiece of "war communism." Yet there exists no adequate treatment of the *razverstka* in the scholarly literature, and indeed there is widespread confusion about the nature and purposes of the *razverstka* policy as well as about the circumstances of its introduction and its replacement in 1921 by a food-supply tax (*prodnalog*). A closer look at the actual *razverstka* reveals some surprising features and in the end casts doubt on the validity and usefulness of the war communism notion itself.

The *razverstka* was introduced in the second half of 1918 as a result of experience in trying to enforce a state grain monopoly by means of the food-supply dictatorship decreed in spring 1918. To understand the *razverstka* method we must first look at the more ambitious aims of the previous policy of a full-fledged grain monopoly. The grain monopoly had already been decreed by the Provisional Government in March 1917, and even this decree was only a step beyond the stage the tsarist government had reached by September 1916 when a fixed price had been made mandatory for all grain sales and when state officials were given de facto control over all grain transport. The Provisional Government's legislation declared that all grain above a fairly modest consumption norm had to be sold to the state at a fixed price. This measure was one of the most radical attempted by the Provisional Government.

The growing claims of the state over disposition of the nation's grain supply was of course a practical response to the intensifying food-supply crisis. But many also had ideological hopes pinned on the grain monopoly as a step toward full government control of the economy. These hopes were not confined to the Bolsheviks, as can be seen from the arguments of V. G. Groman, the staunchest advocate of the grain monopoly both in tsarist governmental councils and in the Petrograd soviet during 1917.[1] Lenin's own view of the matter is found in his 1918 doctrine of state capitalism, since the grain monopoly was a prime example of state capitalism in practice.

What Lenin meant by *state capitalism* in 1918 was not what the term came to mean later, a mixed-economy toleration of private capitalists, but a situation in which a bourgeois state (impelled by immanent capitalist development as accelerated by wartime demands) takes over actual control of the economy even while respecting legal ownership of the capitalists. Even before the revolution Lenin had argued in *Imperialism* that this situation was the threshold to socialism. In 1918 he argued further that the substance of his "organizational task" remained

This article is partly based on research done under an IREX grant in 1980–1981 at the Central State Historical Archive in Leningrad. Further discussion can be found in my *Bread and Authority in Russia, 1914–1921* (University of California Press, forthcoming).

1. During the Menshevik trial in 1931 N.S. Sukhanov stated that "Groman was the author of War Communism. When did he proclaim it? He proclaimed it soon after the February Revolution. . . . He took the Kadet Shingarev by the throat and squeezed out of him the basic element of War Communism, namely, the grain monopoly"; cited in Naum Jasny, *Soviet Economists of the Twenties: Names to be Remembered* (Cambridge: Cambridge University Press, 1972), p. 100.

the same even when a proletarian state had taken power. The grain monopoly in particular was a measure that had already been adopted by such advanced capitalist states as Germany but could be enforced in Russia only over the vociferous opposition of the "uncultured" petty capitalists and other assorted "disorganizers" of town and country. Thus in 1918 the goal of state capitalism was hardly moderate either in terms of its ideological ambitions or in the demands made on the Russian people.[2]

The practicality of the grain monopoly is also called into question by the extreme demands it made on state administrative resources. To carry out the grain monopoly a state needed full information about everyone's grain holding so that a proper determination of each individual's surplus could be made. An organizational structure capable of receiving and distributing the grain had to be created, and material and coercive incentives had to be provided. The original plan of the Provisional Government relied almost completely on voluntary action for all three of these requirements—information, organization, and incentives—and the predictable result was disaster. The Bolshevik food-supply dictatorship of spring 1918 was an effort to supply these prerequisites. Information would be obtained through the village-splitting tactics embodied in the Poor Peasants Committees that were intended to be the "alert eyes" of the food-supply apparatus.[3] This apparatus would be based not on a voluntary hierarchy of committees, such as the one the Provisional Government had created, but on strict centralization supplemented by an infusion of new proletarian talent and dedication. The workers would also provide "real force" in the form of requisition and blockade detachments that would supplement efforts to provide the village with industrial items at low fixed prices. Thus the food-supply dictatorship was not a rejection of Lenin's policy of state capitalism but an attempt to carry it out.

The food-supply dictatorship cannot be considered simply an improvised response to the deepening food-supply crisis of 1918 since it drew on a policy tradition that dated back even before the February Revolution. Top food-supply officials, then and later, argued that the methods of the food-supply dictatorship did not contain anything new in principle but were simply the logical culmination of methods already proposed.[4] While this argument may be exaggerated, it is true that the Provisional Government's Ministry of Food Supply was moving toward much tougher methods in the fall of 1917 and that the Bolsheviks did set themselves the same problem as their predecessors: enforcing a state grain monopoly.[5]

2. See the discussion in chapter 10 of *Imperialism*, especially the passage found in *Polnoe sobranie sochinenii*, 5th ed., 27:425. From the 1918 polemic with the Left Communists to which Lenin referred in 1921: "We still have too little of the mercilessness necessary for the success of socialism. And not because of a lack of decisiveness. . . . But we don't have the ability to *catch* sufficiently quickly a sufficient number of speculators, predators, capitalists—destroyers of Soviet undertakings. And this ability can only come about as a result of the organization of registration and monitoring [*uchet i kontrol'*]. [And] there is not enough firmness in our courts, where bribe takers are given six months in jail rather than being shot. Both of these defects have one social root: the influence of the petit bourgeois element [*stikhiia*] and its flabbiness" (PSS, 36:305).

3. This phrase was used by A. D. Tsiurupa in a speech at the Fifth Congress of Soviets (*Piatyi Vserossiiskii s"ezd Sovetov*, stenographic report [Moscow, 1918], pp. 135–145).

4. Such arguments are made by A. Sviderskii in *Chetyre goda prodovol'stvennoi raboty* (Moscow: People's Commissariat of Food Supply, 1922) and A. B. Khalatov in *Vnutrenniaia torgovlia soiuza SSR za X let* (Moscow: Narkomtorg, 1928).

5. Material on the proposed changes by the Provisional Government can be found in the Central State Historical Archive, Leningrad, fond 1276, opis' 14 , delo 483.

The genuine rethinking of the food-supply procurement problem came later in 1918 after the failure of the food-supply dictatorship had become evident. The village-splitting tactics succeeded more in outraging the peasants than in obtaining grain; the government's attack in the name of the monopoly on independent grain-purchasing delegations sent by individual factories and towns irritated the workers more than they were pleased by the opportunity to take grain by force; the lawlessness of the blockade detachments that enforced the monopoly exceeded all bounds. The political liability of a policy that created rebellion in the country-side and despair in the towns was made even less tolerable by the outbreak of the civil war. In early August Lenin demanded a change in direction and his propos-als rapidly became legislative policy.

The extent of the retreat from the food-supply dictatorship can be gauged by looking at an appeal issued in May 1918 by the Council of People's Commis-sars. The appeal ended with these ringing words that set forth the principles of the grain monopoly:

> Not one step away from the grain monopoly! Not the slightest increase in fixed prices for grain! No independent procurement! All that is steadfast, disciplined, and conscious in a single organized food-supply order! Unhesi-tating fulfillment of all directives of the central authority! No separate actions! War to the kulaks![6]

But by September 1918 these brave slogans could not have been repeated. The fixed price for grain had been tripled. The grain monopoly had been officially relaxed to such an extent that workers in Moscow were temporarily allowed to go to the countryside to buy one and a half poods of grain for each traveler to the countryside—a measure referred to by disgusted food-supply officials as "legalized sackmanism [*meshochnichestvo*]." On a more permanent basis, the worker detachments were allowed to give half of the food they obtained directly to the organization that sent them; this practice was in reality heavily taxed independent procurement rather than state monopoly purchases. Although the kulaks were still treated as deadly enemies of the people, the emphasis of peasant policy had been switched very heavily to neutralization of the peasant producer, that is, the middle peasant who had not been so much as mentioned in the May appeal. Attempts had been made to restrain the blockade detachments that harassed the sackmen, and the Poor Peasants Committees were on the verge of being disbanded. The only plank that remained of the food-supply dictatorship was insistence on a centralized food-supply apparatus.

The *razverstka* method that came to the fore in the second half of 1918 must be seen in the context of this general retreat from the grain monopoly strategy, so ambitious both in aim and method.[7] The *razverstka* method itself was not an

6. *Dekrety sovetskoi vlasti* (Moscow, 1959) 2:353–354.

7. Because of this general retreat, it is misleading to see the *razverstka* as just a systemization of the food-supply dictatorship. Alec Nove, *An Economic History of the USSR* (London: Penguin, 1969), p. 59. Silvana Malle notes the retreat in food-supply policy in the second half of 1918 but sees the *razverstka* as an indication of the failure of that retreat (*The Economic Organization of War Commu-nism, 1918–1921* [Cambridge: Cambridge University Press, 1985], p. 373). Malle stresses the ill effects of collective commodity exchange, an element of continuity in food-supply policy not discussed in this article. The distribution of scarce exchange items to those without a grain surplus was defended both as a welfare measure and as a material incentive for help in collecting the *razverstka*. Martin

invention of the central authorities but developed from the experience of lower-level officials as they struggled to do their jobs. The *razverstka* supplied the requirements of organization, information, and incentives in a more modest but practical way.

How did the *razverstka* work? The word is itself almost impossible to translate: perhaps "quota assessment" is closest.[8] The method was essentially based on the old tsarist method of collective responsibility: an assessment was given to a collectivity, whose members were then free to decide how to divide the burden further. The outside authority was not concerned as long as the assessment was paid in full. This technique was applied from the top to the bottom of the food-supply hierarchy. At the top the People's Commissariat of Food Supply determined a total amount for the entire area controlled by the Bolsheviks. Quotas were then signed to the provinces through negotiations among top provincial officials. The provincial assessment was distributed in the same way among the *uezdy*, and so on down the hierarchy until the individual peasant household was presented with an assessment.

This method recommended itself to the Bolsheviks for the same reason it did to tsarist officials: it economized on administrative resources. Instead of the gleaming organization dreamed of by the enthusiasts of the grain monopoly, the *razverstka* got along with the tried and true methods of collective responsibility. The same is true of information requirements. The grain monopoly had required all grain supplies to be put on register (*uchet*) so that the government could tell how much was surplus and how much was to be left to the individual producer. Here as elsewhere, the *uchet* became the battle cry of the state's drive for information as a prelude to full control. In translations of some famous passages in Lenin's *State and Revolution, uchet* is usually misrendered as "accounting" and taken as a symbol of Lenin's naive view of the simplicity of modern ecnonomic management. This interpretation overlooks the fact that in 1917 and 1918 the *uchet* was seen as a major task and a basic political challenge. The *uchet* was central to socialist ambitions because the first task in nationalization was simply for the state to know what was going on.[9]

Sotsializm—eto uchet: Registration is socialism.[10] This statement may be typical Leninist hyperbole, but it does show the intimate connection between the practical demands of the grain monopoly, the nature of state capitalism ("all-

---

Malia is one of the few historians who see civil war food-supply policy as a retreat from earlier policy: *Comprendre la revolution russe* (Paris: Editions du Seuil, 1980), pp. 132–134.

8. Sometimes *razverstka* or a translation is not used at all, and civil war food-supply policy is simply described with the term *grain requisition* or with the redundant *forcible requisition*. E. H. Carr, who barely alludes in passing to the *razverstka* itself as one of many "constantly changing expedients," uses this last term in *The Bolshevik Revolution*, 3 vols. (New York: Macmillan, 1952), 2:150–151, 227–228). This term, however, is unfortunate because it completely slides over the question of the terms of the forced sale and, indeed, seems to be understood by some writers simply as confiscation. The term *requisition* is best restricted to individual acts of forced sale or provision of services, if only because the burden of these (as distinct from the general obligation of the *razverstka*) became a major source of peasant discontent on the eve of NEP.

9. In Bukharin and Preobrazhenskii's *Azbuka Kommunizma* (Moscow, 1920), pp. 209–210, it is asserted that "the fulfillment of this task [of laying the foundations of a *planomernyi* economy] begins in practice with an *uchet*."

10. Lenin, PSS, 35:63 (November 1917).

embracing *uchet i kontrol'* "), and the possibility of socialism. The task of actually putting grain supplies on register, however, proved to be an impassable obstacle to grain collection; as A. G. Shlikhter, one of the pioneers of the *razverstka* method, put it, "either registration or grain."[11] The monopoly had begun with a determination of the individual's needs with the residual going to the state. The *razverstka* economized vastly on information requirements by beginning with a determination of the state's needs with the residual going to the individual. In this crucial respect, the *razverstka* was closer to a tax than to a state monopoly.[12]

Given the fearsome reputation of the *razverstka* as the symbol of war communist radicalism, it is something of a shock to learn that when the *razverstka* was introduced by Bolshevik food-supply officials in 1918 and 1919 they viewed it as a concession to the peasantry. The *razverstka* represented a switch from village-splitting tactics to an attempt to work with the village. The original aim in 1918 was that even the amount of the assessment would be negotiated with peasant representatives, and, although this procedure could not be maintained during the civil war, the *razverstka* still implied peasant control over distribution of the burden of the assessment. The *razverstka* was also supposed to include distribution of whatever industrial items could be spared, and the failure to do this was due simply to their unavailability.[13] The formula of the *razverstka* was with material incentives if possible, without material incentives if necessary.

The *razverstka*, which became official policy in January 1919, was certainly no "assault on full socialism" but rather was viewed by food-supply officials as a compromise adjustment to civil war conditions and an enforced transitional measure to monopolization—itself only a first step toward a socialist organization of the economy. The word *razverstka* itself implies a lack of ideological ambition. For anyone associated with food-supply policy, the term *razverstka* recalled the tsarist minister of agriculture A. A. Rittikh who introduced a *razverstka* policy in the last months of the tsarist regime. Rittikh's policy was based on a conscious rejection of the movement toward a state grain monopoly, and as such it was scornfully rejected by both liberals and socialists and abandoned by the Provisional Government the moment it took power. Thus the term *razverstka* was associated with neither socialism nor even the highest stage of capitalism, but with "reactionary" tsarist bureaucrats.

Of course, under civil war conditions the *razverstka* policy was even further distorted. The grain assessments were high relative to available supplies, the lack of industrial items removed any economic incentives for fulfillment, and local administrative abuses were a constant source of profound peasant irritation.[14] Bolshevik food-supply officials themselves were under few illusions about the inherent desirability of these methods and were little prone to utopian flights of fancy.

11. A. G. Shlikhter, *Agrarnyi vopros i prodovol'stvennaia politika v pervyi gody sovetskoi vlasti* (Moscow: Nauka, 1976), pp. 411–414. The cited statement was written in 1920.

12. The necessity of improving the statistical base through better registration was not forgotten, since state needs could not be the sole determinant of the *razverstka* total. On this see Iu. K. Strizhkov, "Priniatie dekreta o prodovol'stvennoi razverstke i ego osushchestvlenie v pervoi polovine 1919 g.," in *Oktiabr i sovetskoe krest'ianstvo, 1917–1927 gg* (Moscow: Nauka, 1977), pp. 131–163.

13. N. A. Orlov, *Sistema prodovol'stvennoi zagotovki* (Tambov, 1920).

14. The evolving nature of the *razverstka* is stressed by V. M. Andreev in "Prodrazverstka i krest'ianstvo," *Istoricheskie Zapiski* 97 (1976): 5–49.

If anyone could represent the war communist bureaucrat in all his splendor, it would be A. D. Tsiurupa, the people's commissar of food supply, the man in charge of the *razverstka*. Tsiurupa was a hard-working official who rarely made public speeches, but he did lead the debate on food-supply policy at the Seventh Congress of Soviets in December 1919.[15] Perhaps we can learn something about civil war attitudes of the Bolsheviks by examining his speeches. Tsiurupa made no bones about the necessity of the *razverstka*, the necessity of using force, or the necessity of taking "surpluses" (a term that only meant high grain quotas, given the scarcity of accurate information and the improbability of fulfillment). But his discussion hardly smacked of utopianism. Although he stated that the long-term goal was state procurement monopolies of all the major agricultural products, he noted that this must be done "with extreme [*velichaishii*] gradualness and circumspection." His defense of the goals of monopolization was that it was the only way to ensure even the possibility of correct distribution, since otherwise disorganizing speculation would get out of hand. Tsiurupa was confident, however, that awareness of the necessity of the *razverstka* was growing among the peasants, even if slowly. What was this awareness based on? On the realization that in order to get needed industrial items, the peasant had first to give agricultural products to the city in the form of a loan—in other words, the logic of the peasant-worker alliance, the *smychka* under wartime conditions.

The complaints voiced in the ensuing debate by peasants and local officials about the incompetence and arbitrariness of the food-supply apparatus and the intolerable pressure of the assessments were strongly and uncompromisingly stated. It is these phenomena—completely undesirable from the point of view of the Bolshevik leadership—that were mainly responsible for the bad reputation of civil war policy (especially when they threatened to become a "civil war culture," a habitual and preferred mode of political work even in peacetime conditions). The response of Tsiurupa to these complaints was equally forthright. Tsiurupa admitted the many abuses and failures and went on to say:

> I can say about myself that I am at fault as well. I've worked for five years on food-supply procurement, but that is not enough in such a difficult moment. It must be admitted that we do not know how to work—but the fact that we are aware of this is also important.

Is this the *komchvanstvo*, the communist arrogance, that is often associated with war communism?[16]

Tsiurupa and his colleages would only listen to specific complaints if the general line of the *razverstka* policy was accepted. One official, P. K. Kaganovich, admitted that the norm allowed for peasant horses (2 funts of oats and 12 funts of hay a day) was very low but responded that 5 funts a month for a working man was also too low. "What do you think, the People's Commissariat of Food Supply does this for its own satisfaction? No, we do it because there's not enough

15. Food-supply policy was not debated at any party congress until the tenth in 1921. It evidently did not raise any matter for principled debate. The subject did come up regularly at the congresses of soviets, where the Boslheviks tried to make contact with the nonparty peasants.

16. Compare this to Victor Serge's portrait of Tsiurupa as a fanatic blind to reality in *Memoirs of a Revolution* (Oxford: Oxford University Press, 1965), p. 113. Tsiurupa's speech is found on pp. 121–131, 163–166 of *Sed'moi vserossiiskii s'ezd Sovetov* (Moscow, 1920).

food." The same with coercion: the people's commissariat would much rather have sent the food-supply detachments to the front instead of to the countryside, but it simply could not rely on the peasants sending in the grain by themselves. Both Kaganovich and Tsiurupa were perfectly aware of the damage done to the productive base, but they felt little could be done during the wartime emergency. In Tsiurupa's words: "There are only two possibilities: either we perish from hunger, or we weaken the [peasant] economy to some extent, but [manage to] get out of our temporary difficulties."[17]

In the latter half of 1920, the *razverstka* did become associated in the popular mind with policies that seemed to be based on ideological militancy: the closing of local bazaars and a supposed leap into a money-less economy. Had food-supply officials finally succumbed to utopian illusions?

For people living in Soviet Russia at the time, the renewed crackdown on local bazaars was a more vivid demonstration of Bolshevik ideological ambition on the eve of NEP than efforts at economic reorganization, such as VSNKh's nationalization decree of November 1920.[18] The crackdown was based on the long-standing prohibition of free trade in grain and the steadily increasing list of other agricultural products banned from private trade. But the prohibition against private trade was no more effective than liquor prohibition was in the United States, and the underground market in Russia was probably larger in total volume than legal state procurements.

In 1920, as the war came to a close, the Bolsheviks had to decide what to do about this immense black market. The Bolsheviks perforce had to tolerate this market since everybody, including government and party officials, relied on it in order to survive. As the sour parody had it, "he who does not speculate, neither shall he eat." The Bolsheviks hoped to eliminate the illegal market by combining "administrative" persecution of the illegal market with a steady organizational and economic strengthening of the state food-supply apparatus. But the repression of the black market dwindled steadily in intensity until by 1920 there was almost de facto toleration.[19] This situation, however, was not satisfactory, if only because of the corruption and demoralization involved. Officials denied that the markets brought new goods into circulation, since the local markets thrived mainly on embezzled state property. Legalization was still not considered a possible solution. Some voices in the People's Commissariat of Food Supply argued that sackmanism could no longer be extended even de facto toleration because the disorganization it created was proving stronger than the organizing influence of the food-supply apparatus. One official, Miron Vladimirov, advocated early in 1920 that the illegal market be eliminated in one fell swoop in order to let the food-supply apparatus show what it could do when not faced with this corrupting competition. "All it needs is the courage and daring to carry the experiment through, if only for the space of one month."[20]

17. Kaganovich's speech is in *Sed'moi vserossiiskii s"ezd Sovetov*, pp. 158–159.

18. Secondary accounts seldom mention this crackdown. The following description is based primarily on M. K. Vladimirov, *Meshochnichestvo i ego sotsial'no-politicheskoe otrazhenie* (Kharkov, 1920); A. M. Terne, *V tsarstve Lenina* (Berlin: A. Terne, 1922), pp. 253–259; A. E. Badaev, *X let bor'by i stroitel'stvo* (Leningrad: Priboi, 1927), pp. 87–90.

19. S. Bychkov, "Organizatsionnoe stroitel'stvo prodorganov do NEPa," *Prodovol'stvie i revoliutsiia*, no. 5–6 (1923), p. 192.

20. Vladimirov, *Meshochnichestvo*.

Later in 1920 A. E. Badaev, head of the Moscow food-supply organization, felt the situation allowed the closing of the famous Sukharevka market. According to his later account, he was motivated not only by the disorganization caused by the flourishing illegal market, but also by irritation with the popular argument that Moscow could not survive without it. The idea was then taken up by other urban soviets (with how much central prodding it is difficult to say). The policy was far from popular; in Rostov, for example, even after many of the tradespeople had been expropriated, the workers managed to keep the food bazaar open until the NEP turn-around.[21]

The crackdown on the bazaars showed that there was still some bite left to the Bolshevik commitment to the principle of a state monopoly of the grain trade. Given the refusal to compromise on this principle, a crackdown on corruption was necessary to make the system work at all (as Brezhnev's successors have found). But it is hard to see the crackdown as evidence of an acceleration of ideological militancy, since it was not based on any new governmental legislation but on local enforcement of existing law. Even such officials as Vladimirov who advocated a renewed crackdown conceded it was utopian to expect to eliminate "the petit bourgeois, huckstering, speculative outlook gripping wide sections of the population."[22]

Were the food-supply officials also interested in eliminating money? Was the growing reliance on payment of wages in kind based on a commitment to a "naturalized," money-less economy? Did officials actually believe that the financial chaos of the civil war was a prelude to full communism?

The absence of money was in fact seen as an essential feature of a socialist economy. This belief (securely grounded in the Marxist classics) was not affected by the transition to NEP and decayed only slowly. But it should be said that the reports of the death of the monetary economy in Russia in 1920–1921 are greatly exaggerated. Despite the general economic disorganization that led to a great volume of barter transactions, the Russian economy was at all times essentially a monetary economy. For the food-supply apparatus, the transition to payment of wages in kind was only one part of a much larger picture. Perhaps the point was best made by Evgenii Preobrazhenskii, who is said to have "hymned the virtues of inflation" in his book *Paper Money in the Epoch of the Proletarian Dictatorship.*[23] It is true that the book is dedicated to the printing press as an honored weapon against the bourgeois economy, but this is the only compliment given to the inflation. Preobrazhenskii demonstrates that, although the inflation was meant to act as an unpaid tax on the peasant, the real loser was not the peasant but the workers and the state employees who had to buy a significant amount of their sustenance on the free market. The state employees were especially hard-pressed for cash and were forced to moonlight, to register for fake jobs, and to accept bribes in order to get it. Even the peasant found he could not accumulate wealth, and the only real beneficiary from the inflation was the rapacious speculator

---

21. Badaev's account is in *X let bor'by i stroitel'stvo*, pp. 87–90. The events in Rostov are recounted in Terne, *V tsarstve Lenina*, pp. 253–259.

22. Space does not permit any discussion of the "sowing committee" legislation of December 1920. This legislation was explicitly based on the long-term predominance of the single-owner peasant farm.

23. Carr, *Bolshevik Revolution*, 2:345.

whose entire aim was a quick turnover and high living. Far from advocating the abolition of money, Preobrazhenskii argued for a silver-backed currency. He noted that the People's Commissariat of Food Supply was not likely to meet its *razverstka* target for 1920–1921, and this meant that, if the peasants lost their money illusion, the town dweller would be in a quandary.[24] Even if the state did collect enough grain to pay wages in kind, a more secure currency would still be necessary for the many products the workers had to obtain themselves.[25]

In 1920 food-supply officials repeatedly affirmed their loyalty to the *razverstka* as a basis for the further development of food-supply policy. This policy did not mean that they were also committed to the forced extraction of grain without equivalent exchange beyond the wartime emergency. The food-supply officials had always referred to the grain taken from the peasants as a loan and they were in fact looking forward to peacetime economic reconstruction so that the *razverstka* could work properly on the basis of equivalent exchange. Force was required only when proper exchange was not possible. In 1918, one food-supply official (D. E. Gol'man) contrasted the usual economic method of obtaining grain with the extraordinary "revolutionary" methods of the food-supply dictatorship:

> In order to receive grain by the economic method, we must get our industry in order, provide the market with a vast number of different commodities necessary for the peasant [and so forth]. When we have succeeded in getting to that stage, we can say with assurance that the peasants will bring grain voluntarily and turn it over to the state. [But] we need grain immediately, right now, and we must have all of it.[26]

Hostility to free trade was never hostility to equivalent exchange or to material incentives.

So far we have set forth the meaning of *razverstka* as seen by the professionals, but we should remember that those outside the ranks of food-supply officials had little understanding or interest in these technical developments. The disjunction between the *razverstka* as the symbol of civil war harshness and the *razverstka* as a method of food-supply policy was thus particularly great. The popular hatred of the *razverstka* was due to the burden that any collection method would have imposed under civil war conditions, not to any real appreciation of the technical logic behind the *razverstka*. When we hear our neighbor say "this damned income tax," we do not suppose he is cursing the *income* tax as opposed to a sales tax or a capital gains tax, but simply the tax burden as such. The rhetorical aura of the *razverstka* became indelibly marked by civil war hardships—high grain assessments and lack of material exchange equivalents—that were not inherent in the method itself.[27]

24. Lenin also worried about this; see PPS, 41:146–147 (June 1920).

25. *Bumazhnye den'gi v epokhu proletarskoi diktatury* (Moscow: Gosizdat, 1920), pp. 48–58, 78–84.

26. Internal memorandum cited in Strizhkov, *Prodovol'stvennye otriady v gody grazhdanskoi voiny i inostrannoi interventsii, 1917–1921* (Moscow: Nauka, 1973), p. 106. In Bukharin's words, "The exhausted towns cannot *at first* give an equivalent for grain and services [*povinnosti*]. . . . *Therefore* coericon is also here an absolute and imperative necessity" (*Ekonomika perekhodnogo perioda* [Moscow: Gosizdat, 1920], p. 146; emphasis added).

27. E. G. Gimpel'son adopts this popular understanding of the *razverstka* as taking grain without

This popular understanding of the *razverstka* would not have gone as unchallenged as it has if the Bolsheviks themselves had not become interested in fudging some important distinctions. This occurred as a result of the policy changes of spring 1921. The exact nature of these changes is obscured by describing them simply as the replacement of the *razverstka* by a food-supply tax.[28] But, in and of itself, the substitution of a tax for a *razverstka* only meant that the government no longer recognized even a commitment to provide industrial products in return for the grain assessment. Although the amount of the 1921 tax was lower than that of the 1920 *razverstka*, this comparison is somewhat misleading since the *razverstka* represented the total amount delivered to the state organs, while the tax represented only the unpaid part that was supposed to be supplemented by grain obtained through the cooperatives in exchange for whatever industrial items could be found (which would have been given to the peasants under the *razverstka* as well). The tax was still an extremely heavy burden in a year of famine and economic disorganization, and its collection required much coercion and loss of life. It is paradoxical that NEP should be symbolized by that part of the policy changes of 1921 that was most redolent of civil war conditions.[29]

Another feature of a tax system is the declaration by the state of an exact grain obligation so that the peasant could make his plans accordingly: once the peasant has fulfilled this obligation, nothing further would be required of him. The *razverstka* was midway between this system and a monopoly system that asserted a claim to the entire surplus, whatever it might be. On the one hand, food-supply officials wanted to promise the peasant that if he paid his obligation, he would be left in peace.[30] On the other hand, there was still a rhetorical commitment to delivery of the entire surplus and many local officials were all too willing to translate this into reality through the supplementary requisitions and arbitrary exactions that irritated the peasants more than the *razverstka* itself.

All in all, however, these changes were not so alien to the spirit of the *razverstka* as it was meant to operate in peace. This fact is shown by the speech given at the Tenth Party Congress by a food-supply official, M. I. Frumkin, who supported all the proposed changes except one—the legalization of the free market in grain. *This* was the real change not only from civil war policy, but even from policy before the civil war and before October. The Bolsheviks were embar-

compensation. Although he can easily show that this procedure was only a temporary necessity, his account cannot explain why Bolshevik officials defended the *razverstka* as such. He also goes too far in dismissing the monopoly principle, as well as the *razverstka* method, as merely a dispensable emergency response ("*Voennyi kommunizm*" [Moscow: Mysl', 1973], pp. 48–56). Paul Craig Roberts also fails to distinguish between the monopoly principle and the *razverstka* method but draws the opposite conclusion: principled approval of the monopoly is used as evidence for similar devotion to the *razverstka* ("'War Comunism'—A Product of Marxian Ideas," *Slavic Review* 29 [June 1970]: 238–261).

28. The usual translation of *prodnalog* as *tax-in-kind* is in one respect unfortunate: the reader has a tendency to read it as tax-in-*kind*, that is, as opposed to a money tax. In 1921, however, the *prodnalog* was opposed to the *prodrazverstka*, so that the term should be read as *tax*-in-kind as opposed to a *razverstka*-in-kind.

29. Gimpel'son is thus mistaken in pointing to the ineffectual civil war tax-in-kind as a forerunner to NEP. In reality, the *razverstka* itself, with its stress on using material incentives to the extent possible, is closer to NEP than this early tax-in-kind.

30. Iu. A. Poliakov, *Perekhod k NEPu i sovetskoe krest'ianstvo* (Moscow, 1967), pp. 94–96.

rassed by this shift, and with good cause. In 1919 Lenin had ringingly declared "if you want freedom to trade in grain in a devastated country—then go back, try Kolchak, try Denikin! We will fight against this to our last drop of blood. Here there will be no concessions."[31] In 1921 the country was economically in even worse shape and yet Lenin was making exactly this concession. To make matters worse, the Mensheviks and Socialist Revolutionaries had for a long time been calling for liberalization of food-supply policy and could now gleefully claim they had been vindicated. It was to cover up this embarrassment that the Bolsheviks tended to refer to the whole package of policy changes as "introduction of a food-supply tax." This euphemism was simply a way of referring to legalization of the market without actually saying "legalization of the market."

The confusion was compounded by Lenin's attempts to justify NEP through his characterization of the *razverstka*. Since Lenin was speaking to people not directly concerned with the details of food-supply policy, he mainly used *razverstka* in its popular sense of taking grain without compensation. Before 1921, he had seen this as only a temporary wartime necessity.[32] Lenin repeated this point in spring 1921: "People represent the matter as if the transition were from communism in general to bourgeoisness [*burzhuaznost'*]. [But in reality] the food-supply tax is one of the forms of transition from a peculiar 'war communism,' [a policy] compelled by extreme need, destruction and war, to sound socialist product-exchange."[33] What is misleading in this statement, however, is Lenin's characterization of the views of his opponents. It is implied that people like Frumkin who saw the legalization of the market as a retreat did so because they saw the *razverstka* as something akin to full communism and saw the introduction of state-organized commodity-exchange as a form of *burzhuaznost'*. It is not difficult to defeat opponents who advocate taking grain without compensation when there was no need for it and who refuse to give the peasants material goods that were actually available.

It is hardly necessary to comment on how unfounded this picture is. No one held these views. The food-supply officials had always been in favor of providing material equivalents; under peacetime conditions they were now willing to grant the necessity of voluntary and individualized exchange—but why should this exchange not be restricted to the state and its authorized agents? Why abandon the ideal of a monopoly just when the state could actually look forward to acquiring some goods to trade with the peasants and thus make the monopoly a reality?

By the fall of 1921, the spread of market forms had gone too far to cover up with references to the introduction of a tax system, and so Lenin had to admit that NEP was a strategic retreat. He tried to make retreat palatable by claiming that the retreat was from an advanced position back to state capitalism. If the

31. PSS, 39:408 (July 1919).
32. For example, see PSS, 41:359–360 (October 1920). Moshe Lewin claims that during the civil war, Lenin saw the *razverstka* as the essence of socialism (*Political Undercurrents in Soviet Economic Debates* [Princeton, N.J.: Princeton University Press, 1974], p. 79). Lewin cites two texts from 1919 (PSS, 39:167, 274). But the *razverstka* is not mentioned in either of these texts: what Lenin sees as essential to socialism is the replacement of free trade with state distribution—a position Lenin never repudiated.
33. "*O prodnaloge*," PSS, 43:219–223.

razverstka in its civil war form represented progress, then indeed most people would welcome a retreat.

> We decided that the peasant would give us the necessary quantity of grain according to the *razverstka*, and we would distribute [*razverstaem*] it to factories and workshops—and then we would have communist production and distribution. . . . The *razverstka* in the village—that immediate communist approach to the tasks of construction in the town—interfered with the increase in productive forces and became the basic reason for the profound economic and political crisis with which we collided in spring 1921.[34]

This statement shows not a development but a complete reversal of Lenin's position in the spring. In the spring, the *razverstka* was not an ideal but a bitter necessity; in the fall, it is mandated by ideological extremism. In the spring, the *razverstka* was praised for preserving the Soviet republic in a time of crisis; in the fall it is responsible for a crisis that nearly toppled the republic. The only comment that can be made on the fall version is that it is an even worse distortion than the spring version.[35]

Lenin's obfuscations sealed the fate of proper historical understanding of the *razverstka*. The plausibilty of Lenin's rhetoric has been enhanced by his air of admitting a mistake (although it is unclear to what extent Lenin included himself in the "we" who made mistakes) as well as by the natural sympathy of most scholars for the NEP policies Lenin was defending. Even though the fall version with its "strategic retreat" directly contradicts what was said in spring 1921 about the *razverstka* as a successful emergency measure, the two versions have lived in uneasy coexistence ever since.

Does the concept of war communism help us put the *razverstka* into its proper context? We should remember that the Lenin texts we have just looked at are also the birthplace of the concept of war communism as well as of the term itself. At the least it is dangerously anachronistic to imply that the concept played any role in attitudes and motivations before 1921.[36]

The term *war communism* (strengthened by the image of the besieged fortress) almost inescapably suggests a coincidence between what was mandated by civil war pressures and what was mandated by ideological radicalism. This possibility is reflected in the many accounts that point to a moderate policy of state capitalism that was disrupted by the outbreak of the civil war, which in turn led to a radicalization of Bolshevik policy.

In the case of food-supply policy, the actual relation between military necessity and ideological radicalism is the reverse of this supposed chain: the outbreak of civil war caused a conscious retreat from ideological ambitiousness. The phase of state capitalism could hardly be called moderate, either in its policy goal (a state grain monopoly) or its methods (the food-supply dictatorship). When war

34. PSS, 44:157, 159 (October 1921). Even here Lenin does not claim that the *razverstka* itself was a communist method.

35. Compare Gimpel'son's discussion of the fall version ("*Voennyi kommunizm*," pp. 229–233).

36. For example, Lewin writes "There was even a stronger sedative for whoever might have had qualms about . . . harsh practices: the belief that something more than the war economy justified them. The term 'war communism' implied that the most progressive system on earth was just installed *deus ex machina* by the most expedient, unexpected, but irreversible leap to freedom (*Political Undercurrents*, pp. 78–79).

did break out in the summer of 1918, the immediate effect was to reinforce a retreat from the methods of the food-supply dictatorship that had already started. This effect is shown by two memorandums from Lenin in this period. On 26 May 1918—the same day on which in distant Siberia the Czechoslovak soldiers rose in revolt—Lenin proposed: "Change the War Commissariat into a War-Food-Supply Commissariat—that is, concentrate nine-tenths of the work of the War Commissariat on remaking the army for the war for grain and on conducting this war for three months." In this statement Lenin thus puts a nine-to-one ratio between the urgency of food supply and the urgency of all other military pressures. Six weeks later, in early August, Lenin insisted that food-supply policy had to be revised: precisely because of the war it was necessary to "neutralize the peasantry" (especially the newly discovered middle peasant).[37]

The other radical phase of food-supply policy—the crackdown on local markets in late 1920—also came in a period when military pressures seemed to be relaxed.[38] Thus the term *war communism* seems particularly inappropriate: the war part of the food-supply policy was not communist and the communist part was not appropriate for war.

The coincidence thesis is often put in subjective terms: the Bolsheviks themselves confused pragmatism and revolutionary vision, owing to a habit of baptizing necessary emergency measures with ideological labels.[39] But in the case of the *razverstka*, we see that the Bolsheviks were able to distinguish deeply held principle from temporary compromise. The commitment to a state monopoly was unswerving. Even bourgeois governments, such as Germany and the Provisional Government, had advanced to the point of adopting such a monopoly, and surely a socialist government could do no less. The grain monopoly was part of a wider ideological program of extending state organization over the economy as a basis for socialism—a program that predated the October Revolution and survived the civil war. War conditions, particularly the scarcity of administrative resources and the lack of material exchange equivalents, made a proper grain monopoly impossible and so Bolshevik food-supply officials consciously accepted a practical compromise in the form of the *razverstka*. (Food-supply officials less willingly accepted a host of other compromises that must also be seen as part of civil war food-supply policy.)

No one deceived himself into thinking that the harsh emergency methods of the *razverstka* were actually socialism in disguise. Wartime conditions did indeed strengthen what we would now consider to be illusions about nonmarket methods of distribution, but they did so in a way opposite to that suggested by the concept of war communism. Precisely because wartime methods were so distorted and so far from socialist ideals, the food-supply officials had good grounds to believe that nonmarket methods would work according to expectation under proper peacetime conditions.

The use of war communism as an interpretive framework also leads to an overstatement of the contrast between the *razverstka* and the NEP policy that

37. PSS, 36:374; 37:31–33.

38. Similarly, the only attempts to conduct commodity exchange without money came in 1918 and 1921. M. I. Davydov, "Gosudarstvennyi tovaroobmen mezhdu gorodom i derevnei v 1918–21 gg," *Istoricheskie Zapiski* 108 (1982):55–56.

39. Nove, *Economic History*, p. 47; Carr, *Bolshevik Revolution*, 2:55.

followed. War communism in general and the *razverstka* in particular are seen as expressing a principled disdain for peasant interests that was replaced by the *smychka* orientation of worker-peasant alliance.[40] This contrast cannot stand; it gains whatever plausibility it has only from the contrast between wartime deprivation and relative peacetime prosperity. The *razverstka* method was part and parcel of a general retreat from "class war in the villages" to "neutralization of the middle peasantry." Undoubtedly, beneath the surface of official policy, anti-peasant feelings were exacerbated by the food-supply crisis—but these feelings also continued throughout the 1920s. At no time in the 1920s was the middle peasant *as he was* seen as a completely solid or reliable ally; the only question was how peacefully he would let himself be transformed. But transformed he had to be.[41]

Bolshevik food-supply officials never denied that the worker-peasant alliance required a material base in equivalent exchange. Here we may cite Iurii Larin, archetypal war communist, writing in 1920: "The actual exchange of services and material values between the village and the town, between peasant and proletarian, is in general one of the basic problems of contemporary Russia, [and] one of the bases of the political union between workers and peasants as well."[42] The assertion that during war communism the Bolsheviks not only took grain without compensation but approved of this procedure ideologically seems to result from a confusion between market exchange (which the Bolsheviks did oppose) and exchange in general, including state-organized exchange. Only this confusion can account for E. H. Carr's statement that the Soviet leaders were "obstinately slow to recognize the hard fact" that "the main difficulty in securing supplies of food for the towns was . . . that no adequate return could be offered to the peasants" or for Alec Nove's argument that "the policy of requisitions and armed detachments" came to be seen as good in itself.[43] Bolshevik food-supply officials were so far from denying the importance of material exchange that in 1920 they were thrown into a panic by the imminent disappearance of even the meager goods fund that had earlier been at their disposal.

The contrast between war communism and NEP also suggests that the *razverstka* represented an attitude of coercive voluntarism aimed at immediate elimination of the market, as opposed to the gradualism of NEP. Certainly there is a switch of emphasis from the semipersecution of the civil war years to the semitoleration of the 1920s, but it should be remembered that "crowding-out" (*vytesnenie*) of the free market was an axiomatic goal in both periods, whether

40. Stephen Cohen, for example, calls the problem of the peasantry "the blind side of war communism"; *Bukharin and the Bolshevik Revolution* (New York: Vintage, 1971), p. 95. See also Merle Fainsod, *How Russia is Ruled*, 1st ed. (Cambridge: Harvard University Press, 1953), pp. 93 and 98, and Charles Bettelheim, *Class Struggles in the USSR, 1917–1923* (New York: Monthly Review Press, 1976), pp. 352-355.

41. In 1925, Bukharin distinguished between two methods for the overcoming (*preodolenie*) of bourgeois elements: towards the NEPmen, the method would be crowding out, but towards the peasants, it would be reworking (*pererabotka*). *Kritika ekonomicheskoi platformy oppozitsii* (Leningrad: Priboi, 1926), pp.45–51.

42. *Ocherk khoziaistvennoi zhizni* . . . (Moscow: Gosizdat, 1920), p. 23.

43. Carr, *Bolshevik Revolution*, 2:169; Nove, *Economic History*, p. 66. In similar fashion, Cohen argues that because Bukharin in 1920 rejected the commodity market, he was therefore reduced either to hoping that the peasants would volunteer grain out of revolutionary enthusiasm or to supporting "a system of permanent requisitioning" (*Bukharin*, p. 95).

the market was legal or illegal. The contrast between the two periods can be compared to two methods of conquering a continent. One way is to stick a flag on the coast, declare it the property of Queen Isabella or whomever, and then proceed to the slow work of making that control real. The other method is to regularize relations with the natives through various treaties and then proceed to the slow work of establishing hegemony and finally annexation. Despite the important differences involved, the choice is a matter of tactics and form. Before 1921, the grain market had been declared illegal at the outset, but the Bolsheviks were still aware that the market not only existed but flourished; they did not believe that they could expediently abolish the market before the state was organizationally capable of replacing it. The food-supply officials—who better?—had been aware of the immense difficulties they faced and the great distance they still had to travel through long and patient organizational work. The same criterion of expediency and the same difficulty in restraining overeager local officials remained throughout the NEP period.

It is tempting, but quite misleading, to see a continuity between the *razverstka* and Preobrazhenskii's theory of "unequal exchange" between town and country.[44] This comparison is unfair to both parties. Nikolai Bukharin's claim that Preobrazhenskii's proposal to use indirect taxation to support industrialization was a throwback to civil war coercion cannot be called an exaggeration, for there was no reality behind this claim at all. On their side, food-supply officials before NEP did not base the need for coercion as opposed to material incentives on elaborate theories about the need to "exploit" the petit bourgeois sector, but on the clear and present danger of a collapse of the economy that would involve the peasant along with everybody else. It is worthy of remark that many top food-supply officials (Tsiurupa, Frumkin, Vladimirov) were associated with the right during the 1920s.

In the case of food-supply policy, then, we have seen that the war communism concept originated in Lenin's obfuscatory rhetoric of 1921, that it suggests a coincidence between emergency measures and militant principles that did not exist, and that it overdramatizes the contrast between civil war policy and NEP. In my view, there are no compensating interpretive advantages and the term *war communism* should be dropped.

The genuine difficulty in interpreting the *razverstka* comes from its status as a holding operation for the state grain monopoly under the difficult circumstances of the civil war. There is no ambiguity about the Bolshevik commitment to abolish free trade in grain or about the sacrifices they were ready to impose in the name of that principle. Those critics within and without the Bolshevik party who called in 1920 for a replacement of the *razverstka* by a food-supply tax never went so far as to suggest legalization of the market.[45] But while the monopoly principle implied equivalent exchange, the *razverstka* method was designed to operate, if necessary, with only a minimum of industrial exchange

44. Malle so argues in *Economic Organization*, pp. 453, 514. While it is true that fixed prices during the civil war were slanted toward the towns, a distinction should be made between manipulation of the terms of trade and a principled reliance on coercion as opposed to exchange.

45. For example, David Dallin at the Eighth Congress of Soviets in December 1920 explicitly denied that his critique of Bolshevik food-supply policy was a defence of free trade. *Vos'moi vserossiiskii s'ezd sovetov*, stenographic report (Moscow, 1921), pp. 197–199.

items. This characteristic of the *razverstka* led to the contrast between the understanding of the food-supply professional and the understanding of everyone else. The nonprofessionals tended to identify the *razverstka* with the rigors of the civil war and to define it as taking grain without compensation. When the food-supply officials defended the *razverstka*, they were understood by others to be advocating taking grain without compensation not only as a temporary necessity but as a long-term principle. It is appropriate therefore to repeat the words of the food-supply official Kaganovich: "What do you think, the People's Commissariat does this for its own satisfaction? No, we do it because there's not enough food."

[4]

The Bolsheviks and the Peasantry: the Land Question During the First Eight Months of Soviet Rule

JOHN CHANNON

RECENT years have witnessed a welcome increase in the number of Western publications devoted to the study of the Russian peasantry in the years before and after 1917, although none has focused specifically on the peasantry during the early period of Bolshevik rule, the first eight months or so before the onset of all-out civil war. This is in stark contrast to the detailed researches on urban labour, where the micro-focus of such studies is reflected in their concentration on workers in individual factories, confined albeit to the two major industrial centres of tsarist Russia, Moscow and Petrograd.[1]

In an attempt to understand better the manner in which the majority of the Russian population related to the Bolsheviks during these first eight months, it is the object of this paper to examine the relationship (or lack of one) between the Soviet government and the peasantry — predominantly in the central regions of Russia — before the emergence of full-scale civil war in May–June 1918. Attention will be concentrated on one issue, the land question, and chiefly with regard to its distribution, though some consideration will also be given to distribution of the product of the land, the notorious food supply problem. This not only provides a focal point for examining the interaction between the peasantry and the Bolsheviks on a key issue but it also permits investigation of whether the experience of the central provinces provides support for an argument that frequently appears in the literature: namely, that the peasants were prepared to accept the Bolsheviks because of the land decree but turned against them from the spring to early summer 1918 with the move towards widespread

John Channon is Lecturer in Russian History at the School of Slavonic and East European Studies, University of London.
The author wishes to express his thanks to participants at the conference on the early months of Bolshevik rule held at the University of Essex, May 1984 who commented on an earlier version of this paper, particularly to Bob Service, Maureen Perrie, Terry Cox, Ronald Kowalski, Alan Wildman, Brian Pearce, and to an anonymous reader, for their suggestions and help.

[1] The conference organized by the University of Essex in May 1984 at which an earlier version of this paper was given focused specifically on this question, although the conference papers reflected the bias towards the urban sector and the industrial working class.

594   JOHN CHANNON

coercion and forcible requisitioning in the face of an ever-deepening
food crisis.

The focusing of attention on the land question needs little justification.
The 'accursed' land issue had proved a perennial problem for Russian
governments before 1917. The failure to redistribute land before
October had remained the chief peasant grievance while a major cause
of the downfall of the Provisional Government had been its inability to
resolve the land issue in the face of an ever-growing agrarian
revolution. Lenin showed how well he appreciated the political
significance of such inaction by incorporating into one of the first
legislative acts of the new Bolshevik régime the major peasant demand
for land.[2] Not only did this provide legal sanction to a process already
under way but it undoubtedly proved popular in areas where *pomeshchik*
land still remained to be seized and divided after October.[3]

Although the land question was a key issue facing the Bolsheviks in
relation to the peasantry, there was no unanimity within the party on
how to resolve it after the October seizure of power. It was to prove, in
fact, one of the most contentious issues within the party during this first
period of Bolshevik rule. The divergence of opinion on the agrarian
question was most clearly highlighted by the division between the
views of Lenin on the one hand and those of the Left Communists on the
other. Outside the central areas, moreover, the situation was even more
complex.[4] The situation was further complicated by the fact that
Bolshevik agrarian policies after October cannot be viewed in isolation
from the influence of the Left SRs, since the eight months covered in
this paper encompassed the period of the Bolshevik–Left SR alliance.
And in the central regions during this period it is arguably more
Left SR land policy with which we are concerned. By May 1918 Left SR
strength within *Narkomzem* had certainly been weakened, though it was
still significant. Yet from March to the end of June the Moscow
Regional (*Oblast'*) Commissariat of Agriculture was just as influential,
if not more so, in land policy at the heart of European Russia: the
Commissariat was solidly Left SR and had under its jurisdiction the

---

[2] This was the demand as noted in the Instructions from 242 local peasant resolutions of
May 1917. The main points of the 'Land Decree' were taken from an SR newspaper and
helped to gain Left SR support.

[3] Khar'kov guberniya in the Ukraine provides a good example where by autumn 1917,
less than one fifth of all *pomeshchik* land in the province had been transferred to the peasantry.
P. F. Reshod'ko, 'Bor'ba krest'yan kharkovskoy gubernii za zemlyu v 1917 godu' (*Trudy
Kafedry Istorii KPSS Khar'kovskogo ordena trudovogo Krasnogo znameni gosudarstvennogo universiteta
imeni A. M. Gor'kogo*, vyp. 2, 1964, p. 178).

[4] In late 1917/early 1918, for instance, the Left Communists' position in the Ukraine was
similar to that of Lenin's in central Russia, though their position changed later. (I am
grateful to Dr R. Kowalski for this point.)

THE BOLSHEVIKS AND THE PEASANTRY 595

fourteen *gubernii* at the centre of the country. The Commissariat, moreover, evidently saw itself, in its own words, as 'the central organ for executing the land reform' and, as such, posed a direct challenge to Narkomzem.[5]

Such disagreements between the Commissariats shed interesting light on relations between the Bolsheviks and Left SRs, although the vying for power between the organizations appears to have had no noticeable impact on the peasantry. In fact there was probably little difference between them as far as implementing the land reform was concerned. Both appear to have had access to equipment and agricultural specialists necessary for implementing the reform while the specialists themselves were of similar persuasion regarding their tasks. On the other hand, it is often claimed that the Left SRs were more openly sympathetic to wealthier peasants than the Bolsheviks. In truth there is little evidence at present to suggest that policies of one commissariat were more acceptable to the peasants than those of another.[6] To most peasants the Bolsheviks, inasmuch as they were known at all in the countryside, had been the party which had given them the land, although peasants often failed to perceive differences between Bolsheviks and Left SRs at local level since both seemed to espouse similar policies. Since the peasants were essentially single-issue voters — on the key question of land — they undoubtedly gave their support to whichever party was prepared to implement the radical agrarian reform they desired.[7] As has recently been pointed out, where Bolsheviks were known in rural areas in 1917 they competed with the SRs for votes and may well have obtained far more popular support in the country at large than is revealed by the returns to the Constituent Assembly.[8] Since peasants were sceptical of all such central bodies it probably mattered little to peasants in the localities which was the main organ of agrarian power (the Narkomzem or the Moscow Oblast' Commissariat) or who controlled it (the Bolsheviks or

[5] By the beginning of 1918 several *oblast'* commissariats of agriculture had been established to direct the execution of the land reform in their respective oblasti, although the largest was in Moscow with some 400 workers. See V. G. Lomovtseva, 'Organizatsiya Narodnogo Komissariata Zemledeliya RSFSR v 1917–1918 gg.' (*Trudy Moskovskogo Gosudarstvennogo Istorikoarkhivnogo Instituta*, vol. 19, 1965, p. 88).

[6] For further details of this conflict between Narkomzem and the Moscow Oblast' Commissariat, see J. Channon, 'The Bolsheviks, Land Reform and the Peasantry', conference paper presented at the University of Essex, May 1984, pp. 5–7. Differences do emerge between the two commissariats on agrarian issues other than land, such as food supply, although by the time this was reaching its nadir the Moscow Oblast' was already in the process of being disbanded.

[7] It is well to remember Trotsky's comment that a saying familiar among the peasantry following the Bolsheviks' change of name to Communist after March 1918 ran as follows: 'We supported the Bolsheviks because they gave us the land; we oppose the Communists because they take it away again'. See M. Shachtman, *The Struggle for the New Course* (Ann Arbor, 1972), p. 134.

[8] S. Fitzpatrick, *The Russian Revolution* (Oxford, 1982), p. 59.

596   JOHN CHANNON

the Left SRs) as long as the land policies corresponded to their own aspirations.

On the fundamental question of land Lenin changed course from the summer of 1917 and sought policies which had wide popular support (see below, pp. 614–15). It was a recognition, as one recent writer so aptly put it, that the party had to operate 'in accordance with the fundamental aspirations of the broad masses'.[9] In relation to the land issue such aspirations meant seizure and redistribution of land. This explains Lenin's enthusiasm for publishing the land decree, based after all on a summary of resolutions supposedly indicating what the peasants wanted, and for ostensibly promoting the SR idea of land socialization in the 'Basic Law' of February 1918 with only passing reference to more orthodox Marxist notions of land reform. As Lenin himself claimed, the Bolsheviks agreed to the 'law' because 'we did not want to oppose the will of the majority'. To do so would have been 'to betray the revolution'.[10]

Some historians, however, have doubted whether Bolshevik legislation did accurately reflect peasant aspirations, citing as evidence contradictions between the peasant 'model' mandate and the Bolshevik land decree, chiefly in relation to which lands should be redivided. But this apparent contradiction reflected in practice the division of feeling on the issue among peasants between and within different regions of the country. Local conditions varied tremendously and the peasants desired to solve the land issue themselves according to the needs specific to their own localities.[11]

More problematic perhaps for the Bolsheviks were the compromises this forced. Such an attempt to appease the peasants and accept the implementation of an SR-type land reform forced Lenin to agree to points in the agrarian legislation to which earlier he had been openly opposed. In the 'Basic Law' for instance considerable importance was attached to the land norm yet one of the major problems for the land departments which awaited further guidance on the implementation of such norms was the total lack of conviction of their usefulness on the part of the Bolsheviks. Even though the Left SRs in 1918 accepted that the land norm provided a basis for a future land reform, Lenin had always been hostile to the suggestion that such a norm could provide a

---

[9] L. Colletti, 'The Question of Stalin' cited in R. Blackburn (ed.), *Revolution and Class Struggle* (Glasgow, 1977), p. 174.
[10] See *Bednota*, no. 185, 10 November 1918.
[11] For Lenin's comments see *Izvestiya*, no. 209, 28 October 1917 and *Pravda*, no. 171, 10 November (28 October) 1917. For a more detailed discussion of the issue see Channon, op. cit., pp. 8–9.

THE BOLSHEVIKS AND THE PEASANTRY   597

solution to the agrarian problem.[12] The peasantry, on the other hand, had traditionally divided land in accordance with 'allocation units' (such as the number of 'eaters' or 'workers'), apportioning each unit a share of land. In both cases the Bolshevik government accepted inclusion of these units of measurement in the legislation simply because they had popular support.[13]

Although the Bolsheviks never expected their decrees of 1917–18 to provide a final solution to the agrarian problem, these reflected the revolutionary changes in landownership and land distribution the peasants expected. In the early days of the October revolution the Bolsheviks gave free rein to the peasants on the land issue. Not only was legislation passed seemingly supporting the kind of land reform desired by the peasants, but the Bolsheviks established an organizational apparatus (often adapted from the pre-October period) for planning, guiding and executing it. To this end they also enlisted the aid of former tsarist agricultural specialists. This apparatus however was just one facet of an organizational structure planned to facilitate the transmission of information and assistance between the centre and the localities. Yet government efforts were not limited to administrative–organizational change. Much attention was devoted to communicating the objectives of the new régime in the sphere of land reform. Speeches and slogans proclaimed its intentions, news-sheets and pamphlets were distributed to help publicize the agrarian laws, while instructors and other emissaries were despatched to the countryside to inform peasants about such policies and provide assistance with their implementation. In the first months of 1918 a total of 1,294 agitators were directed to the localities by the agitational-propaganda department of the Peasant Section of VTsIK: 603 of these were Bolsheviks and 691 Left SRs.[14] For the entire eight months following the October revolution it has been estimated that some 47,550 emissaries were despatched around the country for such purposes. The bulk of these were apparently agitators, mainly demobilized soldiers and unemployed workers.[15] Although the Bolsheviks had used propaganda to good effect in 1917 their task was nevertheless made difficult by their lack of a base in the countryside before October. Doubtless some activities of these emissaries aroused

[12] At the First All-Russia Congress of Peasant Deputies in May 1917, Lenin had argued that: '. . . even if you establish norms, they would remain at best a disadvantage . . . because they do not consider the factor of chief importance, that ownership of implements, cattle and money is distributed unequally; they do not take account of the reasons that produced hired labour, which is responsible for exploitation' (cited in E. A. Lutskiy, 'Leninskiy dekret o zemle' in I. I. Mints (ed.), *Leninskiy dekret o zemle v deistviy* (Moscow, 1979), p. 39). For a discussion of what land reform meant for the various political parties see my *Peasant Revolution and Land Reform in Russia, 1917–1924*, forthcoming.

[13] Lutskiy, op. cit.; V. V. Kabanov, 'Razrabotka osnovnogo zakona o sotsializatsii zemli', *Oktyabr' i sovetskoye krest' yanstvo. 1917–1927 gg.* in I. M. Volkov *et al.* (eds) (Moscow, 1977).

[14] *Doklad o deyatel' nosti krest' yanskogo otdela VTsIk* (Moscow, 1918), p. 9.

[15] J. L. H. Keep, *The Russian Revolution* (London, 1976), pp. 450, 451–54.

598   JOHN CHANNON

distrust of the Bolsheviks among the peasants, yet their impact should
not be seen as entirely negative since some did provide assistance with
the land reform.[16] Apart from the limited help with land distribution,
the Bolsheviks did very little to assist the peasants in the spring of 1918.

Yet peasants in the localities had already taken full advantage of the
freedom given them to organize their own affairs, well before Soviet
power took root in the countryside. Most estates were confiscated and
inventories of their property drawn up — in central Russia at least —
before the creation of the majority of *volost'* soviets during January–
March 1918.[17] It was during the same winter months that heated
discussions ensued as to how the spring redivision of land should best
proceed. Furthermore, there seemed to be little peasant discontent with
either the process of confiscation or the new rural organizations
established in the spring of 1918. The organizational forms of these
volost' soviets did vary but on many occasions sections of former
volost' *zemstva* simply changed their name to soviets, either without
new elections or with only individual members being re-elected.[18]
Similarly one can note the inclusion of volost' land committees — often
in toto — as land departments in the soviets. Generally this transfer
seems to have been achieved with relatively little disruption. Under the
circumstances, this should come as no surprise. The ease and readiness
with which former volost' zemstva and land committees were assimilated into volost' soviets were frequently the result of the paucity of
technical personnel. This compelled soviets to adopt the existing
apparatus irrespective of the party and social allegiances of its
workers.[19] To many peasants the differences between the former
volost' organizations and the soviets seemed little indeed; and their

[16] The assistance appeared in a variety of ways: through organizing short courses which
gave guidance on how to execute the law on the socialization of land, or by helping to train
peasants to acquire greater technical expertise for undertaking some of the more complex
land measuring and dividing. See, for example, *Zemlya* (the newspaper [hereafter *Zemlya*
(np)]), no. 27, 7 June (25 May), 1918; P. N. Pershin, *Agrarnaya Revolyutsiya v Rossii*, 2 vols
vol. 2 (Moscow, 1966), p. 326. For more negative aspects of emissaries' activities see Keep,
op. cit, ch. 33; and for examples of lack of Bolshevik help, see Roy Medvedev, *The October
Revolution* (New York, 1985 edn (1979)), p. 157.
[17] S. L. Makarova, 'Kvoprosu o vremeni likvidatsii pomeshchich'ego zemlevladeniya', in
Oktyabr' i sovetskoye krest'yanstvo, pp. 112, 117; Makarova, 'Agrarnye preobrazovaniya
oktyabr'skoy revolyutsii v tsentralnykh rayonakh Rossii (analiz anket sostavlennykh vesnoy
1918 g.' (*Istoricheskiye zapiski*, 1977, 100, p. 296); for a more detailed discussion of the
confiscation of estates and the creation of rural soviets see J. Channon, '"Peasant Revolution" and "Land Reform": Land Redistribution in European Russia, October 1917–20',
unpublished PhD thesis, University of Birmingham, 1983, ch. 2. In practice there was little
change in the peasant organizations themselves apart, that is, from the adoption of a new
name, while the composition of the soviets depended on the criteria applied locally for their
elections.
[18] Makarova, 'K voprosu . . .', p. 117; *Zemlya* (the journal [hereafter jo]), no. 1, 13 March
1918; T. Emmons and W. S. Vucinich, eds, *The Zemstvo in Russia. An Experiment in Local Self
Government* (Cambridge, 1982), p. 409.
[19] Makarova, 'K voprosu . . .', p. 118.

THE BOLSHEVIKS AND THE PEASANTRY 599

attitudes towards the volost' soviets depended to a great extent on their relations with the former zemstva and land committees. If zemstva workers had assisted peasants with land affairs there was little cause for confrontation.

Although elected by popular assembly, the soviets were none the less not dominated by the rural poor, as the Bolsheviks had hoped. Data for almost 60% of volosts in the Central Black-Earth and Central Industrial regions showed that virtually all soviets at this level had been elected on a 'general' basis, that is, without any particular class bias.[20] Gerasimenko similarly notes that 'originally peasants from all social groups were elected to the volost' soviets. No limitations existed in this period on the right to elect or be elected.'[21] Notwithstanding regional variations, the volost' soviets at this time assumed a broad social composition and the situation changed little before the summer.

The experience of self-government peasants had acquired in previous decades proved particularly useful during and after 1917 when the removal of former constraints gave them greater freedom to control their own affairs. A vital part of this new freedom was their taking over of the land. Their attitudes towards this often conflicted with those of the chief agrarian land authorities. Before 1917 peasant demands for a redistribution of land were linked not only to a basic economic objective — the extension of the cultivable area under peasant control — but just as much to 'natural right' and 'social justice', as understood within the context of their millenarian aims. The demand for greater equality and social justice was manifested most frequently through demands for a more just and equitable distribution of the land. Realizing such equalization, however, proved a difficult task. The peasantry had their own idea of what equalization involved. It would be executed in the localities in a decentralized way. The staff in the Narkomzem, however, desired a centrally organized reform to achieve the goal of equalization and this would inevitably take time. Narkomzem's solution was to consider that the land had been distributed among the peasantry in 'temporary equal use' (*vremennoye uravnitel'noye pol'zovaniye*).[22] This temporary distribution was regarded as a preliminary to a change in

[20] T. V. Osipova, 'Razvitiye sotsialisticheskoy revolyutsii v derevne v pervyy god diktatury proletariata', in *Oktyabr' i sovetskoye krest'yanstvo*, p. 45.

[21] G. A. Gerasimenko, *Nizovye krest'yanskiye organizatsii v 1917 g. — pervoy polovine 1918 g.* (Saratov, 1974), p. 225. For a more detailed discussion of volost' soviets see John Channon, 'The Peasantry in the Revolutions of 1917', a paper presented to the conference on 'The Revolutions of 1917: 70 Years After', The Hebrew University of Jerusalem, Israel, January 1988.

[22] See for example, P. N. Pershin, op. cit., vol. 2, p. 233. Since the 'Basic Law' could not be realized for some time transitional measures were to be introduced in the meantime, guided by the Provisional Instructions, passed by *Narkomzem* on 11 April 1918. Although the term 'equalization' was frequently used during the period 1917–21, in practice of course full equality was not achieved but only a situation which approximated to one of less inequality in land use than before 1917.

600   JOHN CHANNON

the future to a more equitable distribution — a complete and final equalization which would include the recently assimilated former non-peasant lands.[23] Most reasons given for assigning this newly distributed land for provisional use only were linked to the fact that the land reform that was being prepared revolved around the gathering and processing of a mass of detailed information. Since this information was not readily available and immediate redistribution of land was vital to allow peasants to commence the spring sowing, such a distribution could only be approximate and provisional until accurate data existed for working out a more equal distribution.[24]

Moreover, the Bolsheviks in 1918 were content to posit a final solution to the land reform at some unspecified time in the future but were unable to give the SR notion serious consideration since no-one in the party believed that a solution was possible via reforms to improve small-scale peasant agriculture.[25] Thus by labelling the division 'provisional' the Bolsheviks were partly appeasing their own consciences and partly answering the reproaches of their critics that the division was incomplete.[26]

None of this though did much to reinforce peasant certainty about the security of the new land received. And on the assumption that the single most important peasant demand was for more land — even though there were widespread differences of opinion as to the sources of such 'additions' — the peasant may well have expected to judge the success of the new régime during the first months by its ability to solve the land issue or rather, by its willingness to let the peasants solve it. Any attempt at assessing whether peasant aspirations were realized during this period requires discussion of the land redistribution which occurred before the early summer of 1918.

On many occasions before October, peasants focused their attention on issues other than land redistribution, such as setting their own rent

---

[23] See for example *Materialy po zemel'noy reforme*, vyp. 1, Raspredeleniye zemli (Moscow, 1919), p. 2; Pershin, op. cit., vol. 2, pp. 542, 560, 569; for such reports from localities in Kursk, Penza and Oryol see *Golos trudovogo krest'yanstva* [hereafter *GTK*], no. 97, 9 April 1918, and no. 113, 28 April 1918; *Orlovskiy vestnik*, no. 48, 27 February (12 March) 1918.

[24] For a more detailed discussion of this see J. Channon '"Peasant Revolution" and "Land Reform"', pp. 213–15, 273–74. Land was also considered in temporary use until such time as organized migration could resume.

[25] For the Bolsheviks the temporary distribution was to last until a final solution to the agrarian problem had been found, and in 1918 this was of unspecified duration. In the long term, of course, all Bolsheviks were committed to collectivization of agriculture (in a general sense) as such a final solution. Moves towards the final socialization for the Bolsheviks commenced in early 1919 with the new emphasis on 'socialist land reorganization' and special provisions for the development of collective agriculture.

[26] Victor Chernov, 'Chornyy Peredel v 1918 godu' (*Zapiski instituta po izucheniyu Rossii*, vol. 2, Prague, 1925, p. 107).

THE BOLSHEVIKS AND THE PEASANTRY 601

levels, while peasant 'seizure' of non-peasant land often meant preventing the landowner from using the land or its products (whether ploughland or meadow) by establishing peasant boundary markers. On other occasions, redivisions of land were considered only provisional or were postponed indefinitely, frequently because husbands and sons were still to return from the war.[27] Elsewhere redivisions in 1917 were opposed because the communal peasants (*obshchinniki*) felt that those wishing to use the division to separate from the community would gain an unfair advantage. Some peasants even opposed such methods of acquiring land because they claimed that they contradicted their belief of what was right and just (see below, p. 608). Furthermore, the peasantry was still aware that the consequence of such 'illegal' acts as land seizure might be confrontation with government troops. Sometimes troops were despatched to 'troublesome' localities, and in such uncertain times as these, many peasants probably recalled the aftermath of the events of 1905–07 and the harsh vengeance wreaked by both landlords and government authorities. True, relatively few such reprisals seem to have occurred in practice though in the midst of war and revolution it would have been virtually impossible to despatch anything like sufficient troops to quell all such disturbances.[28]

Things were to change in the months following October. Before that date peasants had been optimistic that improvements in their conditions would follow and now the Bolshevik seizure of power appeared to confirm this, sanctioning the redistribution of land. As noted above, on the distribution itself the Bolsheviks played an essentially passive role before the summer of 1918 which gave peasants freedom to carry out their own redistributions of land and through the Narkomzem attempted to provide assistance with land reform wherever possible. But over the years the peasantry had accumulated a wealth of experience in distributing land within their communities and were thus

[27] This was clearly a continuation of a process begun during the First World War. In 1917 communal peasants turned to the Provisional Government with petitions (as they did to the Tsar before 1914) to save them from the effects of land reorganization. Thus they opposed land redivisions if these were for the purpose of separation. See A. M. Anfimov (ed.) *Krest'yanskoye dvizheniye v Rossii v gody pervoy mirovoy voyny, iyul' 1914 g. — fevral' 1917 g.*, *Sbornik dokumentov* (Moscow–Leningrad, 1965), pp. 152–53, 232–34, 251–56; *Ekonomicheskoye polozheniye Rossii nakanune Velikoy Oktyabr'skoy sotsialisticheskoy revolyutsii. Dokumenty i materialy*, vol. 3, pp. 325–37.
[28] For examples of troops being used against peasants, land committees etc., see A. D. Malyavskiy, *Krest'yanskoye dvizheniye v Rossii v 1917 g. mart-oktyabr'* (Moscow, 1981), pp. 21–35, 244–48; *Krest'yanskoye dvizheniye v 1917 godu. Dokumenty i materialy* (Moscow–Leningrad, 1927), pp. 154, 416–21, 427; *Revolyutsionnaya bor'ba krest'yan Kazanskoy gubernii makanune Oktyabrya. Sbornik dokumentov* (Kazan', 1958), pp. 43–50, 68, 417, 431–34, 441; J. Bunyan and H. Fisher, (eds), *The Bolshevik Revolution, 1917–18* (Stanford, 1964); Roy Medvedev, op. cit., p. 32. For the argument that such 'illegal' acts contradicted peasant understanding of the government and its intentions because some peasants still trusted the Provisional government, seeing its members as legitimate heirs of the tsar and Duma, see Ya. A. Yakovlev, 'Krest'yanskaya voyna 1917 goda', in *Agrarnaya Revolyutsiya*, vol. 2 (Moscow, 1928), p. 84.

amply capable of redividing much of the land themselves. With regard to technical and organizational matters, moreover, communal land redivisions after October appear little different from those that took place in the pre-October period of the revolution (or even before 1914).[29] Widespread reliance on these communal mechanisms for redistributing land was one factor which acted to strengthen the *mir* and heighten the importance of those individuals responsible for measuring and dividing the land, factors that were to prove so inauspicious for the Bolsheviks.[30] At least during the first half of 1918 'outside' help was on hand when procedures for land reapportionment happened to be more complex. Even though resources were limited, a number of land surveyors (*zemlemery*) were available to assist with the measuring and dividing of land, as well as with various other matters. Although the situation was to change dramatically from the summer of 1918, some 7,000 surveyors were registered with Narkomzem at the end of March and in the spring a significant number of these were dispersed around the more central gubernii of European Russia.[31] The peasants' reactions to these specialists was predictably mixed and was determined largely by their relations with the surveyors in the period before 1917.

I have considered in some detail elsewhere the problems facing researchers when attempting to discover what actually happened with respect to the distribution. Trying to separate what was *planned* from what occurred *in practice* is only one, albeit perhaps the most important of such problems.[32] One of the most difficult exercises is attempting to assess how widespread were the redistributions of land during the spring of 1918. The paucity of relevant materials necessitates reliance on two surveys, one carried out in 1918 and the other in 1922. There are problems in using these sources although both surveys provide very similar results.[33] There was a marked contrast between the black-earth

[29] See, for example, P. A. Butylkin, *Krest'yanskoye dvizheniye v Nizhnem Povolzh'e letom i osenyu 1917 g.* (Saratov, 1983).
[30] For a good example of individuals involved in measuring and dividing the land in 1918 see Yakov Sadovsky, 'Kak ya delil zemlyu' (*Russkaya Mysl'*, bks., 9–12, 1923–24, p. 331).
[31] According to a Narkomzem report at the end of March 1918 (signed by both Kolegayev and Meshcheryakov) there were 7,000 surveyors registered at the Commissariat with another 5,000 in training (TsGANKh, f. 478, op. 4, ed. khr. 5, 1.8).
[32] For a more detailed discussion of this problem see Channon, 'The Bolsheviks . . .', pp. 13–14.
[33] The survey of 1918 covered 16 gubernii at the centre of the country and was based on replies to two sets of questionnaires sent to the volost' soviets in the spring, one distributed by Narkomzem and the other by the Executive Committee of the Moscow Oblast' Soviet. See S. L. Makarova, 'Agrarnyye preobrazovaniya oktyabr'skoy revolyutsii v tsentral'nykh rayonakh Rossii' (*Istoricheskiye zapiski*, 100, 1977). The replies to the former questionnaires are located in TsGANKh, f. 478, op. 6, ed. khr. 224. A summary of the 1922 survey is in Yu. Blyakher, 'Sovremennoye zemlepol'zovaniye po dannym spetsial'noy ankety Ts.S.U. 1922 g.' (*Vestnik Statistiki*, bk. 13, nos. 1–3, March 1923). For a discussion of the problems of using these surveys see Channon, 'The Bolsheviks . . .', pp. 14–17 and 37–38.

and non black-earth regions, with three-quarters or more of the volosts surveyed experiencing redistribution in the former region but only about one-half or less in the latter, notwithstanding some exceptions: reports from village level would seem to confirm this.[34]

How then did all this relate to peasant perceptions of the Bolsheviks and can the number and nature of such redivisions be used to measure the realization of peasant expectations on the land issue? *Prima facie*, the above evidence on land distribution suggests that the peasant objective of acquiring more land had been only partially attained. And this is reinforced when we come to examine the type of redivisions that occurred. In fact, it was relatively uncommon to find that land redistribution had led to a radical transformation of land holding or land relations at village or mir level. 'General' redivisions (*obshchiye* or *polnyye peredely*) — or in the parlance of rural Russia, 'black repartitions' (*chornyye peredely*) — where *all* land was pooled and redivided anew and *all* households were involved in the process, were a relatively rare occurrence. For the Bolsheviks *chornyye peredely* were perceived as an expression of the rural poor. Within such an analysis, the rarity of such redivisions would suggest the poor still had much to gain after the spring of 1918.

But such an analysis overlooks the real reasons why these 'general' or 'black' repartitions were so rare and why their incidence was restricted to the more central regions. It also ignores the reasons for *chornyye peredely* in earlier periods. In early 1918, moreover, other economic and social factors at this particular conjuncture of Russian rural history combined to heighten the pressure for land redivision. 'General' redivisions of land in these regions were chiefly the result of the mir having to cope with a sudden influx of returning *otkhodniki*, permanent urban workers (some, though, still having retained links with the countryside) and peasant soldiers.[35] The strain on land resources was considerable yet 'all' were now eligible to claim a share in the land. Although there were local variations and interpretations of the land decree, the eater unit was the most popular criterion for allocating land, overwhelmingly so in the Central Black-Earth region. Thus, this included not only women and girls (frequently excluded in earlier

[34] The results of a survey of 163 villages in 10 volosts (out of 11) in Sviyazhsk uezd of Kazan' province revealed that redivision occurred in almost 72% of villages. See M. A. Kibardin, *Bolsheviki kazanskoy gubernii vo glave agrarnykh preobrazovanii 1917–1918 godov* (Kazan', 1963), p. 140.

[35] As before 1917, the only way in which 'newcomers' could enforce their right to a share in land was by means of completely new allocation. *Chornyy peredel* also occurred when, as was traditionally the case, two-thirds of all inhabitants were in favour of such a division. Yet even before 1917, simple majorities or even significant minorities had pushed through 'full redivisions'. Thus it would not be surprising to discover similar occurrences under less stable conditions and especially when the 'significant minorities' could be young, aggressive, and armed.

604   JOHN CHANNON

periods), but also teachers, shopkeepers, smiths and the like, and on some occasions even former *pomeshchiki* and clergy.[36] The effect of all this in the spring of 1918 was a dramatic increase in the man-to-land ratio, especially since this related only to the spring crop area. Such pressure on resources forced the mir with repartitional experience to 'equalize' land distribution through a black repartition. And one could argue that the mir in the Central Black Earth region where the redivisional function had never become dormant was actually in the best position for coping with this phenomenon. Thus the repartitional community responds to the economic and social circumstances of 1918–21 in precisely the same way that it had done in the past under similar conditions. Whenever the man-to-land ratio changed dramatically the repartitional community activated its function of land repartition.[37] Although some general redivisions may have been accepted by the village gathering (*skhod*) after the more aggressive actions of the returning soldiers (*frontoviki*), it is clearly not necessarily the case that such redivisions were the result of poor peasants' endeavours. Hence it would be too simplistic to view the type of land redivision executed as a good indicator of the satisfaction of peasant demands. Such redivisions were more the result of the Bolsheviks' decision to let the peasants sort out their affairs in the way they knew best. Although the unique situation of early 1918 was not of the peasants' making, the mir coped with the situation in the 'traditional' manner.

Inevitably, though, such redivisions provoked conflict within the mir or village. Frequently these disputes centred on which lands were to be included in the redivision. In virtually all areas of the country those peasants who had separated from the community before 1917 lost some or all of their land before the summer 1918. Although some such 'separators' seem to have returned willingly to the community — and there were good reasons for doing so — those who were compelled to return doubtless felt resentment towards the new government for the destruction of their farms, even though some were eligible for a share in

---

[36] For examples of the latter see Channon, 'Former landlords (*pomeshchiki*) in rural Russia after the Revolution: some economic and social aspects', *Discussion Paper*, no. 85/6, Dept of Economics, University of Lancaster, 1985, pp. 12–21.

[37] This had been the case, for instance, in the late 1870s and early 1880s when many communities, tired of waiting for the expected revision of the 'census', carried out their own local censuses before proceeding to a new repartition of all the land. With the increase in taxation pressure in the late 1880s and 1890s such communal redivisions continued, reallocating land so that the tax burden could be distributed more equitably between households. (For more details, see Channon, 'The Bolsheviks...', p. 38, n. 65; for information on the upsurges of land redivisions between 1889–1904, see A. M. Anfimov, *Ekonomicheskoye polozheniye i klassovaya bor'ba krest'yan yevropeyskoy Rossii, 1881–1904 gg.* (Moscow, 1984), esp. ch. 4). It should also be noted that the reasons for repartition before and during the revolution could be more complicated and varied than simple changes in the man–land ratios.

THE BOLSHEVIKS AND THE PEASANTRY 605

the new allocation.[38] And most disputes within communities arose over those now deemed eligible for a share in the land. As noted above, land allocations according to eaters or consumers predominated where all individuals were included, such as' those born outside the locality', or women, girls and adopted sons; in some cases clergy and former pomeshchiki were included too and allotted land on the same basis as the peasants.[39] The adoption of alternative criteria for redividing land — for example, on the basis of seed, implements and livestock possessed — would also provoke conflicts. Sometimes the land was not redistributed in 1918 because of such disputes, resulting in continued use of land on the old basis and in a few cases leading to the postponement of redivision for many years.[40]

The mir was the vehicle for land acquisition and redistribution and its ruling body, the skhod, determined which lands would be included. This is where the composition of the skhod became important. Where the skhod had been broadened in early 1918 to include representation from outsiders, the lands of separators and wealthier peasants might be included for redivision because of the relative land scarcity; alternatively other skhody tried to prevent these 'outsiders' acquiring land.[41] Yet these land conflicts were resolved locally, by mirs, as in the past. The same people within the mir were responsible for overseeing the land distribution and use 'tried and tested' methods to resolve conflicts. If these failed, moreover, peasants could always turn to the new agencies established under the new régime, such as the local conflict

[38] In such uncertain times as these the community provided a relatively safe haven in contrast to exposed and isolated separated farms. Far fewer peasants separated from the community in the centre than in the south and south-east, for example, though it is significant to note that the impact of individual farming had been correspondingly greater in the industrial centre than in its agricultural zone.

[39] In some cases allegedly wealthier peasants resisted distribution of land and armed force was then used to execute the division. For examples see Igritskiy, *1917 goda v derevne* (Moscow, 1967), p. 184; K. A. Bodrenkov, 'Voronezhskiye bol'sheviki v bor'be za provedeniye v zhizn' leninskogo dekreta o zemle v 1917–18 gg.', unpublished dissertation, Moscow, 1951, p. 146 citing archives.) Since such resistance often went unchecked, however, it becomes difficult to gauge the effects of such incidents on peasant attitudes towards the régime.

[40] *GTK*, no. 179, 24 July 1918; *Zemlya* (np), no. 12, 21 (8) May 1918, and no. 37, 20 May (7 June) 1918. In areas of the country where there was no landlord land to divide and hence greater pressure from poorer peasants for the redivision of land in the possession of other peasants, conflicts also remained unresolved and redivision prohibited.

[41] Undoubtedly new voices were heard at communal and volost' gatherings (*skhody*) during 1917–18 though this does not seem to have undermined pre-revolutionary representative customs. For a recent discussion of the broadening of the *skhod* during 1917–18 see V. V. Kabanov, 'Oktyabr'skaya revolyutsiya i krest'yanskaya obshchina (*Istoricheskiye zapiski*, II, Moscow, 1984); see also L. Kritsman, *Klassovoye rassloyeniye v sovetskoy derevne* (Moscow, 1926).

commissions, for help in resolving the problems.[42] But such land conflicts were not confined to a mir or village and also occurred between mirs and villages within a volost'. Leaving villages, communities, or even on occasion volosts to implement their own distributions made it possible for those individuals or groups with the greatest influence and power to obtain the best quality land, a sizeable proportion of it and that located most favourably. Thus many of the land disputes which arose in the first half of 1918 developed because of the means employed by one mir or volost' to obtain advantages over another. And this was yet another manifestation of the Bolshevik acceptance that the peasants would undertake the land reform themselves. But were such disputes over land distribution important in terms of Bolshevik-peasant relations?

One way of ascertaining an answer to this question is to examine the nature and number of such conflicts and their resolution. Although disputes over land in the spring of 1918 are well documented, other evidence suggests that there were fewer conflicts than might have been anticipated under such volatile conditions and that, when disputes did arise, in general they were not particularly serious in nature.[43] Several studies of individual provinces by Soviet scholars have reached this conclusion while approximately 85% of all volosts surveyed in the spring 1918 registered no conflicts at all.[44] Some account must be taken of the problems inherent within the latter survey, although such an outcome must also reflect the way in which peasants perceived the distribution at this time. Many peasants believed it to be only provisional (especially if it was not a chornyy peredel, as had always been the case), a point constantly emphasized by Narkomzem (though for different reasons) and confirmed in resolutions of the local land authorities. This certainly engendered caution in the peasants and introduced an element of uncertainty into their future position regarding the land. Yet peasants who were dissatisfied with the distribution which had just occurred accepted that failure to solve the land problem was only temporary and that the final 'repartition' of the future would produce the great chornyy peredel they had been

[42] In an attempt to resolve land disputes as impartially as possible a variety of agencies from guberniya down to volost' level were created, with the sole purpose of attempting to achieve a settlement acceptable to all the participants. One such conflict commission was active in Ryazan province in early 1918, for instance, while similar such commissions existed in other provinces attached to uyezd and volost' soviets. In Voronezh an *instruktorskiy otdel* was established to settle land disputes and inter-uyezd commissions created for the same purpose. In yet other cases so-called 'conciliatory commissions' were set up attached to the land departments of the soviets. For a detailed discussion of the attempts to resolve land disputes see my *Peasant Revolution and Land Reform in Russia, 1917–1924*, forthcoming.

[43] Channon, thesis, ch. 9. Although there were some serious conflicts over land in the spring some of the most violent clashes appear to have arisen over meadows in the summer 1918, particularly during July (see Channon, "Peasant Revolution", pp. 608, 620).

[44] Ibid., pp. 601–06.

THE BOLSHEVIKS AND THE PEASANTRY 607

expecting. Thus any dissatisfaction with the spring redivision could be remedied through the subsequent redistribution.[45] Not all peasants wished for the latter, however. Peasants who were reasonably satisfied with their lot and wished to retain what they had only recently acquired, appear to have shared little faith in promises of yet another distribution — and in the future were to oppose attempts to redivide their land.[46] By late spring, however, this was not yet a problem.

A subsequent survey, however, published in 1922 suggested that a far greater number of peasants were dissatisfied with the redistribution of land than reflected above. Just over half (54%) of all villages surveyed expressed discontent with the redivision and the highest percentages were in both the central regions (the Black Earth — 62% and the Industrial — 63%) as well as the Lakes (64%).[47] One possible explanation for the apparent discrepancy between the evidence in the previous paragraph and the 1922 survey is that such dissatisfaction was not manifested in disputes during early 1918 but only surfaced later, perhaps when peasants realized that the expected subsequent distribution was not forthcoming and that shortcomings from the spring redivision would not be ameliorated. Another possibility is that the survey represented peasant views four years after the event which, as such, were prejudiced by experiences other than the initial redivision.[48] Moreover, not all groups of peasants were equally dissatisfied according to the survey. A breakdown of responses from the different strata of peasants revealed that the poor and middle peasants were most dissatisfied in the more peripheral regions — namely, the north-west, the north and the Urals. Because of the existence of more capitalistically organized estates in the first region, wealthier peasants were able to purchase equipment and machinery from pomeshchiki during 1917–18 and were then aided by land allocations according to the number of workers or the amount of equipment. In the Urals during the spring of 1918 many places lacked grain and seed for sowing and this mainly affected poor and middle peasants who lacked reserves.[49] Other factors can also be adduced. Redivisions in these more outlying regions were sometimes executed in accordance with the number of 'old

[45] For example, incomplete information and bias on the part of those reporting plus the fact noted earlier, that most reports come from volost' and not village authorities. For a discussion of why the division was considered provisional see above, pp. 599–600.
[46] See for example *Ekonomicheskaya zhizn'*, nos. 77 (10 April 1919) and 103 (15 May 1919).
[47] Blyakher, op. cit., p. 146.
[48] In some of the Central Black Earth areas by the early 1920s the increase in rural population together with the marked upsurge in the number of peasant households had virtually eliminated the earlier increases in land use per household that had accrued from the redistribution of land during 1917–18. (See A.N. Tatarchukov (ed.), *Materialy po izucheniyu voprosa o vosstanovlenii khozyaystva TsCho*, Trudy Planovoy Komissii TsChO, vol. I (Voronezh, 1926), pp. 142–43).
[49] Blyakher, op. cit., p. 147; Sylvana Malle, *The Economic Organization of War Communism* (Cambridge, 1985), ch. 7; Medvedev, op. cit., ch. I.

608   JOHN CHANNON

revision souls' — a particularly contentious factor if there was little
pomeshchik land to provide 'additions' (such as the Urals) and where
the existence of the non-repartitional community before the revolution
had produced considerable inequalities in land use and thus increased
pressure for inter-peasant redivisions of land.[50] Thus regional differences in terms of agricultural organization and practices help to explain
the differences between peasant attitudes towards the land redistribution. That the central regions differed in such respects is further
attested by other evidence.

The two surveys discussed above revealed an absence of redistributions in some areas. On the periphery this was due to the volatile
political situation. In some provinces redistribution failed to occur
because of their proximity to the war zones and in some cases due to
actual foreign occupation. The north-west gubernii provide a good
example of this although Pskov seems to have suffered the most. In
other areas in 1918 peasants refused to seize pomeshchik land and other
property because they feared German reprisals. Elsewhere land was
not divided because peasants feared the return of the former government.[51] These cases suggest potential sources of support for the
régime's policies outside the centre since the Bolsheviks could encourage peasants to seize pomeshchik land and try to increase confidence in
the new government by pointing to peasants who had successfully
redistributed non-peasant lands in the centre.

On the other hand, there are cases which include some from the
central regions where the failure to redivide land provided a basis for
peasant resentment and the development of future grievances. Sometimes peasants refused to distribute land in the spring of 1918 because
such a method of acquiring land failed to conform to their expectations
of what constituted a genuine land reform.[52] In other cases peasant ire
was directed against land authorities who exerted pressure to prevent
redistribution — justified usually by the lack of statistical preparations
or the shortage of personnel — especially if these were to be 'black

[50] For greater pressure to redivide peasant land, see also p. 604 above. Traditionally, land
had been divided in accordance with the number of males in each household at the time of
the taxation census (or revision), hence the term 'revision souls'. The last revision on which a
distribution of land was based was 1858. Thus the minimum age for males included in this
census would have been sixty years in 1918, presumably affecting only a small number in
each community or village. Land censuses were also taken in 1877–78, 1887, 1905, and 1917
(incomplete), though none of these were used as the basis for a new nationwide
redistribution. In some cases, during and after 1917, the term 'revision soul' referred to all
males as opposed to consumers (or 'eaters') or workers (of both sexes), though the sources
are not always clear on this point.
[51] E. P. Redakova, 'Provedeniye dekreta o zemle v Pskovskoy gubernii' (*Uchonyye zapiski
Pskovskogo gosudarstvennogo pedagogicheskogo instituta im. S. M. Kirova*, 1958, no. 6, p. 25); *GTK*,
no. 152, 19 June 1918; E. P. Ivanov, 'Polozheniye krest'yan i bor'ba s agrarnym perenasel-
eniyem na Severo-Zapade RSFSR v 1917–1930 gg.', unpublished dissertation, Leningrad,
1969, pp. 96–97; *Zemlya* (np), n. 19, 26 (16) May 1986.
[52] Chernov, op. cit., p. 87.

THE BOLSHEVIKS AND THE PEASANTRY   609

repartitions' although in practice this troubled the peasants little and they usually went ahead with such redivisions, irrespective of such pressure.[53] On other occasions the Bolsheviks had little to offer the peasantry when redistribution failed to occur because of the absence of pomeshchik estates in a locality, the lack of seed for spring sowing or because the land had already been set aside for collective cultivation. Not surprisingly, peasant hostility was aroused where estate land had been registered and inventoried by the land authorities but remained undivided because the managers were former pomeshchiki.[54] Thus, in some respects, peasants in the central regions shared common grievances with those in other regions of the country. But the important point to emphasize is that such discontent over the land never spilled out into mass disaffection and was dealt with at the local level.

Since the land redistribution continued throughout 1918 and into later years it is impossible to state what had been achieved in quantitative terms by the early summer, even though the abolition of non-peasant landownership and other tsarist burdens had removed an important constraint on peasant agriculture. Yet differentials existed between and within volosts and there were certainly inequalities in land-use: some communities and volosts were better supplied with land than others; some were in closer proximity to pomeshchik estates (while there were no estates in other localities); some were more successful in land disputes; while others had a more favourable population-to-land ratio. This highlighted a major problem with a land reform determined locally: some communities and volosts gained but only at the expense of others. Yet this gave to the peasants a greater feeling of being able to decide their own affairs. And Bolshevik indifference to the land reform consolidated this with disastrous consequences since control over land affairs was only one aspect of the importance of local decision making. The skhod was still the focus of this and, as noted above (p. 605), there were new influences on it and in some cases its composition broadened. And it was the mir or village that had to resolve problems resulting from the land distribution and the situation in general in early 1918. Thus solutions to local problems were resolved by 'looking inwards'.

It is clear that the distribution of land created more subsistence households (although the number is uncertain) less involved with the

---

[53] *Za zemlyu i volyu*, no. 104, 31 (18) May; *Zemlya* (np), no. 12, 21 (8) May 1918.

[54] *GTK*, no. 88, 29 March 1918. There were no pomeshchik estates in 10% of volosts in the sixteen provinces covered in the 1918 survey (Markarova, 'Agrarnye . . .', pp. 293–94.) See the example from Kadnikovsk volost' of Vologda guberniya where some monastical and pomeshchik lands were not divided because they were to be used for collective cultivation. (*Severnaya kommuna*, 1918, 5, 7 June). See also *GTK*, no. 102, 14 April 1918; *GTK*, no. 88, 29 March 1918, no. 95, 5 April 1918, no. 109, 24 April 1918; *Zemlya* (np), no. 1, 1 May (18 April) 1918; *Zemlya* (jo), no. 6, 2 May 1918, pp. 29–30.

610   JOHN CHANNON

market. Yet peasants still required implements and tools to work their
farms. The fall-off in production and the chaotic distribution system in
late 1917/early 1918 meant that peasants had to become less dependent
anyway on manufactured goods from urban areas. In 1918 they
produced more of these themselves. Peasant kustar industry did not
experience a great decline and village production of agricultural
implements (such as scythes and ploughs) and bricks, rope and iron —
not to mention such common agricultural activities as milling grain —
continued, often substituting goods earlier produced from urban
areas.[55] Clearly some of the 'newcomers' to the countryside at this time
would have been welcomed, if only for the skills and experience they
brought with them (in metal working for instance). They found
employment opportunities in the villages and probably established
their own households — as well as enterprises and manufactories — in
this way. This is one explanation for the large numbers of such
'newcomers' accepted into the central areas at this time and often
included in the redistribution of land.[56] Other grievances arising from
the land revolution were similarly resolved locally. The redivision of
land was not accompanied by the same degree of redistribution of other
property such as equipment and livestock. Peasants sometimes lacked
seed for sowing and so land remained unsown in the spring, reducing
the potential harvest. Lacking implements for cultivation some
landless labourers refused allotments, others rented out such land
apportioned to them while yet others were forced to return land
received in the distribution to its former owners.[57] In some cases the
area allocated was too small to be of much use, a consequence of the
potential area available being reduced by the additional numbers now
requesting land. Even so, the poor and landless were not attracted in
great numbers to the new forms of collective agriculture favoured
(though little promoted) by the Bolsheviks, and we need not look far to
discover the reasons for this. Since distribution had occurred within the
mir then it was the community that attempted to resolve the land

[55] See Malle, op. cit., p. 78 who notes only a small decrease in the number of kustars
between 1913 and the beginning of 1919 (citing *Narodnoye Khozyaystvo*, 1919, nos. 1–2, p. 36).
Another estimate claims there were some 350,000 rural kustar establishments (with more
than 1.2 million people employed in them) in 1918. These craftsmen and artisans organized
their own exchanges at free market prices with the villages (O. Kuperman, *Sotsial'no-
ekonomicheskiye formy promyshlennosti v SSSR* (Leningrad, 1929), p. 97 cited in R. Medvedev,
op. cit., p. 138.
[56] For data indicating that such 'newcomers' predominated in the Central Black Earth
region and were also most readily accepted/assimilated here see Blyakher, op. cit.,
pp. 142–44. See also note 35 above.
[57] One Soviet source has noted that out of 1,316 volosts in 18 gubernii: equipment remained
on estates in 41.6% of volosts; was distributed between all peasants in 26.9% of volosts; and
was distributed between the poor peasants in only 14.8% of volosts (Pershin, op. cit., vol. 2,
pp. 355–56); *Zemlya* (np), no. 11 (19), 8 May 1918 and no. 23, 3 June (21 May) 1918: M. N.
Shumilov, *Oktyabr'skaya sotsialisticheskaya revolyutsiya i istoricheskiye sud'by batrachestva*
(Moscow, 1967), p. 110.

THE BOLSHEVIKS AND THE PEASANTRY 611

shortage with recourse to traditional practices for overcoming such problems: hiring of labour and leasing of land (even though in theory the revolution had abolished all such transactions) whether these assumed monetary or non-monetary forms.[58] Some land was even leased by former pomeshchiki at this time and provided more grounds for yet further peasant discontent,[59] though this was too sporadic to have any major significance.

Leaving peasants in the localities to sort out land affairs had implications for how the various social strata of peasants fared. Although it is still unclear whether class differentiation in the Marxist sense was operating before the revolution, there seems little doubt that a wealthy stratum of peasants had emerged. On the whole the wealthy in these first eight months seem to have survived within the communities and if their position did change, it was not until the second half of 1918 or even later. How were they able to do this? To avoid recriminations, internally from neighbours and externally from groups seeking food surpluses, the wealthier wished to display openly that they had levelled down their holdings. This might be achieved through family divisions which enabled the preservation of the household's overall share of land, or even an increase in it. This was also a less provocative way for a larger household to retain its advantages. It further ensured that all could take full advantage of the free timber now available.[60] The widespread incidence of these 'general' redivisions in the Central Black Earth region had another important effect. Ever since the late nineteenth century such redivisions in the region had been accompanied by allocations of land by eaters, irrespective of sex. Thus, during 1917–18 there was an incentive to retain large families so as to claim a larger share of land (and other property if this was divided too) even though splitting might occur subsequently. One way to increase a family's share of land was to 'adopt' or take in new members, a practice noted before 1917 and one that would continue into the 1920s.[61] Where no general pooling of land occurred,

---

[58] Hiring of labour was generally practised, frequently 'permitted' by local regulations, and explained by the absence of equipment, unemployment, the food crisis, and large families where there were many children (consumers) but few workers (*Ekonomicheskaya zhizn'*, no. 89, 27 April 1919). The live- and dead-stock of estates had often been sold/auctioned off thus depriving poorer peasants of the seed and implements they lacked. The latter then leased their land to others and themselves became hired labourers. For an example of the continuation of such practices into the summer of 1919, see Shumilov, op. cit., p. 111. Rates were also set for the leasing of land as witnessed by the examples from the provinces of Moscow and Tula (*Zemlya* (np), nos. 38 and 39, 21 (8) June 1918 and 22 (9) June 1918).

[59] See Channon, 'Former landlords . . .', pp. 19–21.

[60] Malle, op. cit., p. 327 citing Yu. Larin, 'Ocherk khozyaystvennogo razvitiya sovetskoy Rossii', p. 63.

[61] Narkomzem reported instances where the inclusion of adopted children who were registered with the community became the subject of disputes over the redivision of land (see *Zemlya* (np), no. 44, 29 (16) June 1918). For other similar reports see *GTK*, no. 109, 24 April 1918; *Zemlya* (jo), no. 6, 1 May 1918, p. 30. Such 'adoption' was practised in the pre-revolutionary period and in the 1920s.

612   JOHN CHANNON

but only partial redivisions of land took place, the wealthier clearly
benefited since they usually retained their allotment and purchased
lands and also received additions from non-peasant land.[62] Such
better-off peasants in some cases acted judiciously in relinquishing
their former position of authority within the community (such as land
measurers, dividers, or scribes) or more usually, because of the need of
their skills, merely became compliant vehicles for the execution of
chornye peredely, often contrary to their own interests.[63]

Yet the wealthy may also have helped the local peasant economy.
Since they no longer had to pay state taxes we might assume there
would have been more cash available for them to put into agriculture
and for purchase of goods from local kustars. To what extent they were
able to do this is a moot point, not least because local taxes still existed
in 1918 and proved an additional burden on peasant communities
generally. Volost' soviets received no central funding for their activities
before the middle of the year and one estimate notes that by November
1918, volost' soviets had collected some 7.9 million roubles (from
57 gubernii). And this of course excludes mir levies. Local taxes were
deemed necessary for several reasons: the volost' soviets required funds
to pay officials and workers (and their land departments for financial
assistance with the land reform) but perhaps more important was the
need, in the face of growing food shortages, for volost' soviets to
purchase grain and seed, frequently on the open market amidst soaring
inflation. Conflict developed when the taxation burden fell on the more
well-to-do (*sostoyatel'nyye*) or they were the subject of the predations of
the requisitioning commissions established by the volost' soviets.[64] Yet

[62] They might well have retained land earlier improved and might have received
'compensation' for land transferred.
[63] This was in accordance with a kind of pragmatic survival strategy. See Sadovsky,
op. cit., pp. 331, 548. For evidence that poor and middle peasants were chairmen of the
sel'sovety during the 'War Communism' period (though replaced by more prosperous
peasants thereafter), see S. P. Dunn and E. Dunn. *The Peasants of Central Russia* (USA and
London, 1967), p. 25; Y. Taniuchi, *The Village Gathering in Russia in the Mid 1920s*, CREES,
monograph no. 1 (Birmingham, 1968); *Kritsman and the Agrarian Marxists*, ed. Terry Cox and
Gary Littlejohn (London, 1984), p. 103 and Ya. A. Yakovlev, *Derevnya kak ona yest'* (Moscow,
1923), pp. 112, 116.
[64] For lack of central funding until mid 1918 see *Ekonomicheskaya zhizn'*, no. 89, 27 April
1919. The November 1918 figure is cited by V. P. Danilov in *Oktyabr' i sovetskoye krest'yanstvo*,
p. 167. While admitting that land was not subject to tax in accordance with the spirit of the
'Basic Law', guberniya congresses still levied land taxes. Local land departments justified
such taxes on the grounds of extreme shortage of funds (*Zemlya* (np), no. 28, 8 June (26 May)
1918; *Zemlya* (jo), no. 1, 13 March 1918) and used some of this to pay those who worked in
committees (*Zemlya* (np), no. 11, 19 (8) May 1918). A variety of taxes were levied covering
all land, and even water resources in some cases, or just individual categories of land (such as
arable, meadow, gardens). (*Zemlya* (np), no. 30, 11 June (29 May) 1918.) Some volost'
soviets created their own commissions to requisition grain and seed within their respective
localities. If recourse to purchasing on the open market became necessary, prices might be as
much as 20 to 30 times the fixed prices. Of 105 volosts in Nizhnii-Novgorod province (out of
a total of 286) between January and April 1918, grain was acquired by requisitioning

when taxes were distributed between *all* inhabitants poor peasants doubtless felt aggrieved too, not least because they believed that the revolution had brought freedom from such impositions. This was in addition to the fact that many poor peasants had benefited little from the distribution. Although in some central regions the area sown by poor peasants in 1918 did increase, most if not all of this area was given over to subsistence crops, rye in the Central Black Earth and potatoes in the Central Industrial.[65] Yet land additions could be too small to be of much practical use, while lack of seed, implements, and livestock often prevented the poor from farming independently. Thus they might rent out or sell land allocated to them to other peasants and themselves continue to work as hired labourers. Then, as was customary, hiring rates were controlled locally.[66]

Thus, through Bolshevik eyes, seeds for future social differentiation might appear to have been sown during this period, giving important implications for a pro-kulak/NEP-type solution to the food crisis of the spring.[67] But it did not necessarily turn the poor peasants against the Bolsheviks. True, Narkomzem's (and the land authorities') insistence on the temporary nature of the land distribution failed to provide peasants with any security of tenure over their newly acquired strips. But the promise of a new redivision in the future did give them hope of something better still to emerge. After all, peasant communities were used to considering partial redivisions as temporary until the next chornyy peredel. The Bolsheviks' land policies had the effect of strengthening the communities and it was this that was to prove most dangerous for them when other policies were instituted. Before

commissions in 42.9% of cases, through taxes levied on the better-off (*zazhitochnyye*) in 20.9% and all the local population in another 12.4%. On the other occasions they relied on imports from other provinces and assistance from the uyezd and guberniya organizations. See E. P. Titkov, 'Prodovol'stvennyy vopros i volostnyye sovety Nizhegorodskoy gubernii v dokombedovskom periode' in *Velikiy Oktyabr' i sotsialisticheskiye preobrazovaniya v sovetskoy derevne* (Gor'ky, 1983), pp. 56–69.
[65] P. Zakharov, *Usloviya obsemeneniya yarovykh poley v Kostromskoy gubernii v 1918 godu po dannym spetsial'noy ankety* (Kostroma, 1918).
[66] This was a frequent practice in 1918 with the setting of daily and piece rates. See for example: *Zemlya* (np), no. 7, 15 (2) May 1918; no. 31, 12 June (30 May) 1918; no. 16, 25 (12) May 1918; *GTK*, no. 179, 24 July 1918. (The latter gives an example of hiring on the basis of 'natural' exchange, at the rate of 1 *pud* of grain for work on the summer harvest.) For a comparison of 1918 and 1917 hiring rates see P. Zakharov, op. cit., pp. 12–13. See also note 58 above.
[67] Such a case has recently been argued by Medvedev (op. cit., ch. 11) though it rests on an optimistic appraisal of the grain situation in the Bolshevik-controlled territories by the spring of 1918 (see note 87 below for the problems of such an assumption) and on continued Left SR support (see C. Sirianni, *Workers Control and Socialist Democracy. The Soviet Experience* (London, 1982), pp. 194–97.) For the analogy between the 'First Eight Months . . .' and the NEP, see Lenin, *Collected Works*, vol. 23, p. 63 and on problems with it see Stephen F. Cohen, *Bukharin and the Bolshevik Revolution* (New York, 1973), p. 135 and Susan G. Solomon, *The Soviet Agrarian Debate* (Boulder, 1977), pp. 82, 240–41, no. 23, 24.

614   JOHN CHANNON

examining these issues more consideration is necessary of how the
Bolsheviks perceived the land redivision of early 1918.

In conceding to peasant demands and SR notions of land reform, Lenin
was following the logic of his earlier argument. In the years leading up
to the revolution, Lenin had increasingly seemed to sympathize with
the view that the large landed estates were essentially feudal and not
capitalist in nature.[68] Thus, he assumed the revolutionary task in
Russia was to liberate the peasantry from these 'feudal encumbrances'
and enable capitalism to develop freely in agriculture. Consequently, a
future redistribution of land would provide an environment in which
small producers could compete freely for land and allow a widespread
development of petty-peasant farming. Such unfettered small-scale
capitalist production would lead to further economic differentiation
resulting in the classic Marxist polarization into the rural bourgeoisie
and the rural poor. The marked inequalities that would emerge would
then reveal to the mass of the peasantry that the only solution to their
problems lay in collective agriculture, and by definition, socialism. Yet
this would take a long time. At the same time, Lenin hoped that the
Bolsheviks would be able to establish such collective farms on the
landed estates, thereby providing successful models for the peasants to
imitate.

Such an analysis was given support in the summer of 1917 when
Lenin realized that it was vital politically to accept that the peasants
wanted a chornyy peredel, a mass redistribution of land. The 242
peasant resolutions now made this clear, he argued, contrary to his own

[68] Much recent discussion has focused on Lenin's apparent change of views on this question
since the appearance of his *Development of Capitalism in Russia*. Some writers have seen Lenin's
work on the peasantry after 1905 as an extension of that in the *Development* ... (e.g. Neil
Harding, *Lenin's Political Thought*, vol. 2, *Theory and Practice in the Socialist Revolution* (London,
1981), pp. 213–17) while others have argued that by 1917, Lenin himself was admitting that
he had overstated the degree of capitalist development in Russian agriculture in the late
nineteenth century, though he was careful not to deny that such a trend was present (Esther
Kingston-Mann, *Lenin and the Problem of Marxist Peasant Revolution* (Oxford, 1983), p. 98).
Accepting that Lenin's thinking on the matter had changed substantially, the most recent
Western examination of Lenin concludes that in 1907 he '... at last conceded that his early
writings had exaggerated the level of Russian capitalist development; and that feudalistic
practices were stronger than he had once imagined'. R. Service, *Lenin: A Political Life*,
vol. 1 (London, 1985), p. 220, note 56; V. I. Lenin, *Polnoye Sobraniye Sochineni* [hereafter *PSS*];
vol. 16, pp. 268–89. Lenin's pessimistic analysis of estate development before 1917 would
suggest that there were few large efficient estates to serve as the basis for his 'model'
collectives anyway. On occasion he even admitted that large estates were not always more
efficiently cultivated and therefore their preservation was not so vital (Kingston-Mann,
op. cit., pp. 94, 108).

THE BOLSHEVIKS AND THE PEASANTRY 615

thinking of March and April.[69] Thus, as Bukharin had allegedly professed soon after October, apart from arresting millions of peasants, the Bolsheviks had 'little choice but to bow to the reality of the Russian countryside'.[70] Yet Lenin appreciated that this measure would secure the backing of the mass of the peasantry when the Bolsheviks seized power. This was consonant with the belief that, on the international front, economic assistance could be expected from the more advanced, industrialized countries which would have already staged successful proletarian revolutions.[71] Such concessions to the peasants, such as the granting of land to them, were further intended by Lenin as a kind of *quid pro quo*: in return for the land the peasants would be expected to hand over their grain for the feeding of the towns and the army.[72]

The initial outcome of the land revolution was to reveal that Lenin had been close to the mark in his anticipation of events. The reality of the countryside by the early summer of 1918 mirrored in many respects his earlier expectations. In his own words, the post-October period was characterized by 'petty commodity production' which could form an 'extremely broad and very sound, deep-rooted basis for capitalism'.[73] This was supported by evidence showing the continuation of exploitation and differentiation. Although deemed illegal according to Soviet legislation, hiring of labour and leasing of land (in some cases even by pomeshchiki), and use of wage labour in kustar industry, were all rife. (See above pp. 611–12.) For Lenin this was the inevitable consequence of a nonsensical equal division of land which could lead only to kulak domination and ruination for the poor,[74] with the implication that kulak farms producing surpluses provided at least one path along which Russia could travel in resolving the food supply issue.

For Lenin, moreover, such processes were proof that the mir was gradually being destroyed from within, though he continually emphasized the lengthy period that would have to expire before collective

[69] Both Kalinin and Stalin had published articles calling for the immediate seizure (and, by implication, partition) of estates by the peasantry before Lenin's *April Theses* — in which he opposed the redivision of large estates — were discussed at the VII Party Conference. Without mentioning the division of estates, the latter accepted Lenin's basic position on the land issue although the VI Party Congress in July–August failed to agree an official party programme. Lenin appears to have been persuaded that peasants must be immediately granted the land in the light of the 242 peasant instructions (*nakazy*) which were known to him in May and published on 19–20 August (O.S.). According to Holubnychy this then formed the basis for the central committee resolution of 31 August (13 September) calling for the immediate transfer of estate land to land committees. V. S. Holubnychy, 'The 1917 Agrarian Revolution in Ukraine', in I. S. Koropeckyj (ed.), *Soviet Regional Economics: Selected Works of Vsevolod Holubnychy* (Edmonton, 1982), p. 46.
[70] D. Koenker, *Moscow Workers and the 1917 Revolution* (Princeton, 1981), p. 345.
[71] Lenin, *PSS*, vol. 29, pp. 198–215. This rested on Lenin's commune-state philosophy of summer 1917 as well as on his understanding of the international situation.
[72] Lenin, *PSS*, vol. 29, pp. 198–215: *Pravda*, no. 272, 14 December 1918 and no. 250, 7 November 1919; *Izvestiya*, no. 219, 8 November 1917 and no. 250, 7 November 1919.
[73] *Pravda*, no. 250, 7 November 1919; *Izvestiya*, no. 250, 7 November 1919.
[74] *Bednota*, no. 185, 10 November 1918.

farming could be developed. Even in November, Lenin was to admit that poor peasants were only *beginning* to agree about the negative consequences of the land redivision.[75] Thus it seems absurd to suggest, as Lenin did at the time, that by the summer of 1918 poor peasants were prepared for the revolution against the wealthy. Except in only the vaguest of terms, it was impossible to assess the class forces in the countryside by the late spring. Lenin seems to have admitted as much in March 1919.[76] A year earlier, the situation had been even more confused. And the land division was partially responsible for this by seemingly weakening the class alliance of the proletariat and the rural poor on which Lenin had placed so much reliance. Through the redivision of land of former non-peasant owners plus some belonging to wealthy peasants, many poor and some landless now obtained more land. Thus, according to popular consensus, the basically subsistence-oriented middle peasantry was strengthened at the expense of the other social strata. The poor peasant base in particular had been weakened at the very point when Lenin was about to advocate class war in the countryside. Simultaneously there had been a weakening of the rural bourgeoisie and, notwithstanding the uncertainty that remains over the extent of this decline, the implications are still important for any assumption that in the middle of 1918 there was sufficient for a 'kulak' strike, with the wealthy hoarding grain. The extent of the reduction in the poor and the concomitant increase in middle peasants is also debatable since, in practice, some of those who had received land had still not received the necessary means of production to establish their own farms.[77] Whatever the absolute size of the poor peasantry there was still no reason to assume that they would or could immediately transfer *en masse* to collective farming. Nine months later (March 1919) Lenin made clear an important reason why the peasantry resented these collectives: the large-scale farms were all too reminiscent in peasants minds of the large estates they had only just succeeded in eliminating.[78] And such emotions doubtless ran higher in the spring of 1918 in the immediate aftermath of the confiscation and distribution of estates. Thus even if collectives had existed poor peasants were unlikely to have appreciated their superiority by the end of the eight months. Lenin admitted both before and after the summer that it would take a *long while* for the peasants to see the benefits of collective farming, and such an objective could only be accomplished by long effort.[79]

[75] Ibid.; *Pravda*, no. 272, 14 December 1918. My emphasis: J. C.
[76] Lenin, *PSS*, vol. 29, p. 184.
[77] N. Harding, *Lenin's Political Thought*, vol. 2, *Theory and Practice in the Socialist Revolution* (London, 1981), pp. 213–17.
[78] Lenin, *PSS*, vol. 29, p. 187.
[79] *Pravda*, no. 272, 14 December 1918. My emphasis: J. C.

THE BOLSHEVIKS AND THE PEASANTRY 617

Whether peasants would have been able to establish more collectives, even if they had so desired, is debatable. While urban dwellers were frequently involved in collectives, very little had been done in practice before the summer of 1918 to encourage such farming. Such a state of affairs cannot be blamed solely on the alliance with the Left SRs since, as even recent Soviet works have shown, some Left SRs were in favour of collectivization too.[80] True, special arrangements for organizing *sovkhozy* were not made within Narkomzem until late July, after the expulsion of the Left SRs, but Bolsheviks had had an important influence in Narkomzem — even if not forming the majority — since the spring.[81] Yet no clear picture existed of the number of large estates left to develop as models of large-scale socialist farming. Clearly, though, not all estates had been redistributed by this time. Many sources mention the existence of an 'undivided' part of land at this period, usually a reference to the former landed estates, while several areas in the Central Black Earth region noted that the intensively-cultivated estates (*kul'turnyye khozyaystva*) were still undivided in the early summer of 1918.[82] In truth, it is extremely difficult to discover the condition of the former estates by the early summer. Even Narkomzem professed ignorance of the situation. On 28 May its collegium frankly admitted that 'the number and conditions of former private properties (*chastnyye vladeniya*) is unknown'.[83] When Lenin admitted in the autumn that the number of agricultural communes and sovkhozy amounted to only 'some hundreds' it is thought that he was including all collective forms of agriculture.[84] Certainly by the end of this eight-month period there were few state farms and probably none corresponded to the image of the huge grain factories he had anticipated.

So, then, did Lenin misunderstand the reality of the Russian countryside? The interlinking issues of differentiation and the mir still posed a problem. Some aspects by which he would judge differentiation to be continuing were clearly evident in the villages. Whether this acted to dissolve the community from within, as Lenin believed, is still a matter of some contention. It may be argued, however, that he failed to appreciate fully the ability of the mir to assimilate the penetration of capitalism, thus countering the polarizing tendencies expected through differentiation. After all, he had not concerned himself with the mir as a

[80] E. H. Carr, *The Bolshevik Revolution* (London, 1972), vol. 2, p. 155; Kabanov, op. cit., p. 98, citing A. Ustinov, *O zemle i krest'yanstve* (Moscow, 1919), p. 21. For a detailed discussion of the authorship of the 'Law' see Kabanov.
[81] On 27 July 1918 the responsibility befell N. M. Petrovsky, a Bolshevik and a member of the *Narkomzem Kollegium*, to prepare for the organization of *sovkhozy* (Lomovtseva, op. cit., p. 82).
[82] This was the case for example in Tula province by early June (*Zemlya* (np), no. 28, 8 June (26 May) 1918).
[83] Knipovich, *Ocherk deyatel'nosti* . . ., p. 11; Lomovtseva, op. cit., p. 82.
[84] Carr, op. cit., p. 156.

concrete basis for peasant unrest during 1905–06. Hence his difficulty during 1917–18 when the community became the vehicle for revolutionary change, adopting both an anti-feudal stance and in several regions an anti-capitalist one too.[85] Besides, collective farms were not the only way of achieving agricultural progress. The community could be the basis for agricultural improvement, as pre-revolutionary developments had shown — and the 'twenties were to verify — although Lenin associated it chiefly with stagnation: 'The peasants fear innovations and tenaciously cling to old habits'. But peasants were and are no less rational than other social groups in seeking the objective of improvement, as long as the requisite assistance was provided.[86] And this, in practice, was what happened in the decade after 1919.

A second problem was that relations between the countryside and the urban sector were different from what Lenin had imagined. We have already noted the weakening of the class alliance of the poorer peasantry with the working class due to the upsurge in the number of middle (subsistence) peasants, but the breakdown in rural/urban relations was to weaken this alliance further. The expected assistance from abroad was not forthcoming, while the Brest settlement and non-Bolshevik forces had removed large grain-producing areas from Soviet control.[87] In addition, peasant agriculture was not as independent or completely unfettered as Lenin had envisaged. The situation in the urban areas was severely disrupting town–country relations and hence any basis for products exchange (the *quid pro quo* envisaged by Lenin).[88] The response of the peasant sector was to assume far more the character of a rural enclave. Peasants negotiated local exchanges of commodities, while the continuing kustar industry provided some of the goods they required for agriculture, at least partially therefore substituting for any fall-off in farm equipment from the urban centres. Volost' soviets often acted independently of one another, and of the centre, attempting to secure sufficient food for the needs of the

[85] Kingston-Mann, op. cit., pp. 43, 98, 107, 115. She questions, in particular, why Lenin ignored peasant demands for the transfer of all land to *communities* in the 1905–06 revolution (my emphasis).

[86] *Bednota*, no. 185, 10 November 1918. For a discussion of how land redistributions were used to achieve improvements in land-use within the communal framework see my *Peasant Revolution and Land Reform in Russia 1917–1924*, forthcoming.

[87] The effects of the loss of territory (especially the Ukraine) on the quantity of grain available to the area under Bolshevik control is still under debate. (See Medvedev, op. cit., ch. 10 citing optimistic views of the surplus over deficit from the Commissariat of Food Supply, as well as figures cited by Trotsky in *How the Revolution Armed*.) For more pessimistic views see P.R.O., London, Foreign Office document 371/3315/18313 (pp. 211–27) and S. G. Wheatcroft, 'Grain Production and Utilisation in Russia and the USSR before Collectivisation', unpublished Ph.D. thesis, University of Birmingham, 1980. I am grateful to B. Pearce for informing me of the F.O. document. See also Sirianni, op. cit., pp. 195–96 citing Jan Meijer, 'Town and Country in the Civil War' in Richard Pipes (ed.), *Revolutionary Russia* (New York, 1969), pp. 343, 356 ff.

[88] For a recent discussion of the issue, see Malle, op. cit.

THE BOLSHEVIKS AND THE PEASANTRY 619

population within their own territories, and this was the focus of peasant ire.[89] It was this rural autarchy that produced a panic response, a foreboding of what was to come in the later 1920s.

Mention has already been made of the practice of levying local taxes to fund the activities of volost' soviets, while the latter we noted also engaged in grain requisitioning independent of the centre to satisfy local needs. The government's continued prohibition on the sale of alcohol only worsened the situation. Introduced in the summer of 1914, the prohibition had shown little success in reducing alcohol consumption by early 1917. Drunkenness was reported to be rife in 1916 while the early months of the following year were to witness soldiers at the front, joined later by local peasants, looting estates and alcohol distilleries in particular. Peasants inevitably turned to various kinds of homebrew (*samogon*). The practice continued into 1918, removing grain from the consumption sphere, although it is difficult to know how much grain was distilled in this way.[90] Harsh punishment, moreover, was meted out to peasants caught producing samogon, such individuals being pronounced counter-revolutionaries to be dealt with harshly as saboteurs.[91] Such actions did little to endear the Bolsheviks to the peasants, and placed vexing limitations on the latter's freedom to do as they pleased with the product of the land — in contradistinction to the use of land itself. As such the samogon problem provides an insight into an important aspect of the issue that was to provoke the final rupture in Bolshevik/peasant relations in 1918, the food supply problem.

Accepting that the peasants would carry out their own land reform served to precipitate such future difficulties for the Bolsheviks in other areas of agrarian policy. The SR land reform would take time and this was precisely what the Bolsheviks lacked, especially with the escalation of the civil war when distribution of the product of the land assumed more immediate significance than distribution of the land itself. Granting the peasants freedom to initiate their own solution to the land problem had done nothing towards solving the problems of food supply.

Yet even on the issue of food supply there is much to suggest that the Bolsheviks from the start tried to avoid confrontation with the peasantry. In December 1917 it was proposed in a draft decree that a

[89] See footnote 64 above.
[90] M. Florinsky, *The End of the Russian Empire* (New York, 1961), pp. 42, 44; A. K. Wildman, *The End of the Russian Imperial Army: The Old Army and the Soldiers' Revolt (March–April 1917)* (Princeton, 1980); Holubnychy, op. cit., p. 21. For a recent discussion of the *samogon* issue see Helena Stone. 'The Soviet Government and Moonshine, 1917–1929' (*Cahiers du Monde Russe et Soviétique*, vol. 28, 1986, 3–4, pp. 359–80).
[91] Holubnychy, op. cit., p. 54, for examples.

progressive tax in kind be collected from the peasants, with 40% of the harvest remaining with rural soviets to meet local requirements.[92] The proposal was adopted by Sovnarkom and published in several newspapers but withdrawn after opposition from the Peasant Section of VTsIK. Not wishing to antagonize the peasantry (or Left SRs?), the Bolsheviks resolved to abandon the idea.[93] The wisdom of such a move was later confirmed by a report in May 1918 concerning the violent peasant resentment at local contributions.[94] From the outset the new Soviet government had clearly been hoping to obtain the requisite supplies of grain through the market, even though some element of 'control' was to be practised — as under the Provisional Government — through the curbing of increases of grain prices.[95] To alleviate the growing urban food shortages the peasants were to be induced to hand over their grain through an exchange of goods. Several actions during December bear witness to this.[96] At the end of the month, Shlikhter noted in VTsIK that the Commissariat of Supply had 'taken over from the army quartermaster's branch all its stocks of manufactured goods for despatch to the countryside where they will be exchanged [for food]'. By all accounts he was exceedingly optimistic.[97] Numerous organizational squabbles were already impeding practical efforts at providing sufficient food yet, only two days later, he was revealing further details of the products exchange due to commence from early 1918.[98]

Such Bolshevik efforts have not passed unnoticed in the literature. Attempts to send manufactured goods to the countryside were

---

[92] James G. Nutsch, 'Bolshevik Agrarian policies' (*Modern Encyclopaedia of Russian and Soviet History*, 1976, pp. 73–74); R. W. Davies, *The Development of the Soviet Budgetary System* (Cambridge, 1958), p. 21.
[93] Nutsch, op. cit.
[94] Davies, op. cit., p. 21, no. 1.
[95] M. Dobb, *Soviet Economic Development since 1917* (London, 1972 edn), pp. 83, 88; see also Lenin's speech at the Fifth session of VTsIK, 4 November 1917; John L. H. Keep, *The Debate on Soviet Power* (Oxford, 1979), pp. 81, 87–88.
[96] To help induce peasants to hand over grain, a Sovnarkom decree of 13 December 1917 declared a state monopoly over agricultural equipment with its distribution among the peasantry to be supervised by the land committees and soviets. (Nutsch, op. cit., pp. 73–74.)
[97] See Keep, op. cit., pp. 252–53 (and p. 408 for criticism).
[98] For organizational squabbles see Keep, op. cit., p. 408; at the twenty-third session of VTsIK 29 December 1917 Shlikhter stated: 'At present the Commissariat (of Supply) is about to send 120 wagon loads of manufactured goods — footwear, metal objects and the like — to the grain growing areas. For each yard of cloth the peasants will be asked to supply ten pounds of grain, and the difference will be made up by cash payments. In this way we shall get the amount of grain we need. In pursuit of this policy the People's Commissariat of Supply has deprived Petrograd, Moscow and (other) cities of manufactured goods that are very badly needed there' (Keep, op. cit., pp. 254–55).

THE BOLSHEVIKS AND THE PEASANTRY   621

evidently in progress during the first few months of the new year,[99] the best known of these being the expedition to Siberia by Shlikhter in February.[100] An exchange of products seemingly went ahead involving manufactured goods to the value of 10 million roubles, though less than 10% of the grain at the transportation points in Siberia actually reached the Central Industrial region.[101] Thus some progress was made in delivering goods to the peasants though the amount of grain obtained clearly fell short of that required by Moscow and Petrograd.[102] None the less, one thing seems clear. The main problem lay as much in transporting as in obtaining the grain. And it was clearly to assist the *shipment* of grain from Siberia (especially Omsk) to Petrograd that force was applied.[103]

Yet the Siberian exchange appears to have comprised only a small proportion of the total exchange of goods undertaken during the period before the early summer of 1918. Of 60,000 wagons of industrial goods (valued at well over 350 million roubles) distributed by the Supply Commissariat between November 1917 and August 1918, no fewer than 42,000 wagons (or 72% of the total) were despatched to peasants in the major grain producing regions. In exchange, however, only 35,831 wagons arrived with agricultural produce. More important perhaps are data showing the disparity between the quantity of metal and agricultural equipment planned for distribution to the villages and

[99] Between December 1917 and April 1918 the government sent 163,839,000 roubles worth of goods to the countryside, whereas on 25 March Sovnarkom passed a resolution sending goods to the value of 1,162 million roubles (Osipova, op. cit., pp. 65–67 citing *Izvestiya Narodnogo komissariata po prodovol'stviyu*, 1918, no. 10–11, p. 3 and TsGANKh, f. 1943). From another source, however, we discover that only 50% of the manufactured goods required were actually produced. E. V. Gimpel'son, '*Voennyy kommunizm': politika, praktika, ideologiya* (Moscow, 1973), p. 38. I am grateful to Bob Service for this last reference.

[100] Shlikhter was a Siberian Bolshevik. Ever since July 1917 Lenin had been aware of the large grain reserves in Siberia, Russell E. Snow, *The Bolsheviks in Siberia, 1917–1918* (New Jersey, 1977).

[101] Yu. P. Alekseyev, 'Ekspeditsii A. G. Shlikhtera i A. P. Sereda za khlebom v 1918 g.' (*Istoriya SSSR*, May–June 1966, 3, p. 137).

[102] See Alekseyev, op. cit., p. 137. Yet, as Yaney has observed, other writers have suggested that the campaign was relatively successful (E. M. Kayden and A. N. Antsiferov, *The Cooperative Movement in Russia during the War* (New Haven, 1929), pp. 180–86; G. Yaney, *The Urge to Mobilize* (Urbana, Chicago, and London, 1982), p. 488.

[103] On 13 January a delegation from Omsk brought shipments of grain to Petrograd. They reported that 1,000 wagon loads remained in Omsk because the railwaymen refused to despatch them. This might have been due to Menshevik influence; problems of 'labour discipline' and local disorganization due to decentralization; hoarding until prices had risen; and delay in the arrival of manufactured goods. SR influence was certainly strong in Siberia and SRs and Mensheviks were blamed elsewhere for sabotaging food transports as well as the guberniya food committees. D. S. Baburin, 'Narkomprod v pervyye gody sovetskoy vlasti' (*Istoricheskiye zapiski*, vol. 61, 1957, p. 344). At the end of January a 20-strong detachment of the best Latvian troops left Petrograd to help move this grain from Siberia. This seems to have completed general Cheka measures to increase the amount of grain shipped from Omsk to Petrograd between December 1917 and March 1918. A. Ezergailis, *The Latvian Impact on the Russian Revolution* (Boulder, 1983), pp. 334–35. It is also of interest to note here the use of Lettish troops generally renowned for their loyalty.

622   JOHN CHANNON

the amount of goods actually despatched. Thus, although a start, the amount in fact distributed was insufficient to meet peasant needs, the full extent of which moreover was still unknown by the authorities at the centre.[104]

Yet in order to acquire more grain, coercion was applied too. The relatively small amounts of grain achieved through products exchange in Siberia led to grain requisitioning there, provoking peasant hostility.[105] Force had been used earlier in the year in a few other instances too, as the various armed detachments despatched to the countryside to extract grain bear testimony.[106] And such force naturally met with resistance. Certainly most of the so-called 'armed uprisings' in the central areas during the first half of 1918 appear to have concerned the question of food supply.[107]

Who was involved in these conflicts is less clear, however. Hostilities between peasants and local organs of *Narkomprod* — acting independently of the centre — as with volost' soviets acting autonomously in grain requisitioning, had little to do with central Bolshevik policy, while many reports tell of conflicts between the detachments and groups of private speculators, such as bagmen (*meshochniki*), rather than peasants directly.[108] How then did all this square with Bolshevik economic policy? Even in January Lenin had declared that detachments were to be sent out to expedite grain freights and collect and store grain, while speculators were to be severely punished and their grain requisitioned.[109] On this same day Sovnarkom adopted a resolution based on Lenin's draft.[110] Concern about food rations for the army and urban areas had evidently led to these sporadic forays into the countryside during the winter months (and even before the Sovnarkom

---

[104] N. Orlov, *Devyat' mesyatsev prodovol'stvennoy raboty sovetskoy vlasti* (Moscow, 1918), pp. 219–23, 279, 350.

[105] Yaney, op. cit.; Carr, op. cit., pp. 55–56.

[106] In January, for instance, a food requisitioning *druzhina* composed of Lettish troops was sent to search for grain in the countryside to feed Petrograd (Ezergailis, op. cit., p. 334) and the northern military food *druzhina* was established to supply food for the army (Baburin, op. cit., p. 342). In the same month, the People's Commissar for Supply proposed, in addition to encouraging products exchange, to send armed detachments into villages to extract grain by force (*Izvestiya*, 18/31 January 1918). At the end of 1917/beginning of 1918 congresses of the rural poor were organized in Voronezh guberniya with the aim of obtaining grain supplies. 48 detachments of Bolsheviks and Red Guards were also despatched for the same purpose (Osipova, op. cit., p. 57).

[107] Osipova, op. cit., p. 58 who notes that conflicts developed over the grain monopoly, fixed prices and demands for free trade. Elsewhere works refer to so-called 'kulak' uprisings in spring 1918: 54 'large' uprisings (Tambov, Kursk, Oryol, and Voronezh) and in four uezds of Nizhniy-Novgorod guberniya, again over the grain monopoly and fixed prices. (A. V. Shestakov, *Klassovaya bor'ba v derevne TsChO v epokhu voennogo kommunizma* (Voronezh, 1930), vyp. 1, p. 69).

[108] In some cases for instance 'bagmen' had organized themselves into detachments (Osipova, op. cit., p. 55.)

[109] *PSS*, vol. 35, pp. 312–13.

[110] See *PSS*, vol. 35, p. 315.

resolution).[111] Yet the Bolsheviks were cautious in such moves, not wishing to provoke the peasantry. The danger of such actions was already patently clear. The few incursions into the villages for grain had given rise to peasant resentment. At the end of March peasant dissatisfaction over the food issue was noted at several guberniya congresses while peasant opposition to the requisitioning of both grain and horses before June 1918 was noted in the Urals and the Lower Volga regions.[112] And nowhere was the significance of this peasant disquiet appreciated more than at local level. Between March and May soviets in several gubernii abolished fixed prices, and permitted free trade in grain, ignoring central legislation but in effect sanctioning *de facto* practices. The local soviets, moreover, were powerless to do otherwise.

In sum, the essence of the Bolshevik government's food policy between the October revolution and the passing of the so-called 'Food Dictatorship' decree of early May was an exchange of goods, though sporadic forced collections of grain (and other items) were in evidence too.[113] This is not to deny that Lenin's policy was problematic: his actions in satisfying the peasant demand for land had a destructive internal logic of their own with regard to the food supply issue. Requisitioning and coercion only *gradually* came to the fore as other non-coercive means proved unsatisfactory. Much of the confusion that exists in the literature on the food issue can probably best be explained by the various local practices and/or exchanges that emerged. Doubtless the government had little clear idea about what was happening in the localities. In some instances, in effect, a free market did operate and was even sanctioned by local soviets. Thus, in *practice*, one can notice similarities between the first half year of Bolshevik rule and the early NEP. It was in terms of *central policy*, however, that the contrasts between the two periods are most marked.

In conclusion, the evidence from the more central regions in 1918 shows that there were conflicts over the distribution of land but that these were not sufficiently serious to provoke widespread unrest among the peasantry. The Bolshevik policy of 'non-intervention' in the countryside, of leaving peasants to sort out their own land affairs, meant that such disputes were generally resolved locally, while

[111] See Robert Service, *The Russian Revolution* (London, 1986).
[112] Osipova, op. cit., p. 59; 'Narodnoye Soprotivleniye Kommunizmu v Rossii', M.S. Bernshtam (ed.), *Ural i Prikam'e noyabr' 1917 – yanvar' 1919*, vol. 3 (Paris, 1982), pp. 60, 106–08, 154–55. We are informed that in Perm' guberniya in March 1918 the frontoviki sided with the peasants against the requisitioning detachments.
[113] In March–May 1918 soviets of many gubernii including Astrakhan', Vyatka, Kazan', Samara, Simbirsk, Saratov and Tambov, abolished fixed prices and permitted free trade in grain. (Osipova, op. cit., p. 56.)

'outside' agencies to help resolve conflicts were on hand if their arbitration was sought. Even if the conflicts failed to be resolved, postponing their resolution still gave the peasants hope of a solution in the future. Peasant anxieties were further appeased by the fact that many regarded the spring redivision as only temporary anyway — a point reinforced by Narkomzem and the local land authorities though for different reasons; most partial divisions had often been considered temporary in the countryside, to be followed in the future by a chornyy peredel, a more just and equitable distribution of land.

But the Bolsheviks' policy of leaving peasants to sort out land affairs themselves had the effect of strengthening the mir and thus consolidating opposition to the Bolsheviks when they instituted other agrarian measures such as the continuation of the alcohol prohibition and finally the move towards more coercion in obtaining grain. Although it was noted that the Bolsheviks from the start wanted to avoid confrontation with the peasantry, such confrontation eventually developed as a consequence of their own land policy, or perhaps more accurately, their lack of one: under the specific circumstances of early 1918 the breakdown of urban/rural relations undermined the Bolsheviks' attempts at 'exchange of goods' while the loss of the major grain-producing areas to non-Bolshevik forces after Brest–Litovsk gave to the food supply problem a greater urgency. Just as the peasants were retreating into a rural enclave economy, so the Bolsheviks were demanding more grain. And their assumption that grain was in kulak hands seemed to ignore their understanding of the land redistribution where there had been an increase in the number of middle peasants. The reaction in the late spring appeared to be a panic move in the face of a perception of a worsening of the food situation which threatened the entire régime.

Certainly such harsh measures seem to fly in the face of Lenin's earlier logic. Poorer peasants needed time to become 'conscious' of the eventual cul-de-sac of 'land redivision' and to support socialized farming, and especially, to overcome their association of the latter with the former large estates. Collective farms themselves required time and support to develop (the latter so obviously lacking), and eight months was clearly too soon for all this to happen. But, one must remember, Lenin was a politician too. He often changed his views and was not always consistent. Giving land to the peasants disposed them favourably in the central regions towards the party responsible for this; forcibly taking from them the produce of the land only months later cost the Bolsheviks dearly.

[5]

Urbanization and Deurbanization in the Russian Revolution and Civil War*

Diane Koenker
University of Illinois at Urbana-Champaign

Urban Russia in 1917 was the crucible of revolution. The collapse of the tsarist government began first in the capital city of Petrograd; the appeal of the Bolshevik party among the urban populations of Petrograd, Moscow, and other cities (along with its influence among troops at the front) was critical in ensuring the successful seizure of power by the Soviets in October 1917. Indeed, the city, and especially its urban work force, had long been central to Marxist theorists, who opposed their vision of a proletarian revolution centered in the city to that of the populists, who believed that rural peasants would provide the spark of revolution in Russia.

It was not only a historical irony, then, but also a critical threat to the future course of the revolution, that from the very moment of Bolshevik success in late 1917, thousands and thousands of urban residents, workers and nonworkers, were abandoning the cities for the relative security of provincial towns and rural hamlets. Between May 1917 and April 1918, the city of Moscow lost 300,000 of its 2 million inhabitants. From 1918 to 1920, the city lost another 700,000 people. Moscow's population toward the end of the civil war was thus half of what it had been in the midst of the 1917 revolution. An even more catastrophic fall occurred in Petrograd: its population plummeted from 2.5 million in 1917 to 700,000 in 1920.[1]

Between 1917 and 1920, nearly every city in the former Russian empire had suffered similar population losses. Of the ten largest cities in 1910,

* An earlier version of this article was presented to the Yale University Interdisciplinary Colloquium, "The City and Urbanization in Comparative Perspective." I am grateful to William Chase for sharing with me his work in progress and to Lewis Siegelbaum, David Ransel, James Barrett, and this *Journal*'s anonymous referees for valuable criticisms and suggestions. Errors in fact or judgment remain my own. I also wish to thank the International Research and Exchanges Board for sponsoring a visit to Moscow that allowed me to collect some of the materials used in this article.

[1] *Statisticheskii ezhegodnik goroda Moskvy i moskovskoi gubernii* (hereinafter *Stat. ezhegodnik g. Moskvy*), vyp. 2 (Moscow, 1927), p. 15; Tsentral'noe statisticheskoe upravlenie (TsSU), *Trudy*, vol. 8, vyp. 1, part 32, p. 342.

Russian Urbanization and Deurbanization   425

TABLE 1
CHANGE IN SIZE OF MAJOR RUSSIAN CITIES FROM 1910 TO 1920

City	1910 Population	1920 Population
St. Petersburg	1,962,000	722,000
Moscow	1,533,000	1,028,000
Odessa	506,000	435,000
Kiev	505,000	366,000
Khar'kov	236,000	284,000
Saratov	206,000	190,000
Ekaterinoslav	196,000	164,000
Tiflis	188,000	327,000
Kazan	188,000	146,000
Baku	167,000	256,000
Astrakhan	150,000	123,000
Rostov-on-Don	121,000	177,000
Nizhnyi Novgorod	109,000	70,000
Ufa	103,000	93,000
Minsk	101,000	104,000
Samara	96,000	177,000
Tsaritsyn	78,000	81,000
Perm	50,000	74,000

SOURCES.—For 1910, B. R. Mitchell, *Abstract of European Historical Statistics*, abridged ed. (New York, 1975), pp. 12–15; Baedeker, *Russia* (1914; New York, 1970). For 1920, Tsentral' noe statisticheskoe upravlenie, *Trudy*, vol. 8, vyp. 1, part 1, table 3, and Mitchell.

the decline in Kiev came closest to Moscow's and Petrograd's: Kiev's population dropped by 28 percent in the years spanning the revolution and civil war. Only a handful of cities gained in population between 1910 and 1920: two, Baku and Tiflis, were politically independent after 1917 and as such were havens for refugees from the destitution and conflict of revolutionary Russia. The other cities that grew were all located on the periphery of European Russia, close to sources of grain but also at one time or another centers of White Army activity as well. Samara and Tsaritsyn on the Volga, Perm in Western Siberia, and Rostov-on-Don all recorded marked increases in population at a time when cities everywhere were contracting (see table 1).[2]

Bolshevik leaders feared they were losing their working-class base of support, that the proletariat that demonstrated such revolutionary class

[2] For 1910 population, B. R. Mitchell, *European Historical Statistics, 1750–1970*, abridged ed. (New York, 1975), pp. 12–15; Baedeker, *Russia*, facsimile of the 1914 ed. (New York, 1970). For 1920, TsSU, *Trudy*, vol. 8, vyp. 1, part 1, table 3.

426   *Koenker*

consciousness in 1917 was becoming "declassed" as a result of the economic pressures and dislocations of the civil war. Menshevik leaders used this same fear to argue that since the social base of Bolshevik legitimacy had withered away, the Bolsheviks themselves should reconsider the assumptions on which they based their right to rule.[3]

Nikolai Bukharin spoke in March 1918 of the disintegration of the proletariat; Ian Rudzutak reported to the second All-Russian Congress of Trade Unions in January 1919: "We observe in a large number of industrial centers that the workers, thanks to the contraction of production in the factories, are being absorbed in the peasant mass, and instead of a population of workers we are getting a half-peasant or sometimes a purely peasant population."[4] And Lenin reiterated this theme at the Tenth Party Congress in March 1921: "People have run away from hunger; workers have simply abandoned their factories, they set up housekeeping in the countryside and have stopped being workers."[5]

Western scholars, too, citing the contemporary record, describe the "withering away of the proletariat." John Keep writes: "The men who made the October revolution, in so far as they were civilians and not soldiers, were soon dissipated to the four winds. . . . their place would eventually be filled by men who came straight from the village and were cast in a different mold."[6]

In this light, it becomes extremely important to examine the reality of this postulated decline of the working class and to ask how the demographic and social changes that took place between 1917 and 1921 affected the set of factors that had propelled the Bolshevik party to power in the first place.

It is one thing, however, to examine concrete indices of economic and social change, particularly demographic data, and quite another to link such changes to more elusive concepts that usually go under the name of "revolutionary" or "class" consciousness. For example, it can be argued that there existed, among Bolshevik supporters in late 1917, a "revolutionary consciousness," a common sense of purpose and commitment to replacing the old regime with something new and more socially just. Some of the elements of this revolutionary consciousness have been

[3] See E. H. Carr, *The Bolshevik Revolution* (Harmondsworth, 1966), 2:196; Leopold H. Haimson, ed., *The Mensheviks: From the October Revolution to World War II* (Chicago, 1974), pt. 2.

[4] Quoted in Carr, 2:196.

[5] V. I. Lenin, *Polnoe sobranie sochenenii*, 5th ed. (Moscow, 1963), 43:42 (my translation).

[6] John L. H. Keep, *The Russian Revolution: A Study in Mass Mobilization* (New York, 1976), pp. 261–62. See also Sheila Fitzpatrick, *The Russian Revolution* (Oxford, 1982), pp. 85–86.

identified in recent studies of the revolution and working class by S. A. Smith, David Mandel, and Rex Wade, among others.[7] It was a consciousness shaped by short-term factors, most notably the specific economic and political experience of 1917, and by long-term factors as well. These include the ideology of Marxism itself, which fostered a tendency among workers to interpret their experience in terms of social class and class conflict. Another long-term factor was the workplace and the relations it engendered: an autocrat-subject relationship between management and labor, and solidarity among workers who labored and suffered together in such close proximity. Still other factors have to do with social attributes of workers—education, skill, maleness, and youth—which predisposed them first to develop a sense of politics and then to respond in a calculated, conscious manner, rather than in a visceral way, to the visions of revolution posed by the Marxist parties and by events leading up to 1917. Finally, the location of workers in cities also helped to shape revolutionary consciousness, in ways that will be detailed below. Suffice it here to say that urban working-class culture reflected several important attributes of the urban milieu, such as individual autonomy, utilization of a wide array of cultural and educational opportunities, and a social heterogeneity that enriched the perceptions and experience of urban residents.

All these factors helped to shape a specific kind of revolutionary consciousness pertinent to the specific conditions of 1917. It was a consciousness strongly influenced by ideas of class and of socialism. It does not follow, however, that these attitudes or this revolutionary consciousness was necessarily permanent and unchangeable. If some elements influencing this consciousness were changed, it is completely plausible that different attitudes might emerge. Kin, neighborhood, or possession of skill, for example, might be placed above class as the immediate source of a worker's identity. In such a case, the party whose popularity was based on its appeal to class interests, the Bolsheviks, might not command the same loyalty they had enjoyed under earlier conditions.

Of course, conditions did change after 1917. Of the factors important in shaping the consciousness of 1917, perhaps the only constant was Marxist ideology, which remained a powerful mediator of experience

[7] S. A. Smith, *Red Petrograd* (Cambridge, 1983); David Mandel, *The Petrograd Workers and the Fall of the Old Regime* (London, 1983), and *The Petrograd Workers and the Soviet Seizure of Power* (London, 1984); Diane Koenker, *Moscow Workers and the 1917 Revolution* (Princeton, N.J., 1981); Israel Getzler, *Kronstadt, 1917–1921* (Cambridge, 1983); Rex A. Wade, *Red Guards and Workers' Militias in the Russian Revolution* (Stanford, Calif., 1984); Ronald G. Suny, *The Baku Commune* (Princeton, N.J., 1972); William G. Rosenberg, "The Democratization of Russia's Railroads in 1917," *American Historical Review* 88, no. 5 (December 1981): 983–1008.

428   *Koenker*

and whose appeal cannot be dismissed. But factory relations were dramatically transformed, the political and economic context of public life was also fundamentally different from what it had been before the revolution, and the cities, instead of representing the attractions of modernity and culture, became after 1917 places from which to flee.

There were many signs, by early 1918, that the Bolshevik party did not command the same allegiance that had brought it to power. Although the Bolsheviks had not completely lost their mandate to rule, there were uncomfortable signs of an independent factory movement in Petrograd in early 1918 and a string of Menshevik successes in local Soviet elections in the summer of 1918.[8] By 1921, amidst discontent and strikes among Petrograd workers, and a growing Workers' Opposition movement within the Communist party, sailors at the Kronstadt naval fortress rebelled, demanding Soviet reelections without Communist participation. The revolt was crushed by loyal Red Army troops, but the alienation it reflected prompted the party to search for a new economic policy to placate frustrated workers and peasants alike.

The party assessment of this debacle depended upon its interpretation of the social composition of its former supporters. The old Kronstadt revolutionary sailor had left the fortress, and his place was occupied by peasants and other unrevolutionary elements. The "true" working class had been driven away from the cities by hunger, to be replaced, presumably, by new workers from cottage industry, agriculture, and white-collar jobs eliminated by the revolution.[9] (This was the same argument used to explain the Bolsheviks' lack of success among workers in the early months of 1917—that the cadres of conscious proletarians were diluted by nonproletarian elements.) In addition, Bolshevik ideology assumed that large factories were an essential component of proletarian consciousness; with the shrinking of the work force in these plants, with the decision by skilled workers to manufacture cigarette lighters that could be more easily exchanged for grain than machine tools, party officials believed that Russian workers were losing their class consciousness: this could only be restored by the resumption of production in large-scale plants.[10]

The questions of support and of working-class consciousness are critical in interpreting this period and in understanding the sources of the Soviet political and social system, and they deserve a prominent place on the

[8] Mandel, *Petrograd Workers and Soviet Seizure*, pp. 390–413; see Vladimir Brovkin, "The Mensheviks' Political Comeback: The Elections to the Provincial City Soviets in Spring 1918," *Russian Review* 42 (1983): 1–50.

[9] *Istoriia rabochikh Moskvy 1917–1945 gg.* (Moscow, 1983), p. 93.

[10] Lenin, 43:42.

research agenda. This article will investigate just one aspect of changing social relations during the civil war, the problem of social composition in the former urban strongholds of the Bolshevik party. Given the obvious social dislocations indicated by the drastic decline of Russia's urban population, the question who stayed and who departed becomes important in identifying the nature of the available constituency for Soviet power during its early period of rule. In particular, this article will address the question of the nature of the deurbanization of Russia and the relationship between this deurbanization, the "declassing" of the proletariat lamented by the Communist party, and the formation of a new and possibly different set of attitudes among workers—working-class consciousness—during these years.

URBANIZATION AND REVOLUTION

A discussion of Russian urbanization is inevitably a tale of two cities, St. Petersburg (after 1914, Petrograd) and Moscow. In large part, this is because of their political prominence and relative magnitude. St. Petersburg, with 2 million residents in 1910, and Moscow, with 1.5 million, were four times and three times the size of their nearest competitors.[11]

Other Russian cities had grown as well since the early 1860s, when Russia's emancipation of its serfs loosened the bonds that restricted economic growth. But urban growth did not necessarily produce urbanization, in the sense of the adoption by the society of values associated with cities and with urbanism. Proportionally, Russia's urban population was dwarfed by the countryside. In 1860, cities accounted for 11.3 percent of the total population; this share had not quite doubled by 1917, to 21.6 percent. St. Petersburg and Moscow provinces, however, were the two most urban in the empire: 75 percent of Petrograd province's population lived in cities in 1915, and 53 percent of Moscow's did.[12] By contrast, Riazan province, an agricultural region that sent many migrants to Moscow, could claim an urban population of only 7 percent of its total in 1915.[13]

[11] Mitchell, pp. 12–15.

[12] Gaston Rimlinger, "The Expansion of the Labor Market in Capitalist Russia, 1861–1917," *Journal of Economic History* 21 (1961): 208–15, esp. 211; E. G. Gimpel'son, *Sovetskii rabochii klass, 1918–1920* (Moscow, 1974), p. 51.

[13] (There shall be occasion to refer to Riazan again later in this essay.) *Statisticheskii ezhegodnik Rossii* (Petrograd, 1915). The 1915 definition of "urban" is not clear. One study of Russian urbanization restricts the term to settlements of at least 15,000 people, or 20,000 in some cases (Robert A. Lewis and Richard H. Rowland, "Urbanization in Russia and the USSR, 1897–1970," in *The City in Russian History*, ed. Michael Hamm [Lexington, Ky., 1976], p. 206). Using these criteria, Lewis and Rowland claim that 9.4 percent of the population was urban in 1897, a figure that is considerably lower than those used here. Therefore, the definition of "urban" used by Russian census officials must include cities

430   *Koenker*

The social composition of Russian urban dwellers defies the strict definitions of census categories. Although urban growth was fueled largely by migration, the passage to the city was not one way, and an inhabitant did not acquire all the facility and characteristics of urban residence as soon as he or she passed the city barriers. The research of R. E. Johnson has shown that migrants themselves traveled back and forth many times during their years in the city; their families also tended to be distributed between city and village. It was not unusual for a working-class wife to bear her children in the city and then send them back to the country to live with relatives until they were old enough to work. Even more common, married male migrants lived and worked in the city while their wives and children remained home in the country.[14]

Such characteristics suggest that there existed a number of types of workers in Russian cities on the eve of revolution and that workers responded in different ways to the opportunities and pressures of 1917 and the years that followed. To clarify the following discussion, it is useful to rank these urban types in terms of a hypothetical "level of urbanization," in which "urbanization" is defined as the complete adoption of urban values, culture, and experience:

type A: most urbanized, parents permanent city residents, children born and raised in city;

type B: parents in city, children move back and forth (consecutively as much as all together);

type C: father in city, mother in country, children (especially boys) move back and forth;

type D: father in city, mother and children in country;

type E: sons and daughters come to city as first-generation migrants, parents remain in country.

The working-class memoir literature provides examples of all five types, although it is impossible to assign numerical weights to each category.[15]

---

smaller than 15,000. See also Chauncey D. Harris, *Cities of the Soviet Union* (Washington, D.C., 1972), chap. 7.

[14] R. E. Johnson, *Peasant and Proletarian* (New Brunswick, N.J., 1978); *Pervaia vseobshchaia perepis' naseleniia 1897 goda* (St. Petersburg, 1903).

[15] A classic memoir of the genre is S. I. Kanatchikov, *Iz istorii moego bytiia* (Moscow, 1929); see an abridged translation of this and other memoirs in *The Russian Worker*, ed. Victoria E. Bonnell (Berkeley, 1983). See also Reginald E. Zelnik, "Russian Bebels: An Introduction to the Memoirs of Semen Kanatchikov and Matvei Fisher," *Russian Review* 35 (1976): 249–89, 417–47; and L. M. Ivanov, "Preemstvennost' fabrichno-zavodskogo truda i formirovanie proletariata v Rossii," in *Rabochii klass i rabochee dvizhenie v Rossii*, ed. L. M. Ivanov (Moscow, 1966), p. 105.

Families of type A, however, were clearly in the minority, although growing in numbers; barely 10 percent of the Moscow working class in 1912 had been born in the city, although the percentage of workers whose parents had also been workers (types A through D) was greater. For all of Moscow province in a 1908 study, about 40 percent of workers had parents who were workers, a figure that rose to 45 percent for workers aged fifteen to twenty-five years.[16]

In assessing the impact of the urban crisis on urbanized workers after 1917, two questions arise. First, it is important to inquire whether and in what ways the city acted upon its inhabitants, especially those of the working class, to produce a particular cast of mind (*oblik* is the Russian term), a set of characteristics and values that can be labeled "urban working-class culture." The second question concerns the link between such culture and propensities to revolutionary activism.

Among the city's special contributions to the creation of a working-class culture were the ways in which city life encouraged workers to act together, such as in food supply and dining cooperatives and in sick funds. The necessities of communal living developed the practice of cooperation, and of course, as the Marxists argued, the experience of working in large mechanized factories also taught cooperation. On the other hand, the diversity of the urban work force also provided opportunities for individual mobility and encouraged separatism as well as cooperation; typesetters, highly skilled urban workers, were notorious for setting themselves apart from other workers and often rejected participation in a wider labor movement in favor of helping themselves.[17]

In addition to these competing values of cooperation and individualism, the city offered its working-class residents cultural opportunities that in turn encouraged workers to value culture and education. Evening schools, public schools, neighborhood clubs and libraries, theater, and an active publishing industry offered workers a wide range of opportunities for self-improvement. Many workers used their reading ability to familiarize themselves with basic political issues, which were far more accessible in the cities than anywhere else, thanks to the concentration there of publishers and political activists.[18]

Among the ways in which these urban values were transmitted, three deserve special mention. The first of these is family. The typology offered

[16] I. M. Koz'minykh-Lanin, *Ukhod na polevye raboty fabrichno-zavodskikh rabochikh moskovskoi gubernii* (Moscow, 1912).

[17] *Istoriia Leningradskogo soiuza rabochikh poligraficheskogo proizvodstva*, vol. 1 (Leningrad, 1925); V. V. Sher, *Istoriia professional'nogo dvizheniia rabochikh pechatnogo dela v Moskve* (Moscow, 1911); Koenker, *Moscow Workers*, chap. 2; Mandel, *Petrograd Workers and the Fall of the Old Regime*, chap. 2.

[18] Koenker, *Moscow Workers*, pp. 45–46.

432   *Koenker*

above might suggest that the nuclear family was a rare phenomenon in urban Russia. Yet the children who grew up in such families quickly absorbed the values of their parents and used these values to define for themselves a distinct subculture of their own. The attributes of an urban youth culture are complex and have been discussed at greater length elsewhere;[19] moreover, there is surely room for further investigation into the entire problem of urban culture, both of the young and the old. However, there did exist an urban youth subculture based on substantial personal autonomy deriving from the absence at home of working parents, from the less restrictive control by heads of urban families, from the availability of culture, recreation, and work away from the family's strict tutelage. Youths in the city were thus relatively free to gravitate toward associations of their teenage peers, which reinforced a special sense of local identity. The favorite activities of such groups—literary discussions, drama, politics—also helped to forge an identity that was seen to be distinctly modern and distinctly urban.[20] Further, perceptions and experiences of social relations interpreted in the light of Marxist class ideology were surely an important lesson imparted by working-class fathers.[21] Thus the urban working-class family was perhaps weaker as an institution than the archetypical patriarchal peasant family, but this weakness gave members of urban families a flexibility and freedom not easily found in the countryside.

A second important medium for transmitting new values was the city's concentration of workplaces and the proximity of plants in different industries, of different sizes, and representing different types of work. In contrast to laborers in single-industry towns such as Ivanovo-Voznesensk or the mining communities of the Urals, city workers could share a variety of experiences, among family members employed in different places, or in local taverns and dining halls, or in the activities of youth groups. The political and social attitudes that developed among urban workers who assimilated diverse experiences reflected the interaction of workers of different types.

[19] Diane Koenker, "Urban Families, Working-Class Youth Groups, and the 1917 Revolution in Moscow," in *The Family in Imperial Russia*, ed. David L. Ransel (Urbana, Ill., 1978), pp. 280–304.

[20] V. Iu. Krupianskaia, "Evoliutsiia semeino-bytovogo uklada rabochikh," in *Rossiiskii proletariat: oblik, bor'ba, gegemoniia*, ed. L. M. Ivanov (Moscow, 1970), p. 283; Anna Litveiko, "V semnadtsatom," *Iunost'*, no. 3 (1957), pp. 3–18; I. V. Babushkin, *Vospominaniia, 1893–1900* (Moscow, 1951), p. 39. On the role of theater, see Gary Thurston, "The Impact of Russian Popular Theatre, 1886–1915," *Journal of Modern History* 55 (1983): 237–67.

[21] See the memoir by Eduard Dune, "Zapiski krasnogvardeitsa," MSS in the Nicolaevsky archive, Hoover Institution, Stanford, California.

The exemplary working-class neighborhoods of the two capital cities were Vyborg in Petrograd and Zamoskvorech'e in Moscow. Both districts were dominated occupationally by highly skilled metalworkers, but they also housed workers of other industries, especially women in textiles and food processing. The two districts shared a physical isolation from the upper-class and political culture of their cities, but were not so homogeneous that residents never came into contact with nonworkers or with workers of different social backgrounds. In 1917, both districts were far more politically active than other working-class neighborhoods of more homogeneous industrial composition.[22]

A third means by which the city fostered a special working-class culture was through the concentration of political power and activity. Newspapers ranging from government gazettes to sensationalist tabloids were printed in the cities, and they were read avidly by urban workers.[23] The world of politics easily became the stuff of conversation in working-class neighborhoods, and urban workers had much better access to political information than workers scattered in provincial factory and mining towns. Furthermore, as political centers, both cities (although St. Petersburg more than Moscow) attracted opposition and underground activists. Socialists naturally sought to organize among workers, and their participation as evening-school teachers as well as professional political activists helped to give a socialist cast to ideas of political opposition. The city's particular advantage was to make available to workers a mixture of theory and a variety of experience that made a revolutionary socialist world view seem especially valid.

But how did this urban working-class culture contribute to the outcome of the two revolutions of 1917? It is indeed difficult to prove that working-class supporters of Soviet power were somehow more "urban" in attitudes than those who supported other parties or none at all. Recent research by Heather Hogan, Victoria Bonnell, and others[24] has demonstrated that organized workers—those active in trade unions, factory committees, Soviets—tended to be urban, skilled, and predominantly male. Craft unions were especially successful in organizing in the first few weeks after February 1917, as they had been after 1905. Although the attribute

[22] On neighborhoods, see Laura Engelstein, *Moscow, 1905* (Stanford, 1982); and Mandel, *Petrograd Workers and the Fall of the Old Regime*.

[23] Reading habits before and after the 1917 revolution were surveyed by E. O. Kabo in 1923, and reported in *Ocherki rabochego byta* (Moscow, 1928).

[24] Heather J. Hogan, "Labor and Management in Conflict: The St. Petersburg Metal-working Industry, 1900–1914" (Ph.D. diss., University of Michigan, 1981); Victoria E. Bonnell, *Roots of Rebellion: Workers' Politics and Organizations in St. Petersburg and Moscow, 1900–1914* (Berkeley, 1983); Smith (n. 7 above).

of skill rather than urban experience may have been more important in facilitating such organization, the union ideology reflected values fostered by urban working-class life: socialism, collectivism, organization, and culture.[25] It is also true that maleness was a more important factor in organization than urban experience per se; women did not organize themselves effectively either in 1917 or before, even though the proportion of urban-born women in the work force was generally higher than that of urban-born men.[26] The contributions of urban women to the development of working-class culture, as wives, mothers, and workers, are largely uncharted, in part because they did not participate in the unions that provide much of the published record of working-class life before and during 1917, but their role deserves further study.

The future of the urban working class was represented by its youth, the children chiefly of families of type A and to a lesser extent of types B and C. These youths espoused urban and socialist values: education and culture, collectivism and comradeship, sobriety, sexual equality (apparently on a level higher than that of their parents), class pride, and solidarity.[27] In 1917, working-class youth and others organized for the first time on a large scale; fragmentary biographical information suggests the leaders of their youth groups came from urban rather than from migrant families.[28] By October, and even earlier, many working-class youth groups were enthusiastic if undisciplined supporters of the Bolshevik party. By contrast, young workers who had come recently from the countryside, as a young Moscow metalworker recalled, "were still weakly developed, and after the February revolution wavered among the Mensheviks, Socialist Revolutionaries, and Bolsheviks. The other and large part of the youth— products of worker families—already had experienced hard factory labor, had received the tempering of a worker. This worker youth after the February revolution very quickly organized around Bolshevik party cells, joined in protest meetings against the policies of the Provisional Government, fought for the eight-hour working day."[29]

[25] Bonnell, *Roots of Rebellion*, p. 263; Koenker, *Moscow Workers*, chap. 2.

[26] In 1912, 11 percent of women in factories and 23 percent in nonfactory manufacturing were urban born, compared to figures of 9 percent and 7 percent for urban-born men. Since many replacements for drafted workers after 1914 were wives of factory workers, the percentage of urban-born women in the work force was probably even higher in 1917.

[27] Litveiko; *Krasnaia Presnia 1905–1917 gg.* (Moscow, 1930), pp. 455–57; *Prechistenskie rabochie kursy* (Moscow, 1948).

[28] Koenker, "Urban Families," p. 301.

[29] *Moskovskie bol' sheviki v ogne revoliutsionnykh boev* (Moscow, 1976), pp. 275–76 (my translation).

Although youth organizations as such played only a supporting role in the actual seizure of power, the energy and commitment of youth were tapped by the revolution in other ways. Armed worker militias and Red Guards recruited members predominantly from among young and unmarried workers between the ages of seventeen and twenty-four.[30] Moreover, Bolshevik party electoral candidates, in Moscow at any rate, tended to be substantially younger than those of the other two socialist parties. Alexander Rabinowitch also suggests indirectly that Petrograd Bolsheviks were attractive to and perhaps composed of young workers, particularly those under thirty years old. Although he does not dwell on the social composition of the party rank and file, he indicates that the Bolsheviks in Petrograd were a highly autonomous group of activist workers (a characteristic also of the Red Guards), who shaped the policy of the leadership, sometimes against Lenin's wishes.[31] Their political independence and self-confidence reflected the advantages of urban culture: education and individualism, underscored by the strong sense of class separateness and consciousness that characterized the Bolshevik program in 1917. But although the revolutionary activists were dominated by skilled young male urban workers, more recent migrants were also brought into the revolutionary arena in Moscow and Petrograd precisely because of their location in the urban centers: here the urban working class gave its special stamp to the revolutionary outlook of the nonurban elements it was able to mobilize.

The evidence is only circumstantial that young workers of urban families supported the radical Bolsheviks more than other parties, and that their radicalism was conditioned by prior attitudes shaped by urban life. But there is little evidence for the contrary argument that urban radicalism in 1917 was fueled by the rawest and least politically experienced elements of urban society. As for the Bolsheviks themselves, they had no doubts about the social composition of their supporters; they read the results of the elections to the Constituent Assembly in November 1917, when they received 36.5 percent of the urban vote to 24 percent overall (and 47 percent in Petrograd and Moscow).[32] And even though the army gave nearly half its votes to the Bolsheviks, the army would soon be demobilized. Thus their urban supporters were all-important, and the Bolshevik reaction to the urban depopulation following the revolution suggests they feared that the loss of their urban proletarian cadres would seriously

[30] Wade (n. 7 above); V. I. Startsev, *Ocherki po istorii Petrogradskoi krasnoi gvardii i rabochei militsii* (Moscow-Leningrad, 1965).
[31] Alexander Rabinowitch, *The Bolsheviks Come to Power* (New York, 1976).
[32] L. M. Spirin, *Klassy i partii v grazhdanskoi voine v Rossii* (Moscow, 1968), pp. 59–60.

436   *Koenker*

undermine their legitimacy, if not their ability to govern. "Without such an economic base," argued Lenin in March 1921, in advocating the New Economic Policy, "there can be no lasting political power for the working class."[33]

Indeed, when the cities collapsed after 1917, among those who departed were the same urban and skilled young male workers who had fought for Soviet power in October, now leaving to fight in the civil war. Bolshevik hegemony was threatened in two ways: by the loss of these supporters and others like them who rusticated themselves outside the cities, and by changing social and economic conditions that might have served to alter the components of urban culture that had produced such firm Bolshevik support in October. Bolsheviks thus feared "declassing" in two senses, both in changes in social composition and in changing attitudes.

DEURBANIZATION IN MOSCOW: DEMOGRAPHIC CHANGES

Given the tremendous transformation that occurred in Russia between 1910 and 1920, it is not surprising that statistical sources can only hint at the dimensions of that transformation. Nonetheless, published census results permit us to trace the movement of the overall population of Moscow by size, age, sex, and precinct from its peak in 1917 through 1918 and up to 1920. Specific divisions by occupation were reported only in the 1918 and 1920 censuses, so a detailed study of changes in population by employment categories can be made only for the shorter period.

Over the entire period from February 1917 to August 1920, Moscow's population dropped by almost one million, a loss of 520,000 males, and 470,000 females. During the same period, there were roughly 110,000 births and 200,000 deaths, a natural decrease of 90,000.[34] Thus about 900,000 people must have left the city by the summer of 1920. Further, William Chase estimates from the 1926 census that about 100,000 people moved into Moscow during the civil war,[35] so the task becomes to account for one million lost Muscovites. Who were they? The sober, urban, most class-conscious workers? Or the politically marginal recent recruits from the Russian countryside? The answer to this question should provide a new appreciation of the nature of the social base underlying the political decisions made during these years, decisions that were to have a critical formative influence on the subsequent shape of the Soviet state and society.

To develop a profile of the changing social composition of Moscow, ideal indices would be place of birth, length of residence in the city,

[33] Lenin, 43:311.

[34] *Stat. ezhegodnik g. Moskvy*, pp. 15, 88.

[35] William Chase, *Workers, Society, and the State: Labor and Life in Moscow, 1918–1928* (Urbana, Ill., forthcoming), chap. 3.

occupation, length of time in that occupation, education, parents' occupation, and so forth. Most of these are unavailable, so it is necessary to estimate changes in social composition using age, sex, and occupational indices only.

Because occupational data were published only in the 1918 and 1920 census reports, it is difficult to determine who were the first 300,000 people to leave Moscow. The actual outflow did not begin until after May 1917, since a population count made for electoral purposes showed a slightly higher population in May than in February. By September, there were 195,000 fewer inhabitants in the city; about 163,000 of these were aged fifteen or over. Yet over the same period, the number of registered voters in the city—adults over twenty—increased slightly. It is unlikely that fifteen- to nineteen-year-olds (of whom there were 250,000 in September)[36] would have left in such disproportionate numbers. Therefore, the adults who had left by the autumn of 1917 may have been so marginal to the urban community that they had not bothered to participate in the electoral process in 1917. Most of those who departed were men (103,000 to 60,000 women); the evidence is suggestive that these were men and women most closely connected to the countryside, abandoning the city to make sure they would share in the expected redivision of land.

From September 1917 to April 1918, another 120,000 people left, 83,000 of them adults, 42,000 of them adult males. (Men and women over sixty did not participate in this exodus; their numbers actually increased from February 1917 to April 1918, a phenomenon that raises intriguing questions about the position of the aged in Russian society during this period.) By early 1918, Moscow had lost a considerable number of adults, especially adult males. Men left in the greatest numbers from the industrial suburbs to the east of the city center and from the southern Zamoskvorech'e. Some of these losses may have been due to relocation, as the city Soviet commandeered large private houses and reassigned them to workers' families.[37] But the decline in the female population was uniform throughout the city, and this reaffirms the suggestion that the men who left the factory districts were the marginal and single men, those of type D, who had only recently come to the city from the countryside.[38]

Where exactly did the refugees go? Scattered evidence suggests that they returned to the countryside, both in the north and in the grain-

[36] The published February census groups fifteen- to fifty-nine-year-olds, without further division.

[37] G. S. Ignat'ev, *Moskva v pervyi god proletarskoi diktatury* (Moscow, 1975), p. 281.

[38] The census by geographic districts—precincts and later commissariats—was reported in *Biulleten' Tsentral'nogo Statisticheskogo Upravleniia*, no. 33 (1920).

producing districts far beyond Moscow. Already in April 1918 four train-loads of women and children, accompanied by extra cars of food for the journey, were en route to Syzran on the Volga, an evacuation sponsored by the local trade union council.[39] A comparison of the rural population between 1917 and 1919 indicates that the farming population of agri-culturally nonproductive Moscow province declined from 72,000 in 1917 to 64,000 in 1919, echoing the urban pattern. Moscow city workers with ties to nearby regions may have preferred to trust their chances in the city rather than to return home, even if home were nearby. On the other hand, the agrarian population of more fertile Riazan province, the source of many Moscow migrants, increased from 175,000 in 1917 to 192,000 in 1919.[40] The northernmost regions of Russia around Arkhangel, Vologda, and Tver also increased in population during the civil war, and surely substantial population gains went unrecorded in the southern regions beyond the limit of the twenty-two provinces of the Russian Soviet Fed-erative Socialist Republic. Once again, as in the Time of Troubles in the early seventeenth century, town-dwelling Russians escaped to the forest and to the steppe. What is most curious about the changes in rural pop-ulation is that the overall rural growth of about 8 percent was accounted for entirely by men; the female rural population remained constant, so the destination of the female out-migrants from Moscow remains something of a mystery.[41]

Between 1918 and 1920, Moscow's net loss was about 690,000 people.[42] Of these 690,000 missing persons, only 190,000 were economically self-supporting; the remaining 490,000 or so were dependents. Thus 70 percent of the missing Muscovites were children, nonworking women (and men, about 34,000 of them) between the ages of twenty and fifty-nine, and those too old to work. Little else is known about these refugees, neither whom they depended on, nor whether the women were workers' wives, factory workers themselves made redundant by the return of their husbands from the front, grandes dames of society, or shopkeepers' spinster daughters. But by and large, for a whole series of cultural reasons, nonworking women had not played a significant role in political activity in 1917,[43] and their absence after 1918 probably had little effect on the

[39] *Professional'nyi vestnik*, April 20, 1918, p. 18.

[40] TsSU, *Trudy*, vol. 6, a study of the economic stratification of the peasantry in 1917 and 1919.

[41] *Ekonomicheskaia zhizn'*, December 1, 1920, p. 3.

[42] The natural decrease in this period was 56,000, but since mortality statistics were not provided by sex, net out-migration must be calculated without regard to sex. In order to preserve the value of sex-ratio information, it is preferable here to refer to net loss of population rather than net out-migration.

[43] See the worker families reported on in Kabo (n. 23 above).

Russian Urbanization and Deurbanization   439

TABLE 2

Net Change in Moscow Working Population by Occupational
Group from 1918 to 1920

Group	Male	Female	Total
Workers	−90,760	−9,680	−100,440
Servants	−25,390	−56,270	−81,660
Employees	−59,460	+24,400	−35,060
Free professions	−720	+1,340	+620
Proprietors	−46,960	−14,530	−61,490
Other	+65,690	+14,320	+80,010

Source.—*Statisticheskii ezhegodnik goroda Moskvy i moskovskoi gubernii*, vyp. 2
(Moscow, 1927), pp. 46–51.

political and social consciousness of the Muscovite supporters of Soviet
power. The children who left, on the other hand (especially some 100,000
teenagers), were now removed from a formative urban experience. But
their absence, too, would little affect current political life in the city. If
the city was "declassed," in other words, it was not because of the
departure of women and children.

To evaluate the impact of Moscow's depopulation on its political life,
it is important to know which *self-supporting* individuals left the city.
The net loss of 194,000 economically independent residents can be accounted for in table 2.

Among the largest groups of absentees were workers, domestic servants,
and proprietors. Workers will be examined in more detail below. Domestic
servants were a rural class, cut off from city life and from one another;
most worked as single maids of all work in middle-class households.
(These and cooks disappeared most completely between 1918 and 1920.)
Nor did domestic servants produce dependents for future urban generations.[44] Their disappearance would have little negative effect on urban
political life; furthermore, if they were reabsorbed into the urban work
force in other occupations, their exposure to political culture might actually
increase.

The departure of individual proprietors for Paris, Berlin, Odessa, Vladivostok, or wherever else they escaped to, like the departure of their
servants, probably did not directly affect socialist political relationships

[44] *Stat. ezhegodnik g. Moskvy*, p. 73. In 1912, 4 percent of domestic servants
were urban born (the city average was 29 percent). Among servants, there were
sixteen self-supporting individuals for every one dependent, while the overall
ratio was about two dependents to one independent (p. 74).

440   *Koenker*

in Moscow. Note also that 60,000 male employees left; their leaving was partially balanced by an influx of 24,000 women employees, primarily typists and other clerical personnel (messengers and couriers were classified as servants). Many of these office workers presumably worked for Soviet institutions, the biggest growth sector in Moscow, but others replaced departed or drafted men in business, factory, or cooperative society offices. Finally, an additional 80,000 residents in other categories came to the city, including 14,000 wards of the state (orphans, invalids, prisoners), and 50,000 people classified simply in "other occupations." Since these were almost all males, this large group of newcomers certainly represents the Moscow Red Army garrison. Many of these may not have been newcomers at all, but workers reassigned from Moscow factories to Moscow barracks.

Returning to the change among workers between 1918 and 1920, note that 90 percent of the decline is accounted for by men. Working women did not leave the city, unlike their economically dependent counterparts; from 90,000 in 1918, their numbers dropped only to 80,000 in 1920, whereas the number of male workers fell from 215,000 in 1918 to 124,000. In Petrograd, too, women dominated the labor force after 1918, especially in the age group fifteen to twenty-five.[45] During the civil war, Moscow women continued to work in the same occupations they had held during the war and in 1917: textiles, clothing manufacture (especially army uniforms), and food and tobacco production.

Among men, skilled workers suffered the greatest numerical losses (although in percentages, these losses were less than among semiskilled or unskilled workers). It is this group that included the most committed of the revolutionary activists of 1917. Indeed, a different set of figures that permits comparison of 1920 and 1917 shows that the number of metalworkers, the quintessential urban proletarian activists, declined in Moscow by almost 40,000, or 66 percent: 25,000 of these left between 1917 and August 1918, a loss therefore only marginally represented in the comparison of 1918 and 1920.[46] By virtue of their scarce and flexible skills, these metalworkers were among the most employable men in Russia, and many of them traveled the countryside during these years, finding work at the big state munitions plants in centers such as Sormovo, Tula, and Izhevsk; here they received the same food ration as Red Army men and were closer to sources of food supply.[47]

[45] TsSU, *Trudy*, vol. 26, vyp. 2, tables 3 and 4.
[46] *Fabrichno-zavodskaia promyshlennost' g. Moskvy i moskovskoi gubernii 1917–1927 gg.* (Moscow, 1928), p. 1. These industrial figures presumably derive from the August 1918 industrial census, taken four months after the urban population count that provides most of the occupational information used here.
[47] D. A. Baevskii, *Rabochii klass v pervye gody sovetskoi vlasti (1917–1921 gg.)* (Moscow, 1974), p. 250.

Like Moscow's, Petrograd's losses included large numbers of skilled and valuable longtime workers. In fact, none left in such great numbers, both absolute and relative, as the skilled metalworkers, so that by October 1918, when the Red Army's need for armaments caused metal production to revive, metal union officials pleaded for a return of workers to the city: "We still have raw materials, coal, and iron. We still have machines. We can and know how to work. But few of our metalworkers have stayed in Petrograd. Some died in the fight for freedom, others have gone to the front, still others have left the red capital during the evacuation, and still others have dispersed all over the country in search of bread for themselves and their families. Many, after the closing of their factories, moved to other branches of industry, joined the militia, or engage now in petty trade."[48]

But despite the allegations of declassing, of workers returning to their native villages, statistical evidence suggests that the overwhelming majority of Moscow's skilled workers were lost to the Red Army itself. And the loss of such activists surely diminished the reserves of Bolshevik agitators and Bolshevik supporters. On the other hand, of more than 300,000 Muscovites mustered into the army,[49] not all were hereditary proletarian cadres—workers of the family types A, B, and C. Scattered evidence compiled from biographies and from figures on aid to army dependents suggests that many recruits came directly from tsarist army units on active or reserve status in Moscow, and from families of white-collar employees as well as of workers.[50] However, recruits were overwhelmingly young, unmarried, and childless; workers of this type had enthusiastically supported Soviet power in 1917, and their physical absence from the city would clearly affect the political climate.

Not all eligible workers joined the Red Army, however. Reports about the initial May 1918 mobilization suggest that from 15 to 25 percent of those called were too ill to report; others were rejected upon initial examination, so it is likely that only half of those called up left the city. Many other workers also remained in Moscow in reserve units, working their jobs during the day and training evenings and on weekends.[51] Still others, especially skilled workers, received permanent assignments as army instructors in Moscow. A young printer who volunteered for duty in May 1920 was trained as an instructor and spent the remainder of the civil war training reserve units of printers in his original Moscow neigh-

---

[48] V. Z. Drobizhev, A. K. Sokolov, and V. A. Ustinov, *Rabochii klass sovetskoi Rossii v pervyi god proletarskoi diktatury* (Moscow, 1975), p. 91 (my translation).

[49] *Krasnaia Moskva 1917–1920 gg.* (Moscow, 1920), p. 618.

[50] Ibid., pp. 435–38.

[51] *Uprochenie sovetskoi vlasti v Moskve i moskovskoi gubernii* (Moscow, 1958), pp. 443–52.

442   *Koenker*

borhood.[52] Finally, just as had happened in 1914 and 1915, skilled workers were deemed too valuable for production to be used as soldiers, and beginning in late 1918, they began to return to their original industrial occupations.[53]

It is important now to evaluate the nature of the change in the social composition of Moscow during the civil war years, and especially to suggest something about the fate of the politically active urban workers who helped make the revolution in 1917. First of all, they did not rusticate themselves in large numbers. Those that returned to the countryside were those with the closest ties there—unskilled recent migrants, servants, and nonworking dependents. Second, although many of the urbanized workers served in the Red Army, many also remained in the city. Moscow experienced what a Soviet analysis of the 1918 census called a "middling-out" of the working class.[54] Many of the most politically committed workers left the work force for military service or for posts in the Soviet government. The least politically active workers (e.g., the nonvoters in 1917) returned to their villages, leaving the middle strata, including women, in the labor force. But the skilled workers whose class consciousness and revolutionary zeal had helped win the October revolution did not entirely disappear, and the women who remained were likely to be family members of these veterans of 1917.

Unquestionably, the population was older; the median age of Moscow residents rose by a year between 1917 and 1920, and other evidence confirms the commonsense assumption that the skilled workers who stayed in the city and continued to work were older family men. They were less likely to have been Bolshevik supporters than their younger brothers or sons. Eduard Dune's father, a skilled worker and a family man, sympathized with his son's determination to fight for Soviet power in October 1917, but he himself chose to stand aside. Thus it was the loss of young activists rather than of all skilled and class conscious urban workers that caused the level of Bolshevik support to decline during the civil war. Older workers had tended to support the Menshevik party in 1917;[55] the Menshevik resurgence in 1918 was made possible in part by the Red Army's mobilization and removal from the urban political scene of the activist young workers. Such an analysis suggests that revolutionary consciousness may have been based as much on generational as on class

---

[52] *Leninskii zakaz: sto let tipografii 'Krasnyi proletarii'* (Moscow, 1969), p. 97.
[53] Baevskii, pp. 246–48.
[54] Drobizhev et al., p. 151.
[55] Koenker, *Moscow Workers*, chap. 5.

distinctions, a fact which was not part of the Bolshevik canon of revolutionary theory.

The changed social composition of the Moscow work force can be summarized by returning to the five types of urban workers described above. Urban type A workers had no place to go except the Red Army. Young men from this group may have disappeared during the civil war; their parents and sisters remained. Type D workers, husbands and fathers alone in the city without families, were the first to leave in search of land even before the serious crises began. Many workers of types B and C, whose attachment to the countryside depended on the length of the family's stay in the city and on the economic viability of their village property, may have chosen to stay in the city; young sons in these groups would also provide Red Army recruits. Finally, some young workers of type E, the first-generation migrants, may have also chosen to stay on, especially those who had begun to take advantage of city life. A number of Red Army veterans came from this stratum, and some recalled having attended evening schools while in the city.[56] Workers of this type who were least assimilated would have returned home with the first wave of refugees in 1917, but social origin is an especially poor predictor of the outlook of such young unattached workers. Further research on the formation of the Soviet working class after 1921 would do well to observe the career paths of similar young workers who migrated from the countryside without the baggage of strong rural ties. It is likely that some of these type E workers would interact with and be assimilated into the urban core of the working class that had remained in the city.

DEURBANIZATION IN MOSCOW: CULTURAL CHANGES

The prevailing analysis of the "declassed" proletariat in 1920–21 by Mensheviks and Bolsheviks was based on two assumptions: one was the physical disappearance of former proletarians, and the other was the changing consciousness of the proletarians who remained. The demographic data for Moscow reveal that a sizable core of veteran urban proletarians remained in the city; they did not all disappear. Lenin assumed that a worker who manufactured cigarette lighters in his darkened former factory was less class conscious than his neighbor who used his skills to manufacture machine guns or locomotive parts. And while one may argue with Lenin's rather narrow definition of consciousness, there is no question that the dislocations of the civil war produced changing attitudes and caused workers to rearrange the priorities of their value systems. The question is, Were urban workers' values, their political consciousness,

[56] *Geroi grazhdanskoi voiny* (Moscow, 1974).

444   *Koenker*

declassed or deurbanized? Did workers forget the class origins and class pride that had been so important in 1917? How did the dislocation of the civil war alter the specific elements that had contributed to the prevailing political consciousness as of October 1917?

Urban workers were especially likely to participate in political activity because of four factors: the educational and cultural opportunities afforded as part of an urban upbringing; the awareness of class interests fostered by ideology, employment patterns, and the settlement of workers in specific neighborhoods; the ease of organization for workers whose education and skills gave them resources with which to act; and the fact that the cities themselves were centers of political life.

The civil war exodus from Moscow affected some of these factors and not others. Education and culture continued, although at reduced levels. All children, regardless of social class, were given free noon meals, provided they attend city schools for an hour each day. The city could not afford to heat the school buildings, but the idea, explained Moscow Soviet chairman M. N. Pokrovskii, was to feed them and at the same time to teach the habit of attending school. The city's cultural life, especially its theaters, seemed to visitors more vibrant than ever before. The number of libraries in Moscow nearly tripled and in Petrograd doubled between 1917 and 1919; educational institutions, especially for workers, expanded at the same rate.[57] The theater, always one of the most popular Russian art forms, was especially lively. An American visitor in 1918 wrote, "In the days before the war, the cheaper seats at the Moscow Art Theatre and at the opera and ballet were fought for by long queues of students and workmen in blouse and belt. The only difference today, with the ascendency of the proletariat, is that the workman's greater comparative wealth has enabled him to move down into the parterre."[58] A year later, Arthur Ransome attended a performance of *Uncle Vanya* at the Art Theatre, and was "struck by the new smartness of the boy officers of the Red Army, of whom a fair number were present."[59] Factory theaters were also springing up, twenty of them by late 1920.[60]

---

[57] Arthur Ransome, *Russia in 1919* (New York, 1919), pp. 187–88, 183–84.

[58] Oliver M. Sayler, *Russia, White or Red* (Boston, 1919), p. 87.

[59] Ransome, p. 139.

[60] *Rabochii klass sovetskoi Rossii v pervyi god diktatury proletariata. Sbornik dokumentov i materialov*, ed. D. A. Chugaev (Moscow, 1964), p. 322. Indeed, the broad popularity of drama among the Russian working populace raises the heretical notion of the revolution as theater. Angelica Balabanoff suggests as much in her recollections of 1919, although she did not seem to appreciate the importance of drama in Russian popular culture: "I had already been shocked by the display and theatricality of public life in revolutionary Russia (the Bolsheviks seemed to be masters of stage direction), which seemed to me unsuited to the

Russian Urbanization and Deurbanization   445

Working-class neighborhoods continued to exist through the civil war and became ever more autonomous units of public and daily life. Workers in these neighborhoods often became responsible for maintaining their factories, domestic safety, and housing: as landlords fled, more and more apartment buildings, for example, became "wild"—that is, were managed on an ad hoc basis by residents themselves.[61] Unemployment and even cooptation of workers into official Soviet positions would not necessarily have taken workers away from these neighborhoods, and thus their proletarian character was not likely to change despite the social changes going on in the city at large. There were substantial population shifts within the city, as workers resettled in formerly middle-class residential areas. On the other hand, because of the breakdown of local transport and the strong sense of neighborhood and district loyalty that appears again and again in workers' memoirs, it is unlikely that workers moved very far from their original places of residence.

The neighborhood may well have replaced the factory as the focus of working-class identity during these years. And the consolidation of these neighborhoods may have been aided by a curious new phenomenon appearing in the statistical record: the absolute number of marriages began to climb in 1918, doubled in 1919, and remained at a high level well into the 1920s (see table 3).[62]

A number of explanations were proposed and dismissed at the time by Soviet officials. First, only a small part of the increase represented marriages deferred from the war years; these had been "made up," based on prewar rates, by mid-1919. More influential was the award of cloth and later cash to wedding couples, and some marriages may have been fictitious, made to qualify women for the special Red Army ration.[63] But even when these nuptial incentives were repealed in mid-1920, the rate remained high.[64] It is more pertinent that early in 1918 civil marriage replaced church ceremonies; one might guess that urban workers most likely preferred to marry outside the church and that such urban couples accounted for much of the marital increase.[65] A British Labour party

---

Revolution's proletarian character" (Angelica Balabanoff, *My Life as a Rebel* [Bloomington, Ind., 1973], p. 219).

[61] Kabo, p. 78.

[62] *Stat. ezhegodnik g. Moskvy*, p. 88.

[63] *Krasnaia Moskva*, p. 65.

[64] Nor were easy divorces a significant factor, since the divorce rate was low during this period. *Otchet Moskovskogo gubernskogo ekonomicheskogo soveshchaniia na 1-e oktiabria 1921 g.* (Moscow, 1921), p. 8.

[65] G. V. Zhirnova, "Russkii gorodskoi svadebnyi obriad kontsa XIX-nachala XX vekakh," *Sovetskaia etnografiia*, no. 1 (1969), pp. 48–58.

TABLE 3

MARRIAGES AND MARRIAGE RATES IN MOSCOW FROM 1912 TO 1923

Year	Marriages	Marriages per 10,000 Population
1912	9,564	58
1913	10,093	60
1914	9,679	55
1915	7,478	41
1916	7,623	39
1917	9,918	54
1918	12,650	75
1919	24,693	174
1920	21,363	191
1921	19,863	169
1922	21,072	153
1923	25,342	156

SOURCE.—*Statisticheskii ezhegodnik goroda Moskvy i moskovskoi gubernii*, vyp. 2 (Moscow, 1927), p. 88.

delegate to Russia was told in 1920 (probably by Inessa Armand) that such people before the revolution preferred to live together without benefit of clergy rather than submit to the institution of the church; now, "as a rule, they prefer to be legally married."[66] Urbanized workers rather than peasants strongly preferred a secular culture; the rise in the civil marriage rate was thus surely facilitated by the fact that the women remaining in the city were relatively more urban than peasant, as were the men. They were the children of type A and B families; and in marrying they were not only expressing hope in the future, but helping to perpetuate the elements of urban culture that had been evolving since well before the revolution. The families they would produce (slowly, because the number of births continued to fall during these years) would be purely urban, too. Consequently, this surge of marriages (equaled elsewhere in Russia only in Petrograd) represented a consolidation of urban working-class society in the midst of what otherwise has been portrayed as urban collapse. One might also expect that the frequency of marriages added a new element of kinship ties to reinforce or to rival the existing bonds of class and neighborhood.

The advantage of urbanism most negatively affected by the crisis of 1917–20 was the urbanized worker's special reservoir of resources and

[66] *Report of the British Labour Delegation to Russia* (London, 1920), p. 21.

organizational facility. Economically, the period was a nightmare. Real wages plummeted, and nominal wages became meaningless as more and more compensation came in the form of uniform food rations. On the other hand, Moscow workers all had a great deal of time off work, which they might have used for culture, political activity, and organization. In 1919, the darkest year of the civil war, the average worker spent eighteen days a month at work and twelve days off. Of those twelve, six were missed for personal reasons; the figure was even higher (9.5 days) for the stalwart metalworkers: for every two days on the job, they took one off.[67] Most of these days were not spent in political activity, however, or in idle carousing, but in the search for food, on personal trips to forage in the countryside. Thus the city's advantage as a cultural center was offset in this period by the total absorption of its residents in the struggle for daily existence.

Still the workers who remained in the city were among the most urbanized elements, and although the urban propensity toward working-class activism may have been slowed, it was not reversed. But activism, even working-class activism, was not necessarily identical to Bolshevism, and other short-term changes occurred during the civil war years that may have helped to alter the class consciousness and Bolshevik support of 1917. They were probably not the changes blamed by Lenin for the deterioration of workers' consciousness, such as trading homemade cigarette lighters on the Moscow black market.

What then were the changes? First of all, Bolshevik consciousness in 1917 had been reinforced by a sense of class separateness and class identity. Separate neighborhoods remained after 1917, but there was a tendency toward more interclass mingling, not less. For example, British labor delegates visited a nine-room apartment occupied in 1920 by its former sole resident, a rich widow, plus a factory worker, a tram conductor, a military student from rural Smolensk, and a former lawyer now employed in a Soviet bureau, all with wives and children.[68] Moreover, once the government had chased out its class enemies, the need for a class-pure government might not remain as essential as it had in 1917. With the departure of so many manufacturers, bankers, and traders, perhaps the Bolsheviks' extremist vision of class struggle no longer seemed so important. This may be why party membership dropped in 1918.[69] On the other hand, William Chase argues with some evidence that the place of the big bourgeoisie was taken by petty traders selling foodstuffs and

[67] *Krasnaia Moskva*, p. 65.
[68] *Report of the British Labour Delegation*, p. 138.
[69] Ignat'ev (n. 37 above), p. 91.

448   *Koenker*

manufactured goods on the Sukharev market.[70] Moreover, the class enemy
was alive and well and fighting in the White Armies, as newspapers
stressed throughout the period, although, despite the appeals for Sunday
work to produce more arms and all-out drives such as "Front Week,"
this confrontation was removed from the direct daily experience of most
workers.

A second short-term factor in the Bolsheviks' success in 1917 had
been their identification as a peace party. Once Russia had withdrawn
from the international war, this appeal must have been diminished, too.
Careful research in the varied periodical press of the period may help to
determine how the populace felt about the civil war that their boys were
mobilized to fight, but memoir sources give the strong impression that
the civil war was perceived as a just and necessary conflict: Mensheviks,
Bolsheviks, and nonparty citizens all volunteered to defend the social
revolution.

The economic situation had unquestionably been a major critical factor
in the formation of the particular class consciousness of 1917. Factories
closed, workers were laid off, and the devastating supply crisis haunted
the cities throughout 1917. If the economic crisis was due to sabotage,
as workers believed, then the socialists in the Provisional Government
had been powerless to stop it. The Bolsheviks received a great deal of
support precisely because they had not been implicated in the economic
debacle of 1917.

But the economy continued to collapse in 1918, 1919, and 1920. Did
the urban cadres of 1917 face the continuing crisis with the same sense
of class consciousness that they had shared in October? Ralf Dahrendorf
has argued that under varying conditions, class identity can lose its power
as a focus of unity, and that other factors — workplace, neighborhood,
skill, kin — may become more important.[71] The struggle for existence
that workers in 1917 tried to solve as a class, through the Soviets, was
not solved, and to survive, workers turned to other sources: individual
trading and foraging for food, local institutions, workplace control. The
result was that the Bolshevik party had to scramble politically to keep
the backing of its former supporters. That no other organization arose
to challenge them successfully may be ascribed in some measure to the
utter lack of resources that workers had for any new mobilization of their

[70] William Chase, "Moscow and Its Working Class, 1918–1928: A Social
Analysis" (Ph.D. diss., Boston College, 1979), pp. 36–39; Marguerite Harrison,
Marooned in Moscow (New York, 1921), pp. 151–57.
[71] Ralf Dahrendorf, *Class and Class Consciousness in Industrial Society*
(Stanford, Calif., 1959), and *Conflict after Class* (London, 1967).

energy and support, but also to Bolshevik control of the means of repression, including control over food distribution, housing, and of course the Cheka—the new government's secret police.

CONCLUDING REMARKS

This examination of the civil war years, particularly in Moscow, suggests that the deurbanization of those years represented a change in quantity but not entirely in quality in the cities. The proletariat declined in the city, but it did not wither away. Thus its basic urban character remained, reinforced in marriage and in the location if not the quality of its experience. Despite substantial turnover and the presumed influx of new generations of nonurbanized peasants after 1921, a core of the city's working class remained to impart its own brand of urban culture.

If the relationship between the urban working class and its representative Bolshevik party changed during these years, it changed not entirely because the cadres of 1917 left the factories for the front, the villages, the black market, or the commissariats. Rather, it changed because the political and economic conjuncture of these years called for different responses and fostered a different set of priorities from those of the preceding revolutionary years. If Lenin's perceptions of the situation were at all representative, it appears that the Bolshevik party made deurbanization and declassing the scapegoats for its political difficulties, when the party's own policies and its unwillingness to accept changing proletarian attitudes were also to blame.

A number of writers have suggested that the civil war years be viewed as a generational experience, in Karl Mannheim's sense, during which new values are acquired that are retained by members of a generation throughout their active lives.[72] What characteristics were acquired during these years that might have become part of a new Russian urban culture? One must look to the many negative elements of the period: the atmosphere of political emergency and terror against opposition; the prevalence of crime and utter lawlessness in working-class districts; the collapse of any semblance of a market economy; the erosion of industrial discipline and of productivity; the decline of the workplace as the center of one's life; the experience of unemployment, of living on the dole, and later in the period, of labor mobilization; and the wholesale militarization of society. But we should not ignore, in assessing the formative elements

---

[72] Fitzpatrick (n. 6 above), pp. 64–65; Robert C. Tucker, "Stalinism as Revolution from Above," in *Stalinism*, ed. Robert C. Tucker (New York, 1977), pp. 91–92; Stephen F. Cohen, "Bolshevism and Stalinism," ibid., pp. 3–29; see also Alan B. Spitzer, "The Historical Problem of Generations," *American Historical Review* 78, no. 5 (December 1973): 1353–85.

450   *Koenker*

of the period, the continuing positive aspects of urban life: theater, libraries, schools, recreation, family formation, associations, newspapers, political participation, and the sense that a new society was being created even in these dark years.

The demographic and social evidence presented here thus modifies the hypothesis that Russia "deurbanized," that its workers were "declassed" during the years from 1917 to 1921. Just as urban growth and urbanization are not synonymous, so too we should distinguish between the numerical decline of the urban population, or "urban contraction," and "deurbanization," which suggests a reversal of all of the elements of the urbanization process. Despite the years of hunger, cold, and disease in the cities, despite the antiurban utopian dreams that these years encouraged,[73] urban life and urban culture were not extinguished during the Russian civil war, but only transformed. The full nature of this transformation remains to be explored.

[73] See, e.g., the pseudonymous work of the agricultural economist A. V. Chaianov: Ivan Kremnev, "The Journey of My Brother Alexei to the Land of Peasant Utopia" (Moscow, 1920), reprinted in the *Journal of Peasant Studies* 4, no. 1 (October 1976): 63–117.

Part II
Stalin and Stalinism

[6]

New Perspectives on Stalinism

SHEILA FITZPATRICK*

The nature of Stalinism[1] has always been a highly contentious question, charged with political significance for almost all disputants. In the early Cold War period, when the political charge was most explosive, Soviet and Western commentators shared the assumption that what had emerged in the Soviet Union in the 1930s was both the historically inevitable outcome of the Bolshevik Revolution and a basically permanent and immutable new "Soviet system," though they disagreed vehemently about its nature. From the Soviet standpoint, the revolution had produced socialism. From the western standpoint (excluding a small group of Soviet sympathizers), the product was totalitarian dictatorship. From both, the system was the antithesis of Western democracy and was its major ideological competitor on the international scene.

In the decades after Stalin's death, changes in the Soviet Union led both sides to reassess their judgments, particularly on the immutability of the Soviet system. Some features of Stalin's regime were repudiated or criticized in the Soviet Union, and there were Soviet attempts to separate the legitimate "Leninist" outcome of the Revolution from the temporary "excesses" of the Stalin period. In the West, revision of Cold War premises in other areas finally prompted Sovietologists to reexamine the totalitarian model, which now came under criticism for inherent political bias as well as for inappropriateness to contemporary Soviet reality.[2] At the Bellagio conference organized by Robert C. Tucker in 1975, the term "Stalinism" was preferred to "totalitarianism," although the most vigorous objections to the totalitarian model related to the *pre*-Stalin period.[3] Since then, political scientists have tended to move away from a totalitarian image of the Soviet Union before and after Stalin, while tacitly accepting its applicability to the Stalinist system.

---

* An earlier version of this article was presented at the Third World Congress of Slavic Studies in Washington, DC, November 2, 1985.

[1] I use "Stalinism" here as a convenient term for the new political, economic, and social structures that emerged in the Soviet Union after the great break associated with collectivization and the First Five-Year Plan.

[2] For an excellent discussion of this reexamination, see Abbott Gleason, " 'Totalitarianism' in 1984," *Russian Review*, vol. 43, 1984, pp. 145-159.

[3] See Robert C. Tucker, ed., *Stalinism: Essays in Historical Interpretation*, New York, 1977, especially the article by Stephen F. Cohen, "Bolshevism and Stalinism," pp. 3-29.

Apart from the argument about models, however, there have been other developments affecting the direction of Western Soviet scholarship in recent years. The most relevant, for our purposes, is the entry of historians into a field long dominated by political scientists, the study of the Soviet Union from the Revolution of 1917 to the end of the Stalin period. Of course, there were always some historians in the field, including some very good ones. But the new cohort is larger, with more sense of itself as a group and, in particular, a much stronger desire to assert an identity *as historians*. That assertion of professional identity is a way of making two points. First, the new cohort is telling other historians that Soviet history is a legitimate field (earlier a controversial issue among Russian historians), drawing attention to the recent improvement in access to Soviet archives and other primary sources, and emphasizing its own professional qualifications. Second, it is distinguishing itself from the older generation of Sovietologists, dominated by political scientists' main interpretative framework, the totalitarian model.

Social history is a major focus of interest for the new cohort of historians. This choice also involves assertion of separate identity and implicit criticism of the earlier Sovietological preoccupation with politics and ideology. Without going too deeply into the chicken-and-egg question, social historians have particularly good reason (or a particularly good excuse) for dissatisfaction with the totalitarian model: the model's assertion of the primacy of politics made social history seem a backwater, remote from the real dynamics of post-revolutionary Soviet development. In addition, the new cohort's identification with a broader community of *social* historians has the effect (intended or otherwise) of providing external reinforcement to its struggle against the perceived "Cold War bias" of earlier Sovietology. This particular bias is generally disliked by social historians in other fields, whose instincts are often more radical than that of the historical profession as a whole.

My purpose in this essay is to investigate the likely impact of historians, particularly social historians, on the study of the Stalin period. This is a participant's report, as I am currently working on a social history of the 1930s, but it should not be read as a New Cohort manifesto. It is both descriptive and prescriptive, and the prescriptions are largely addressed to other social historians, who may well disagree with them. The question of interest to the broader audience of scholars in Soviet studies is what the new social historians may have to say on one of the big traditional issues of Sovietology—the nature and dynamics of Stalinism.

General Interpretations of Stalinist State and Society

The overarching theme that Western historians have commonly used for interpreting the Stalin period is state against society, *nachal'stvo* against *narod*. This is a familiar framework in Russian historiography. According to this view, the state acts on society, trying to change and mold it in ways that serve state purposes; society acts primarily by *re*-acting to state pressure, which it tries to resist, evade, or subvert by passive resistance. In scholarship on the Soviet period, particularly the Stalin era, the state-school approach established by Russian historians in the nineteenth century has been reinforced by a compatible concept of twentieth-century American political scientists, the totalitarian model. In this model, the Soviet totalitarian state seeks to transform society according to Marxist-Leninist ideology, using the Communist Party as an agent of mobilization and reinforcing its dictates with police coercion and terror. The society is reduced to an object, inert and featureless, which is shaped and manipulated by the energetic action of the totalitarian regime.

This view of state/society relations obviously encourages scholars to investigate state mechanisms rather than social processes. Soviet studies, consequently, have focussed strongly on state and party, dealing with society almost exclusively in a context of state and party intervention. The scholarly literature on the Stalin period is full of studies of such intervention: forced collectivization, subordination of trade unions, labor discipline laws, the development of the Stakhanovite movement under party sponsorship, harassment of the old intelligentsia, the establishment of party controls over culture and scholarship, censorship, the Great Purge (seen as Stalin's "war against the nation," in Ulam's phrase),[4] and so on. Some of these studies also deal with resentful social responses to state intervention, as in the case of peasants and collectivization or the intelligentsia and cultural controls. But this is the only kind of social response that is generally discussed, and social processes unrelated to state intervention are virtually absent from the literature.

In the interventionist episodes, society is seen as a victim of state action, and its reaction is a mixture of covert hostility and passive acceptance of *force majeure*. Scholars have explained the lack of more effective societal resistance (both to the tsarist and Soviet state) in terms of the traditional "underdevelopment" of social classes and social organization in Russia, and the state's ruthless use of coercion and terror. In addition, some theorists like Hannah Arendt have argued that totalitarian regimes "atomize" society, destroying or subordinating all the institutions and associational forms that might lend themselves to active social resistance.

"Society" is often an undifferentiated whole in Sovietological writing, since internal social relationships and processes have little relevance to the totalitarian model. For practical expository purposes, however, it is necessary on occasion to identify parts of the whole to which specific state interventionist acts are addressed. The terminology used usually corresponds to Soviet usage, namely, "workers," "peasants," and "intelligentsia." These are the two "non-antagonistic classes" and the "stratum" identified as the basic groupings of Soviet society in the Stalin Constitution of 1936. An earlier Soviet usage, more rigorously Marxist, subdivided the peasantry into class groups ranging from "kulak" to "poor peasant," and also distinguished between an old

---

[4] Adam B. Ulam, *Stalin*, New York, 1973, title of ch. 8.

"bourgeois" and new "proletarian" intelligentsia. Although Sovietologists generally dislike these classifications and put the terms in quotation marks, it is virtually impossible to avoid using them when describing state policies: "kulaks," for example, may be an ambiguous social group, but what other label can be used for the targets of the "dekulakization" policy? Thus, perhaps ironically, Sovietologists have fallen into the habit of dealing with Soviet society in terms of Marxist—and even Stalinist-Marxist—class categories.

At times, reading Western scholarship on the Stalin period, one might also conclude that Sovietologists have accepted Stalinist premises about the disappearance of class antagonisms in Soviet society. Inter- and intra-class conflicts and tensions are as rare in the Western "totalitarian" model as they are in the Soviet "socialist" one. However, there is one notable exception to this rule. In following Trotsky (*The Revolution Betrayed*) and Djilas (*The New Class*), Sovietologists sometimes refer to an antagonistic relationship between an oppressed society and an exploiting, privileged bureaucratic elite. This is essentially a Marxist version of the old state-against-society image (from which, in fact, Trotsky probably derived it).[5] Its appeal to Sovietologists is no doubt related to its congenial political implications, since both Trotsky and Djilas were indicting the Stalinist system as well as analyzing it. All the same, its place in the conventional wisdom of Sovietology is somewhat anomalous. This may be the point of origin of another curious Sovietological habit in writing about Soviet society, which is to attach negative connotations to the term "bourgeois" and generally positive ones to "proletarian." Marxist prejudice, as well as Marxist and Stalinist-Marxist analysis, have found a modest place in the interstices of Sovietology's totalitarian model.

Social History Approaches

a) *Problems of structure and social interaction*

It is too early to report on current work in progress in this field, since such work on the Stalin period is only just beginning. Nevertheless, it is important to consider these problems, as the sketchy existing analytical framework outlined above is clearly inadequate, being the product of casual borrowing from Soviet and other Marxist sources by Sovietologists whose main attention was elsewhere, and its revision may have significance for our understanding of the nature of Stalinism. I have drawn to some extent on my own experience of the problems of structure in planning a book on the social history of the 1930s,[6] and

---

[5] Earlier, in his analysis of the 1905 Revolution, Trotsky had portrayed the tsarist state as an essentially free-standing entity, not representative of any class in the society but opposed to the society as a whole. In a review of the last volume of Trotsky's *1905* (*Krasnaia nov'*, 1922, no. 3), Pokrovsky accused him of borrowing this non-Marxist concept from one of the historians of the state school, the liberal P. N. Miliukov.

[6] The working title of this book, which should be finished in 1986, is *Stalin's Russia: A Social History of the 1930s*.

on relevant discussions at recent meetings of Soviet social historians in the United States.[7] But it is also possible to make deductions about likely directions of future work on the basis of social history's own logic.

Social historians are in the business of *analyzing* society, which among other things means breaking it down into constituent parts. They are unlikely to be satisfied with hypotheses involving an undifferentiated "society," as in the state-against-society dichotomy discussed earlier. They will probably want to make finer distinctions than those of Stalinist-Marxist analysis, with its three categories of "working class," "peasantry," and "intelligentsia"; they are bound to object in particular to the last, hybrid category, which puts lowly office-workers in the same group as professionals and administrators. They will surely find it difficult to accept the idea of a society without significant internal tensions and conflicts (as in the "non-antagonistic" class relationships of Stalinist Marxism), or of a society so inert that all the dynamics are external (as in the totalitarian model).

The first challenge for social historians of the Stalin period will be to decide what kind of social breakdown is most appropriate. The Stalinist-Marxist breakdown is clearly simplistic, especially when compared with the complex class analysis used by Soviet Marxists in the 1920s. On the other hand, it is hard to avoid the conclusion that Soviet society actually underwent a Great Simplification in the course of Stalin's "revolution from above" at the beginning of the 1930s. Kulaks, nepman, and small traders disappeared from the roster, groups like artisans and peasant craftsmen were dispersed, and collectivization levelled old distinctions within the peasantry. Perhaps the result of this was to produce a very simple social structure, as well as a damaged one. But it is also reasonable to assume that, as the society recovered from the blows of the First Five-Year Plan period, it became more complex.

Trotsky and other Marxist critics have drawn our attention to the emergence of a new social hierarchy in the 1930s. At the top of the hierarchy, in Trotsky's view, was the "bureaucracy," a quasi-ruling class by virtue of its control (though not ownership) of the means of production, possessing material privileges that set it apart from the rest of society. This idea has been quite influential among Western social historians.[8] However, some of scholars have already noted that the bureaucracy itself was hierarchical, so that the social position and class interests of those at the bottom were quite different from those at

---

[7] I have in mind particularly the last two meetings of the National Seminar on the Social History of Russia in the Twentieth Century (Philadelphia, 1983 and 1984), the two workshops on Social History of the Stalin period that I organized as a Senior Fellow at the Harriman Institute for the Advanced Study of the Soviet Union, Columbia University, in the spring of 1985, and the third workshop in this series, held in Austin in March 1986 under the joint sponsorship of the International Studies Program, University of Texas at Austin, and the Harriman Institute.

[8] See, for example, Moshe Lewin, "The Social Background of Stalinism," in Tucker, ed., *Stalinism*, pp. 111-136.

the top, perhaps at times directly opposed to them.[9] Trotsky, to be sure, had in mind the higher level of bureaucracy when he talked of a new ruling class. But how high, and on what basis can a cut-off point be drawn? Soviet statisticians in the Stalin period sometimes used a category of "leading cadres and specialists,"[10] based on *nomenklatura* distinctions, which might coincide with Trotsky's group (though state/party *nomenklatura* is an unsatisfactory criterion for class membership in Marxist terms). But there is also the problem of the professional and technical intelligentsia, whose members were often but not necessarily employed by state institutions, sometimes in a "bureaucratic" (administrative) role and sometimes simply as specialists. This whole group shared the material privileges of the higher stratum of the bureaucracy and had a high level of education and other elite characteristics. When social historians come to grips with the problem of social hierarchy, they will have to decide what kind of elite they are looking for—a Marxist "ruling class," or simply the group with highest status and economic advantages in the society. The answer has great significance for our understanding of the social dynamics of Stalinism.

There are other forms of emerging hierarchical stratification that call for close investigation. The position of Stakhanovites within the working class is a particularly interesting issue, but there are also a multiplicity of distinctions to be made between unskilled and skilled labor, "new" workers (fresh from the villages) and "old" ones, and workers in different occupations and branches of industry, not to mention the distinctions among convict,[11] semi-free, and free labor to be found on the new construction sites. The collectivized peasants and rural society in general present an even more promising field of investigation for those interested in emerging social hierarchies. The *kolkhoz* itself was a hierarchical structure, with a top stratum of white-collar workers (chairman, accountant, and so on), a middle stratum of skilled blue-collar workers like tractor drivers and mechanics, and, at the bottom, the rank-and-file *kolkhozniki* who did the actual field work and had only traditional peasant skills. Rural society in a broader sense underwent significant changes after collectivization, as the numbers and proportional weight of white-collar and administrative personnel and blue-collar workers increased, while those of peasants (*kolkhozniki* and *edinolichniki*) diminished. Class differentiation, that favorite subject of the agrarian Marxists in the 1920s, is really a much more appropriate theme for the

[9] This point was strongly made by Arch Getty at the first and third workshops on Social History of the Stalin Period (see above, note 7). The approach is employed in Getty's publications and in the work of Gabor Rittersporn.

[10] For definition and data on this category, see *Sostav rukovodiashchikh rabotnikov i spetsialistov Soiuza SSR*, Moscow, 1936.

[11] In his comment on this paper as presented at the Third World Congress of Slavic Studies, Stephen F. Cohen suggested that convict laborers should be considered the bottom stratum in the general hierarchy of Soviet society in the Stalin period. I am inclined to agree with him and with the implied criticism of social historians for disregarding this group.

1930s. Indeed, it is arguable that Russia's long-awaited "rural bourgeoisie" finally materialized in the 1930s, albeit not in the expected form.

Of course the discovery that Stalinist society was hierarchically stratified is scarcely unexpected (what society is not?) and in itself is unlikely to change anyone's thinking about the nature of Stalinism. But on what principles was the stratification based? What kind of relations existed between different strata and classes? How could individuals improve their social and economic status, or protect themselves from the sudden reversals of fortune that often overtook those who were successful in this society? The answers to such questions, if social historians can find them, may well be highly relevant to our general understanding of Stalinism.

We already have certain general notions about status in Stalinist society: that the *kolkhoz* peasantry ranked lowest, both for economic reasons and because the *kolkhozniki* were not issued internal passports, which implied second-class citizenship; that rural in general ranked lower than urban; and that the white-collar professional and administrative group was accorded highest status, which is often held to indicate the "embourgeoisement" of the Stalinist regime. The last premise, of course, begs a question that is relevant to all status issues, namely, whether the regime was imposing its values on the society or *vice versa*.

Privileged access to material goods and services was a concomitant of elite status in Stalinist society.[12] This point may be carried further. It is possible that, in this society where scarcity and privation were the norm, the degree of preferential access to deficit commodities was the major determinant of status distinctions, or rather, of those status distinctions that were peculiarly "Stalinist," being products of the "revolution from above" and its aftermath rather than reflecting Bolshevik-revolutionary or traditional Russian values. While some aspects of this question are difficult to investigate because various forms of elite privilege were concealed from the public eye (in contrast to the highly publicized privileges of Stakhanovite workers and peasants), the task of determining degrees of preferential access for different social and occupational groups is greatly facilitated by the existence of formal rationing systems that had exactly this function. Urban rationing was in force for approximately half the Stalin period—from 1929 to 1935, and again from 1941 to 1947—as well as earlier, during World War I and the Civil War years. A comparison of the changing ration priorities of social and occupational groups over this period should contribute a great deal to our understanding of the regime's changing sense of status hierarchies. Moreover, the 1929-35 rationing system was a peculiar hybrid of industrial working-class and white-collar elite priority access via "closed distribution points" (*zakrytye raspredeliteli*) serving specific groups of factory workers, engineers, government officials, and so on; here social

---

[12] See Mervyn Matthews, *Privilege in the Soviet Union: A Study of Elite Life-Styles under Communism*, London, 1978.

historians will find much to illuminate the genesis and evolving organizing principles of Stalinist social structure and privilege.

Of course, formal priority of access cannot be equated with actual access.
In practice, everyone working in state and cooperative trade, or in the supply-
and-procurements departments of industrial enterprises and other state institutions, had informal privileges of access to goods that exceeded those of their
counterparts working outside the commercial sphere. This fact points up the
importance of making vertical as well as horizontal distinctions in our social
analysis. So far, scholars have noted only a few significant vertical distinctions,
for example, between administrators and technical specialists in the white-collar
elite. But the vertical distinctions between commercial and non-commercial
occupations at all levels are of great interest, not only because the commercial
sector was large but also because it had many unusual characteristics.

Because of its "second economy" (black·market) connections and residual "NEP spirit," employment in the commercial sector carried low prestige
despite its material advantages; it constituted an exception to our general
hypothesis linking social status with preferential access to goods. Low prestige
was most noticeable at the bottom of the commercial hierarchy, with jobs like
sales clerk. At the top, managers of large department stores, commercial directors of enterprises and the like clearly had entree to the broader social elite,
though this advantage was partly related to the services they could render other
elite members. Advancement in the commercial sector was evidently much less
dependent on education and party membership—the two standard criteria for
upward mobility in the Stalin period—than was the case in other spheres. All
this suggests more than an interesting special case, understandably neglected by
Soviet historians, for study by Western social historians. It raises the possibility
that we are still greatly underestimating the diversity and complexity of Stalinist
society, partly because we have implicitly accepted some of the limitations and
prejudices of Stalinist-Marxist analysis of it.

b) *Implications of High Social Mobility*

Until recently, social mobility was a neglected theme in Soviet studies.
Western Sovietologists often assumed that the process was irrelevant in a totalitarian society, or for that matter a society that claimed to be building socialism.
Marxists analyzing Soviet society were equally uninterested, since social mobility is not a traditional Marxist concept. My discussion of regime-sponsored
upward mobility into the elite in *Education and Social Mobility* and elsewhere[13]
drew attention to the subject, but some scholars were uneasy about the positive
value-loading of the term in American usage (where upward mobility is closely
linked with ideas of democracy and opportunity), and others were more struck
by the aspect of regime sponsorship than the process itself.

---

[13] Sheila Fitzpatrick, *Education and Social Mobility in the Soviet Union, 1921-1934*, Cambridge,
1979, and "Stalin and the Making of a New Elite, 1929-1938," *Slavic Review*, vol. 38, 1979.

However, it is the process itself and its remarkable dimensions that are likely to preoccupy social historians of the Stalin period. This society is impossible to analyze adequately in purely static terms because of the exceptional social and geographical mobility of the population. Tens of millions of peasants moved to towns and became workers in the 1930s. A large segment of the old working class moved into white-collar and managerial occupations. Private traders and businessmen were forced out of their old occupations and had to find new ones; "kulaks" were deported from the villages and resettled in distant regions, where many became workers in the new industrial enterprises. The World War II and postwar demobilization of the army led to further large-scale mobility. But war and specific regime policies encouraging various types of mobility explain only part of the general phenomenon. More than anything else, it was a necessary by-product of the Soviet Union's rapid industrialization, which created more white-collar, professional, and managerial jobs, at the same time expanding the blue-collar labor force and drawing peasants into the towns.

For this reason, the general trend of mobility in the Stalin period was upward, despite the occurrence of downward mobility from the privileged classes after the Revolution and dramatic episodes of elite purging in the 1930s. As I have argued elsewhere, the phenomenon of large-scale upward mobility needs to be incorporated into our interpretation of Stalinism, because the Stalinist regime claimed and almost certainly received credit for enabling members of the lower classes to improve their social position.[14] But this is not the only way in which recognition of high social mobility may affect our generalizations about Stalinism.

One familiar generalization concerns the weakness of social classes and associational bonds, and the consequent inability of society to resist state power or curb its expansion. Many scholars have regarded this "atomization" or social fragmentation as part of the dynamics of totalitarianism. But it can be linked equally—and not necessarily incompatibly—with the enormous social mobility of the early Stalin period, which inevitably weakened traditional associational bonds and reduced class consciousness and the capacity for social organization. To take an obvious example, a working class consisting largely of yesterday's peasants (as was the case of the Soviet working class in the 1930s) is unlikely to generate assertive labor unions. A peasantry whose young men are leaving to work in the towns may offer comparatively little aggressive resistance to state initiatives, even when the policy is as unpopular as collectivization appears to have been in the countryside. A new elite, such as that emerging in the Soviet Union in the 1930s, will not have the same *esprit de corps*, independence and, habits of collective self-assertion as one that is long established and firmly entrenched.

---

[14] In *Education and Social Mobility*, pp. 16-17 and 254, and in "Stalin and the Making of a New Elite," pp. 401-402.

The high level of state coercion characteristic of the Stalin period is another basic Sovietological theme that deserves reconsideration in the context of high social mobility. These two phenomena clearly had a complex interdependent relationship, and neither can be adequately treated without reference to the other. The casual connections worked both ways. On the one hand, state coercion produced involuntary social mobility, as in the deportation of kulaks, the expropriation of nepmen, the Great Purge and the deportation of "class enemies" from the newly acquired western territories in the 1940s. On the other hand, spontaneous social mobility on the scale of the early '30s created organizational and control problems for the state that prompted further coercive actions, as in the case of the labor discipline measures and the 1932 passport law (originally introduced to prevent mass exodus from village to town as famine gripped large areas of the countryside).

While the "totalitarian" view of Stalinist rule correctly emphasizes the regime's transformationalist aspirations in explaining coercion and terror, it is surely misleading to imply that, in the absence of effective societal resistance to the state, the coercion was gratuitous and unrelated to any social problem. It *was* related to an acute social problem but that problem was excessive mobility rather than resistance. Moreover, the mobility of the population was as much an impediment to the regime's efforts at social engineering as a consequence of them. For all its "totalitarian" ambitions and repressive policies, the actual control exercised by the Stalinist regime was often limited, as social historians looking from the bottom up have begun to point out.[15] One of the limitations was that controls were difficult to apply to rootless and unpredictably mobile segments of the population. Another was that the same rootlessness and mobility were characteristic of the Communists and bureaucratic cadres who were supposed to implement the regime's policies and controls.[16]

A related theme in the literature on totalitarianism, the importance of "indoctrination" in the Stalinist system, may also be seen from a new perspective by social historians. The regime was undoubtedly disposed to indoctrinate its citizens, not just in the sense of teaching Marxist-Leninist dogma but also and more significantly in the broader sense of inculcating new social and cultural norms. However, this disposition need not be regarded solely as totalitarian imperative: the stress on indoctrination and education had a practical social justification as well, and could even be interpreted as a response to societal demands, in addition to meeting a perceived state interest.

In Stalinist society, large numbers of citizens needed to learn new skills and master new social roles because they had recently changed their social position through upward mobility. These needs were a responsibility for the regime, on the one hand, and a burden on individuals, on the other. Factories had to

[15] See below, pp. 367-372.
[16] J. Arch Getty, *Origins of the Great Purges: The Soviet Communist Party Reconsidered, 1933-1938*, Cambridge, 1985, especially pp. 34, 61.

assimilate and train new workers, but at the same time new workers fresh from the villages needed to learn the rules of urban and factory life in order to survive. The same imperatives applied at all levels of society starting with the *kolkhoz*, where new conventions had to be mastered by officials and peasants alike. At the top level of society, new elite members had to learn technical and managerial skills as well as acquiring the *kul'turnost'* appropriate to their status.

The term "indoctrination" is clearly too narrow for the process of social and political *vospitanie*, not to mention basic education and technical training, that absorbed so much of the regime's and society's attention in the 1930s. But the subject, however labelled, is important; and social historians are unlikely to restrict it to transmission of ideology or accept the notion that society's role was purely passive. A more promising approach is suggested by Vera Dunham, who describes the emerging "middleclass values" of the Stalin period as the result of negotiation ("the Big Deal") between the regime and the society's elite.[17] A similar process of negotiation might be discerned in the development of norms for the new *kolkhozy*, for the regime's original intentions were clearly modified in response to village realities and the traditional patterns of peasant life. In some cases—perhaps including that of the Stalinist elite—negotiation of values might be seen as a three-way process, with the *arrivistes* (new workers, new elite members, and so on) learning from their precursors (old workers, "bourgeois" intelligentsia) under regime supervision, while adding their own contribution to the cultural mix.

c) *The View "from Below": Social Initiatives and Responses*

Social historians are generally inclined to prefer the perspective "from below"—that is, from within the society, or even from the grass-roots viewpoint of ordinary lower-class citizens—to the governmental and elite perspective "from above." Those who are now working on the Soviet period are no exception; indeed, their interest in history from below may be accentuated because of the reaction against totalitarian-model scholarship, which imposed an extreme version of the perspective "from above" on Soviet studies. "Revisionist" social and political historians of the younger generation like Arch Getty, Roberta Manning, and Gabor Rittersporn[18] counterpose local pictures-from-life (often drawn from the Smolensk Archive, which is our major accessible source of primary data on conditions outside the center in the 1930s) to the

---

[17] Vera S. Dunham, *In Stalin's Time: Middleclass Values in Soviet Fiction*, Cambridge, 1976.

[18] See Getty, *Origins of the Great Purges*, and "Party and Purges in Smolensk, 1933-1937," *Slavic Review*, vol. 42, 1983; Roberta T. Manning, "Government in the Soviet Countryside in the Stalinist Thirties: The Case of Belyi Raion in 1937," *Carl Beck Papers in Russian and East European Studies*, no. 301, Pittsburgh, n.d.; Gabor T. Rittersporn, "The State Against Itself: Social Tensions and Political Conflict in the U.S.S.R. 1936-1938," *Telos*, no. 41, 1979, and "Société et appareil d'état soviétiques 1936-1938: Contradictions et interférences," *Annals E.S.C.*, no. 4, 1979.

generalizations earlier derived from central policy pronouncements and laws, and note the vast discrepancies between them.

Of course, the perspective from below inevitably differs from that from the top; policies are never implemented exactly in the manner that policy-makers intend; local conditions vary, so that the experience of one region or locality cannot be assumed to be typical. I think, however, there is little doubt that the accumulation of local and specific case studies will significantly change some of the conventional wisdom on the Stalin period. Stalinist policy-makers, like Western Sovietologists, were far removed from Soviet society, and probably therefore exceptionally prone to schematic error in their perception of it.

But the interesting question is how far revisionism based on the perspective "from below" can take us on the Stalin period. In the accepted Sovietological view, the great social changes of this era were products of radical policies initiated by Stalin's regime without significant social support and ruthlessly implemented without regard to society's responses. The paradigm is "revolution from above," Stalin's own term for forced-pace industrialization, collectivization, and other similarly ambitious and socially disruptive policies of the First Five-Year Plan period. The same framework is applied to the Great Purges of the late 1930s. A perspective "from below" might suggest alterations of greater or less magnitude or lead scholars to abandon the framework altogether.

Three types of alternative explanations can be distinguished in published revisionist work and informal discussions. The first emphasizes that the regime had less actual control over society than it claimed, that its actions were often improvised rather than part of a grand design, that implementation of its radical policies often diverged from the policy-makers' intentions, and that the policies had many unplanned and unanticipated social consequences. The second, taking revisionism a step further, sees the regime's policies as appealing to definite social constituencies, responding to social pressures and grievances, and liable to be modified in practice through processes of informal social negotiation. The third and most challenging approach would describe such policies as the product of initiative from below rather than attributing them to the regime's initiative from above.

The first approach is not necessarily incompatible with the concept of "revolution from above" or even the totalitarian model, if totalitarianism is taken as an ideal type rather than a literal description of historical reality. It is, after all, impossible to imagine an actual historical situation in which political control was absolute, laws were implemented to the letter and in complete accordance with the legislators' intentions, and the political leaders had a grand design detailed enough to cover every contingency. Such hypotheses (though not absent from past Sovietological scholarship) fly in the face of common sense.

However, a number of recent scholarly works emphasizing improvisation, accident, inefficiency, and practical failures of regime planning and control[19] conclude that the accumulation of such evidence undermines the totalitarian model of the Stalinist system to the point where it is no longer worth using. This is the import of Arch Getty's study of party organization, which stresses the tenuousness of central control over local organs and the party's inability to keep accurate membership files in the 1930s.[20] Roberta Manning's work on Belyi raion makes a similar point, noting that there were far too few control personnel (including NKVD) in the Western Oblast, particularly the countryside, to perform the functions usually attributed to them.[21] Peter Solomon's research on local judicial and administrative organs points in the same direction,[22] and his description of the evolution of Soviet penal policy in the early 1930s offers a striking refutation of any simple notion of Grand Design in a sphere of particular relevance to totalitarian theory.[23]

The implications for the "revolution from above" framework[24] are not so clear. In principle, "revolution from above" can accommodate a fair amount of improvisation, disorganization, and unanticipated consequences, even though it has not always been seen in these terms in the past. It could be argued, indeed, that the concept is essentially incompatible with notions of detailed planning and rigorous supervision by central authorities. An interesting recent paper on the collectivization campaign of the winter of 1929-30 makes a convincing case that local improvisation of various kinds abounded, and radical initiatives often came from lower-level officials *before* they were sanctioned by top-level party decisions.[25] This finding may mean—as the author seems to conclude—that the process was not "revolution from above," or at least not revolution from the very top. But such a conclusion sheds little light on the reasons why lower-level officials took these apparently risky initiatives. If they did so because they were getting radical "signals" from above (as they certainly were in this case), we are left with the old "revolution from above" framework, but perhaps gain a new insight into the process by which it was carried out. It may be that Stalinist "revolution from above" not only permitted but actually *required* lower-level officials to respond to urgent but imprecise "signals" by improvising and taking initiatives that, if unsuccessful, could always be disavowed by the leadership.

[19] These themes are not totally new in the literature. They are prominent, for example, in Merle Fainsod's *Smolensk under Soviet Rule*, Cambridge, MA, 1958.

[20] Getty, *Origins of the Great Purges*, especially pp. 31-37.

[21] Roberta T. Manning, "The Collective Farm Peasantry and the Local Administration: Peasant Letters of Complaint in Belyi *Raion* in 1937," paper presented at the 1983 meeting of National Seminar for the Study of Russian Society in the Twentieth Century, pp. 7-12, 15.

[22] Peter H. Solomon, "Local Political Power and Soviet Criminal Justice 1922-1941," *Soviet Studies*, vol. 37, no. 3, July 1985.

[23] Peter H. Solomon, "Soviet Penal Policy, 1917-1934: A Reinterpretation," *Slavic Review*, vol. 39, 1980.

[24] The best statement on this is Robert C. Tucker, "Stalinism as Revolution From Above," in Tucker, ed., *Stalinism*, pp. 77-108.

[25] Lynne Viola, "The Campaign to Eliminate the Kulak as a Class, Winter 1930: A Note on the Legislation," paper presented at XVI National Convention of AAASS, New York, 1984.

The second revisionist approach puts regime policy in a social context, and assumes that the social context (grievances, pressures, sources of support, responses) must to some degree shape, constrain and modify the actions of the party leadership. The pioneering work was Vera Dunham's thesis of "the Big Deal" between the new elite and the regime as a source of Stalinist "middleclass values."[26] This was followed by work on the Cultural Revolution[27] and upward mobility into the elite via the education policies of the First Five-Year Plan, which, I argued, were both an appeal to one of the regime's basic social constituencies and a source of future social support.[28] The regime's relationship with the working class during the First Five-Year Plan has since been investigated in several studies,[29] and there is work in progress on the social context of collectivization.[30] Rittersporn and Getty have suggested new perspectives on the Great Purges, linking them in different ways with tensions within the bureaucracy and with popular grievances against the new Soviet bosses.[31]

This approach challenges the totalitarian-model assumption that society is irrelevant to an understanding of Stalinist political processes. It also tends to reduce the role of terror and coercion, if only by suggesting that other factors are relevant as well, and this has been one of the most controversial aspects of the revisionist argument. Critics have asserted that any reduction of the traditional emphasis on terror amounts to white-washing of the Stalinist regime, or at least unacceptable abdication of moral judgment.[32] This is a complicated issue, since historians usually do not accept such *a priori* limitations on interpretation, and in this case are likely to dismiss the criticisms as manifestations of Cold-War bias. However, leaving aside the question of moral judgment[33] and

[26] Dunham, *In Stalin's Time*, ch.1. For a discussion of the technical intelligentsia and the regime that also touches questions of values, see Kendall E. Bailes, *Technology and Society under Lenin and Stalin: Origins of the Soviet Technical Intelligentsia, 1917-1941*, Princeton, 1978.

[27] Sheila Fitzpatrick, ed., *Cultural Revolution in Russia 1928-1931*, Bloomington, IN, 1978.

[28] Fitzpatrick, *Education and Social Mobility*.

[29] For example, Lynne Viola, "The Campaign of the 25,000ers: A Study of the Collectivization of Soviet Agriculture, 1929-1931," Ph.D. dissertation, Princeton, 1984; Hiroaki Kuromiya, "Politics and Social Change in Soviet Industry during the 'Revolution from Above,' 1928-1931," Ph.D. dissertation, Princeton, 1985.

[30] Roberta Manning is interested in the question of social support and antagonisms within the village community at the end of the 1920s. In a paper on "Peasants After Collectivization" presented at the second workshop on Social History of the Stalin Period (Columbia University, April 1985), I suggested that the modifications in *kolkhoz* policy in 1930-35 were the outcome of informal "social negotiation" between the regime and the peasantry.

[31] Getty, *Origins of the Great Purges*; Rittersporn, "The State Against Itself."

[32] See, for example, L. Kolakowski's note on Sovietological revisionists in *Survey*, vol. 21, no. 4, 1975, pp. 87-89, or Leonard Schapiro's review of my *Russian Revolution* in *Times Literary Supplement*, March 18, 1983, p. 269.

[33] A good deal of criticism on avoidance of explicit moral judgment has been directed at me— and correctly, in a sense, since I have an idiosyncratic position on this issue that is no more congenial to most other revisionists than it is to our critics. My original, and somewhat naive, notion was that historians and social scientists were bound by a kind of Hippocratic oath to be as objective and non-partisan as was humanly possible. I retreated from this position after being deluged by counter-

political bias, there is a real problem here for social historians, namely, how to deal with state coercion and terror in the Stalin period. The first reaction probably was (as the critics suspected) to steer clear of the subject on the grounds that it had been sufficiently or even excessively emphasized by the previous generation. But the more recent trend[34] has been toward reworking the subject—this time, it is hoped, without some of the earlier polemical excesses—in the context of social history.

The controversies surrounding the second revisionist approach tend to obscure the fact that it is relatively cautious in its revisionism and leaves much of the traditional structure of Sovietological interpretation intact. Virtually all the work is compatible with the idea of Stalinist "revolution from above," although it adds the new and very important concept of supporting or responsive social constituencies. A frequent image is that of the regime "unleashing" social forces[35] to accomplish its purposes. It is generally not argued that social pressures were strong enough to *force* the regime into radical action or that subsequent policy modifications or "concessions" to aggrieved social groups were regime responses to assertive social resistance. The new scholarship adds social voices and interests to the picture and it portrays the bureaucracy as a complex social entity, not a mere transmission belt, but at least some of the older Sovietological interpretations could assimilate these changes without too much trouble.

The third revisionist approach, substituting initiative from below for initiative from the regime at the great turning points of the Stalin era, would be much more difficult for other schools to incorporate. This makes it very attractive in principle to Young Turks, but in practice there are not many examples in the published or unpublished literature. The idea comes, I think, from my introduction to *Cultural Revolution in Russia*,[36] where I suggested "revolution from below" as an alternative hypothesis to "revolution from above." The argument in my article in that volume was more cautious, suggesting participation "from below" rather than any decisive revolutionary initiative from that quarter. None of the other contributors actually excluded regime initiative or asserted that

---

examples, and am now half persuaded that those who incline to take the role as detached observer do so (like the "alien, indifferent, and polemically-disposed" Sukhanov) mainly because of quirks of personality and temperament. But I still think the Sukhanovs make good historians.

[34] "State Coercion and Social Responses" was the subject of the third workshop on the Social History of the Stalin Period, held in Austin, Texas, on March 7-8, 1986.

[35] The image, borrowed from the Bolshevik *literateur* Voronsky, is used in Sheila Fitzpatrick, "Cultural Revolution in Russia, 1928-1932," *Journal of Contemporary History*, 1974, no. 1, p. 35. See also Getty, *Origins of the Great Purges*, p. 155, passim.

[36] Fitzpatrick, ed., *Cultural Revolution*, pp. 6-7. In this passage, which has been widely interpreted as a revisionist manifesto, I contrasted a traditional "revolution from above" interpretation of Cultural Revolution with a new interpretation that found "important elements of 'revolution from below.'" Although my own preference for the latter was clearly indicated, I had to concede "initiative" to the party leadership even while suggesting that the process was "generated by forces within the society." It will be noted that I have since shifted toward Tucker's position on the importance of "revolution from above."

social pressures for Cultural Revolution were irresistible.[37] A scholar who may come close to this position is Rittersporn on the Great Purges: he states that "the struggles of 1936-1938 were *unleashed by popular discontent* [my emphasis] with the arbitrariness, corruption and inefficiency of the ruling strata."[38] This statement seems to promise more than his subsequent argument delivers, since he concedes that the masses were passive and "incapable of organized resistance,"[39] and does not show how or why, under these circumstances, their discontent should have acted so powerfully on the rulers.

How are we to account for the absence of specific, documented cases of revolutionary "initiative from below" in recent scholarship? One possibility is that scholars are being prudent, having discovered that even modest social-support hypotheses arouse indignation and controversy. Another possibility is that they are having trouble making this particular argument fit the data on such major episodes as Cultural Revolution, collectivization, and the Great Purges. It is always tempting to turn conventional wisdom on its head, but this approach may actually do less than justice to the real revisionist contribution to understanding of the Stalin period. What has emerged from the recent scholarship is an appreciation that no political regime, including Stalin's, functions in a social vacuum. There were social pressures and constituencies influencing Stalinist policy formation, though these were comparatively weak during the "revolution from above" phase. More importantly, there were social constraints, social responses and informal processes of negotiation between the regime and social groups that had a very significant impact on policy implementation—that is, on the nature and outcome of Stalin's "revolution from above" in practice.

Social historians have made their debut in studies of the Stalin period by challenging the totalitarian model and arguing that it gives a one-sided and simplistic picture of the interaction of state and society. The new data presented appear to bear out this claim, although in my opinion they do not yet significantly change the old picture of the Stalinist regime as *initiator* of social change in the 1930s. They do show, however, that the regime had only limited control over the *outcome* of the radical policies it had initiated. The regime's unusual capacity and inclination for generating "revolution from above" was something quite different from a capacity and an inclination for planned social

---

[37] In my article "Cultural Revolution as Class War" in Fitzpatrick, ed., *Cultural Revolution*, I identified a number of social constituencies actively or passively supporting Cultural Revolution, but located the actual initiative—the "signal" that launched the movement—in the party leadership. Of the other contributors, Frederick Starr and Katerina Clark emphasized the radical utopian spirit of architects and writers and the absence of day-to-day party control and direction of their activities. However, while they saw these groups as taking the initiative in their own professions, they also saw them as responding to opportunities and a favorable climate that were external to their professions and not created by their activity.

[38] "The State Against Itself," p. 87.

[39] "The State Against Itself," p. 103.

engineering. It could set off explosions that destroyed or damaged certain features of the social landscape, but its ability to rebuild according to preselected blueprints appears much more doubtful.

It is perhaps surprising that, despite its interest in social history, the new cohort of historians has concentrated so heavily on the old Sovietological questions—framed by an earlier generation of social scientists—about the political system. We have not yet discarded the assumption that the only significant social relations in the Soviet Union are those in which society relates to government. This tendency may be understandable, given the Stalinist context, and even legitimate, given the recent trend in social history to "bring the state back in." But surely there is a special problem in the case of Soviet social history: we seem to be bringing the state back in without ever having removed it from center stage. We may risk losing an opportunity to formulate new questions and develop a real social-history perspective on the Stalin period.

It seems to me that social historians have made their point on the totalitarian model and should now try turning their attention elsewhere. We are starting to investigate a society with, for example, a remarkably high level of social and geographical mobility, a new pattern of social stratification, and (according to a rather suspect piece of conventional wisdom) no internal class or social conflicts worth discussing. We have a lot to work on. We might even find, before bringing the state back in, that Stalinism had some *social* as well as political dynamics—which would, after all, be both the most logical and the most original contribution social historians could make to the field.

[7]

Victims of the Soviet Penal System in the Pre-war Years: A First Approach on the Basis of Archival Evidence

J. ARCH GETTY, GÁBOR T. RITTERSPORN, and
VIKTOR N. ZEMSKOV

THE GREAT PURGES OF THE 1930s were a maelstrom of political violence that engulfed all levels of society and all walks of life. Often thought to have begun in 1934 with the assassination of Politburo member Sergei Kirov, the repression first struck former political dissidents in 1935–1936. It then widened and reached its apogee in 1937–1938 with the arrest and imprisonment or execution of a large proportion of the Communist Party Central Committee, the military high command, and the state bureaucracy. Eventually, millions of ordinary Soviet citizens were drawn into the expanding terror.[1]

Debate in the West about the precise numbers of victims has appeared in the scholarly press for several years and has been characterized by wide disparity, often of several millions, between high and low estimates. Using census and other data, scholars have put forward conflicting computations of birth, mortality, and arrests in order to calculate levels of famine deaths due to agricultural collectivization (1932–1933), victims of the Great Terror (1936–1939), and total "unnatural" population loss in the Stalin period. Anton Antonov-Ovseenko, Robert Conquest, Steven Rosefielde, and others have posited relatively high estimates (see Table 1).[2] On the other hand, Stephen Wheatcroft and others working from

We are grateful to Nina I. Abdullaeva and Elena N. Orlova of the reading room of the Central State Archive of the October Revolution of the USSR (TsGAOR) and to Tatiana F. Pavlova, whose mediation allowed us to consult files of the judiciary at an early stage of our project. We are indebted to State Archive of the Russian Federation (GARF) Director Sergei V. Mironenko's energetic intervention permitting us to explore the most interesting sources and to the assistance of Dina N. Nokhotovich and her colleagues, who facilitated our work in the former "special" collections (*fondy*) of TsGAOR. Our colleague Andrei K. Sokolov has supported us throughout. We greatly benefited from his criticism of a first version of this article. We also express our gratitude for the help of Irina V. Rogacheva. This research was supported by the French Ministry of Research, IREX, and research funds of the University of California.

[1] Standard works are Robert Conquest, *The Great Terror: Stalin's Purge of the Thirties* (New York, 1968); and *The Great Terror: A Reassessment* (New York, 1990); Roy A. Medvedev, *Let History Judge: The Origins and Consequences of Stalinism* (New York, 1989); Aleksandr I. Solzhenitsyn, *The Gulag Archipelago 1918–1956: An Experiment in Literary Investigation* (New York, 1973); J. Arch Getty, *Origins of the Great Purges: The Soviet Communist Party Reconsidered, 1933–1938* (New York, 1985); Robert W. Thurston, "Fear and Belief in the USSR's 'Great Terror': Response to Arrest, 1935–1939," *Slavic Review*, 45, no. 2 (1986): 213–34; Gábor T. Rittersporn, *Stalinist Simplifications and Soviet Complications: Social Tensions and Political Conflicts in the USSR, 1933–1953* (Philadelphia, 1991); see also J. Arch Getty and Roberta T. Manning, eds., *Stalinist Terror: New Perspectives* (New York, 1993).

[2] For the most significant high estimates, see S. Rosefielde, "An Assessment of the Sources and Uses of Gulag Forced Labour, 1929–56," *Soviet Studies*, 33, no. 1 (1981): 51–87; and "Excess Mortality

1018   *J. Arch Getty, Gábor T. Rittersporn, and Viktor N. Zemskov*

the same sources have put forth lower totals.[3] Both "high" and "low" estimators have bemoaned the lack of solid archival evidence and have claimed that should such materials become available, they would confirm the author's projection. The debate, along with disputes on the "totalitarian" nature of the Stalinist regime, the importance of Joseph Stalin's personality, and the place of social history in Soviet studies, has polarized the field into two main camps, perhaps unfortunately labeled "Cold Warriors" and "revisionists."[4] Revisionists have accused the other side of using second-hand sources and presenting figures that are impossible to justify, while the proponents of high estimates have criticized revisionists for refusing to accept grisly facts and even for defending Stalin. Both sides have accused the other of sloppy or incompetent scholarship.

Now, for the first time, Soviet secret police documents are available that permit us to narrow sharply the range of estimates of victims of the Great Purges. These materials are from the archival records of the Secretariat of GULAG, the Main Camp Administration of the NKVD/MVD (the USSR Ministry of the Interior). They were housed in the formerly "special" (that is, closed) sections of the Central State Archive of the October Revolution of the USSR (TsGAOR), which is now part of the newly organized State Archive of the Russian Federation (GARF).[5] A few Moscow scholars (among them V. N. Zemskov) had access to some of them in the past but were not allowed to cite them properly. Now, according to the liberalized access regulations in Russian archives, scholars are able to consult these documents and to publish exact citations.[6] (See "A Note on Sources" at the end of this article.)

We propose to deal here only with quantitative elements of the terror, with what we can now document of the scale of the repression. Of course, such a cold numerical approach risks overshadowing the individual personal and psychological horror of the event. Millions of lives were unjustly taken or destroyed in the Stalin period; the scale of suffering is almost impossible to comprehend. The horrifying irrationality of the carnage involves no debatable moral questions— destruction of people can have no pros and cons. There has been a tendency to

---

in the Soviet Union: A Reconstruction of Demographic Consequences of Forced Industrialization, 1929–1949," *Soviet Studies*, 35 (July 1983): 385–409; Robert Conquest, "Forced Labour Statistics: Some Comments," *Soviet Studies*, 34 (July 1982): 434–39; and his *Great Terror: A Reassessment*, 484–89.

[3] R. W. Davies and S. G. Wheatcroft, "Steven Rosefielde's 'Kliukva,'" *Slavic Review*, 39 (December 1980): 593–602; S. G. Wheatcroft, "On Assessing the Size of Forced Concentration Camp Labour in the Soviet Union, 1929–56," *Soviet Studies*, 33, no. 2 (1981): 265–95; and "Towards a Thorough Analysis of Soviet Forced Labour Statistics," *Soviet Studies*, 35, no. 2 (1983): 223–37; Jerry F. Hough and Merle Fainsod, *How the Soviet Union Is Governed* (Cambridge, Mass., 1979), 176–77; Barbara Anderson and Brian Silver, "Demographic Analysis and Population Catastrophes in the USSR," *Slavic Review*, 44, no. 3 (1985): 517–36.

[4] For a discussion of "revisionist" research, see Sheila Fitzpatrick, "New Perspectives on Stalinism," *Russian Review*, 45, no. 4 (1986): 357–73; and the replies in *ibid.*, 375–413; and in *Russian Review*, 46, no. 4 (1987): 382–431.

[5] Even though TsGAOR no longer exists, the GARF documents referenced here are numbered according to the old TsGAOR system. Because GARF now includes other formerly independent archives with their own numbering system, we cite numbered documents below as "GARF (TsGAOR)."

[6] See *Vremennoe polozhenie: O poriadke dostupa k arkhivnym dokumentam i pravilakh ikh ispol'zovaniia* (Moscow, 1992), 3, 6, 8, for the new provisional rules of access.

accuse "low estimators" of somehow justifying or defending Stalin (as if the deaths of 3 million famine victims were somehow less blameworthy than 7 million).

Scholars and commentators will make use of the data as they choose, and it is not likely that this new information will end the debates. Still, it seems a useful step to present the first available archival evidence on the scale of the Great Terror. Admittedly, our figures are far from being complete and sometimes pose almost as many questions as they answer. They nevertheless give a fairly accurate picture of the orders of magnitude involved and show the possibilities and limits of the data presently available.

THE PENAL SYSTEM ADMINISTERED BY THE NKVD (Peoples' Commissariat of Internal Affairs) in the 1930s had several components: prisons, labor camps, and labor colonies, as well as "special settlements" and various types of non-custodial supervision. Generally speaking, the first stop for an arrested person was a prison, where an investigation and interrogation led to conviction or, more rarely, release.[7] After sentencing, most victims were sent to one of the labor camps or colonies to serve their terms. In December 1940, the jails of the USSR had a theoretical prescribed capacity of 234,000, although they then held twice that number.[8] Considering this—and comparing the levels of prison populations given in the Appendixes for the 1930s and 1940s—one can assume that the size of the prison system was probably not much different in the 1930s.[9]

Second, we find a system of labor camps. These were the terrible "hard regime" camps populated by dangerous common criminals, those important "politicals" the regime consigned to severe punishment, and, as a rule, by other people sentenced to more than three years of detention.[10] On March 1, 1940, at the end of the Great Purges, there were 53 corrective labor camps (*ispravitel'no-trudovye lageri*: ITL) of the GULAG system holding some 1.3 million inmates. Most of the data cited in this article bear on the GULAG camps, some of which had a multitude of subdivisions spreading over vast territories and holding large numbers of people. BAMLAG, the largest camp in the period under review, held more than 260,000 inmates at the beginning of 1939, and SEVVOSTLAG (the notorious Kolyma complex) some 138,000.[11]

Third came a network of 425 "corrective labor colonies" of varying types. These

[7] Release became increasingly rare in the 1930s. Even though the number of convicts in the Russian Federation declined from more than 2 million in 1933 to 1,217,309 in 1935, the proportion of custodial sentences increased from 24.3 percent in 1933 to 37.8 percent in 1935 to 44 percent by the first six months of 1936; GARF (TsGAOR), fond 9474, opis' 1, delo 97, listy 19, 59; and delo 104, list 8. (Subsequent archival citations will use abbreviations: f. = fond, op. = opis', d. = delo, l. and ll. = list and listy.)

[8] GARF (TsGAOR), f.9474, op.1, d.6, l.123.

[9] It must be noted, however, that in May 1933, 800,000 inmates were held "at places of detention . . . with the exception of camps." The all-time high came in early 1938, when 910,307 people were held in such places (548,756 of them in prisons, notwithstanding a theoretical "limit" of 155,439 places). "Smolensk Archive," WKP 178, 134; GARF (TsGAOR), f.9414, op.1, d.1139, l.88.

[10] This rule must have changed over the years, because the proportion of labor camp detainees serving terms of less than three years exceeded 18 percent by 1940 and 28 percent in January 1941; GARF (TsGAOR), f.9414, op.1, d.1155, l.7.

[11] GARF (TsGAOR), f.9414, op.1, d.1155, l.20.

1020   *J. Arch Getty, Gábor T. Rittersporn, and Viktor N. Zemskov*

colonies were meant to confine prisoners serving short sentences, but this rule varied with time.[12] The majority of these colonies were organized to produce for the economy and housed some 315,000 persons in 1940. They were nevertheless under the control of the NKVD and were managed—like the rest of the colony network—by its regional administrations. Additionally, there were 90 children's homes under the auspices of the NKVD.[13]

Fourth, there was the network of "special resettlements." In the 1930s, these areas were populated largely by peasant families deported from the central districts as "kulaks" (well-to-do peasants) during the forced collectivization of the early 1930s. Few victims of the Great Purges of 1936–1939 were so exiled or put under other forms of non-custodial supervision: in 1937–1938, only 2.1 percent of all those sentenced on charges investigated by the political police fell into this category.[14] This is why we will not treat exile extensively below.

Finally, there was a system of non-custodial "corrective work" (*ispravitel'no-trudovye raboty*), which included various penalties and fines. These were quite common throughout the 1930s—they constituted 48 percent of all court sentences in 1935[15]—and the numbers of such convictions grew under the several laws on labor discipline passed on the eve of the war. Typically, such offenders were condemned to up to one year at "corrective labor," the penalty consisting of work at the usual place of one's employment, with up to 25 percent reduction of wage and loss of credit for this work toward the length of service that gave the right to social benefits (specific allocations, vacation, pension).[16] More than 1.7 million persons received such a sentence in the course of 1940 and almost all of them worked in their usual jobs "without deprivation of freedom."[17] As with resettlements, this correctional system largely falls outside the scope of the Great Terror.

Figure A provides the annual totals for the detained population (GULAG camps, labor colonies, and "kulak" resettlements, minus prisons) in the years of the Great Purges. It shows that, despite previously accepted—and fairly inflated—figures to the contrary, the total camp and exile population does not seem to have exceeded 3.5 million before the war. Were we to extrapolate from the fragmentary prison data we do have (see the Appendixes), we might reasonably add a figure of 300,000–500,000 for each year, to put the maximum total detained population at around 3 million in the period of the Great Purges.[18]

[12] Some 17.9 percent of the political prisoners and 41.7 percent of those convicted for the theft of public property were held in colonies, not camps, by 1951, although the overwhelming majority of them were serving terms of more than five years; GARF (TsGAOR), f.9414, op.1, d.1356, ll.1–3.
[13] The 1940 data on the camps, colonies, and children's homes come from GARF (TsGAOR), f.9414, op.1, d.28, ll.2–3.
[14] Between 1930 and 1936, the figure had been 32.6 percent; GARF (TsGAOR), f.9401, op.1, d.4157, ll.202–03. Detailed statistical information on the resettlements can be found in V. N. Zemskov, "Spetsposelentsy: Po dokumentatsii NKVD-MVD SSSR," *Sotsiologicheskie issledovaniia*, no. 11 (1990): 3–17. The numbers of "special settlers" quoted below come from this article.
[15] GARF (TsGAOR), f.9474, op.1, d.97, l.19.
[16] *Ugolovnyi kodeks RSFSR—Kommentarii* (Moscow, 1944), 36–38.
[17] GARF (TsGAOR), f.8131sch, op.27, d.540, ll.9–22; f.9492, op.6, d.14, ll.10–11. In this and certain other categories of punishment, it was possible to be sentenced without having been arrested.
[18] See GARF (TsGAOR), f.9414, op.1, d.1139, l.88, for what is likely to be the record number of prison inmates at the beginning of 1938, and GARF (TsGAOR), f.9401, op.1, d.4157, ll.202, 203–05,

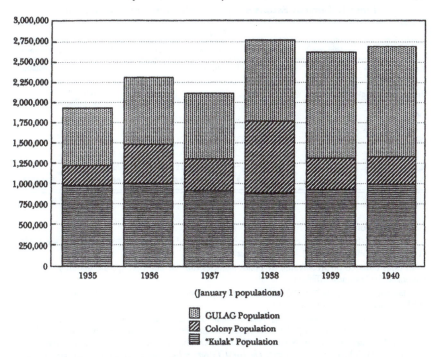

(January 1 populations)

GULAG Population
Colony Population
"Kulak" Population

FIGURE A: **Camp, Colony, and "Kulak" Exile Populations, USSR, 1935–1940**

Mainstream published estimates of the total numbers of "victims of repression" in the late 1930s have ranged from Dmitrii Volkogonov's 3.5 million to Ol'ga Shatunovskaia's nearly 20 million. (See Table 1.) The bases for these assessments are unclear in most cases and seem to have come from guesses, rumors, or extrapolations from isolated local observations. As the table shows, the documentable numbers of victims are much smaller.

We now have archival data from the police and judiciary on several categories of repression in several periods: arrests, prison and camp growth, and executions in 1937–1938, and deaths in custody in the 1930s and the Stalin period generally. Runs of data on arrests, charges, sentences, and custodial populations in the 1930s unfortunately reflect the simultaneous actions of several punitive agencies including the secret police, procuracy, courts, and others, each of which kept their own records according to their own statistical needs. No single agency (not even the secret police) kept a "master list" reflecting the totality of repression. Great

---

for figures on exile, which may nevertheless contain a certain number of people banished in the wake of collectivization. Even though the number of exiles other than "kulaks" was relatively significant until the mid-1930s, it decreased to around 28,000 by the end of the decade. "Spravka ob administrativno-ssyl'nykh i vyslannykh, sostoiashchikh na uchete v organakh NKVD–UNKVD s 1-go avgusta 1939 g. po 1 ianvaria 1940 g.," document photocopied in the Archive of the USSR Ministry of the Interior by the society Memorial, to which we are indebted for having put it at our disposal.

1022   *J. Arch Getty, Gábor T. Rittersporn, and Viktor N. Zemskov*

Table 1. Current Estimates of the Scale of Stalinist Repression

	1937–38 total arrests	1938 camp population	1938 prison and camp population	1952 camp population	1937–38 camp deaths	1937–38 executions	1921–53 executions
Anton Antonov-Ovseenko	18.8 million[1]		16 million				7 million
Roy A. Medvedev	5–7 million					0.5–0.6 million	
Ol'ga Shatunovskaia	19.8 million[1]					7 million	
Dmitri Volkogonov	3.5–4.5 million						
Robert Conquest	7–8 million	~7 million	~8 million	12 million	2 million	1 million	
Documentable	**~2.5 million**	**1.9 million[2]**	**2.0 million[2]**	**2.5 million[2]**	**160,084[3]**	**681,692**	**799,455[4]**

NOTES:

[1]1935–1940

[2]includes labor colonies

[3]in GULAG (hard regime) camps, in labor colonies, and in prisons (For the latter, see GARF [TsGAOR], fond 9414, opis' 1, delo 2740, list 52.)

[4]in cases initiated or investigated by police agencies that include perhaps the majority of people sentenced for "political offenses"

Another source indicates 786,096 executions for "counterrevolutionary crimes" between 1930 and 1953 (*Pravda* [February 14, 1990]: 2).

SOURCES: A. Antonov-Ovseenko, *The Time of Stalin: Portrait of a Tyranny* (New York, 1980), 212; Roy A. Medvedev, *Let History Judge: The Origins and Consequences of Stalinism*, rev. edn. (New York, 1989), 455; *Moskovskie novosti*, November 27, 1988; O. Shatunovskaia, "Fal'sifikatsiia," *Argumenty i fakty*, no. 22 (1990); Robert Conquest, *The Great Terror: A Reassessment* (New York, 1990), 485–86; GARF (TsGAOR), fond 9401, opis' 1, delo 4157, listy 201–02; see also Appendixes and Note on Sources, below.

care is therefore needed to untangle the disparate events and actors in the penal process.

A 1953 statistical report on cases initiated or investigated by the NKVD provides data on arrests and on the purported reasons for them. According to these figures, 1,575,259 people were arrested by the security police in the course of 1937–1938, 87.1 percent of them on political grounds. Some 1,344,923, or 85.4 percent, of the people the secret police arrested in 1937–1938 were convicted.[19] To be sure, the 1,575,259 people in the 1953 report do not comprise the total of 1937–1938 arrests. Court statistics put the number of prosecutions for infractions unrelated to "counterrevolutionary" charges at 1,566,185,[20] but it is unlikely that all persons in this cohort count in the arrest figures. Especially if their sentence was non-custodial, such persons were often not formally arrested. After all, 53.1 percent of all court decisions involved non-custodial sentences in 1937 and 58.7

[19] GARF (TsGAOR), f.9401, op.1, d.4157, ll.203, 205. The contrast is striking with the period 1930–1936, when 61.2 percent were arrested for political reasons, and 61.7 percent of all those arrested by the political police were eventually convicted, and especially with the years from 1920 through 1929, when 58.7 percent of security police arrests were for political reasons, but only 20.8 percent of all those arrested were convicted. A handwritten note on this document tells us that 30 percent of those sentenced between 1921 and 1938 "on cases of the security police" were "common criminals," and their number is given as 1,062,000. Since the report speaks of 2,944,879 convicts, this figure constitutes 36 percent; 30 percent would amount to 883,464 persons (l.202).

[20] GARF (TsGAOR), f.9492, op.6, d.14, l.14.

percent in 1938, and the sum total of those who were executed or incarcerated yields 647,438 persons in categories other than "counterrevolution."[21] Even if we remember that during the Great Purges the authorities were by far more inclined to detain suspects than in other times, it seems difficult to arrive at an estimate as high as 2.5 million arrests on all charges in 1937–1938.

Although we do not have exact figures for arrests in 1937–1938, we do know that the population of the camps increased by 175,487 in 1937 and 320,828 in 1938 (it had declined in 1936). The population of all labor camps, labor colonies, and prisons on January 1, 1939, near the end of the Great Purges, was 2,022,976 persons.[22] This gives us a total increase in the custodial population in 1937–1938 of 1,006,030. Nevertheless, we must add to these data the number of those who had been arrested but not sent to camps, either because they were part of a small contingent released sometime later or because they were executed.

As Table 1 shows, popular estimates of executions in the Great Purges of 1937–1938 vary from 500,000 to 7 million. We do not have exact figures for the numbers of executions in these years, but we can now narrow the range considerably. We know that between October 1, 1936, and September 30, 1938, the Military Board of the Supreme Court, sitting in 60 cities and towns, sentenced 30,514 persons to be shot.[23] According to a press release of the KGB, 786,098 persons were sentenced to death "for counterrevolutionary and state crimes" by various courts and extra-judicial bodies between 1930 and 1953.[24] It seems that 681,692 people, or 86.7 percent of the number for this 23-year-period were shot in 1937–1938 (compared to 1,118 persons in 1936).[25] A certain number of these unfortunates had been arrested before 1937, including exiled and imprisoned ex-oppositionists who were summarily killed in the autumn of 1937.[26] More important, however, our figures on 1937–1938 executions are not entirely comparable to those quoted in the press release. Coming from a 1953 statistical report "on the quantity of people convicted on cases of NKVD bodies," they also refer to victims who had not been arrested for political reasons,[27] whereas the communiqué concerns only persons persecuted for "counterrevolutionary offenses." In any event, the data available at this point make it clear that the number shot in the two worst purge years was more likely a question of hundreds of thousands than of millions.[28]

[21] Calculated on the basis of GARF (TsGAOR), f.9492, op.6, d.14, l.29, by subtracting the number of "counterrevolutionaries" indicated on l.14. The actual figure is nevertheless somewhat smaller, since the data on death sentences include "political" cases.

[22] Unless otherwise noted, data quoted in the text are drawn from the Appendixes, "USSR Custodial Populations, 1934–1953."

[23] Dmitrii Volkogonov, *Triumf i tragediia: Politicheskii portret I. V. Stalina* (Moscow, 1989), vol. 1, part 2, 246.

[24] *Pravda* (February 14, 1990): 2.

[25] *Pravda* (June 22, 1989): 3; *Kommunist*, no. 8 (1990): 103; GARF (TsGAOR), f.9401, op.1, d.4157, l.202.

[26] *Izvestiia TsK KPSS*, no. 10 (1989): 75, 77–78; no. 1 (1990): 52–53.

[27] "Spravka o kolichestve osuzhdennykh po delam organov NKVD"; GARF (TsGAOR), f.9401, op.1, d.4157, l.202. Judiciary statistics mention 4,387 death sentences pronounced by ordinary courts in 1937–1938, but this figure also includes a certain number of "political" cases; GARF (TsGAOR), f.9492, op.6, d.14, l.29.

[28] The only period between 1930 and the outbreak of the war when the number of death sentences for non-political crimes outstripped the ones meted out to "counterrevolutionaries" was

Of course, aside from executions in the terror of 1937–1938, many others died in the regime's custody in the decade of the 1930s. If we add the figure we have for executions up to 1940 to the number of persons who died in GULAG camps and the few figures we have found so far on mortality in prisons and labor colonies,[29] then add to this the number of peasants known to have died in exile, we reach the figure of 1,473,424. To be sure, of 1,802,392 alleged kulaks and their relatives who had been banished in 1930–1931, only 1,317,022 were still living at their places of exile by January 1, 1932. (Many people escaped: their number is given as 207,010 only for the year of 1932.)[30] But even if we put at hundreds of thousands the casualties of the most chaotic period of collectivization (deaths in exile, rather than from starvation in the 1932 famine), plus later victims of different categories for which we have no data, it is unlikely that "custodial mortality" figures of the 1930s would reach 2 million: a huge number of "excess deaths" but far below most prevailing estimates. Although the figures we can document for deaths related to Soviet penal policy are rough and inexact, the available sources provide a reliable order of magnitude, at least for the pre-war period.

Turning to executions and custodial deaths in the entire Stalin period, we know that, between 1934 and 1953, 1,053,829 persons died in the camps of the GULAG. We have data to the effect that some 86,582 people perished in prisons between 1939 and 1951.[31] (We do not yet know exactly how many died in labor colonies.) We also know that, between 1930 and 1952–1953, 786,098 "counter-revolutionaries" were executed (or, according to another source, more than 775,866 persons "on cases of the police" and for "political crimes").[32] Finally, we know that, from 1932 through 1940, 389,521 peasants died in places of "kulak" resettlement.[33] Adding these figures together would produce a total of a little more than 2.3 million, but this can in no way be taken as an exact number. First of all, there is a possible overlap between the numbers given for GULAG camp deaths and "political" executions as well as between the latter and other victims of the 1937–1938 mass purges and perhaps also other categories falling under police jurisdiction. Double-counting would deflate the 2.3 million figure. On the other hand, the 2.3 million does not include several suspected categories of death in custody. It does not include, for example, deaths among deportees during and

from August 1932 to the last quarter of 1933. This year saw the heavy-handed application of a particularly harsh decree against the theft of public property (the "Law of August 7, 1932"), and 5,338 people were condemned to death under its terms in 1932 and a further 11,463 in 1933; GARF (TsGAOR), f.9474, op.1, d.76, l.118; d.83, l.5. It is highly probable that far from all these people were executed (d.97, ll.8, 61). At any rate, the campaign began to lose its momentum by the closing months of 1933. On the uncertainty of our 1932–1933 data on thieves of public property, see below.

[29] At least 69,566 deaths were recorded in prisons and colonies between January 1935 and the beginning of 1940; GARF (TsGAOR), f.9414, op.1, d.2740, ll.52, 60, 74. The other data are 288,307 for strict regime camps and 726,030 for people executed "on cases of the political police."

[30] Zemskov, "Spetsposelentsy," 6; A. N. Dugin, "Neizvestnyi Gulag: Dokumenty i fakty," unpublished manuscript, 112.

[31] The available records do not include a figure for 1945. And 76.6 percent of these victims fall to the war years. V. N. Zemskov, "Gulag: Istoriko-sotsiologicheskii aspekt," *Sotsiologicheskie issledovaniia*, no. 7 (1991): 7.

[32] *Pravda* (February 14, 1990): 2; GARF (TsGAOR), f.9401, op.1, d.4157, ll.201–03, 205.

[33] See Zemskov, "Spetsposelentsy," 6, for detailed data on exiled "kulak" populations.

Table 2. Age and Gender Structure of GULAG Population
(as of January 1 of each year)

AGE/SEX	Percent of GULAG Population			Percent of USSR Population	
	1934	1937	1940	January 1937	January 1939
up to 18 years of age	1.2	0.7	0.5*	5.0‡	—
19–24	23.8	12.0	9.6	10.3	—
25–30	26.2	47.0	34.8	11.7	33.0
31–40	28.1	26.3	30.0	13.8	—
41–50	16.0	10.7	16.7	8.7	9.0
50+	4.7	3.3	8.4†	11.9	13.0
Women	5.9	6.1	8.1	52.7	—

NOTES: 1939 categories do not exactly match those of 1937. Respectively, the 1939 groupings are: 20–39, 40–49, and 50+.

*close to 1.2 percent by March 1940 (see GARF [TsGAOR], fond 9414, opis' 1, delo 28, list 14) and 4.5 percent by January 1, 1941

†7 percent for the age group of 51–60 versus 3 percent in 1937 and 4.5 percent in 1934—6.2 percent of the USSR population as of January 1, 1937

‡ages 16–18 (ages 12–15 = 7.5 percent)

SOURCES: GARF (TsGAOR), fond 9414, opis' 1, delo 1155, listy 9–10 (camp population); Rossiiskii gosudarstvennyi arkhiv ekonomiki (RGAE) [TsGANKH], f. 1562, op. 329, d. 144, ll. 2–10 (1937 data); Frank Lorimer, *The Population of the Soviet Union* (Geneva, 1946), 143 (1939 data—estimated distributions).

after the war as well as among categories of exiles other than "kulaks."[34] Still, we have some reason to believe that the new numbers for GULAG and prison deaths, executions as well as deaths in peasant exile, are likely to bring us within a much narrower range of error than the estimates proposed by the majority of authors who have written on the subject.

WE NOW HAVE SOME INFORMATION about the demographic composition of the GULAG's prisoners. In terms of gender, there are few surprises. As Table 2 shows, women constituted a minority of hard regime camp inmates, although their share reached almost 13 percent by 1943 and 24 percent by 1945. They accounted for no more than 11 percent of the people prosecuted by the court system until the late 1930s, then the demographic situation of the war years increased their part to more than 40 percent by 1944; and, even though this proportion diminished afterward, it did not descend below 20 percent until 1955.[35]

As we look at Table 2, the prominence of persons between 25 and 40 years of age among labor camp inmates is not surprising. A shift can be observed between 1934 and 1940. The generation that grew up in the tumult of war, civil war, and

[34] To mention only one example, we have information to the effect that 17 percent of Crimean Tatars who had been banished to Uzbekistan died before the end of 1945, some 27,000 people. A. Nekrich, *The Punished Peoples: The Deportation and Fate of Soviet Minorities at the End of the Second World War* (New York, 1978), 113–15.
[35] GARF (TsGAOR), f.9492, op.6, d.14, l.19; f.9474, op.1, d.97, l.6.

1026   *J. Arch Getty, Gábor T. Rittersporn, and Viktor N. Zemskov*

revolution and came of age in the New Economic Policy era continued to
constitute a cohort more exposed to penal sanctions than the rest of society. Thus
people between ages 19 and 24 in 1934 are likely to account for the large
over-representation of the age group 25 to 30 in 1937 and of the 31 to 35 cohort
on the eve of the war. Those in the 51 to 60 and especially 41 to 50 age ranges,
however, seem to be most vulnerable to repression in the wake of crises like
collectivization and the Great Purges. The presence of persons between ages 18
and 21 also becomes notable in the camps by March 1940, when they made up 9.3
percent of the inmates (their share in the 1937 population was 6.4 percent).

In fact, it gives one pause to reflect that 1.2 percent of strict regime camp
detainees were 18 or younger in 1934 and that, by 1941, their share nearly
reached the proportion of those between 16 and 18 in the country's population.
From mid-1935 to the beginning of 1940, 155,506 juveniles between the ages of
12 and 18 passed through the labor colonies. Some 68,927 of them had been
convicted of a crime and 86,579 had not.[36] The large proportion of unconvicted
young detainees indicates that they were likely to be incarcerated by extra-judicial
bodies, as was a high proportion of adult inmates not sentenced by courts between
1938 and 1940.[37] Nevertheless, political reasons did not play a predominant role
in the conviction of minors. The ordeal of collectivization and the ensuing famine
as well as the turmoil of mass migration from countryside to cities dramatically
increased the number of orphans, abandoned children, and single-parent households and weakened the family as well as the social integration of some categories
of youth. Juvenile delinquency became a serious concern for the authorities by the
spring of 1935, when they ordered that the courts were entitled to apply "all penal
sanctions" to children having reached 12 years and guilty of "theft, violence,
bodily harm, mutilation, murder and attempted murder."[38]

Records show that 10,413 youngsters between 12 and 16 years of age were
sentenced by the courts of the Russian Federation in the second half of 1935 and
the first half of 1936; 77.7 percent of them were accused of theft (as opposed to
43.8 percent of those in the 16 to 18 group) and 7.1 percent of violent crimes.[39]
At this time, when the overall proportion of custodial sentences did not exceed 44
percent in the republic, 63.5 percent of the youngest offenders (and 59.4 percent
between 16 and 18) were sent to detention.[40] In addition, there was a tendency to
apply the 1935 decree to infractions it did not cover; thus, despite instructions to
the contrary, 43 juveniles were sentenced for alleged misconduct in office [!] by
mid-1936 and 36 youngsters under 16 were so sentenced between 1937 and

[36] GARF (TsGAOR), f.9414, op.1, d.28, l.15. The latter category of juveniles in custody but not
convicted of a crime may represent in part the children of arrested "enemies of the people." Some
13,172 family members of alleged "traitors to the Motherland" were held in GULAG camps alone as
of January 1, 1939; GARF (TsGAOR), f.9414, op.1, d.1155, l.4.

[37] See Table 8.

[38] *Sobranie zakonov i rasporiazhenii Raboche-Krest'ianskogo Pravitel'stva SSSR,* chast' I (1935), 262;
A. Shliapochkinov, "Prestupnost' i repressiia v SSSR," *Problemy ugolovnoi politiki,* kn. 1 (Moscow,
1935), 80; *Ugolovnyi kodeks RSFSR* (Moscow, 1937), 105; *KPSS v rezoliutsiiakh i resheniiakh s"ezdov,
konferentsii i plenumov TsK,* vol. 5 (Moscow, 1971), 206–11.

[39] Compared to an analogous 7.7 percent of convictions among their elders for violent crimes;
GARF (TsGAOR), f.9474, op.16, d.79, ll.45, 73.

[40] GARF (TsGAOR), f.9474, op.1, d.97, l.6; d.104, l.8.

Victims of the Soviet Penal System in the Pre-war Years 1027

Table 3. Data on 10,366 Juvenile Camp Inmates, April 1, 1939*

	No.	Percent of All Sentences	Adults: Percent of All Sentences January 1, 1939
Sentenced for:			
"Counterrevolutionary offenses"	160	1.6	34.5
Dangerous crimes against the administrative order,	929	9.0	14.8
including Banditry	97	0.9	1.4
Misconduct in office	60	0.6	6.1
Crimes against persons	434	4.2	4.8
Crimes against property	2,507	24.4	12.1
Theft of public property†	22	0.2	2.1
Being "socially harmful and dangerous elements"‡	5,838	56.9	21.7
Violating the law on internal passports	115	1.1	2.1
Other crimes	204		

NOTES:

*of a total of 10,371 juveniles in the GULAG system.

†In reality, a great number of thieves of public property were not sentenced under the terms of the decree sanctioning this type of crime.

‡The meaning of this category is explained in the text below.

SOURCES: GARF (TsGAOR), fond 9414, delo 1140, opis' 1, listy 151, 153; d. 1155, ll. 3–6, 9 (see also d. 1140, ll. 190, 193–94, for somewhat different proportions concerning adults on January 1, 1939).

1939.[41] The sources show, incidentally, that the procuracy suggested that people below 18 years of age should not be confined in ordinary places of detention, and there is reason to believe that it also vainly protested against a directive of the camp administration stipulating that "the stay of minors in labor colonies is not limited by the terms of court sentences."[42]

At any rate, 24,700 children and adolescents up to 16 years of age appeared in courts in 1938 and 33,000 in the course of the following year,[43] an increase that reflects a hardening penal practice. Table 3 indicates, however, that even if juveniles could be detained for political reasons, this motive did not account for a high proportion of the youngest camp inmates, even in the wake of the Great Purges. Although these data denote a tendency to imprison juveniles almost in the same proportions as adults if they were accused of the most serious crimes, they also show the penal system's proclivity to impose custodial sentences on youngsters more readily than on grown-ups.

Table 4 shows the national origin of the majority of labor camp inmates on January 1, 1937–1940, alongside the ethnic composition of the USSR according to the working materials of the (suppressed) 1937 and (published) 1939 censuses. In comparison with their weight in the general population, Russians, Belorussians, Turkmen, Germans, and Poles were over-represented in the camps by 1939;

[41] *Ugolovnyi kodeks RSFSR* (1937), 105; GARF (TsGAOR), f.9492, op.6, d.14, l.23; f.9474, op.16, d.79, l.45.

[42] GARF (TsGAOR), f.8131sch, op.27, d.71, ll.104–05.

[43] GARF (TsGAOR), f.8131sch, op.27, d.239, ll.115–16; 78.1 percent of them were convicted of theft and 5.3 percent of robbery.

1028   *J. Arch Getty, Gábor T. Rittersporn, and Viktor N. Zemskov*

Table 4. Ethnic Groups in GULAG Camps, January 1, 1937–1940

Ethnic Group	1937	1938	1939	1940	1937 camps %	1937 census %	1939 camps %	1939 census %	over (+)/under (−) representation (camps and census) 1937	1939
Russians	494,827	621,733	830,491	820,089	60.28	58.07	63.05	58.09	+2.21	+4.96
Ukrainians	138,318	141,447	181,905	196,283	16.85	16.33	13.81	16.47	+0.52	−2.66
Belorussians	39,238	49,818	44,785	49,743	4.78	3.01	3.40	3.09	+1.57	+0.31
Tatars	—	22,916	24,894	28,232	—	1.35	1.89	2.52	—	−0.63
Uzbeks	29,141	19,927	24,499	26,888	3.55	2.81	1.86	2.84	+0.74	−0.98
Jews	11,903	12,953	19,758	21,510	1.45	1.65	1.50	1.77	−0.20	−0.27
Germans	—	998	18,572	18,822	—	0.71	1.41	0.84	—	+0.57
Kazakhs	—	11,956	17,123	20,166	—	1.77	1.30	1.82	—	−0.52
Poles	—	6,975	16,860	16,133	—	0.39	1.28	0.37	—	+0.91
Georgians	4,351	6,974	11,723	12,099	0.53	1.24	0.89	1.32	−0.71	−0.43
Armenians	5,089	6,975	11,064	10,755	0.62	1.22	0.84	1.26	−0.60	−0.42
Turkmen	—	4,982	9,352	9,411	—	0.46	0.71	0.46	—	+0.23
Latvians	—	1,191	4,742	5,400	—	0.04	0.58	0.07*	—	+0.51
Finns	—	997	2,371	2,750	—	0.09	0.29	0.08*	—	+0.21

*In some cases, and especially in those of Latvians and Lithuanians, the 1937 and the available 1939 data show notable discrepancies (see also Gerhard Simon, *Nationalismus und Nationalitätenpolitik in der Sowjetunion* [Cologne, 1986], 422–24). This inconsistency perhaps precludes refined analysis but does not prevent visualization of magnitude.

SOURCES: GARF (TsGAOR), fond 9414, opis' 1, delo 1155, listy 1, 11 (camp population: d. 1139, ll. 178–81; and d. 1140, ll. 191–92, give slightly different figures for January 1, 1938 and 1939); RGAE (TsGANKH), f. 1562, op. 329, d. 144 (1937 census data); Frank Lorimer, *The Population of the Soviet Union* (Geneva, 1946), 138–39 (1939 census data).

Germans and Poles being especially hard-hit. On the other hand, Ukrainians, Jews, Central Asians (except Turkmen[44]) and people from the Caucasus were less represented in the GULAG system than in the population of the country; as national groups, they suffered proportionately less in the 1937–1938 terror.[45]

If ethnic groups for whom camp figures are unavailable in 1937 were too weakly represented to be counted, then Table 4 accurately demonstrates the statistical impact of the terror on different nationalities. Because we know that the party/state administration was heavily staffed by Russians and that many members of the party elite and economic leadership were of Polish and German background, the changes in the ethnic composition seem to indicate a terror aimed

[44] We shall see that the case of the Turkmen can be explained by the particular cruelty of the purge in their republic.
[45] Ukrainians seem to have been more heavily repressed before 1934, when their share in the camp population had reached 19 percent. It is probable that a certain number of Ukrainian inmates were listed as Russians, Belorussians, or Poles. Data about the ethnic origin of executed people are unavailable at this writing, and these may modify the picture for the national background of the victims of the 1937–1938 terror but not that of previous and subsequent years, when many fewer persons were shot. Even after the occupation of the Western Ukraine, however, the share of Ukrainians in hard regime camps was 14.6 percent in 1940 and 12.6 percent in 1941 (versus 61 percent and 59 percent of Russians). Nevertheless, by 1951, the proportion of Ukrainians was 23.6 percent in the population of camps and that of Russians 52.6 percent, and 20 percent and 55.6 percent respectively in the combined population of camps and colonies. See GARF (TsGAOR), f.9414, op.1, d.1356, l.4.

more at the elite than at particular national groups per se.[46] To be sure, a sizable proportion of citizens of Polish and German origin living in border areas suffered several waves of "cleansing" for their alleged unreliability.[47] In addition, wherever they resided, they were likely to be accused of political sympathies with states with which relations were strained, especially at a time when the authorities suspected fifth columns throughout the country and ordered a clampdown on "spies and nationalists."[48] This circumstance must have contributed to the fact that, in early 1939, when GULAG inmates made up 0.77 percent of the country's population, some 2.7 percent and 1.3 percent of these ethnic groups were in hard regime camps, as well as about 1.3 percent of all Koreans, 1.7 percent of all Estonians, 1.9 percent of all Finns, and 3.2 percent of all Lithuanians, compared to approximately 0.85 percent of all Belorussians, 0.84 percent of all Russians, 0.65 percent of all Ukrainians, and 0.61 percent of all Jews. The national group suffering the most in proportional terms was the Latvians, who were heavily represented in the party and state administration and of whose total census population a staggering 3.7 percent was in strict regime camps alone.

The hypothesis of an increasingly anti-elite orientation of the penal policy is supported by data on the educational levels of labor camp inmates. Table 5 shows the educational background of hard regime camp inmates on January 1, 1937, alongside educational levels for the population as a whole in 1937. Even allowing for the rise in educational levels in the general population between 1937 and 1940, it seems clear that the purge hit those with higher educational levels more severely. Although less educated common folk heavily outnumbered the "intelligentsia" in the camps, those who had studied in institutions of higher or secondary education were proportionally nearly twice as numerous in the GULAG system as they were in society at large, while those with elementary (or no) education were under-represented.

Moreover, in the years spanning the Great Terror, the proportion of the camp population with some education rose significantly, while that of less educated people declined. From 1934 to 1941, the segment of the camp population with higher education tripled and the proportion with secondary education doubled. Again, however, care must be used in interpreting these data, because educational levels in the population as a whole were increasing steadily during the decade of

[46] The under-representation of those of Jewish background is somewhat surprising, given the relatively high proportion of Jews in the party membership and in responsible positions. At the beginning of 1937, they constituted the third largest ethnic group in the party, with 5.3 percent of all members. Rossiiskii tsentr khraneniia i izucheniia dokumentov noveishei istorii, hereafter, RTsKhIDNI, f.17, op.120, d.278, l.10. (This is the recently renamed Central Party Archive [TsPA], Institut Marksizma-Leninizma. We cite this collection below as RTsKhIDNI [TsPA]). It is possible, however, that in many cases the figures for the national composition of the camp population were based on the declarations of the inmates themselves and that a great number of Jewish communists felt sufficiently assimilated to identify with other ethnic groups.

[47] Political Archive of the Foreign Office, Bonn, Botschaft Moskau, A2 Innerpolitische Verhältnisse der Sowjetunion, vol. 8: the Leningrad Consulate General to the Embassy, June 30, July 20, and August 3, 1935, p.1; vol. 13: the Vladivostok Consulate to the Embassy, September 14, 1937; Botschaft Moskau, A4 Militär- und Marineangelegenheiten: the Leningrad Consulate General to the Embassy, May 28, 1935; Botschaft Moskau, A21 Kiew, Kurze Meldungen: the Kiev Consulate to the Embassy, May 27, 1936.

[48] Compare GARF (TsGAOR), f.8131sch, op.27, d.140, l.25; f.9401, op.1a, d.20, l.54; op.2, d.1, l.3.

1030   *J. Arch Getty, Gábor T. Rittersporn, and Viktor N. Zemskov*

Table 5. Educational Levels of the GULAG Population versus the USSR as a Whole, 1937

	GULAG Population, 1937 (%)	USSR Population, 1937 (%)
School Achievement		
higher	1.0	0.6
secondary	8.9	4.3
elementary	49.3	38.3*
semi-literate	32.4	—
illiterate	8.4	39.0

NOTE: *given as *gramotnye* (literate) in census
SOURCES: GARF (TsGAOR), fond 9414, opis' 1, delo 1155, list 10 (camp population); RGAE (TsGANKH), f. 1562, op. 329, d. 144, ll. 11–13 (1937 data).

the 1930s. We lack detailed annual education data for the period and especially statistics on the share of people with college and high school instruction in the population of the late 1930s and early 1940s. Thus it would be dangerous to draw firm conclusions, even though the available evidence strongly suggests that the terror intensified against the educated elite. It comprised 12.8 percent of the population of hard regime camps by 1941, compared to 6.3 percent in 1934. As Table 6 indicates, the number of detainees with higher and secondary education grew much faster than the rest of the GULAG population.

IT IS COMMONLY BELIEVED THAT MOST OF THE PRISONERS of the "Gulag Archipelago" had been arrested and sentenced for political offenses falling under one of the headings of "counterrevolutionary offenses" (Article 58 in the criminal code). It is also common wisdom that many people arrested for other reasons were accused of political crimes for propaganda value. The available evidence does not bear out this view, but it does suggest considerable ambiguity in definitions of "political crimes." Table 7 shows the breakdown of labor camp inmates for selected years, according to the offense for which they were sentenced. Although the presence of alleged counterrevolutionaries is impressive, it turns out that ostensibly non-political detainees heavily outnumbered "politicals."

In view of the murderous campaign of 1932–1933 against pilferers of state and

Table 6. Percentage of Increase in Detainees by Educational Background in GULAG Camps

	1934–1936	1936–1939	1939–1941
Education			
higher	+47.5	+69.6	+25.6
secondary	+54.1	+48.0	+23.5
elementary and less	+37.9	+34.4	+7.9

SOURCE: GARF (TsGAOR), fond 9414, opis' 1, delo 1155, list 10 (d. 1140, l. 190, gives slightly different figures for 1939).

Table 7. Offenses of GULAG Population
(by Percent as of January 1 of each year)*

	1934	1936	1940
Sentenced for:			
"Counterrevolutionary offenses"	26.5	12.6	33.1
Dangerous crimes against the administrative order,	15.2	17.7	3.6
including Banditry	3.9	3.2	2.4
Other crimes against the administrative order,	1.3	—	13.9
including Speculation	1.3	1.1	2.4
and "Hooliganism"	—	—	7.3
Misconduct in office, Economic crimes	7.5	10.6	7.3
Crimes against persons	4.7	5.5	5.2
Crimes against property	15.9	22.3	12.1
Theft of public property	18.3	14.2	1.9
"Socially harmful and dangerous elements"	8.0	11.5	18.9
Violation of the law on internal passports	—	2.3	1.3
Military offenses	0.6	0.8	0.7
Other delicts	2.0	2.6	3.3

NOTE: *The percentages do not add up to 100 because of rounding.
SOURCE: GARF (TsGAOR), fond 9414, opis' 1, delo 1155, listy 3–6.

collective farm property, and of the fact that in 1951 the number of prisoners convicted for this offense largely outstripped that of all categories of "counter-revolutionaries,"[49] their share seems at first glance suspiciously low in Table 7, especially in 1940. One explanation for the relatively low proportion of inmates convicted under the "Law of August 7, 1932"—which had prescribed the death penalty or ten years of hard labor for theft of state property—is an unpublished decree of January 1936 ordering the review of the cases of all inmates convicted under the terms of this Draconian law before 1935.[50] The overwhelming majority of these people had been condemned between 1932 and 1934, and four-fifths of this cohort saw their sentences reduced by August 1936 (including 40,789 people who were immediately released).[51] Another possible explanation is that many people benefited from a directive reorienting the drive against major offenders and from reviews of their convictions that led by the end of 1933 to modifications of 50 percent of the verdicts from the previous seventeen months.[52] This state of affairs seems to account for the considerable confusion in the records concerning the implementation of the "Law of August 7" and for the fact that, while claiming that the number of persons sentenced under its terms was between 100,000 and 180,000, officials were reluctant to advance exact figures even as late as the spring of 1936.[53]

[49] That is, 709,348 detainees—28 percent of all camp and colony inmates—versus 579,918—22.9 percent; GARF (TsGAOR), f.9414, op.1, d.1356, ll.1–3.
[50] GARF (TsGAOR), f.3316, op.2, d.1754, ll.2–3.
[51] GARF (TsGAOR), f.3316, op.2, d.1837, ll.88–89.
[52] *Sovetskaia iustitsiia*, no. 24 (1934): 2–3; *Sotsialisticheskaia zakonnost'*, no. 8 (1937): 38; *Ugolovnyi kodeks* (1937): 131–32.
[53] See, for example, GARF (TsGAOR), f.3316, op.2, d.1534, ll.87, 112; d.1754, ll.21, 26; f.9474, op.16, d.48, ll.15, 17, 35–36, 42; d.79, ll.6, 16. In January 1933, even the people's commissar of justice, N. V. Krylenko, had no exact idea how many people had been sentenced to death and how many of them were in fact shot under the terms of the decree (compare GARF [TsGAOR], f.9474,

The category of "socially harmful and dangerous elements" and the manner it was put to use must also warn us not to accept the definitions of "counterrevolutionaries" in our sources. Article 7 of the penal code stated that "to persons having committed socially dangerous acts or representing danger through their relation[s] with the criminal milieu or through their past activities, measures of social defense of a judicial-corrective, medical or medico-pedagogical character are applied." Nevertheless, it failed to specify penalties except to indicate in Article 35 that these persons could be subjected to internal exile, without giving the slightest hint of the sentences courts were entitled to pass.[54] The definition of the offense and the corresponding penalty were more than vague, but this did not prevent extra-judicial bodies of the secret police from singling out "harmful" and "dangerous" people among "recidivists [and] persons associated with the criminal milieu conducting a parasitic way of life etc."[55] This information comes from an appeal to the top leadership by the procurator general, who was proposing to restrict the sentencing powers of the NKVD Special Board at the beginning of 1936 but not insofar as "dangerous elements" were concerned.

Although the procurator of the USSR, Andrei Vyshinskii, valued procedural precision, his office does not appear to have objected to the launching in August 1937 of a lethal "mass operation" targeting "criminals (bandits, robbers, recidivist thieves, professional smugglers, recidivist swindlers, cattle thieves) engaged in criminal activities and associated with the criminal milieu"—whether or not they were actually guilty of any specific offense at the moment—and connecting these common criminals to a wide range of supposedly "anti-Soviet" and "counter-revolutionary" groups, from "kulaks" to former members of forbidden political parties, former oppositionists, and alleged terrorists.[56] Clearly, the regime saw a political threat in the conduct, and indeed in the sheer existence, of "dangerous" persons. The secret directive of 1937 was no dead letter: the records suggest that it led to the arrest of a great number of people, some of whom were hardly more than notorious hooligans and yet were sometimes sent to the firing squad.[57]

Some 103,513 "socially harmful and dangerous elements" were held in hard regime camps as of January 1937, and the number grew to 285,831 in early 1939, when, as Table 3 shows, they made up a record 21.7 percent of all detainees (and 56.9 percent of juvenile detainees). But the proportion (and also the number) of "dangerous" persons began to decline by January 1940 and that of "hooligans" started to rise, until the size of their contingent came close to that of the "harmful

---

op.1, d.76, l.118; and V. P. Danilov and N. A. Ivnitskii, "O derevne nakanune i v khode sploshnoi kollektivizatsii," in Danilov and Ivnitskii, eds., *Dokumenty svidetel'stvuiut* [Moscow, 1989], 41–42).

[54] Although an addendum in 1930 forbade the exile of juveniles below 16 years of age, the widespread practice of deporting "kulak" families made short shrift of it. A 1946 decision of the Supreme Court explained that "socially dangerous elements" could be sent to exile "also in the case when they would be acquitted by the court for the accusation of having committed a specific crime"; *Ugolovnyi kodeks RSFSR* (Moscow, 1956), 138.

[55] GARF (TsGAOR), f.8131sch, op.27, d.70, l.103.

[56] *Trud* (June 4, 1992): 4.

[57] See, for example, GARF (TsGAOR), f.7523, op.65, d.557, ll.29–30, 42–45, 49, 53. In some cases, the sentence was reviewed after the spring of 1938, which led to the release of a certain number of people.

elements" by 1941, in part because of toughened legislation concerning rowdies.[58] A total of 108,357 persons were sentenced in 1939 for "hooliganism"; in the course of the next year, 199,813 convicts fell into this category. But by 1948, the proportion of "hooligans" among camp inmates was 2.1 percent, whereas that of "dangerous elements" fell to 0.1 percent.[59] No doubt the same offense in the 1930s could be regarded as "socially dangerous" and in the 1940s as "hooliganism."[60]

"Socially harmful" people may have been victims of political repression, but it would be far-fetched to presume that the unjust punishment they received was a response to conscious acts of opposition to the regime. Having observed this, we must remember that the great majority of those sentenced for "counterrevolutionary offenses" had never committed any act deliberately directed against the Soviet system and even continued to remain faithful to the Bolshevik cause, notwithstanding their victimization. From this point of view, the regime's distinction between "political" and "non-political" offenders is of doubtful relevance. Unless we are prepared to accept broad Stalinist definitions of "counterrevolutionary" offenses or the equally tendentious Western categorization of *all* arrests during Stalin's time (even those for crimes punishable in any society) as political, we should devise ways to separate ordinary criminality from genuine opposition to the system as well as from other reasons for which people were subjected to penal repression.

At any rate, the Appendix figures show that from 1934 to 1953, a *minority* of the labor camp inmates had been formally convicted of "counterrevolutionary crimes." Our data on sentencing policy are incomplete for the period before 1937, but they permit us to advance some estimates of orders of magnitude. Thus we can calculate that only about 11 percent of the more than 5.3 million persons sentenced by courts and extra-judicial bodies between 1933 and 1935 represented "cases of the OGPU/NKVD"[61] of which, as we have seen, a relatively high proportion had not been considered "political." Some 28 percent of the almost 5 million people convicted by various courts and NKVD boards in 1937–1939 were sentenced "from cases of the security police," mostly under the pretext of "counterrevolutionary offenses." But while the judiciary and the Special Board of the NKVD/MVD subjected nearly 31 million persons to penalties in the period 1940–1952, only 4.8 percent (though a sizable 1.5 million persons) fell under Article 58. By contrast, more than twice as many (11 percent) of all people sentenced in these years were charged with appropriating public property.[62]

It turns out that by far the largest group of those sentenced between 1940 and 1952 consisted of people accused of violating laws devised to strengthen labor

---

[58] GARF (TsGAOR), f.9414, op.1, d.1155, l.5; *Ugolovnyi kodeks RSFSR* (Moscow, 1947), 154; *Ugolovno-protsessual'nyi kodeks RSFSR* (Moscow, 1947), 196–97.

[59] GARF (TsGAOR), f.9414, op.1, d.1155, ll.5–6; f.9492, op.6, d.14, l.14.

[60] See the injunction to courts to clamp down on "hooligan misbehavior of a counterrevolutionary character" in *Sovetskaia iustitsiia*, no. 18 (1935): 10.

[61] Calculated on the basis of GARF (TsGAOR), f.9401, op.1, d.4157, l.203; and f.9474, op.1, d.97, l.59. Having combined court statistics with police data referring also to certain persons condemned by the judiciary, we must concede that it is possible a small number of them figure twice in our computation.

[62] Compared to some 9 percent in 1937–1939.

1034   *J. Arch Getty, Gábor T. Rittersporn, and Viktor N. Zemskov*

Table 8. GULAG Population according to Sentencing Authority (Percentages as of January 1)*

	1934	1935	1936	1937	1938	1939	1940	1941
Jurisdiction								
Police bodies	42.2	41.3	33.7	30.9	49.8	59.4	54.5	38.7
Including:								
the Special Board of the NKVD					3.7	8.3	9.4	8.2
the "Special Troikas" of 1937–1938						23.3	25.4†	17.2
Courts and Tribunals	57.8	58.7	66.3	69.1	50.2	40.6	45.5	58.6

NOTES:

*There was no corresponding information on some 2.6 percent of the detainees for 1941.

†The increase of this cohort, despite the abolition of this jurisdiction in November 1938, was no doubt due to the transfer of inmates who had been in colonies before the end of 1939.

SOURCE: GARF (TsGAOR), fond 9414, opis' 1, delo 1155, list 8 (see also f. 8131sch, op. 27, d. 70, l. 141, where similar though not entirely identical data can be found for 1934–1935).

discipline, ranging from unauthorized absence from work to dodging mobilization for work in agriculture, to failing to meet the compulsory minimum of work in the collective farm. Although the judiciary jargon called them "wartime decrees," most of them remained in force until 1956. More than 17 million people had been convicted under their terms between 1940 and 1952 (albeit "only" 3.9 million of them were sentenced to detention), comprising half (55.3 percent) of all the period's sentences.[63] One may wonder if acts infringing on proprietary prerogatives and labor relations in a state that is virtually the only proprietor and practically the only employer do not bear some relation to politics. But if we leave aside this dilemma as well as the year 1936, for which our data are too fragmentary, we can conclude that, on the whole, only about 8.4 percent of the sentences of courts and extra-judicial bodies were rendered "on cases of the secret police" and for alleged political reasons between 1933 and 1953.

From 1934, when many believe the terror was mounting, to 1937–1938, the camp proportion of "counterrevolutionaries" actually declined. Table 8 shows that so did the proportion in the strict regime camp population of those who had been sent there by specific police bodies.

Even though the number of people convicted "on cases of the NKVD" more than tripled from 1934 to 1935, a careful look at the sources shows that many sentences had hardly anything to do with "political" cases. Data on the arrested "counterrevolutionaries" show a 17 percent growth due to an increase in the number of people accused of "anti-Soviet agitation" by a factor of 2.6.[64] As for

[63] GARF (TsGAOR), f.9401, op.1, d.4157, ll.201–02; f.9492, op.6, d.14, ll.6–8, 10, 14; d.15, ll.12–13. To avoid double-counting, we used NKVD figures for the number of "politicals" sentenced in 1937–1938, which are higher than those of the judicial statistics. Our data for 1940–1952 are on "counterrevolutionaries." As for the numbers of pilferers and violators of labor discipline, they certainly include the same persons more than once in some cases, since these offenses were likely to be committed repeatedly. For some legal dispositions that account for the high number of custodial sentences under the "wartime decrees," see *Ugolovnyi kodeks RSFSR—Kommentarii*, 282, 284–85.

[64] GARF (TsGAOR), f.9401, op.1, d.4157, l.203.

sentences in 1935, 44.6 percent of them were rendered by regional NKVD "troikas" (tribunals), which did not deal with "political" affairs.[65] Another 43 percent were passed by regular courts, but fewer than 35,000 of the more than 118,000 people concerned had been "counterrevolutionaries."[66] To be sure, the quantity of "political" sentences increased, compared to the previous year. In 1936, however, the NKVD arrested the same number of "counterrevolutionaries" as in 1934, which does not seem to show steadily intensifying political repression. Similarly, the continually decreasing number of people shot in cases initiated by the secret police[67] and the constantly diminishing share (as well as aggregate number) of "counterrevolutionaries" in hard regime camps between 1934 and 1937 casts doubt on the idea of "mounting" repression in this period.

The abolition of the OGPU, a degree of uncertainty concerning the sentencing privileges of the new NKVD, and attempts to transfer the bulk of "political" cases to the jurisdiction of military tribunals as well as to the special boards of regional courts and the Supreme Court[68] suggest that the penal policy of more or less ordinary judicial instances, whose statistics are available, is indicative of the general trend of 1935–1936. The data are unfortunately incomplete, but we have information on at least 30,174 "counterrevolutionaries" who were sentenced by civilian and military courts in 1935, in the wake of the Kirov assassination, and on 19,080 people who were prosecuted by the same courts for supposedly political offenses in the first half of the next year.[69] Most of this growth is attributable to the increased frequency of "anti-Soviet agitation," which accounted for 46.8 percent of the cases before the courts of the Russian Federation in the first six months of 1935, and 71.9 percent in the corresponding period of the next year.[70] The loose application of this charge did not always sit well in high places, and the people's commissar of justice along with the prosecutor general warned top decision-makers of the consequences of an excessive use of the more than vague legislation on "counterrevolutionary agitation."[71] The prosecutor general had a heated exchange of letters with the head of the security police that raised the possibility of limiting NKVD jurisdiction in this matter.[72]

There was a tendency to *diminish* rather than inflate the share of "political" cases in 1936. Even the chairman of the ominous Military Collegium of the Supreme Court noted in December 1936 that the number of "counterrevolutionaries" convicted by his bench and its subordinate courts in the first nine months of the year was 34.4 percent *less* than in the same period of 1935. The number of prosecutions had grown only for two categories of crimes. Characteristically

[65] GARF (TsGAOR), f.8131sch, op.28, d.6, l.62.

[66] GARF (TsGAOR), f.9474, op.1, d.97, l.21.

[67] Some 2,056 such executions are on record in 1934 versus 1,229 in 1935 and 1,118 in 1936; GARF (TsGAOR), f.9401, op.1, d.4157, l.203.

[68] GARF (TsGAOR), f.8131sch, op.27, d.73, l.228; f.9474, op.1, d.85, l.7; *Sovetskaia iustitsiia*, no. 19 (1934): 4; *Sobranie zakonov i rasporiazhenii* . . . (1935): 139–40.

[69] GARF (TsGAOR), f.9474, op.1, d.97, l.21; d.104, ll.123, 133, 146.

[70] GARF (TsGAOR), f.8131sch, op.27, d.71, l.127; f.9474, op.1, d.104, ll.123, 126, 130; op.16, d.97, l.113. The crime did not seem to have entailed the hardest penalties at this time, since about half the convicts were sentenced to terms of between two and five years.

[71] GARF (TsGAOR), f.8131sch, op.27, d.71, ll.127–33; d.73, ll.228–34.

[72] GARF (TsGAOR), f.8131sch, op.27, d.70, ll.103–06, 134–36, 138–42.

1036   *J. Arch Getty, Gábor T. Rittersporn, and Viktor N. Zemskov*

enough, these were espionage and sabotage, and their frequency increased, especially in the third quarter of 1936.[73]

It is from that time, late 1936, and not from late 1934 that the number of "counterrevolutionaries" (as well as the cohort sentenced by the NKVD) began to swell dramatically, above all in the wake of the launching of wholesale "mass operations" during the summer of 1937 that victimized "socially harmful" people alongside a wide range of purported political delinquents. The documents that ordered the mass "repression of former kulaks, criminals, and anti-Soviet elements" through decisions of newly organized "Special Troikas" of the secret police specified that the operation had to be completed within four months and even set "control figures" for the numbers of people to be shot and imprisoned. The relevant instruction foresaw 72,950 executions and 186,500 new detainees as the outcome of the drive and stipulated that the numerical targets were not to be exceeded without authorization of the Moscow headquarters of the NKVD.[74]

Nothing indicates that the operation enjoyed a more orderly implementation than any other campaign in the Soviet system of planning. Available documentation on the course of the action is fragmentary, but it shows that after mid-February 1938, when according to the initial orders the operation should have been over for more than two months, the chief of the NKVD requested additional funding for the detention and transportation of about twice the number of people spoken about in the original directives.[75] Moreover, the "Special Troikas" had largely "overfulfilled plans" by this time, having doomed 688,000 people before the end of 1937. Similarly, the expectations of the NKVD boss proved equally low compared to the 413,433 persons actually subjected to the jurisdiction of the local "troikas" in 1938.[76] Local enthusiasm outstripped the expectations of the center.

In general, the leadership of the terror was not very good at predicting events. In December of 1936, NKVD chief N. I. Ezhov issued a secret order to the effect that the number of inmates at SEVVOSTLAG (Kolyma) should be 70,000 in 1937 and 1938.[77] (This was its population as of July 1936.) But this "plan" was overfulfilled by 20,000 in the second half of 1937, and by the end of 1938 the camp housed 138,170, twice the planned level.[78] Characteristically, as late as February 1938, the GULAG administration was at a loss to give the exact number of victims falling under its authority nationally.

Some local camp commandants found the numbers of convicts modest by the early months of 1938 and bombarded Moscow with telegrams asking for a larger

[73] GARF (TsGAOR), f.9474, op.1, d.104, ll.144, 146. For other documents suggesting that in 1936 the prevailing line was not to find "enemies" at all cost, see d.86, ll.85, 91; d.97, l.17; d.99, ll.10–11, 91; f.8131sch, op.27, d.62, ll.62, 69, 78–81; d.70, ll.103–06, 134–36, 138–42; f.9492, op.1s, d.1, l.1.
[74] *Trud* (June 4, 1992): 4. It also provided a breakdown by republics. There are few reasons to doubt the authenticity of these documents, since some of the measures they enumerate reappear in a source we have consulted; GARF (TsGAOR), f.5446, op.57, d.52, l.26. For a sudden increase in the number of people among "kulak" exiles listed as "sentenced" in 1937–1938, see Zemskov, "Spetsposelentsy," 6.
[75] GARF (TsGAOR), f.9414, op.1, d.15, ll.59–60, 192.
[76] GARF (TsGAOR), f.9401, op.1, d.4157, l.202; f.9414, op.1, d.1138, l.20. It is highly probable that our sources indicate only an approximate figure for 1937 "troika" victims.
[77] GARF (TsGAOR), f.9401, op.1a, d.9, l.341.
[78] GARF (TsGAOR), f.9414, op.1, d.1155, l.20.

"labor force,"[79] probably because their production plans were calculated on the basis of larger contingents than the ones at their disposal. Still, hundreds of thousands of new inmates arrived after the summer of 1937 to camps unprepared to accommodate them. At the moment when the head of the secret police was applying for an increase in the NKVD budget to receive a new influx of prisoners, reports of the procurator general—who was supposed to supervise penal institutions—painted a dreary picture of the lack of elementary conditions of survival in the GULAG system as well as of starvation, epidemic disease, and a high death rate among those already there.[80] The year 1938 saw the second highest mortality in hard regime camps before the war and probably also in prisons and labor colonies, where 36,039 deaths were recorded, compared to 8,123 in 1937 and 5,884 in 1936.[81]

Returning to the question of plan and control over the purge, we find a letter in which the NKVD chief promised to improve the poor camp conditions, yet he reported figures for the increase in GULAG population different from the data reported by his own administration.[82] Evidence also suggests that the NKVD and the Central Committee issued directives during the drive that were incompatible with each other.[83] In addition, there is at least one republic on record, that of Belorussia, where vigilant local officials continued mass shootings for a time even after an order was dispatched calling for an end to the wholesale purge.[84]

Although the theoretical capacity of the prisons in Turkmenistan was put at 1,844 places, 6,796 people had been locked up in them at the beginning of 1938, and 11,538 by May; this was clearly unanticipated in Moscow.[85] The dimensions the campaign reached in the republic explains the over-representation of Turkmen among camp inmates. Other ethnic groups also suffered—at one time, all of Ashkhabad's 45 Greek residents were arrested as members of an "insurrectionary organization."[86] The NKVD chief of the republic prescribed "control figures for cases of espionage [and] sabotage" as well as specific "limits" for the number of arrests to celebrate May Day,[87] which suggests that after a while, the operation was farmed out to regional heads of the secret police. A fire at a factory became an occasion to meet "quotas" for sabotage by arresting everybody who happened to be there and forcing them to name their "accomplices" (whose number soon

[79] GARF (TsGAOR), f.9414, op.1, d.1139, ll.118–22.
[80] GARF (TsGAOR), f.8131sch, op.27, d.111, ll.5–6, 34.
[81] About 6.9 percent of the yearly average population of GULAG camps perished in 1938 and 15.2 percent in the famine year of 1933; GARF (TsGAOR), f.9414, op.1, d.1155, ll.1–2; d.2740, ll.52–53.
[82] GARF (TsGAOR), f.9414, op.1, d.15, l.190; d.1138, ll.6, 70. It is unlikely that Ezhov's intention was to conceal the real figure, because the number he furnished was within the same range as the two other series of data we have on new arrivals. By the way, they were compiled at different times and are not identical.
[83] GARF (TsGAOR), f.8131sch, op.27, d.145, ll.109–10, 125.
[84] GARF (TsGAOR), f.8131sch, op.27, d.118, ll.74–78.
[85] GARF (TsGAOR), f.9414, op.1, d.1138, ll.122–23. Some 148 people died in Turkmenistan's jails and labor colonies in the course of May 1938 alone.
[86] GARF (TsGAOR), f.8131sch, op.27, d.145, ll.72–73.
[87] GARF (TsGAOR), f.8131sch, op.27, d.145, ll.53, 57.

exceeded one hundred persons).[88] If nothing else worked, it was always possible to round up people having the bad luck to be at the marketplace, where a beard made one suspect of the "crime" of being a mullah and where more than 1,200 "counterrevolutionaries" were seized in a matter of five months.[89] Mock executions and incredibly savage torture were used in Turkmenistan to wring out confessions to all sorts of "subversive acts" and "organizations."[90] To be sure, neither torture nor trumped-up cases was a Turkmen monopoly: the records show that both became widespread in the wake of the wholesale purge the "Special Troikas" spearheaded.[91]

This state of affairs illustrates the problems posed by our sources on the question of "politicals." A person arrested for his "suspicious" Polish origin or shot because of having been married to a Pole in the past was no doubt accused of being a "counterrevolutionary."[92] We can also only wonder how many victims shared the fate of namesakes and were sentenced to long terms or shot as alleged former members of defunct parties.[93] How many people were like the peasant who had been condemned "merely" to ten years but whose paperwork slipped in among that of people slated for capital punishment? (He was shot with them.)[94] Probably, most such people figure in our data on "politicals," even if some of the mistakenly executed were listed under the heading of their original "nonpolitical" sentences.

Last but not least, there was the purge of the purgers: how "counterrevolutionary" were the great number of officials of the NKVD and the judiciary who were denounced for "anti-Soviet activities" after November 1938, when the Central Committee abolished the "troikas," called off the purge, and decided that "enemies of the people and spies having made their way" into the secret police and the procuracy had been responsible for the terror of the preceding period?[95] Many of these "hostile elements" were sentenced as "politicals," just as the majority of those they had cruelly mistreated, although they continued to protest their fidelity to the regime until the very end.[96]

But whatever we think about "counterrevolutionaries," their identified cohort constituted 34.5 percent of the camp population by 1939. This was not their largest share in the pre-war period: at the beginning of 1932, people sentenced for "political" reasons in what corresponded then to hard regime camps comprised 49 percent of the inmates.[97] The widespread recourse to capital punish-

[88] GARF (TsGAOR), f.8131sch, op.27, d.145, ll.73–74.
[89] GARF (TsGAOR), f.8131sch, op.27, d.145, ll.46, 56–57.
[90] GARF (TsGAOR), f.8131sch, op.27, d.145, ll.46–47, 52–53, 58–60, 62, 67–70.
[91] See, for example, GARF (TsGAOR), f.8131sch, op.27, d.145, ll.24, 190–91; d.118, ll.19–20, 25–26, 32–33, 35–36, 57–59; d.139, ll.26, 36–40, 42, 95, 119; d.140, ll.24–25; d.240, ll.172, 249–50; d.244, ll.19–20.
[92] GARF (TsGAOR), f.7523, op.65, d.567, l.23; f.8131sch, op.27, d.145, ll.76–77.
[93] GARF (TsGAOR), f.8131sch, op.27, d.145, l.65.
[94] GARF (TsGAOR), f.8131sch, op.27, d.139, l.12.
[95] RTsKhIDNI (TsPA), f.17, op.3, d.1003, ll.85–86; GARF (TsGAOR), f.8131sch, op.27, d.118, l.32; d.140, l.25; d.145, ll.50, 101; d.239, l.45.
[96] RTsKhIDNI (TsPA), f.17, op.3, d.1003, l.84; GARF (TsGAOR), f.7523, op.65, d.568, ll.49–52, 60–66; f.8131sch, op.27, d.240, ll.173–74.
[97] "Svedenie o sostave zakliuchennykh, soderzhaiushchikhsia v ispravit.-trudovykh lageriakh NKVD," 1, 2. (We are again grateful to the society Memorial for putting documents at our disposal.)

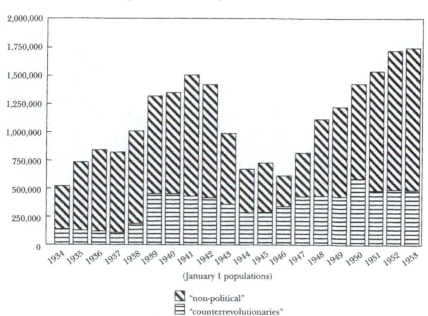

(January 1 populations)

◼ "non-political"
⊟ "counterrevolutionaries"

FIGURE B: "Political" Crimes as Proportion of GULAG Population, 1934–1953

ment in 1937–1938 is responsible for holding the proportion of "counterrevolutionaries" under 50 percent until 1946. The percentage then declined again, probably as the result of a renewed offensive against pilferers of public property.[98] If we superimpose the numbers of purportedly political inmates on the oscillating population of the labor camps from year to year, we find that while the proportion of "counterrevolutionaries" fluctuated, their aggregate numbers remained remarkably constant from 1939 until Stalin's death (Figure B). This suggests that, numerically, a cohort of "politicals" was taken into the camps at the time of the Great Terror and remained relatively constant in future years.

THE TIME OF THE GREAT PURGES (1936–1939), as Figure C indicates, was numerically not the period of greatest repression, even if we take into account the masses of people shot in 1937–1938 and the much less frequent recourse to capital punishment from the late 1940s. Annual numbers of detainees were

[98] Rittersporn, *Stalinist Simplifications and Soviet Complications*, 273–74. The steep rise of the share of prisoners listed under the heading of "counterrevolutionaries," from 41.2 percent in 1945 to 59.2 percent by January 1, 1946, was in part due to the amnesty of July 1945 that freed a large number of detainees and was not applicable to "politicals"; *Sbornik dokumentov po istorii ugolovnogo zakonodatel'stva SSSR i RSFSR, 1917–1952 gg.* (Moscow, 1953), 426–27. It seems that their share in the combined population of camps and labor colonies was 36.4 percent or, according to another source, 34.1 percent on January 1, 1947, and 25.8 percent at the beginning of 1948; Dugin, "Neizvestnyi Gulag," 42, 49.

1040   *J. Arch Getty, Gábor T. Rittersporn, and Viktor N. Zemskov*

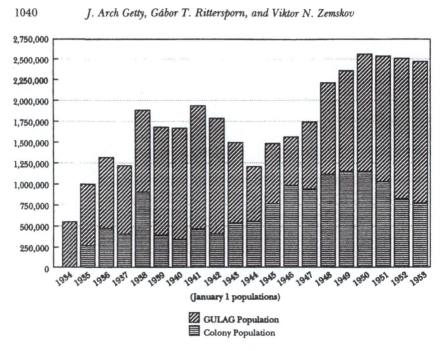

(January 1 populations)

GULAG Population
Colony Population

FIGURE C: GULAG and Colony Populations, 1934–1953

greater after World War II, reaching a peak shortly before Stalin's death.[99] If we extract the war years from the trend, we find that the picture is one of steadily increasing repression throughout the 1930s and 1940s.

Looking specifically at the hard regime camp populations (Figure C and the Appendixes), we find that in the twenty years from 1934 through 1953, the annual population increased in fourteen of the years and dropped in six. Of the six declining years, four were wartime; we know that approximately 975,000 GULAG inmates (and probably also a large number of persons from labor colonies) were released to military service.[100] Nevertheless, the war years were not good ones for the GULAG. First, many of those released to the army were assigned to punitive or "storm" formations, which suffered the heaviest casualties. Second, at the beginning of the war, prominent political prisoners were transferred and isolated in the most remote and severe camps in the system and most "politicals" were specifically barred from release to the military. Third, of the 141,527 detainees who had been in jails and evacuated during the first months of the war from territories soon to be occupied by the enemy, 11,260 were

[99] The unprecedented growth of the camp population after early 1947 was less a result of the increasing prosecution of "counterrevolutionaries" than of the imprisonment of other categories of offenders and a general rise from 1947 of the average length of sentence for a number of offenses having little to do with Article 58; GARF (TsGAOR), f.9492, op.6, d.14, ll.29–31.
[100] GARF (TsGAOR), f.9414, op.1, d.68, l.8.

executed.[101] Fourth, in the first three years of the war, 10,858 inmates of the GULAG camps were shot, ostensibly for being organizers of underground camp organizations.[102]

Finally, wartime life became harder for the remaining camp residents. More than half of all GULAG deaths in the entire 1934–1953 period occurred in 1941–1943, mostly from malnutrition. The space allotment per inmate in 1942 was only one square meter per person, and work norms were increased.[103] Although rations were augmented in 1944 and inmates given reduced sentences for overfilling their work quotas, the calorie content of their daily provision was still 30 percent less than in the pre-war period.[104] Obviously, the greatest privation, hunger, and number of deaths among GULAG inmates, as for the general Soviet population, occurred during the war.

The other years of significant population decrease in the camps were 1936 and 1953–1954. In 1936, the number of persons in both the GULAG system and labor colonies declined, as did the proportion of those incarcerated for "counterrevolution" and on sentences of the NKVD. Similarly, while the aggregate numbers of detainees were generally increasing between 1934 and 1937, the rate of increase was falling. In 1953, the year that saw the deaths of both Stalin and his secret police chief L. P. Beria, more than half of the GULAG inmates were freed.

We have fairly detailed data about the internal movement of persons—arrivals, transfers, deaths, and escapes—inside the strict regime camp network (see the Appendixes and Figure D). They confirm Solzhenitsyn's metaphor that this was a universe in "perpetual motion." Large numbers of persons were constantly entering and leaving the system. During the 1934–1953 period, in any given year, 20–40 percent of the inmates were released, many times more than died in the same year. Even in the terrible year of 1937, 44.4 percent of the GULAG labor camp population on January 1 was freed during the course of the year.[105] Until 1938–1939, there were also significant numbers of escapes from the hard regime camps. In any year before 1938, more of the GULAG inmates fled the camps than died there. A total of about 45,000 fugitives were on record in the spring of 1934,[106] a year when a record number of 83,000 detainees took flight. Between 1934 and 1953, 378,375 persons escaped from the GULAG camps.[107] Of them, 233,823 were recaptured, and the remaining 38 percent made good their escape.

---

[101] Dugin, "Neizvestnyi Gulag," 29–30. It is specified that 9,817 of them were shot in the prisons, 674 allegedly for "revolt[s] and resistance" while in transit, and 769 "illegally," also while being transported.

[102] GARF (TsGAOR), f.9414, op.1, d.68, ll.8–10.

[103] GARF (TsGAOR), f.9414, op.1, d.68, l.18.

[104] GARF (TsGAOR), f.9414, op.1, d.68, l.21.

[105] Some 53,778 inmates were released from the labor camps in the first quarter of 1940; 66.5 percent of them had served their full sentences. Another 30.6 percent had seen their sentences reduced or quashed; GARF (TsGAOR), f.9414, op.1, d.1155, l.28.

[106] GARF (TsGAOR), f.8131sch, op.27, d.28, l.32.

[107] We lack comparable data for labor colonies. One of the few available sources relates to a colony in the Smolensk area with 431 inmates in the spring of 1934, of whom 193 were condemned to detention and 238 to corrective labor and from which 507 persons had escaped in the last three months of 1933—including 156 people serving prison terms—and 433 in the first quarter of 1934, of whom 188 had been sentenced to confinement. "Smolensk Archive," WKP 351, 52, 55. For indications that this colony was not an exception, see GARF (TsGAOR), f.8131, op.11, d.106, l.73; d.109, ll.120, 125; op.28, d.5, l.2.

1042   *J. Arch Getty, Gábor T. Rittersporn, and Viktor N. Zemskov*

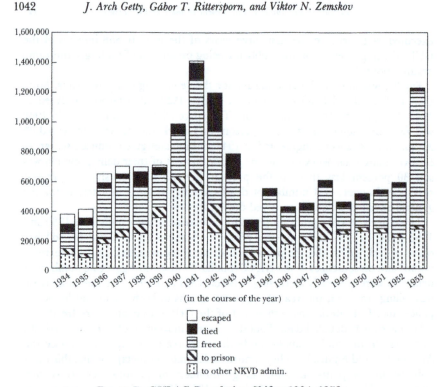

(in the course of the year)

☐ escaped
■ died
▤ freed
◣ to prison
⊡ to other NKVD admin.

FIGURE D: GULAG Population Shifts, 1934–1953

The data show, however, that the number of escapes fell sharply beginning in 1938, as Stalin with Ezhov and then with Beria tightened camp regimes and security.[108]

The data also indicate that the average length of sentence increased in the last years before the war. The longer terms "counterrevolutionaries" were likely to receive must have contributed to the growth of the proportion of people serving more than five years. However, Table 9 suggests that—despite a notable drop in the share of long terms meted out by the courts—the sentencing policy for inmates of hard regime camps came closer by the late 1930s to the one applied to "politicals" around mid-decade.

Even if most camp convicts were "non-political," were only serving sentences of up to five years, and hundreds of thousands were released every year, the GULAG camps were horrible places. Work was hard, rations were barely adequate, and living conditions were harsh. The inmates were exposed to the exactions of fellow prisoners and especially to the cruelty of the guards.[109] Behind our figures lies the suffering of millions of people.

[108] Volkogonov, *Triumf i tragediia*, vol. 1, part 1, 43; RTsKhIDNI (TsPA), f.17, op.2, d.577, l.9.
[109] See, for example, GARF (TsGAOR), f.8131sch, op.27, d.28, ll.29–31.

Victims of the Soviet Penal System in the Pre-war Years   1043

Table 9. Length of Sentences during Stalinist Repression, 1935–1940 (by percent)

Length	RSFSR courts for common crimes, first half of: 1935	RSFSR courts for common crimes, first half of: 1936	USSR civilian courts for political crimes, first quarter of: 1936	USSR courts 1939	in GULAG camps, January 1940
10+ years	—	—	—	0.1	1.0
5–10 years	20.0	17.6	50.7	4.0	42.2
up to 5 years	80.0	82.4	44.2	95.9	56.8

NOTE: The data on penalties concerning common crimes and for 1939 summarize only custodial sentences. Detention for more than 10 years was introduced in October 1937.

SOURCE: GARF (TsGAOR), fond 9474, opis' 1, delo 104, listy 8, 126 (1935 and 1936 data); f. 9492, op. 6, d. 14, l. 29 (1939 data); f. 9414, op. 1, d. 1155, l. 7 (camp population).

THE LONG-AWAITED ARCHIVAL EVIDENCE ON REPRESSION in the period of the Great Purges shows that levels of arrests, political prisoners, executions, and general camp populations tend to confirm the orders of magnitude indicated by those labeled as "revisionists" and mocked by those proposing high estimates.[110] Some suspicions about the nature of the terror cannot be sustained, others can now be confirmed. Thus inferences that the terror fell particularly hard on non-Russian nationalities[111] are not borne out by the camp population data from the 1930s. The frequent assertion that most of the camp prisoners were "political" also seems not to be true. On the other hand, the new evidence can support the view, reached previously by statistical study and evidence of other types, that the terror was aimed at the Soviet elite.[112] It also confirms the conclusions of authors who had studied the available sources and shown the uncertainties of legal theory and penal practice in the 1930s.[113] In addition, it seems that much of the process was characterized by high-level confusion and by local actions in excess of central plans.

The Stalinist penal system can be profitably studied with the same sociological tools we use to analyze penal structures elsewhere. It contained large numbers of common criminals serving relatively short sentences, many of whom were released each year and replaced by newly convicted persons. It included a wide variety of sanctions, including non-custodial ones. For most of those drawn into it,

[110] See Hough and Fainsod, *How the Soviet Union Is Governed*, 177; and S. G. Wheatcroft, "More Light on the Scale of Repression and Excess Mortality in the Soviet Union in the 1930s," in Getty and Manning, eds., *Stalinist Terror: New Perspectives*, 275–90.

[111] See, for instance, Bohdan Nahaylo and Viktor Swoboda, *Soviet Disunion: A History of the Nationalities Problem in the USSR* (London, 1990), chap. 6.

[112] Sheila Fitzpatrick, "The Impact of the Great Purges on Soviet Elites: A Case Study from Moscow and Leningrad Telephone Directories in the 1930s," 247–60, and J. Arch Getty and William Chase, "Patterns of Repression among the Soviet Elite, 1936–1939: A Biographical Approach," 225–60, both in Getty and Manning, eds., *Stalinist Terror: New Perspectives*.

[113] Peter H. Solomon, "Soviet Penal Policy, 1917–1934: A Reinterpretation," *Slavic Review*, 39, no. 2 (1980): 196–217; Solomon, "Soviet Criminal Justice and the Great Terror," *Slavic Review*, 46, nos. 3–4 (1987): 391–413; Solomon, "Local Political Power and Soviet Criminal Justice, 1922–1941," *Soviet Studies*, 37, no. 3 (1985): 305–29; Eugene Huskey, "Vyshinskii, Krylenko and the Shaping of the Soviet Legal Order," *Slavic Review*, 46, nos. 3–4 (1987): 414–28.

1044   *J. Arch Getty, Gábor T. Rittersporn, and Viktor N. Zemskov*

it was in fact a penal system: a particularly harsh, cruel, and arbitrary one, to be sure, but not necessarily a one-way ticket to oblivion for the majority of inmates.

Yet it is also important to highlight three specific features. For the first, the use of capital punishment among the "measures of social defense" sets Soviet penal practices apart from those of other systems, even though the number of executions shows a sharp decrease after the dreadful dimensions in 1937–1938. Second, the detention system in the second half of the 1930s (and perhaps at other times) was directed against educated members of the elite. Third, it had a clearly political purpose and was used by the regime to silence real and imagined opponents.

Our attempt to examine the repression of the Stalin period from the point of view of social history and penology is not meant to trivialize the suffering it inflicted or to imply that it was "no better or worse" than in other authoritarian states. Although repression and terror imply issues of politics and morality, above all for those who perpetrate or justify them, we believe that scholars can also study them as a question of historical precision. The availability of new data permits us to establish more accurately the number and character of victims of the terror and to analyze the Stalinist repressive system on the basis of specific data rather than relying on the impressions and speculations of novelists and poets.[114] We are finally in a position to begin a documented analysis of this dismal aspect of the Soviet past.

[114] See Stephen Cohen, "Stalin's Terror as Social History," *Russian Review*, 45, no. 4 (1986): 375–84.

A Note on Sources

The GARF (TsGAOR) collection we used was that of the GULAG, the Main Camp Administration of the NKVD/MVD (the USSR Ministry of the Interior). This collection consists of nine inventories (*opisi*), the first of which, that of the Secretariat, contains the main body of accessible data on detainees. To be sure, it was not possible to scrutinize the more than 3,000 files of this *opis'*, so we restricted ourselves to those that promised to tell the most about camp populations.

Accurate overall estimates of numbers of victims are difficult to make because of the fragmentary and dispersed nature of record keeping. Generally speaking, we have runs of quantitative data of several types: on arrests, formal charges and accusations, sentences, and camp populations. But these "events" took place under the jurisdiction of a bewildering variety of institutions, each with its own statistical compilations and reports. These agencies included the several organizations of the secret police (NKVD special tribunals, known as troikas, special collegia, or the special conference [*osoboe soveshchanie*]), the procuracy, the regular police, and various types of courts and tribunals.

For example, archival data on sentences for "anti-Soviet agitation" held in different archival collections may or may not have explicitly aggregated such events by the NKVD and the civilian courts. Summary data on "political" arrests or sentences may or may not explicitly tell us what specific crimes were so defined. Aggregate data on sentences sometimes include persons who were "sentenced" (to exile or banishment from certain cities) but never formally "arrested"; when we compare sentencing and arrest data, therefore, we do not always have the information necessary to sort apples from oranges. Similarly, our task is complicated, as shown above, by the fact that many agencies sentenced people to terms in the GULAG for many different types of crimes, which were variously defined and categorized.[115] We believe, however, that despite the lack of this information, we now have enough large chunks of data to outline the parameters and to bring the areas for which we lack data within a fairly narrow range of possibility.

Further research is needed to locate the origins of inconsistencies and possible errors, especially when differences are significant. We must note, however, that the accuracy of Soviet records on much less mobile populations does not seem to give much hope that we can ever clarify all the issues. For instance, the Department of Leading Party Cadres of the Central Committee furnished different figures for the total party membership and for its ethnic composition as of January 1, 1937, in two documents that were nevertheless compiled about the same time.[116] Yet another number was given in published party statistics.[117] The conditions of "perpetual movement" in the camp system created even greater

[115] It is only after the organization of a People's Commissariat of Justice for the whole of the Soviet Union that country-wide judicial statistics become more or less trustworthy from 1937.

[116] Compare RTsKhIDNI (TsPA), f.17, op.120, d.278, ll.8, 10; and TsKhSD (the Central Committee Archive), f.77, op.1, d.1, l.8.

[117] *Spravochnik partiinogo rabotnika*, vyp.18 (Moscow, 1978), 1.366. Since this figure corresponds to that calculated by Thomas H. Rigby, one wonders if the editors did not decide to rely more on the painstaking research of this scholar than on their own records. See *Communist Party Membership in the U.S.S.R., 1917–1967* (Princeton, N.J., 1968), 52.

1046   *J. Arch Getty, Gábor T. Rittersporn, and Viktor N. Zemskov*

difficulties than those posed by keeping track of supposedly disciplined party members who had just seen two major attempts to improve the bookkeeping practices of the party.[118]

At times, tens of thousands of inmates were listed in the category of "under way" in hard regime camp records,[119] although the likelihood that some of them would die before leaving jail or during the long and tortuous transportation made their departure and especially their arrival uncertain. The situation is even more complicated with labor colonies, where, at any given moment, a considerable proportion of prisoners was being sent or taken to other places of detention, where a large number of convicts served short terms, and where many people had been held pending their investigation, trial, or appeal of their sentences.[120] The sources are fragmentary and scattered on colonies, but it seems that A. N. Dugin's attempt (see the Appendixes) to find figures for the beginning of each year— which was checked by V. N. Zemskov—yielded rather accurate results. Even so, we are not certain that errors have not slipped in.

Moreover, we do not know at the time of this writing if camp commandants did . not inflate their reports on camp populations to receive higher budgetary allocations by including people slated for transfer to other places, prisoners who were only expected to arrive, and even the dead. Conversely, they may have reported low figures in order to secure easily attainable production targets.

We made extensive use of a series of statistics that were compiled about 1949 and that followed the evolution of a great number of parameters from 1934 up to 1948.[121] We indicated some instances in which current periodic reports of the accounting department furnished slightly different figures from those of 1949 (see the notes to Tables 3, 4, and 6) and one case in which an NKVD document in 1936 gave data similar to but not entirely identical with those calculated after the war (note to Table 8). In these as well as in most other instances, the gaps are insignificant and do not call into question the orders of magnitude suggested by the postwar documents, whose figures are, as a rule, somewhat higher than the ones recorded in the 1930s. A notable exception concerns escapes, because a 1939 report mentioned almost twice as many fugitives for 1938 as the relevant table of 1949.[122] Although we have no explanation for this discrepancy at this moment, we can speculate that the fact that a 1939 medical report showed lower mortality figures in hard regime camps in the years between 1934 and 1939 than the 1949 account may be because the latter also includes people who had been executed.[123]

Another source we relied on consists of four tables concerning people arrested and sentenced "on cases of the secret police" from 1921 through the first half of

[118] Getty, *Origins of the Great Purges*, 58–64, 86–90.
[119] See, for example, GARF (TsGAOR), f.9414, op.1, d.1138, l.6.
[120] See, for instance, GARF (TsGAOR), f.9414, op.1, d.1139, ll.88–89; d.1140, l.161.
[121] GARF (TsGAOR), f.9414, op.1, d.1155. For unknown reasons, the file is listed among those of 1940.
[122] GARF (TsGAOR), f.9414, op.1, d.1140, l.53.
[123] GARF (TsGAOR), f.9414, op.1, d.2740, l.53. The hypothesis seems all the more tempting, since the gap widens in 1937, becomes yawning by 1938, and remains considerable in 1939. See also ll.63 and 75 with a different figure for deaths in 1939 than on l.53 and lower mortality rates in 1939–1940 than the ones given in the 1949 table.

1953.[124] A peculiarity of the document is that while enumerating sentences and arrests up to 1938, it lists fewer people arrested in 1935 and 1936 than sentenced. All the while quoting the same figure for 1935 detentions as does our source, a letter signed by the head of the NKVD also speaks of more persons against whom "proceedings [had been] instituted" than those arrested.[125] We know that some of the victims of the "cleansing" of border zones and major urban centers of "socially alien elements" had been arrested before being banished to faraway localities, although most of them seem to have been exiled without arrest by decisions of the NKVD jurisdiction.[126] We also have information in this period about defendants in affairs of "anti-Soviet" agitation who had been left free pending their trial, as well as instances of the judiciary asking the police to "resolve by administrative order" cases in which there was no legal ground for conviction,[127] a good many of which were not necessarily initiated by the NKVD.

We cannot stress enough the fact that this is only the first exploration of a huge and complex set of sources; little more than scales, ranges, and main trends of evolution can now be established. Although the above-mentioned circumstances cannot guarantee exactitude, there are good reasons for assuming that the data are reliable on the population of strict regime camps, on orders of magnitude, and on the general orientation of penal policy. There is a remarkable consistency in the way numbers, from different sources, evolve over the period under study and a notable coherence among the figures to which different types of documents refer at particular moments.[128]

Moreover, figures produced by researchers using other archival collections of different agencies show close similarities in scale. Documents of the People's Commissariat of Finance discuss a custodial population whose size is not different from the one we have established.[129] In the same way, the labor force envisioned by the economic plans of the GULAG, found in the files of the Council of People's Commissars, does not imply figures in excess of our documentation.[130] Last but not least, the "NKVD contingent" of the 1937 and 1939 censuses is also consistent with the data we have for detainees and exiles.[131]

[124] V. P. Popov published part of these tables ("Gosudarstvennyi terror v sovetskoi Rossii, 1923–1953 gg.," *Otechestvennye arkhivy*, no. 2 [1992]: 28). Besides combining several columns that masked many significant details, this publication lists eight executions for 1949, although none are given in the source for that year. Capital punishment was abolished in May 1947 and reintroduced in early 1950 (*Vedomosti Verkhovnogo Soveta SSSR*, no. 17 [1947]: 1; no. 3 [1950]: 1).

[125] GARF (TsGAOR), f.8131sch, op.27, d.70, l.138. Nevertheless, this document gives slightly higher figures for the number of convictions by different police bodies than the 1953 table. An explanation for this circumstance may be that the letter was written in early 1936, when the outcome of certain appeals was not clear.

[126] GARF (TsGAOR), f.8131sch, op.27, ll.135, 139; d.58, l.138; d.59, l.187.

[127] GARF (TsGAOR), f.9474, op.1, d.97, l.7; "Smolensk Archive," WKP 237, 55.

[128] See, for example, GARF (TsGAOR), f.8131sch, op.27, d.70, ll.104, 141; f.9414, op.1, d.20, ll.135, 149.

[129] V. V. Tsaplin, "Arkhivnye materialy o chisle zakliuchennykh v kontse 30-kh godov," *Voprosy istorii*, nos. 4–5 (1991): 157–60.

[130] See Oleg V. Khlevniuk, "Prinuditel'nyi trud v ekonomike SSSR, 1929–1941 gody," *Svobodnaia mysl'*, no. 13 (1992): 73–84.

[131] See E. M. Andreev, L. E. Darskii, and T. L. Khar'kova, *Istoriia Naseleniia SSSR 1920–1959 gg.* (vypusk 3–5, chast' I, of *Ekspress-informatsiia, seriia: Istoriia statistiki*) (Moscow, 1990), 31, 37; V. N. Zemskov, "Ob uchete spetskontingenta NKVD vo vsesoiuznykh perepisiakh naseleniia 1937 i 1939 gg.," *Sotsiologicheskie issledovaniia*, no. 2 (1991): 74–75.

Appendix (a). USSR Custodial Populations, 1934–1943

	1934	1935	1936	1937	1938	1939	1940	1941	1942	1943
GULAG CAMPS										
Jan. 1 population to the	510,307	725,483	839,406	820,881	996,367	1,317,195	1,344,408	1,500,524	1,415,596	983,974
GULAG from:										
NKVD camps	100,389	67,265	157,355	211,486	202,721	348,417	498,399	488,964	246,273	114,152
Other places of detention	445,187	409,663	431,442	636,749	803,007	383,994	644,927	840,712	544,583	355,728
Recaptures	46,752	45,988	35,891	35,460	22,679	9,838	8,839	6,528	4,984	3,074
Other	1,374	1,412	1,381	-1,116	7,758	7,398	6,237	7,459	10,207	4,221
from the GULAG to:										
NKVD camps	103,002	72,190	170,484	214,607	240,466	347,444	563,338	540,205	252,174	140,756
Other places of detention	17,169	28,976	23,826	43,916	55,790	74,882	57,213	135,537	186,577	140,093
Freed	147,272	211,035	369,544	364,437	279,966	223,622	316,825	624,276	509,538	336,153
Died	26,295	28,328	20,595	25,376	90,546	50,502	46,665	100,997	248,877	166,967
Escaped	83,490	67,493	58,313	58,264	32,033	12,333	11,813	10,592	11,822	6,242
Other	1,298	2,383	1,832	2,725	16,536	13,651	6,432	16,984	12,917	7,344
Dec. 31 population:	725,483	839,406	820,881	996,367	1,317,195	1,344,408	1,500,524	1,415,596	983,974	663,594
Annual change	215,176	113,923	-18,525	175,486	320,828	27,213	156,116	-84,928	-431,622	-320,380
death rate/1000	52	39	25	31	91	38	35	67	176	170
"Counterrevolutionaries":										
Jan. 1 population	135,190	118,256	105,849	104,826	185,324	454,432	444,999	420,293	407,988	345,597
Annual change	-16,934	-12,407	-1,023	80,498	269,108	-433	-24,706	-12,305	-62,591	-76,536
Percent of GULAG population	26.5	16.3	12.6	12.8	18.6	34.5	33.1	28.7	29.6	35.6
LABOR COLONIES										
Jan. 1 population	—	240,259	457,088	375,488	885,203	355,243	315,584	429,205	360,447	500,208
Dec. 31 population	—	457,088	375,488	885,203	355,243	315,584	429,205	360,447	500,208	516,225
Annual change	—	216,829	-81,600	509,715	-529,960	-39,659	113,621	-68,758	139,761	16,017
PRISONS										
Jan. 15 population	—	—	—	—	—	350,538	190,266	487,739	277,992	235,313

Appendix (b). USSR Custodial Populations, 1943–1953

	1944	1945	1946	1947	1948	1949	1950	1951	1952	1953
GULAG CAMPS										
Jan. 1 population	663,594	715,506	600,897	808,839	1,108,057	1,216,361	1,416,300	1,533,767	1,711,202	1,727,970
to the GULAG from:										
NKVD camps	48,428	59,707	172,844	121,633	213,102	564,800	561,660	657,557	603,093	393,504
Other places of detention	326,928	361,121	461,562	624,345	482,498	88,235	71,339	55,291	14,849	16,853
Recaptures	1,839	953	1,203	1,599	2,494	1,733	1,723	1,341	905	415
Other	2,394	2,136	579	1,043	870	1,054	1,329	833	5	—
from the GULAG to:										
NKVD camps	64,110	96,438	182,647	153,899	203,938	239,762	258,269	250,836	221,619	278,240
Other places of detention	39,303	70,187	99,332	58,782	100,901	16,344	16,882	21,845	15,836	8,934
Freed	152,131	336,750	115,700	194,886	261,148	178,449	216,210	254,269	329,446	937,352
Died	60,948	43,848	18,154	35,668	27,605	15,739	14,703	15,587	10,604	5,825
Escaped	3,586	2,196	2,642	3,779	4,261	2,583	2,577	2,318	1,253	785
Other	7,590	6,105	9,771	2,388	2,162	3,006	333	295	578	1,949
Dec. 31 population:	715,506	600,897	808,839	1,108,057	1,216,361	1,416,361	1,533,767	1,711,202	1,727,970	
Annual change	51,912	−114,609	207,942	299,218	108,304	199,939	117,467	117,435	16,768	−830,919
death rate/1000	92	61	30	44	25	13	10	10	6	3
"Counterrevolutionaries":										
Jan. 1 population	268,861	283,351	333,833	427,653	416,156	420,696	578,912	475,976	480,766	465,256
Annual change	14,490	50,482	93,820	−11,497	4,540	153,216	—	4,790	−15,510	—
Percent of GULAG pop.	40.7	41.2	59.2	54.3	38.0	34.9	22.7	31.0	28.1	26.9
LABOR COLONIES										
Jan. 1 population	516,225	745,171	956,224	912,794	1,091,478	1,140,324	1,145,051	994,379	793,312	740,554
Dec. 31 population	745,171	956,224	912,794	1,091,478	1,140,324	1,145,051	994,379	793,312	740,554	463,252
Annual change	228,946	211,053	−43,430	178,684	48,846	4,727	−150,672	−201,067	−52,758	−277,302
PRISONS										
Jan. 15 population	155,213	279,969	261,500	306,163	275,850	—	—	—	—	—

NOTE: The 1938 data for the population of colonies also includes prison inmates, who numbered 548,417 on February 10, 1938, and the 1946 population, which contains 444,500 persons sentenced to "corrective work" without detention; GARF (TsGAOR), fond 9414, opis' 1, delo 330, listy 55; d. 1139, l. 88; d. 1259, l. 18). The 1950 figure for "politicals" includes detainees in labor colonies. Camp and colony data are unavailable for December 31, 1953, and are here replaced by the numbers for April 1, 1954, when 448,344 "counterrevolutionaries" were held at these places of detention.

SOURCES: GARF (TsGAOR), fond 9414, opis' 1, delo 1155, listy 2-3 (camps and "counterrevolutionaries," 1934–47); d. 1190, l. 36; d. 1319, ll. 2-15, d. 1356, ll. 2-3 (camps and "counterrevolutionaries," 1948–53); f. 9413, op. 1, d. 11, ll. 1-10 (prisons); A. N. Dugin and A. Ia. Malygin, "Solzhenitsyn, Rybakov: Tekhnologiia lzhi," *Voenno-istoricheskii zhurnal*, no. 7, 1991, 68–70 (for colonies: calculations verified by V. N. Zemskov on the basis of GARF (TsGAOR), f. 9414, op. 1, d. 330, l. 55). See also A Note on Sources.

[8]

Бабьи Бунты and Peasant Women's Protest during Collectivization

LYNNE VIOLA

Bab'i bunty were an integral part of the rural landscape during the years of wholesale (or сплошная) collectivization. The term could be translated roughly as "women's riots," yet this translation does not begin to do justice to its specific cultural and historical evocations. "Бабий" (the adjective) is a colloquial expression for women that refers in particular to country women with country ways. The "баба" (singular noun) is most often perceived as illiterate, ignorant (in the broader sense of "некультурная"), superstitious, a rumor-monger, and, in general, given to irrational outbursts of hysteria. The *baba*, might best be seen as a colorful combination of the American "hag," "fishwife," and "woman driver" all rolled into a peasant mold. The element of stereotype is evident. Accordingly, the modifier colors and reinforces the noun that follows. A "бунт" is a spontaneous, uncontrolled, and uncontrollable explosion of peasant opposition to authority. Not quite a demonstration, it is often aimless (at least in the mind of official observers), generally unpredictable, and always dangerous. A "*babii bunt*," then, is a women's riot characterized by female hysteria, irrational behavior, unorganized and inarticulate protest, and violent actions.

Such, in any case, were the denotation and connotation of the term as used by Communist Party leaders, local activists, and other observers during collectivization. Rarely, if ever, were *bab'i bunty* described or evaluated in political or ideological terms. The causes of the *bab'i bunty* were generally attributed either to the instigation of agitators, the "kulaks" and "*podkulachniki*" (kulak henchmen), who supposedly exploited the irrational hysteria of the *baba* for their own counterrevolutionary purposes, or else blamed on the reckless and lawless actions of the cadres who implemented collectivization and had succumbed to "dizziness from success." *Bab'i bunty* appear to have been tolerated to a far greater extent than were similar protests led by peasant men. They also seem to have been dealt with less harshly in cases when criminal charges ensued, the women escaping prosecution under the RSFSR penal code article 58 for counterrevolutionary crimes. The *baba* was not perceived as the fairer sex, but as the darker sector

24   *The Russian Review*

of the already dark peasant masses; consequently, like an unruly child or a butting goat, she was often not held responsible for her actions although sometimes subject to reprimand and punishment.

Officials' perceptions of peasant actions are generally based on assumptions about peasant ways and mores. As Daniel Field has demonstrated, however, peasants appear at times to have exploited these official assumptions about themselves for their own ends. Field suggests that peasants manipulated their reputation for naive monarchism as a means of deflecting punishment and as a rationalization for confrontations with officials who, according to peasant claims, were violating the will of the tsar.[1] Although the *baba* was no longer a naive monarchist during the First Five-Year Plan period (despite some cases of a Soviet-style naive monarchism that pitted Stalin and the Central Committee of the Communist Party against local officials after the publication of Stalin's article "Dizziness from Success"), it may well be that the *bab'i bunty* belied the official perception of peasant women's protest and were neither as irrational nor as hysterical as they appeared to outside observers.

This article is an exploration of the anatomy of the *bab'i bunty* and the protest of peasant women during collectivization. It is an attempt to examine the basis of peasant women's protest, the forms that such protest assumed, and the influence of official perceptions of and government reactions to the women's actions. The article is not intended as a comprehensive treatment of peasant women during collectivization. Nor is it meant to imply that *all* peasant women were opposed to collectivization. Due to the inevitable source problems connected with a topic such as this, the article will necessarily be somewhat impressionistic and the conclusions tentative. It is based on cases of protest in (ethnically) Russian and Ukrainian villages where the *bab'i bunty* occurred; the responses of women to collectivization in Central Asia and in non-Slavic villages are not explored, due to the very different cultural styles of women there and the absence of any overt or exclusively female peasant protest in these areas.

The collectivization of Soviet agriculture gave rise to a massive wave of peasant protest and violence in the countryside during the late 1920s and early 1930s. Peasant unrest began on the eve of wholesale collectivization in 1928 during the implementation of "extraordinary measures" (i.e., forced requisitions) in state grain procurements. It continued, at varying levels of intensity, to the end of the First Five-Year Plan, by which time wholesale collectivization was basically

---

[1] Daniel Field, *Rebels in the Name of the Tsar*, Boston, 1976, pp. 23, 209-210, 214.

completed.[2] The largest waves of peasant protest appear to have occurred in the second half of 1929 and in the years 1930-31. In 1929, for example, 30,000 fires were registered in the RSFSR alone and many, if not most, were attributed to arson, or the *krasnyi petukh*.[3] The number of cases of rural mass disturbances prosecuted under article 59[2] of the RSFSR criminal code increased in 1929 from 172 in the first half of the year to 229 in the second half of the year.[4] Although similar statistical data for 1930-31 are more difficult to extract from the sources, there is little doubt that the wave of violence and unrest in those years far surpassed that of the second half of 1929.[5] Peasant violence and protest were an inevitable byproduct of forced grain requisitions, collectivization, and dekulakization and were shaped by the traditional peasant approach to radical politics.

The Communist Party was aware of the dissatisfaction of the peasantry on the eve of and during the collectivization drives of 1930-31. Party concern over the extent of peasant unrest, moreover, appears to have played a significant role in shaping policy. Olga Narkiewicz has concluded that "it was the fear of a full-scale peasant revolution (whether real or imagined)" that induced the party leadership to pursue the policy of all-out collectivization in the late autumn of 1929.[6] R. W.

---

[2] By the end of 1931, approximately 60% of peasant households were collectivized. See I. E. Zelenin, "Kolkhoznoe stroitel'stvo v SSSR v 1931-1932 gg.," *Istoriia SSSR*, 1960, no. 6, p. 23.

[3] V. P. Danilov, M. P. Kim, and N. V. Tropkin, eds., *Sovetskoe krest'ianstvo. Kratkii ocherk istorii (1917-1970)*, 2nd ed., Moscow, 1973, p. 280.

[4] "Doklad o rabote UKK Verkhsuda RSFSR za vtoruiu polovinu 1929 g.," *Sudebnaia praktika*, no. 8, 10 June 1930, p. 12.

[5] For a rough indication of the scope of peasant unrest in the early part of 1930, see R. W. Davies, *The Socialist Offensive: The Collectivisation of Soviet Agriculture, 1929-1930*, Cambridge, MA, 1980, pp. 257-258. According to one Soviet article (which, unfortunately, provides no source), there were 1,678 armed uprisings in the countryside in the period January to March 1930 alone. See B. A. Abramov and T. K. Kocharli, "Ob oshibkakh v odnoi knige. (Pis'mo v redaktsiiu)," *Voprosy istorii KPSS*, 1975, no. 5, p. 137. In the Lower Volga, there were 165 riots (волынок) in March 1930 and 195 in April 1930 according to V. K. Medvedev, *Krutoi povorot (Iz istorii kollektivizatsii sel'skogo khoziaistva Nizhnego Povolzh'ia)*, Saratov, 1961, p. 119. In the Middle Volga, there were 319 uprisings in the first four months of 1930, as compared to 33 for the same months of 1929 according to F. A. Karevskii, "Likvidatsiia kulachestva kak klassa v Srednem Povolzh'e," *Istoricheskie zapiski*, vol. 80, 1967, p. 92. And, finally, in Siberia, in the first half of 1930, there were 1000 "registered terrorist acts" according to N. Ia. Gushchin, "Likvidatsiia kulachestva kak klassa v Sibirskoi derevne," *Sotsial'naia struktura naseleniia Sibiri*, Novosibirsk, 1970, p. 122. Data on 1931 are more scarce, but according to Zelenin, in the spring of 1931, there were open attacks (e.g., arson, destruction of livestock and agricultural equipment, etc.) in 15.8% of all collective farms; see Zelenin, "Kolkhoznoe stroitel'stvo," p. 31.

[6] O. A. Narkiewicz, "Stalin, War Communism and Collectivization," *Soviet Studies*, vol. 18, no. 1, July 1966, p. 37.

26 *The Russian Review*

Davies has linked the March 1930 "retreat" from breakneck collectivization inaugurated by Stalin's 2 March article, "Dizziness from Success," and the Central Committee decree of 14 March to the widespread peasant unrest of the first months of 1930.[7] This second contention is, in fact, frankly expressed in the later editions of the official history of the Communist Party of the Soviet Union.[8] The party publicly acknowledged the extent and dangers of peasant dissatisfaction in the months following the March retreat and, in particular, at the Sixteenth Congress of the Communist Party in late June and early July of 1930. This acknowledgement was to be the most explicit admission of the extent of the threat to the state posed by peasant unrest during collectivization.

Speakers at the Sixteenth Party Congress noted the key role played by women in the protest against collectivization and the collective farm. Although the extent and intensity of the women's protest were not specified, they were serious enough for Lazar Kaganovich to make the following remark:

We know that in connection with the excesses [перегибы] in the collective farm movement, women in the countryside in many cases played the most "advanced" role in the reaction against the collective farm.[9]

A. A. Andreev, the first secretary of the North Caucasus Regional Party Committee, seconded Kaganovich, claiming that women were in the vanguard in the protests and disturbances over collectivization.[10] These claims received concrete substantiation in reports written by workers and officials who served in the countryside during collectivization.[11] The reasons for the "vanguard" role of peasant women in the protest against collectivization were considered to be the low cultural and political level and backwardness of peasant women, the "incorrect approach" of rural officials, "dizzy from success," to the volatile women, and, finally, the exploitation of the women's irrational fears and potential for mass hysteria by the kulak and the omnipresent *podkulachnik*.

[7] Davies, *The Socialist Offensive*, pp. 255-256. For Stalin's article and the Central Committee decree, see I. Stalin, "Golovokruzhenie ot uspekhov. K voprosam kolkhoznogo dvizheniia," *Sochineniia*, vol. 12, Moscow, 1952, pp. 191-199; and *KPSS v rezoliutsiiakh i resheniiakh s"ezdov, konferentsii i plenumov TsK*, 7th ed., part 2, Moscow, 1953, pp. 548-551.

[8] *Istoriia KPSS*, 2nd ed., Moscow, 1962, p. 444; and 3rd ed., Moscow, 1969, p. 405.

[9] *XVI s"ezd VKP (b). Stenograficheskii otchet*, Moscow-Leningrad, 1930, p. 70.

[10] *XVI s"ezd VKP (b)*, p. 123.

[11] For example, M. N. Chernomorskii, "Rol' rabochikh brigad v bor'be za sploshnuiu kollektivizatsiiu v Tambovskoi derevne," *Materialy po istorii SSSR. Dokumenty po istorii Sovetskogo obshchestva*, fasc. 1, Moscow, 1955, pp. 347-348, 350, 354, 364-366, 369, 375; and examples cited below, pp. 30, 35-37.

Бабьи бунты   27

The party's response to women's protest against collectivization was different from its response to (male) peasant protest in general, which was usually labeled kulak opposition and dealt with by increasing the level of repression. Instead of repressive measures (although these were not always excluded), the party emphasized a more "correct approach" to peasant women—an end to the excesses—on the part of rural officials and the need to improve work among women.[12] The importance of work among women, in fact, had been a concern from at least the time of the grain procurement crisis when the potential dangers of female-led opposition to Soviet policy became clear.[13] Work among women basically had two objectives. First, it was held necessary to educate women and expand political indoctrination among them. A second task was drawing more women into active involvement in the political life of the village through participation in the women's delegate meetings, soviet elections, and membership in local soviets and the Communist Party. And, indeed, during the years of collectivization, there was a gradual, but noted improvement in such work as local officials were implored to pay more attention to women and increasing numbers of women were recruited to the party and elected to the boards of local soviets.[14] The state's response and its emphasis on the need to improve work among women were predicated upon the official conception of peasant women's protest as essentially non-political and a function of the ignorance and backwardness of the *baba*.

[12] *XVI s"ezd VKP (b)*, pp. 70, 457. Also see similar statements in *Kollektivizatsiia sel'skogo khoziaistva na Severnom Kavkaze (1927-1937 gg.)*, Krasnodar, 1972, pp. 262-264, 266; and *Zapadnyi oblastnoi komitet VKP (b). Vtoraia oblastnaia partkonferentsiia (5-12 iiunia 1930 g.). Stenograficheskii otchet*, Moscow-Smolensk, 1931, pp. 164-165.

[13] To cite just two examples of such concern, at the Fourteenth All-Russian Congress of Soviets in May 1929, a peasant woman activist and delegate from Siberia stressed the need to improve work among women in light of a series of *bab'i bunty* during grain requisitioning. This plea then was echoed by A. V. Artiukhina, the last head of the *Zhenotdel* before its dissolution in 1930, at the Second Session of VTsIK (All-Russian Central Executive Committee of the Soviets), Fourteenth Convocation, in November 1929. Artiukhina warned that if such work was not improved, "backward" peasant women would not support collectivization and would be exploited by the kulak. See *XIV Vserossiiskii s"ezd sovetov. Stenograficheskii otchet*, Moscow, 1929, Biulleten' no. 3, pp. 11-12; and *II sessiia VTsIK XIV sozyva. Stenograficheskii otchet*, Moscow, 1929, Biulleten' no. 7, pp. 25-28.

[14] See, for examples, *Chto nuzhno znat' kazhdomu rabotniku kolkhoza? (Dlia 25000 tov., edushchikh v kolkhozy)*, Moscow, 1930, p. 7; *Derevenskii kommunist*, no. 1, 12 January 1930, p. 32; and M. Kureiko, *25-tysiachniki na kolkhoznoi stroike*, Moscow-Leningrad, 1931, pp. 44-45. For information on the expanding role of women in political life in the countryside, see Dorothy Atkinson, *The End of the Russian Land Commune, 1905-1930*, Stanford, CA, 1983, pp. 367-368; and Ethel Dunn, "Russian Rural Women," in Dorothy Atkinson, Alexander Dallin, and Gail Warshofsky Lapidus, eds., *Women in Russia*, Stanford, CA, 1977, p. 173.

Nevertheless, the party's efforts were too little and too late. Moreover, and despite periodic waves of party and government expulsions and purges to offset local excesses, the party's contradictory demands of a "correct approach" to the peasantry and the timely implementation of often brutal policies made it highly unlikely that the rough, civil-war methods of rural officials would be or could be tempered or civilized. Nor could the party mitigate the effect that it perceived the kulak and *podkulachnik* had in sparking women's opposition and the *bab'i bunty*. As a consequence, the party failed to quiet the fears of many peasant women or to prevent the wave of *bab'i bunty* that erupted in the countryside as a reaction to both rumor and reality.

The Communist Party claimed that the underlying basis of women's protest during collectivization was irrational female hysteria unleashed by the "kulak *agitprop*," or the rumor-mill, and reinforced by the women's *petit bourgeois*, small landholder instincts. It was true that the rumor-mill often played a very important role in sparking *bab'i bunty* and women's protest; it was also true that peasant women's "*petit bourgeois* instincts" played a central role in their opposition to collectivization and the transformation of the life of the village that it entailed. However, the protest engendered by the rumor-mill and by some of the policies of collectivization was not always "irrational" or the manifestation of a *petit bourgeois* class consciousness.

Rumors about collectivization and the collective farm raged through the countryside. Heated discussions took place in village squares, at the wells, in the cooperative shops, and at the market.[15] At one and the same time, there were tales of the return of the Whites and the *pomeshchiki* (landlords), the coming of Antichrist, Polish *pans*, and the Chinese, the arrival of commissars, Bolsheviks, Communists, and Soviet gendarmes, and impending famine and devastation.[16] Among the rumors were many that struck a particular resonance in the minds and hearts of peasant women. These rumors, broadly speaking, touched upon questions of religion, the family, and everyday life.

---

[15] Sadovnikov, "Shefstvo nad kolkhozom 'Revoliutsii'," *Sovetskaia iustitsiia*, no. 6, 28 February 1930, pp. 5-6.

[16] These rumors were widespread and have been gleaned from many different sources. See, for examples, TsGAOR (Central State Archive of the October Revolution, Moscow), *f.* 5470, *op.* 14, *d.* 204, *l.* 54 (trade union of chemical workers, *svodka* on the work of Leningrad 25,000ers in the countryside); I. A. Ivanov, "Pomoshch' leningradskikh rabochikh v kollektivizatsii sel'skogo khoziaistva podshefnykh raionov," *Rabochie Leningrada v bor'be za pobedu sotsializma*, Moscow-Leningrad, 1963, p. 219; N. A. Ivnitskii and D. M. Ezerskii, eds., "Dvadtsatipiatitysiachniki i ikh rol' v kollektivizatsii sel'skogo khoziaistva v 1930 g.," *Materialy po istorii SSSR. Dokumenty po istorii Sovetskogo obshchestva*, fasc. 1, Moscow, 1955, pp. 425-426; and *Sotsialisticheskoe zemledelie*, 31 December 1930, p. 3.

Бабьи бунты   29

Some of them assumed fantastic dimensions; others—whether fantastic or not—were sometimes based on actual occurrences.

Rumors concerning the Apocalypse were widespread at this time. During the initial stages of collectivization, there was a wholesale attack on religion and the Church, which, although largely the result of actions of local crusaders and militant atheists, was not officially condemned by Moscow until after March 1930. At this time, churches were closed down and transformed into clubs or offices, church bells were removed, village priests were hounded and imprisoned, and icons were burned. Both the onslaught on religion and the scale of the general offensive on traditional ways of life in the village served to encourage an apocalyptic mindset among the peasantry.

The collective farm became the symbol of the Antichrist on earth. In one village, old women asked, "Is it true or not?—they say that all who join the collective farm will be signed over to the Antichrist."[17] On the eve of collectivization, reports from the North Caucasus claimed that a certain personage assuming the identity of Christ was wandering through the villages proclaiming the coming of the Last Judgment. He had in his possession a document from the Virgin Mary calling for everyone to leave the collective farm prior to Judgment Day or else to face the wrath of God. The Christ of the North Caucasus also had a blacklist of collective farmers for use on Judgment Day.[18] When, in the autumn of 1929, the church was closed in the Ukrainian village of Bochkarko, it was claimed that a miraculous light issued from the church and a sign appeared on the cupola, which read: "Do not join the collective farm or I will smite thee."[19] In the village of Brusianka (Bazhenskii *raion*, Sverdlovskii *okrug*, in the Urals), tickets to the next world went on sale; they were sold in three classes and prices ranged from 50 kopeks to 2 rubles 50 kopeks.[20]

Peasant women were especially susceptible to rumors about the Apocalypse and Antichrist and to news of events like those described above. The peasant woman was the upholder of religion within the village and household, so it was natural that the attacks on religion and the Church often affected women most acutely. The peasant woman,

---

[17] L. Berson, *Vesna 1930 goda. Zapiska dvadtsatipiatitysiachnika*, Moscow, 1931, pp. 18-19.

[18] TsGAOR, *f.* 5469, *op.* 13, *d.* 123, *ll.* 28-40 (*Dokladnye zapiski* on the activities of metal workers in the North Caucasus countryside in the fall of 1929; compiled by the metal-workers union).

[19] TsGAOR, *f.* 5469, *op.* 13, *d.* 123, *ll.* 78-91 (*Dokladnye zapiski* on the activities of metal-workers in the Ukrainian countryside in the fall of 1929; compiled by the metal workers union).

[20] A. Angarov, "Sel'sovet i likvidatsiia kulachestva kak klassa," *Bol'shevik*, no. 6, 31 March 1930, p. 25.

however, was also said to be particularly responsive to tales of the supernatural. It may be that women's protest sparked by such fantastic rumors was based on a combination of devotion to the faith and superstition. It may also be that tales of the Apocalypse, which forecast an imminent cataclysm in which God destroys the ruling powers of evil and raises the righteous to life in a messianic kingdom, served as a religious justification (either perceived to be real or exploited as a pretext) for peasant resistance to the state or provided a peasant vocabulary of protest.[21] Whether a particular form of peasant protest, a pretext for resistance, or an irrational impulse, peasant women's protest raised by religious rumors and the attack on the Church derived at least in part from legitimate concerns over the fate of the Church and the believers.

There were also rumors that touched upon questions of the family and everyday life and that were especially troubling to peasant women. Some of these rumors were in the realm of the absurd, such as the rumor that spread through the countryside that four thousand young peasant women were to be sent to China to pay for the Far Eastern railroad or the variation of this rumor, which stated that only women weighing over three and one half *puds* (approximately 126 pounds) would be sent to China.[22] Mikhail Sholokhov in the novel *Virgin Soil Upturned* provides another example of rumor in the category of the absurd, most probably a variation of a rumor in actual circulation. Sholokhov writes:

> There was a nun in the village the day before yesterday .... She spent the night at Timofei Borshchov's and told them the fowls had been got together so we could send them to town for the townsfolk to make noodle soup with, then we would fix up little chairs for the old women, a special shape, with straw on them, and make them sit on our eggs until they hatched, and any old woman who rebelled would be tied to her chair.[23]

This rumor clearly verged on the fantastic, but it should be noted that it was based on two real grievances that women held during collectivization. These concerned the socialization of domestic livestock—the economic mainstay of a peasant woman's existence—and the introduction of incubators, opposition to which was due either to the fact that

---

[21] During the Schism, the Old Believers often expressed protest in similar terms. Moreover, an apocalyptic mindset among peasants seems to be a characteristic response at times of momentous upheaval and transformation. See, for example, Michael Cherniavsky, "The Old Believers and the New Religion," in Michael Cherniavsky, ed., *The Structure of Russian History*, New York, 1970, pp. 140-188.

[22] Angarov, "Sel'sovet i likvidatsiia," p. 25.

[23] Mikhail Sholokhov, *Virgin Soil Upturned*, tr. by Robert Daglish, vol. 1, Moscow, 1980, p. 176.

their use was predicated on the socialization of poultry or else the perhaps frightening novelty of their appearance.

In addition to these rumors, there were a series of rumors of equally fantastic dimensions, which claimed that collectivization would bring with it the socialization of children, the export of women's hair, communal wife-sharing, and the notorious common blanket under which all collective farmers, both male and female, would sleep.[24] These rumors were of obvious concern to women and, moreover, very possibly were inspired by cases when local officials either attempted to implement similar practices or told peasants that such practices were in the offing. For example, the 25,000er Gorbunevskii, working in the Crimea, announced on 1 March 1930 that his collective farm would become a commune and that all of the peasant children would be socialized. When the parents of the soon-to-be socialized children heard this, they began a massive slaughter of their also soon-to-be socialized livestock, fortunately sparing the children.[25] The RSFSR Commissar of Justice, N. M. Ianson, told of a case involving an "aesthetic deviation" that may have been the basis of tales of the export of women's hair. According to Ianson, there was a local Communist in the Urals—a former partisan and party member from 1917 or 1918—who made all the village women cut their hair short. Ianson claimed that the Communist took seriously (and literally) the propaganda centering on the need to create a new life (быт) in the village and to bring the countryside closer to the city. The Communist felt that short hair—as well as the introduction of short skirts—would give the *baba* a more urban look. One *baba*, who felt differently, wrote in a letter of complaint, "he has shamed us for all of our life, only death remains ...."[26] Rumors of the common blanket, which were probably the most pervasive of all, also may have derived from one or two cases when local activists discussed the promise of communism. One *Rabkrin* (Workers' and Peasants' Inspectorate) plenipotentiary told women that they would all have to sleep, along with all of the men, under one common blanket.[27] In the North Caucasus, local activists in one village actually went so far as to confiscate all blankets. They told the peasants

[24] Berson, *Vesna 1930 goda*, pp. 18-19; *Bastiony revoliutsii. Stranitsy istorii leningradskikh zavodov*, fasc. 3, Leningrad, 1960, p. 241; and see note 16 above.

[25] *Trud*, 28 March 1930, p. 3.

[26] This local Communist was originally sentenced to six years for his "aesthetic excess" but later the term was lowered. Ianson claimed he was extremely progressive, given his social conditions. See N. M. Ianson, "O peregibakh i ikh ispravlenii," *Sovetskaia iustitsiia*, no. 11, 20 April 1930, p. 3; and "Rech' t. Iansona na 3-om soveshchanii sudebno-prokurorskikh rabotnikov," *Sovetskaia iustitsiia*, no. 24/25, 10-20 September 1930, pp. 7-8.

[27] *Sovetskaia iustitsiia*, no. 13, 10 May 1930, p. 10 (Editorial by P. I. Stuchka).

that henceforth there would be no more individual blankets; all would
sleep on a 700 meter-long bed under a 700 meter-long blanket.[28]

Many of these rumors clearly played upon the real fears of peasant
women concerning issues of family and everyday life. Moreover, given
the enormity of the transformation implemented by the state at this
time along with the "excesses," the horrendously low level of rural
officialdom, and the actual occurrence of any number of bizarre
instances such as those described above, one can only say with difficulty
that peasant women's protest was irrational. One could perhaps claim,
as Petro Grigorenko suggests in his memoirs, that women often simply
exploited the rumors of the absurd, without really believing them, as a
way to attack the collective farm under the guise of irrational, nonpolitical protest and, consequently, as a way to avoid the suppression of
resistance by outside forces (armed civilian forces, security troops, or
the militia) as might have been the case in an overtly anti-Soviet village
uprising.[29] The plausibility of this suggestion will be examined below.
For now, it is sufficient to conclude that, whether pretext or actual
belief, the rumor-mill struck a deep chord among peasant women who
saw many of their most cherished beliefs and domestic interests under
attack.

Rumors, however, were not always the spark behind the *bab'i
bunty*. Quite often, protest was triggered directly by clearly articulated
opposition to the implementation of radical policies. This opposition
raises the issue of the "*petit bourgeois* instincts" of peasant women.
Such "instincts," indeed, formed a part of the basis for resistance and
figure largely in the rumor-mill, but opposition to policy deriving from
so-called "*petit bourgeois*" concerns was often less motivated by
"instinct" than by a set of rational interests, revolving around the family and the domestic economy. For example, peasant women led the
protest against attempts to socialize domestic livestock because the
domestic livestock was generally the basis and justification of the
woman's economic position within the household. Women also protested directly and without recourse to the rumor-mill over issues concerning their children. Once again, the socialization of domestic livestock could be a threat because the loss of a milch cow could very well
mean that peasant children would be without milk.[30] In later years,

---

[28] Angarov, "Sel'sovet i likvidatsiia," p. 21.

[29] Petro G. Grigorenko, *Memoirs*, tr. by Thomas P. Whitney, New York, 1982, p. 35.

[30] Anna Louise Strong, *The Soviets Conquer Wheat*, New York, 1931, p. 37. It should
be noted that Beatrice Farnsworth briefly mentions the rational content of the *bab'i bunty*
of collectivization in an essay that appeared as this article was being revised. See her
interesting "Village Women Experience the Revolution," in Abbott Gleason, Peter
Kenez, and Richard Stites, eds., *Bolshevik Culture: Experiment and Order in the Russian
Revolution*, Bloomington, 1985, p. 254.

Stalin even admitted how important an issue the loss of a cow had been in provoking women's opposition to the collective farm when he said, "in the not too distant past, Soviet power had a little misunderstanding with the collective farm women. The issue was cows."[31] In one village, a *babii bunt* occurred over the proposed closing of a mill. The women's concern here was that, "we cannot feed our children" if the mill closes down.[32] Some women also objected to the introduction of nurseries. According to Maurice Hindus, the Ukrainian-born American reporter, this was due to the high infant mortality rate in the village. Hindus claimed that there was not a woman in the village that he visited who had not lost a child in infancy, so it was natural that these women were reluctant to entrust their children to the care of others. (This reluctance, moreover, was particularly appropriate, given the experience of caring for socialized livestock.)[33] None of these concerns derived from "instinct"; rather, they were legitimate and articulate protest against specific policies and practices associated with the initial stages of collectivization.

It is evident that official perceptions of the basis of peasant women's protest were at least in part misconceived and that the *content* of women's protest was rational and based on legitimate concerns. The question that now arises is the extent to which official perceptions about the *form* of women's protest, the *babii bunt*, were accurate?

The *bab'i bunty* were depicted as spontaneous outbursts of mass hysteria marked by indiscriminate violence, disorder, and a cacophony of high-pitched voices all shouting demands at once. Groups of women assembled at the village square became "milling crowds." And behind every *babii bunt* could be found a kulak or *podkulachnik* agitator who exploited the ignorant, irrational *babas*. Instead of calmly discussing grievances in an organized, "cultured" manner, reports describing women's protest claimed, for example, that, at soviet meetings, the women would simply vote against *all* measures of Soviet power regardless of content or that, at secret meetings against the collective farm in March and April 1930, the women (who formed the majority of those in attendance and were the most active participants) would all talk at once with neither chairman or agenda, in an atmosphere of bedlam.[34] Women often physically blocked the carting away of requisitioned grain

---

[31] Stalin, "Rech' na pervom vsesoiuznom s"ezde kolkhoznikov-udarnikov," *Sochineniia*, vol. 13, p. 252.

[32] V. Denisov, *Odin iz dvadtsati piati tysiach*, Krasnoiarsk, 1967, pp. 19-21.

[33] Maurice Hindus, *Red Bread*, New York, 1931, p. 14.

[34] Berson, *Vesna 1930 goda*, p. 73; S. Leikin, "Raskulachennyi kulak i ego taktika," *Bol'shevik*, no. 13, 15 July 1930, p. 74; Sadovnikov, "Shefstvo nad kolkhozom 'Revoliutsii'," *Sovetskaia iustitsiia*, no. 6, 28 February 1930, pp. 5-6.

34   *The Russian Review*

or the entrances to huts of peasants scheduled to be exiled as kulaks, forcibly took back socialized seed and livestock, and led assaults on officials. The response of officials was frequently to hide or run away and to allow the *bab'i bunty* to take their course until the women ran out of steam—for the most part without recourse to the use of force. In the first half of 1930, the end result was generally the dissolution of the collective farm. The women were seldom held responsible for their actions, thanks to official perceptions of the basis of such actions. The *bab'i bunty* thus accomplished what they set out to accomplish and the state held strong in its perceptions of peasant women's protest.

There is a most illuminating case, rare in its detail, of a *babii bunt* in the Russian village of Belovka in Chistopol canton in the Tatar ASSR in 1929 which perfectly illustrates official perceptions of and reactions to the *bab'i bunty*. The cause of the *babii bunt* in Belovka was a decision made by the local soviet in August 1929 to introduce a five-field system of crop rotation in the village and to carry out a redistribution of peasant lands. Behind the *babii bunt*, according to the description of the case, loomed the "local kulaks" and, in particular, the insidious figure of one Sergei Fomin, the "kulak" miller. The case report read:

> As a result of kulak agitation among the *dark, illiterate* [italics mine—L.V.] peasant women, a crowd of 100 people ... firmly demanded the repeal of the decree on the introduction of the five-field system.

Despite warnings to disperse, the crowd, "supported by the general din," continued its protest, knocking to the ground and beating a member of the local soviet. At this point, other soviet activists entered the fray and, according to the report, prevented the crowd from realizing its presumed intentions of beating the activist to unconsciousness. The case was brought to the attention of the regional court, which prosecuted the ten most active *babas* and the miller Fomin, who was described as the "ideological instigator" of the disturbance. Fomin, who was also charged with setting fire to the local soviet secretary's home, was prosecuted separately, according to "special consideration." The women, prosecuted under article 59² of the criminal code for mass disturbances, were given sentences of imprisonment with strict isolation ranging from two to three years.

The Belovka case was reexamined by the Supreme Court in January 1930, at which time the decision of the regional court was overturned. The Supreme Court held Fomin *exclusively* responsible for the women's actions, describing him as the "ideological inspiration," the "ideological leader [вожак ' and main "culprit" in the disturbance. Fomin's "counterrevolutionary organizational role" in the disturbance was the "actual root" of the *babii bunt* and, according to the Supreme

Court, the regional court had failed to discern this clearly enough. In addition, the Supreme Court accused the local soviet of Belovka of insufficient preliminary preparatory work among women, something that could have mitigated the effects of Fomin's propaganda. Finally, the sentences of the women, all described as illiterate, middle and lower-middle peasants, and representative of the "most backward part of the peasantry" (i.e., women), were lessened to forced labor within the village for periods ranging from six months to one year. The purpose of the sentences was to serve as a warning and an educational measure and *not* as punishment.[35]

This case is instructive in illuminating official views of and reactions to peasant women's protest. In Belovka, the women were viewed as no more than naive dupes of the local kulaks who served as a figurative battering ram against Soviet power. The local soviet's failure to work among the women and prepare them for the new policy transformed them into ammunition, which the kulak could fire at the Soviet regime. However, the Belovka case may not tell the whole story of the *bab'i bunty*. Petro Grigorenko, in his memoirs, described the *bab'i bunty* as a kind of "tactic." The women would initiate opposition to the collective farm or other policies and the men would remain on the sidelines until the local activists attempted to quell the disorder. At that point, the more vulnerable peasant men could safely enter the fray as chivalrous defenders of wives, mothers, and daughters rather than as anti-Soviet *podkulachniki*.[36] Descriptions of *bab'i bunty* by cadres in the field offer confirmation of Grigorenko's findings and appear to belie the official image as presented in the Belovka case.

A riot that occurred in the village of Lebedevka in Kursk at the Budennyi collective farm may serve as an example. A 25,000er by the name of Dobychin, serving as a plenipotentiary for collectivization, arrived in the collective farm on 7 March. Dobychin called a meeting of the peasant women and was greeted with cries of "We do not want a collective farm" and "You want to derail the *muzhik*." Dobychin responded, "We will not hold such types in the collective farm, good riddance .... [s]leep it off and you'll see that we will let the *bedniak* [poor peasant] derail him who made you drunk and sent you here." Dobychin's tactic led to a general uproar and an assault on Dobychin. The women, with one Praskov'ia Avdiushenko in the lead, approached the stage where he stood. Praskov'ia said to Dobychin, "Ah well, come nearer to us." With this, she grabbed the worker by his collar and

---

[35] "Nepravil'noe vydelenie dela ob ideinom vdokhnovitele massovykh bezporiadkov," *Sudebnaia praktika*, no. 3, 28 February 1930, pp. 11-12.

[36] Grigorenko, *Memoirs*, p. 35. Also see Atkinson, *The End of the Russian Land Commune*, pp. 367-368, for support of Grigorenko's conclusion.

36   *The Russian Review*

dragged him off the stage. Dobychin somehow managed to escape, but the unrest continued and even escalated when the church watchman's wife began to ring the church bell. With this, all of the peasants entered the fray. They seized their recently socialized livestock and prepared a collective declaration requesting permission to quit the farm. This disturbance, like many others, was not suppressed, but simply ended with the collapse of the collective farm.[37]

A similar situation was described by the worker Zamiatin who was among those workers recruited from the city soviets in early 1930 to work in the local rural soviets. Zamiatin depicted the situation faced by the 25,000er V. Klinov. Zamiatin said that the approach to Klinov's village resembled an "armed camp"; on his way, he saw a sign nailed to a bridge that read: "Vas'ka [Klinov] you scum, get out. We will break your legs." When he arrived, Zamiatin found the village alive with rumors of the approach of a band of riders who were coming to kill all the Communists and collective farmers. In this village, dekulakization had already been implemented but, as happened elsewhere, the kulaks were not yet removed from the village. This omission, according to Zamiatin, had led to the crisis that existed. With Zamiatin's arrival, Klinov set about preparing for the exile of the kulaks. He began by removing the church bell, which traditionally served as tocsin to gather together the peasants in case of emergency. The heads of kulak families were exiled, and all went well until one of the exiled kulaks returned to announce that the other kulaks would soon be coming back to seek vengeance. This led to the decision to exile the families of the exiled kulak heads of households. The announcement of this decision led to an uproar. The peasant women, in an attempt to forestall this action, blocked the entrances of the huts of the kulak families. Several days later, the women also led the opposition to the attempt to cart away the village's grain by blocking the grain warehouse. This led to a *babii bunt*, followed quickly by a general free-for-all in which all the peasants participated in a pitchfork battle. The disturbance was suppressed by the militia, which was called in after all of the peasants had joined the rebellion.[38]

In both of these cases, peasant women were responsible for initiating the resistance and were soon joined by the peasant men in a general village riot. In a classic depiction of a *babii bunt* in a Cossack village in *Virgin Soil Upturned*, the Cossack men stood at the back of the crowd of women urging them on when they attacked the chairman of the local soviet. Here, the women led the attack on the grain warehouse "with

[37] G. I. Arsenov, *Lebedevka, selo kolkhoznoe*, Kursk, 1964, pp. 43-44.

[38] S. Zamiatin, *Burnyi god. Opyt raboty piatitysiachnika v Rudnianskom raione na Nizhnei Volge*, Moscow, 1931, pp. 9-16.

the silent approval of the menfolk at the back." And while the women were dragging the chairman of the collective farm through the village, the Cossack men broke the locks of the grain warehouse and seized their grain.[39] The women served both as initiators and decoys in this disturbance.

Lev Kopelev has provided yet another description of a *babii bunt*, and one that closely conforms to Grigorenko's hypothesis. Kopelev described a disturbance in a Ukrainian village:

A "riot" also broke out in Okhochaya. A crowd of women stormed the kolkhoz [collective farm] stables and barns. They cried, screamed, wailed, demanding their cows and seed back. The men stood a way off, in clusters, sullenly silent. Some of the lads had pitchforks, stakes, axes tucked in their sashes. The terrified granary man ran away; the women tore off the bolts and together with the men began dragging out the bags of seed.[40]

Here, as elsewhere, the *babii bunt* was the first stage in a general peasant riot. Here too the women had specific aims and, whether the riots were intended to dissolve the collective farm, halt dekulakization, or retake socialized seed and livestock, they accomplished their aims.

Women tended to lead the village riots because they were less vulnerable to repression than peasant men. There were even reports of *bab'i bunty* in 1929 when the women brought their children with them into battle or laid down in front of tractors to block collectivization.[41] In the *bab'i bunty*, the men stood to the side. In non-violent protest, the situation was similar. Peasant men frequently allowed their female relatives to express opposition to policy. According to a report of a worker brigade in Tambov, in the Central Black Earth Region, the men did not go to the meetings on collectivization, but sent the women instead. When asked why they did not attend the meetings, the men replied, "They [the women] are equal now, as they decide so we will agree ...."[42] In this way, it was easy for a peasant to claim that he had not joined the collective farm or surrendered his grain because his wife would not let him or threatened him with divorce. The 25,000er Gruzdev was told by one peasant, "my wife does not want to socialize our cow, so I cannot do this."[43] One peasant man explained the power of

---

[39] Sholokhov, *Virgin Soil Upturned*, vol. 1, pp. 311, 316, 321.

[40] Lev Kopelev, *Education of a True Believer*, New York, 1980, p. 188.

[41] *II sessiia VTsIK XIV sozyva*, Biulleten' no. 7, p. 28.

[42] Chernomorskii, "Rol' rabochikh brigad," p. 325.

[43] Denisov, *Odin iz dvadtsati piati tysiach*, p. 27. It should be noted that in many cases peasant men were sincere about their wives' resistance and that there were reports of divorce and family strife over the collective farm. See Strong, pp. 114-115; and R. Belbei, *Za ili protiv. (Kak rabochii ispravliaet peregiby v derevne)*, Moscow, 1930, p. 50.

the women in the following way:

> We dared not speak at meetings. If we said anything that the organizers
> didn't like, they abused us, called us *koolaks*, and even threatened to put
> us in prison .... We let the women do the talking .... If the organizer
> tried to stop them they made such a din that he had to call off the
> meeting.[44]

It is clear here that at least some peasant men recognized both their
own vulnerability and the far greater leverage that peasant women had
in speaking out against state policies.

Peasant women were able to get away with a great deal more than
their male counterparts in resisting collectivization and the other policies of the times. Force was generally not used to suppress *bab'i bunty*.
Furthermore, it would appear that women tended not to be prosecuted
under article 58 of the criminal code for counterrevolutionary crimes in
cases when opposition to policy led to court actions: in reports of court
cases in *Sudebnaia praktika* (supplement to *Sovetskaia iustitsiia*, the
organ of the RSFSR People's Commissariat of Justice) in 1930 and
1931, only men appear as defendants in cases prosecuted under article
58. This tendency, along with the infrequent use of force to suppress
bab'i bunty, was a function of both official images of women's protest as
irrational and the fear and inability of rural officials to respond
effectively to the type of bedlam created by disgruntled peasant women.
And, if actions reveal motives, it is likely that peasant women who
rebelled against the policies of collectivization clearly understood how
they were perceived and appreciated the power of their "irrational
behavior."

The *bab'i bunty* that occurred during the years of collectivization
were neither as irrational nor as spontaneous as the official accounts
tend to conclude. The anatomy of the *bab'i bunty* and the content of
peasant women's protest contained several consistent features, which
belie the official images. First, the *bab'i bunty* often revealed a relatively high degree of organization and tactics. Following the initial articulation of protest, which could frequently resemble a mob scene, the
peasant women would endeavor to disarm local activists or plenipotentiaries by one means or another, sound the church bell to alert the village and mobilize support, and, finally, approach directly the resolution
of the problem that had given rise to the protest.[45] Moreover, the

---

[44] Hindus, *Red Bread*, pp. 169-170.

[45] See the case described in Lynne Viola, "Notes on the Background of Soviet Collectivisation: Metal Worker Brigades in the Countryside, Autumn 1929," *Soviet Studies*, vol.
36, no. 2, April 1984, p. 216, in which the women organizers of a rebellion called upon

women's protest frequently had a specific goal in mind (dissolving the collective farm, seizing socialized seed or livestock, halting grain requisitions or dekulakization, etc.). Second, the women's protest was frequently based upon opposition to specific policies and, whether inspired by seemingly irrational rumors, rumors used as a pretext for resistance, or direct opposition to the implementation of policy, it derived from rational and legitimate concerns and socio-economic interests, which were under attack by the state. Third, peasant women's protest seems to have served as a *comparatively* safe outlet for peasant opposition in general and as a screen to protect the more politically vulnerable male peasants who could not oppose policy as actively or openly without serious consequence but who, nevertheless, could and did either stand silently, and threateningly, in the background or join in the disturbance once protest had escalated to a point where men might enter the fray as defenders of their female relatives. Finally, an important feature distinguished women's protest from protest (generally led by males) officially branded as "counterrevolutionary." Many of the counterrevolutionary cases prosecuted under article 58 of the criminal code in late 1929 and early 1930 occurred while the defendants were drunk. Women's protest, on the other hand, appears to have been, with few exceptions, sober and, consequently, perhaps, more rational than male protest[46]

Several other conclusions about official perceptions of the *bab'i bunty* and women's protest supplement direct observations on the nature of peasant women's opposition during collectivization. First of all, the *bab'i bunty* were very much a part of the traditional peasant approach to political protest. Peasants rarely resisted the state through organized political action. Their resistance often assumed the aspect of a spontaneous, disorganized, irrational *bunt*. However, peasant rebellions frequently merely *appeared* irrational to outside observers, who were powerless to cope with massive explosions of discontent and who, in the case of the *bab'i bunty*, were reluctant to resort to armed force to quell riots.[47] The outside observers who wrote about the *bab'i bunty* tended, in addition, to be city people or, at the very least, of a higher cultural level than the peasants and, consequently, had a very different conception of the forms that protest and rebellion were expected to

all women to join the protest or face a fine of three rubles.

[46] "Direktiv UKK Verkhsuda RSFSR," *Sudebnaia praktika*, no. 5, 10 April 1930, pp. 4-6.

[47] Roberta Manning has analyzed peasant rebellions during the 1905 revolution and its aftermath and has concluded that, "however spontaneous and chaotic they [riots] might have appeared, they display signs of organization and prior planning and a rudimentary sense of strategy." See her description of peasant protest in Roberta Thompson Manning, *The Crisis of the Old Order in Russia*, Princeton, 1982, pp. 148-158.

assume. The rudimentary organization behind the *bab'i bunty* and the specific grievances articulated in protest were often, in the eyes of outside observers, overshadowed or impossible to discern against the backdrop of apparent pandemonium.

Second, and of equal importance, there is a real possibility that the Communist Party was aware of the true nature and dynamics of the *bab'i bunty* and women's protest during collectivization. As Field has argued, the "myth of the tsar" was as useful to the tsarist government as it was to the peasantry. It was based on the "myth of the peasant" and provided the regime with a rationalization for any problems leading to peasant disturbances.[48] In the Soviet context, the myth of the peasant could serve several purposes. First, official images of the *bab'i bunty* and peasant women's protest could be manipulated to minimize the true nature and extent of the opposition engendered by collectivization. Second, it served a particularly useful purpose when women's protest engulfed entire villages, including poor and middle peasant women. In these cases, the party had a ready rationalization for the contradictions of the class struggle in the village, for its failure to capture the support of its poor and middle peasant allies among the peasantry. Finally, particular injustices could be attributed to officials who, it was said, were violating the essentially correct policy of the center. In this way, Moscow could, and often did, seek to divert grievances from the state to local officials, who were frequently used as scapegoats. Moreover, it is clear that, at least in the months following the March 1930 retreat, peasants also adhered or pretended to adhere to this rationalization, displaying a Soviet-style naive monarchism which pitted rural officials against Stalin and the Central Committee of the Communist Party.[49]

Peasant women played an important role in the protest that consumed many Russian and Ukrainian villages during the First Five-Year Plan, and it is important to attempt to understand the nature of this protest and the state's response to it. Yet, one cannot claim that all women were united, on the basis of similar interests, in opposition to the collective farm. Dorothy Atkinson has suggested that there were also women (widows, heads of households, wives of seasonal workers) who supported collectivization because of the difficulties of working their land alone and women, mostly young, who were genuinely

---

[48] Field, *Rebels in the Name of the Tsar*, pp. 2, 213-214.
[49] See Lynne Viola, "The Campaign of the 25,000ers. A Study of the Collectivization of Soviet Agriculture, 1929-1931," Ph.D. Dissertation, Princeton University, 1984, chapters 4 and 5.

enthusiastic about collectivization.[50] Furthermore, the general scale of peasant resistance to the state during collectivization should not be exaggerated. Although the exact dimensions of peasant resistance are not known, it is quite clear that the opposing sides in the rural conflicts caused by collectivization were unevenly matched. With the possible exception of the early months of 1930, the state always retained the ability to respond to peasant unrest in an organized fashion with a show of force. And—again with an exception, that of Central Asia—the confrontation between state and peasantry in no way approached the scale of a full-fledged civil war with troop formations and organized national or regional resistance. Despite these qualifications, however, the peasant unrest of these years was of sufficient scale and ferocity to force the state to take notice. And notice it did. The Party admitted that the "retreat" of 1930 came about as a response to peasant unrest, and Stalin even made note of the opposition of peasant women to the attempt to socialize domestic livestock when, in 1933, he promised a cow for every collective farm household. This was clearly not a retreat from collectivization, but it was a retreat—and a retreat that proved permanent[51] —from many of the most objectionable policies and practices of those times, such as the open attack on the Church, the attempt to socialize domestic livestock, and the unsanctioned "dizziness" of local cadres who sought to impose upon the peasantry their ideas of socialist construction in the realm of everyday life. It is plausible and logical to suggest that the protest of peasant women played an important role in the amendment of policies and practices in these spheres.

[50] Atkinson, *The End of the Russian Land Commune*, pp. 367-369.

[51] As R. W. Davies has demonstrated in *The Soviet Collective Farm*, Cambridge, 1980, the basic shape of collectivized agriculture took form in the years, 1930-31, as a compromise (albeit unbalanced) between the state and the peasantry, between socialist fortress-storming in the village and traditional ways. The state was forced to settle for a program minimum, in which the peasantry was allowed to maintain a private plot, domestic livestock, and limited direct access to the market. After 1930-31, the compromise would be maintained of necessity, and no longer on the basis of peasant protest, by what E. J. Hobsbawm has labeled the "normal strategy of the traditional peasantry"— passivity—which, he adds, "is not an ineffective strategy, for it exploits the major assets of the peasantry, its numbers and the impossibility of making it do some things by force for any length of time, and it also utilises a favourable tactical situation, which rests on the fact that no change is what suits a traditional peasantry best." See E. J. Hobsbawm, "Peasants and Politics," *Journal of Peasant Studies*, vol. 1, no. 1, October 1973, p. 13. For further information on the shape of collective farming in the 1930s, see Roberta T. Manning, *Government in the Soviet Countryside in the Stalinist Thirties: The Case of Belyi Raion in 1937*, Carl Beck Papers in Russian and East European Studies, no. 301, Pittsburgh, 1984.

The *bab'i bunty* and the outspoken protest of peasant women do not appear to have continued beyond the First Five-Year Plan. Nevertheless, during the early years of collectivization, the *bab'i bunty* and women's protest proved the most effective form of peasant opposition to the Soviet state. Peasant women played an important role in the resistance to collectivization, defending their interests and demonstrating a degree of organization and conscious political opposition rarely acknowledged.

[9]

How the Mice Buried the Cat: Scenes from the Great Purges of 1937 in the Russian Provinces

SHEILA FITZPATRICK

> The ground trembled under him, he was feared, he was hated. "Brigand" was what the population always called him. People learned to go out of their way to avoid him, so as not to catch his eye more often than necessary. They say that even little children ran away screaming when they saw him. And when he disappeared, the whole street breathed a sigh of relief behind their gates.
>
> He enjoyed his notoriety and was proud of it. Showing off the "education" acquired who knows where, he often pronounced with a grim, self-satisfied smirk: "Where I go, the grass will not grow for ten years."
>
> Kochetov behaved toward the citizenry exactly like a conqueror toward the conquered. He exacted tribute and called it "fines for the state treasury." . . . And people paid up. People preferred to pay because it was safer than not paying. If anyone dared doubt that, Kochetov himself appeared with his "activists"—and then the floors shook, dishes rattled and children cried. . . . "If you don't deliver, I'll dig it out of you like God scooping out a turtle."
>
> *Sovetskaia iustitsiia*, no. 20 (1937): 22.

The villainous Kochetov was a small-time Soviet boss in a rural district (*sel'sovet*) in Russia's agricultural heartland. In 1937 he fell victim to the Great Purges that swept the Soviet bureaucracy. Along with his immediate superior, the chairman of the *raion* soviet, he was one of a group of local officials indicted for "counterrevolutionary" crimes and put on trial in Aleshki, the administrative center of an obscure rural *raion* in the Voronezh region.

The Aleshki trial was one of dozens held in *raion* centers in the Soviet Union in the autumn of 1937.[1] These trials were not products of the normal workings of the judicial system. They were show trials with a political message. Nineteen thirty-seven

---

[1] This account is based on reports of thirty-five show trials held in rural *raion* centers in the Russian Republic (thirty-two trials), the Ukraine (two trials) and Belorussia (one trial) reported in the regional and central press from March to November 1937. The great majority of trials occurred from August to October 1937, and almost all the reports were published in oblast newspapers.

was the height of the Great Purges, in which hundreds of thousands of members of the Soviet Communist elite—party and government officials, industrial managers, military officers—as well as members of the intellectual elite were arrested and subsequently sent to labor camps or shot as "enemies of the people." In the notorious Moscow trials of August 1936, January 1937 and March 1938, Bukharin, Zinoviev and other former leaders of the Soviet Communist Party astonished the world by confessing that they had long been secret counterrevolutionaries, wreckers, terrorists, agents of the exiled "Judas-Trotsky," and spies for hostile capitalist powers.

But Moscow was a long way from Aleshki, and the Aleshki version of the Great Purge was both rhetorically and substantively worlds apart from the Moscow trials that inspired Arthur Koestler's famous novel, *Darkness at Noon*. The petty bureaucratic tyrants and oppressed citizens we meet in reports of the Aleshki and other *raion* trials of 1937 could have come straight from the pages of such nineteenth-century Russian satirists as Saltykov-Shchedrin and Chekhov, who chronicled the follies and abuses of local officials and the dreariness of provincial life. These officials are corrupt, venal, illiterate and almost invariably drunk. They are often ludicrously ill-equipped for their positions, like the head of the *raion* sector of animal husbandry who had formerly been a ladies' hairdresser, or his assistant who had been manager of the local public bathhouse.[2] They make pompous but only semiliterate speeches full of Soviet malapropisms. They invite young female tractor-drivers into their offices and tell them to strip for "medical inspection."[3]

In contrast to the Moscow trials, highly stylized productions involving fantastic scenarios of conspiracy and treason, the *raion* trials were relatively down-to-earth and straightforward. The former officials on trial in the *raiony* were described as "enemies of the people" or under the influence of "enemies." But only rarely were political offenses like espionage or contacts with the Trotskyists or other party oppositionists suggested in the *raion* trials; and only in a few cases did the prosecution argue that the indicted officials had intentionally sabotaged agriculture (by acts like infecting animals with disease, laming horses and so on) because they were counterrevolutionaries who wanted a return to capitalism. The accused officials were encouraged to confess their guilt, as in the Moscow trials, but in fact they often recanted in court and tried to defend themselves, so that the *raion* trials had little of the sinister, mysterious atmosphere of their Moscow counterparts.

Another important difference between the Moscow show trials and their provincial counterparts was that in rural *raion* trials the core of the indictment was not treason and political conspiracy but *exploitation and abuse of the peasantry* by Communists holding official positions at the *raion* and *sel'sovet* levels. These accusations, in contrast to their Moscow counterparts, were almost always completely plausible. In many instances, what the officials were accused of doing (for example, dictating unrealistic sowing plans or extracting so much grain after the harvest that the peasants went hungry) was simply what their jobs and their superiors required them to do. In other instances, the behavior that was condemned in court (for example, bribe-

---

[2] *Krest'ianskaia pravda*, 2 September 1937.
[3] Ibid., 3 September 1937.

taking, bullying or forcing through appointments of kolkhoz chairmen against the objections of kolkhozniki) was standard practice for Soviet rural officials in the 1930s.

Finally, a distinctive feature of the rural *raion* trials was that the state's case usually rested largely on the evidence of peasant witnesses. Their passionate and circumstantial testimony in court against former *raion* and *sel'sovet* leaders was generally the dramatic centerpiece of the show trials, which were held in the largest auditorium of the *raion* center before large audiences of kolkhozniki who had been brought in from all over the *raion* for the occasion. This was political theater, no doubt, but it was a participatory political theater in which peasant witnesses and auditors appeared to revel in the humiliation of their former bosses. My title, reflecting the *Schadenfreude* (*zloradstvo*) that seems the dominant mood of the rural *raion* show trials of 1937, is that of a popular eighteenth-century Russian woodcut showing the funeral of a large cat, long believed to represent Peter the Great, whose corpse, firmly tied down, is being carried to the grave by a group of dancing and celebrating mice.[4]

THE MASTER PLOT

If the show trials are to be viewed as theater, we have to ask who was writing the plays. At one level, this question has a simple answer: the texts at our disposal were almost all written by journalists of oblast daily newspapers.[5] The newspapers ran long and detailed reports of local show trials, often including allegedly verbatim reports of particularly exciting testimony and court exchanges; they generally appeared sequentially in three or four issues. These reports belong to the Soviet version of the genre of exposé journalism, generally focused on local bureaucratic abuses or court cases, whose ostensible function of political (moral) instruction was combined with an unacknowledged but unmistakable entertainment function. They tended to be written with verve and literary flair, pouring sarcasm and scorn on the delinquencies and hypocrisy of the "bureaucrats" who were their most frequent targets. These "exposé" stories and feuilletons were oases in the desert of the Soviet press in the 1930s, which was otherwise largely devoted to unrelenting and mendacious boosterism of Soviet economic achievements, official communiqués and the publication in full of long speeches by party leaders.

But the journalistic texts were only representations of other "texts," namely the show trials themselves. While it is unlikely that the *raion* trials were scripted with anything like the same care as the central Moscow trials, they were still very far from spontaneous events. At a minimum, they had had the same kind of detailed advance planning in the oblast prosecutor's office and local NKVD branch that any major

---

[4] On the provenance of the woodcut "The Mice Bury the Cat" see Dianne Ecklund Farrell, "Medieval Popular Humor in Russian Eighteenth-Century Lubki," *Slavic Review* 50 (Fall 1991): 560–62.

[5] Virtually all my sources are newspaper reports of rural *raion* show trials, not court records or memoir accounts. If any court records of the trials have survived in Soviet oblast archives, they have yet to be discovered. The Smolensk Archive (available in the West) includes no court records, though it contains valuable related material, some of which has been analyzed by Roberta Manning in her unpublished article, "The Case of the Miffed Milkmaid." In A. I. Solzhenitsyn, *The Gulag Archipelago,* vols. 1–2 (New York, 1973), 419–31, there is an account of one show trial (held in Kady *raion,* Ivanovo oblast) which appears to be based on information from one of the indicted officials or a family member.

criminal trial in the United States would be given by the prosecuting counsel—with the important difference that, in the absence of any significant opposition from defense counsel, the prosecutors' plans were less likely to go awry.[6]

The trials' "scripts," moreover, were drawn from two additional sources. One was the set of signals from Moscow that provided what I will call the "master plot"[7] of the rural *raion* show trials of 1937—that is, the generic model on which local variants were based. The other source, on whose identity I will speculate a little later, provided the detailed information on local abuses and crimes that was used in a particular *raion* trial. Despite the existence of a "master plot," Moscow's hand in the framing and controlling of local show trials should not be exaggerated. The virtually unanimous failure of local trials to take up the hint that Stalin should be lauded for correcting local abuses, or indeed to mention Stalin at all, provides persuasive evidence of the limitations of Moscow's control.

The word "signal" had a special meaning in Stalinist discourse. It referred primarily to information about important policy shifts that was transmitted from the center to lower-level officials via a nonbureaucratic channel such as the central party newspaper, *Pravda*. A signal was not the same thing as a law or an administrative order, although it might coexist with an explicit instruction given privately by a superior authority to a subordinate one. It was essentially a message about political mood and current priorities, transmitted in the form of a slogan ("The Five-Year Plan in four years!"), a remark (Stalin's interjection at a conference that "a son does not answer for his father"), an exemplary story, or—as in the cases we are concerned with—an exemplary or "show" trial (*pokazatel'nyi sud*) that received national publicity. The reception of signals was treated as an instinctive rather than an intellectual act, and people who were not tuned into the right Communist wave length were likely to miss them.[8] In the case of the flood of rural *raion* show trials in the fall of 1937, the signals came in a series of reports and commentaries in *Pravda* highlighting the mistreatment of peasants by local Communist officials.

The first report—perhaps more of a forerunner than one of the series—concerned a show trial of former party and soviet leaders in Lepel' *raion* in Belorussia that was held in March. The accused were charged with illegally confiscating peasant property as payment for tax arrears, despite the recent law forgiving arrears in the light of the exceptionally poor harvest of 1936. According to *Pravda*'s report, the Lepel' investigation was sparked by letters of complaint from local peasants, and the Belorussian state prosecutor took action on instructions from Andrei Vyshinsky, state prosecutor of the USSR. Peasant witnesses testified at the trial, which was held at the Lepel' municipal theater, and the court had reportedly received dozens of letters from peasants grateful for deliverance from their former oppressors.[9]

---

[6] There were defense counsels in some and conceivably most of the rural *raion* trials (see, for example, the Lepel' trial, as reported in *Pravda*, 13 March 1937) but, as was usual in the Stalin period, their role was limited to asking for a more lenient sentence for their clients.

[7] I have borrowed this term from Katerina Clark's discussion of the "master plot" of Socialist Realism in *The Soviet Novel: History as Ritual* (Chicago, 1981), 5–15.

[8] Note that, in accordance with this metaphor, it was also possible for signals to be sent "from below" and received by the top party and government leadership. The peasant complaints and petitions discussed below fall into this category.

[9] *Pravda*, 9–12 March 1937.

Three months later, *Pravda* reported a similar show trial from the Shiriaevo *raion* of Odessa oblast in the Ukraine. There, top *raion* officials had been found guilty of "outrageous" treatment of kolkhozniki and routine violations of the 1935 Kolkhoz Charter,[10] including illegal confiscation of peasant property, extortion, night-time searches, arbitrary exaction of taxes and of subscriptions to state loans, imposition of impossibly high grain procurement quotas in 1936, and "insulting behavior" toward kolkhozniki.[11] These crimes had come to the attention of the party's Central Control Commission, which had instructed the Ukrainian state prosecutor to take action. The main evidence against the accused in the Shiriaevo trial came from peasant witnesses, more than thirty of whom were called to testify.[12]

A few weeks later, *Pravda* reported similar show trials in Novominsk, a Cossack *raion* in the Black Sea oblast of Rostov, and in the Danilov *raion* of Iaroslavl oblast. The Novominsk trial featured severe economic exploitation by local officials that had provoked thousands of peasants to leave the collective farms.[13] In the Danilov trial, the *raion* leadership was charged with illegally liquidating the "New Life" kolkhoz and confiscating all its property when officials were unable to resolve a dispute with kolkhoz members.[14] *Pravda*'s coverage of the Danilov affair was notable for its report that at the end of the trial, after stiff sentences had been handed down, local kolkhozniki sent thanks to Stalin for defending them against their enemies—a signal that seemed to fall on deaf ears.[15]

Early in August, *Pravda* elaborated the message of Shiriaevo and Danilov trials in an editorial warning local officials not to mistreat the peasantry. *Raion* officials had been condoning all kinds of violations of the rights of kolkhozniki, *Pravda* stated. Officials had disposed arbitrarily of kolkhoz land and property, behaving as if it were "their own private property, their own little kingdom (*votchina*)"; they had even liquidated entire collective farms, as in the Danilov case. This was to forget the golden rule that "kolkhozniki are the masters of their own kolkhoz."[16]

Emerging from all this was a master plot on the theme of abuse and exploitation of the collectivized peasantry by Soviet officialdom at the *raion* level that formed the basis for the thirty-odd show trials held in rural *raions* of the Soviet Union in September-October 1937. It may be summarized as follows:

[10] By 1937 the great majority of Soviet peasants were members of a collective farm (kolkhozniki). The Model Charter of the Agricultural Artel (*Primernyi ustav sel'skokhoziaistvennoi arteli*), approved by the Second Congress of Kolkhoz Shockworkers, was issued as a law by the Soviet government on 17 February 1935. It was in effect the kolkhoz constitution, defining the rights and obligations of kolkhoz members and kolkhozy.

[11] TASS dispatch, "Delo nad byvshimi rukovoditeliami shiriaevskogo raiona," *Pravda*, 16 June 1937.

[12] Reports on the Shiriaevo trial appeared in *Pravda*, 15–19 June 1937. Information on the trial also appeared in the national agricultural newspaper, *Sotsialisticheskoe zemledelie*, 18 June 1937 and 21 July 1937, as well as in some oblast papers.

[13] See *Pravda*, 2 July 1937 and 5 July 1937.

[14] The Danilov case was reported in *Pravda*, 15 July 1937, 29 July 1937, 30 July 1937, and 31 July 1937. More detailed reports also appeared in the local oblast paper, *Severnyi rabochii* (Iaroslavl), in daily installments from 26–30 July 1937.

[15] *Pravda*, 31 July 1937.

[16] Ibid., 3 August 1937.

Enemies of the people, linked in a mutual-protection and patronage network, had wormed their way into key positions in the *raion* and used their
official positions to plunder the peasantry mercilessly. Because of the officials' stupidity and ignorance of agriculture, their incessant orders and
interference had done great harm to the collective farms. The peasants,
outraged and indignant, had done their best to resist unlawful demands.
They had brought suits and written letters of complaint to higher authorities, but these had often been blocked by the mutual-protection ring. Finally, however, the news of the scandalous behavior of local officials got
out, and the guilty parties were brought to justice. The simple people—
who demanded the severest punishment for their former oppressors—had
triumphed over the officials who had cheated and insulted them.

While it is not possible to establish with certainty who were the "authors" of variants
of the master plot used in specific local show trials, the evidence points strongly to
a natural (but perhaps, to Sovietologists, unexpected) source—the local peasantry.

Peasants were inveterate letter-writers, complaining about and denouncing
those in immediate authority above them in the 1930s. They wrote to party and
government leaders like Stalin and Mikhail Kalinin; they wrote to the highest organs
of the Soviet and republican governments; they wrote to oblast party committees,
prosecutors' offices and NKVD branches; they wrote to oblast newspapers and central newspapers, especially the mass-circulation peasant newspaper, *Krest'ianskaia
gazeta.* They wrote letters and complaints with or without cause, for good reasons
and bad, and they generally sent them outside their own *raion,* to the oblast center
or even to Moscow, because of their belief that the bosses in any given *raion* would
back each other up.[17]

Such peasant complaints often triggered the investigations of official wrong-
doing at the *raion* level that led to the rural *raion* trials of 1937. Local complaints
are mentioned as a stimulus in three out of the four "model" trials reported in
Pravda: in the Lepel' case, Vyshinsky's attention was alerted by "complaints from
the toilers of Lepel' *raion*";[18] "complaints from kolkhozniki" are mentioned in the
Shiriaevo case;[19] and in Danilov, "letters of *sel'kory*" (correspondents from the village) disclosed the abuses of the *raion* leadership, which consequently did its best to
suppress them.[20] Similar references to complaints and petitions from the village
abound in the *raion* show trials that took place in the autumn.[21]

[17] For a more extended discussion of peasant letters see my "Peasant Letters to *Krest'ianskaia gazeta,* 1938" (Paper presented to the AAASS National Convention, Washington, DC, October 1990).

[18] *Pravda,* 9 March 1937. The term "toilers" covered peasants as well as workers, and other honest
wage-earners, but in this case it probably refers to peasants.

[19] Ibid., 16 June 1937.

[20] Ibid., 30 July 1937. In the 1920s the term "sel'kor" was usually reserved for the small group of
villagers that had consciously taken on the role of "the eyes and ears of Soviet power" in the village. By
the latter part of the 1930s, however, it was used more broadly to refer to any villager who wrote to a
newspaper complaining about or giving information on fellow peasants.

[21] In the Andreevsk trial, for example, peasant witnesses mentioned that they had sent a telegram
of complaint to the people's commissar of agriculture (*Rabochii put',* 8 September 1937). In Shchuche
the complaint had been sent to the Central Executive Committee of Soviets of the Russian Republic
(VTsIK) (*Kommuna,* 6 October 1937). In Aleshki peasant complaints against Kochetov were forwarded
to the Central Commission of Soviet Control in Moscow by a sympathetic secretary of a neighboring
sel'sovet (ibid., 1 September 1937).

Since the general tenor and substance of the grievances aired by peasant witnesses at the *raion* show trials of 1937 correspond remarkably closely to those of the peasant letters of complaint received by *Krest'ianskaia gazeta* at the same period, the hypothesis that the scenarios of rural *raion* show trials were often directly based on local peasant complaints seems extremely plausible.[22] This raises the intriguing possibility that the peasants who appeared as witnesses in the trials were not only full-fledged actors in this political theater but were also (to pursue the theatrical metaphor) *playing themselves.*

THE DEFENDANTS

The standard cast of characters under indictment at the rural *raion* trials consisted of the former secretary of the *raion* party committee (the top-ranking official in a *raion*), the chairman of the *raion* soviet (the second-ranking official), the heads of the *raion* agriculture department and sometimes the taxation (finance) and procurement agencies, along with other agricultural officials, and a sprinkling of *sel'sovet* and kolkhoz chairmen.

The typical defendant—and, indeed, the typical Soviet official at *raion* or *sel'sovet* level in the 1930s—was a poorly educated man of peasant origin, probably in his thirties or forties, who was a member of the Communist Party. The senior *raion* officials were likely to have spent a year or so at Soviet party school in addition to their basic primary schooling, and they had usually seen something of a broader world through service in other *raion* centers within the oblast and perhaps its immediate neighbors. *Sel'sovet* and kolkhoz chairmen, by contrast, were lucky to have completed primary education, rarely had job experience outside the *raion*, and seem usually to have been natives of the *sel'sovet* in which they served.[23]

If accusations of participation in "counterrevolutionary Trotskyite conspiracies" were rare in the rural *raion* trials, this surely reflected the fact that few Communists at this low level of the Soviet bureaucracy had ever had personal contact with an actual member of any Communist opposition group.[24] Nevertheless, it became standard practice in these trials to charge at least the senior defendants with counterrevolutionary crimes, using Article 58 of the Criminal Code—although, interestingly enough, Article 58 does not seem to have been used in any of the "model" trials reported in *Pravda* in the period March-July 1937.[25] The sentences, accordingly, were

[22] That is, the letters expressing criticism of local bosses that are filed in the newspaper's archive under the heading "Abuses of power" (Tsentral'nyi gosudarstvennyi arkhiv narodnogo khoziaistva SSSR, f. 396, op. 10–11).

[23] For unusually detailed biographical data on defendants see the report of the Krasnogorsk *raion* trial in *Rabochii put'*, 29 August 1937.

[24] My sample of thirty-two *raion* trials discloses not a single actual Oppositionist among the defendants. The closest to a serious accusation of Trotskyite conspiracy was in the Shchuche trial (which was also unusual in combining industrial and kolkhoz/agricultural themes and personnel), where one of the defendants, director of a sugar plant, admitted that he had been influenced by a Trotskyite he met after graduating from a party technical school in Moscow in 1928 (*Kommuna*, 3 October 1937). In another trial the former *raion* party secretary was accused of softness on Trotskyites (but not membership of a Trotskyite conspiracy) because he let the director of the local veterinary school, a former Trotskyite, go into hiding to avoid arrest (ibid., 3 September 1937).

[25] In the Lepel' trial the accused were indicted under Art. 196 of the Belorussian Criminal Code (violation of Soviet law and abuse of power), and in the Danilov trial they were accused of destruction of socialist property under the law of 7 August 1932.

more severe in the autumn trials than in the spring, and became still harsher in the course of the autumn. Ten years' imprisonment with confiscation of property was the harshest sentence handed down in any of the "model" trials, while some defendants got off with as little as six months. In the autumn trials, by contrast, it was usual for two or three of the top-ranking defendants to be sentenced to death while other defendants received eight- to ten-year sentences.[26]

In two instances (the Andreevka trial in the Western oblast and the Aleshki trial in Voronezh oblast), second hearings were held in order to impose stiffer sentences.[27] The Andreevka case is of particular interest because the new Smolensk *obkom* secretary, Korotchenko, had made the mistake of sending a rather boastful message to Stalin *before* the verdict was brought in informing him of the success of the Andreevka trial in educating the peasantry and raising vigilance. Stalin responded the next day with a curt instruction that all the Andreevka "wreckers" should be shot, but by that time the court had brought in its verdict sentencing them to various terms of imprisonment. The oblast prosecutor had to lodge a protest that resulted in an immediate rehearing of the case, which presumably resulted in death sentences for the accused.[28]

The defendants in the rural *raion* trials were strongly encouraged to confess their guilt, as in the central Moscow trials, but they were a good deal less cooperative than their Moscow counterparts, especially where charges of counterrevolution were concerned.[29] In the Aleshki trial, none of the main defendants made a confession that was satisfactory from the prosecutors' standpoint. While the top-ranking defendant (Kolykhmatov, the *raion* party secretary) had admitted to counterrevolution under pretrial interrogation, he recanted in court and maintained that he was guilty only of failing to curb his subordinates' overzealous actions that showed poor judgment and offended the local population. Seminikhin, the former chairman of the *raion* soviet, was similarly recalcitrant, constantly attacking the credibility of the witnesses on the grounds that they were venting personal grievances: "Every few minutes he

[26] Sentences were reported for ten of the trials and can be deduced for an eleventh. See *Krest'ianskaia pravda*, 29 August 1937 (Ostrov), 2 September 1937 (Krasnogvardeisk), and 20 October 1937 (Kirillovo); *Kurskaia pravda*, 4 September 1937 (Borisovka); *Rabochii put'*, 29 August 1937 (Krasnogorsk) and 18 October 1937 (Sychevka); *Kommuna*, 6 September 1937 (Aleshki), and 6 October 1937 (Shchuche); *Moskovskaia kolkhoznaia gazeta*, 3 November 1937 (Malin and Konstantinovo); and footnote 28 below (Andreevka).

[27] In the Aleshki trial (Voronezh oblast) in September, only two death sentences were imposed, though the prosecutor asked for four. This verdict, too, was subsequently appealed by the oblast prosecutor, resulting in a retrial in November at which three additional death sentences were imposed (*Kommuna*, 6 September 1937 and 20 November 1937).

[28] See coded telegrams from Stalin's personal archive (currently held in the "Presidential" or "Kremlin" Archive) recently published in *Izvestiia*, 10 June 1992 (I am indebted to Arch Getty for informing me of this publication); and the report in *Rabochii put'* (Smolensk), 2 September 1937. Surprisingly, although Stalin instructed that an announcement of the defendants' execution should be placed in the local press, *Rabochii put'* reported neither the new sentences imposed by the court after the prosecutor's protest nor the execution of the Andreevka defendants that presumably followed.

[29] In his account of the Kady trial (see above, footnote 5), Solzhenitsyn suggests that a defendant's withdrawal of his pre-trial confession unhinged the whole proceedings and even caused the *raion* show trial as a genre to be abandoned. In my sample of *raion* trials, however, recanting in court on earlier admissions was not unusual and did not have a devastating effect on proceedings, since most *raion* cases were built more on peasant testimony than on confession by the accused.

would jump up and announce to the court that the witness was personally antagonistic towards him." As for Kochetov, the villainous *sel'sovet* chairman, he stub-
bornly asserted that while he might be guilty of abuse of power, he was not guilty of
counterrevolution.[30]

In the Andreevka trial, two defendants persistently denied their guilt for any
counterrevolutionary crimes, even at the retrial held as a result of Stalin's unpubli-
cized intervention. One of the defendants (K. V. Rumiantsev, the former senior *raion*
land-surveyor) was particularly obdurate when questioned about his role in the
raion's decision to merge collective farms against the will of their members:[31]

RUMIANTSEV. Not guilty. I didn't know that forced merging was a counterrevolution-
    ary crime.
PROSECUTOR. Did you know you were committing crimes?
RUMIANTSEV. I knew I was carrying out the will of the head of the *raion* agriculture
    department and the party committee.
PROSECUTOR. That is, consciously carrying out wrecking work.
RUMIANTSEV. (keeps silent)[32]

THE CHARGES

Many of the actions for which officials were indicted in the *raion* trials were not crimes
in the ordinary sense. In some cases officials were clearly being made scapegoats for
local economic disasters. In others they were being held to account for behavior that
was really part of their job description (as in the Rumiantsev case cited above) or
for state policies that were unpopular with the local peasants. An interesting subset
of offenses had to do with treatment of kulaks, a subject on which opinion at village
level seemed to be distinctly at odds with Moscow. Overall, the most striking common characteristic of the "criminal" behaviors attributed to the defendants was that
they were harmful to peasants, especially kolkhozniki, and offended the peasants'
sense of fairness and propriety.

Abuse of Power

The many accusations made by peasant witnesses under this heading are among the
most colorful and bitter. Curses, insults, beatings, humiliation, intimidation, and
unjustified arrests were described as commonplace in the behavior of rural officials
toward peasants. In one trial, an eighty-year-old peasant woman related "with tears"
how the *sel'sovet* chairman beat her husband and dumped him in a wheelbarrow; he
died two weeks later as result of his injuries.[33] Another witness described how a *raion*
official once made four kolkhoz brigade-leaders climb on the stove and stay there,
guarded by the local policeman, for four hours. "When people asked the kolkhoz

---

[30] *Kommuna*, 29 August 1937, 3 September 1937, and 4 September 1937. For other similar denials
and protestations see, for example, the reports of the Borisovka and Danilov cases in *Kurskaia pravda*,
29 August 1937; and *Severnyi rabochii*, 30 July 1937.

[31] It is not known whether this Rumiantsev was related to a major political figure in the region, Ivan
Petrovich Rumiantsev, long-time first secretary of the Western oblast party committee until his disgrace
and disappearance in the Great Purges in the summer of 1937.

[32] *Rabochii put'*, 5 September 1937.

[33] *Kommuna*, 30 August 1937.

chairman . . . why he countenanced this, he said 'What could I do? After all, [he] was the boss, he could have made me get onto the stove too.'"[34]

The wild behavior of Radchuk, a *sel'sovet* chairman, was described by many peasant witnesses in the Novgorod *raion* trial. Radchuk's specialty was physical assault and forced entry (connected with various forms of extortion) into the homes of kolkhozniki. One witness described how Radchuk began breaking down the door of her house.

> "Now," he cried, "I'll chop down the door with an axe, you just watch." I took fright, jumped out the window, and ran to the post office to telephone my husband in Novgorod. But when he came home, Radchuk had already gone, and the door was broken down with an axe.[35]

Peasants frequently complained about the imposition of arbitrary fines and money levies (sometimes described as "taxation" or "contributions to state loans") by *sel'sovet* authorities. In Shiriaevo, for example, it was said that "a night brigade" had been organized for the purpose, descending on peasants in dead of night to conduct house searches and take inventories of property that might be seized.[36] From the standpoint of peasant witnesses, this was extortion regardless of whether the money went to the state or to individual officials, but they frequently implied that the latter was the case. It was alleged that in Aleshki Kochetov had imposed fines on kolkhoz members totalling sixty thousand rubles in 1935 and 1936: "He imposed the fines on any pretext and at his own discretion—for not showing up for work, for not attending literacy classes, for 'impolite language,' for not having dogs tied up."[37]

The *raion* soviet chairman indicted in the same trial, Seminikhin, was reportedly even more creative in his fund-raising from the population:

> In 1936, two hundred kolkhozniki recruited for construction work went off from Aleshki to the Far East. They were already on the point of boarding the train when three militiamen appeared, read out a long list of names and took all those on the list off under guard to the *raion* soviet and the offices of the chairman.
> "Aha, tax delinquents!" Seminikhin greeted them. "You thought you could get away? Pay up and look lively about it. Pay up, or I won't let you out of the office and will not permit you to get on the train. And I'll take your suitcases."
> He posted a militiaman at the door and gave the order to let out only those who showed a receipt for payment.
> In this manner, the *raion* soviet chairman "squeezed" seven hundred rubles of their last savings from the kolkhozniki.[38]

In many areas, kolkhozniki had extremely little money to take, so the main form of extortion was seizure of property. There were many and varied accounts of *sel'sovet* and *raion* officials behaving "as if in their own little kingdoms" and "exacting tribute

---

[34] Ibid., 4 September 1937.
[35] *Krest'ianskaia pravda*, 3 September 1937.
[36] *Sotsialisticheskoe zemledelie*, 21 July 1937.
[37] *Sovetskaia iustitsiia*, no. 20 (1937): 22.
[38] Ibid., 24.

from the population." One country chairman took four or five kilograms of meat from each calf or pig slaughtered, plus vodka whenever he visited the village.[39] A second "opened unlimited 'free credit' for himself on products [at the local store]. On occasion, he even roused the manager of the store from his bed at night, demanding immediate issue of vodka and snacks for himself. And when he needed potatoes, he simply sent to the nearest kolkhoz for them with an accompanying note to the person in charge of stores."[40] Kolkhoz chairmen were also accused of treating kolkhoz property as if it were their own private property, selling buildings and (illegally) leasing land on their own initiative and pocketing the profits.[41]

In Aleshki, *raion* chairman Seminikhin had established a so-called "auxiliary farm" of the *raion* soviet containing thirty sheds, ten cows, seven horses, and other items commandeered from various parts of the *raion*, feeding his herd with feed taken from the kolkhozy. He was particularly successful in raising pigs, selling pork at the local peasant market as well as earning fifteen hundred rubles by selling pigs to the state procurement agency. The ironic comment going the rounds among the peasants was: "The *raion* soviet has built up a real kulak farm!"[42]

A more malign variant of extortion than regular, small-scale "tribute" was to strip a kolkhoznik of *all* his possessions in one swoop. In one case cited in the Shchuche trial, a country chairman, coveting the flourishing kitchen garden of a kolkhoznik, "abruptly dekulakized him and took away all his property." When he discovered that the victim's wife had managed to sell some small household items before he could confiscate them, "he took away the money and behaved so abusively that she was reduced to a state where she was sent to a psychiatric hospital."[43]

Expulsions and Liquidations

Complaints by peasants about their expulsion or forced departure from the kolkhoz were among the most frequent of all peasant grievances, judging both by the 1937 *raion* trials and the letters received at the same period by *Krest'ianskaia gazeta*. This may seem paradoxical, given the peasantry's hostility to collectivization less than a decade earlier. But by this time it had become clear that, as a result of heavy state taxation and other factors, peasant farming outside the kolkhoz was not a viable long-term option. Besides, when a member of a kolkhoz was expelled, he not only lost his share of the kolkhoz assets but also risked losing his private plot and even his house. Expulsion conflicts most frequently arose when members of the kolkhoz departed to work for wages elsewhere, usually leaving wives and families in the village. Departure for wage-work was a traditional cause of struggle between the Russian village commune (of which the kolkhoz was in many respects the heir) and individual peasants. It was often in the peasant's interest to depart, either temporarily or on a long-term basis, but in the village's interest to keep him (that is, retain his labor power and tax-paying capacity). After collectivization, as in the old days of serfdom and post-Emancipation redemption payments, peasants needed permission to de-

---

[39] *Kommuna*, 28 September 1937.
[40] *Sovetskaia iustitsiia*, no. 20 (1937): 22.
[41] *Krest'ianskaia pravda*, 17 August 1937.
[42] *Sovetskaia iustitsiia*, no. 20 (1937): 24; *Kommuna*, 4 September 1937.
[43] *Kommuna*, 28 September 1937.

part, which now had to be obtained from both the kolkhoz and the *sel'sovet*. In the narratives of the 1937 *raion* trials, however, the kolkhoznik's right to depart was usually taken as a given, and conflicts over departure were thus represented as struggles between righteous peasants and power-abusing kolkhoz and *sel'sovet* chairmen.

Almost twenty witnesses testified in the Aleshki trial that they had been unjustly expelled from the *"Path to Socialism"* kolkhoz. Among them was Matrena Okuneva, who said:

> They expelled me from the kolkhoz because I married a worker on the railways, although I continued to live in Lipiagovka and work in the kolkhoz. I never complained, because I thought that's how it was supposed to be. Soon after that Kachkin and Kabanov [kolkhoz chairman and party organizer respectively] appeared in my yard and demanded that I go to weed the beets. I refused because I considered myself expelled from the kolkhoz. Then Kachkin said that the *sel'sovet* would fine me fifty rubles. . . . They took a man's jacket from me, and Kabanov said: "Be grateful to us, we could have burned [your house] down, only we took pity on the neighbors."[44]

Other "expulsion" cases cited seem essentially to have been cases of unauthorized departures of kolkhozniki who were on the brink of starvation because of the harvest failure of 1936. In the Ostrov trial (Pskov oblast), for example, witnesses stated that more than one thousand households had left collective farms in the *raion* in 1935–1936 because they could not survive on the meager amount of grain the kolkhoz was giving them.[45] In the Nerekhta trial (Iaroslavl oblast), peasants blamed the *raion* leadership for "mass expulsions and forced departures from the collective farms" at the same period. These witnesses clearly felt that the *raion* bosses, like the old estate-owners in the time of serfdom, owed it to their peasants to help them out in time of trouble. For example, they related with indignation how

> after there was a fire in a kolkhoz and sixteen houses burned down, [the kolkhoz chairman] appealed to accused Begalov [chairman of the *raion* soviet] for help, saying that otherwise the kolkhozniki would all leave. In answer to the request, the accused Begalov said: "To hell with them, let them go." As a result, twenty households left the kolkhoz.[46]

The liquidation of an entire collective farm by order of *raion* officials was an extreme (and illegal) action that can best be understood from the peasant standpoint as expulsion of *all* the households that constituted the kolkhoz, resulting in the total loss of all village assets including land. In the case of the "New Life" kolkhoz in Danilov, *raion* officials followed the formal announcement of liquidation by swiftly confiscating all collective property and animals—and then, adding insult to injury, demanded that the former kolkhozniki immediately pay the heavy tax that was levied on noncollectivized peasants.[47] When the "Forward" kolkhoz in Kirillovo *raion* was liquidated, its land was distributed among neighboring collective farms in what was

[44] Ibid., 2 September 1937.
[45] *Krest'ianskaia pravda*, 28 August 1937.
[46] *Severnyi rabochii*, 22 September 1937.
[47] *Sotsialisticheskoe zemledelie*, 26 July 1937.

officially described as a "voluntary renunciation." The *raion* authorities went on to confiscate the kolkhoz's horses, agricultural equipment, stock of seed potatoes, and other collective property. From the standpoint of the kolkhozniki, who had owned this same property as individual households before collectivization, the liquidation of the kolkhoz must have seemed a second and definitive seizure of their assets. No wonder that, as witnesses related, the Kirillovo peasants wept when their kolkhoz was dissolved.[48]

Only one of the reported instances of kolkhoz liquidation came from the fertile Black Earth region of the country, and it occurred several years earlier than the non-Black Earth liquidations. Witnesses at the 1937 trial in Ivnia *raion* (Kursk oblast), stated that in 1933—that is, during the famine—the "Lenin" kolkhoz was liquidated by order of the local Machine-Tractor Station (MTS) and its lands given to the neighboring state farm, despite the fact that twenty-eight of thirty-one households voted against it. As a result of the transfer, the peasants were reduced overnight to the status of landless agricultural laborers working for a wage on the state farm.[49]

In both the Danilov and Kirillovo cases, conflict between local officials and kolkhozniki preceded the liquidation of the kolkhoz. In Kirillovo, it was a violent confrontation over the spring sowing plan in 1936, which the kolkhoz general assembly refused to accept, to the outrage of the *sel'sovet* chairman. The Kirillovo trial narrative implies that liquidation of the kolkhoz was essentially a punitive response by local authorities to the peasants' insubordination. In the narrative of the Danilov trial, however, there are suggestions that the *raion* leadership may have had more venal motives for liquidation, perhaps wanting to get hold of kolkhoz property for their own use or that of their friends.

Agricultural Disasters

There was nothing new about blaming Soviet rural officials for harvest failures. The accusations made against officials in the *raion* trials of 1937 differed from earlier charges in one important respect, however: the officials were not being blamed for failing to meet state grain procurements targets, as had frequently happened in the early 1930s. This time, they were being blamed for failing to meet the *peasants'* needs—that is, allowing so little grain to be distributed among kolkhoz households after the harvest that the kolkhozniki were brought to the brink of starvation.

Most charges of this kind related to the exceptionally bad harvest of 1936, whose consequences had been felt most acutely in the spring and summer of 1937 before the next harvest came in.[50] In the Krasnogvardeisk trial, a kolkhoz chairman, Alekseev, admitted that he had brought the kolkhoz to economic ruin and described his reaction.

> In 1936 the kolkhozniki received zero payments per labor-day [that is, no grain was distributed after the harvest]. When I saw it all, I decided to run

---

[48] *Krest'ianskaia pravda*, 20 October 1937.

[49] *Kurskaia pravda*, 2 October 1937 and 16 October 1937.

[50] In one exceptional case from the Nerekhta *raion* trial, the accusations made against a *raion* soviet chairman included his treatment of peasants during the 1933 famine (*Severnyi rabochii*, 22 September 1937).

away from the kolkhoz. I told the chairman of the *raion* soviet, Gornov.
He said: "Get away as fast as you can."

Alekseev took this friendly advice, but not fast enough (probably because he made
the mistake of trying to take his house with him, using kolkhoz horses), and he was
arrested, together with Gornov, by the NKVD.[51]

In Ostrov *raion,* as a result of the 1936 harvest failure, average kolkhoz earnings
dropped by 20 to 50 percent, it was reported at the Ostrov trial. But because state
grain procurements took precedence over peasant needs, many collective farms cut
their payments in kind to members much more drastically, and this was treated as a
crime in the 1937 *raion* trials. The indicted officials were held responsible for the
departure of large numbers of hungry kolkhozniki who went to work for wages in
the towns or the state farms in order to survive.[52]

A number of *raion* trials featured charges from kolkhozniki about inept agricultural instructions from *raion* authorities that had caused hardship to peasants and
damaged agricultural productivity. "Unrealistic sowing plans" figured prominently
in these complaints, and, despite the fact that it was part of the *raion* agriculture
departments' duty to give orders to the collective farms about what crops to sow and
where and when to sow them, the rhetorical conventions of the trials allowed peasant
witnesses to speak of such instructions with undisguised resentment and contempt.
In the Krasnogvardeisk trial, the testimony of a peasant from "Thirteen Years of the
Red Army" kolkhoz was reported to have "left an enormous impression on all present at the court":

> [The witness] talked about how kolkhozniki tried to protest against wreck-
> ing plans and went specially to Manninen, [head of] the *raion* agriculture
> department. With contemptuous effrontery, that enemy of the people an-
> nounced to the kolkhozniki: "If you go to the oblast to complain about our
> plans, we will add more."[53]

Peasant witnesses cited many instances of agriculturally illiterate instructions
from the *raion* authorities and MTSs. One kolkhoz, for example, was ordered to turn
water-meadow and shrubbed area into plowland, leaving nowhere to pasture cattle.
In another kolkhoz, the *raion*'s sowing instructions were predicated on the false assumption that its hayfields covered over two hundred hectares, which according to
the peasants was double their actual extent ("Under the heading of hayfield, the
wreckers included pastureland for cattle, quicksands, and the private plots of
kolkhozniki").[54]

Another kind of agricultural disaster that figured prominently in a few *raion*
trials was the large-scale loss of livestock. In the trial in Shchuche *raion* (Voronezh
oblast), which lost almost one thousand horses in the first half of 1937, this was
attributed to lack of fodder associated with the 1936 harvest failure, compounded
by an epidemic that started in a Shchuche horse-breeding state farm and spread rap-

[51] *Moskovskaia kolkhoznaia gazeta,* 5 October 1937.
[52] *Krest'ianskaia pravda,* 28 August 1937.
[53] Ibid., 2 September 1937.
[54] Ibid., 26 August 1937 and 2 September 1937.

idly throughout the *raion*. The defendants in Shchuche were charged with gross negligence in the livestock losses, not intentional malice.[55]

In two other cases (the Kresttsy and Sychevka trials), however, officials in *raiony* with heavy livestock losses were accused of intentionally infecting animals with diseases.[56] Of all the charges made in the rural *raion* show trials of 1937, these are the least plausible and most reminiscent of the fantastic accusations of conspiratorial counterrevolutionary sabotage that characterized the Moscow trials of the Great Purges. The director of the Sychevka state farm (a former member of the Social-Revolutionary Party, one of the Bolsheviks' political competitors in 1917) was charged with leading a conspiracy to destroy the farm's livestock, using the prevailing unsanitary conditions as a cover for infecting 80 percent of the animals with diseases. Then, it was alleged, the *raion* veterinarian had done his bit to spread the epidemic throughout the country by sending animals from the infected herd to be shown at the All-Union Agricultural Exhibition in Moscow.[57]

A somewhat similar accusation was made against *raion* leaders in the Porkhov trial, although in this case the actual sabotage had been performed by aggrieved peasants. One of these was a noncollectivized peasant who allegedly poisoned kolkhoz cows and horses with arsenic at the behest of the *raion* party secretary. The other was a former kulak who, working as a kolkhoz stablehand after his return from exile, was said to have intentionally lamed the kolkhoz horses.[58]

Favoritism toward Former Kulaks

Kulaks (prosperous peasants, regarded by Communists as exploiters of poor peasants and potential capitalists) had been "liquidated as a class" by the Soviet regime at the beginning of the 1930s. What this meant in practice was that a good proportion of kulaks had been sent to labor camps or deported along with their families to distant areas of the Soviet Union, while others had been expropriated and evicted from their homes without arrest or deportation. Of the former group, some had returned from labor camps to the villages by the late 1930s (though the deportees were still forbidden to return). Of the latter group, many had left the countryside and gone to work in the towns, but some were still living in the area, and a few had even joined the collective farms. Official policy toward the group softened around 1936, when the Stalin Constitution restored full citizenship and voting rights to former kulaks and other old "class enemies." In the villages, however, the presence of former kulaks often produced conflicts because of their efforts to recover the property that had been confiscated from them and the new owners' and occupiers' efforts to hang on to it.

Peasant witnesses in the trials made many accusations that officials had done favors for former kulaks, presumably often as a result of bribes. It was said that kulaks had managed to get houses and horses back, that they had been given good

[55] *Kommuna,* 28 September 1937 and 3 October 1937.
[56] On the Kresttsy trial see *Krest'ianskaia pravda,* 28 October 1937. On the Sychevka trial see *Rabochii put',* 12 September 1937 and 16 October 1937.
[57] Roberta Manning, "The Case of the Miffed Milkmaid," gives a fascinating account, drawn from the Smolensk Archive, of the events in Sychevka leading up to the show trial.
[58] *Krest'ianskaia pravda,* 30 July 1937.

314   *The Russian Review*

jobs in the collective farms, and that, once admitted to the kolkhoz, they had taken revenge on peasants who were Soviet activists.[59] In Borisovka *raion* (Kursk oblast) the prosecutor claimed that in 1936 and the first half of 1937, 75 houses were returned to the kulaks who were their former owners, and 134 kulaks had their voting rights restored.[60] Returning the houses meant that schools, kindergartens, kolkhoz clubs, and other communal institutions had to be evicted, but the *raion* leaders were unmoved by their plight. This was held to be the more offensive since the party secretary, Fedosov, had behaved so brutally toward ordinary peasants in the *raion*: "Everything was taken from the population down to their socks, but [the *raion* party leaders] returned to the kulaks the property that had been legally confiscated from them."[61]

When kolkhozniki complained to the Borisovka party leaders about the concessions being made to former kulaks, it was reported that the party leaders "oriented those present at the meeting toward reconciliation with the class enemies."[62] This is not surprising, since reconciliation was the party's general line at the time in connection with the promulgation of the new constitution.[63] What is more surprising is that in 1937, without any overt change in the party line and with the constitution still in force, this could be treated in Kursk as a political crime.

Kursk was not the only place where this happened. At the trial in Sychevka *raion,* the two senior *raion* officials were also charged with distorting party policy on kulaks by announcing that it was time to forget about the whole idea of class enemies and make appointments and judgments of individuals on the basis of merit. They had instructed *sel'sovet* chairmen to destroy all the existing lists of kulaks and other persons who had earlier been disenfranchised or subject to other forms of discrimination—a reasonable interpretation, on the face of it, of the spirit of the new constitution. But then they had gone further—probably further than the new party line required, and certainly further than public opinion in Sychevka would stand for—and appointed a landlord's son as director of the school and several former kulaks as kolkhoz chairmen, as well as put former merchants in charge of village co-ops. According to peasant witnesses at the trial, the former kulaks who were appointed as kolkhoz chairmen "caused enormous damage," "persecuted Stakhanovites and beat them up," and "destroyed the horses."[64]

"Suppression of Kolkhoz Democracy"

According to the Kolkhoz Charter of 1935, collective farms were self-governing bodies whose chairmen were freely elected at the kolkhoz general meeting. But this was not in practice the way chairmen were selected. The normal custom was for local

[59] See, for example, *Sotsialisticheskoe zemledelie,* 26 July 1937, 28 December 1937; *Kurskaia pravda,* 14 October 1937; and *Rabochii put',* 16 October 1937.

[60] This is anomalous because the 1936 Constitution had in fact already restored voting rights to kulaks, priests and other former "class enemies."

[61] *Kurskaia pravda,* 23 August 1937, 26 August 1937, 29 August 1937, and 2 September 1937.

[62] Ibid., 26 August 1937.

[63] For a discussion of the changing policy on class in the 1930s see Sheila Fitzpatrick, "L'Usage Bolchévique de la 'Classe': Marxisme et Construction de l'Identité Individuelle," *Actes de la Recherche en Sciences Sociales,* no. 85 (November 1990): 75–80.

[64] *Rabochii put',* 16 October 1937.

authorities (the *raion* agriculture department or the local MTS) to nominate a chairman, whom the kolkhozniki then duly "elected." In the early 1930s the chairman was often an outsider—a Communist or worker sent out from the towns. But by the second half of the 1930s it was becoming increasingly common for locals (kolkhoz members or peasants from elsewhere in the *sel'sovet*) to be nominated as chairmen. It remains uncertain how seriously the central political leaders meant the charter to be taken with regard to democratic election of kolkhoz chairmen, but it seems clear at any rate that *peasants* wanted this provision taken seriously, and that newspapers were willing to endorse and publicize their complaints.

"Suppression of kolkhoz democracy" was one of the standard charges brought against *raion* officials in the rural show trials of 1937. In the Kazachkin trial in Saratov *krai*, for example, the *raion* authorities were accused of forcing a kolkhoz to accept a former *raion* official as chairman despite the protests of the kolkhozniki. This man subsequently robbed the kolkhoz of its assets, proving that the kolkhozniki had been right all along.[65]

Sometimes it was alleged that *raion* or *sel'sovet* authorities applied extreme measures of coercion in conflicts with kolkhozniki over chairmen. The liquidation of the "New Life" kolkhoz in Danilov *raion* was said to be the result of such a conflict.[66] In the Aleshki trial,

> witnesses I. N. Goltsev and V. A. Mishin related how, when they and other kolkhozniki got up at the general meeting in the "First of May" kolkhoz and criticized the work of the [kolkhoz] administration, demanding that the kolkhoz chairman be fired for failure to carry out his duties, the *sel'sovet* chairman, Kochetov, disbanded the meeting. Four of the most active kolkhozniki, including the two witnesses, were arrested on the basis of his provocative and false statement.[67]

In reporting the trials, oblast newspapers often played up the democracy theme. The Voronezh newspaper, commenting on the revelations of the Shchuche *raion* trial, added its own editorial flourish:

> Ask any kolkhoznik of the "Red Bitiug" kolkhoz why they elected Zazadravnykh chairman, and they will answer: "But we didn't elect him. Kordin [the *sel'sovet* chairman] foisted him on us. We protested and didn't want to accept him, but they made us." And that is completely true. That was the system there.[68]

VIRTUOUS PEASANTS AND EVIL BOSSES

In the narratives of the *raion* trials, evil bosses exploit and abuse, and peasants are their victims. The relationship of peasants and bosses was presented in clear antithetical terms; there was scarcely any shading of the stark black-and-white contrast between victimizers and victims. Rarely if ever did peasant witnesses mention a good boss at the *raion* level—one who, say, interceded for them or understood their prob-

---

[65] *Kommunist*, 14 September 1937.
[66] *Severnyi rabochii*, 30 July 1937.
[67] *Kommuna*, 4 September 1937.
[68] Ibid., 4 October 1937.

316   *The Russian Review*

lems. By the same token, in only a few instances did the gallery of defendants include a peasant who was not an office-holder of some kind, and in those instances the evil peasant was usually a kulak returned from exile.[69]

These same conventions prevailed in peasant letters of complaint to *Krest'ianskaia gazeta,* no doubt reflecting peasants' general disinclination to look anywhere but on the dark side. In real life, however, the dichotomy between rulers and ruled in the Soviet countryside was by no means so straightforward. In the first place, there was a gulf in real life between the status and powers of the *raion* authorities and those at *sel'sovet* and kolkhoz level. In the second place, *sel'sovet* and kolkhoz chairmen were not far removed from the local peasantry. The majority were local peasants themselves by origin—natives of the *sel'sovet* or even, in the case of many kolkhoz chairmen, of the village. There was considerable turnover in these lower offices; and, as we have seen, peasants were pushing with some success for veto power over appointments of kolkhoz chairman. The kolkhoz chairmen, moreover, were not salaried: they were paid (like other kolkhozniki, albeit more generously) with a proportion of the kolkhoz's harvest and income.

The premise that an impassable divide separated evil rulers from virtuous peasants was dramatized many times in the *raion* trials, and not only by peasant witnesses. For example, in the Shchuche trial, which is unusual in the context of *raion* trials for the defendants' willingness to participate in their own indictment, two defendants gave the following answers when the prosecutor asked why they did not try to recruit peasants and workers into their anti-Soviet activities:

SEDNEV (plant director). Undoubtedly if they [the workers] had known that I was a Trotskyist wrecker, they would have torn me limb from limb.

POLIANSKII (MTS director). Well, if I had even hinted of wrecking, they [the peasants] would have beaten me up if I was lucky, but more likely would simply have killed me.[70]

The peasant testimony at the trials presented many vivid images of the local "masters" taunting peasants with their powerlessness.

—So you went to VTsIK [that is, laid a complaint with the Russian Republican government in Moscow]! But we are the people in power here. I do what I want.[71]
—I am a Communist and you don't belong to the party. However much you complain about me, you won't be believed.[72]
—You should have shot the bastard; you wouldn't have got into any trouble for it [a *raion* official's comment to a subordinate, who had beaten a peasant].[73]
—If five people croak, that will teach you how to work, you idle bastards [a *raion* official's remark to kolkhozniki during the 1933 famine].[74]

[69] For the exceptions (in the Porkhov, Malin and Zolotukhino trials) see *Krest'ianskaia pravda,* 30 July 1937; *Moskovskaia kolkhoznaia gazeta,* 27 October 1937; and *Kurskaia pravda,* 14 October 1937.
[70] *Kommuna,* 3 October 1937.
[71] Ibid., 6 October 1937.
[72] *Krest'ianskaia pravda,* 27 August 1937.
[73] *Kommuna,* 28 September 1937.
[74] *Severnyi rabochii,* 22 September 1937.

—Grain has to be given to the horses. The kolkhozniki can survive without grain.[75]
—The clever ones left the collective farms long ago, and all that remain are the fools.[76]

Reports of the trials stressed the "deep hatred" with which peasants spoke of their former oppressors in courtroom testimony.[77] Before and during the trials, newspapers reported, resolutions and petitions came in from neighboring collective farms demanding the death sentence for the accused, who were referred to with such epithets as "contemptible swine" and "rotten bastards."[78] The halls where the trials were held were always described as packed, with the audience listening intently, full of indignation against the accused.

> Each evening, crowds of kolkhozniki gather near the school. . . . During the trial, as many as fifty statements indicating new facts of abuse and illegality performed by Seminikhin, Kolykhmatov and the others were personally handed by citizens to the oblast prosecutor, who is attending the trial.[79]

In one of the most dramatic confrontations reported in the press, a peasant witness, Natalia Latysheva, turned on the former leaders of Novgorod *raion* as soon as she took the stand.

LATYSHEVA. Comrade judges! Are these really human beings? They are ogres, swine.
  (*Movement in the hall, cries of approval, confusion on the bench of the accused.*)
CHAIRMAN. Witness, it is facts that are asked of you.
LATYSHEVA. Forgive me, comrade judges, but when I saw those swine, I couldn't contain myself. And it is a fact that they are scoundrels! . . . There they sit, damn them. The kolkhozniki will never forgive them for what they did.[80]

In Latysheva's story, as in those of many other peasant witnesses in the trials, the district's interference in agriculture (for example, in the giving of sowing plans) was completely unjustified and stupid, since the officials had no idea what they were doing. On Latysheva's kolkhoz, for example, the *raion* had tried to discourage the peasants from developing a stud farm and forced them to grow unprofitable and inappropriate crops. But the kolkhozniki were not to be browbeaten.

LATYSHEVA. We did not give up. We decided to breed trotters. And we did—those enemies of the collective farms did not break our spirit. To the astonishment of all, we built up a horse farm, and now we have twenty-one horses of pure Orel stock. (*Spontaneous applause breaks out in the hall, cries of "Good for you!" and "Well done!" are heard.*)

---

[75] *Krest'ianskaia pravda*, 2 September 1937.
[76] Ibid.
[77] Ibid.
[78] Ibid., 26 August 1937. See also the report of the Pavlograd trial in *Zvezda* (Dnepropetrovsk), 20 September 1937.
[79] *Kommuna*, 4 September 1937.
[80] *Krest'ianskaia pravda*, 3 September 1937.

CHAIRMAN. Witness, have you anything more to add?

LATYSHEVA. I have. (*The peasant woman turns to the accused, and stands face to face with the enemies of the people. . . .*) All the same, our side won, not yours. We were victorious![81]

Our side won! It would be tempting to end the story on this note of populist triumph. But had the peasant mice really won a significant victory over the oppressor cats? After all, the death of a cat does not change the essential relationship of cats and mice; and in Stalinist Russia the downfall of a Kochetov or even many Kochetovs in 1937 does not seem to have produced any lasting changes in an exploitative system of collectivized agriculture and a rural administrative structure that tended to generate petty local despots. To be sure, 1935–37 was a period of relatively conciliatory state policies toward the peasantry, in contrast to the harsh conflicts of collectivization at the beginning of the decade, but by 1938–39 the screws were being tightened again.

In the woodcut "The Mice Bury the Cat," as in the real world of the Soviet Union in 1937, it is not at all clear who killed the cat that the mice are so gleefully burying. It is hard to believe that the mice themselves were the killers—that is, that peasants had the political strength to take revenge on corrupt bosses without outside encouragement, or, if they had had the strength, that this would have been their chosen form of revenge. It is more plausible, certainly, that the peasant mice should have helped bigger predators locate their prey by writing letters of complaint and denunciation against particularly unpopular cat bosses. But peasant denunciations against local bosses were a constant feature of life; moreover, to say that they were probably used in constructing the show trials is not to say that the show trials could not have been constructed without them.

One thing we can be fairly sure of is that once the cat was dead, the mice danced at the funeral. The *raion* show trials of 1937, it seems, were a kind of Soviet carnival[82]—not just an outing for the local peasants, when they got a trip into the *raion* center where vodka was probably on sale, but a real *prazdnik* in which for a few days the world was turned upside down and mice could taunt and mock cats with impunity. Of course, this was not exactly a Bakhtinian Carnival: the mockery had a sly, malicious, almost corrupt quality that is alien to Bakhtin's notion of popular revelry. But then it is likely that real-life medieval carnivals were always a bit crueler and less innocently joyful than they appear in the retrospective view of twentieth-century intellectuals.

If carnival is the appropriate metaphor for the rural *raion* trials, this throws a disconcerting light on the big show trials in Moscow, and perhaps on the Great Purges as a whole. In the familiar *Darkness at Noon* picture of the Moscow trials, victims such as Nikolai Bukharin—the Marxist theorist whom Lenin called the party's fa-

---

[81] Ibid.

[82] On carnival see Natalie Zemon Davis, "The Reasons of Misrule," in her *Society and Culture in Early Modern France* (Stanford, 1975), 99–123; Peter Burke, *Popular Culture in Early Modern Europe* (London, 1978), chap. 7; and Mikhail Bakhtin, *Rabelais and His World*, trans. Hélène Izwolsky (Bloomington, 1984).

vorite—are revolutionary martyrs, tragically destroyed by the cause to which they have devoted their lives. From within this paradigm it seems inconceivable that anybody could see a similarity between the idealistic intellectual Bukharin and the crude and brutal Kochetov. From the standpoint of peasants, however, was one Communist boss any different from another, except in degree of rank and power? If there was reason to dance at Kochetov's funeral, was there not also reason to dance at the funeral of a Kochetov-writ-large such as Bukharin?

Almost certainly the potential carnival appeal of the Great Purge trials was not lost on Soviet political leaders. We can see signs that efforts were made by Stalin and on his behalf to tap into ordinary people's envious resentment of power and privilege. One of these is *Pravda*'s early report in connection with the Danilov trial that kolkhozniki of the *raion* had sent thanks to Stalin for restoring their kolkhoz (which the *raion* leaders had liquidated) and protecting them from their enemies.[83] Another is Stalin's toast to "the little people" at a reception for Stakhanovite workers in October, when he said that "leaders come and go, but the people remains. Only the people is eternal."[84]

It should have worked. According to the conventional wisdom of historians, Russian peasants have always been "naive monarchists," eager to believe that if the Tsar only knew of the injustices perpetrated by his nobles and officials, he would come riding to the people's rescue.[85] This "naive monarchism" of the Russian peasant, many Russian intellectuals believe, lay at the root of the Stalin cult, which allegedly could have developed only in a peasant country.[86]

Remarkably, the "naive monarchism" ploy failed. Ignoring *Pravda*'s hint, peasant witnesses in later trials did *not* credit Stalin with bringing corrupt lower officials to justice. They did *not* report that he had responded to their letters of complaint or attribute to him any guiding role, and they steadfastly avoided such "naive monarchist" formulations as "If Stalin had only known what was going on." In fact, in reported testimony at the trials there are virtually no references to Stalin at all.

This reticence must surely be understood in terms of the peasants' hostile reaction to collectivization and their strong belief that Stalin personally was the man mainly responsible for their sufferings in the early 1930s.[87] That these attitudes had not disappeared in the mid-1930s is shown by the striking reaction of peasants in the Western oblast to the murder of Sergei Kirov, the Leningrad party leader, in December 1934. Although Kirov is usually described by historians as a relatively popular leader, peasants evidently regarded his death as a fortunate event (on the general grounds that the mice had one less cat to worry about) that called for rowdy cele-

[83] *Pravda*, 31 July 1937.
[84] I. V. Stalin, *Sochineniia*, 14 vols., ed. Robert H. McNeal (Stanford, 1967), 1:254. Although eminently quotable, Stalin's aphorism was not widely quoted and does not appear in any of the *raion* trial reports I have read (though admittedly it came too late for many of the trials).
[85] For a skeptical examination of the idea of "naive monarchism" see Daniel Field, *Rebels in the Name of the Tsar* (Boston, 1976).
[86] For a rebuttal of this argument see the comments by the distinguished historian of the Russian peasantry, V. P. Danilov, in *Voprosy istorii*, 1988, no. 12:11.
[87] See, for example, OGPU reports of rumors and stories circulating in the countryside in the Smolensk Archive, WKP 166, pp. 216, 399.

bration. A ditty that appeared in more than one region of the oblast had as its concluding lines: "They killed Kirov; we'll kill Stalin" (*Ubili Kirova, ub"em Stalina*).[88]

Could it be, then, that Latysheva's "*Our side won!*" was not so far from the
mark after all? Were the mice at the cat's funeral really dancing to Stalin's tune? Or
was that their own subversive ditty, "Ubili Kirova," that they were singing?

---

[88] For one scandalous incident involving this ditty see the Smolensk Archive, WKP 355, pp. 36–39.
Note that the Russian verb in the first clause is ambiguous as to person: it could mean either "They killed
Kirov" or "We killed Kirov."

[10]
"Us against Them": Social Identity in Soviet Russia, 1934–41

SARAH DAVIES

According to Stalin, by the mid-1930s the Soviet Union had evolved into a socialist society without private property or antagonistic classes, in which workers, peasants and intelligentsia shared common interests. Since then, much energy has been expended on debates over whether the USSR could be considered a class society in the Marxist sense.[1] This theoretical question will not be addressed directly here. Instead, the focus will be upon the subjective perceptions of ordinary workers and peasants from 1934 until World War Two, and, in particular, on the *language* they employed to construct representations of their social identity.[2]

As this is a vast subject, the article will consider only identities articulated as "us against them" in the sense of the "people" (in various guises) against those perceived as power-holders. This image coexisted and competed with many others. David Hoffmann's work on Moscow in this period reveals the existence of identities based on cleavages between new and cadre workers, men and women workers, and workers of different nationalities. Stephen Kotkin suggests that workers sometimes articulated their identity through the use of the official "Bolshevik" language. Sheila Fitzpatrick shows how some peasants continued to define themselves as *bedniaki*, in

The author is grateful to those who commented on earlier versions of this article presented at the conference "Rossiiskaia povsednevnost', 1921–1941 gg.," St. Petersburg, 1994, and at the panel "Popular Opinion in Soviet Russia in the 1920s and 1930s" (ICCEES World Congress, Warsaw, 1995). She also thanks Sheila Fitzpatrick, David Hoffmann, Mary McAuley, David Priestland, Chris Ward, and two referees for their criticisms and suggestions. The British Academy and the Leverhulme Trust provided the financial support that made this research possible.

[1] For example, Alec Nove, "Is There a Ruling Class in the USSR?" *Soviet Studies*, vol. 27, no. 4 (1975): 615–38; idem, "The Class Nature of the Soviet Union Revisited," *Soviet Studies*, vol. 35, no. 3 (1983): 298–312; and David Lane, *Soviet Economy and Society* (Oxford, 1985), 163.

[2] On language and social identity see Gareth Stedman-Jones, *Languages of Class: Studies in English Working-Class History* (Cambridge, 1983), 22, 101; Lewis Siegelbaum and Ronald Suny, eds., *Making Workers Soviet: Power, Class and Identity* (London, 1994); and Sheila Fitzpatrick, "Ascribing Class: The Construction of Social Identity in Soviet Russia," *Journal of Modern History*, vol. 65 (1993): 745–70.

implicit opposition to kulaks.[3] Divisions also existed between peasants and workers, Stakhanovite and ordinary workers, and so on. People were rarely consistent in their self-identification. Cleavages among workers or between workers and peasants were not incompatible with broader solidarities based on identification with "the people" against "them," the power-holders. Simply, different identities were articulated on different occasions and for different purposes.

The "us/them" (*nizy/verkhi*) identification was typical of language that was "popular," in the sense of nonofficial. While the official language of the Soviet regime under Stalin stressed the harmony of social interests, popular language emphasized conflict. Although the categories of "official" and "popular" cannot be absolutized, since both emerged from a common culture, shared a frame of reference, and appropriated each others' terms, it is also clear that the conflictual image was characteristic of unauthorized, or what the regime termed "anti-Soviet" and "negative" expressions, and the following analysis is based entirely on comments and letters highlighted by the regime for their unorthodoxy.

Party and NKVD informants recorded the comments in highly classified reports on the popular mood. These reports, and the letters written by ordinary citizens, are problematic sources, partly because their representativeness and authenticity are difficult to ascertain,[4] and partly because there is little indication of the context of the views enunciated in them, apart from a few sparse details contained in the opinion reports about the originators of pronouncements (their name, place of work, party affiliation, occasionally their job). The lack of contextual information makes it hard to attribute meaning to particular statements. Therefore, the article will try to focus as much as possible on the language itself, and to identify recurring themes and images. In particular, it will reveal the way in which the sense of cleavage between "us and them" drew on a variety of repertoires—traditional, nationalist, populist, and Marxist—as well as from the official propaganda.

This dichotomous image of society is common to many cultures, as Ralf Dahrendorf shows. It is articulated as "them" and "us," "die da oben" and "wir hier unten," "ceux qui sont en haut" and "en bas."[5] Stanislaw Ossowski maintains that the spatial metaphor of vertical stratification of people into two main groups—those above and those below—has an ancient lineage stretching back to biblical times.[6] In Russia this perception of social polarization was acute in the prerevolutionary period, partly because of the sharp division between state and society, "official Russia" and the people, which gave rise to an image of "dual Russia."[7] During the revolutionary

[3] David Hoffmann, *Peasant Metropolis: Social Identities in Moscow, 1929–1941* (London, 1994); Stephen Kotkin, *Magnetic Mountain: Stalinism as a Civilization* (London, 1995); Sheila Fitzpatrick, *Stalin's Peasants: Resistance and Survival in the Russian Village after Collectivization* (Oxford, 1994).

[4] This is a question that I have dealt with at greater length elsewhere. See S. R. Davies, "Propaganda and Popular Opinion in Soviet Russia, 1934–1941" (Ph.D. diss., Oxford University, 1994). Most of my sources are from the former Leningrad Party Archive (now TsGAIPD). Equivalent material in other archives suggests that Leningrad was not a particularly special case: workers and peasants in different regions used similar language, although perhaps less frequently and less articulately.

[5] Ralf Dahrendorf, *Class and Class Conflict in Industrial Society* (Cambridge, 1959), 285.

[6] Stanislaw Ossowski, *Class Structure in the Social Consciousness* (London, 1963), 19–37.

[7] Robert Tucker, *The Soviet Political Mind: Stalinism and Post-Stalin Change* (London, 1972), 122.

72   Sarah Davies

period, Leopold Haimson has shown, workers felt this sense of polarization very keenly. Ronald Suny suggests that the 1917 Revolution was a "struggle between classes in the inclusive sense of the *verkhi* . . . versus the *nizy.*"[8] According to Lenin, "the whole world [of the workers] is divided into two camps: 'us,' the working people, and 'them,' the exploiters."[9] This sense of polarization did not vanish with 1917: it continued in a modified form throughout NEP, found a partial outlet during the Cultural Revolution, and reemerged in the 1930s, when the social divide became pronounced and egalitarianism was officially denounced.

In the period 1934–41 the "us/them" conflict was signified by a variety of means. Ordinary people defined themselves with such categories as "we," "the workers," "the people," "the *nizy,*" "the peasants," "the Russians," and "the masses." These categories tended to overlap and be used rather indiscriminately to identify the whole stratum of people excluded from power. They reveal the influence of SR, nationalist, populist, as well as Bolshevik language. Likewise, the categorization of the "other," the "enemy," drew on a number of sources in both pre- and postrevolutionary discourse.[10] The "other" was defined most commonly as "they," "the *verkhi,*" "responsible workers," "party members," "the state," "the rulers," "the new bourgeoisie," "the new capitalists," "engineers and technical workers" (ITR), "Jews"; and, less commonly, "rotten intelligentsia," "academics," and "tsar'ki." Popular self-identification had a rather negative quality in that it often appeared to rely on identification *against* more than identification *with.* The role played by the "them" in defining "us" therefore assumed a disproportionate weight.

The fundamental dichotomy between elite and people, us and them, was represented and explained in different ways, but rarely involved Marxist criteria. One common interpretation of the conflict was that it lay in an unequal distribution of political power. This was articulated through the use of analogies such as slaves and masters. Another means of representing the divide was in terms of ethical criteria, of good versus evil. A final representation was of a division based on economic power, the cleavage between rich and poor. Often representations of the social dichotomy relied on more than one explanatory factor: however, in the following analysis, each type of explanation will be examined separately.

It seems likely that this sense of dichotomy did much to legitimize certain aspects of the terror in the eyes of the ordinary people, and that the regime may have to a certain extent deliberately manipulated and promoted the us/them thinking, partic-

---

[8] Ronald Grigor Suny, "Toward a Social History of the October Revolution," *American Historical Review* 88 (February 1983): 51. See also Leopold Haimson, "The Problem of Social Stability in Urban Russia 1905–17," *Slavic Review* 23 (Autumn 1964): 619–42, and 24 (Winter 1965): 1–22; and idem, "The Problem of Social Identities in Early Twentieth-Century Russia," *Slavic Review* 47 (Winter 1988): 1–20.

[9] Cited in Timothy McDaniel, *Autocracy, Capitalism and Revolution in Russia* (London, 1988), 389.

[10] On representations of enemies in the Soviet period see William Chase, *Workers, Society and the Soviet State: Labor and Life in Moscow, 1918–1929* (Urbana, 1987); Diane Koenker, "Class and Class Consciousness in a Socialist Society: Workers in the Printing Trades during NEP," in *Russia in the Era of NEP: Explorations in Soviet Society and Culture,* ed. Sheila Fitzpatrick, Alexander Rabinowitch, and Richard Stites (Bloomington, IN, 1991); and Hiroaki Kuromiya, *Stalin's Industrial Revolution: Politics and Workers, 1928–1932* (Cambridge, 1988).

ularly in 1936–37.[11] In official discourse, the terror was portrayed as a battle between the "people" and the "enemies of the people." This opposition, people/enemy of the people, shared many similarities with the us/them dichotomy. Both were directed against those in positions of responsibility (although of course the terror targeted other groups as well, including ordinary workers and peasants), and both highlighted the political, economic and moral corruption of those in power. However, it is also clear that popular understandings of the official representation of "people" versus "enemies of the people" could differ from those intended by the regime. As Fredric Jameson points out, "the dialogue of class struggle is one in which two opposing discourses fight it out within the general unity of a shared code."[12] The same code could be used for divergent purposes. While the regime intended this language to mobilize support, subordinate groups could use it to indicate disaffection: to highlight inequality, the powerlessness of ordinary people, and distrust of *all* those in power, not simply the officially designated enemies.

THE POLITICAL DICHOTOMY

According to the propaganda, power in the USSR belonged to the people, namely, the workers and peasants. This power was vested in the people's representatives: the *vozhdi naroda*. In practice, and in the perceptions of many of the supposed power-holders, it actually rested in an elite of officials, Jews, and so on. Ordinary people felt that they were excluded from power, that those in power did not consult with the masses and ignored their opinions. The repurcussion of this was indifference to politics among some people, although others adopted a more positive stance, considering it necessary to take action to put "their own people" in power. The predominance of "higher-ups" implicated in the show trials encouraged the perception that all power-holders must be "enemies" and "wreckers" and that this would only be remedied when the government contained a higher proportion of workers and peasants.

The imagery employed to represent the distribution of political power derived from the traditional language of power relationships: "We nonparty workers are slaves"; "Workers were slaves and remain slaves"; "The Communists have white bones, and the nonparty people, black. If you look at it in the old way: the Communists are the nobility and the nonparty people, the workers"; "The masses are the manure of history"; "The people are pawns, they understand nothing, you can do what you want with them"; "The workers are lumps, drop them where you like"; "Workers are treated like dogs." Those in power were bosses (*khoziaeva*), "Soviet directors," "our gentlemen Bolsheviks."[13]

[11] See Sheila Fitzpatrick, "Workers against Bosses: The Impact of the Great Purges on Labor-Management Relations," in *Making Workers Soviet*, 312.

[12] Fredric Jameson, *The Political Unconscious: Narrative as a Socially Symbolic Act* (London, 1981), esp. 83–89. For more on the idea of "dialogue" and in general on Bakhtin's philosophy of language and culture see Mikhail Bakhtin, *The Dialogic Imagination* (Austin, 1981); idem, *Tvorchestvo Franzua Rable i narodnaia kul'tura srednevekov'ia i renessansa* (Moscow, 1965); and V. N. Voloshinov, *Marksizm i filosofiia iazyka* (Leningrad, 1930).

[13] Tsentral'nyi gosudarstvennyi arkhiv istoriko-politicheskikh dokumentov Sankt Peterburga (TsGAIPD), f. 25, op. 5, d. 46, l. 109 (p/34), f. 24, op. 2v, d. 1914, l. 58 (p/36), d. 2286, l. 12 (p/37), d.

74   *Sarah Davies*

A concerted propaganda campaign tried to portray the country's leaders in a populist guise as *vozhdi naroda,* an image that clearly had the potential to resonate with the people's own representations of the "ideal" leader. Although this propaganda undoubtedly worked to an extent, as the popularity of the leader cult demonstrates, others questioned the veracity of the image. Leaders were perceived as being nonproletarian: "Our leaders are not from the workers, Stalin is from an artisanal family. How could Kirov get an education if he was a *bedniak?*" Kalinin, who had been a worker at Krasnyi Putilovets (later, the Kirov Works) before his rise to power, was distrusted for having lost his proletarian roots: "Kalinin has broken away from the masses and does not want to know the working class." It was felt that most of the *vozhdi* were afraid of the people. Stalin and his *soratniki* "are afraid of us, and do not trust us workers." Zhdanov too was a "leader without the people."

The people did draw distinctions between the behavior of leaders. Kirov was sometimes represented as the ideal leader, perceived as being on the side of Leningrad workers: "Kirov was close, simple, completely one of us (*tselikom nash*)."[14] He set the standard against which others, particularly his successor, Zhdanov, were compared. Thus at a *kruzhok* of Krasnyi Treugol'nik at the end of 1935, workers complained that while Kirov often used to visit the factory, Zhdanov had not been there once, and they asked that he rectify this.[15] A cadre worker expressed a similar comparison between Kirov and Zhdanov in a letter of 1938, maintaining that Zhdanov knew about events at the grassroots only from reports:

> You do not hear stories about [workers'] lives, or ask questions of thousands of ordinary Communists, Komsomols and nonparty people which they could answer directly in their own words, and that is very bad. It's bad that you are never at factories and in the districts. In this you are not like the late Sergei Mironovich Kirov. He was close to the people. It was impossible for all the workers not to love him; it was impossible for his enemies to hate him. The party always relied and relies on the working class. Therefore it was and is victorious. There is no other way. Therefore there's no need to fear the workers, but you must come to us at the factories. The tsar was afraid to come to the people—and they killed him. . . . You must come to the factories, that will be more useful than your presence at the academic theater in Moscow.[16]

It was indeed the case that, unlike Kirov, Zhdanov was heavily involved with work in Moscow and had little time for ordinary factory workers in Leningrad.

This feeling that those in power ignored grassroots opinions was quite widespread. Thus, a smith, speaking at a soviet election meeting in December 1934, de-

---

1914, l. 3 (p/36), d. 4306, l. 176 (n/40), d. 3563, l. 32 (n/39), and d. 4313, l. 279 (n/40), op. 5, d. 2696, l. 90 (p/35), and op. 2v, d. 4306, l. 213 (n/40), and d. 4300, l. 275 (n/40). The information in parentheses that follow archival citations indicate the type of source and the year it was produced; for example, (p/34) denotes a party report, (n/34) an NKVD report, (l/34) a letter and (k/34) a Komsomol report, all from 1934.

[14] Ibid., f. 24, op. 5, d. 2288, l. 100 (p/34), f. 25, op. 5, d. 53, l. 59 (p/34), and d. 2288, l. 61 (p/34), and op. 2v, d. 2286, ll. 97, 78 (p.37).

[15] Ibid., f. 25, op. 10, d. 17, l. 80 (p/35).

[16] Ibid., f. 24, op. 2g, d. 149, l. 129 (l/38).

nied that popular suggestions and amendments to the soviet had any influence, because "the bourgeoisie and landowners (*pomeshchiki*) are in power . . . poor peasants have been exiled, kulaks remain, and there are only Jews in power."[17] This feeling emerged especially when decisions were taken which seemed quite contrary to popular wishes, and it was accompanied by demands for ordinary people to be given a consultative role. For example, at the end of 1934, when the decision to abolish bread rations was announced, a worker asked why they could not have a plebiscite in order to find out about popular opinion, as had been done in Germany. Another said that the party was "handful of people ruling not in 'our' interests. They ought to first of all ask the workers' opinion, have a meeting, and only if we agreed, only then sign a government decree." Similarly, after the publication of the labor decree of June 1940, supposedly at the workers' behest, there were complaints at several factories that in the USSR, in contrast to Britain and America, the government never *asked* the people for help in improving the national economy, it simply issued a decree.[18]

Despite the considerable social mobility of this period, the power elite was often represented as inaccessible to workers and peasants, no doubt because when any of the latter did move up the hierarchy, their lifestyle changed radically.[19] Elections were regarded as a formality, for it was believed that ordinary people were never elected. The 1937 elections to the Supreme Soviet provoked remarks that the existing power-holders had already arranged matters so that they would be elected—"Who was in power, will be again, we won't get in"—and that once they had grown accustomed to the good life they were unlikely to give it up.[20] This system was effective because it relied on fear, as one worker explained:

> It's just talk that the people will take part in the Supreme Soviet elections. It's nothing like that. Some person suggests the candidacy of Stalin or Kalinin and everyone begins to vote for them. They are afraid not to vote for them, because those who don't want to get arrested. After the elections to the Supreme Soviet, the situation will not change because the same people will remain.[21]

In practice, few workers and peasants were elected in party or soviet elections. Of the deputies elected to the Supreme Soviet of the USSR in 1937, only 11.5 percent were workers and 8.5 percent kolkhozniks.[22] Likewise, in the elections to primary party organizations in Leningrad in 1938, only 20 percent of those elected were workers, prompting one old worker to ask, "Why do they not elect us, but only engineers?"[23]

[17] Ibid., f. 25, op. 5, d. 49, l. 117 (p/34).
[18] Ibid., f. 24, op. 5, d. 2286, ll. 67, 93 (p/34), and op. 2v, d. 4306, l. 128 (n/40).
[19] When workers did move up the ladder, there was some resentment, as in the case of some leading Stakhanovites. For example, in 1936 one worker asked, "Why did Stakhanov develop the Stakhanovite movement, and does not work himself, but is a boss (*nachal'nik*)?" (ibid., f. 25, op. 10, d. 36, l. 68 [p/36]).
[20] Ibid., f. 24, op. 10, d. 303, l. 162 (p/37), and op. 2v, d. 1855, l. 210 (n/36), and d. 2499, ll. 24, 26 (n/37).
[21] Ibid., f. 24, op. 2v, d. 2499, l. 27 (n/37). See also ibid., ll. 48, 79, 105 (n/37).
[22] *Rossiiskaia Federatsiia*, 1993, no. 2:55.
[23] TsGAIPD, f. 24, op. 2v, d. 3179, ll. 110–13 (p/38).

While for this worker "engineers" epitomized "them," for others the target was the Jews. Jews more than any other ethnic group were singled out, not only because of the tenacity of Russian anti-Semitism but also because the largest ethnic minority in Leningrad was Jewish. According to the 1939 census Jews comprised 6.3 percent of the city's population (compared with 1.7 percent Ukrainians, the next largest nationality), and Leningrad had the highest proportion of Jews in the RSFSR.[24] Persistent stereotypes connecting Jews with positions of power were partly based on the fact that few Jews worked in factories, and even fewer in agriculture. For example, in Leningrad in 1924, at nineteen industrial enterprises whose ethnic composition is known, out of six hundred non-Russian workers, only sixteen were Jews. In the 1930s the proportion of Jewish workers remained small.[25] A disproportionately large number of Jews had always been leading members of the party, although this number declined a little in the 1930s. They also came to be identified with state power, since state service was one of the few outlets for Jews after NEP, when many had been engaged in trade and commerce. They dominated the Leningrad intelligentsia, comprising, in 1939, 18 percent of scientists and teachers in higher education, 20 percent of engineers, one-third of writers, journalists and editors, 31 percent of store managers, 38 percent of physicians, 45 percent of lawyers, and 70 percent of dentists.[26]

As a result, Jews were naturally identified with the (non-Russian, nonworker) "other." Leningrad Party Secretary Irklis received a letter shortly after the murder of Kirov which implicated Jews in the murder and declared that "the sacred revolutionary Smolny is full of the Jewish nation." According to the letter, this fact was well known to all workers and was causing unrest among them:

> All the traders' sons have set themselves up well with you in Smolny and behave brutally toward the old party members and toward the masses in general. . . . They shelve valuable applications and arrange responsible jobs for Jews and Jewesses at a fast pace, and now you can meet people of all nations among the unemployed with the exception of Jews, as they are all sitting in the leading jobs.

The letter went on to report conversations indicative of a desire to get rid of the Jews, warning Irklis, "a valuable worker and and old party member," so that he should not suffer like Kirov. The masses were apparently planning a St. Bartholomew's Night Massacre to eliminate Jews, or preparing for a new revolution.[27]

Another letter expressed similar feelings that Jews had taken over all the positions of power. The letter, signed by "A Russian," referred to the party organization of the Leningrad Industrial Institute, whose leader, Zakhar Zabludovskii, was apparently "not indifferent to people of Jewish extraction." The writer claimed that Jews "with dark pasts" occupied 80 percent of the apparat, and that Jews were given priority in housing, stipends and other privileges, and never excluded from the party.

[24] Iu. A. Poliakov et al., eds., *Vsesoiuznaia perepis' naseleniia 1939 goda: Osnovnye itogi* (Moscow, 1992), 62–63.

[25] Michael Beizer, "The Jewish Minority in Leningrad, 1917–1939" (paper presented to BASEES conference, Cambridge, Eng., March 1995), 8–10.

[26] Ibid., 10.

[27] TsGAIPD, f. 24, op. 2v, d. 727, l. 367 (l/34).

Zabludovskii allegedly had once drunkenly shouted, "For one Jew, we'll expel a thousand Russians from the institute."[28]

The Jewish dream of world domination was the subject of another anonymous letter, sent to Zhdanov. The letter argued that the Jews advocated world revolution because Russia was too small for them. Reflecting on the fall in the real standard of living since the Revolution, the writer concluded that socialism and communism were not viable, and simply a mask for the Jews to gain equal rights. The Jews organized 1917; Russians and other nationalities were simply pawns. Stalin, Kirov and other leaders had been bought up by the Jews and forced to subscribe to the doctrines of Comintern, the "international Yiddish cabal." Zhdanov was warned that he too would be sucked in, bought products from Torgsin, given cars, flattered, and have his speeches and portraits printed, all so that the Jews could realize their dream of world power.[29]

Although these three letters to party secretaries referred specifically to Jews, the sentiments they professed reveal a more general hostility toward the existing power structure, an anxiety that power was in the hands of a self-seeking alien group with its own interests and rules. Similar sentiments were expressed about other power-holders, although without the particular language associated with anti-Semitism. Jews were often associated with Bolsheviks, as in the assertion that "the Bolsheviks and Yids will destroy us."[30] The term "Jew" was sometimes applied indiscriminately, simply as a general term of abuse; for example, "Better had they killed Stalin than Kirov—Stalin is a Jew, but Kirov was Russian."[31] The letters were therefore part of a wider phenomenon of hostility to and resentment of power and privilege by impotent groups, rather than purely a manifestation of ethnic hostility.[32]

The sense of impotence, of being superfluous to the workings of power, generated some apathy and alienation from politics on the part of workers. The show trials were designed to mobilize the population, but when asked about their reactions to the trial of Piatakov and others, cleaners at Proletarskaia Pobeda replied, "We sweep the floor, that does not concern us."[33] Even the more politically literate expressed their alienation:

> The working class never fought for political rights. Only unconscious workers took part in the October Revolution. For the worker it is all the same who is in power, as long as he lives well. Each lives only for himself, and is not bothered about the rest.

> Workers were slaves and remain slaves. For us it makes no difference what kind of power there is, Soviet or fascist.[34]

[28] Ibid., d. 1543, l. 10 (l/35).
[29] Ibid., d. 1518, ll. 9–10 (l/35).
[30] Ibid., op. 5, d. 3202, l. 109 (p/36).
[31] Ibid., f. K598, op. 1, d. 5343, l. 17 (k/34).
[32] The tendency for class and nationalist languages to overlap in Russia has been noted by Ronald Suny, "Nationalism and Class in the Russian Revolution: A Comparative Discussion," in *Revolution in Russia: Reassessments of 1917*, ed. E. Frankel, J. Frankel and B. Knei-Paz (Cambridge, 1992).
[33] TsGAIPD, f. 24, op. 2v, d. 2267, l. 27 (p/37).
[34] Ibid., d. 1914, ll. 56, 58 (p/36).

78   *Sarah Davies*

The traditionally indifferent peasant also took the line of least resistance: "It's all the same to us, who's for Stalin, who's for Trotsky; better if they demanded fewer deliveries after the trials, but as it is they hurt each other, and the muzhik takes the rap."[35]

While these people ignored the machinations at the top, others appear to have considered the show trials and purges an opportunity to express their disaffection with the "other." The officially sanctioned punishment of authority figures in 1936–38 merely accentuated preexisting popular hostility toward power-holders. The scapegoating intention and/or effect of the terror against officialdom is clear and has often been highlighted.[36] Like the Cultural Revolution of 1928–31, the terror served as an outlet for popular hostility and hitherto thwarted social mobility. However, rather than deflecting criticism from Stalin and the evils of the system itself, it seems, in some cases, to have stimulated the already existing hostility toward all those in power, including Stalin.[37]

That the terror against those in power met with popular enthusiasm from some quarters is beyond doubt. Complaints that Kamenev and Zinoviev had been treated too leniently in 1934–35 were legion. It was felt that workers in such a situation would have been treated far worse, and that Zinoviev and Kamenev had been spared only because they were famous leaders.[38] One soldier described the situation in a letter to his parents in February 1935:

> The old counterrevolutionaries—Zinoviev, Kamenev and Evdokimov—have been sentenced as follows: Zinoviev ten years, Evdokimov eight years, Kamenev five years, and the rest they don't describe who, where and how long, previously they wrote—shooting for this one and that one, and there is no sense in it at all, and a simple worker gets ten years for nothing.[39]

After the trial, a worker asked a question that would, as the terror developed, become ever more common: "Why is it only the educated (*uchenye*) who are involved in all these affairs, and not workers?" The fall of Enukidze in mid-1935 led to demands that all the *verkhi* be checked, including those in the Central Committee, since the real root of the country's problems lay with them and not with the *nizy*.[40] These sentiments grew more pronounced as the regime itself encouraged vigilance toward those in positions of power and Stalin recommended listening to the voices of the "little people."[41]

During the August 1936 trial of Zinoviev and Kamenev, fears were expressed that once again they would be let off: "If a worker does something, then he is sent to court for trifles, but if the *verkha* does something, he is treated less strictly":[42]

[35] Ibid., op. 10, d. 163, l. 141 (p/37).
[36] For example, by Rittersporn and Fitzpatrick in much of their work.
[37] Fitzpatrick also argues this in *Stalin's Peasants*, 312.
[38] For example, TsGAIPD, f. 25, op. 5, d. 48, ll. 1, 3 (p/34).
[39] Ibid., f. 24, op. 2b, d. 33, l. 43 (l/35). I have opted to retain the original grammar and punctuation in this and subsequent quotes.
[40] Ibid., f. 25, op. 5, d. 48, l. 12 (p/34), f. 24, op. 2v, d. 1367, ll. 71–72 (p/35).
[41] I. Stalin, *Sochineniia* (Stanford, 1967), 1:253–55.
[42] TsGAIPD, f. 24, op. 2v, d. 2061, l. 115 (p/36).

More likely they'll shoot us fools. Nikolaev killed Kirov, and do you think he was shot, no, they sentenced him but only on paper. They have covered the eyes of us dark people. If they are shot, the Communists will get it from the capitalists.[43]

The news of the death sentences handed down to Zinoviev and Kamenev was therefore greeted with some jubilation and regarded as yet another blow against authority. One peasant commented: "All the leaders in power and Stalin should be shot," while a worker said in a similar vein, "Let them sentence the Zinovievites to shooting, and anyway the *vozhdi* will be stifled one by one, especially Stalin and Ordzhonikidze."[44] Another noted the number of Jews featuring in the trial. This became quite a common observation at the successive trials. At the trial of the "Anti-Soviet Trotskyite Center" at the beginning of 1937, there were many questions and observations of this type, including one by a Komsomol: "There are many Jews in this trial, because the Jewish nation loves power, and so they struggled for power so strongly."[45] Not only Jews but also "big people" and *sluzhashchie* stood out: "Look at the people sitting there. They are *sluzhashchie*, and *sluzhashchie* create these things. Now if only they would send old workers from the Karl Marx Factory and a couple of young ones to tell Stalin to rebuild and change things."[46] The reputation of party members continued to decline, particularly in the wake of the turnover in party personnel of 1937–38 and the Bukharin-Rykov trial, when workers observed that only Communists were involved, and one even asked if all members of the party had been accused.[47]

By the time of elections in 1937–38 the cumulative effect of the official and unofficial attacks on authority was often popular distrust of anyone in a position of power. The fall from grace even of the "hero" Tukhachevskii caused particular shock. Everywhere people asked, "Whom do we trust now?" for the old regime and its servants had been discredited in the eyes of many at the grassroots. Stalin, Molotov or any member of the Central Committee might turn out to be a "Trotskyist" or a "wrecker." As one engineer put it, "Now being in power means to wreck."[48] It was felt that those in power had been corrupted "because among the *verkhi* there is not one worker."[49] The us/them feelings were thus exacerbated, and there was a tendency to blame the authorities for every misfortune. A kolkhoznik explained: "That's why life is bad in the kolkhoz; wreckers destroy and we have to try to pay for it. We achieve nothing, they wreck and we restore with our backs."[50]

The popular representation of society as split between the people on one side and the "powers" on the other legitimized the terror against the *verkhushka* since it

[43] Ibid., d. 1851, l. 74 (n/36).
[44] Ibid., l. 72 (n/36).
[45] Ibid., d. 2061, l. 141 (p/36), and d. 2267, ll. 14, 25ob (p/37), and f. K598, op. 1, d. 5423, l. 11 (k/37).
[46] Ibid., f. 24, op. 10, d. 291, l. 77 (p/37), and f. K598, op. 1, d. 5423, l. 65 (k/37).
[47] Ibid., f. 24, op. 2v, d. 3178, ll. 19, 23, 29 (p/38).
[48] Ibid., d. 2664, ll. 1–8 (p/34), d. 2498, ll. 1–2, 150 (n/37), d. 2286, l. 13 (p/37), d. 2665, ll. 2–4 (p/37), d. 3178, ll. 23, 28–29 (p/38), and d. 2499, l. 24 (n/37), and op. 10, d. 291, l. 78 (p/37).
[49] Ibid., op. 2v, d. 2499, l. 24 (n/37).
[50] Ibid., op. 10, d. 163, l. 68 (p/37).

already predisposed them to regard power-holders as ipso facto guilty. To a certain extent the popular hostility toward "them," and the regime's image of the "enemy" coincided. However, it is clear that this popular hostility was directed not simply toward officially sanctioned enemies, but sometimes also toward Stalin, his colleagues and the whole party leadership. Likewise, some of those officially denounced as enemies, such as kolkhozniks and workers, clearly did not fall within the category of power-holders despised by the ordinary people. Nevertheless, the construction of the image of the enemy was not simply a one-way process.

THE MORAL DICHOTOMY

In their characterization of the social divide, people often had recourse to moral metaphors. The importance of the moral and religious dimension as a source of legitimacy in popular struggles against authority has been widely noted.[51] Mark Steinberg has shown how workers in the Russian printing industry rarely used Marxist language, preferring to define their opponent using ethical criteria:

> Although workers often accepted the notion of irreconcilable conflict between labor and capital, they viewed it less as a structural conflict of interest between classes than as a moral battle between, to use their own vocabulary, good and evil, light and darkness, honour and insult.[52]

This practice, Steinberg shows, continued after 1917. Ideas of suffering, redemption and salvation enabled the worker to make sense of his own experience in a more comprehensible way than the unfamiliar language of Marxism—capital, accumulation, labor value—would allow.[53]

The moral dimension was always a part of the idealist populist language. This, and the influence of the church, left its impact on the language of ordinary workers and peasants in the 1930s. It appealed both to the more literate and also to those who only had elementary ideas about good and evil. It emerged in the practice of attributing positive moral characteristics to the "people," and negative ones to their oppressors. The people were represented as naturally honest, defenseless and child-like. They were the innocents. Those in power were by contrast dishonest, sinful, drinkers of blood (*krovopiitsy*), hangmen, and murderers. They were unequivocally guilty. Their relationship to the people was based on deception and mockery or insult (*izdevatel'stvo*). An important distinction between the two groups was that the people worked, while "they" lived off them in a morally reprehensible way.

The moral superiority of the toiler was contrasted with the immorality of those who had made it into the ruling elite using dishonest means, or who had become corrupted as a result of being in power. In its most idealist form, this notion emerged in the populist belief that truth resides only in the people. An anonymous letter sent to the head of the Leningrad NKVD, Zakovskii, after the death of Kirov illustrates

---

[51] For example, by N. Cohn in *The Pursuit of the Millennium: Revolutionary Millenarians and Mystical Anarchists of the Middle Ages* (London, 1970).

[52] Mark Steinberg, *Moral Communities: The Culture and Class Relations in the Russian Printing Industry, 1867–1907* (Berkeley, 1992), 234.

[53] Mark D. Steinberg, "Workers on the Cross: Religious Imagination in the Writings of Russian Workers, 1910–1924," *Russian Review* 53 (April 1994): 213–39.

this view. The letter criticized the government for being unaware of the people's real feelings behind the facade of peace:

> It does not see that every destroyed church resounds with the most terrible echo throughout the whole country. It does not hear the curses of millions of people every day. It does not hear what the tortured people say in the queues created by Soviet power. It does not hear that *people's truth*. . . . Soviet power is "blat" plus bureaucratism, boorishness and vandalism. No Soviet "truths" can wipe out this genuine *people's truth*. . . . Soviet power is racing toward its destruction. The more and the quicker it does so, the faster does the cup of the people's patience fill up.[54]

Because of this stereotype of the innate honesty of the people, and the corresponding dishonesty of those in power, the official discourse on wreckers and sabotage within the leadership found a resonance in the minds of ordinary people, who already assumed that they must be guilty. The words of a worker, Kuznetsov, seem representative:

> I do not trust your VKP(b)—they are all wreckers. I believe only in the worker, who works in production. None of the Communists are honest. You get together on your own at your meetings, and what you are sorting out is a mystery. You don't tell the workers about it.[55]

Those in power were constantly represented as deceiving the people, as breaking their promises, pulling the wool over people's eyes, saying one thing and doing another. This feeling was particularly profound in a period when the media was saturated with stories of happiness and prosperity which contradicted sharply with the reality of everyday life. An "honest worker" from the Samoilov Factory expressed this feeling:

> What is there to say about the successes of Soviet power. They're lies. The newspapers cover up the real state of things. I am a worker, wear torn clothes, my four children go to school half-starving, in rags. I, an honest worker, am a visible example of what Soviet power has given the workers in the last twenty years.[56]

"Deception" and "betrayal" were some of the most commonly employed words in this period. The Constitution was a deception, the elections were a deception, the government's economic policies were a deception. The people's enemies had deceived them and betrayed their trust.

In 1935 workers from the Kirov Works wrote a lengthy letter to Zhdanov, full of strong words against the regime and the "soap-bubble comedy" it was enacting: "The time of respect for the Bolsheviks has passed, for they are traitors and oppressors of everyone except their *oprichniki*." The end of rationing was "Molotov's vile deception," especially as the leadership was well aware of the conditions in which workers lived, particularly those with a family: "Oh, how criminal, how base to de-

---

[54] TsGAIPD, f. 24, op. 2v, d. 1518, l. 1 (I/37).
[55] Ibid., d. 2664, l. 265 (p/37).
[56] Ibid., d. 2282, l. 109 (p/37).

ceive the toilers (*truzheniki*), especially his family. And the children, about whom you shout a lot in the press, constant deceivers and scoundrels." With reference to the party's attention to youth in mid-1935, they wrote:

> And you Bolsheviks—fighters for the people (*narodnoe delo*), for liberty, equality and fraternity, you still shout at the present time, speak about the education of contemporary youth, and in the spirit of communism as well. Are you not embarrassed to deceive the young so shamefully, surely you Bolsheviks can see, and how can it be educated and be a genuine reserve and helper of your treacherous party.[57]

The feeling that "you are deceiving us" recurs time and time again.[58] The deception of the people was represented as a constant attribute of power: "The tsarist government deceived the people and Soviet power deceives them." The people were easy to deceive because of their naive and trusting nature: "We have been deceived for nineteen years, and, fools, we understand nothing, like sheep." "We are deceived like fools."[59]

The moral distinction between the honest people and the dishonest rulers was often based on the perception that the people, unlike their rulers, actually worked. The assumption behind this was that toil in itself is redemptive, and suffering is good. Since those in power did not actually work, they became morally corrupt. The characteristics applied by the people to their rulers suggest moral degeneration—they were lazy, fat, drinkers of blood, cowardly, thieving. Sloth is a sin, and those in power did no real work, but just sat in offices and issued decrees: "Party members lead and nonparty members work."[60] Sometimes this representation was given a nationalist coloring. Georgians and Jews were portrayed as loafers (*lodyri*) living at the expense of the Russians.[61]

The much-vaunted moral precept in the new Constitution, "He who does not work shall not eat," was treated with irony by many ordinary people, who argued that, on the contrary, "he who works does not eat, and he who does no work [those in power] eats."[62] The greed of those in power was constantly emphasized: "Look at the military, responsible workers, the GPU, they live well, just get fatter"; and, on Kirov's corpse, "Kirov is so fat lying there. No doubt he didn't get the pay a worker does."[63] Attributing the sin of greed to "them" was one way ordinary people coped with the fact that they themselves were hungry, for hunger was associated with moral virtue. This sense of moral righteousness can be discerned in a letter from a group of domestic workers to the Leningrad Soviet in 1936. Among their demands was one that cafes selling vodka should be reduced by 80 percent, and serve tea and

---

[57] Ibid., d. 1518, ll. 184–88 (l/35).

[58] For example, ibid., op. 5, d. 2696, l. 90 (p/35), and d. 3202, l. 92 (p/36), and op. 2v, d. 1833, l. 185 (n/36).

[59] Ibid., op. 2v, d. 2499, ll. 77, 104 (n/37), and op. 5, d. 3202, l. 109 (p/36).

[60] Ibid., op. 2v, d. 3720, l. 339 (p/39). See also ibid., d. 3563, l. 32 (p/39).

[61] Ibid., op. 2v, d. 2286, l. 137 (p/37), and f. 25, op. 10, d. 17, l. 80 (p/36).

[62] Also, "There are many intelligentsia, and they live off us, they say that he who does not work does not eat, but we work and there is nothing to eat" (ibid., f. 24, op. 2v, d. 1914, l. 92 [p/36], and d. 1846, l. 123 [n/36], and op. 5, d. 3732, l. 88 [p/36]).

[63] Ibid., op. 2v, d. 1049, l. 20 (p/35), and op. 5, d. 47, l. 31 (p/34).

coffee instead, for "we see how responsible workers with briefcases wait at eight o'clock for the opening of the cafe with vodka and beer; having drunk a couple of pints of beer, the *sluzhashchii* goes to work. Is that normal?"[64]

Since those in power did no work themselves, they lived off the labor of others. This idea of exploitation was often expressed through the use of the concept of theft: "They" robbed the workers with loans and deprived them of what was theirs by right, the fruits of their labor: "Soviet power robs the peasants, takes eveything, while people are left to go hungry. You won't build socialism that way." Other nationalities were innately predisposed to theft: "There is not one sensible person in power, they are all Yids, Armenians and other *zhuliki*" (thieves, swindlers).[65]

In contrast to those in power, the laboring people were by definition good and free from sin. The idea of redemptive suffering was an essential aspect of the moral superiority of the worker. He suffered because his work was so hard and life so difficult. In contrast to the official doctrine of work in the USSR as creative, joyful and liberating, people continued to see labor as a curse to be endured. The writer of a letter to Zhdanov in 1935 signed off as "Stradalist pravdist" (roughly, sufferer for truth), and described his life as a poor worker in Leningrad, his miserable, exhausting day at the factory with little to eat but bread and water:

> That, dear comrade Zhdanov, is how we Leningrad workers work and suffer
> and torture ourselves in our lives. Our life is very tortured and suffering,
> what else can one say, when living people begin to envy the dead, that they
> sleep without any torture, while we live and suffer terribly.[66]

The idea of suffering was often expressed in terms of torture and blood—those in power "drink the blood" of the worker and "have become carried away with exaggerated successes at the expense of the blood and sweat of the Russian people." There was a tendency to equate this suffering and patience with Russianness. Only "workers in the USSR can bear such difficult torture, for the Russian can be patient for long," but not forever: "The Russian people have waited for a long time, but even Russian patience has an end." This view of the Russian people was often, but not exclusively, the product of the more literate and it was associated with a certain amount of idealization: The Russian had "a large and broad soul," according to one party member writing to Zhdanov.[67]

The final aspect of the moral dichotomy that should be considered is that of the authorities' insulting attitude to the people. As Steinberg points out, some workers firmly believed in the idea of the dignity and equality of all men, partly because of the influence of Christian teaching.[68] This belief provided a vocabulary with which to protest against the behavior of the *verkhi*. The millions of petitions sent to the highest party leaders were full of complaints about the rude, boorish and insulting behavior of individual bureaucrats. The comments and letters also indicate that *iz-*

---

[64] Ibid., op. 2v, d. 1748, l. 171 (l/36).

[65] Ibid., d. 3563, l. 61 (n/39), d. 1049, l. 23 (p/35), and d. 4306, l. 198 (n/40).

[66] Ibid., d. 1518, l. 183 (l/35).

[67] Ibid., l. 184 (l/35), d. 2500, l. 62 (n/37), and d. 2499, l. 29 (n/37), and op. 2g, d. 47, l. 197 (l/37).

[68] Steinberg, *Moral Communities*, 112–22.

84   *Sarah Davies*

devatel'stvo was considered morally unacceptable. One letter sent to the Leningrad Executive Committee shortly after the end of bread rationing stressed this idea several times:

> Better first to bury all our rulers of Soviet power, so that they do not insult the working class. . . . That's enough watching the mockery of the working class. So here's a task for you, the bosses, if prices on food are not lowered and on bread by 40 percent, it will be bad for you. . . . No, that's enough slavery and mockery of the working class.[69]

Another anonymous letter to Zhdanov from the end of 1935 echoed this theme: "That's enough laughing at the workers, enough starving, enough teasing them like dogs, who suffers like the poor worker, our enemies are our aristocrats who harm the working people."[70] This objection to the people being treated like dogs also emerges in a comment in 1940 that, under Catherine II, landowners exchanged their peasants for dogs, while now Soviet directors sell workers to each other over drinks in restaurants.[71]

Underlying many of these representations of a moral dichotomy were often questions of political and economic difference. Nevertheless, the moral dimension should not be underestimated. The moral difference between "us" and "them," between good and evil, was for many ordinary people as valid as the more obvious political and material inequality. Official representations of the "enemies of the people" in 1937–38 also played up the moral degeneracy of those concerned, portraying them as the embodiment of evil. Gábor Rittersporn, echoing Moshe Lewin, argues that the "conspiracies" of the 1930s relied on the "allegorization of an ineffable evil that came to possess the world of every social category, the projection of the regime's elusively hostile universe in identifiable deeds and agents," and that this corresponded with traditional popular beliefs.[72] In the official discourse, moral turpitude was criticized, not only that of Trotsky (the "Judas") but also of ordinary Communists. Thus, in September 1937, *Pravda* in its leader, "The Moral Aspect of a Bolshevik," attacked the "bourgeois" morality of some Communists and Komsomols and their excessive drinking.[73] Once again, the official and popular languages echoed each other.

THE ECONOMIC DICHOTOMY

While inequalities of power were frequently articulated using political and moral language, the reality of economic difference was the most immediately perceptible and intelligible facet of everyday life. As one peasant put it succinctly, "They say that everyone is equal, but in fact not everyone is equal—some are well dressed, and others badly."[74] The fact that one family had 150 rubles a month, while another had

[69] TsGAIPD, f. 24, op. 2v, d. 1518, l. 14 (l/35).

[70] Tsentral'nyi gosudarstvennyi arkhiv Sankt Peterburga, f. 7384, op. 2, d. 49, l. 432 (n/35).

[71] TsGAIPD, f. 24, op. 2v, d. 4306, l. 213 (n/40).

[72] Gábor Rittersporn, "The Omnipresent Conspiracy: On Soviet Imagery of Politics and Social Relations in the 1930s," in *Stalinist Terror: New Perspectives,* ed. J. Arch Getty and Roberta Manning (Cambridge, 1993), 115.

[73] *Pravda,* 20 September 1937.

[74] TsGAIPD, f. 24, op. 2v, d. 1914, l. 92 (p/36).

3,000, that leaders were chauffeured around in cars and shopped in Torgsin, that the state bought grain from peasants for one price and sold it for twenty times more—all these basic inequalities were the most visible signs of the existence of two groups in society. Popular interpretations of economic difference were not usually related to questions concerning the relationship to the means of production; they did, however, use Marxist concepts such as exploitation and capitalism. More often, though, they focused on inequality in income and lifestyle, and in particular on access to privileges. The main observation was that those in power seemed to get a lot more money or privileges than the people, and hence that the people were being exploited in order to keep the privileged in power.

This theme was replayed hundreds of times. A sophisticated version emerges in the words of a worker at the Lenin Works in the middle of 1934:

> How can we liquidate classes, if new classes have developed here, with the only difference being that they are not called classes. Now there are the same parasites who live at the expense of others. The worker produces and at the same time works for many people who live off him. From the example of our factory it is clear that there is a huge apparat of factory administrators, where idlers sit. There are many administrative workers who travel about in cars and get three to four times more than the worker. These people live in the best conditions and live at the expense of the labor of the working class.[75]

This refrain was powerful after 1934, a period that witnessed the turn toward the market and greater income differentials. Despite Stalin's denunciation of egalitarianism at the Seventeenth Party Congress, demands for leveling persisted. Referring to the congress, one cleaner commented that

> the speeches are good, but there's no bread, at the factory there are three bones: pure white, they have a canteen of a closed type; whitebone, they have their own one; and black [workers], they have a general one where there is nothing. We are all workers and we should be fed equally.[76]

Likewise, a request to the Leningrad Soviet in 1934 highlighted the need to improve children's food "and not open various better canteens for ITR [technical specialists]. They should have achieved equality of food for all."[77] The end of rationing in 1935 seemed to signal the end of the preferential treatment of workers, and it provoked many comments that prices would be only accessible to "craftsmen and businessmen" (*kustari i chastniki*), *sluzhashchie*, "white guards," "Stalin's shockworkers and Red Partisans," "scientists," "kulaks and bourgeois," and "alien elements."[78] Many women feared that the more highly paid and the technical specialists would buy up everything, leaving nothing for the rest. Interestingly, certain academics regarded the end of rationing in a similar light. The orientalist Krachkovskii, for example,

[75] Ibid., f. 25, op. 5, d. 38, l. 46 (p/34).
[76] Ibid., d. 38, l. 44 (p/34).
[77] Ibid., f. 24, op. 5, d. 2286, l. 6 (p/34).
[78] Ibid., f. 25, op. 5, d.. 48, l. 52 (p/34), d. 46, l. 141 (p/34), d. 54, l. 27 (p/34), and d. 49, l. 116 (p/34), and f. 24, op. 2v, d. 1200, l. 70 (n/35), and op. 5, d. 2286, l. 80 (p/34), and d. 2691, l. 35 (p/35).

86   *Sarah Davies*

interpreted the decree abolishing rations on meat, fish and other food as a regression to a new class system:

> This decree, like all recent measures is aimed mainly at high-paid groups. For those who get 1000–1500 a month the reduction is very important. For the average Soviet citizen, in particular for a young academic, the decree is useless. It does not even provide a meager minimum, that ration which used to be given. In a word, however much we shout about socialism, in fact we're moving to new classes.[79]

A common perception existed that the elite made policies that promoted their own economic interests rather than those of the workers and peasants. Many workers interpreted the end of rationing in this way: "Power sees that the people have begun to live only on rations, and no one buys bread at the expensive price, and it gets little profit, so they have to sell unrationed bread, as it will be more profitable. Power only worries about its own profit, and does not want to bother about the people." A similar reaction greeted all price rises during this period—it must be good for the "new capitalists," responsible workers, Communists, and so on. One worker even thought that price reductions were "a fiction carried out for the benefit of the higher class." Likewise, such labor policies as the Stakhanovite movement and the laws of 1938–40 were regarded as a way of extracting more profit from the worker in order to benefit the elite. Typical of comments was, "The Stakhanovite movement has been thought up by our rulers in order to squeeze the last juice from the toilers."[80]

The Stakhanovite movement was accompanied by the public promotion of consumer values and a status revolution.[81] This made the growing economic inequality glaringly obvious to the *nizy*. A question addressed to propagandists in a region of Western Siberia in 1936 summed up the economic disparity between elite and people: "Isn't what is prevailing in practice in the USSR the principle of socialism for the masses and the principle of communism for the *vozhdi*?"[82]

The privileged lifestyle of the elite, symbolized by holidays, cars, servants, special closed shops, flats, and clothes, was one of the most visible signs of social injustice, of a two-tier system. Ordinary people tended to associate this visible wealth with enemies; that is, with those in power. At an election meeting in 1934 at Krasnyi Putilovets, someone complained that "trips to resorts and rest homes are given to alien (*chuzhdye*) people, lawyers, *sluzhashchie* travel with their wives, and there is no room for the worker." At another meeting at the Munzenberg Factory, the complaint was similar: "Our children never get to go to rest homes, it costs 112 rubles, a female worker cannot afford it, and only the children of responsible workers go."[83]

There were constant complaints about those with cars, the ultimate status sym-

[79] Ibid., f. 24, op. 2v, d. 1200, l. 71 (n/35).

[80] Ibid., d. 1049, l. 22 (p/35), f. 25, op. 10, d. 74, l. 11 (p/37), and f. 24, op. 2v, d. 1829, l. 63 (n/36).

[81] See Sheila Fitzpatrick, *The Cultural Front: Power and Culture in Revolutionary Russia* (London, 1992), 216–37.

[82] Gosudarstvennyi arkhiv Novosibirskoi oblasti, Novosibirsk, f. 3, op. 10, d. 926, l. 52 (p/36).

[83] TsGAIPD, f. 25, op. 5, d. 46, l. 180 (p/34), and d. 49, l. 11 (p/34).

bol.[84] The insinuation—again—was that those with cars were enemies. Remarking on the fall of Enukidze, a chauffeur said, "How many are there of his kind in Leningrad. They go out to the dacha at the weekend in cars, bought with the people's money, wasting petrol, which we lack." Some people interpreted the new phenomenon as symptomatic of the development of middle-class values: "A new bourgeoisie has appeared in our country, they travel around in cars, go around the workshops, grow paunches"; "Soviet power is bad because it has created many Soviet bourgeois, for example . . . the secretary of the RK VKP(b) Osip. He travels round in cars, while the kolkhoznik doesn't have that chance."[85]

The Torgsin stores, which during 1930–36 sold goods for gold and hard currency, were particularly reviled. Although Torgsin stores were not in fact as luxurious and opulent as they have sometimes been portrayed, they nevertheless had great symbolic significance, epitomizing the inequities of the system.[86] In jokes and leaflets, which relied on transmitting ideas in a symbolic and concentrated form, the symbol of the Torgsin stores frequently appeared. One leaflet of 1934 read, "Comrades! Unite. Russia is perishing. Stalin is wearing the people out. Torgsin caters for Russian gentlemen, who served the emperor Nicholas."[87] A joke was made by deciphering Torgsin as "Tovarishchi opomnites', Rossiia gibnet, Stalin istrebliaet narod" (Comrades remember, Russia is perishing, Stalin is exterminating the people).[88] At the time of the end of rationing, another joke ran, "There are four categories: (1) *Torgsiane*, (2) *Krasnozvezdiane*, (3) *Zaerkane*, (4) *Koe-kane.*"[89] There was some popular pressure for the shops to be closed. An anonymous letter with just such a demand landed on Zhdanov's desk in 1935 from a group of workers at the Kirov Works. The letter clearly reveals how workers tended to associate class with privilege.

> Comrade Zhdanov. At all the meetings they speak of a classless society, but in fact it turns out not like that, we have a handful of people, who live and forget about communism. It's time to stop the fattening-up of responsible workers. It is time to close the Soviet Torgsins . . . for they are a disgrace, the worker must buy expensive products with his pennies, while the responsible worker, who receives 600–750 rubles a month, gets butter in this shop for 7 rubles per kg., and they give him 4 kilos a month, while the worker for his pennies gets butter for 27 rubles, in general it's a disgrace to have such shops now, it's simply squandering the people's resources, if they get everything there virtually gratis. It's clear that responsible workers cost the state a lot, they get dachas, even those without children, they go to resorts, and get benefits, take our factory director, he doesn't come to our shop, why should he, it's expensive there. No, we've still got along way to go before a classless society if this carries on.[90]

[84] Fitzpatrick, *Cultural Front*, 230.
[85] TsGAIPD, f. 24, op. 2v, d. 1367, l. 71 (p/35), f. 25, op. 5, d. 83, l. 24 (p/36), and f. 24, op. 2v, d. 1851, l. 124 (n/36).
[86] E. A. Osokina, "Za zerkal'noi dver'iu Torgsina," *Otechestvennaia istoriia*, 1995, no. 2:97–98.
[87] TsGAIPD, f. 24, op. 2v, d. 772, l. 15 (n/34).
[88] Tsentr khraneniia dokumentov molodezhnykh organizatsii, Moscow, f. 1, op. 23, d. 1128, l. 64 (k/35).
[89] TsGAIPD, f. 25, op. 5, d. 46, l. 73 (p/34) (this translates roughly as, "the Torgsiners, the Red Stars, the Closed Workers' Cooperative people, the Somehow or others").
[90] Ibid., f. 24, op. 2v, d. 1518, l. 32 (l/35).

88   *Sarah Davies*

There are numerous examples of such attitudes berating those in power for their economic privileges, but one that stands out is the letter already mentioned, written by a group of low-paid domestics. These workers were barely mentioned in the official press or statistics, but they were most exposed to the glaring differences in lifestyle between rich and poor in this period. In the letter they described how they earned about 125 rubles for fourteen hours' work for employers who were receiving anything from four to twenty times as much. Their bosses (doctors, engineers, directors) also had access to free cars, holidays and luxury flats. They particularly resented the wives of these people who engaged in "light work for amusement," such as being school directors, and whom they considered worse than the "former ladies," since they demanded so much work (up to eighteen hours a day) from their servants. They directly stated that they felt themselves to be the *nizy,* and they resented the fact that the press ignored them, that, according to responsible workers, there were no longer any *nizy,* only "low-paid groups."[91]

Although the writers of this letter were more directly exposed to the privileged lifestyle of the new elite, many others shared their views and were keen to accord enemy status to those enjoying a life so conspicuous in its opulence. The terror clearly had popular support because it was perceived as hitting those with economic privileges. The expulsion of "former people" and other undesirables from Leningrad in early 1935 was greeted with satisfaction by those who hoped that workers would be the beneficiaries: "Finally all the parasites will be expelled from Leningrad and the working class will have at least a little improvement in housing at their expense."[92]

It is revealing to compare the type of criticism made by workers in 1937 with official accusations against "enemies," since both highlighted the material excesses of the elite. Popular complaints tended to be more vehement and to articulate more general grievances about, for example, the low standard of living and the state loans. Workers said to agitators, "What are you saying that life has become better; in our hostel the stoves have not been lit for three days, there's no food and linen. In the administration of the artel they say there's no money, while fifteen-twenty thousand are being spent on the chairman's office alone." Likewise, old cadre workers and Communists at the Kirov Works complained during the loan campaign that "the people who demand loans are those who decorate their flat for twenty thousand, like the head of the factory committee, Podrezov."[93] Fitzpatrick cites some of the official accusations leveled against the accused, such as the director of Molodaia Gvardiia, who "ripped off the state shamelessly. In the rest houses that the publishing firm is building, a luxurious apartment has been equipped for Leshchintser. Furniture of Karelian birch has been bought for that apartment. He is a bourgeois degenerate."[94] These words echo the unofficial language of workers and peasants, with the difference that the latter tended to blame all those in power, or the entire system, as well as concrete individuals. As one party worker explained in a letter to Stalin of 1937:

[91] Ibid., d. 1748, ll. 166–68 (l/36).
[92] Ibid., op. 5, d. 2714, l. 106 (p/35).
[93] Ibid., op. 2v, d. 2665, ll. 61–62 (p/37).
[94] Fitzpatrick, *Cultural Front,* 230.

The logic of the peasant is very simple. For him, all leaders are plenipotentiaries of the regime, and correspondingly, he considers that the regime is responsible for all his woes. . . . And the situation of the kolkhozniks is such that mentally they have sent us all to the devil.[95]

Despite the official representation of a socialist society without antagonistic classes, some people continued to view their world as polarized between two groups, those with power, and those without. For these, the dream of socialism seemed far away. As one person wrote in a note to a speaker at an election meeting at the end of 1934, "Comrades, how can you say this, we are enserfed, hungry and cold. This is called a classless socialist society. It's all lies."[96] People felt divided from the elite on political, economic and moral grounds. The way these divisions found expression owed as much to traditional conceptions of social justice as it did to the ideas of Marx and Lenin. The terror of 1937 was one way in which the people could satiate their appetite for revenge against at least some of those in power.

For a while, the officially sanctioned image of the enemy and that constructed by the people partially coincided. However, by early 1938 the "quasi-populist" aspect of the terror was already receding, with the stress henceforth on stability of cadres.[97] In its wake came a new policy of appeasing and extolling the intelligentsia, one symbol of which was the award of Stalin Prizes worth thousands of rubles. Those disbursed in March 1941 for science, technology, art, and literature provoked such comments from workers as, "We agree that they should get prizes, but why do they need such big sums when they are well off? We ourselves are creating capitalists living off interest, and then those millions will be squeezed out of us workers as loans."[98] Such feting of the intelligentsia in the difficult years 1938–41, when harsh laws were being applied to workers and peasants, probably ensured that the latter groups' sense of social polarisation, if anything, increased in this period. Possibly, only the appearance in 1941 of an external enemy provided the necessary stimulus for at least some of the disaffected *nizy* to feel part of a "united people."

---

[95] TsGAIPD, f. 24, op. 2g, d. 49, l. 114 (l/37).

[96] Ibid., f. 25, op. 5, d. 48, l. 53 (p/34).

[97] Sheila Fitzpatrick, "Stalin and the Making of a New Elite, 1928–1939," *Slavic Review* 38 (Summer 1979): 396.

[98] TsGAIPD, f. 24, op. 2v, d. 4814, ll. 116–17 (n/41), and d. 5134, ll. 30–36 (p/41).

Part III
War and Post-War Recovery

[11]

THE SOVIET RESPONSE TO SURPRISE ATTACK:
THREE DIRECTIVES, 22 JUNE 1941

By J. Erickson

The artificiality and contrivance of the conundrum, demonstrably a device more Delphic than Clausewitzian for divining complex strategic issues, seems to have a relevance all its own in examining the situation which prevailed both on the eve and during the first few hours of the German invasion of the Soviet Union in 1941: when is a surprise not a surprise? This is the riddle-me-ree which has plagued Soviet historians and commentators for the past two decades at least, with the unravelling of it complicated not only by military technicalities but also by the vicissitudes of Soviet politics. The abrupt banishment of the relevance of 'surprise' as a factor of any significance during the heyday of Stalinist historiography made nonsense of any attempt to reconstruct the historical actuality of the situation; the simplistic approach of the Khrushchev period, which sought to personalize blame and load it mostly on Stalin made fresh distortions inevitable; and, finally, the most recent period of Soviet writing has sought with varying degrees of success to insist that 'the government' duly prepared the country yet 'unpreparedness'—of a kind which must never be allowed to repeat itself—inflicted serious damage and loss on the Soviet Union. It is not to be wondered at, therefore, that for all the mass of writing which touches on or skirts over the events of 1941 Soviet historians have avoided dealing directly with the issue of 'surprise attack' in terms of a strict historical narrative: only two specific studies exist in the open literature, those by V. A. Anfilov (the first edition of which was published in 1962 followed by a revised version put out by 'Nauka' in 1971)[1] and A. M. Nekrich's small but incisive study *1941 22 iyunya* published in 1965[2]—though the fate of Professor Nekrich at the hands of the party authorities can scarcely have encouraged others to take up

[1] V. A. Anfilov. *Nachalo Velikoi Otechestvennoi voiny* (22 iyunya-sredina iyulya 1941 goda) ('Voenizdat', 1962), 222 pp.: republished as *Bessmertnyi podvig: Issledovanie kanuna i pervogo etapa Velikoi Otechestvennoi voiny* ('Nauka', 1971), 245 pp. (in an edition of 25,000 copies, half that of the 1962 print).
[2] A. M. Nekrich, *1941 22 iyunya* ('Nauka', 1965), 175 pp. (Though by no means an official Soviet publication, it is perhaps not out of place to mention Major-General P. Grigorenko's essay on 1941: for one text, see *Der sowjetische Zusammenbruch 1941* (Possev-Verlag, 1969), with an introduction by Michel Garder.)

this line of investigation and research.[3] For the rest, in terms of serious historical investigation, it is still a matter of searching out recondite but revealing minutiae.[4]

One distinctive advance, however, has been the comparatively recent Soviet publication of German military documents and records, the unavailability of which seriously hampered any realistic analysis of German plans and preparations and the Soviet response (or lack of it). Wildly inaccurate or grossly exaggerated statements about German 'superiority', which became the *obiter dicta* of so many accounts, explained nothing save in terms of historical absurdities. Now no serious Soviet historian can ignore Colonel Dashichev's documentary compilation *Sovershenno sekretno! Tol'ko dlya komandovaniya* (published in 1967 and reproducing some of the 'Barbarossa' directives),[5] or the present production of a Soviet version of the 'Halder Diary',[6] or yet again Colonel Proektor's analysis of German intelligence appreciations of (and operations against) the Soviet Union, and his substantial section on German strategic planning.[7] As well as being the greatest land operation in the history of the world to date (that is, 1941), Operation Barbarossa was also one in which deception was designed to play a major role, with the 'surprising' of the enemy as a deliberate objective, an obvious fact which is all too frequently ignored. Intelligence and 'deception' (*dezinformatsiya*) assume, therefore, crucial significance: there is the well-established narrative of the 'warnings' delivered to Stalin, but it was Professor Nekrich who first publicly probed beneath the surface to ascertain (not least in his interview with F. I. Golikov, who was head of Military Intelligence (GRU) at that time) the nature of the 'gap' between the information received and the interpretation

---

[3] Cf. text of Soviet discussion of the Nekrich book, *Survey*, April 1967, no. 63, pp. 173–80. See also Vladimir Petrov, *June 22, 1941. Soviet Historians and the German Invasion* (University of South Carolina Press, 1968), *passim*.

[4] For a most recent item of this type, crammed with significant material, see Lt.-Col. A. Khor'kov, 'Boevaya i politicheskaya podgotovka voisk Kievskogo Osobogo Voennogo Okruga nakanune Velikoi Otechestvennoi voiny' in *Voenno-istoricheskii zhurnal*, 1971, no. 11, pp. 76–81 in the section on 'Nauchnye soobshcheniya i informatsiya'.

[5] See *Sovershenno sekretno! Tol'ko dlya komandovaniya: Strategiya Fashistskoi Germanii v voine protiv SSSR. Dokumenty i materialy*, ed. Col. V. I. Dashichev ('Nauka', 1967). (For original material, see *Kriegstagebuch des Oberkommandos der Wehrmacht 1940–1945*, Band I, 1940–1941, ed. Hans-Adolf Jacobsen (Frankfurt am Main, 1965); see also German Military Documents, *OKH* (Generalstab des Heeres), Operationsabteilung, "Aufmarschanweisung 'Barbarossa'", also 'Aufmarsch Barbarossa 1941', US National Archives, Microcopy T-78, Rolls 335 and 336, the latter also containing material for 1942.) Cf. P. A. Zhilin, *Kak Fashistskaya Germaniya gotovila napadenie na Sovetskii Soyuz* ('Mysl', 1966, second edition) and a recent English-language version, *They sealed their own doom* (M., Progress Publishers, 1970).

[6] See *Voennyi dnevnik* (General-polkovnik F. Gal'der), vol. 1, ed. V. I. Dashichev ('Voenizdat', 1968); vol. 2, ed. D. Proektor ('Voenizdat', 1969).

[7] See D. M. Proektor, *Agressiya i katastrofa: Vysshee voennoe rukovodstvo Fashistskoi Germanii v vtoroi mirovoi voine 1939–1945* ('Nauka', 1968); see especially pp. 178–92 (on intelligence) and pp. 192–211 on German strategic planning.

TO SURPRISE ATTACK 521

placed upon it.[8] A recent publication of immense value with respect to this 'information-intelligence' problem—what kind of information did the Soviet command have at its disposal and when?—is *Pogranichnye voiska SSSR. 1939-iyun' 1941*[9] which incorporates many of the reports of the Soviet frontier detachments bearing on the build-up of German forces in the east. Data such as this amply confirm the statements made by Marshal Bagramyan, among others, that it was known that 'an attack was being prepared against the Soviet Union'; nevertheless, this scarcely comprehends the vital point of when, where and how such an 'attack' would materialize.[10]

It is to this latter consideration, the materialization of the 'threat' in its final form, that the present paper is briefly addressed, using the framework of the three Soviet operational 'directives' issued on 21/22 June 1941, in order to examine the 'profile' of response at various levels and under a variety of conditions. What emerges in sum is that Stalin was by no means alone in thinking that the attack of 22 June was a form of 'provocation' and this verdict emanated from soldiers who could not be described as either complacent or incompetent, all of which is to say that the excellent planning put in by the German command to achieve tactical surprise to a large degree worked. Equally vivid is the impression that though the 'system', Stalin's system, could be blamed for failing to take due precautions, the 'system' was not wholly proof against a commander with the energy and with insight enough to think a little ahead. This, then, is not a study in great stratagems and military wiles, but rather a glance at the role of personal responsibility and the importance of professional competence—not to say common-sense and level-headedness—in a vast, if murky crisis.

The Directive of 21/22 June 1941

Not all Soviet soldiers invited their own destruction. From Minsk at 0240 hours on the morning of Saturday, 21 June, Major-General V. E. Klimovsky (Chief of Staff in the Western Special Military District), in

---

[8] See Nekrich, *op. cit.*, pp. 124–5. See also *The Memoirs of Marshal Zhukov* (Jonathan Cape, 1971 edition) (hereafter Zhukov, *Memoirs*), p. 216 for a comment on what Golikov relayed to the Soviet General Staff, though Marshal Zhukov adds: 'I don't know what intelligence F. I. Golikov personally reported to him [Stalin].' In this connection, the point is clarified by Gnedin (the individual who for two years delivered to Stalin and Molotov intelligence reports) who asserts that Golikov was a 'misinformer' and that Stalin was interested only in the material classified as 'doubtful' by Golikov: see *Survey*, April 1967, no. 63, p. 177.

[9] *Pogranichnye voiska SSSR 1939-iyun' 1941*; Sbornik dokumentov i materialov, collective editorship ('Nauka', 1970).

[10] Cf. Zhukov, *Memoirs*, p. 228: 'was it possible for the military leadership, acting independently, to detect in good time the movement of the enemy troops to the areas from which they launched their attack on June 22? In those conditions it was extremely difficult.' If there was a 'single' fatal mistake, Marshal Zhukov avers that it was the failure to fix the 'probable date' of the German attack with any certitude.

one more effort to impress Moscow with the seriousness of the situation, sent this signal:

> German aircraft with loaded bomb-racks violated the frontier 20 June. According to the report of 3rd Army commander, wire barricades along the frontier on the Augustovo, Seina roads though in position during the day are removed towards evening. From the woods, sounds of engines.

All through Friday Klimovsky had received information about German activity on the frontier; like the rest, this was given to Pavlov and sent on to Moscow, to the General Staff. General Klich, district artillery commander, and already worried enough about his untrained gunners and his immobilized guns, summed up the results so far: 'Always the same reply—"Don't panic. Take it easy. 'The boss' knows all about it." '[11] Commissar Pimenov, head of the political propaganda section of 6th Rifle Division, had already been branded 'panic-monger'; he had written to Pavlov asking for permission to take up defensive positions and to evacuate the wives and children from the Brest fortress. The staff of the NKVD frontier troops in Bialystok had put the frontier posts on alert on 18 June and all were standing by at noon on 21 June. But the orders about no firing on German aircraft still stood; when this order was confirmed in May, all personnel had to sign their receipt and understanding of it. The commander of the 97th Detachment who did open fire on aircraft was himself very nearly shot for it. No further orders were forthcoming, though the commander of the Soviet frontier troops, Lieutenant-General G. G. Sokolov was at that time in Bialystok. Another senior officer from Moscow in the area was Lieutenant-General D. M. Karbyshev, a considerable expert on military fortifications, who had since early June carried out an inspection of the western defences—but not the most forward defensive positions, from which he was barred. Some of his fellow engineer officers, present at the field exercises of Red Army engineers supervised by General Vasiliev, saw with their own eyes that things were not quite so peaceful as was thought in *Building No. 2* of the Defence Commissariat.

What happened on the frontier, however, and what was made to happen (or not to happen) in its most immediate vicinity had become and still remained the exclusive prerogative of Stalin. Responsive to this will, the General Staff had once again between 15 and 18 June circulated a directive to the frontier commands, forbidding any

[11] For a useful personal memoir, confirmed from a variety of other sources, see Col. I. T. Starinov, *Miny zhdut svoego chasa* ('Voenizdat', 1964), especially pp. 186–91; Colonel-General L. M. Sandalov's invaluable memoir, *Perezhitoe* ('Voenizdat', 1966), pp. 70–90 supplies much important detail and this has been expanded in his latest work, *Na Moskovskom napravlenii* ('Nauka', 1970), especially pp. 65–73.

concentration of troops in the frontier areas and continuing the ban on action against German aircraft.[12] Scattered the troops undoubtedly were, both by deployment and because of training plans; many in the Western Special District were on field exercises, like the 28th Rifle Corps (responsible for the Brest fortress and its area) with nine rifle, three artillery and all engineer battalions at work on defences, its anti-aircraft guns and their crews away at Minsk on practice shoots, and its signal battalions in camp. The corps commander had reported that 'not less than 1–1½ days' would be needed to assemble the corps. Meanwhile, in the old, historic, crenellated fortress of Brest, the Germans could see Soviet soldiers carrying out their routine drills, complete with ceremonial band. Elsewhere on the Soviet side, the frontier appeared quiet and without alarms.

The situation in the Baltic district was not much different. Denied permission to concentrate, Kuznetsov had managed a few precautionary measures; some of his artillery was on its way to its positions, but the lack of gun-towing equipment slowed everything down and even when some of the guns reached their sites, they still needed ammunition. An anti-aircraft alert to AA guns had gone out on 18 June, operative to 21 June, but the gun-sites were short of crews and trained officers; black-outs in Riga, Kaunas, Vilna, Dvinsk and Libau had been ordered after the evening of 19 June, but all this took time and organization.[13] The bomber forces continued with their night-training programme from 20–22 June; in most of the bomber regiments, the machines were undergoing their post-flight checks round about dawn—their fuel expended and their crews exhausted. The activation and laying of mine-fields had come to a sudden halt on 21 June; Major-General V. F. Zotov, chief of the Baltic military engineers, had begun to call out the civilian population to dig trenches and positions in the frontier areas, but he called off his engineers when cows from a collective farm had detonated some of the mines—an order given to prevent 'the spread of panic'.

In Leningrad, Andrei Zhdanov, member of the Military Soviet and Secretary of the regional Party Committee, left on 19 June for the Black Sea resort of Sochi. The day after Zhdanov left for his summer

---

[12] See Anfilov, *Nachalo . . . voiny*, pp. 45–46; in *Bessmertnyi podvig* (see footnote 1). pp. 181–5, Colonel Anfilov considerably modifies his earlier version, insisting that between 14–20 June a number of important precautionary moves were taken—for example, the order of the Baltic MD command on 15 July, stipulating that 'today as never before we must be at full combat readiness. Many commanders do not understand this fact . . . .' Cf. Marshal A. A. Novikov, *V nebe Leningrada*, Zapiski komanduyushchego aviatsiei ('Nauka', 1970), p. 41, reporting conversation with P. G. Tikhomirov (Chief of Leningrad MD Operations Staff) who referred to a special General Staff directive forbidding movement of troops to the frontier and banning flights in a 10-kilometre frontier zone.

[13] Anfilov, *Nachalo . . . voiny*, p. 47.

holiday, the Leningrad command received instructions from the General Staff to mine the frontier areas; the Finns on the Karelian Isthmus were in the process of 'activating themselves'. For more than a month, the General Staff had pressed for the completion of the fixed frontier defences to the north of Leningrad.[14] But to the south, where in 1940 the Leningrad command had handed over the Pskov-Ostrov 'fortified district' to the Baltic district, nothing at all had been done to plan any defences. The only troops in this area, which was so soon to become a terrible danger-spot, was an armoured formation located near Struga. Otherwise, the military cupboard was bare. As for moving troops, permission was impossible to come by. On the morning of 21 June, Lieutenant-General V. A. Frolov, commander of 14th Army (Leningrad MD) asked to be allowed to start the movement of his rifle and armoured troops; the Defence Commissariat refused him, but in the afternoon, 'at his own risk'—which was considerable—Frolov began to move the 52nd Rifle Division to its positions in the Murmansk area. The 42nd Rifle Corps (Kandalaksha) was similarly alerted.[15] No doubt the terrain, grim and demanding as it was for man and machine alike, and the subsequent confusion, helped Frolov to get away with what turned out to be a sensible insubordination.

What Frolov had accomplished with part of his army Kirponos at Kiev, in spite of repeated efforts, had so far failed to manage for his whole command. The signs of impending German attack were taken very seriously; the military observed the German build-up and attack preparations, the frontier guards reported on the frontier violations for intelligence and sabotage purposes.[16] In the ten days from 10–21 June, NKVD guards intercepted eight agents of the OUN, the Ukrainian nationalist movement fallen increasingly under German auspices; in German-occupied Poland, the special regiment *Nachtigall*, officially German-officered but with Ukrainian 'officers' also, had been training under the *Wehrmacht* for many months. For the moment, the scattered frontier forces, alerted by the cipher-signal of 18 June about the 'mass' of German troops, were under orders to observe further German movement and to stand by. The Red Army, however, lacked any such preliminary instruction. Kirponos's covering formations remained dispersed, his mobile reserves retained in the interior and his general reserves—31st, 36th and 37th Rifle Corps, 15th, 9th and 19th Mechanized Corps—located in the Zhitomir-Kiev area.

On the morning of 21 June, the naval patrols reported nothing of significance, although the movements of three German transports,

[14] Lt.-Gen. B. V. Bychevsky, *Gorod-Front* ('Lenizdat', 1967, second edition), p. 8.
[15] See G. K. Kozlov, *V lesakh Karelii* ('Voenizdat', 1963), pp. 20–21.
[16] Cf. V. V. Platonov, *Oni pervymi prinyali udar* ('Voenizdat', 1963), pp. 15–17. Detailed documentation can be found in *Pogranichnye voiska SSSR* ... (see footnote 9).

moving from Rumanian ports, caused some mystification in the Black Sea fleet command. Black Sea Fleet warships were coming in to Sevastopol; their crews required some rest after the training exercises, and no sailings were planned for the 22nd. Only a few aircraft were up, and no night flying had been scheduled.[17] In the Baltic, the officers stood to, though no order had as yet been issued.

At the Soviet Embassy in Berlin, where 'only a small group of Soviet diplomats was obliged to remain behind', most made ready to enjoy the promise of a fine day on 21 June. Ambassador Dekanozov had received another report about a German attack on 22 June; while this fell upon the Ambassador's disbelieving ears, the information was transmitted to Moscow, which, during the morning of the 21st instructed the Embassy to arrange an interview with Ribbentrop. The Soviet diplomat charged with this duty, V. Berezhkov, found that Ribbentrop was 'out of town' and everybody else was 'out'. In the early afternoon, Director Wörmann promised to pass any message, but Berezhkov was instructed to communicate directly only with Ribbentrop. The 'communication' was 'a demand for an explanation from the German government of the concentration of German troops on the Soviet frontier'. Moscow telephoned several times to hurry delivery of the message, but Berezhkov learned only that 'Ribbentrop was out and no one knew when he would be back'.[18] In a diplomatic sense, he never returned. It was left to Molotov to summon Ambassador von Schulenburg to his office at 9.30 p.m., there to repeat this hitherto unanswered and miserably plaintive query:

> There were a number of indications that the German Government was dissatisfied with the Soviet Government. Rumours were even current that a war was impending between Germany and the Soviet Union. They found sustenance in the fact that there was no reaction whatsoever to the TASS report of 13 June; that it was not even published in Germany. The Soviet Government was unable to understand the reasons for Germany's dissatisfaction. ... He would appreciate it if I (von Schulenburg) could tell him what had brought about the present situation in German-Soviet relations.

Von Schulenburg, uninformed himself of the German attack plans, could give no answer.

In the Soviet military commands, there was nothing as yet—apart from private premonitions—to distinguish this Saturday evening, 21 June, from any other; it promised to be, as Colonel Sandalov (Chief of Staff to 4th Army) described it, 'quite ordinary'.[19] Red Army officers,

---

[17] Cf. Vice-Admiral I. I. Azarov, *Osazhdennaya Odessa* ('Voenizdat', 1966, second edition), pp. 10–11.
[18] See V. Berezhkov, *S diplomaticheskoi missiei v Berlin 1940–41* (M., 'Novosti', 1966), pp. 93–94.
[19] Sandalov, *Perezhitoe*, p. 89.

senior and junior alike, made their way to the numerous garrisons shows and theatres; many, among Red Army men also, were actually at home. In the Minsk Officers Club a popular comedy 'The Wedding at Malinovka' was playing to a full house, with Colonel-General Pavlov, his chief of staff Klimovsky and the district deputy commander, Lieutenant-General V. I. Boldin, in the audience. These evening pleasures were briefly interrupted by Colonel Blokhin, head of intelligence in the Western Special Military District, who reported to Pavlov that 'the frontier was in a state of alarm'; German troops had been brought to full combat readiness and firing had been reported in some sectors. Pavlov, who passed this on to Boldin, dismissed it as 'some kind of rumour'. Boldin, however, could not help recounting the latest intelligence summary to himself; by the evening of 21 June, German troops had been fully concentrated on the East Prussian, Warsaw and Deblin axes, and the bulk of the forces were now packed into a 30-kilometre zone in the frontier areas. In Olshanka, south of Suvalki, heavy and medium tanks, heavy artillery, AA guns and 'many aircraft' had been reported. The Germans were setting up positions on the Western Bug; at Byalaya Podlyaska, 40 train-loads of bridging equipment and large quantities of ammunition had been unloaded.[20]

At about the time when Pavlov was interrupted in his box at the play, near Sokal (Kiev district command) a German deserter, Alfred Liskow, subsequently confessing himself a communist and a worker from Munich, crossed the Soviet lines at about 9 p.m. He was taken at once to the area officer, Major M. S. Bychkovsky, who heard him say that his commanding officer announced a German attack at 0400 hours on 22 June; German guns had taken up their fire positions, and tanks and infantry were at their start lines. Bychkovsky at once informed the commander of the Ukrainian Frontier District, Major-General V. L. Khomenko, of this information and passed it to 5th Army commander, Potapov. Further down the line, it went to the commanders of the 87th Rifle Corps and the 41st Tank Division. That having passed out of Bychkovsky's hands, he nevertheless ordered the guard to be doubled, and a close watch to be kept. Somewhat later, on his own initiative—dangerous enough—he ordered preparations for the blowing of the bridge into Sokal; he sent one of his officers into the Strumilov 'fortified district' to get more explosives, but this was far from easy, since most of the Red Army officers had gone to Lwow for their free day on Sunday,[21]

At the other end of what with devastating speed was so soon to

---

[20] See Colonel-General I. V. Boldin, *Stranitsy zhizni* ('Voenizdat', 1961), pp. 81–82.
[21] See Platonov, *op. cit.*, pp. 19–20; in view of Beria's strict orders, the author describes Major Bychkovsky's decision as *'neslykhannyi'*, 'unprecedented'.

become a colossal battle-front, the staff of the 5th Rifle Division was interrogating a Lithuanian deserter, who, with but faintly disguised relish, informed them that the German Army would attack at 0400 hours and planned to 'finish you off pretty quickly'. The Germans were acutely well-informed about the Soviet disposition: they knew that the bulk of the corps to which the 5th Division was attached had its location at Kozlovo-Rudo, which they would bomb at dawn. Colonel Ozerov, divisional commander, was not himself in any two minds about whether 'war' or 'provocation' was afoot—he pointed to the evidence of the past week, with 'whole armadas' of German planes criss-crossing the Soviet lines in the Baltic. Corps Commissar Dibrov, a senior political officer who was also the third, 'political member' of the major command organ, the Military Soviet of the Baltic district, had already telephoned twice from Riga, intimating that rifle sections should be left in the forward positions, but that their ammunition was to be withdrawn. Major-General M. S. Shumilov, 16th Corps commander, raged at this 'incitement to hysteria', but, with a sensible disregard for Dibrov, went ahead and issued ammunition. All this took place a little before midnight; not much before, the frontier troops reported to the military that they had received orders to evacuate their families. Had the Red Army, they asked, any contingency plan like this? Ozerov contacted corps HQ, which relayed this reply by telegraph:

> You exhibit unnecessary nervousness. The families of the frontier troops live on the actual frontier, necessary to remove them from zone of possible provocation. As for your families who live in Kaunas, as far as is known nothing threatens them. Their evacuation would produce needless alarm among civilian population.[22]

For the moment, Ozerov had his answer. As for deserters, the sardonic Lithuanian hardly disposed of the entire significance of their information. Stalin, who took the final decisions, was told of the attack news brought by 'a German deserter' (possibly Liskow, but elsewhere identified as one Wilhelm Korpik), a German communist labourer from Berlin, who crossed the Soviet lines after hearing the orders read to his unit. For his 'disinformation', Stalin ordered him to be shot forthwith. Liskow's interrogation had continued through the night and into the small hours of 22 June and was not complete when German guns opened fire at dawn.

As Molotov in Moscow summoned von Schulenburg to his office at 9.30 p.m., Dekanozov, denied access all day to Ribbentrop, finally

[22] See Major-General P. V. Sevastyanov, *Neman-Volga-Dunai* ('Voenizdat', 1961), p. 11.

528   *THE SOVIET RESPONSE*

called on von Weizsäcker to deliver a protest about German over-flights; stiffly, the German diplomat terminated Dekanozov's attempts 'to prolong the conversation somewhat' and Dekanozov did not refer to those 'few questions' which he later explained were meant for the *Reich* Foreign Minister only, and from whom alone could come 'the clarification' which Moscow so avidly sought.   Moscow's urgent telephone calls throughout the day had so far gone for nothing.   That afternoon, from his East Prussian headquarters in the *Wolfsschanze* at Rastenburg, Hitler wrote to Mussolini at the end of 'the hardest decision of my life', to terminate 'the hypocritical performance in the Kremlin'.   Now, on the eve of the 'final decision'—to be made at 7 p.m., that evening—Hitler felt himself once more 'spiritually free', since the partnership with the Soviet Union had appeared 'a break with my whole origin, my concepts and my former obligations'; 'these mental agonies' were over.   In this letter, useful for its summary of Hitler's strategic ideas but nauseating in its fake and forced moralizing, the Führer referred to the latest situation map of Soviet forces, whose 'concentration . . . is tremendous'.[23]   The latest compilation put Red Army strength at 154 rifle divisions, 10 armoured divisions and 37 mechanized brigades in European Russia.   The *Lageberich Ost* for 21 June noted some Soviet re-deployment, the transport of tanks along the Minsk-Smolensk stretch of railway in the previous week and troop movements from the Far East and from the Urals in particular.   Strong concentrations of Soviet parachute troops had been noted in the Ukraine (in fact, the exercises of the 6th and 212th Parachute Brigades had been reconnoitred on 20 June by a high-flying aircraft 'with Rumanian markings . . . which made off in a westerly direction').   The general situation, however, remained substantially unchanged, with no major modification in Soviet strength, dispositions and apparent intentions.[24]

What German officers had themselves seen and could still see, crouched and waiting as they were on the Soviet frontiers, with their armour, artillery, assault and bridging units at the ready, merely confirmed the *Lagebericht*.   Guderian's personal reconnaissance on 17 June convinced him, as he scrutinized the unoccupied Soviet strong-points on the Bug, that the Russians suspected nothing.   After midnight on 21 June, the Berlin-Moscow express, cleared and checked without any deviation from normal practice, passed over the rail bridge and on to Brest-Litovsk without a hitch.   (Even later, a goods train with grain trucks was passed on to the German side.   Not until dawn did the

[23] For a Soviet text of this document, see *Sovershenno sekretno!* . . . (see footnote 5), pp. 186–90; also *Voenno-istoricheskii zhurnal*, 1965, no. 5, pp. 89–92.
[24] *OKH* (Generalstab des Heeres) Qu IV, Abt. Frd H Ost (II) Nr. 1036/41, dated 21.6.41:   German Military Documents.

TO SURPRISE ATTACK   529

Soviet transport administration send out a telegram to all track chiefs to 'hold all transit and export trucks destined for Germany'. A statement of the tally of such traffic was to be submitted by 1800 hours, 22 June.) To the north, nothing disturbed the tranquillity of the East Prussian frontiers.   Southwards, in Army Group South's attack area, 48th Motorized Corps commander reported at midnight that 'Sokal is not blacked out. The Russians are manning their posts which are fully illuminated. Apparently they suspect nothing'.

That the Russians lacked suspicions was far from true. The Soviet naval command, both regional and central, was definitely uneasy. In the Baltic, Soviet patrol boats had reported nothing of significance (except noticeably less German shipping), but on the evening of 21 June the Military Soviet of the Baltic Fleet did not leave its staff headquarters. At 2240 hours, Admiral Tributs summoned Panteleev, his chief of staff, and announced that he had talked to Admiral Kuznetsov in Moscow; Panteleev at once summoned the senior staff officers, and at three minutes to midnight, in accordance with Kuznetsov's instruction, the Baltic Fleet went over to 'Readiness state No. 1', a fully operational state. Promptly at midnight, the staff transferred itself to the advanced command post, where, sitting at a table drinking tea, Operations officer Captain Pilipovsky and Mobilization Chief Colonel Illin quickly reviewed their preparations. The patrol line, with the sweeper *Krambol* in the lead, was strengthened, but as yet nothing had been reported.   Panteleev ordered the Libau base commander to move his submarines to Ust-Dvinsk, and the Hango base commander to shift his submarines and torpedo-boats to Paldisk. A number of warships currently undergoing trials were now placed under operational command and would be 'accepted' for the fleet as from 22 June; others, tested but unfitted, were rushed back to the Leningrad yards.[25]

Kuznetsov sent the same signal on operational readiness to the Black Sea Fleet at three minutes to midnight. (It went out subsequently to the Northern Fleet, to the Pinsk and Danube Flotillas.)   At the Sevastopol naval base, the immediate concern of the duty officer had been to see to the movements of a tug towing barges laden with refuse. After midnight, duty officer Rybalko handed over to a subordinate in order to take a short rest—from which he was, however, shortly roused and summoned to a senior officer, Eliseev, who had him read Kuznetsov's signal.   The fleet commander, Vice-Admiral F. S. Oktyabrsky, was alerted and very soon the warning signals went out to ships and shore installations. The base and its warships began to

[25] For personal memoir, see Vice-Admiral Yu. A. Panteleev, 'Na Baltike pogoda portitsya', in *Voyuet Baltika* ('Lenizdat', 1964), pp. 54–55.

'black out'. Within the hour (at 0155 hours on 22 June) the officers and ratings of the fleet tumbled to a 'general muster' as the sirens wailed over Sevastopol.[26]

Even so, these were but single alerts; as yet not a single order had been issued to either the Red Army or the Navy. Of Stalin's own activity at this juncture there are indications that his mind had begun to grasp a part of the danger which loomed over the Soviet Union. On Saturday, 21 June, Tyulenev, commander of the Moscow Military District, had been summoned to the telephone, out of which issued 'the muffled voice' of Stalin to put this question: 'Comrade Tyulenev, what is the position concerning Moscow's anti-aircraft defences?' Tyulenev duly reported the readiness state, at which he was told: 'Listen, the situation is uncertain and therefore you must bring the anti-aircraft defences of Moscow up to 75% operational readiness.'[27] This order Tyulenev passed to Major-General Gromadin, the AA air defence commander in Moscow, without delay. Somewhat later that evening (Saturday), Tyulenev went to the Defence Commissariat where he met Marshal Timoshenko, who informed him now that signs of a very tense situation on the frontier were growing and were fully 'confirmed'. In Moscow itself, the German Embassy appeared to be on the alert and officials on the move. The General Staff reports indicated that so far it was 'all quiet' on the frontier itself but information from district commanders, fully borne out by intelligence reports, emphasized the possibility of a German attack. The gist of all this Marshal Timoshenko had conveyed to Stalin, who so far was inclined to dismiss it as 'panicking to no purpose'.

Exactly what Stalin did think remains a mystery. He certainly wanted no premature moves and was bent on steering wide of any 'provocation'. But during the late afternoon of 21 June he had begun to act as if he sensed greater danger. He summoned the Moscow party leaders, A. S. Shcherbakov and V. P. Pronin, who made their way to the Kremlin in the evening; here Stalin instructed them to warn all party raikom (district) secretaries not to leave their posts and under no circumstances to leave their particular towns. '*Vozmozhno napadenie Nemtsev*'—'A German attack is possible'—was the cryptic formula Stalin used to cover all his instructions. Some little time before this, he had seen Timoshenko and Zhukov to convey to them that a German attack might be in the offing, at which these officers hurried back to the Defence Commissariat to begin some feverish, last-minute work

---

[26] See Vice-Admiral I. I. Azarov, 'Nachalo voiny v Sevastopole', in *Voenno-istoricheskii zhurnal*, 1962, no. 6, pp. 77–83; see also Zhukov, *Memoirs*, p. 235 on signal about Sevastopol.

[27] General of the Army I. V. Tyulenev, *Cherez tri voiny* ('Voenizdat', 1960), p. 141.

drafting orders and signals.[28] If Stalin actually intended this as actual precaution, it was all far too little and all catastrophically late. What seems to have been at the forefront of Stalin's mind was not war but that fantasy of 'provocation'; with the civilian leaders he might be somewhat more forthright, for they could do nothing but stand and wait, while the soldiers had to be kept on some leash lest they succumb to 'panic' and were unnerved to the point of opening fire.

Tyulenev, having checked with Timoshenko and the General Staff (who intimated that as far as they knew the Germans did not enjoy 'overall superiority'), took his leave and made for his *dacha* on the outskirts of Moscow. Shortly after midnight (21–22 June) German troops were moving to their battle-stations, closing inexorably on the Soviet frontier. At 0100 hours on 22 June, the German army commands sent out their own call-signs indicating full and final readiness: '*Kyffhäuser*' from 4th Army, '*Wotan*' from von Rundstedt's command.

The time and place of the forthcoming offensive—22 June at 0330 hours—had become known in the German commands on 15 June: code-words to activate operations were designated, with final dispositions to proceed after 18 June. Security requirements and the initiation of sabotage operations received the finishing touches and armour moved at night towards the start lines. (From time to time Soviet frontier guards caught the sound of this movement, but by day German forces lay hidden.) The code-word *DORTMUND* transmitted to German commands in the east (as outlined in the warning order of 14 June) would signify that Operation 'Barbarossa' would proceed, whereas the transmission of *ALTONA* indicated cancellation or postponement, but in any event all preparations were to be basically complete by 15 June. Since late in May German infantry had moved closer to the Soviet frontier (and always by night), but only after mid-June did the armour and motorized formations start towards their final positions. Out of the 3,800,000 of the German *Feldheer*, almost 3,200,000 now faced the Soviet Union: 148 divisions, including 19 *Panzer* divisions, 12 motorized infantry divisions, nine line of communications divisions (the *Sicherheitsdivisionen*), all reinforced by anti-aircraft, anti-tank, engineer heavy artillery units of the *Heerestruppen*, supported by 3,350 tanks, 7,184 artillery pieces, 600,000 lorries and more than that number of horses. The three German *Luftflotten* disposed of over 2,000 combat aircraft.[29]

---

[28] It is by no means easy to fix the detailed chronology of this late afternoon/evening section of 21 June: see Zhukov, *Memoirs*, p. 231 for version that has him going to Stalin. Tyulenev has a somewhat different timetable with more comings and goings.
[29] Cf. Generaloberst Halder, *Kriegstagebuch*, Band II, ed. Hans-Adolf Jacobsen (Stuttgart, 1963), p. 461.

Guderian proceeded at this point to his command post, which he reached at 0210 hours, as the first German assault squads moved into their attack positions, infesting the thick green banks of the river Bug. German officers had read or were now reading the Führer's personal order to his armies, 'To the soldiers of the *Ostfront*'. One order was not read out to the assembled companies, the 'Commissar Order' which prescribed death for Red Army military commissars when captured. One other directive, that concerning the rules governing the conduct of German troops in the east, had previously had a very stormy passage and was not even circulated in some commands. The specialists of *Regiment 800* (the 'Brandenburgers' of the special service regiment), many of them Russian-speaking, were already operating by their own laws. *Abwehr II* had long evinced close interest in key Soviet objectives, 45 of which were marked down for special attack either by *Regiment 800* or by *Widerstandgruppen* drawn from disaffected elements in the national minorities. *Regiment 800* was to be concerned in the first instance with targets lying within 15 kilometres of the frontier, operating to paralyse the Soviet defence and the enemy's will to fight (*Wehrwille*). Army Group Centre also prepared a list of targets which were to be struck by the bombers of *Luftflotte II*—headquarters installations in Kobrin, Volkovysk, Bialystok, Lida, Slutsk, Baranowicze, Minsk and the air force signals centre, as well as Gomel, Mogilev, Orsha and Smolensk.[30]

The 'Brandenburgers' infiltrated or were dropped by parachute behind the Soviet lines and once there proceeded to blow up or sabotage power and communications facilities, activate the selected agents of the *Widerstandgruppen*, secure bridges vital for German movement and spread confusion by sending out fake orders and messages. Men of *Regiment 800* dressed in Red Army uniform were by now making for the Brest fortress or for the bridges over the Bug: advance parties, smuggled in on Saturday in goods trains or hidden under loads of gravel in railway trucks, had been in the town of Brest for some hours. Meanwhile, at 0220 hours the staff at Soviet 4th Army had just finished the interrogation of yet another German deserter who had crossed into the Soviet lines west of Volchin, and were about to circulate this latest confirmation of a German attack which was due in less than two

[30] See planning papers and instructions, *Abwehr II*/Abschnittstab Ostpreussen (for May-June 1941): Besprechung OKW/Abw, u. OKH, Berlin, 5–6 June 1941; see also special target list: Abwehr II/Abschnittstab Ostpreussen, describing nature of target, importance and whether guarded ('Objekte im Aufgabenbereich des V.O./Abw. II bei Abschnittstab Ostpreussen'); also target list 17.6.41 (Abw. II/Nr. 574/41).
    Cf. comments in an important new study *Bor'ba Latyshskogo naroda v gody Velikoi Otechestvennoi voiny 1941–1945* (Riga, 1970), pp. 78–81 on 'diversionist' operations.

TO SURPRISE ATTACK

hours.[31] It was a good try, but the news never got out, for the telephone lines had been cut for some time.

This interruption of Soviet signal traffic was of the greatest significance, coupled with the fact that very late (in fact, too late) the Defence Commissariat finally stirred from a strange kind of torpor. At 1700 hours on 21 June Stalin had summoned Timoshenko and Zhukov to the Kremlin, where it seems that he disclosed something of the full menace of the situation, but it does not appear that a decision was taken to bring the Red Army up to a state of full readiness in order to 'repel any attack, should it occur'. (There seems to be, nevertheless, no small amount of confusion about the chronology of this evening contact with Stalin.) General Zhukov was evidently contacted 'in the evening' by Lieutenant-General Purkaev, Chief of Staff in the Kiev Special Military District), who informed Moscow that a German NCO deserter had brought confirmation of an impending German attack timed for the morning of 22 June: Timoshenko, Zhukov and Vatutin then went at once to the Kremlin, having agreed to get permission 'at all costs to alert' Soviet troops. Stalin, though worried, still emphasized the point about a 'provocation' organized by the German generals. Timoshenko spoke up for an immediate alert and Stalin asked for the draft directive already written out by Zhukov: it was not to his liking—'it is too soon to issue such a directive; perhaps the question can still be settled peacefully'—and he instructed Zhukov and Vatutin to prepare a shorter document.[32] Having made some further amendments, Stalin authorized Timoshenko to send it to all commands: transmission was completed by 0030 hours on the morning of 22 June:

*To Commanders of Frontier Military Districts**
1. In the course of 22–23.6.41 a surprise attack by the Germans on the fronts of the Leningrad, Baltic Special, Western Special, Kiev Special and Odessa Military Districts is possible. The German attack may begin with provocative actions.
2. The assignments for our forces—not to give way to provocative actions of any kind which might produce major complications.

* The directive had the following designation: 'O razvertyvanii voisk s sootvetstvii s planom prikritiya mobilizatsii i strategicheskogo sosredotocheniya.'[33]

[31] Cf. Sandalov, *Perezhitoe*, 'Tak nachinalas' voina', p. 91 ff.; also Sandalov in *Bug v ogne* (Minsk, 1965), pp. 14–17.
[32] Zhukov, *Memoirs*, pp. 231–2.
[33] *Ibid.* The text here is taken from Anfilov, *Nachalo . . . voiny*, pp. 48–49. Cf. Sandalov, *Na Moskovskom napravlenii*, p. 77 for the directive as it came through from the command. (See also Anfilov, *Bessmertnyi podvig*, p. 186.)

THE SOVIET RESPONSE

At the same time troops of the Leningrad, Baltic Special, Western Special, Kiev Special and Odessa Military Districts to be at full combat readiness to meet a surprise attack by the Germans or their allies.

3. I thereby order:

a) during the night of 22.6.41 secretly to man the fire points of the fortified districts (URs) on the state frontier;

b) before dawn 22.6.41 to disperse on field aerodromes all aircraft including Red Army support aviation, and thoroughly camouflage the machines;

c) all units to be put at combat readiness without additional drawing on personnel on mobilization lists. Preparation of all measures for the blacking-out of towns and installations.

No other measures to be taken without special authorization.

The district commands, depending in no small degree upon the competence and shrewdness of their chiefs, reacted with varying speeds to this order, though Military Soviets were authorized to transmit 'analogical orders' by 0225 hours. Colonel-General Kuznetsov in the Baltic instructed his army commander in the following terms:

During the course of the night of 22.6.41 secretly man the defences of the basic zones. In the forward zone move in field sentries to guard the pill-boxes, but the sections assigned to occupy the forward zone to be held back. Cartridges and shells to be issued. In the case of provocation action by the Germans, fire *not* to be opened. In the event of flights by German aircraft over our territory, make no demonstration and until such time as enemy aircraft undertake military operations, *no fire* to be opened on them.

In the event of strong enemy forces undertaking offensive operations, destroy them.

Position anti-tank mines and minor obstacles without delay.[34]

Not a line of this gave the formation commanders any real notion as to what they should do or just how they might decide between 'war' and 'provocation'. With dawn as the deadline, some tasks were beyond fulfilment; in the Western and Kiev military districts, the fighters and some bombers were still neatly lined up on the runways on airfields thoroughly pinpointed by the Germans. Not hundreds but thousands of machines were thus displayed in a style best fitted to ensure their destruction. Only Major-General M. V. Zakharov, commander in Odessa where the 9th Army was being formed, had ordered his aviation to disperse by dawn on 22 June to the field aerodromes; this he did on the evening of 21 June, when he also instructed his corps commanders to move their troops from populated centres and to organize close contact between covering detachments and frontier

[34] Anfilov, *Nachalo ... voiny*, p. 49.

troops. Elsewhere, with communications being severed or shattered, the chances of a rapid dispersal had already vanished.

It was at 0300 hours that Pavlov, following his general 'instruction' from Timoshenko, issued orders for the formations to be put at full combat readiness, and for units to man the fire points in the 'fortified districts'. This order (vague as it was) lost even marginal utility since it failed to reach many formations. The 4th Army in Pavlov's command had been isolated for some time, but not before it heard from the Brest fortress that the electric power had gone, that the water supply was damaged and the telephone lines cut. Colonel Litvinenko, signals officer, sent out repair squads and at 0330 hours 4th Army was again in contact with Minsk and Brest. At that point Pavlov came on the telephone, to say that a 'provocationist raid by Fascist bands on to Soviet territory' was likely; there was to be no response to the 'provocation', the 'bands' were to be taken prisoner but the frontier *must not be crossed*. Major-General Korobkov asked for precise orders: Pavlov told him to bring all troops to full readiness, to move elements of 42nd Rifle Division from the Brest fortress to take up defensive positions and to disperse the aviation regiments to the field aerodromes.[35] Just before 0400 hours, Korobkov got through to the staff of 42nd Rifle Division—just as the German guns opened fire. At 0530 hours 4th Army received its copy of Timoshenko's first order. The 4th Army also guarded the six bridges across the Bug—two rail, four road bridges, and only the railway bridge at Brest was mined. The others were not, and there was no order about the Brest bridge.

One hour after Timoshenko's order to Red Army district commanders, Admiral Kuznetsov sent a signal in almost identical terms to senior Soviet naval officers. Admiral Tributs in the Baltic found himself baffled by trying to resolve the contradiction in 'not responding to provocation' and 'responding to a surprise attack by the Germans or their allies with all available forces'. His ships were manned and at the highest state of readiness (No. 1) and had been put under the articles of war by their captains. They were, however, short of fuel, in nearly every case by as much as 50% of their operational requirements. The commander of the Hango base, Major-General Kabanov, without declaring any 'official' alert status, had meanwhile moved two regiments up to the land-frontier with Finland during the evening of 21 June; he deployed his forces and also put into operation Admiral Tributs' personal 'recommendation' to him that the 6,000 women and children should be evacuated by fast passenger ship. The light forces under Drozd cruised in the Gulf of Riga; submarines and torpedo

---

[35] For detailed narrative, see Sandalov, *Perezhitoe*, pp. 92–99 and *Na Moskovskom napravlenii*, pp. 74–81; also Boldin, *op. cit.*, pp. 82–85.

boats were on the move, and so were a number of Soviet merchant ships, like the Latvian steamer *Gaisma*. (At 0320 hours, off Gotland, the *Gaisma* was shelled by four German torpedo-boats; after the shells came torpedoes, which broke the ship in two; an hour later (0415 hours) her captain sent this last signal 'Torpedoed, *Gaisma* sinking. Goodbye'.)[36]

At the moment when the *Gaisma* came under fire, the Black Sea Fleet had manned its ships in Sevastopol and had reported the approach of unidentified aircraft towards the blacked-out city. It had been difficult to signal to the lighthouses to extinguish their lamps; with communications once again widely cut, Major-General Morgunov, garrison commander, suggested sending motor-cyclists up from the nearest gun-batteries to have the lights cut off. The Upper Inkermann Light, however, could not be contacted and blazed out into the night, even as the German bombers and mine-layers came on. At 0313 hours, as the German aircraft—loaded with magnetic mines—made their approaches at no great height, Soviet searchlights switched on and AA guns, ashore and on ship, opened fire. Vice-Admiral Oktyabrsky had already given permission (after getting confirmation that no Soviet planes were up) to open fire: 'Follow the procedure.' Colonel Zhilin, fire control officer, was evidently sceptical about the order which was passed through the duty officer; he insisted on recording in the war-diary the fact that he was not responsible for this order. Almost at once, the parachute mines floated down; hearing no explosions but seeing the parachutes, the intelligence officer, Colonel Hamgaladze, assumed that an airborne attack on the base was imminent. The general duty officer Colonel Raev was ordered to 'take measures' to defend the staff headquarters, but he replied that he had no men. A company of sailors from a training squad was hastily organized. Many, servicemen and civilians alike, thought this an exercise, designed to increase 'vigilance'. The Black Sea Fleet, however, had begun its war; the Fleet aviation commander, Rusakov, was summoned to Oktyabrsky and at 0413 hours Soviet fighters were patrolling the base.[37]

Admiral Golovko, in command of the Northern Fleet, also had trouble with his orders. Two days previously, on 19 June, the Main Naval Staff had instructed him to prepare his submarines for sea. Golovko had consulted Admiral Isakov about the operational tasks assigned to the submarines in the event of war; Golovko had plans of his own for using his larger submarines (the so-called 'pikes') against German communications, and even using the 'babies', the smaller

---

[36] See S. F. Edlinsky, *Baltiiskii transportnyi flot v Velikoi Otechestvennoi voine 1941–1945 gg.* (M., 'Morskoi Transport', 1957), p. 11.
[37] Azarov, 'Nachalo voiny v Sevastopole', *loc. cit.* (see footnote 26).

craft, in this role. Now, in the early hours of 22 June, he had no clear orders at all; the operational-readiness alert had been radioed to him, followed after 20 minutes by Kuznetsov's directive which puzzled Golovko as much as it baffled Tributs, followed by a third signal at 0300 hours ordering the Northern Fleet to despatch at 0700 hours two submarines (the Naval Staff did not specify the type), the mine-layers *Groznyi* and *Sokrushitel'nyi* and a flight of MBR-2 bombers to guard the mouth of the White Sea. The Northern Fleet was alerted but bereft of actual orders which had any bearing on those 'unidentified' planes and ships whose movements greatly concerned Golovko.[38]

These probes and clashes round the giant periphery waxed and waned. But on the enormous land front, where the German Army lay massed on its selected approaches, the final moments had begun to tick away to zero-hour — 0330 hours. To eliminate the possibility of the Russians having time to recover themselves between the air and artillery blows, German bombers operating against the Belorussian airfields made high-altitude approaches under cover of night, betraying no mass movement of aircraft over the Soviet frontiers. They were already sweeping down with open bomb-doors to obliterate at the first light Soviet fighters, massed on their 66 aerodromes, with one savage, unexpected and disastrously wounding blow. In a wider arc the bombers of the *Luftflotten* spread out and with the approach of dawn Soviet cities, towns and a cluster of select targets came under sustained attack—Kowno, Rowno, Odessa, Sevastopol, Minsk, the Baltic bases, rippling across Western Russia in flashes of fire and destruction.

The reports of German air attacks followed thick and fast. At the Defence Commissariat Voronov, Air Defence commander, was giving Marshal Timoshenko the information his command possessed on German air movement; without making any comment, Timoshenko handed Voronov a large signal pad and asked him to present this information 'in written form'. Lev Mekhlis (whose presence as Stalin's watch-dog usually boded ill for Soviet military commanders) scrutinized Voronov as he wrote, and when Voronov had finished suggested that he sign it, at which Voronov was ordered back to his own command post—but without orders to activate Soviet AA defences and without an operational assignment of any kind. Zhukov at the General Staff had passed the news of the German air onslaught to Stalin shortly after 3.30 a.m., which only elicited the response that the attacks were 'a provocation on the part of the German generals'. Tyulenev, called suddenly from his *dacha* to the Kremlin, paused to consult Zhukov on

[38] B. A. Vainer, *Severnyi Flot v Velikoi Otechestvennoi voine* ('Voenizdat', 1964), pp. 14–23. See also Admiral A. G. Golovko, *Vmeste s flotom* (M., 1960), pp. 18–26, diary entries for 18–22 June.

his way and learned of the German bombing and of Stalin's reaction; he left Zhukov trying to make contact with the military district commanders.   In the Kremlin Marshal Voroshilov made a hurried appearance on the heels of the commandant who met Tyulenev. Voroshilov straightaway asked Tyulenev: 'Where has the Supreme Commander's command centre been set up?' Tyulenev was taken aback.   No such centre existed.   All he could suggest was that the 'Supreme Commander'—whoever he might be—make use of the Moscow Military District or Moscow AA Command HQs, both of which were at least guarded.[39]

Admiral Kuznetsov was similarly bemused. It had been about 11 p.m. (21 June) when Marshal Timoshenko ordered him to report at once and in person: 'very important information' had just come into the Defence Commissariat.   Within the past hour Kuznetsov had also lighted upon some important information of his own; the Soviet attaché Vorontsov, whom Admiral Kuznetsov had ordered back from Berlin to make a personal report in Moscow, had finally made his appearance and reported at once to Kuznetsov as ordered. This time there could be no doubting the importance of Captain Vorontsov's report—for almost an hour he gave details of what was happening on the German side and repeated that a German attack could be expected any hour. No one was left in any doubt of the Naval Attaché's emphatic statement: 'It's war.'[40]

Kuznetsov left for the Defence Commissariat, the building next to his own and at no great distance; the sudden summer storm which had intruded on his talk with Vorontsov, with a sudden roll of thunder and gusting winds, had now subsided and the pavements had dried. Once inside the Defence Commissariat, Admiral Kuznetsov found Timoshenko and Zhukov seated and busily occupied writing, and the Admiral could not but notice the lengthy, three-page telegram which Zhukov was on the point of despatching to Military District commanders.   Kuznetsov asked Zhukov if 'resort to weapons' was authorized 'in the event of armed attack'.   Zhukov replied somewhat tersely that this was indeed the case, whereupon Kuznetsov sent Alafuzov, head of the Naval Staff, racing to send out signals authorizing 'No. 1 Readiness' state. That was the night, Kuznetsov recalls, when Soviet admirals ran helter-skelter down the street, signal-pad in hand. Twenty minutes later Kuznetsov sent out his directive:

[39] Cf. Tyulenev, *op. cit.*, p. 142.
[40] Admiral N. G. Kuznetsov, *Nakanune* ('Voenizdat', 1966), pp. 326–7. This is a controversial personal memoir with some controversial interpretations, to say the least; a revised edition has evidently been prepared, but I have not so far been able to obtain it.

TO SURPRISE ATTACK 539

> In the course of 22 and 23 June there is the possibility of a German surprise attack. The German attack may begin with provocations. Our task is not to respond to any provocations which may bring complications. Simultaneously fleets and flotillas will come to full combat readiness, to meet surprise attacks by the Germans or their allies. I order: transition to Readiness State No. 1 to be carefully camouflaged. Reconnaissance in foreign territorial waters categorically forbidden. No other measures without special authorization. KUZNETSOV.[41]

One by one the fleet commanders reported to Moscow: by 0240 hours, 22 June, Kuznetsov recorded all fleets, ships and stations at full readiness. Half an hour later it was growing light in Moscow. For a moment Kuznetsov stretched out on a settee, only to be roused by the telephone with Oktyabrsky reporting the air attacks on Sevastopol. Kuznetsov checked the time: 0315 hours. On trying to raise Stalin by telephone, Kuznetsov could only reach the Kremlin duty officer, who did not know Stalin's whereabouts. Kuznetsov telephoned Timoshenko to report 'a state of war' and tried Stalin again, whereupon the duty officer put him through to Malenkov, who greeted the Admiral's news with utter disbelief: 'Do you know what you are reporting?' Kuznetsov replied that indeed he did and took full responsibility for it, at which Malenkov put the telephone down.[42] (A little later a Kremlin officer contacted Sevastopol naval HQ separately.)

Under attack by German bombers the Red Army had also been struck some swift and secret blows even before the German guns opened up. At Koden, where the bridge over the Bug was vital for the rapid deployment of German armour (all in the Soviet 4th Army's sector), Soviet frontier guards were summoned from their posts by their German counterparts, shouting that they had 'important business'. German assault parties quickly machine-gunned the Russians as they made their appearance and then seized the bridge, which was not mined. Across the railway bridge at Brest (which also spanned the Bug) German assault infantry and combat engineers cut down the Soviet sentry, machine-gunned the Soviet detail in their guard post and, after a rapid inspection of the structure, tore out the demolition charge from the central pier.[43]

At 0315 hours on the morning of 22 June German guns along the sector facing the river Bug opened fire. From that moment onwards the huge arc of the Soviet land frontier was lit in this short summer

[41] For the timing and sequence of signals, see *ibid.*, pp. 327–36.
[42] *Ibid.*, p. 337.
[43] See appendix to *Geroicheskaya oborona*, Sbornik vospominanii ob oborone Brestskoi kreposti v iyune-iyule 1941 g. (Minsk, 1961), pp. 597–600, operational narrative; see also eye-witness accounts in *Bug v ogne* and also *Geroicheskaya oborona*.

night by the gun flashes of multiple German batteries hammering Soviet frontier defences. German assault troops, equipped for their river crossings with rubber dinghies, submersible tanks and with the bridging equipment at the ready behind them, fought their first engagements with Soviet frontier guards who replied with their light armament, rifles and machine-guns. To the north there was appreciably less of an artillery preparation. Aided by the mist and the half-light, the German infantry and supporting armour slid out of their concealment and advanced towards the Soviet field defences. At the other extremity of the Soviet-German front, in the south, von Rundstedt's armies first used their artillery against the Soviet defences and then raced for their appointed crossing points on the lower Bug and the San.

Directive No. 2: 0715 hours, 22 June 1941

The most urgent of multiple crises came at the centre, in Pavlov's command. In Minsk, relying on communications which worked only fitfully, Pavlov heard the commanders of the 3rd, 10th and 4th Armies report German penetrations of the frontiers at Sopotskin, as far as Augustovo, continued German bombing, and the fracture of the signals lines; the two radio stations on which army commanders could have relied had also been put out of action. Shortly after 4 a.m., Timoshenko telephoned and Pavlov reported on the situation; all the while, information seeped into Pavlov's HQ—bombing, sabotage, shelling, German attacks along the frontier. Colonel Blokhin produced another report: Pavlov's command was being assailed by 13 German infantry divisions, five tank divisions, two motorized divisions and airborne units, supported by 40 artillery and five aviation regiments.[44] Now the German bombers attacked Bialystok, Grodno, Lida, Volkovysk, Brest and Kobrin. The staff of 4th Army was located at Kobrin: Korobkov had put the Brest and Vysoki garrisons on the alert, but the Brest fortress was already fully engaged:

> The buildings and stores in the fortress, the military installations and also the railway station at Brest were swept by shelling, and at the same time fire broke out as a result of the continuation of the intensive bombardment. All communications were cut at once.

What 28th Rifle Corps (Major-General Popov) recorded was similar to the entry in 4th Army's war-diary:

> . . . like thunder from a clear sky, throughout the depth of the frontier zone, unexpectedly, the roar of a barrage. The surprise

[44] Figures as cited in Boldin, *op. cit.*, p. 84.

> Fascist artillery-fire burst on those points where the rifle and engineer units building fortifications were spending the night, on sections located on the Brest training ground and on the frontier guards' posts. The most intensive artillery fire was directed against the military cantonments of Brest and especially on the Brest fortress. The latter was literally covered all over with uninterrupted artillery and mortar fire.[45]

The 4th Army command tried hard to get to Brest to direct the operations; failing this, the danger loomed of losing contact with mechanized and aviation formations, with the flank divisions of 4th Army, and with Minsk itself. But Korobkov first needed permission to move, and he was for the moment stuck fast in Kobrin. At 0530 hours, just as 4th Army received a copy of Timoshenko's midnight warning order about the possibility of a 'surprise blow', German dive-bombers blew the Kobrin HQ to pieces; the staff moved some three miles away, to Bukhovich. Before communications went completely dead, Korobkov received a telegram from Minsk (timed 0525 hours): 'In view of the large-scale military operations proceeding from the Germans I order you: mobilize your troops and proceed as with combat operations (*po-boevemu*).'[46] Through Kobrin, already evacuated by 4th Army staff and battered by German dive-bombers, walked those engineer officers who had just the day before been inspecting the district exercises. They were searching for the senior officers who were due to attend the exercises, and who might have operational orders of some kind. In the town itself, shattered by bombing, the populace listened amazed to the Moscow news broadcast relayed over the loudspeakers, with breezy keep-fit exercises followed by news of socialist triumphs in Soviet factories (the same items heard by the stupefied Soviet listeners in the Berlin Embassy).[47] The engineer officers also saw a shot-up Soviet aerodrome, with crews salvaging what they could from the burning wrecks. What they did not know was that the *Luftwaffe* had carried out a widespread aerial massacre, strafing and bombing the neatly parked aircraft on the ground: in just a few hours (up to noon, 22 June), the Western Military District lost 528 planes on the ground and 210 in the air. The Soviet Air Force lost in all 1,200 machines (many of them newly delivered) by that same noon.[48] At 0430 hours, 28 Soviet fighters had taken off to intercept

[45] Extract from 4th Army War Diary (Armeiskii zhurnal boevykh deistvii), *Bug v ogne*, p. 17.
[46] Text quoted in Sandalov, *Na Moskovskom napravlenii*, p. 79. (Korobkov, 'freely confessing' his thoughts, went on to say that even after German bombers had blown his HQ to pieces he still entertained the hope that war might be a 'local', limited affair.)
[47] Berezhkov, *op. cit.*, p. 103.
[48] Figures as cited by Anfilov, *Bessmertnyi podvig*, pp. 199–200; Western MD losses amounted to 38% of total strength, which was 1,909 aircraft on 22 June, the

the German bombers and fighters—to engage and even to ram the enemy—but the German bombers cruised largely unmolested.

In Minsk, which Timoshenko telephoned from Moscow for a fourth time, Boldin, Pavlov's deputy, gave him a report. Timoshenko then instructed Boldin—'I am telling *you* this and I wish you to pass it on to Pavlov'—that no operations against the Germans were to be undertaken without Moscow's express permission. 'Comrade Stalin will not permit artillery fire to be returned against the Germans.' All that was permitted was reconnaissance but for no more than 60 kilometres into German territory. Boldin apparently argued, pointing to the threat already developing to Soviet communications, and the need to activate the mechanized forces and in particular the AA defences, but all to no avail. Boldin scarcely thought that this was a German 'provocation'; on the other hand, Korobkov of the 4th Army confessed to his chief of staff that he was not entirely convinced. At last Timoshenko gave permission for the 'red packets' (the cover plans) to be opened; but even then in the 3rd and 4th Army the staffs were able to decipher only a part of their orders,[49] and the 10th Army, already in a tight spot, had some heavy fighting on its hands, so that 'cover plans' meant nothing. German bombers had hit fuel dumps and signal points with persistent accuracy in the 10th Army area, wounding and unnerving the formation from the very first moments. Within a few hours it began to break to pieces, thus uncovering Bialystok. The Soviet 3rd Army under Lieutenant-General Kuznetsov on Pavlov's right flank, and covering the junction with the Baltic district, found itself attacked at its front and in its right flank; in the first hour, 3rd Army communications were cut and stayed out of action, since there were no radio sets in use. Pavlov received only one signal from Kuznetsov: the rest was silence.

After 5 a.m., fierce fighting began to develop in the area of the Brest fortress. The fire from Russian guns, small and medium, denied the Germans effective use of the railway bridges: the Brest bridge came under fire from the fortress, the bridge at Semyaticha was covered by the machine-guns of the 'fortified district'. The Russians, at first disorganized, suffered heavy losses, but seven battalions of the 6th and 42nd Rifle Divisions (28th Rifle Corps) though far from fully manned began to fight back. The Political Section of the 6th Rifle Division

---

bulk of them older types of machines—1,022 fighters and 887 bombers): by contrast, thanks to some judicious planning, the Odessa MD lost only 10 machines.

[49] Cf. Anfilov, *Bessmertnyi podvig*, p. 197; the Western MD transmitted the warning signal 'GROZA' at 0300 hours (22 June), which activated the 'red packets' ('*Krasnyi paket*') detailing the cover plan for the frontiers. See also Boldin, *op. cit.*, p. 86, on permission to activate the '*Krasnyi paket*' and the failure to decipher: the instructions were presumably coded.

reported that it was not possible to concentrate properly—men 'arrived in dribs and drabs, half-dressed . . . .' Worst of all, the German bombardment had put much of the Soviet artillery out of action. And the seven battalions were mere shadows of their establishment; the combat report of the Political Section of 42nd Rifle Division underlines that,

> of the troops quartered in the Brest Fortress were two battalions of the 44th and 455th Rifle Regiments, part of which had no weapons; that complement, and also the independent reconnaissance battalion with its seven armoured cars and a motor-cycle company, proceeded to Zhabinki and took up defensive positions; 393rd Independent AA Battalion brought up three guns but no shells.

The defence plan could not now be put into operation. Scratch units, augmented by sections falling back on the fortress, took up the defence— which, long after the battle rolled eastwards, continued from the shattered turrets and ruined emplacements, and finally from lone rifles in underground rooms and tunnels, from tombs of debris.[50] This resistance, which initially denied the Germans easy access to the Bug and Muchavets rivers, became a ghastly but epic illustration of how Russian infantrymen could fight in traditionally ferocious style.

In the north-west, in the Baltic District, German bombers did a thorough job on signals and communications centres, on naval bases, and on the Soviet aerodromes in particular. From Riga to Kronstadt, and on Shauliya, Vilna and Kaunas the bombs fell on the pre-selected targets. Soviet fighter aircraft had been on a one-hour alert, but were held on their airfields after the first wave of German bombers, they had no authorization to cross their own frontiers. Along the frontier, many of the defence positions were unmanned. The 11th Army (which covered the vital junction between the Baltic Special and the Western Special Military Districts) deployed 11 battalions of the 5th, 33rd and 188th Rifle Divisions covering the approaches to Vilna along a 50-mile sector: to the north 8th Army covered the Shauliya-Riga approaches. In the air attacks, both armies lost not only an appreciable amount of equipment but also had their communications shattered. With German attacks in full swing against its sectors, 11th Army still received no orders; towards 6 a.m., the 5th Rifle Divisions (11th Army) did receive some orders from corps headquarters, namely, *not* to engage in operations, since this was merely a 'provocation'. From the high ground the officers of this division could see German units on the move and with binoculars pick out exact details. Divisional commander Ozerov,

544   *THE SOVIET RESPONSE*

practically pleading with Corps for orders, was admonished: 'We
advise you not to engage in combat operations, otherwise you will
answer for the consequences.'[51] The German troops bored into the
Soviet positions and overwhelmed the frontier guards, relentlessly
opening passages for the motorized and armoured formations poised
to pour in.

From the naval base at Libau the base commander reported just
before 5 a.m.: 'Bombs falling on military installations and in the
region of the aerodromes; no serious damage.' Straight on the heels
of this came the report of the Chief of Staff of the Kronstadt base that
magnetic mines—16 at least- –had been dropped but that the fairway
was still clear. Into the Baltic Fleet headquarters a 'cascade' of reports
flooded in; the intelligence officer, Colonel Frumkin, reported that the
German radio had broadcast *en clair* the information that the whole of
the southern Baltic had been mined. This, the Soviet officers assumed,
was to inhibit Soviet submarine operations. In Leningrad itself, the
Chief of Staff of the district, General Nikishev, summoned the
commanders of the various armies at 5 a.m., and authorized the
implementation of the 'mobilization plan'. From the safes the officers
drew the 'red packets', but the engineers, among others, got a rude
shock. The 'engineering war plan' consisted of a single injunction:
to form two engineering and one bridging regiments into independent
battalions and to distribute them as reinforcements to the district
armies. This was ludicrously irrelevant. A little later the intelligence
staff reported its latest news: a *Ju-88* had been shot down over the
Karelian Isthmus, and interrogation of the two survivors showed that
this had been a photo-reconnaissance mission from East Prussia to
cover the southern part of the Leningrad district. The object was to
search for Soviet movement to the south of Leningrad and in the
Karelian Isthmus.[52]

At the other geographic extremity, on the southern flank in Army
Group South's attack area, the same pattern of heavy bombing attacks,
unexpected and punishing artillery fire and the assault on the Soviet
frontier positions unfolded with the same fury. Ranging over the
Soviet airfields, German bombers inflicted more serious losses: by
noon on 22 June, these amounted to 277 machines. On the frontier
airfield at Stanislav 36 machines were destroyed on the ground, and 21
on the forward field at Gernauti (though General Zakharov's aircraft

[51] See operational narrative in *Bor'ba Latyshskogo naroda . . .*, p. 94 ff.; also Anfilov,
Bessmertnyi podvig, pp. 212–13; on lack of orders to 5th Division see Sevastyanov,
op. cit., p. 14.
[52] See account in Bychevsky, *op. cit.*, pp. 9–10; at the same time the Soviet command
wondered if and when the Finns would 'come in', though Finnish participation in
the war was considered inevitable.

in the Odessa district, thanks to timely dispersal, escaped this aerial blast with minute loss, only three fighters). From the Soviet frontier to Odessa and Sevastopol the German bombers went in search of their targets. In Lwow, the city where the non-Russian population had gleefully whispered 'the Germans are coming to get you' to the Russians, the 'uninterrupted bombing created panic' among the civilians; German-trained 'diversionists', in addition to blowing up fuel and ammunition dumps, added to the havoc as much as possible, not least by signalling the bombers and guiding them to special targets. The city commandant of Lwow was obliged to call out his military patrols and to augment them with the few tanks at his disposal in an effort to restore order.

As the bombers passed over the frontier, Soviet guards, already alerted by the noise of the engines, saw bursts of white rockets from the German lines and responses from the aircraft. This and other information the frontier troops passed back to the staffs of the nearest military units; in the Rava-Russki 'fortified district', Colonel Eremin, chief of staff, 41st Rifle Division, received a running commentary on 'unusual German movement' on the other side of the frontier. Precisely at 0415 hours (Moscow time), the German guns opened fire on the frontier posts and defence positions, targets long since accurately pin-pointed. Army Group South faced three river barriers to brave from the outset, the Western Bug, the San and the Prut; the German command was also aware of the strong Soviet defences and the deep echeloning of Kirponos's armies in the northern part of this front.[53] But there were gaps in these defences, which Army Group South proceeded to exploit by committing the German 6th Army and von Kleist's *Panzergruppe 1* at the junction of the Rava-Russki and the Strumilov 'fortified districts', against the left flank units of the Soviet 5th Army and part of the right flank of the Soviet 6th Army.

Supported by their artillery fire the German assault boats were launched into the Bug, which was on average some 70 metres wide in these southern reaches and made for the Soviet bank. Soviet frontier troops armed with their rifles, light machine-guns and grenades put up what resistance they could. Where possible, the unfortunate families of the frontier guards crowded into a block-house or took shelter in basements; at Sokal, Captain Bershadsky's detachment fought to defend the wooden bridge over the river, though his wife

---

[53] The most authoritative and the most detailed study is Marshal I. Kh. Bagramyan's *Tak nachinalas' voina* ('Voenizdat', 1971), which supersedes his earlier brochures and essays; Marshal Bagramyan's memoir (which is also partly a monograph) is assuredly one of the most important books on 1941 and likely to remain so. See 'Osobyi voennyi okrug', pp. 49 ff., and 'Prigranichnoe srazhenie', as from *"KOVO-41" vstupaet v sily*, pp. 87 ff.

546   *THE SOVIET RESPONSE*

and 11-year son lay dead in the shattered buildings of the frontier post.[54] In the Krystynopol area German assault troops seized the bridge, while units of the Soviet 124th Rifle Division rushed up from five miles away to support the frontier troops. At Vygadandka the railway bridge over the Bug was guarded by the 128 NKVD Railway Regiment, with a strength of 20 men; here, a German motor-cycle assault troop tried to rush the bridge. Within an hour the frontier on the Western Bug was the scene of scores of furious engagements and the Soviet frontier guards, lacking heavy weapons and short of ammunition, called for support from the Red Army.

Von Stülpnagel's 17th Army, operating on the Tomashov-Przemysl sector and aiming at Lwow, struck straight at the junction between two 'fortified districts', those of Rava-Russki and Przemysl; the former was defended by the 41st Rifle Division, 3rd Cavalry Division, 97th Rifle Division and a second echelon formation, 159th Rifle Division (6th Rifle Corps), and the latter by the 99th Rifle Division, with the 72nd Rifle and 173rd Rifle Divisions (8th Rifle Corps: 26th Army) in support. As the German guns fired off their opening barrages, these formations were removed from their camps and barracks and sent racing to the frontier. The alert system here functioned, in the opinion of the chief of staff of the 41st Rifle Division, 'without fuss'. The lightly armed frontier troops meanwhile kept the Red Army informed of the local developments on their sectors, and also sent out requests for immediate reinforcements.

This efficiency, which cost the Germans dear and which contrasted so sharply with the chaos of the western and north-western districts, had a particular explanation. The district commanders each played specific parts in the unfolding of the calamities at the frontiers. Pavlov at the centre had simply not believed in the imminence of a German attack; on that vital Saturday evening he was at the theatre. Kuznetsov in the Baltic acted in a confused and half-hearted manner, disorganizing much of his command. Colonel-General Kirponos at Kiev had more than once tried to rouse Moscow to the urgency of the situation; as late as 15-16 June, he suffered a rebuff, but he persisted. Though absolutely forbidden to move troops on the frontier, on 17 June he obtained permission from Timoshenko to start five rifle corps in the interior moving westwards. After more persuasion, Kirponos finally prevailed upon Timoshenko (sometime during the afternoon of 19 June) to allow the command to be decentralized and to man his operational command headquarters at Tarnopol by 22 June. The

[54] See 'Na Sokal'skom napravlenii' in Platonov, *op. cit.*, pp. 102–5; the Sokal detachment consisted of about 130 men, armed with light weapons.

stubbornness and persistence of Kirponos paid off, for the German armies had to smash through his defences.[55]

Initial reverses and confusions, however, could not be wholly avoided. The first bombings brought considerable havoc among the military and civilians alike. As the officers of the 41st Rifle Division took up their operational command post at Height 305 in the Rava-Russki 'fortified district', they watched a long column of dishevelled women and weeping children, many the families of divisional personnel, leaving the exposed village for Rava-Russki itself. As for the frontier guards their families either died with them or vanished as the battle swept over them. The German 17th Army had also to reckon on the difficulties of forcing the river San, whose bare banks provided the attackers with neither cover nor concealment. To the north-east of Przemysl, however, German assault troops seized the railway bridge over the San with a swift blow, but since the Soviet rifle divisions had manned the Przemysl 'fortified district' by 0600 hours and as the frontier guards fought on, this was merely the prelude to long and determined Soviet resistance.[56]

Timoshenko had meanwhile alerted two more rifle corps in the Kiev district, those commanded by the generals Zlobin and Chistyakov. Shortly after the German attack, these corps commanders reported to Kiev that they lacked the necessary equipment for full operations; they were told that the district had no adequate reserves itself, but that a request for more weapons had gone out to Moscow. The 'centre' (Moscow) was already being inundated with pleas of this kind, to which the several administrations of the General Staff returned totally unresponsive answers. From the Leningrad command, now committed to an urgent and emergency programme of frontier mining, came a request for more mines and for engineering equipment, since the dumps could supply only a tenth of the armies' needs. The 'centre' abruptly dashed any hope of outside help: 'To cover your requirements from the centre or from the centre's own dispositions is out of the question. There are more important commands than yours. Organize the exploitation of local resources.'[57]

With communications shattered or working only fitfully, with the disordered situation beyond many local comprehensions and com-

[55] For the background to these preparatory moves, see Bagramyan, *op. cit.*, 'Poslednie prigotovleniya', pp. 76–86 (note also the instructions given by Kirponos to Ponedelin on 19 June governing opening fire on German aircraft, p. 83); for General Staff instruction to organize 'in deepest secrecy' Front administration at Tarnopol, see also p. 83. Cf. Anfilov, *Bessmertnyi podvig*, pp. 181–2 for discussion of creation of 'Front administrations' under order of 18 June, Tarnopol for the 'South-West', Panevezius for 'North-West' and Obuz-Lesna for the 'West'.

[56] Cf. Bagramyan, *op. cit.*, pp. 108–9.

[57] Quoted by Bychevsky, *op. cit.*, p. 11.

petences, the 'centre' had scarcely an idea of what was happening on the frontiers. By 6 a.m., nothing less than the whole gigantic battle stretching from East Prussia to the Ukraine had been joined. In little more than 120 minutes, the situation—above all, in the centre—had developed dangerously. Of all the *coups de main* which the Germans had planned against the vital rail and road bridges, not one had failed to succeed. Now, south of Brest, German armour crossed over captured bridges and newly-built pontoon bridges; to the north of it, a German engineer battalion laboured to finish the first pontoon bridge in 4th Army's area near Drohiczyn. Nevertheless, with fuel and ammunition dumps blown to pieces, towns and bases bombed, raked airfields littered with burning planes, tank and vehicle parks in flames, with German troops advancing by columns upon and across the frontiers, the Soviet Union was still not at war and the Red Army lacked any specific orders to deal with the attacks.

After consultation with Stalin, Timoshenko at 0715 hours, 22 June, issued to the frontier artillery district commanders *Directive No. 2*, signed also by Zhukov as chief of the General Staff, stipulating 'active offensive operations' (though hastily mobilized units were fighting desperate holding actions against increasingly powerful thrusts) and proposing limited air attacks, even as Soviet bombers and fighters were being pounded to pieces as they lay stranded on the ground. The directive read:

> 22 June 1941 at 0400 hours in the morning German aircraft without any cause whatsoever carried out flights over aerodromes and towns along the length of the frontier and proceeded to bomb them. Simultaneously in a number of places German troops opened fire with artillery and penetrated the frontier.
>
> In connection with the unprecedented attack by Germany on the Soviet Union, I issue these orders:
>
> 1. Troops in full strength and with all the means at their disposal will attack the enemy and destroy him in those places where he has violated the Soviet frontier.
>   In the absence of special authorization, ground troops will not cross the frontier line.
> 2. Reconnaissance and attack aircraft will locate the concentration areas of enemy aircraft and the deployment of his ground forces. Bomber and ground-attack aircraft will destroy with powerful blows the aircraft on enemy aerodromes and will bomb the main concentrations of his ground forces. Aviation strikes will be mounted to a depth of 100–150 kilometres in German territory. Königsberg and Memel will be bombed.
>   No flights over Finland and Rumania to take place without special authorization.[58]

[58] See text in Anfilov, *Bessmertnyi podvig*, p. 210; it is worth noting that Anfilov attributes the issuing authority for this order to the Glavnyi Voennyi Sovet (created

TO SURPRISE ATTACK   549

There was no mention of a state of war or of any move to general mobilization.

From 'the centre', confused and ill-informed as it was, unrealistic orders went out across a communications net which had already been seriously impaired. Frontier units were desperately trying to assemble often under heavy enemy attack. For many, this was still a 'provocation', for no announcement of war or general mobilization had been made nor did one come for several hours. Only at noon did the Soviet government, through the limping phrases and halting tone of Molotov, announce to the Russian people in a radio broadcast that the Soviet Union was at war with Germany. The fiction of a 'provocation' could no longer be maintained, however much the wish might be father to the thought. Stalin, who had persistently refused to face the truth, or who thought that truth was and must be what he promulgated, now had no option but to admit 'a state of war'.

Directive No. 3: 2115 hours, 22 June

Sixteen hours after the opening of Operation 'Barbarossa' the formidable divisions of the German *Ostheer* had virtually unhinged two of the three Soviet Fronts, the North-Western and the Western: at the junction of these two strategic entities the Soviet 11th Army had been pulverized and the right flank of its neighbour on the Western Front—3rd Army—also laid bare. North of Kaunas German tanks were over the river Dubissa and south of the city German armour was astride the broad Niemen. With the right flank of the Western Front battered in, the left was simultaneously flapping feebly, for Korobkov's 4th Army was in no position to put up an effective defence—thus imperilling the flank of 10th Army at the centre of Pavlov's Front and also threatening the right flank of 5th Army on the South-Western Front (with 5th Army having also to face the danger created by the German penetration of the junction of the 5th and 6th Armies). Struck at their joints and hinges, the three Soviet Fronts were buckling and swaying alarmingly even after a few hours of military operations.[59]

Of the nature and extent of this catastrophe 'the centre' seemed largely unaware. Neither the Defence Commissariat nor the General Staff disposed of any accurate information about the situation in the frontier districts. At noon, however, Stalin appeared to make up his mind that the Soviet field commanders were simply 'not up to it' and

---

in 1938)—there was no Soviet 'C-in-C', this was more than a Defence Commissariat instruction and the *Stavka* was not formally brought into being until 23 June, so that the 'Main Military Soviet' technically initiated combat operations.

[59] Cf. A. Philippi and F. Heim, *Der Feldzug gegen Sowjetrussland 1941–1945* (Stuttgart, 1962), pp. 54–55; Albert Seaton, *The Russo-German War 1941–1945* (London, 1971), pp. 98 ff., 116 ff., 133 ff. on the early actions on the three Fronts.

lacked both the skill and experience to mount 'powerful counter-blows' against the German forces, whereupon he ordered that senior officers be sent to assist the Front commands—Colonel-General O. I. Gorodovnikov to the North-Western Front, the Marshals Kulik and Shaposhnikov to the Western Front, and General Zhukov to the South-Western Front, all in the capacity of *'predstaviteli Glavnogo Komandovaniya'*.[60] Tyulenev in Moscow was also ordered to assemble a staff and to take command of the newly activated Southern Front (based on the Odessa MD):[61] the Moscow MD staff hurriedly furnished him with a field staff and organized a command train which set off southwards on the evening of 22 June, by which time the other senior officers had already left by air for the battle fronts. The orders for a full-scale counter-stroke mounted by the Red Army—designed to hurl the German Army back with one massive attack—followed on their heels: *Directive No. 3* issued by Marshal Timoshenko at 2115 hours on 22 June. All three Soviet Fronts *were to take the offensive*: the North-Western and Western Fronts, each using their rifle troops plus two mechanized corps, were to mount coordinated operations from Kaunas and Grodno, to carry the war on to enemy territory and by the evening of 24 June, having encircled and destroyed the enemy, would invest the Suwalki area. Front operations would be supported by the long-range bomber air force (ADD); the South-Western Front was ordered to employ the 5th and 6th Armies supported by 'several' mechanized corps to destroy by means of 'concentric blows' those enemy forces operating on the Vladimir-Volynsk/Krystynopol front and by the evening of 24 June Front forces would invest the area of Lublin, having also 'secured itself' from the direction of Cracow and also defending the state frontier with Hungary. On the flanks of the Soviet German front Soviet forces were restricted to 'defensive assignments'—to cover the state frontier and to inhibit enemy penetrations.[62]

The Front commanders, struggling desperately to maintain the cohesion of their forces, had no option but to prepare the massive offensive operations, envisaged to a depth of some 50–75 miles, which *Directive No. 3* demanded. All three looked to their mechanized corps for salvation. Kuznetsov in the north-west proceeded with his plan to strike at the flank of *Panzergruppe 4* from north-west Kaunas;

[60] See Anfilov, *Bessmertnyi podvig*, p. 237; cf. Zhukov, *Memoirs*, p. 238.

[61] Tyulenev, *op. cit.*, p. 142; for important background material, see Anfilov, *Bessmertnyi podvig*, p. 182, which explains that on 20 June Odessa MD command proposed setting up 'Southern Front' administration (based on Odessa MD), approved by the Politburo on 21 June after accepted by Glavnyi Voennyi Sovet, but new 'Front' would be organized by the Moscow MD.

[62] See *Istoriya Velikoi Otechestvennoi voiny Sovetskogo Soyuza 1941–1945*, Tom Vtoroi (Iyun' 1941 g.—Noyabr' 1942 g.) ('Voenizdat', 1961), p. 30.

TO SURPRISE ATTACK 551

Pavlov, having first sent his 'shock group' into what he imagined was the attack, planned to employ his mechanized forces south of Grodno and near Brest; Kirponos, aware that he had yet to concentrate the bulk of his armour, decided to employ the formations immediately at hand (15th and 8th Mechanized Corps) to strike at the German spearheads. The odds against any chance of success, however, were enormous. Aircraft which might have covered the units during their concentration had long ago been shot to pieces on the ground; the artillery, like much of the infantry, was stuck fast for lack of transport; where transport existed, as with so many of the tanks, it stood stalled for lack of fuel: where there was fuel, there was little or no ammunition. And even where all these requirements were met there was no time to prepare.

The night came at last. For Lieutenant-General Boldin, as for so many in the beleaguered or hard-pressed Soviet divisions, it was 'lit by hundreds of flashes—from raging fires, from the tracer of the machine-gun units, from shells and bombs exploding nearby'. Under the cover of darkness officers struggled to put their units into some semblance of order. The scanty supplies of food and ammunition salvaged from the burning dumps were distributed. Boldin knew now beyond all doubt that Pavlov's orders could never be accomplished; he hoped, nevertheless, that Khatskilevich's 6th Mechanized Corps and the 36th Cavalry Division might hold off the enemy. By night 10th Army units were to take up the defensive positions behind the Narev which 6th Mechanized had been holding; the tanks and motorized infantry would concentrate by dawn in the thick woods north-east of Bialystok. Pulled in from Slonim to Sokulka, 29th Mechanized Divisions would cover the concentration of the 6th Corps, which Boldin intended to commit in attack towards Grodno, to the south of which he presumed 11th Mechanized Corps under Mostovenko was already fighting. Golubev himself had been very slow in deploying the 6th Mechanized Corps; he had split up the tanks and used the infantry to hold the Narev crossing. That was how Protaturchev's 4th Tank Division (6th Mechanized Corps) came to be chasing its own tail for too long. Even so, Khatskilevich's corps, unlike the 13th, had a strong complement of T-34 and KV tanks, though it was short of fuel and ammunition; its divisions were under-manned, but Boldin, struggling to make up for the time lost by Golubev, could hardly wait. In the end, wholly ignorant of the whereabouts of 11th Mechanized Corps and disastrously robbed of 36th Cavalry Division, Boldin proceeded to attack.[63]

The night which brought momentary respite to parts of the frontier commands also brought the first operational digest (*svodka*) from the

[63] See Boldin, *op. cit.*, pp. 92–97.

Soviet General Staff, compiled at 2200 hours on 22 June. Of the urgency of the situation it contained not the slightest trace. Blatant with complacency and swelled with ignorance, it read:

> Regular troops of the German Army during the course of 22 June conducted operations against frontier defence units of the USSR, attaining insignificant success in a number of sectors. During the second half of the day, with the arrival of forward elements of the field forces of the Red Army, the attacks by German troops along most of the length of our frontiers were beaten off and losses inflicted on the enemy.[64]

In the course of the next few hours the '*predstaviteli Glavnogo Komandovaniya*' were to see for themselves just what this 'insignificant success' amounted to, and all of them, even the brash and bumptious Kulik, were aghast at what they found on the battlefronts. General Zhukov, however, had few illusions, if only because Vatutin (now placed in charge of the General Staff) quickly exploded them: he informed Zhukov that same evening (22 June) that the General Staff lacked 'accurate information' about either Soviet or German strength and movement, that there were no data on losses and that there was no contact with Kuznetsov or Pavlov (the North-Western and Western Front commanders). Nevertheless, Stalin still stuck by *Directive No. 3* and ordered Zhukov's signature to be added to the document: from Kiev Zhukov asked Vatutin just what the Directive prescribed, and on being told that it envisaged a 'counter-offensive' to 'rout the enemy in all major directions' and then an advance into enemy territory, the former could not contain himself and burst out with the remark that the Soviet command had no knowledge of just where the German Army was attacking and in what strength. Vatutin pointed out ruefully that he too, would wait for the morning to issue an operational directive but that the matter had been 'decided', hence there was no choice.[65] It was at midnight when *Directive No. 3* arrived at South-Western Front HQ and the Chief of Staff (M. A. Purkaev) objected in strong terms, but the order had to be carried out: at least Kirponos and his staff had Zhukov's considerable professional skill and experience behind them, a factor which exerted its influence in the skilful armoured counter-attacks mounted by the South-Western Front. But elsewhere the outcome of *Directive No. 3* was uniformly disastrous. Kulik could do little or nothing, a combination of his own ineptitude and a situation which was slipping beyond the grasp of any one man. When he finally arrived in full flying kit at Boldin's command post (not far from Bialystok), the best he could manage was to tell Boldin 'to get on with

[64] See *Istoriya Velikoi Otechestvennoi voiny* . . . , Tom Vtoroi, p. 29.
[65] See Zhukov, *Memoirs*, p. 239.

it' and then he flew out abruptly, prompting the terse comment from corps commander Nikitin: 'Strange visit, that'.[66] Nor was the situation in the north-west restored by the arrival of Gorodovnikov: the plight of 11th Army had already passed the point of restoration, Kuznetsov's attempt to attack the flanks of *Panzergruppe 4* with two mechanized corps (the 12th and 3rd) failed for all the whirling tank battles which were fought, and already on 23 June the Leningrad command was casting anxious glances over its shoulder in the direction of a disintegrating Baltic Front. On 23 June the gap prised open between the Soviet North-Western and the Western Fronts had widened to almost 80 miles: 10th Army of the Western Front, faced with the ruination of its flank armies (3rd and 4th), could not long hold out and within 72 hours had ceased to exist as an organized fighting force, its units melting away into the thick woods south of Minsk.

Within three days, with the same catastrophic tale repeated elsewhere, Timoshenko was forced to recognize that the great counterstroke envisaged by *Directive No. 3* had failed: the Soviet frontier armies were for the most part broken and shattered, leaving them wholly incapable of checking the German advance. The shock of 'surprise' had begun to wear off, only to be superseded by an awareness of what a fearsome project lay ahead.

University of Edinburgh

[66] Boldin, *op. cit.*, p. 98.

[12]

Stalin's Cabinet: the Politburo and Decision Making in the Post-war Years

YORAM GORLIZKI

OVER THE 1930S the Politburo was pummelled into an instrument of Stalinist rule: what once had been a crucible of political struggle had turned, by World War II, into a tractable committee of Stalin's friends and accessories.[1] No longer hemmed in by formal procedures or protocol, the cabinet was recast to fit in with Stalin's personal habits and work rhythms. After the war, the cabinet adapted still further to the leader's needs and requirements. From October 1946 the formal Politburo elected at the XVIII Party Congress in 1939 practically ceased to function. The enlarged formal sessions of old, to which Central Committee members and other party officials were invited, had given way to small, loose-knit, kitchen cabinets which were at Stalin's beck and call.[2]

Nevertheless, even at the height of Stalin's dictatorship the Politburo continued to perform a distinct organisational role. By contrast with the Council of Ministers, the Politburo carried out a discrete set of institutional responsibilities which included control of foreign affairs, security matters and organisational issues. For the duration of Stalin's rule these questions remained firmly within the Politburo's domain. In addition, the Politburo also attended to high order party matters. In view of Stalin's control over his Politburo colleagues it may be wondered why the dictator should have persisted with the Politburo at all. Why was Stalin not drawn to a purely dictatorial system of executive rule which, governing in his name, would have dispensed with the Politburo altogether?

The present article examines this question by looking at the functions served by the post-war Politburo. It begins by looking at the internal dynamics of the Politburo and suggests that rather than one Politburo there were in fact a variety of distinct 'politburos' in the late Stalin period. Despite this diversity, each 'politburo' was deployed by Stalin to lock his colleagues into a system of collective responsibility; each offered a flexible yet reliable system by which the dictator could bind his peers. In the second part, the article moves on from the internal dynamics of the Politburo to look at its external relations. Whereas internally the Politburo was fluid and pliable, externally it projected an image of stability and order. The article suggests that a political system as hierarchic as Stalinism required an image of unity and authority at its apex. The Politburo, it argues, served this purpose well. In the third section, devoted to the last six months of Stalin's rule, the article looks at the Politburo as an agency of 'Bolshevik' leadership. Despite Stalin's importance, even at the height of his dictatorship the Soviet system never freed itself entirely from a deep-seated

292   YORAM GORLIZKI

Bolshevik tradition of party 'democracy'. At times, such as the XIX Congress of
October 1952, Stalin himself turned to this tradition in order to kick-start the political
system. It was at this point that the Politburo, now substantially reformed, assumed
a specific party leadership role. The article concludes by suggesting that after the XIX
Congress, one of the 'politburos' under Stalin—the Politburo without Stalin—was
given a decisive impetus.

Internal dynamics

Composition of the Politburo

It was some months after the war, and the formal dissolution of the State Defence
Committee (GKO) on 4 September 1945, when the Politburo began to resume
peacetime operations.[3] Formally the Politburo continued in much the same vein as it
had left off before the war, with a virtually identical membership and a similarly
modest workload. At its meeting of 29 December 1945 the Politburo resolved to meet
every other Tuesday for a short time, from 8 pm to 9 pm. Apart from Andreev, who
was absent, the meeting of 29 December was made up of the same Politburo members
elected at the XVIII Congress in 1939: Voroshilov, Zhdanov, Kaganovich, Kalinin,
Mikoyan, Molotov, Stalin and Khrushchev. The candidate members of 1939, Beria
and Shvernik, were now joined by Voznesensky and Malenkov, who had been
coopted as candidate members in 1941.[4] In the coming years the ranks of the formal
Politburo swelled as a succession of candidates—Malenkov and Beria in March 1946,
Voznesensky in March 1947, Bulganin in February 1948 and Kosygin in September
of that year—were raised to full membership.[5]

Although it did not keep to the schedule set out on 29 December 1945, the full
Politburo did convene with some regularity over the coming months, with sessions on
19 January, 4 March, 13 April and 4 May 1946.[6] Meetings of the Politburo, however,
tailed off following the session of 3 October 1946; over the rest of Stalin's reign there
were only two further formal, enlarged sessions of the Politburo, on 13 December
1947 and 17 June 1949.[7] The official Politburo in fact came to be overshadowed by
the regular conferences of a narrow 'ruling group' (*rukovodyashchaya grupa*) which
met up routinely in Stalin's office. The composition of this circle, sometimes known
as the 'select group' (*uzkii sostav*) or the 'close circle' (*blizhnii krug*), differed
markedly from that of the formal Politburo.[8] Excluded from the *rukovodyashchaya
grupa* were those Politburo members who had either fallen foul of Stalin or who were
cut off from the ruling circle for reasons of location or ill-health. For some time
Stalin's suspicions had fallen on Voroshilov, Andreev and, to a lesser extent,
Kaganovich, all of whom were, despite their formal membership of the Politburo, not
privy to the proceedings of the ruling group in the aftermath of the war;[9] others
excluded were the head of state, Mikhail Kalinin, who had long suffered from
ill-health and who died in 1946, and Khrushchev and Zhdanov, both of whom were
stationed outside Moscow.[10] Although the composition and style of operations of the
rukovodyashchaya grupa deviated, sometimes markedly, from those of the *de jure*
Politburo, to the extent that most resolutions issued in the name of the Politburo in

the late Stalin years were determined by this group, it may be thought of as a 'second' or *'de facto'* Politburo.

With six of the nine full members of the Politburo excluded, the *rukovodyashchaya grupa* at the war's end consisted of a small core of Politburo members who had also served on the State Defence Committee (GKO). Of this 'quintet' *(pyaterka)* three, Stalin, Molotov and Mikoyan, were full Politburo members while the others, Malenkov and Beria, were candidate members.[11] From early October to mid-December 1945 Stalin took a holiday in the south, leaving the affairs of state in the hands of a 'quartet' *(chetverka)* of Molotov, Mikoyan, Malenkov and Beria.[12] Stalin kept closely informed of the decisions of his colleagues and grew quickly impatient with their performance, especially that of Molotov. On coming back to Moscow in December Stalin lessened his dependence on the 'quartet' and altered the balance of forces within it by adding a new member, Andrei Zhdanov, so that, with Stalin, the 'quintet' had now become a 'sextet'. At the same meeting of the Politburo, on 29 December, Stalin also sought to formalise the activities of the ruling group by endowing it with a title, 'the Commission of External Affairs at the Politburo'.[13] Notwithstanding its title, the Politburo 'Commission' by no means confined itself to foreign affairs. Rather, it served Stalin as a procedural ruse for bringing together the *rukovodyashchaya grupa*.[14] On 3 October 1946 Stalin did away with the pretence that the Commission was concerned entirely with external affairs by signing a Politburo resolution which allowed the Commission to engage with questions of 'domestic construction and internal policy'. Stalin also widened the membership of the group by determining that 'the head of Gosplan comrade Voznesensky be added to the sextet and that henceforth the sextet be known as the septet'.[15] In the following year the Commission was further consolidated with the addition of Nikolai Bulganin on 5 March 1947 and Aleksei Kuznetsov on 17 September 1947 so that the septet had now become a 'novenary' *(devyatka)*.[16] Finally, the vacancy within the novenary created on 31 August 1948 by the death of Andrei Zhdanov was filled three days later by Aleksei Kosygin.[17]

Alongside the formal Politburo, which in effect ceased to function in the autumn of 1946, meetings of the *rukovodyashchaya grupa* were held frequently and the bulk of Politburo resolutions were in effect in its hands.[18] Whereas 'neither the Central Committee, nor the Politburo ... worked regularly', Khrushchev recounted later, 'Stalin's regular sessions with his inner circle went along like clockwork'.[19] Indeed, one draft Politburo resolution on the organisation of leadership meetings of December 1948 made no mention of the formal Politburo at all while it accorded the 'novenary' a fixed time, every Wednesday, in the leadership's schedule.[20] Yet while Stalin bestowed on the *rukovodyashchaya grupa* shape and continuity by attaching to it titles (e.g. the 'Commission for Foreign Affairs') and numerical epithets (i.e. 'quartet', 'quintet' etc.) he refrained from encumbering it with rules and procedures. One of the great advantages to Stalin of an informally convened leadership group was its flexibility. For one thing, membership of the full Politburo was not a prerequisite for entry to the group. A succession of leaders, including Malenkov, Beria, Voznesensky and Bulganin, gained admission to the group many months before their formal accession as full members of the Politburo. Stalin hence unilaterally elevated colleagues without having to go through the tedious formality of having them

294   YORAM GORLIZKI

'elected' as full members of the Politburo by the Central Committee.[21] Stalin could also expel members from his group with unseemly ease. This became a particular advantage in the wake of the Leningrad Affair, at which point membership of the ruling group became quite convoluted. Stalin began to whittle down the 'novenary' in the spring of 1949 with the removal of the disgraced Voznesensky and Kuznetsov, and later in the year of Kosygin, partially filling the gap with the rehabilitated Kaganovich.[22] Tracing the contours of the 'leading group' thereafter is something of a puzzle, as it must have been not least for members of the ruling group themselves. Unbeknown to themselves, Mikoyan and Molotov were unceremoniously axed from the ruling circle towards the very end of Stalin's reign.[23] Having grown from a 'quintet' in 1945 to a 'novenary' in 1948, by the very end Stalin's core leadership had once again been reduced to a rump 'quintet' consisting of Malenkov, Beria, Bulganin, Khrushchev and the tyrant himself.[24]

In addition to the formal Politburo and the Politburo's standing 'Commission' of 'quintets', 'sextets' and so forth, there were still other informally convened groups which passed resolutions in the Politburo's name. In the post-war period some decisions, especially those on cadres at the very highest levels, were reached in minute caucuses consisting of no more than four or possibly even three members of the leadership. Thus, for example, the decision of 4 March 1949 to remove Mikoyan and Molotov as ministers of foreign trade and foreign affairs was reached by a supreme council of Stalin, Malenkov, Beria and Bulganin.[25] A minority of Politburo resolutions were even formulated and signed by Stalin alone.[26]

By stark contrast, some sessions of the 'leading group' were convened without the leader at all. It is these meetings which are of greatest interest since they were to set the pattern for high-level interaction within the ruling group after Stalin's death. In the first autumn after the war, Stalin obtained leave from his Politburo colleagues to take a 10-week break in the south from early October to the middle of December. Whilst out of Moscow Stalin left the affairs of state in the hands of a quartet of Molotov, Mikoyan, Malenkov and Beria. Stalin received daily reports on events in Moscow and was quick to stamp his authority on the 'quartet', and especially on his own stand-in, the hapless Molotov, by first forcing the other three to gang up on Molotov and then by extracting a humiliating apology from the latter for what Stalin regarded as his unwarranted independence of action.[27] A year later, again while away in the south, Stalin deployed similar tactics against another erstwhile Politburo member, Anastas Mikoyan.[28] In the years that followed, especially after his 70th birthday in December 1949, as Stalin spent longer stretches outside the capital, he became reliant on manipulating, cajoling and overruling his cabinet colleagues from afar.[29]

There is little evidence that, in meeting without Stalin, the Politburo gained any freedom of initiative. Many decisions formally approved by the Politburo in Moscow in Stalin's absence were in fact carefully monitored and vetted by the leader. On 1 November 1949, for example, a 'quintet' of Malenkov, Molotov, Beria, Kaganovich and Bulganin—without Stalin—issued a Politburo resolution setting up a commission to consider allegations against the Central Committee secretary G. M. Popov.[30] On 4 December a 'sextet' of the same group now joined by Mikoyan—but again excluding Stalin—approved the conclusions of the commission on Popov.[31] Although

STALIN'S CABINET   295

these decisions were formally reached without Stalin, a closer examination reveals that it was Stalin who first set in motion the inquiry in a letter from the south of 29 October and that Malenkov's later amendments to the resolution were all dictated by Stalin.[32] Similarly the sacking of Men'shikov, Mikoyan's replacement at the ministry of foreign trade, on 4 November 1951 was passed as a Politburo resolution in Stalin's absence by a group of six Politburo members.[33] Again, however, a reading of the memoir literature suggests that the decision was made entirely by Stalin while the leader was in Sochi and that, notwithstanding their own reservations, the cabinet were merely implementing Stalin's wishes.[34] On other occasions Stalin simply rejected and overturned the decisions of his cabinet colleagues. Thus Stalin greeted a draft Politburo resolution of 19 August 1950 not to send a delegation to Romania, which had been unanimously agreed by the rest of the cabinet, with a terse message, rendered by Poskrebyshev as: 'Instruction to send the delegation' (*ukazanie poslat' delegatsiyu*).[35]

Some have attributed to the new leaders-in-waiting a conspiracy to pull Stalin away from the levers of power. Evidence for such a thesis is slender indeed.[36] Yet the experience of routine meetings without Stalin over a number of years provided a firm footing for decision making after the dictator's death. Members of the group acquired independent knowledge of the machinery of policy making and of the nature of collective cabinet responsibility. Even where collaborative decision making in effect came down to jointly trying to read Stalin's mind or anticipating his shifts in mood, these cabinet sessions provided the leadership with valuable experience of working together and of operating as a collective. The speed with which this Stalin-less cabinet swung into action on hearing of Stalin's illness—even issuing organisational directives before the dictator's death—indicates a level of common understanding and initiative among the leaders.[37] The operational unity of the ruling group was confirmed by the alacrity with which the group was reconstituted as a cabinet after Stalin's death.[38] Thus a 'third' politburo, one without Stalin, acquired sufficient momentum and coherence to negotiate the gulf represented by Stalin's death with minimum disruption. Of the various politburos under Stalin it was this which best anticipated the decision-making dynamics and policy directions of the post-Stalin cabinet.[39]

After the war Stalin experimented with a variety of organisational forms for the Politburo. This diversity and the diminutive proportions of the smaller politburos enabled Stalin to convert his cabinet into a responsive and flexible instrument of rule. In its most rudimentary form the Politburo comprised a small coterie of Stalin's favourites who were skilled at reading the dictator's mind and implementing his wishes with a minimum of fuss.[40] These narrow and informal Politburo meetings were freed from the schedules and procedures which hamstrung the official or *de jure* cabinet. In the company of a small circle of colleagues, all of whom were well-known to Stalin and to each other, there was all the less reason to follow the inconvenient and time-consuming protocols of formal Politburo sessions.

The Politburo and decision making

An abiding pre-*perestroika* image of decision making in the late Stalin era is of policy issues of national importance being discussed over interminable late-night dinners as Stalin's aide, Poskrebyshev, went round the table collecting signatures off half-drunk party and state leaders.[41] The archives are silent on the state of mind and sobriety of the country's leaders at Stalin's drinking sessions. What they do confirm is the absence of guidelines for putting issues on the agenda or of rules for decision making and conflict resolution. Most decisions, especially on 'political'—as opposed to 'technical'—questions turned simply on Stalin's position, or expected position, on a given matter. Indeed, it was precisely in order to free the Politburo from tedious rules and formalities that the cabinet adopted the more manageable form of a small 'Commission' whose proceedings depended in large part on the personal chemistry between Stalin and its members. This lack of even a rudimentary formality is perhaps most keenly expressed in the absence of transparent or commonly agreed methods for minuting and communicating decisions.

Proceedings of the Politburo were not stenographically recorded or professionally minuted. Instead, decisions were noted down by the head of the special sector, Poskrebyshev, or, in his absence, by a member of the Politburo's inner circle. Stalin routinely entrusted the task of formulating and writing up Politburo decisions to Georgii Malenkov. Many first drafts of Politburo resolutions in the late Stalin years are in Malenkov's hand. Thus, for example, the text of the controversial resolutions to dismiss A. A. Kuznetsov as Central Committee secretary on 15 February 1949 and to sack Molotov as minister of foreign affairs and Mikoyan as minister of external trade on 4 March 1949 were written up by Malenkov, as was the Politburo resolution of 15 April 1950 to appoint Malenkov himself to the Buro of the Presidium of the Council of Ministers.[42] In some cases, Politburo resolutions were relayed down the phone. Thus, for example, at 12.15 pm on 12 June 1949 Malenkov dictated to a secretary at the special sector a Politburo resolution appointing Tevosyan deputy chairman of the Council of Ministers.[43] At other times Poskrebyshev would receive long lists of orders, often scribbled down, which he would be asked to draw up (*oformit'*) as Politburo resolutions.[44]

For the most part the relative formlessness and procedural indeterminacy of decision making was compensated for by the need for one indispensable ingredient: Stalin's consent. Thus, for example, on 21 January 1950 Poskrebyshev received a list of draft Politburo resolutions from Marshal Vasilevsky which, the latter tellingly assured Poskrebyshev, 'has been confirmed by comrade Stalin'. Vasilevsky, it seems, did not even deem it worth mentioning that the decision had been taken at a joint meeting also attended by Molotov, Beria, Bulganin, Malenkov and Mikoyan.[45] Similarly, a draft Politburo resolution 'On the refutation by TASS' of 6 June 1952 was accompanied by a short missive from Vyshinsky to Poskrebyshev: 'Comrade Poskrebyshev please draw up this resolution. Comrade Molotov tells me that it has been confirmed by comrade Stalin. Vyshinsky'.[46]

These ill-defined procedures for drawing up Politburo resolutions were sometimes exploited by members of the leadership. So long as they had obtained Stalin's permission, members of the ruling circle could authorise Politburo resolutions directly, without having to go to the trouble of consulting other members of the cabinet. This was especially true of those low-key issues, such as permission to invite or to send overseas delegations, which the Politburo nevethetheless regarded as its prerogative. Thus, for example, it was in this area that on 21 January 1950 Molotov sought Stalin's permission for a set of 21 Politburo resolutions which, 'by virtue of their clarity do not demand, it seems to me, special discussion'.[47]

For the most part, however, Stalin insisted that all members of his inner circle ratify Politburo resolutions. The precise form of ratification was a matter usually determined by Stalin himself. As in the 1930s one of his preferred means was 'by correspondence' (*oprosom*). On 6 February 1951, for example, the minister of foreign affairs, Vyshinsky, requested of Molotov that 12 questions be voted on by correspondence. 'Comrade Stalin', he wrote, 'has agreed that this type of question may be resolved in this manner'.[48] Obtaining Stalin's consent was at all times the main obstacle to getting a Politburo resolution passed. Nevertheless, Stalin still clung to the notion, inherited from the 1930s, that key decisions receive unanimous support, even if this incurred the inconvenience and delay of having a draft circulated by courier to all members of the Politburo for their signature. The frequency of correspondence votes indeed begs the question of why Stalin should have gone to the length of consulting all other members of the leadership when all knew that it was Stalin's opinion that mattered.[49] Certainly, once Stalin had given the green light to a Politburo resolution it was unthinkable that another member of the committee could have opposed it either at the meeting itself or, where the decision was voted on by correspondence, by refusing to put his signature to the proposal. In view of Stalin's tight grip over the Politburo it may be wondered why the Politburo should have stuck so rigidly to protocol by going through the time-consuming formalities of seeking the opinions of other members of the committee by conducting a vote.

One reason for this insistence was Stalin's need to bind his co-leaders in a system of collective responsibility. Stalin used correspondence votes and Politburo meetings to 'test' the loyalty of his inner circle. The formal device for achieving this goal was to force cabinet colleagues to sign Politburo resolutions, even after the event, thus making them jointly accountable for state policy. Less formally, Stalin would use Politburo meetings as occasions to spring awkward questions on unsuspecting colleagues and then to check their reactions.[50] Politburo meetings thus evolved into an amalgam of formal devices (the demand for co-signatures and correspondence votes) and personalised modes of control (throwing surprise questions and soliciting early opinions on controversial matters) through which Stalin could manipulate his colleagues. The Politburo thus became indispensable as a tool for controlling the leadership.

The Politburo also served a social function for Stalin. By most accounts Stalin was a lonely man who craved company. Much of his time with Politburo colleagues was spent sitting through Westerns or endless dinners marked by a conspicuous lack of policy-oriented discussion. In its increasingly informal settings and style of operations, the post-war Politburo satisfied Stalin's need for social interaction: here the country's ruling group doubled up as Stalin's social circle.[51]

Yet there were also other reasons why the outward 'form' of Politburo decision making was maintained. Internal relations within the Politburo were fluid and sometimes fast-changing. Authority and status within the Politburo depended on access to the leader, on gaining Stalin's trust and confidence. As Politburo members knew to their cost, Stalin's trust could vanish suddenly, without notice. Depending on the state of one's relations with Stalin, normal hierarchies might be quickly inverted. Thus even Poskrebyshev, who was no more than Stalin's aide, was known to shout and to 'snarl viciously' at Politburo members who had lost Stalin's confidence.[52] Outside the ruling circle, however, the Politburo had to project an image of stability and order. Here, in striking contrast to its internal reality, the Politburo was a symbol of steadfast authority.

External relations

The Politburo and the party-state

Although it served as a general cabinet, the Politburo was also the chief executive committee of the party. In view of the long intervals separating party congresses and Central Committee plenums after the war, the party leadership functions of the Politburo became all the more important. This was especially so in the late 1940s when the governmental machinery, the Council of Ministers, led by some of the most senior politicians in the country, had seen its work become better organised and more systematic.[53] As the party's *de facto* chief executive committee, a robust Politburo was needed as a symbol of Bolshevik leadership and, specifically, as a mechanism for keeping an increasingly authoritative Council of Ministers in check.

The division of responsibilities between the Politburo and the Council of Ministers was fairly clearly drawn in the post-war period. On 8 February 1947 the Politburo passed a resolution 'On the organisation of the Council of Ministers' which assigned most economic policies to that body but reserved for the Politburo all decisions relating to the ministry of foreign affairs, the ministry of external trade, the ministry of state security, most currency issues, and all questions relating to the ministry of the armed forces.[54] In addition, the Politburo continued to exercise powers that had been in its remit by tradition. The first of these, exemplified not least by the February resolution itself, was administrative reorganisations. For most of the late Stalin period the Politburo amalgamated, divided and renamed a multitude of state and party organisations.[55] As the party's supreme executive agency, the Politburo also took the most important decisions on appointments. The Politburo controlled all key state and ministerial assignments,[56] while promotions to supreme party posts, including those of Central Committee secretary and republican first secretary, all came before the Politburo and were issued as Politburo resolutions.[57]

Normally members of the Politburo had a clear understanding of what fell within the Politburo's jurisdiction.[58] The dividing line between the Council of Ministers and the Poliburo was not, however, always clear-cut. On occasion, the Politburo was moved to reassert its jurisdiction over contested policy areas.[59] More significantly, the rather convoluted route for deciding some issues, especially those voted on by correspondence, allowed decisions to be 'intercepted' by members of the Politburo and taken to other venues for resolution. On 20 August 1947 an item on sending 44 athletes to the students' olympiad in Paris came before the Politburo. The first Politburo member to consider the matter by correspondence was Beria, who requested that the issue be transferred to the Council of Ministers. The Buro of the Council of Ministers then rejected the Politburo draft, resolving instead to send five observers including, on Beria's insistence, 'a comrade from Abakumov'.[60] Thus, as a consequence of the overlapping membership of the Politburo and Sovmin, an item which, strictly speaking, had been within the Politburo's brief was in fact decided by the latter.

Stalin was well aware of the growing systematisation of affairs at the Council of Ministers. In order to keep that body in check he frequently made use of the Politburo's powers of assignment and reorganisation.[61] Another tactic, used prolifically towards the end of Stalin's reign, was to issue scathing resolutions condemning 'departmentalist' practices within the ministries. The Politburo thus served as an important counterweight to an energetic Council of Ministers apparatus. In addition to shaping the decision-making powers of non-party institutions, however, the Politburo exercised numerous leadership functions within the party itself. One of these consisted of dealing with the steady flow of work from the party's own central bureaucracy. Far from atrophying, as some commentators had once believed, the activities of the Central Committee apparatus flourished in the post-war years.

The Politburo and the Central Committee apparatus

In its relations with the party apparatus the Politburo was supreme: as a matter of course, party officials accepted its authority without question. Yet in view of its numerous other commitments—overseeing defence, state security, foreign affairs and administrative reorganisations, as well as keeping the leader company—the Politburo sought to free itself of its more mundane party responsibilities. In the long run the Politburo's attempts to curtail its own party-based duties, for example by strengthening the powers of auxiliary agencies such as the Orgburo, proved to be futile, however. One reason was that the bureaucratic system continued to throw up demands for authoritative guidance that could, in the end, only be satisfied by the ruling cabinet. In such a context, no attempt to delegate authority to subordinate committees could have been entirely successful.

The first major reorganisation of the Central Committee apparatus took place in the wake of the Central Committee meeting of March 1946, which replaced Andreev and the deceased Shcherbakov with A. A. Kuznetsov and G. M. Popov, who now joined Malenkov and Zhdanov as secretaries at the Central Committee. On 13 April the Politburo adopted a resolution on the Orgburo and secretariat which assigned responsibilities among the new secretaries[62] and attempted to define the relative powers of Orgburo and secretariat, something the leadership had never found it easy to do.[63] The spring 1946 reforms consolidated the power of the Orgburo. The April resolution confirmed that while the secretariat would confine itself to cadre issues, the Orgburo, which would now meet weekly, would exercise broader leadership tasks.[64] In order to meet its new workload, membership of the Orgburo was increased from nine members to 15.[65] The sudden expansion of the Orgburo marked both its growing weight within the Central Committee apparatus and a loosening of Malenkov's grip over affairs there.[66] These tendencies were reinforced over the following months when, on 4 May, Malenkov was ejected from the secretariat (to be replaced as Central Committee secretary by Patolichev) and, on 2 August, when Zhdanov took over the chairmanship of the Orgburo from Malenkov. A Politburo resolution on the latter date declared that, henceforth, the Orgburo would be the 'leading agency' (*direktivnym organom*) of party-organisational work and that it would have the right to 'issue leading directives' on party matters.[67]

The new elevated status of the Orgburo heralded a fresh relationship between itself and the Politburo.[68] In assigning new 'leadership' functions to the Orgburo, the Politburo resolution aimed to relieve the Politburo itself of lesser responsibilities. In fact such a rationalisation addressed a genuine concern within the party bureaucracy. Pressure on the party's top committees had been building up since the end of the war. Demobilisation had brought with it an upsurge in the personnel-assignment functions of the Central Committee, while the campaign for ideological discipline, which reached a head in 1946, entailed a revitalisation of the Central Committee's agitprop functions. The rise in workload at the Central Committee generated issues which, in the absence of meetings of the Central Committee, had to be addressed by the party's executive committees. Rather than taking such questions, especially those of an 'organisational' nature, to the Politburo, many were now siphoned off to the new beefed-up Orgburo. Unburdened of a good portion of its everyday party-based tasks, the Politburo could be left to concentrate on 'political' issues and be better able to slot in to Stalin's nighttime routines. The Orgburo, by contrast, would emerge as a surrogate Politburo devoted entirely to the most pressing and important party-organisational matters.

These arrangements did not, however, last long. The balance struck between the Orgburo and secretariat in 1946 was disturbed by the continued growth in cadre work at the Central Committee.[69] Moreover, the pre-eminence of the Orgburo, which had been a Zhdanov stronghold since the summer of 1946, was eroded with the decline in Zhdanov's own fortunes and his eventual death in August 1948. On 1 July 1948 Zhdanov's arch rival, Malenkov, was re-appointed party secretary.[70] Soon the reinstated Malenkov was chairing sessions of both the secretariat and the Orgburo. Under a new schedule, the secretariat met weekly while the Orgburo convened only twice a month.[71] An increasing share of party work was absorbed by the secretariat while the functions of the Orgburo were gradually eclipsed. These tendencies reached their apogee at the XIX Congress, which determined that the role of the secretariat be further increased, as a result of which the number of secretaries was doubled from five to 10. At the same time the Politburo and Orgburo were also reformed. In the previous years the Orgburo had been unable to perform an authoritative party-based role independently of the Politburo. In recognition of this fact the Politburo and Orgburo were now merged into a single institution.[72] With a total membership of 36 (25 members and 11 candidates), the party 'Presidium' was presented as the Soviet Union's new cabinet.

In terms of its internal mode of decision making and actual membership the Politburo in Stalin's latter years was a malleable institution shaped above all by the inclinations and preferences of the leader. To those outside the inner circle, however, the Politburo assumed an image of unimpeachable authority: Politburo members possessed supreme rank and status, Politburo resolutions took precedence over other commands, and the Politburo as an institution enjoyed automatic jurisdiction over the most important policy issues and cadre questions. Yet by the end of Stalin's reign the discrepancy between a Politburo which, in reality, had become jaded and undisciplined, and the considerable leadership functions which this body was expected to exercise, had become accentuated. It may have been for this reason that Stalin decided to modernise the Politburo. Thus at the XIX Congress the name, membership and operations of the Politburo were all fundamentally changed. This reorganisation of the Politburo was more than a simple 'rationalisation', however. The reforms of October 1952 underlined the cabinet's role as an agency of bolshevik leadership. In fact, the creation of the new presidium resonated closely with the calls for 'party democracy' and the demands for increased accountability and collective decision making which were raised in the run-up to the party congress.

Stalin's cabinet and the XIX congress

The XIX congress stimulated efforts to 'democratise' the party at all levels. Steps to promote 'internal democracy' within the party included more frequent meetings of the party rank and file, mandatory reports of the apparatus to full party committees and a host of protest votes against sitting party officials.[73] Such moves to reactivate party 'democracy' were twinned with steps to regularise the party's decision-making processes at all levels.[74] At the very highest tier, the Politburo and Orgburo were merged into the Presidium, with an enlarged full membership of 25 and 11 candidate members.[75] In contrast to its narrowly constituted predecessor, the new larger Presidium appeared to be more representative of the different sectors of the Soviet party-state and thus more open to outside influences. Underlining its claims to inclusiveness, the new Presidium embraced 12 (of the 13) vice-chairmen of the Council of Ministers, all 10 Central Committee secretaries as well as the most important individual ministers, regional representatives and leaders of other key state and party institutions.[76] One commentator has even suggested that the new Presidium represented an extension of the 'job-slot system'—the principle that seats on the Central Committee were *ex officio*—to the Soviet cabinet.[77]

The full Presidium, however, met only once and never came to exercise regular cabinet-type functions. That position was taken by a newly constituted Buro of the Presidium, for which there was no provision in the new party statutes but which was set up at the Central Committee meeting immediately after the XIX Congress. Unlike the full Presidium, which was supposed to meet once a month—but in fact met only once, on 18 October 1952[78]—the Buro, according to a resolution of 10 November, was to meet once a week on Mondays. The composition of this inner group was close to that of the *rukovodyashchaya grupa* which had met in the previous two years, with the exception that two younger leaders, Saburov and, then, in a revised list, Pervukhin, were added.[79] In meeting regularly, the new Buro regained some of the shape and consistency which had eluded the pre-existing, informally convened, ruling circle.[80] With Stalin's health failing, the new Buro even met in his absence.[81] Indeed, a second resolution, also of 10 November, openly made provision for this by indicating that, should Stalin be away, chairmanship of the Buro be rotated between Malenkov, Khrushchev and Bulganin. In fact, in its latter meetings the Presidium Buro may be regarded as a continuation of the third of the politburo variants identified in the first section of this article—namely the politburo without Stalin—and a forerunner of the cabinet that took over when Stalin died.[82] The Presidium Buro also accorded with the prevailing spirit of the Congress period—again anticipating what would follow Stalin's death—by opening its proceedings to the scrutiny of subordinate party officials.[83]

As with the Presidium, the role of the secretariat was clarified in the 1952 party statutes.[84] The reform of the secretariat mirrored changes taking place across the Central Committee. The appointment of Aristov, Mikhailov, Brezhnev and Ignatov as secretaries assured a rejuvenation of the Central Committee apparatus—something Stalin had apparently contemplated for some years.[85] Moreover, with a doubling in the number of secretaries from five to 10, the secretariat began to handle more material, absorbing a considerable amount of workload from the old Orgburo. Notwithstanding a Presidium Buro decision of 17 November, which determined that the secretariat would meet once a week, with Malenkov, Pegov and Suslov chairing it, the vast amount of post-congress activities forced the secretariat to meet more often.[86] With the Orgburo gone and the secretariat now taking over its everyday administrative duties, there was a clear-cut division of labour between a Presidium which addressed issues of 'political leadership' and a secretariat which handled 'administrative' matters.

One of the major innovations of the XIX Congress was the establishment of new cabinet commissions on foreign affairs, defence and ideology. The commissions, which were attached to the party Presidium, reflected a new turn in the organisation of upper party-state structures.[87] Each commission was headed by a senior party figure—Malenkov, Bulganin and Shepilov—and had other important party leaders as members. Significantly, the commissions signalled a loosening of ties between party and state. Whereas previously Politburo work had been regarded as compatible with service within the Council of Ministers—thereby underlining the view that the party and state were 'interlocking directorates'—a separation between the two hierarchies was now effected. A resolution of 10 November released Malenkov from his work as deputy chairman of the Council of Ministers in order to let him focus on the new Presidium commission on foreign affairs, while on the same day Bulganin was released from his position on the Council of Ministers in order to allow him to concentrate on the new defence commission.[88] The severance of their connections to Sovmin meant that these leaders were now tied exclusively to the Presidium and to its commissions. Further, in a symmetrical move which split the leadership in half, a resolution of 10 November 1952 assigned Malenkov, Khrushchev and Bulganin as chairmen of the Presidium Buro (in Stalin's absence), while chairmanship of the Sovmin Buro was allocated to Beria, Pervukhin and Saburov.[89]

The evolution of the cabinet in Stalin's last months reflected broader developments within the Soviet party-state. Prime among these was the holding of the XIX Congress, which had direct consequences for the Politburo. Apart from its new name, the regular sessions of the Presidium Buro accorded with the new post-congress emphasis on 'collective decision making'. Further, and also in line with the new emphasis on party leadership, the establishment of the Presidium commissions and the transfer of senior leaders and of policy-making powers from Sovmin to party agencies signalled both the incipient separation of party and state hierarchies and, albeit more tentatively, the supremacy of the former over the latter. At the same time the oncoming succession also left its mark on the cabinet, which became less dependent on Stalin than it had been in earlier years and which, in line with Stalin's own wishes, accommodated a new generation of younger leaders, many of whom were from the provinces.[90]

Conclusion

For much of the post-war period Politburo meetings assumed the form of small gatherings in Stalin's office or at his dacha from which were excluded not only specialist third parties such as ministers or Central Committee members but even members of the *de jure* Politburo itself. Decisions at these meetings were rarely taken to a vote and, when they were, the preferences of absent members were registered 'by correspondence' after the meeting itself. Both the composition of meetings and the mode of decision making were determined above all by the dynamics of confrontation and exclusion which were Stalin's preferred methods of inter-personal control. The system of rule, however, never descended into a pure dictatorship where Stalin pursued policies in his own name, bypassing the Politburo altogether. In fact, Stalin approached the Politburo with a measure of caution and reserve. This applied not only to the outward mechanisms of Politburo rule (for example the procedures for electing Politburo members or for passing Politburo resolutions), which remained largely unchanged, but to the handling of Politburo members themselves. Despite frequently being excluded and manipulated by the leader, members of the Politburo under Stalin were treated relatively leniently.[91]

The ability of one capricious individual to determine the composition and to set the agenda of Politburo meetings accounts for the internal fluidity of the Politburo in the late Stalin period. Outwardly, however, the Politburo projected an image of solidity and order. One reason for this appearance of stability was that Stalin himself sought continuity in the Politburo's membership.[92] As much as he tested and intimidated his colleagues at close range, they were all known quantities and, collectively, the easier to control and to manage for that. Irrespective of their usefulness to Stalin, some Politburo members were also key figures for the political system as a whole. More so than anyone who perished during the Great Purges, leaders such as Molotov, Mikoyan, Kaganovich and Voroshilov were acknowledged as Stalin's comrades-in-arms and as architects of the stalinist system. No attempt to discredit these leaders, even one instigated by Stalin, could have failed to weaken faith in the Stalinist system. Stalin himself intimated as much when he was forced to temper his attack on Molotov and Mikoyan at the October 1952 plenum of the Central Committee. 'He had to do so', claimed Mikoyan, 'since, to the extent that all members of the Politburo and participants at the plenum knew us well, the plenum was flabbergasted by his attacks on the two of us'.[93] Both Molotov and Mikoyan continued to carry out important functions not only after they had been sacked as ministers in 1949 but even after they had been condemned by Stalin in the autumn of 1952;[94] indeed, the moment Stalin died both were immediately reinstated in the ruling circle. That this should have been the case is hardly surprising given that the personal authority of these hero-founders continued to be immense, and certainly exceeded that of the institutions which they headed.[95]

Yet the Politburo was more than the sum of its individual member-parts. It was also an institution in its own right. It was as an institution, with its own rules and expectations, that the Politburo enabled Stalin to bind his deputies into a system of collective responsibility. Moreover, the stalinist system was sufficiently hierarchic and bureaucratic to require an image of stability and order at its summit. The outward institutional coherence of the Politburo was a source of authority for functionaries further down the hierarchy. In addition to being the leading executive committee of the party-state the Politburo was also, in the absence of meetings of the Central Committee or of party congresses, the ruling committee of the party. Even at its height, Stalinism had never become an unalloyed personal dictatorship, for it always contained a strong trace of Bolshevik ideology. At times, such as the XIX Congress, this ideology became more robust and the practices of internal 'party democracy' were revived. This had direct consequences for the organisation of the party and its ruling committees. It was because of its claim to be more 'democratic' than any other institution that, at the time of the XIX Congress, party committees were elevated over institutions of the state. This, however, came at a price: the rise of party institutions was conditional on the resuscitation of 'collective decision making' within the party, a commitment that reached to the nerve-centre of the party's power. To the extent that three politburos had co-existed under Stalin—the expanded sessions of the *de jure* Politburo, the closed meetings of the inner circle, and the Politburo without Stalin—it was to be a combination of this drive for collective decision making and the fact of Stalin's death itself that would allow the last of these politburos—the Politburo without Stalin—finally to come into its own.

University of Manchester

[1] Research for this article was generously supported by grant no. 00222676 from the United Kingdom Economic and Social Research Council. I am very grateful to my collaborator on the project, Oleg Khlevnyuk, for sharing his ideas on this topic and for collecting the archival materials. An earlier version of the article was presented at a conference on 'Stalin's Politburo, 1929–1953' at the European University Institute, Florence, March 2000, organised by Arfon Rees. I would like to thank the participants at the conference and Vera Tolz for their comments and suggestions.
[2] In order to blunt the original charge that the creation of the Politburo might demote the rest of the Central Committee to a lower status, the VIII Congress of 1919 required that members of the Central Committee who were not Politburo members be given the right to attend and to participate in Politburo sessions, albeit without full voting rights. This set the precedent for the enlarged Politburo sessions of the 1920s and early 1930s. See Merle Fainsod, *How Russia is Ruled* (Cambridge, MA, Harvard University Press, 1963), p. 178.
[3] It is worth bearing in mind that immediately prior to its effective dissolution during the war and its replacement by GKO the Politburo had met in full session only rarely. Thus, for example, it had met only twice in each of the two years preceding the outbreak of war. See *Sbornik politbyuro v 30-e gody: sbornik dokumentov*, compilers O. V. Khlevnyuk *et al.* (Moscow, AIRO, 1995), pp. 251–255.
[4] Other participants at this session were the members of the Central Committee Bulganin, Kosygin and Shkiryatov, the candidate member of the central committee A. F. Gorkin, a member of the central auditing commission, Shatalin, and the head of the trade union organisation, V. V. Kuznetsov. RGASPI, f. 17, op. 163, d. 1471, ll. 2, 7.
[5] See A. A. Danilov, 'Stalinskoe politbyuro v poslevoennye gody', in *Politicheskie partii Rossii: Stranitsy istorii* (Moscow, Izdatel'stvo Moskovskogo universiteta, 2000), pp. 205, 207, 209.
[6] In addition, there were two further meetings after the summer vacation, on 2 and 6 September 1946. With none of these 1946 meetings attended by fewer than 14 people, each may be regarded as full expanded sessions of the *de jure* Politburo. Following the Politburo meeting of 29 December, attended by eight Politburo members, four candidates and six others (see n. 4), the session of 19 January was attended by five full members (Zhdanov, Kaganovich, Kalinin, Mikoyan and Stalin), four candidates (Beria, Voznesensky, Malenkov and Shvernik) and five Central Committee members (Bulganin,

STALIN'S CABINET 305

Kosygin, Popov, Poskrebyshev and Shkiryatov). Save for Kalinin, who died on 3 June 1946, all the subsequent expanded sessions of 1946 were attended by the same 14 people who were present at the meeting of 19 January. They were joined by, among others, Andreev (who attended all meetings from 4 March onwards), A. A. Kuznetsov (who attended all sessions from 13 April), Molotov (who was present at the meetings of 4 March, 13 April and 2 September), Mekhlis (present at the meetings of 4 May, 2 and 6 September), Khrushchev (there at the 6 September meeting) and Voroshilov, Patolichev and Zverev (each of whom attended the meetings of 2 and 6 September). The largest Politburo meeting in 1946 by some margin was that of 6 September, which was attended by 33 people including nine officials who were not full members of the Central Committee. RGASPI, f. 17, op. 163, d. 1471, ll. 2, 7; f. 17, op. 3, d. 1055, l. 1; f. 17, op. 3, d. 1056, l. 1; f. 17, op. 3, d. 1058, l. 1; and f. 17, op. 163, d. 1489, ll.1–2. Also see Yurii Zhukov, 'Bor'ba za vlast'' v rukovodstve SSSR v 1945–1952 godakh', *Voprosy istorii*, 1995, 1, pp. 24, 26.

[7] In addition to Politburo members and candidates, the Central Committee members Zverev, A. A. Kuznetsov, Mekhlis, Popov, Poskrebyshev and Shkiryatov were invited to the Politburo session of 13 December 1947, as were the candidates Lyubimov and Petrov. RGASPI, f. 17, op. 163, d. 1506, ll. 1–3. The session of 17 June 1949 was attended by the Central Committee members Efremov, Malyshev, Mekhlis, Ponomarenko, Popov, Poskrebyshev, Suslov, Tevosyan and Shkiryatov and by the candidates Zotov, Kruglov and Chernousov. In addition, a further 19 officials were invited to this meeting. See RGASPI, f. 17, op. 163, d. 1525, ll. 1–6. Also see Zhukov, 'Bor'ba za vlast'', pp. 28–29. For a list of expanded 'special' politburo sessions, for example the Stalin prizes, see RGASPI, f. 558, op. 11, d. 418, ll. 1–9.

[8] Reference to the *uzkii sostav* may be found in Anastas Mikoyan, *Tak bylo: razmyshleniya o minuvshem* (Moscow, Bagirus, 1999), pp. 500, 564; the *blizhnii krug* is referred to in Danilov, 'Stalinskoe politbyuro', p. 193.

[9] All three appear to have lost Stalin's trust in the years since the XVIII Congress. Andreev's visits to Stalin's office had fallen off in 1940, Kaganovich's in 1942 and Voroshilov's in 1944. See sheet 2 of S. G. Wheatcroft, 'Stalin and the Soviet Political Elite: The Private Meetings in Stalin's Kremlin Office, 1930–1953', paper presented at conference on 'Stalin's Politburo, 1929–1953', Florence, March 2000, cited by permission. Stalin's exclusion of Voroshilov and Andreev was commented on in the Secret Speech (for the English version, see *The Anti-Stalin Campaign and International Communism* (New York, Columbia University Press, 1956), p. 84). The wartime marginalisation of Kaganovich is more of a mystery but may have been connected to the arrest and suicide of his brother, Mikhail, in July 1941.

[10] For a brief portrait of a senile and near-blind 'Old Uncle Kalinin' being chided and made fun of by Stalin in 1945 see Milovan Djilas, *Conversations with Stalin* (London, Hart-Davis, 1962), p. 97. Zhdanov spent much of the war in Leningrad, while Khrushchev was based in Ukraine.

[11] For reference to this group as the '*pyaterka*' see Danilov, 'Stalinskoe politbyuro', p. 193. Three members of the State Defence Committee, Voznesensky, Kaganovich and Voroshilov (who was replaced by Bulganin in 1944), did not make it on to the ruling group. Danilov writes that 'attempts to expand the membership of the latter by including on it Voznesensky and other members of the leadership were decisively rebuffed (above all by Beria and Malenkov)' (p. 193).

[12] There is a gap in Stalin's Kremlin visitors' book from 8 October to 17 December 1945 (see *Istoricheskii arkhiv*, 1996, 4, p. 113). For references to the remaining leaders in Moscow as the 'chetverka' see Vladimir Pechatnov, 'Soyuzniki nazhimayut na tebya dlya togo, chtoby slomit' u tebya volyu ...', *Istochnik*, 1999, 2 (38), pp. 80, 82, 83; and Danilov, 'Stalinskoe politbyuro', p. 194.

[13] See the Politburo resolution of 29 December 1945 'On preparing functionaries for foreign policy work and on the organisation of the department of foreign policy at the Central Committee and the Commission of External Affairs at the Politburo'. The resolution confirmed that the commission was to consist of Stalin, Molotov, Beria, Mikoyan, Malenkov and Zhdanov. RGASPI, f. 17, op. 163, d. 1471, ll. 2, 6.

[14] One issue of tangential relevance to foreign affairs which was to occupy the Commission in its early months was the so-called 'aviators' affair' in which two air force marshals, Novikov and Khudyakov, were arrested for knowingly accepting faulty planes and defective parts from the aviation industry, thereby endangering the lives of Soviet air pilots. Thus, for example, at the beginning of April 1946 Stalin deemed it appropriate to acquaint the sextet, together with Bulganin, who was closely involved in 'exposing' the affair, with Khudyakov's testimony which had implicated some of the most eminent aircraft designers in the country, such as A. S. Yakovlev, A. N. Tupolev and S. V. Ilyushin, as well as several directors of aircraft factories. See R. G. Pikhoya, *Sovetskii soyuz: Istoriya vlasti, 1945–1991* (Moscow, RAGS, 1998), p. 46.

[15] There is a reference to this resolution in Khrushchev's secret speech. For the English version see *The Anti-Stalin Campaign and International Communism* (New York, Columbia University Press, 1956), p. 83; for the Russian version, see *Reabilitatsiya. Politicheskie protsessy 30–50kh godov* (Moscow, Politizdat, 1991), p. 64.

[16] This at least is Zhukov's reading ('Bor'ba za vlast',' pp. 29–30). A closer examination of the archives however reveals that the Politburo resolution of 17 September 1947 investing Kuznetsov with the right to supervise the work of the security agencies makes no mention of promotion to the '*devyatka*' (RGASPI, f. 17, op. 163, d. 1504, 1. 66). Equally, the Politburo resolution of 5 March 1947 promoting Bulganin as minister of armed forces and deputy head of Sovmin makes no mention of him joining the '*vosmerka*' (RGASPI, f. 17, op. 163, d. 1497, 1. 25). Suspicions on this score are heightened by the fact that a succession of Politburo resolutions to the end of 1947 continue to refer to a 'septet' ('*semerka*') without either Bulganin or Kuznetsov (see the resolutions of 22 May (f. 17, op. 163, d. 1499, 1. 51), 23 August (f. 17, op. 163, d. 1503, 1. 61) and 15 December (f. 17, op. 163, d. 1507, 1. 13)). Although there clearly was a 'novenary' it may be that Bulganin only joined it when he was formally elected to the Politburo on 18 February 1948 and that Kuznetsov never joined it, the ninth member being Kaganovich, who returned to Moscow from Ukraine in December 1947.

[17] Danilov, 'Stalinskoe politbyuro,' p. 209.

[18] We are not yet in a position to compare all Politburo resolutions for this. Nevertheless, a sample of important Politburo resolutions all appear to have been made by the 'Commission'. The decision to abolish the State Defence Committee, for example, was made by the 'quintet' of Stalin, Molotov, Mikoyan, Beria and Malenkov, who met in Stalin's office from 11 to 12 on the night of 4 September 1945. Shvernik, Kalinin, Andreev, Voznesensky and Kaganovich later voted for the motion by correspondence (RGASPI, f. 17, op. 163, d. 1463, 1. 76; *Istoricheskii arkhiv*, 1996, 4, pp. 110–111). The decision on 2 August to rehabilitate Malenkov by appointing him deputy chairman of the Council of Ministers was made by the 'sextet'. The decision was voted on by Stalin, Beria, Mikoyan, Zhdanov and Malenkov himself. Molotov was away from Moscow at the time. Voroshilov, Shvernik, Bulganin, Kosygin, Voznesensky and Andreev later voted on this issue by correspondence. Numerous other high profile cadre decisions were also made by the 'Commission'. Thus, for example, the decision of 15 December 1947 (i.e. two days after the expanded session of 13 December) to appoint Kaganovich as head of Gosplan and 'to recommend' that Khrushchev return to his former post as first secretary of the Ukrainian communist party was made by the 'septet' of Stalin, Beria, Malenkov, Mikoyan, Zhdanov and Voznesensky (Molotov was again out of Moscow) (RGASPI, f. 17, op. 163, d. 1507, 1. 13, cf. *Istoricheskii arkhiv*, 1996, 5–6, p. 23).

[19] See N.S. Khrushchev *Khrushchev Remembers* (London, Andre Deutsch, 1971), p. 299.

[20] 'Proekt postanovleniya Politbyuro o grafike zasedanii rukovodyashchikh partiinykh i pravitel'stvennykh organov', 11 December 1948, RGASPI, f. 82, op. 2, d. 296, 1. 138.

[21] Malenkov and Beria were fully paid up members of the ruling 'quintet' in mid-1945, many months before their formal election as full members of the Politburo on 18 March 1946. Similarly Voznesensky was admitted to the 'septet' on 3 October 1946, almost half a year before his election as a Politburo member on 26 February 1947. If Zhukov is right, it was almost a year after Bulganin's elevation to the 'octet' on 5 March 1947 before he was elected to the full Politburo on 18 February 1948 (RGASPI, f. 17, op. 163, d. 1509, 1. 116; cf Zhukov, 'Bor'ba za vlast'', pp. 29–30 and fn. 16).

[22] On 16 April 1949, before the removal of Kosygin, an exchange between Molotov and Stalin on a draft Central Committee resolution was circulated to Beria, Malenkov, Mikoyan, Kaganovich, Bulganin and Kosygin (RGASPI, f. 17, op. 163, d. 1523, 1. 170). Kaganovich had returned to Moscow from Ukraine at the end of 1947, at which point his visits to Stalin's office picked up. See sheet 2 of Wheatcroft, 'Stalin and the Soviet Political Elite'. For a reference to the 'septet' of 7 April 1950 (i.e. without Kosygin) see Zhukov, 'Bor'ba za vlast'', p. 35.

[23] For a description of how, much to Stalin's disgust, Mikoyan and Molotov turned up uninvited to meetings they had been told about by other members of the inner circle, see for example Mikoyan, *Tak bylo*, pp. 579–580; and Khrushchev, *Khrushchev Remembers*, pp. 280–281.

[24] For references to the 'usual five' see Khrushchev, *Khrushchev Remembers*, pp. 281, 307. Khrushchev appears to have taken Kaganovich's place in the inner circle later in 1950.

[25] The decision was only later confirmed 'by correspondence' by Mikoyan and Molotov themselves as well as by Voznesensky, Kosygin, Shvernik, Voroshilov and Kaganovich (RGASPI, f. 17, op. 163, d. 1521, 1. 78). Stalin's practice of convening at his office select ad hoc meetings of like-minded Politburo members went back to the late 1920s. Oleg Klevnyuk, *Politbyuro*, pp. 45, 46, 48.

[26] The move to de-couple Mikoyan and Molotov from their traditional ministerial responsibilities was reinforced by a Politburo resolution of 9 April 1949, signed only by Stalin, that questions relating to foreign trade and foreign affairs be presented directly to the Politburo, not by Mikoyan and Molotov but by their successors as ministers, Menshikov and Vyshinsky (RGASPI, f. 17, op. 163, d. 1523, 1. 67).

[27] See Pechatnov, 'Soyuzniki nazhimayut', pp. 80–85; and the excellent paper by Oleg Khlevnyuk, 'Zadavlennye oligarkhi: Stalin i ego okruzhenie v poslevoennye gody', presented at the 31st AAASS convention at St Louis, November 1999, cited with permission, pp. 6–9.

[28] Khlevnyuk, 'Zadavlennye oligarkhi', pp. 11–12.

[29] From the collections of long-distance correspondence in the Stalin *fond* at RGASPI it is apparent

that Stalin was out of Moscow at least from 8 September to 20 December 1946, 17 August to 16 November 1947, 8 September to 11 December 1948, 5 September to 7 December 1949, 6 August to 21 December 1950 and 11 August to 21 December 1951. See the Stalin *fond*, dd. 105, 108, 112, 115, 116, 117. Towards the end Stalin also saw fewer visitors in Moscow. In 1950 Stalin did not receive visitors in his Kremlin office for a five-month stretch, from the beginning of August to the end of December; the same was true of a seven-month period from August 1951 to February 1952 (Pikhoya, *Sovetskii soyuz*, p. 56). The meetings in Stalin's office also fall from 227 hours in 1949 to 120 in 1950, 94 in 1951 and 72 in 1952. See Wheatcroft, 'Stalin and the Soviet Political Elite', sheet 2.

[30] RGASPI, f. 17, op. 163, d. 1583, ll. 263–265. The reference to this group as a 'quintet' comes in a telegram from Poskrebyshev in RGASPI, f. 17, op. 163, d. 1523, l. 74.

[31] For reference to this group as a 'sextet' see RGASPI, f. 17, op. 163, d. 1537, l. 100.

[32] RGASPI, f. 17, op. 163, d. 1583, ll. 263–265.

[33] These were Beria, Bulganin, Kaganovich, Malenkov, Mikoyan and Khrushchev (RGASPI, f. 17, op. 163, d. 1607, l. 133).

[34] Mikoyan, *Tak bylo*, pp. 530–531.

[35] Having first voted against, the cabinet of Malenkov, Beria, Mikoyan, Bulganin and Khrushchev complied with Stalin's instruction by issuing a new resolution within two days (RGASPI, f. 17, op. 163, d. 1558, l. 132). On another occasion, a draft resolution by the 'small Politburo' on 6 November 1951 in protest at the violation of Soviet air-space by an American plane was amended by Stalin within a day (RGASPI, f. 17, op. 163, d. 1604, ll. 28–29).

[36] Cf. Zhukov, 'Bor'ba za vlast'', pp. 38–39.

[37] 'Poslednyaya 'Otstavka' Stalina', *Istochnik*, 1994, 1, pp. 106–111. By contrast one should note that Molotov at the January 1955 Central Committee plenum suggested that the resolutions on the partition of power issued while Stalin was still alive were drafted by Malenkov and Beria, not by the ruling collective. See reference in Danilov, 'Stalinskoe politbyuro,' p. 219.

[38] The first post-Stalin presidium announced on 7 March 1953 restored some figures, such as Molotov, Mikoyan and Kaganovich, who had been attacked (Kaganovich to a lesser extent) by Stalin in previous months. The full line up was Malenkov, Beria, Molotov, Voroshilov, Khrushchev, Bulganin, Kaganovich, Mikoyan, Saburov and Pervukhin. Zhukov, 'Bor'ba za vlast,' p. 38, suggests that the last ruling circle under Stalin consisted of Beria, Bulganin, Malenkov, Khrushchev, Saburov and Pervukhin; Khrushchev suggests that the ruling circle consisted of Stalin, Beria, Malenkov, Bulganin and Khrushchev (*Khrushchev Remembers*, pp. 281, 307).

[39] Between 1950 and 1952 there was considerable overlap between the 'Politburo without Stalin' and the Buro of the Presidium of the Council of Ministers. The latter, which always met *without* Stalin, was set up on 7 April 1950 and consisted of seven members (Bulganin, Beria, Kaganovich, Mikoyan, Molotov, Malenkov (from 15 April 1950) and Khrushchev (from 2 September 1950)). The Buro of the Presidium met frequently, convening 39 times in 1950, 38 times in 1951 and 43 times in 1952. For more, see Yoram Gorlizki, 'Ordinary Stalinism: The Council of Ministers and the Soviet Neopatrimonial State, 1945–1953', ms., University of Manchester, 2000, p. 21.

[40] This was especially true of Beria and Malenkov who, as a rule, never opposed Stalin and always tried to prevail on other members of the inner circle not to do anything which might infuriate the leader. See, for example, Mikoyan, *Tak bylo*, p. 522.

[41] Djilas, *Conversations with Stalin*, p. 73, wrote: 'Unofficially and in actual fact a significant part of Soviet policy was shaped at these dinners' (also see p. 144). By contrast, Khrushchev does not overstate the significance of these meetings for policy making. 'It's true', he averred, 'that sometimes state and party questions were decided, but we spent only a fraction of our time on those. The main thing was to occupy Stalin's time so he wouldn't suffer from loneliness' (Khrushchev, *Khrushchev Remembers*, pp. 298–301, at p. 299). It should be noted, however, that Khrushchev is one leader who tends to play up the level of 'disorder' at the Politburo, possibly in order to absolve himself of responsibility for its more reprehensible actions. This tactic was especially significant at the height of de-Stalinisation. Consider the following passages from Khrushchev's secret speech: 'Comrades may ask us: Where were the members of the Political Buro of the Central Committee? Why did they not assert themselves against the cult of the individual in time?' ... Many decisions were taken either by one person or in a roundabout way, without collective discussions. The sad fate of Politburo member, comrade Voznesensky, who fell victim to Stalin's repressions, is known to all. It is a characteristic thing that the decision to remove him from the Politburo was never discussed but was reached in a devious fashion ... The importance of the Central Committee's Politburo was reduced and its work was disorganised by the creation within the Politburo of various commissions—the so-called 'quintets', 'sextets', 'septets' and 'novenaries'. Khrushchev, 'Secret Speech', pp. 81, 83.

[42] RGASPI, f. 17, op. 163, d. 1520, l. 125; d. 1521, l. 78; and d. 1546, l. 106. Similarly, the decision of 21 April 1947 to relieve Voroshilov of supervision over the ministry of health and to hand over this

308   YORAM GORLIZKI

function to Zhdanov was jotted down by Malenkov before being signed by Stalin (RGASPI, f. 17, op. 163, d. 1497, l. 223). Also in Malenkov's hand was the Politburo decision of 26 March 1949 to give Bulganin the right to supervise the ministry of aviation industry and the ministry of armaments (RGASPI, f. 17, op. 163, d. 1522, l. 90).

[43] RGASPI, f. 17, op. 163, d. 1526, l. 166. The decision appears to have been taken the previous night. See *Istoricheskii arkhiv*, 1996, 5–6, p. 55.

[44] E.g. GARF, f. 17, op. 163, d. 1540, l. 187; RGASPI, f. 17, op. 163, d. 1541, l. 7.

[45] Vasilevsky's list also included three Council of Ministers resolutions (GARF, f. 17, op. 163, d. 1540, l. 187; and see *Istoricheskii arkhiv*, 1997, 1, p. 7.

[46] RGASPI, f. 17, op. 163, d. 1622, ll. 43–44.

[47] These decisions, which included an invitation to six Bulgarian writers to visit the USSR for three weeks and the 'arrangement of jobs for three Iranian political immigrants', were confirmed by Stalin and immediately drawn up as Politburo resolutions (RGASPI, f. 17, op. 163, d. 1541, l. 7).

[48] RGASPI, f. 17, op. 163, d. 1576, l. 58.

[49] Correspondence votes applied to high profile cadre decisions, such as the move to elevate Malenkov in August 1946 and to downgrade Molotov and Mikoyan in March 1949. The appointment of Malenkov as deputy chairman of Sovmin on 2 August 1946, first agreed by Stalin with Beria, Malenkov, Mikoyan and Zhdanov, was then sent out to Voroshilov, Shvernik, Bulganin, Kosygin, Voznesensky and Andreev for confirmation. Similarly the decision to sack Molotov and Mikoyan from their ministries on 4 March 1949, though it was first agreed by a small group of Stalin, Malenkov, Beria and Bulganin, was only subsequently confirmed by Mikoyan, Molotov, Voznesensky, Kosygin, Shvernik, Voroshilov and Kaganovich (RGASPI, f. 17, op. 163, d. 1521, l. 78). The post hoc correspondence vote was also used to confirm decisions drafted by sub-groups with specialised expertise where the matter required urgent action. This was true of foreign policy matters, which were normally agreed jointly by Vyshinsky and Molotov and then sent to Stalin in the first instance before being forwarded to other members of the Politburo for ratification. Such was the procedure for validating the response of the head of state, Shvernik, to Truman's address of 7 July 1951. After being agreed by Vyshinsky and Molotov and then sent on to Stalin it was forwarded to other members of the Politburo for approval (RGASPI, f. 17, op. 163, d. 1593, l. 91; also see RGASPI, f. 17, op. 163, d. 1616, l. 131). Similarly, in two notes of 24 and 31 July 1952 Vyshinsky forwarded to Molotov a list of 14 questions relating to the ministry of foreign affairs which, Vyshinsky assured Molotov, Stalin had decided could be voted on by correspondence (RGASPI, f. 17, op. 163, d. 1626, 1.100; and f. 17, op. 163, d. 1627, l. 19).

[50] Both in his secret speech and in his memoirs Khrushchev recalled: 'Sometimes he would glare at you and say, "Why don't you look me in the eye today? Why are you averting your eyes from mine?" or some such stupidity. Without warning he would turn on you with real viciousness'. See Khrushchev, *Khrushchev Remembers*, p. 258; also see Khrushchev, *Secret Speech*, p. 40. On another occasion, recounted by Mikoyan, Stalin reportedly ordered Poskrebyshev to accuse Molotov and Mikoyan of conspiring against the leader, so that Stalin might test their reactions. Mikoyan, *Tak Bylo*, p. 535.

[51] 'The main thing [at those dinners]', Khrushchev recalled, 'was to occupy Stalin's time so that he wouldn't suffer from loneliness. He was depressed by loneliness and he feared it' (Khrushchev, *Khrushchev Remembers*, p. 299).

[52] Examples may be found in Troyanovsky, *Cherez gody*, p. 159; and Khrushchev, *Khrushchev Remembers*, pp. 274–275.

[53] For more on this, see Gorlizki, 'Ordinary Stalinism', pp. 4–11.

[54] By the 'Politburo' the resolution was in fact referring to the Politburo 'Commission' or 'leading group' which, at this stage, consisted of seven leaders. Thus a draft of the resolution referred to 'concentrating these issues in the hands of the septet' (*sosredotochit' v semerke*) (RGASPI, f. 17, op. 163, d. 1495, ll. 129–130).

[55] The Politburo, for example, set up and divided sectoral buros of the Council of Ministers. See its resolution of 6 April 1949 'On the formation of the buro for metallurgy and geology' (RGASPI, f. 17, op. 163, d. 1523, l. 1); Politburo resolutions also formed the buro of chemicals and electric power stations of the Council of Ministers of 26 January 1950 (RGASPI, f. 17, op. 163, d. 1541, l. 70); and, on the same day, united the buros of food industry and trade (l. 141). It was the Politburo, too, which dissolved five of the sectoral buros of the Council of Ministers on 15 March 1951 (RGASPI, f. 17, op. 163, d. 1580, l. 1).

[56] Thus, for example, the sackings of Mikoyan and Molotov as ministers of external trade and foreign affairs were passed as Politburo resolutions. For Mikoyan, see RGASPI, f. 17, op. 163, d. 1521, l. 78. It was also by a Politburo resolution of 8 February 1947 that Saburov was appointed deputy chairman of the Council of Ministers (RGASPI, f. 17, op. 163, d. 1495, l. 119). Similarly, on 17 January 1950 the Politburo appointed Pervukhin and Tikhomirov deputy chairman of the Council of Ministers and minister of chemical industry respectively (RGASPI, f. 17, op. 163, d. 1540, l. 151). The following

STALIN'S CABINET 309

month, on 9 March, it was a Politburo resolution which determined that at the Council of Ministers Beria should oversee the work of the ministry of timber industry (RGASPI, f. 17, op. 163, d. 1497, l. 40). Stalin's right to oversee the ministry of armed forces was also presented as a Politburo resolution; see the Politburo resolution of 26 March 1949 (RGASPI, f. 17, op. 163, d. 1522, l. 91). The Politburo even delved into matters such as the composition of sectoral buros at Sovmin and who should preside over sessions of the Sovmin Presidium. See for example the resolution of 6 April 1949 on the Buro of metallurgy and geology which names the chairman, deputy chairman and four members of the Buro (RGASPI, f. 17, op. 163, d. 1523, l. 3). On 1 September 1949 a Politburo resolution determined that sessions of the Sovmin Presidium would be chaired in turn by Beria, Bulganin, Malenkov, Kaganovich and Saburov (RGASPI, f. 17, op. 163, d. 1530, l. 61).

[57] Strictly speaking, Central Committee secretaries were supposed to have been elected by the Central Committee. This was the case with the election of Kuznetsov and Popov on 18 March 1946. Nevertheless, in the absence of Central Committee meetings, secretaries were appointed directly by the Politburo. Thus, for example, it was by a Politburo resolution that Mikhail Suslov was appointed Central Committee secretary on 22 May 1947. Although the decision was initially taken by the 'septet', it was subsequently voted on by Bulganin, Kosygin and Shvernik ('Postanovlenie Politburo o M.A. Suslove', RGASPI, f. 17, op. 163, d. 1499, ll. 51). Similarly, it was by a Politburo resolution, approved by the 'octet', that Malenkov and Ponomarenko were appointed secretaries on 1 July 1948 (RGASPI, f. 17, op. 163, d. 1513, l. 37). Although issued as Central Committee or Politburo resolutions, some decisions may possibly have been taken by Stalin alone. Of his own appointment as Central Committee secretary Khrushchev later recounted: 'Stalin simply appointed, but as for a vote of the Central Committee, well I don't know. By the way, where could they have voted, since there had long not been either party congress or a meeting of the Central Committee?' (see Russian edition, *Voprosy istorii*, 1994, 11, p. 73). Republican secretaries in Ukraine and Belorussia were approved by the Politburo on 27 February 1947 (RGASPI, f. 17, op. 163, d. 1496, ll. 195, 198). Heads of Central Committee departments were approved in Politburo resolutions of 10 July 1948, 20 July 1949, 30 December 1950 and 3 July 1952 (RGASPI, f. 17, op. 163, d. 1513, ll. 79–80; d. 1528, l. 90; d. 1545, l. 164; d. 1624, l. 152).

[58] See for example the exchange between Stalin and Mikoyan in 1946 on foreign policy where the former is reported to have asked: 'Since when have you started taking decisions in the name of the Politburo on questions of foreign policy?', to which Mikoyan began his reply: 'It is well known that this comes within the competence of the Politburo ...' (Mikoyan, *Tak bylo*, p. 497).

[59] For example, on 25 May 1948 the Politburo ruled that any 'de-reserving' of ferrous and rare metals and strategic raw materials (such as rubber, wool and so on) from the state material reserves could only be effected after a special discussion at the Politburo. This confirmed a procedure which had existed in the 1930s (RGASPI, f. 17, op. 3, d. 1070, 1.43).

[60] Following this intervention a new version, this time drafted at the Council of Ministers, was approved by the 'septet' and issued, finally, as a Politburo resolution (RGASPI, f. 17, op. 163, d. 1503, ll. 61–64).

[61] Thus, for example, Stalin plucked leading figures out of Sovmin and subdivided and liquidated the latter's powerful sectoral buros. For more, see Gorlizki, 'Ordinary Stalinism', p. 23.

[62] According to the 13 April resolution Malenkov would still be in charge of sessions of the Orgburo, while Kuznetsov was to head the cadres administration and to chair sessions of the secretariat (RGASPI, f. 17, op. 163, d. 1480, ll. 4–6).

[63] Under the 1939 party statutes the Orgburo had been supposed to exercise 'general leadership of organisational work' while the secretariat was expected to carry out 'current work of an organisational-executive character' (Art. 34, in Graeme Gill, *The Rules of the Communist Party of the Soviet Union* (Basingstoke, Macmillan, 1988), pp. 172–173). Earlier statutes had not been any clearer. The party statutes of 1922 had stated simply that the Orgburo carried out 'general leadership of organisational work' and the secretariat 'current work of an organisational and executive character'. A Central Committee report of 1923 stated that appointments to the highest party positions came under the jurisdiction of the Orgburo whereas lower-level appointments came before the secretariat. See Gill, p. 120 (art. 25); and Fainsod, *How Russia is Ruled*, p. 182.

[64] These included checking the work of regional and republican party committees and hearing their reports, taking appropriate measures where necessary. See points 2, 3 and 5 of the resolution. An earlier draft, which had proved unacceptable to Stalin, envisaged that Malenkov would preside over both the Orgburo and the secretariat and that Kuznetsov would 'watch over' rather than 'lead' the cadres administration. Compare RGASPI, f. 17, op. 163, d. 1480, ll. 4–6 and APRF, f. 3, op. 22, d. 14, l. 158. Whereas the new draft stipulated that the Orgburo would meet at eight on Wednesdays, the first draft, of 21 March, had stated that the meetings should take place at 2 pm (Danilov, 'Stalinskoe politbyuro', p. 200).

[65] The growth in membership had been decided at the Central Committee meeting of 18 March

310   YORAM GORLIZKI

(Pikhoya, *Sovetskii soyuz*, p. 57). The 15, who included 10 new faces, were Aleksandrov, Andryanov, Bulganin, A. A. Kuznetsov, V. V. Kuznetsov, Malenkov, Mekhlis, Mikhailov, Patolichev, G. M. Popov, Rodionov, Shatalin, Stalin, Suslov and Zhdanov. The nine members of the Orgburo appointed at the XVIII Congress in 1939 were Andreev, Kaganovich, Malenkov, Mekhlis, Mikhailov, Scherbakov, Shvernik, Stalin and Zhdanov. See *Politbyuro, Orgbyuro, Sekretariat TsK RKP (b)—VKP (b)–KPSS* (Moscow, Politizdat, 1990), pp. 32–34; and Danilov, 'Stalinskoe politbyuro', p. 201.

[66] See Danilov, 'Stalinskoe politbyuro', p. 201.

[67] By contrast, in a move which placed it in a directly subordinate position, the secretariat was entrusted with 'preparing questions for consideration by the Orgburo and checking implementation of decisions of the Politburo and the Orgburo'. The resolution also stated that the secretariat, in not having its own plan of work, would 'follow the workplans of the Orgburo and of the Politburo'. Whereas the Orgburo was to meet no less than once a week, the secretariat would 'convene as deemed necessary' (*po mere neobkhodimosti*). See points 1 and 2 of the resolution, RGASPI, f. 17, op. 163, d. 1487, ll. 131–134.

[68] As with the relationship between the Orgburo and the secretariat, the dividing line between the Orgburo and the Politburo had never been clear-cut. Reviewing the relationship between the Orgburo and the Politburo on 29 March 1920, Lenin remarked: 'The practice arrived at was that it became the main and proper function of the Orgburo to distribute the forces of the party, while the function of the Political Buro was to deal with political questions. It goes without saying that this distinction is to a certain extent artificial; it is obvious that no policy can be carried out in practice without finding expression in appointments and transfers. Consequently, every organisational question assumes a political significance; and the practice was established that a request of a single member of the Central Committee was sufficient to have any question for any reason whatsoever examined as a political question'. Cited in Fainsod, *How Russia is Ruled*, p. 179.

[69] The expansion of cadre work at the Central Committee was such that in a draft on the reorganisation of the apparatus even Zhdanov recognised that 'concentrating the distribution of cadres under the leadership of one secretary' was not enough, and recommended as an alternative that 12 new cadres secretaries be appointed (RGASPI, f. 77, op. 3, d. 4, ll. 41–43).

[70] Malenkov's ally, Panteleimon Ponomarenko, was also appointed Central Committee secretary on 1 July (RGASPI, f. 17, op. 163, d. 1513, l. 37). Malenkov also took control of the key department of party, trade union and Komsomol agencies. See Danilov, 'Stalinskoe politbyuro', p. 209.

[71] See especially points 1 and 4, RGASPI, f. 17, op. 163, d. 1513, ll. 79–80.

[72] Although the Presidium is sometimes seen as a straight substitute for the Politburo, it was in fact successor to both the Politburo and the Orgburo. See Fainsod, *How Russia is Ruled*, pp. 216, 323.

[73] See Yoram Gorlizki, 'Party Revivalism and the Death of Stalin', *Slavic Review*, 54, 1, 1995 pp. 5–9.

[74] Thus, for example, plenums of republican and regional party committees were to meet once every two months, as opposed to every three months, and the plenums of district committees were to meet once every month instead of once every month and a half. Gorlizki, 'Party Revivalism', p. 7.

[75] More explicitly than before, the new party statutes of 1952 made plain the leadership function of the Presidium over the Central Committee between Central Committee plenums. Article 34 of the 1952 statutes stated tersely that the Central Committee 'organises a Presidium for leadership of the work of the Central Committee between plenums'. By contrast, the 1939 and earlier statutes had stated only that the Central Committee 'organises a Politburo for political work [and] an Organisational Buro for the general leadership of organisational work'. See Gill, *The Rules of the Communist Party*, pp. 47, 172, 193.

[76] The 12 vice-chairmen of Sovmin included 10 full members of the Presidium (Beria, Bulganin, Voroshilov, Kaganovich, Malenkov, Malyshev, Mikoyan, Molotov, Pervukhin and Saburov) and two candidates (Kosygin and Tevosyan). The only vice-chairman excluded from the presidium was Andreev. The 10 party secretaries included seven full members (Stalin, Aristov, Malenkov, Mikhailov, Ponomarenko, Suslov and Khrushchev) and three candidates (Brezhnev, Ignatov and Pegov). In addition, the Presidium included four of the most important individual ministers (Ignat'ev (state security), Vyshinsky (foreign affairs), Zverev (finance) and Kabanov (Gosplan)); five representatives from the regions (Andryanov (Leningrad), Korotchenko and Mel'nikov (Ukraine), Puzanov (RSFSR) and Patolichev (Belorussia)); and holders of three other top state and party positions (Shvernik (head of state), V. V. Kuznetsov (head of the trade union organisation) and Shkiryatov (head of committee of party control)). An old, though reliable, list may be found in Fainsod, *How Russia is Ruled*, pp. 323–324.

[77] See Evan Mawdsley, 'An Elite within an Elite: Politburo/Presidium Membership under Stalin, 1927–1953', paper presented at conference on 'Stalin's Politburo, 1928–1953', European University Institute, Florence, March 2000, cited by permission, pp. 17–18. For more on the 'job-slot' system see Robert V. Daniels, 'Office Holding and Elite Status: The Central Committee of the CPSU', in Paul Cocks

STALIN'S CABINET 311

et al. (eds), *The Dynamics of Soviet Politics* (Cambridge, MA, Harvard University Press, 1976), pp. 77–95; and Evan Mawdsley & Stephen White, *The Soviet Elite from Lenin to Gorbachev: The Central Committee and its Members* (Oxford, Oxford University Press, 2000), pp. x–xi, 5, 41–50, 98–104.

[78] Danilov also refers to a meeting of the 'expanded presidium' (*rasshirennoe zasedanie Presidiuma*) of 1 December, originally cited in the Malyshev and Simonov memoirs. Confusingly, this meeting is sometimes referred to as a meeting of the 'central committee'. See Danilov, 'Stalinskoe politbyuro', p. 217.

[79] The first list was Stalin, Beria, Bulganin, Kaganovich, Malenkov, Saburov and Khrushchev. For reasons that are unclear, the names of Voroshilov and Pervukhin were later added by hand (Pikhoya, *Sovetskii soyuz*, p. 94). With the establishment of the Buro Stalin also achieved the formal exclusion of Molotov and Mikoyan from the inner cabinet (Andreev, unlike the latter two, was not even on the Presidium). Cf. Mikoyan, *Tak Bylo*, pp. 576–577.

[80] Although it did not meet weekly as initially intended, the Presidium Buro did meet regularly. Thus a first meeting, on 27 October, was followed in quick succession by meetings on 10 and 17 November. Although the last of these meetings was strictly confined to members of the Buro, the meeting of 10 November was also attended by all seven party secretaries who were not members of the Buro while the session of 27 October was also attended by Mikoyan, Molotov and Malyshev.

[81] Thus, for example, on 9 January the Buro, without Stalin, approved a text for publication on the arrest of the 'doctor-wreckers' which came out four days later (Pikhoya, *Sovetskii soyuz*, p. 94).

[82] With the return of Molotov and Mikoyan, whom Stalin had briefly expelled from the ruling circle, the 10-man 'Presidium' that took over upon Stalin's death was identical to the Buro of the Presidium formed the previous autumn. Compare Pikhoya, *Sovetskii soyuz*, p. 94 and *Politbyuro, Orgbyuro, Sekretariat*, pp. 36–37.

[83] Thus, in a departure from existing practice, on 19 December 1952 the secretariat resolved that 10 regional first secretaries be acquainted with the protocols of Presidium Buro meetings. See Gorlizki, 'Party Revivalism', p. 9.

[84] Whereas the 1939 rules had stipulated that the secretariat engage in 'current work of an organisational-executive character' the 1952 version introduced the broader formulation: '[The secretariat exists] for leadership of current work, chiefly the organisation of verification of the implementation of decisions of the party and the selection of cadres'. See Gill, *The Rules*, pp. 172–173, 193.

[85] In an interview, Ponomarenko recalled that in 1948 Stalin had signalled that 'the secretariat should draw in certain younger leaders of regional and republican party organisations who are educated and have work experience'. See G. A. Kumanev, *Ryadom so Stalinom: Otkrovennye svidetel'stva* (Moscow, Bylina, 1999), p. 144. At its sole meeting of 18 October the Presidium determined the following division of labour among the secretaries: apart from the senior secretaries (Stalin, Malenkov and Khrushchev), whose duties were not defined, Pegov was to take charge of a 'unified agency for cadres', Aristov was to supervise regional and republican party committees, Suslov, Ignatov and Ponomarenko were to go on secretariat assignments to the republics and regions, Mikhailov was to be responsible for propaganda and agitation, and Brezhnev was to oversee the chief political administrations of the army and navy. The following week, on 27 October, the Buro of the Presidium introduced a slightly amended division of labour in which Aristov was made head of the crucial department of party, trade union and Komsomol agencies. Aristov's new position facilitated Khrushchev's control of the cadres apparatus. For more on this see Gorlizki, 'Party Revivalism', p. 14.

[86] Gorlizki, 'Party Revivalism', p. 14. The expansion in the number of secretaries had been something that Zhdanov had called for in 1948 (RGASPI, f. 77, op. 3, d. 4, ll. 41–43).

[87] The Politburo had set up ad hoc policy commissions before to look at one-off issues. Stalin had also authorised standing policy commissions. Thus, for example, on 18 April 1949, in the wake of Mikoyan's dismissal as minister of foreign trade, the Politburo had set up a standing 'commission on prices' headed by Mikoyan which included among its members Kosygin, Kaganovich, Saburov and Zverev (RGASPI, f. 17, op. 163, d. 1523, l. 164). On the same day the Politburo approved a lower profile standing 'commission on foreign policy' headed by V.G. Grigor'yan (RGASPI, f. 17, op. 163, d. 1523, l. 165). On 19 January 1950 the Politburo set up a permanent commission on foreign trade, also headed by Mikoyan, which included Kaganovich, Saburov and the minister Men'shikov. The commission was given the right to summon relevant ministers (RGASPI, f. 17, op. 163, d. 1540, l. 183).

[88] It was, similarly, in order to let him focus on the commission on foreign affairs that, on 18 October, Molotov was relieved of oversight of the ministry of foreign affairs and that Mikoyan was released from Sovmin duties in monitoring the ministry of foreign trade. Other recruits to the Presidium commissions included Rumyantsev to the ideological commission (18 November), Brezhnev to the defence commission (19 November) and Beria to the foreign affairs commission (12 December) (Beria, however, retained his position as deputy chairman of the Council of Ministers).

312   YORAM GORLIZKI

[89] APRF f. 3 op. 22, d. 12, 1.3 Zhukov regards these six as the heirs apparent to Stalin in the last phase of the dictator's life. See Zhukov, 'Bor'ba za vlast', p. 38.

[90] This was especially apparent on the Presidium, where, among the relatively new faces from the provinces, were V. M. Andryanov, D. S. Korotchenko, L. R. Mel'nikov and, among the candidates, L. I. Brezhnev, N. G. Ignatov and A. M. Puzanov; on the Presidium Buro itself the younger figures were Saburov and Pervukhin (Pikhoya, *Sovetskii soyuz*, pp. 93–94).

[91] Commentators have long noted the relative durability of Politburo membership and high survival rate in the post-war years. With the notable exception of Voznesensky no member of the formal Politburo was arrested or detained in this period. For the double argument that levels of attrition were lower in the Politburo than in the 'wider circles of the party elite' and 'that stability of [Politburo] membership was greater in the years of Stalin's fully developed despotism [i.e. 1939–1953] than in any other period ... in Soviet history' see T. H. Rigby, 'Was Stalin a Disloyal Patron?', in T. H. Rigby, *Political Elites in the USSR* (Aldershot, Edward Elgar, 1990), pp. 138, 141. Rigby reaches the conclusion (p. 141) that 'the durability of Stalin's inner clientele was truly remarkable'. Khlevnyuk also makes the point that even those, such as Molotov and Mikoyan, who were repeatedly harangued by the aging dictator escaped his onslaughts unharmed and that, even after the attacks of October 1952, they continued to play an important role. For more on this see Khlevnyuk, 'Zadavlennye oligarkhi', pp. 15–17, 23. By contrast, Khrushchev was 'convinced that [had] Stalin lived much longer, Molotov and Mikoyan would have met a disastrous end' (Khrushchev, *Khrushchev Remembers*, p. 310).

[92] The formal Politburo was dominated by figures such as Molotov, Voroshilov, Kaganovich, Mikoyan, Andreev, Malenkov and Shvernik whom Stalin had known since the 1920s; most of the other members, such as Beria, Bulganin and Khrushchev, he had known since the early 1930s. These were leaders whose loyalty Stalin had repeatedly tested and whose strengths and weaknesses the leader knew inside out. Apart from the unfortunate Voznesensky, the only new recruit was Kosygin. These points are made in T. H. Rigby, *Political Elites in the USSR*, pp. 141, 143.

[93] Mikoyan, *Tak Bylo*, p. 558.

[94] Khlevnyuk, 'Zadavlennye oligarkhi', pp. 15–17, 23.

[95] Indeed, as the former diplomat Oleg Troyanovsky recounts, the main consequence of Molotov leaving the ministry of foreign affairs was not that Molotov's stature should have diminished but, rather, that the institutional weight of the ministry itself should have fallen away. He writes: 'After the replacement of Molotov by Vyshinsky [in 1949], who was not a Politburo member, the role of the ministry in determining the course of the Soviet Union in international affairs noticeably decreased, and became all but ancillary' (Troyanovsky, *Cherez gody*, p. 166).

[13]

The Leningrad Affair and
the Provincialization of Leningrad

BLAIR A. RUBLE

The last day of July 1950 should have been a day of celebration in
Leningrad as more than 80,000 sports fans filed into the new Kirov Stadium on Krestovskii Island.[1] The day's events—which featured local
gymnasts ranging from school children to national champions, as well
as a soccer game between local rivals Dinamo and Zenit—dedicated a
massive sports facility at the new Maritime Victory Park. Over the previous seven years the stadium had become a symbolic capstone to
efforts to rebuild the war-ravaged city, and its opening as the premier
sports facility in the Soviet Union should have signified Leningrad's
reemergence as that country's most important city.[2] The weather colla-
borated with the gymnasts to make for a perfect day: the temperature
rose to the upper 60s as nearly every cloud drifted from sight leaving
the spectators to bask in rare northern sunlight. Even the football
rivals cooperated by playing to a tie. There were no losers at Kirov Stadium that day.

Despite the setting of a sundrenched stadium nestled next to the
Gulf of Finland, the day's events were probably somewhat bittersweet
for many of the 80,000 Leningraders in attendance. Seven springs
before, and only six weeks after the Red Army had driven the
Wehrmacht from the city gates, the State Defense Committee in Moscow proclaimed massive plans to reconstruct the Leningrad economy.[3]

---

[1] "Stadion imeni S. M. Kirova otkryt," *Leningradskaia pravda*, August 1, 1950, p. 3.

This article is based upon a paper presented at the Third Annual Conference of the
National Seminar on Russian Social History in the Twentieth Century held at the University of Pennsylvania in January 1983. The author would like to express his gratitude to
Mary McAuley of the University of Essex for her invaluable encouragement and assistance in this and other projects as well as to Timothy Colton, Abbott Gleason, Peter
Hauslohner, Harry Rigby, and two anonymous reviewers for their thoughtful comments
and suggestions.

[2] A. S. Nikol'skii, K. I. Kashin, "Stadion imeni S. M. Kirova," *Arkhitektura i
stroitel'stvo Leningrada*, 1950, no. 2, pp. 5-16; N. F. Khomutetskii, *Peterburg-Leningrad.
Istoriko-arkhitekturnyi ocherk*, Leningrad, 1958, pp. 233-336.

[3] V. I. Kruchina, "O surovykh dniakh blokady," *Leningradskaia panorama*, 1983, no.
3, p. 3; V. A. Kamenskii, *Leningrad. General'nyi plan razvitiia goroda*, Leningrad, 1972,
pp. 36-38; V. I. Pilavskii, *Arkhitektura Leningrada*, Leningrad-Moscow, 1953, pp. 45-46;

Just six weeks after that, Andrei Zhdanov, during his last appearance as Leningrad Regional Party First Secretary, unveiled an even more extensive rebuilding strategy designed not only to "reconstruct" Leningrad but to "resurrect" it as the Soviet Union's only rival to Moscow.[4] By July 30, 1950, as Leningraders filled their new stadium, the physical reconstruction of the city was complete. Leningrad had been saved both from the bombs and artillery shells of the German Army and from the blueprints of pre-war city planners and architects who envisioned the development of a new city center to the south of Leningrad's historic core.[5] Nevertheless, physical reconstruction could not stave off further deterioration in relation to Moscow. The 80,000 Leningraders at Kirov Stadium that summer day in 1950 could not have been unaware of the fact that their city had been losing more ground to Stalin's capital. Indeed, their hometown was then the target of one of the most vicious purges of the Stalin period, the so-called Leningrad Affair. If any in the crowd needed to be reminded of what was going on in their city they had only to look to the city's 'mayor', City Soviet Chairman P. F. Ladanov, as he presided over the opening ceremonies. Only twelve days before he had been elevated from First Secretary of the Kuibyshev District Party Committee to replace Andrei Alekseevich Kuznetsov, who had just been arrested and was about to be shot.[6]

At the close of the war, few observers anticipated Leningrad's failure to reassert its preeminence.[7] After all, the city had survived the longest siege of modern times. Moreover, its political elite appeared to be moving into positions of national prominence from which they could guarantee sufficient resources for Leningrad's resurgence. Stalin's subsequent destruction of that political elite appeared to explain the city's looming provincialization.[8]

Harrison E. Salisbury, *The 900 Days: The Siege of Leningrad*, New York, 1969, pp. 575-576.

[4]Salisbury, *The 900 Days*, pp. 573-575.

[5]N. V. Baranov, "General'nyi plan razvitiia Leningrada," in Leningrad. Arkhitekturno-planirovochnoe upravlenie, *Leningrad*, Leningrad-Moscow, 1943, pp. 65-84; L. A. Il'in, "Plan razvitiia Leningrada i ego arkhitektura," *Arkhitektura Leningrada*, 1936, no. 1, 18-33; I. I. Fomin, "Ansambl' Moskovskogo shosse," *Arkhitektura Leningrada*, 1938, no. 2, pp. 39-44; A. N. Kosygin, "Novoe stroitel'stvo v gorode Lenina," *Arkhitektura Leningrada*, 1938, no. 5, pp. 5-7; L. I. Gal'pern, "Proekty obshchegorodskogo tsentra v Leningrade," *Arkhitektura Leningrada*, 1940, no. 2, pp. 7-15; "Novaia sistema obshchegorodskogo tsentra Leningrada," *Arkhitektura Leningrada*, 1941, no. 1, pp. 2-7.

[6]"Deviataia sessiia Leningradskogo gorodskogo soveta deputatov trudiashchikhsia vtorogo sozyva," *Leningradskaia pravda*, July 19, 1950, p. 2.

[7]See, for example, Alexander Werth, *Leningrad*, London, 1944, and W. L. White, *Report on the Russians*, New York, 1945.

[8]See, for example, Salisbury, *The 900 Days*, pp. 571-583.

The rise and fall of great cities is an eminently complex process, one usually beyond the control of any single elite or despot, no matter how powerful. Stalin undoubtedly undermined efforts to bring about a "renaissance of Leningrad," either out of distaste for the former imperial capital or distrust of that city's powerful political machine. The origins of the city's decline are nonetheless not attributable to Stalin's malevolence alone. Broader social and economic changes affecting the country as a whole, ranging from the development of a Moscow-focused national rail system at the end of the nineteenth century to the eastward relocation of the Soviet Union's industrial base during the Second World War, also contributed to a gradual erosion of Leningrad's stature. Such politically inspired decisions as Lenin's transfer of the capital to Moscow in 1918, Stalin's dispatch of the Academy of Sciences in 1934, and his decapitation of Leningrad's political elite in 1948 and 1949 only intensified a syndrome of decline in relation to Moscow.

The plans for Leningrad's resurgence were hindered further by the impact of broad social changes occurring prior to the German invasion of 1941. A torrent of peasants fleeing collectivization in the countryside poured into every Soviet city during the 1930s. In the case of Leningrad this influx bloated the city's population by nearly 1.5 million souls between 1929 and 1939.[9] Meanwhile, the city bore more than its share of the terror unleashed in the wake of the Kirov assassination in December 1934. The cumulative effect of these events was to erode Leningrad's remaining links with its own past. By the time Hitler's army arrived on the outskirts overlooking the city, Leningrad had become, to paraphrase Alexander Werth, no more Petersburg or Petrograd than Stalingrad was Tsaritsyn.[10]

Stalin's personal animus, the pressures of collectivization, the reorientation of the Soviet industrial system towards Moscow and the East all made their contributions to Leningrad's transformation from a world city to a provincial center; all were apparent before the Second World War. Leningraders nonetheless were confident at war's end that their city would recover both from the ravages of the blockade and from the more subtle erosion of their city's standing.[11] That confidence proved ill-founded.

The 1940s represent a major discontinuity in the history of Leningrad. A city that laid claim to the legacy of both Peter and Lenin was destroyed, only to be reconstituted by new residents with few historic

---

[9]*Malaia sovetskaia entsiklopediia*, Moscow, 1930, vol. 4, p. 572; TsSU SSSR, *Narodnoe khoziaistvo SSSR, 1922-1972 gg.*, Moscow, 1972, p. 19.

[10]Werth, *Leningrad*, p. 24.

[11]Salisbury, *The 900 Days*, pp. 571-583; White, *Report on the Russians*, pp. 89-109.

ties to either founding father. Behind the neo-classical and baroque facades of the Moika and Fontanka came to live, not dispossessed gentry and honored revolutionary heroes, but one more generation of peasants in workers' clothing. The city's new population soon filled up major social and political institutions as well, including the local Communist Party. There were similar developments elsewhere in the Soviet Union, but the northern capital's politically charged atmosphere magnified their significance: the major political struggle of the immediate post-war period—that between Malenkov and Zhdanov—was played out against the backdrop of Leningrad's struggle to reconstitute itself.[12] Once the purges of 1948 and 1949 had run their course, the historic break with the city's past, brought about by a decade of war, social dislocation, and political conflict, only cemented Leningrad's provinciality.

The Transformation of the City's Population

During the German and Finnish armies' stranglehold over the city, Leningrad's only links to the outside world had been by air and by the 237-mile long "Road of Life" across the ice of Lake Ladoga and through surrounding forests to the nearest railhead. The "Road of Life" allowed supplies and materiel to reach the city and, perhaps of equal importance, permitted unnecessary civilian personnel to leave. Between January and March 1942, 554,000 Leningraders left their city, many never to return. Meanwhile, substantial numbers of those civilians left behind and their military defenders were dying of starvation, disease, and constant enemy bombardment. In January 1942, thousands of Leningraders died each day, with as many as 30,000 city residents perishing on the worst days of February. According to official figures, 632,253 civilians died during the siege, a total considered far too low by many Western historians of the period. By March 1943, the once vibrant city of 3.2 million souls—the largest city to be placed under siege since Paris in 1870—was reduced to a militarized encampment of 639,000 inhabitants.[13]

In addition to the unimaginable human loss, the German attacks obliterated the city's physical plant, a process helped along by abandonment and scavenging. The siege totally destroyed over 3.2 million square meters of housing space, 166 kilometers of streets, 75 kilome-

[12]Werner Hahn, *Postwar Soviet Politics*, Ithaca, NY, 1982.

[13]L. D. Leonov, B. K. Peiro, *Leningrad—gorod geroi*, Leningrad, 1957, pp. 28-30; Salisbury, *The 900 Days*, pp. 407-422, 513-518; D. V. Pavlov, *Leningrad 1941: The Blockade*, translated by John C. Adams, Chicago, 1965, pp. 136-167; Leon Gouré, *The Siege of Leningrad: August 1941—January 1944*, New York, 1964, pp. 150-153, 217-218, 239.

ters of sewer lines and 44 kilometers of water lines.[14] By 1944, the city was liberated but lay in shambles.

During the summer of 1944, Eric Johnston, President of the United States Chamber of Commerce, visited Leningrad and reported that only a skeleton force remained in the city. Chief Architect Baranov told Johnston that much of the evacuated population would likely never return to the city. Most of Leningrad's prewar factories and the people to work in them were "hauled halfway across Russia to the Urals, Siberia or the Chinese border."[15] (A year later the Leningrad Regional Party First Secretary reported to the USSR Supreme Soviet that 75% of the city's industrial equipment had been evacuated or destroyed during the war).[16] Leningrad would be repopulated and rebuilt, but not necessarily by the city's prewar residents.

Unfortunately, the available data are not sufficient to establish the social composition of the city's postwar population with any certainty. All one can do is attempt a reconstruction on the basis of scattered and incomplete information. Of Leningrad's prewar population of 3.2 million, nearly 1.4 million are not accounted for by official statistics on wartime population losses.[17] Such a lacuna probably results from the concerns more pressing than data collection that were confronting an overburdened wartime leadership, as well as from the speed with which population shifts were taking place. Between March 1943 and September 1945, for example, the city's population doubled, from 639,000 to 1,240,000.[18] It is unlikely that Leningraders spread halfway to Vladivostok could have made the necessary hundred- and thousand-mile treks across the war-torn Soviet Union to their native city in sufficient numbers to account for this increase. In addition, from the data on Leningrad's postwar population emerge three characteristics that suggest much of the city's postwar population may have been drawn from rural areas rather than from among returning wartime evacuees: the new population was predominantly female, it was relatively undisciplined, and relatively unskilled.[19] Such characteristics were shared by the

[14]V. A. Kamenskii, A. I. Naumov, *Leningrad. Gradostroitel'nye problemy razvitiia*, Leningrad, 1977, p. 144.

[15]White, *Report on the Russians*, pp. 90-93.

[16]"XI sessiia Verkhovnogo soveta Soiuza 1-ogo sozyva, preniia po dokladu o Gosudarstvennom biudzhete SSSR na 1945 god. Rech' deputata A. A. Kuznetsova," *Leningradskaia pravda*, June 28, 1945, p. 2.

[17]As noted above, official data identify a low population of 639,000 in March 1943, as well as 554,000 evacuees and 632,253 civilian deaths. These figures account for approximately 1.8 million persons in a prewar population of 3.2 million. Gouré, *The Siege of Leningrad*, p. 239; Salisbury, *The 900 Days*, pp. 513-518.

[18]Gouré, *Siege of Leningrad*, p. 239; "Iz letopisi sobytii," *Leningradskaia panorama*, 1982, no. 6, p. 7.

[19]V. A. Ezhov, "Izmeneniia v chislennosti i sostave rabochikh Leningrada v

populations of other urban centers. But that is the point: Leningrad was becoming more like other Soviet cities. Its peculiar advantages were eroding quickly so that the consequences of postwar population changes for Leningrad were more radical.

Leningrad had traditionally been a male city. The imbalance between the sexes was caused in part by the heavy-industrial base of the city's economy and in part by the city's historic role as a military center. The male proportion of the population had dropped in the early twentieth century, but risen again because new arrivals during the First Five Year Plan were predominantly male.[20]

A dramatic change occurred after the war. In April 1945, 76.4% of all Leningraders employed in industries traditionally staffed by males were now female, a figure suggesting that women were predominant in the city's population as a whole.[21] Postwar in-migration increased the city's male population, as might be expected in a period of demobilization. Still, the city continued to become more female throughout the postwar period at a rate slightly higher the rates of the USSR and RSFSR general and urban populations.[22] The feminization of the Leningrad population can be attributed to several factors, not the least of which is the high participation levels and losses of Leningrad males in both the Winter War with Finland and the Second World War. The process may well have been augmented by a significant in-migration from already female-dominated rural areas as well.

Local officials bemoaned the relatively undisciplined nature of the postwar Leningrad population during the first months of post-blockade reconstruction. In October 1945, Lt. Gen. N. Shiktorov, chief of the Leningrad MVD, complained to the readers of *Leningradskaia pravda* that the vaunted discipline of Leningraders, so apparent during the blockade, had given way to rising levels of crime, hooliganism, and industrial indiscipline.[23] Shiktorov claimed that these problems were most evident in such public places as movie theaters, restaurants, stores, as well as on trams and buses. He criticized inadequacies in

poslevoennyi period (1945-1950 gg.)," *Vestnik Leningradskogo universiteta. Seriia istorii, iazyka i literatury,* 1966, no. 2, pp. 15-21.

[20]James H. Bater, *St. Petersburg: Industrialization and Change,* Montreal, 1976, pp. 168, 313; Leningradskoe upravlenie narodno-khoziaistvennogo ucheta, *Ekonomiko-statisticheskii spravochnik Leningradskoi oblasti,* Leningrad, 1932, pp. 145, 153.

[21]Ezhov, "Izmeneniia v chislennosti i sostave rabochikh," p. 19.

[22]G. M. Romanenkova, "Sotsial'no-ekonomicheskie posledstviia demograficheskogo razvitiia," in N. A. Tolokontsev, G. M. Romanenkova (eds.), *Demografiia i ekologiia krupnogo goroda,* Leningrad, 1980, pp. 54-55; TsSU SSSR, *Itogi vsesoiuznoi perepisi naseleniia 1970 goda,* Moscow, 1972, vol. 2, Tables 1-2, pp. 5-11.

[23]N. Shiktorov, "Ukrepim obshchestvennyi poriadok i bezopasnost' v Leningrade," *Leningradskaia pravda,* October 23, 1945, pp. 2-3.

general social and Party educational work and insufficient adult supervision for youth, young adults under thirty by then representing over 60% of the city's workers.[24]

The general social indiscipline identified by Shiktorov was apparently even more pronounced within the city's industrial establishments. In December 1946, P. S. Popkov, the wartime Chairman of the Leningrad City Soviet, who had replaced Aleksei Kuznetsov as First Secretary of the Leningrad City and Regional Party Committees earlier in the year, reported to the Leningrad City Party Committee that labor turnover had soared to 58.5% in the city's factories.[25] According to Popkov, the premier Bolshevik and Sevkabel plants hired 11,042 workers between January and October 1946, while 6,692 workers left their positions at those plants during the same period. Meanwhile, the model Izhorsk Factory hired 1,785 workers, as 1,454 workers left their jobs. Popkov also observed that labor turnover contributed to an inordinate overtime at Leningrad factories—45,000 hours of overtime work at the famous Kirov Plant alone during October 1946.

Once again, the data are far from complete and one must infer more than is perhaps advisable. Still, comments by members of the Leningrad political and economic elites point to behavior that could be expected of large numbers of demobilized soldiers, of rural in-migrants to the city's industrial plants, or both.[26] At a minimum, the image offered of the Leningrad proletariat during the period is not that of a highly skilled, long-employed labor elite. Rather, it suggests a work force consisting of fairly substantial numbers of peasant-workers, be they former soldiers or migrants directly from the village.

By January 1946, 148,000 demobilized soldiers returned to the city, of which 88,000 almost immediately went to work in industry. By late 1947, however, Leningrad factories were forced to reach beyond the pool of returning Red Army men. As a result, factories and local Communist Party organizations initiated large-scale programs to train new recruits, most of whom were probably drawn from the countryside.[27] Such programs, however, had been necessary even earlier. Approximately 100,000 new workers entered Leningrad factories in 1944. Local industry, already hard pressed to return to prewar production levels, had to train large numbers of new recruits. During the first half of 1945, 8,105 workers from Leningrad defense plants entered

[24]A. Vasker, "Trudovoi podvig," *Leningradskaia pravda*, January 28, 1983, p. 3.
[25]"Rech' tovarishcha P. S. Popkova na plenume Leningradskogo gorkoma VKP(b). 28 dekabria 1946 goda," *Leningradskaia pravda*, January 1, 1947, pp. 2-3.
[26]V. A. Ezhov, "Izmeneniia v chislennosti i sostave rabochikh."
[27]Z. V. Stepanov (ed.), *Ocherki istorii Leningrada*, vol. 6, pp. 31-34; V. A. Ezhov, "Izmeneniia v chislennosti i sostave rabochikh," p. 16.

courses; 6,530 of them successfully completed programs of instruction.[28]

The immediate postwar period, then, was one of considerable instability and change in the city's population and work force. In May 1948, 65% of the city's machine-construction work force and 87% of employees in the Leningrad textile industry had joined the local labor force since the end of the war. In 1948, 76% of all workers in the Nevskii Machine-Construction Plant and 83% at the Leningrad Metallurgical Plant, two of the city's most important factories, had not completed secondary school. These workers apparently stayed at their jobs for quite some time, so that one-third of the city's industrial workers in the late 1950s had attained their jobs during the late 1940s.[29]

By the time of the 1959 census, Leningrad's population barely surpassed its prewar level of 3.2 million residents.[30] The city had recovered its population and rebuilt its economic base, but the population was now more female than before, less disciplined and in greater need of vocational training. These trends were apparent in other cities as well, but the consequences for Leningrad were especially significant. The highly skilled workers of whom Leningrad politicians had been so proud had been swamped by yet another wave of migrants from the countryside. These changes cannot be explained solely by the 632,253 civilian deaths cited in official Soviet publications. Undoubtedly, more people died during the blockade than Soviet statistical handbooks acknowledge. A large percentage of the half-million evacuees probably never returned to live in Leningrad. The city may have survived the war, but not with its prewar population intact.

Renewal of Party Life

Changes within the structure of the Leningrad Communist Party and the city's governing elite were even more dramatic than those in the population at large. During the first two years of the war, the membership of the city party organization dropped by nearly 75% (see Table 1). Membership in the Leningrad party declined by 26.2% while the party expanded by 190.7% nationwide; the traditional primacy of the Leningrad party organization in national affairs diminished considerably.[31] When Sergei Kirov died, one Soviet Communist in ten was from Leningrad. By the end of World War II, only two percent of the

[28]Iu. Kapustin, "Voprosy vosstanovleniia i razvitiia promyshlennosti Leningrada," *Partiinoe stroitel'stvo*, 1945, no. 17/18, pp. 14-19.
[29]Ezhov, "Izmeneniia v sostave i chislennosti rabochikh," pp. 19-20.
[30]*Itogi vsesoiuznoi perepisi 1970 goda*, vol. 1, table 2, p. 10.
[31]S. S. Dmitriev, et al., *Leningradskaia organizatsiia KPSS v tsifrakh. 1917-1973 gg.*, Leningrad, 1974, p. 70; N. A. Petrovich et al., *Partiinoe stroitel'stvo*, Moscow, 1976, p. 62.

The Leningrad Affair   309

Table 1: Membership in Leningrad City Party Organization, 1939-1954

Date	Full Members	Candidate Members	Total Membership
January 1, 1939	100,610	29,972	130,582
January 1, 1940	114,591	36,737	151,328
January 1, 1941	117,745	34,048	151,793
January 1, 1942	61,842	12,386	74,228
January 1, 1943	30,305	13,588	43,893
January 1, 1944	35,363	14,280	49,643
January 1, 1945	56,982	14,269	71,251
January 1, 1946	95,217	16,452	111,669
January 1, 1947	156,047	23,100	179,147
January 1, 1948	176,741	22,677	199,418
January 1, 1949	189,511	17,318	206,829
January 1, 1950	196,664	13,915	210,579
January 1, 1951	200,213	14,935	215,148
January 1, 1952	204,071	16,658	220,729
January 1, 1953	207,545	15,967	223,512
January 1, 1954	219,965	8,696	228,661

Source: S. S. Dmitriev, et al., *Leningradskaia organizatsiia KPSS v tsifrakh, 1917—1973 gg.* Leningrad, 1974, p. 70.

all-union party membership hailed from Leningrad. Over the course of the post-war period, the national percentage of Communists belonging to the Leningrad party has stabilized around 3% (see Table 2).

While the relative weight of Leningrad party membership within the national Communist Party organization declined, the composition of the Leningrad party itself was undergoing considerable change. For example, 54,000 of the 153,531 Leningrad party members on July 1, 1941 left for the front almost immediately following the outbreak of hostilities.[32] By January 1943, death rolls contained the names of 13,000 party members as party membership plummeted to 43,893.[33] Between 1943 and 1945, 21,608 new members joined the city's Communist Party.[34] Moreover, many of the 368,416 recruits who joined the

[32] Dmitriev, *Leningradskaia organizatsiia KPSS*, pp. 39-45.
[33] *Ibid.*
[34] *Ibid.*, pp. 74-75.

310   *The Russian Review*

Party on the Leningrad front during the war remained in the city,[35] that two-thirds of all the members of the Leningrad City Party Organization in 1947 had not been in the party when fighting broke out.[36]

Table 2: Leningrad Party Membership
as a Percentage of National Party Membership, 1917-1971

Date	Percentage
October 1, 1917	16.6%
January 1, 1927	8.1%
January 1, 1934	10.3%
January 1, 1939	5.7%
January 1, 1941	3.9%
January 1, 1946	2.0%
January 1, 1952	3.3%
January 1, 1956	3.8%
January 1, 1966	3.3%
January 1, 1971	3.1%

Sources: S. S. Dmitriev, et al., *Leningradskaia organizatsiia KPSS v tsifrakh, 1917—1973 gg.*, Leningrad, 1974, p. 70; N. A. Petrovich et al., *Partiinoe stroitel'stvo*, Moscow, 1976, p. 62.

This evolving character of the composition of Leningrad party membership parallels the broader trends within the Leningrad population as a whole as well as within the national Communist Party. Approximately 40% of new Leningrad party officials appointed prior to the Nineteenth All-Union Party Congress in October 1952, were women. From January 1, 1941, until January 1, 1947, the percentage of party members under 25 years of age more than doubled (from 3.6% to more than 8%). By 1947, 35% of Leningrad Communists had received some degree of higher or specialized secondary education, as opposed to 25% before the outbreak of the war. Finally, proletarian representation within the party declined dramatically, from 80% in 1939 to 47.4% in 1954, while white collar membership increased from 13.9% to 46.8% over the same period.[37] Overall, then, the Leningrad party

[35]S. P. Kniazev, "Kurs na vosstanovlenie posle sniatiia blokady (1944-1945 gg.)," in Institut istorii partii Leningradskogo obkoma KPSS—Filial Instituta Marksizma-Leninizma pri TsK KPSS, *Ocherki istorii Leningradskoi organizatsii KPSS*, Part 2: *Noiabr' 1917-1945 gg.*, Leningrad, 1968, p. 649.

[36]Dmitriev, *Leningradskaia organizatsiia KPSS*, pp. 45-51.

[37]"Rech' tov. Kozlova," *Leningradskaia pravda*, October 16, 1952, p. 3; Dmitriev, *Len-*

organization experienced many of the same compositional changes as other party organizations elsewhere in the Soviet Union. The vaunted political machine built by Kirov and nurtured by Zhdanov began to resemble any other provincial party organization.

The make-up of party leadership councils changed even more than did the membership at large. Between May 1945 and March 1953, nineteen men held Leningrad's six major political posts.[38] With the notable exceptions of the purgers V. M. Andrianov and A. V. Nosenko, all had served in low- or middle-level positions in Leningrad throughout much of the 1930s. Most attained some form of post-secondary education in the technical sciences, but none had attended the city's most prestigious educational institutions. Most were in their early 40s and had worked their way up Kirov's and Zhdanov's party *apparat* from working class and peasant backgrounds. Yet, only one among these nineteen, Frol Kozlov, would remain active in Leningrad affairs after 1954 and by the end of the 1950's even he had left for Moscow to become First Deputy Prime Minister of the USSR.

The instability of political personnel cut deep. 663 of 759 delegates elected to the Eleventh Regional Party Conference in September 1952 were serving in such a gathering for the first time, as were 99 alternate delegates.[39] Regional Party First Secretary V. M. Andrianov, who had been brought in from Sverdlovsk in 1949 to supervise the purges during the Leningrad Affair, reported to that gathering that more than 2,000 party leaders (in addition to another 1,500 state, trade union, and Komsomol officials) had advanced in rank during his tenure in office.[40] A month later, Andrianov told the Nineteenth Party Congress in Moscow that such advancement proved necessary as a

---

ingradskaia organizatsiia KPSS, pp. 45-51, 73-75; P. S. Popkov, "O roste partii i vospitanii molodykh kommunistov," *Leningradskaia pravda*, September 6, 1946, pp. 2-3.

[38]REGIONAL PARTY FIRST SECRETARIES: A. A. Kuznetsov (1945-1946), P. S. Popkov (1946-1949), V. M. Andrianov (1949-1953); REGIONAL PARTY SECOND SECRETARIES: I. M. Turko (1945-1946), G. F. Badaev (1946-1949), B. F. Nikolaev (1949-1952), F. R. Kozlov (1952-1953); CITY PARTY FIRST SECRETARIES: A. A. Kuznetsov (1945-1946), P. S. Popkov (1946-1949), V. M. Adrianov (1949), F. R. Kozlov (1950-1952), A. I. Alekseev (1952-1953); CITY PARTY SECOND SECRETARIES: Iu. F. Kapustin (1945-1949), N. A. Nikolaev (1949), F. R. Kozlov (1949), A. V. Nosenko (1949-1953); CHAIRMEN OF THE CITY SOVIET: P. S. Popkov (1939-1946), P. G. Lazutin (1946-1949), An. Al. Kuznetsov (1949), P. F. Ladanov (1949-1954); CHAIRMEN OF THE REGIONAL SOVIET: N. V. Solov'ev (1938-1946), I. S. Kharitonov (1946-1948), I. D. Dmitriev (1948-1950), I. P. Petrov (1950-1952), V. N. Ponomarev (1952-1954).

[39]"Doklad predsedatelia Mandatnoi komissii tov. N. A. Romanova," *Leningradskaia pravda*, September 25, 1952, p. 3.

[40]"Doklad sekretaria Leningradskogo oblastnogo komiteta VKP(b) tov. V. M. Andrianova," *Leningradskaia pravda*, September 28, 1952, pp. 2-4. Frol Kozlov repeated the 2,000-person figure in his report to the Nineteenth Party Congress the following month ("Rech' tov. Kozlova," October 16, 1952).

result of distortions in ideological work, which had led to "toadyism and servility" in personnel practices.[41] One can assume that these new appointees replaced incumbents who had been purged. One might add that such high levels of turnover had not been typical of Leningrad party practice since the last major purge in 1937 and 1938. Of the secretaries of primary Party organizations elected on the eve of the war, 73% had already served at least one term.[42]

Institutions of municipal government proved no more stable than those of the party. In May 1944, the Leningrad City Soviet convened for the first time since the war began. Less than one-third of the Soviet's deputies attended; 708 of 1037 council members were either dead or at the front.[43] When, in 1947, a new city soviet as well as fourteen new district soviets met for the first time, their deputies were, as a group, older and better educated than their prewar counterparts (see Table 3). Finally, the membership of the Regional Soviet was also in a state of flux.

More detailed information is available concerning the Leningrad Regional Soviet than any other Leningrad deliberative body.[44] The average (mean) age of regional soviet deputies increased from 41.6 to 44.9 years over the course of the elections of 1947, 1950, and 1953 (see Table 4). The soviet also embraced a greater number of deputies engaged in agricultural activities[45] The professional profile of soviet deputies shifted away from industrial managers and party *apparatchiki* towards scholars, teachers, military officers, police representatives, and, to a lesser extent, workers (see Table 4).

Any general conclusions about the nature of the Leningrad elite based upon data concerning membership in the regional soviet of this period must remain tentative. The regional soviet functions as only one of several key local institutions and, of all such bodies, is the least concerned with city affairs.[46] More importantly, the council's membership remained extraordinarily unsettled. Of 208 deputies elected to

[41]"Rech' tov. Andrianova," *Leningradskaia pravda*, October 9, 1952, pp. 3-4.

[42]"Vospitanie partiinykh kadrov," *Leningradskaia pravda*, June 10, 1941, p. 1.

[43]A. R. Dzeniskevich et al., *Nepokrennyi Leningrad*, 2nd edition, Leningrad, 1974, p. 455.

[44]Unfortunately, election lists for the City Soviet appear only in the city's evening newspaper, *Vechernyi Leningrad*. That paper remains unavailable in the West.

[45]This shift towards agricultural concerns became more pronounced in later years: Regional Soviet Chairmen G. I. Vorob'ev (1954-1957), N. I. Smirnov (1957-1961), G. I. Kozlov (1961-1963, 1964-1968), V. G. Sominich (Regional Agricultural Soviet Chairman, 1963-1964) and A. N. Shibalov (1968-1980) all graduated from agricultural institutes.

[46]For a discussion of the division of labor between city and regional institutions during this period, see Cynthia S. Kaplan, "The Communist Party of the Soviet Union and Local Policy Implementation," *Journal of Politics*, vol. 45, no. 1, February, 1983, pp. 2-27.

The Leningrad Affair   **313**

Table 3: Composition of Leningrad City and District Soviets, 1939-1947

Category	1939	1947
Sex		
Male	64.1%	64.8%
Female	35.9%	35.2%
Party Membership:		
Party & Komsomol Members	65.0%	63.7%
Non-Party Members	35.0%	36.3%
Education:		
Higher Education	41.0%	54.5%
Secondary Education	30.0%	25.2%
Primary Education	29.0%	20.3%
Age:		
29 or younger	23.2%	4.6%
30-39	48.7%	30.0%
40-49	19.9%	47.2%
50 or older	8.2%	18.2%

Source: Z. V. Stepanov, ed., *Ocherki istorii Leningrada*, Leningrad, 1970, vol. 6, pp. 38-39.

office in 1947, only 4 were re-elected in 1950 and only 70 of the 208 deputies elected in 1950 were re-elected in 1953 (See Table 5). By 1950, the Leningrad Regional Soviet and every other local Leningrad political institution were in a state of turmoil generated by the purges of the Leningrad Affair.

An examination of the leading Leningrad party and municipal institutions during the postwar period suggests a local elite caught in a whirlwind. That whirlwind, generated as it was by national as well as local political and social developments, helped to insure Leningrad's provincial status for the next quarter century.

The Decapitation of a Local Political Elite

Following the death of Andrei Zhdanov in August 1948, his major rivals Malenkov and Beria set in motion a large-scale purge of Zhdanov protégés in Leningrad and elsewhere. Before the end of March 1949, A. A. Kuznetsov, Secretary of the Communist Party's Central Committee, P. S. Popkov, First Secretary of the Leningrad Regional and City Party Committees, N. A. Voznesenskii, Chairman of the USSR State

Table 4: Composition of Leningrad Regional Soviet, 1947-1953

Category	1947	1950	1953
SEX			
Male	159	152	146
Female	49	56	62
PARTY MEMBERSHIP			
Party & Komsomol Member	167	157	162
Non-Party Member	41	51	46
PROFESSION			
National Party/State Official	2	5	4
Regional or District			
Party/State Official	107	62	75
Managers			
Industrial	27	24	9
Agricultural	18	17	18
Workers			
Industrial	18	32	26
Agricultural	7	16	19
Scholars	10	15	20
Military & Police	9	5	14
Teachers	5	21	18
Other	5	11	5
AGE			
20-30	11	14	10
31-40	66	47	50
41-50	116	115	101
51-60	13	27	37
60 or older	2	5	10
Mean age	41.6	43.7	44.9
Total Membership	208	208	208

Source: "Spisok kandidatov v deputaty Leningradskogo oblastnogo soveta deputatov trudiashchikhsia zaregistrirovannykh okruzhnymi izbiratel'nymi komissiiami," *Leningradskaia pravda*, November 21, 1947, p. 3; November 21, 1950, pp. 1, 3-4; January 27, 1953, pp. 3-4.

The Leningrad Affair   315

Table 5: Re-election of Regional Soviet Deputies, 1947-1953

	1947	1950	1953
Elected in 1947	208	4	6
Elected in 1950		208	70
Elected in 1953			208

Source: as Table 4.

Planning Committee, his brother A. A. Voznesenskii, RSFSR Minister of Education, as well as M. I. Rodionov, Chairman of the RSFSR Council of Ministers, had all been removed from their posts never to be seen again.[47] By late summer, the Leningrad Regional Party Committee under its new First Secretary, V. M. Andrianov, supervised the dismissal of all five regional party committee secretaries, all five city party committee secretaries, the four most senior city soviet officials including Chairman P. G. Lazutin, several high level regional soviet officers, including Chairman I. S. Kharitonov, the chairman and deputy chairman of the Leningrad Regional Trade Union Council as well as the directors of several major Leningrad factories.[48] More than one-quarter of all primary Communist Party committees in Leningrad probably changed secretaries with perhaps as many as 2,000 other officials losing their jobs as well.[49] Beyond Leningrad, L. N. Efremov, First Secretary of the Gor'kii Regional Party Committee, would later report that numbers of leading Gor'kii Communists also fell victim of the "provocational Leningrad Affair, fabricated by Malenkov."[50]

[47]Salisbury, *The 900 Days*, pp. 578-579; *Ocherki istorii Leningrada*, vol. 6, pp. 43-44; and Robert Conquest, *Power and Policy in the USSR*, New York, 1967, pp. 96-97. Werner Hahn reports that the main victims of the purge were probably executed in September and October 1950 (Hahn, *Postwar Soviet Politics*, p. 122).

[48]Conquest, *Power and Policy*, pp. 96-97; Salisbury, *The 900 Days*, pp. 578-579.

[49]In September 1952, City Party Committee Secretary A. I. Alekseev indicated to a city party conference that 1,213 officials had been appointed in recent months to primary party posts. Later, Alekseev noted that there were 4,230 such primary party organizations ("Doklad sekretaria Leningradskogo gorodskogo komiteta VKP(b) tov. A. I. Alekseeva," *Leningradskaia pravda*, September 23, 1952, pp. 2-3). At the subsequent regional party conference, Regional Party First Secretary V. M. Andrianov referred to 2,000 new officers having been appointed during his brief tenure in Leningrad, a figure repeated by Regional Party Second Secretary Frol Kozlov at the Nineteenth Party Congress a month later ("Doklad tov. Andrianova," September 28, 1952; "Rech' tov. Kozlova," October 16, 1952).

[50]These remarks were contained in Efremov's report to the Twenty-Second Party Congress in 1961, "Rech' tovarishcha L. N. Efremova," *Pravda*, October 22, 1961, p. 3. Zhdanov had been First Secretary in Nizhnii Novgorod (now Gor'kii) prior to moving to Leningrad.

The purges of the Leningrad Affair consumed a local political elite that had emerged under the sponsorship of Sergei Kirov during the late 1920s and early 1930s. Throughout the 900-day blockade of the city by German and Finnish forces, Leningrad's political leaders remained cut off from the world outside, developing a cohesion reinforced by intense isolation and compulsory cooperation. They also came to identify with the population of the city to a degree not readily apparent during the chaotic years of the initial five-year plans.

Once the Red Army broke the German blockade, Leningrad filled with a new population fleeing a war-ravaged countryside. The city's Communist Party was reconstituted by members who had not belonged to the party when the war began. In a relatively short period, the local political elite once again found itself shut off from both the population and the Communist Party organization it nominally led. As a result, Leningrad's political institutions were particularly vulnerable to decapitation from above.

When Sergei Kirov assumed control of the Leningrad Party in 1926 he began to encourage the promotion of inexperienced activists within the party. Many among these young men and women perished during the purges of the late 1930s. Nonetheless, others survived to control local Party and municipal institutions during those same purges, following Kirov's assassination on December 1, 1934. They were directing the city's major political and economic institutions when the war broke out and they led the city through the trauma of the blockade. They also formed the core of those purged in 1948 and 1949. The career of A. A. Kuznetsov best illustrates the fate of this cohort.

Aleksei Aleksandrovich Kuznetsov was born in the revolutionary year of 1905 to a worker's family living near Novgorod.[51] He went to work in a local saw mill at the age of fourteen. Within three years, he had organized one of the first Young Communist League (Komsomol) cells in his region and quickly emerged as a prominent regional Komsomol activist. In 1930, Kuznetsov, now a Communist Party member and an avid supporter of the collectivization drive, moved to Leningrad to work in the Komsomol organization there. Once in Leningrad, this energetic *komsomolets* caught Kirov's eye and, under Kirov's tutelage, moved from Komsomol to party work. In 1933, Kuznetsov became First Secretary of the city's Dzerzhinskii District *(raion)* Party Committee.

[51]V. N. Bazovskii and N. D. Shumilov, *Samoe dorogoe. Dokumental'noe povestvovanie ob A. A. Kuznetsove*, Moscow, 1982.

The Leningrad Affair   317

Kirov's assassination in December 1934, did not stall Kuznetsov's upward climb. In 1938, he became Second Secretary of the Leningrad City Party Committee under Zhdanov. Kuznetsov also assumed responsibility for local defense industries. This last assignment took on particular significance during the Winter War with Finland.[52]

On June 21, 1941, the Germans invaded the Soviet Union. The central government in Moscow ceased to function as the result of confusion and indecision at the highest levels of Soviet administration. Zhdanov, for his part, was caught vacationing on the Black Sea. The task of mobilizing the Soviet Union's second largest city and industrial center thus fell to Kuznetsov. He quickly gained recognition for his recruitment efforts on behalf of the Red Army as well as for his frequent visits with the troops and besieged Leningrad workers.[53] Kuznetsov served throughout the war on the Leningrad Defense Committee together with Zhdanov, Regional Party Secretary T. F. Shtykov, Chairman of the Regional Soviet N. V. Solov'ev, Chairman of the City Soviet P. S. Popkov, and late in the war, Regional Party Secretary M. N. Nikitin (who was in charge of the region's partisan movement) and City Party Committee Secretary Ia. F. Kapustin.[54] Together with the city's military commanders, this handful of Party leaders organized the defense of the city throughout the 900-day German-Finnish blockade. They were remarkably young leaders, having advanced rapidly through Leningrad Party ranks during the 1930s. By 1950, with very few exceptions (such as Shtykov, who had become Soviet Ambassador to North Korea in 1948), they would all be dead.

Kuznetsov became First Secretary of the Leningrad Regional and City Party Committees in January 1945, as Zhdanov moved to Moscow. Then, in March 1946, Kuznetsov joined Zhdanov on the Secretariat and moved to Moscow where he accepted oversight responsibilities for party personnel policy, the military and police.[55] Just barely past his forty-first birthday, Kuznetsov had climbed to the pinnacle of the Soviet political

[52]"XVIII Vsesoiuznaia konferentsiia VKP(b). Rech' tov. Kuznetsova (Leningrad)," *Leningradskaia pravda*, February 18, 1941, p. 2.

[53]Kuznetsov's visits with the troops are the subject of considerable attention in later efforts to rehabilitate his reputation. For example, in the 1974-1975 film series "Blokada" this aspect of his wartime activities is highlighted. As fate would have it, G. V. Romanov, Regional Party First Secretary from 1970 until 1983, Politburo Member and currently a member of the Central Committee's Secretariat, was probably among a group of soldiers addressed by Kuznetsov as they headed out to battle (Bazovskii and Shumilov, *Samoe dorogoe*, p. 57).

[54]Dzeniskevich, *Nepokrennyi Leningrad*, pp. 30-36; N. R. Ivanov, V. S. Lekhnovich, K. A. Nikitin, *V osazhdennom Leningrade*, Leningrad, 1969, pp. 3-6; Iu. P. Petrov, *Partizanskoe dvizhenie v Leningradskoi oblasti, 1941-1944*, Leningrad, 1973.

[55]Bazovskii and Shumilov, *Samoe dorogoe*, pp. 237-250; Hahn, *Postwar Soviet Politics*, pp. 122-129.

system.

Aleksei Kuznetsov's rise and fall represents the fate of a remarkable group of Leningrad political leaders. As individuals, many proved to be exceptionally successful; aside from Kuznetsov, this generation of Leningrad leaders included a future head of the State Planning Committee—N. A. Voznesenskii, a future RSFSR Minister of Education—A. A. Voznesenskii, a future Premier of the USSR—A. N. Kosygin, as well as a large number of ambassadors, generals, and other high-ranking party and state officials. Western travellers visiting Leningrad soon after German and Finnish armies had withdrawn from the city's edge found these officials to be gracious and proud hosts who were delighted to have opportunities to meet with foreigners.[56] Yugoslav Communist Milovan Djilas would later report that Leningrad's postwar leaders "were all, to a man, simple, educated, hard-working people who had taken on their shoulders and still bore in their hearts the tragic greatness of the city. But they lived lonely lives and were glad to meet men from another clime and culture."[57]

Having survived the purges and the war, this new elite came of age only to fall victim in the Leningrad Affair. Subsequent Leningrad leaders may have been present in the city during the late 1940s; for the most part, however, the Leningrad elite of the 1960s and 1970s did not enter active political life until after the Leningrad Affair had run its course. Those purges, then, mark a sharp demarcation in the city's political history.

The Provincialization of Leningrad

The conventional explanation of the Leningrad Affair interprets the events of 1948 and 1949 as a consequence of Zhdanov's protracted struggle for power with Malenkov. Robert Conquest, for example, observes that the one uncontestable outcome of the Affair was for Zhdanov's men to be replaced by Malenkov's.[58] The few Soviet accounts of the Leningrad purges that have come to light are not strikingly different from that offered by Conquest.

During the Twenty-Second Party Congress in 1961, the Leningrad Affair served as a major theme of attacks on the "Anti-Party Group" (notably, Malenkov, V. M. Molotov, and L. M. Kaganovich). Leningrad Regional Party First Secretary I. V. Spiridonov accused the three and K. E. Voroshilov of complicity in the mass repressions of Leningrad party and governmental personnel.[59] N. M. Shvernik, then

[56]Werth, *Leningrad*; White, *Report on the Russians,* pp. 106-109.
[57]Milovan Djilas, *Conversations with Stalin,* translated by Michael B. Petrovich, New York, 1962, p. 168.
[58]Conquest, *Power and Policy,* pp. 97-111.

The Leningrad Affair   319

Chairman of the Party Control Commission, confirmed Spiridonov's interpretation,[59] as did KGB Chairman A. N. Shelepin.[61] Shelepin even went further than Spiridonov by implicating Molotov and Kaganovich in the Kirov assassination as well. The attack on the perpetrators of the Leningrad Affair and the Kirov assassination ended with a poignant appeal by Leningrad Old Bolshevik D. A. Lazurkina to remove Stalin's body from the Lenin Mausoleum on Red Square.[62]

In his memoirs, Nikita Khrushchev similarly identified Malenkov as the chief beneficiary of the Leningrad Affair.[63] Khrushchev suggests that NKVD Chief Beria and his deputy V. A. Abakumov were motivated by resentment of A. A. Kuznetsov's supervision of the police when Kuznetsov moved from Leningrad to serve as a member of the Central Committee's Secretariat. Khrushchev also records an ill-defined distrust of Leningrad as a city on the part of Stalin, Malenkov, Beria, and Abakumov. Harrison Salisbury emphasizes this anti-Leningrad sentiment in his account of the affair by arguing that, while the Malenkov-Zhdanov rivalry undoubtedly played a central role, such competition does not explain the extent of the purges.[64] Salisbury also notes a charge that the Leningrad Party sought to establish a new RSFSR government centered in Leningrad. The Leningrad Affair thus contributes to the city's further provincialization by undermining plans to upgrade the city's status. Salisbury views the campaign against Zhdanov's clients as a mechanism devised by Malenkov and Beria, in close collaboration with Stalin and his aide A. N. Poskrebyshev, to smash the Leningrad Party organization and to destroy the city's prestige once and for all.

Recently, western analysts have identified policy issues within the personal struggles of the period. For example, Werner Hahn identifies multiple and linked areas of policy concern that might underlie the purges of 1948 and 1949: the nature of Soviet relations with the West, the possibility of a reorientation of the postwar Soviet economy towards consumer industries, and the distribution of a majority of reconstruction funds to front-line regions.[65] The precise role any one of these issues played in the Leningrad Affair is likely to remain uncertain. Nevertheless, one should note that Leningraders' ultimately

---

[59]"Rech' tovarishcha I. V. Spiridonova," *Pravda*, October 20, 1961, p. 4.

[60]"Rech' tovarishcha N. M. Shvernika," *Pravda*, October 26, 1961, pp. 3-4. Shvernik had served briefly as Leningrad Regional Party Second Secretary in 1925 and 1926.

[61]"Rech' tovarishcha A. N. Shelepina," *Pravda*, October 27, 1961, p. 10.

[62]"Rech' tovarishcha D. A. Lazurkinoi," *Pravda*, October 31, 1961, p. 2.

[63]N. S. Khrushchev, *Khrushchev Remembers*, translated by Strobe Talbott, Boston, 1970, pp. 247-258.

[64]Salisbury, *The 900 Days*, pp. 577-583.

[65]Hahn, *Postwar Soviet Politics*, pp. 19-66.

320   *The Russian Review*

unsuccessful plans for a postwar renaissance of their city were tied to
improved relations with the West, a reorientation of the economy
towards consumer-goods production and a disproportionate claim to
postwar reconstruction funds.[66] In this respect Leningrad's resurgence
became inexorably linked to Moscow's leadership struggles in a particularly explosive blend. The final result of this fusion of local and
national politics ultimately proved the undoing not only of several
senior Leningrad political officials but also of their dreams for a revitalized Leningrad. Political as well as social forces at work throughout the
Soviet Union took on unique significance within the Leningrad environment, dashing efforts to stave off the provincialization of a former
world center.

[66]Werth, *Leningrad*, pp. 166-167. These themes were also evident in the speeches during the period of such Leningrad figures as City Party Committee Second Secretary
Kapustin (Ia. Kapustin, "Voprosy vosstanovleniia i razvitiia promyshlennosti Len-
ingrada."); Central Committee Secretary Zhdanov (A. A. Zhdanov, "Na predvybornom
sobranii izbiratelei Volodarskogo izbiratel'nogo okruga g. Leningrada. 6 fevralia 1946 g.,"
Pravda, February 8, 1946, pp. 3-4 and *Partiinoe stroitel'stvo*, 1946, no. 3, pp. 47-53); and
Regional and City Party First Secretary Kuznetsov (A. A. Kuznetsov, "O zadachakh
Leningradskoi partiinoi organizatsii v sviazi s vyborami v Verkhovnyi sovet Soiuza SSR,"
Leningradskaia pravda, December 8, 1945, pp. 2-3).

[14]

The Standard of Living of Soviet Industrial Workers in the Immediate Postwar Period, 1945–1948

DONALD FILTZER

Regime and society at the end of World War II: some analytical premises

THERE IS LITTLE NEED TO RECOUNT THE DEVASTATION which the Soviet Union suffered during World War II. What are less straightforward are the political problems which the postwar period presented to the Stalinist leadership.[1] During the 1930s the social relations of the Stalinist system—the Soviet 'mode of production'—had acquired their definitive form. However tumultuous and traumatic this process had been, by the time of the German invasion of the USSR in June 1941 the Stalinist system had taken on a stable and reproducible—albeit inherently crisis-ridden—form. This nascent stability was badly shattered by the war, and at the war's end it was by no means clear to the leadership how it was to reconstruct the power relations of the system. This was not just a question of repairing the extraordinary damage caused by the fighting. Society had undergone profound changes. Tens of millions had died and tens of millions more had been displaced, either as refugees or evacuees. Politically, the centralisation of decision making at the top of the system was accompanied by a parallel decentralisation to local authorities, and in fact—as is inevitable in war time—to millions of individuals.[2] There was equally the problem of popular expectations. Many of the soldiers who had fought at the front—the so-called *frontoviki*—had marched outside the borders of the USSR, where they saw that even the most devastated parts of Eastern and Central Europe were vastly more prosperous than what they had experienced at home. They returned with contradictory views and aspirations: probably most of them associated the profound patriotism generated by their war-time experiences with a loyalty to Stalin, if not to the Soviet regime as an institution; but many also returned with the idea that life would now become easier and that the regime would not attempt to reimpose the harsh police controls of pre-1941. As one interviewee told us, the returning soldiers approached the tasks of reconstruction 'with enthusiasm, but it was a joyless enthusiasm ... We did everything that we had to do, but not gladly'. The general population shared this attitude, though perhaps more inchoately. People were exhausted by the war and hoped that now they would be left in peace to get on with their lives.[3]

At one level we know the answer to this story. By 1947–48 the Stalinist leadership had reasserted control over virtually all areas of politics and ideology, a process that was accompanied by an intensification of police repression, not just through renewed purges but through mass arrests of the civilian population—over half of which were for violations of labour discipline.[4] We should be clear that this was not a repeat of what had happened during the first five-year plan, when the emerging elite, in order to solidify and consolidate its dominance, had crushed widespread opposition from peasants and industrial workers. In the postwar years there is little evidence of this type of mass resistance, if we leave aside problems of banditry in the newly occupied territories of Western Ukraine and the Baltic states. Yet in 1945, and for most of 1946, the regime's relationship with society was marked by political prevarication and uncertainty over how to react to different social groups.

During the first five-year plan the collapse of the standard of living had played a vital role in subduing popular opposition by atomising the working class and placing the struggle for survival at the centre of people's daily activity. A similar phenomenon occurred in the postwar years. A combination of harvest failure and deliberate regime policy in 1946 and 1947 dashed hopes of improvement and plunged the mass of the population into a renewed desperate struggle for survival. This had two, contradictory effects. At one level, the political passivity which the crisis generated among the population helped the elite to re-secure its domination. In the longer term, however, the depth and severity of the hardship helped solidify that profound popular demoralisation which characterised so-called 'late Stalinism' and which rendered the Soviet system virtually impervious to subsequent attempts at political and social reform.

The regime's attack on the agricultural population in these years has received modest but sufficient attention from historians, so that the story is relatively well known.[5] What is less well known is what happened to industrial workers. The problem goes far beyond that of living standards and 'material provision'. The collapse of agriculture, in particular the famine of 1946–47, set in motion further large-scale population movements which substantially influenced the social composition of the industrial workforce. Within industry and construction chronic poverty provoked high levels of labour turnover, especially among younger workers, which threatened production plans—despite draconian penalties which made so-called 'wilful' job-changing a criminal offence punishable by sentence to a labour camp.[6] More intangibly, it deepened popular alienation from the system. People survived and the struggle for survival eased palpably after 1948. But their expectations were low: if you talk to former Soviet citizens who remember the postwar years they will almost invariably tell you that their greatest aspiration was merely that each year would be a little bit better than the year before. They simply gave up thinking about politics; most, at least in the towns, even wept when Stalin died. But the lack of positive enthusiasm and involvement had already become a brake on the system's further development, a fact which explains the advocacy of 'reform' by virtually all of Stalin's would-be successors.[7] In this sense the problem of living standards is intimately connected with a whole range of other issues which stamped working-class life: working conditions; work discipline; work relations inside the enterprise; political attitudes and political culture; and larger questions such as crime and public health. This article, therefore, is but a small initial contribution to an all-sided analysis of the social history of this period which has still to be written.

SOVIET WORKERS' STANDARD OF LIVING 1945–1948   1015

TABLE 1

REAL WAGES OF WORKERS AND 'EMPLOYEES' IN THE NATIONAL ECONOMY AND REAL PER CAPITA INCOME
OF WORKERS' FAMILIES 1940–1953

	Cost of living index, Moscow, 1940 = 100	Money wages index, all workers and employees, national economy 1940 = 100	Real wages index (col. 3 divided by col. 2), workers and employees, 1940 = 100	Real wage index, workers and employees, 1946 = 100	Real per capita family income, workers, 1946 = 100
1946 (prior to 16 September)	499.5	143.5	28.7	–	–
1947 (prior to 16 December)	439.9	172.0	39.1	136.2	124.4
1948	219.8	181.9	82.7	288.2	n/d
1949	186.8	187.4	100.3	349.5	n/d
1950	154.8	193.1	124.7	434.5	336.2
1951	141.0	199.0	141.1	491.6	n/d
1952	132.3	203.0	153.4	534.5	421.6 (unskilled) 490.6 (skilled)
1953	118.2	212.7	180.0	627.2	n/d

Sources: Calculated from Eugene Zaleski, *Stalinist Planning for Economic Growth, 1933–1952* (London, 1980), pp. 458–459, 535, 668–669; RGAE, f. 1562 (TsSU), op. 15, d. 2129, l. 80 (1946); d. 2475, l. 11 (1947); d. 3086, l. 172, 172ob. (1950); op. 26, d. 25, l. 116, 116ob., 118, 118ob. (1952).

The standard of living: basic contours

It is, of course, difficult to make precise measurements of the standard of living given the uncertain reliability of Soviet data. Nevertheless, we can trace the pattern of recovery of postwar living standards among the non-agricultural population by looking at real wages and family incomes, on the one hand, and the production and availability of basic foods and consumer items, on the other. Both show the same general trend: the crisis of living standards inherited from the war persisted until 1948, after which there was fairly rapid progress back to the levels of 1940. To this end we have constructed two tables, both based on existing Western calculations of real wages and physical output.

Table 1 gives two measures of real income. It uses Zaleski's data for money wages and the Moscow cost of living index to construct real wages indices for all workers and 'employees' for the years 1946–53, taking 1940 and 1946 as base years. It also uses family budget surveys carried out by the Central Statistical Administration to calculate (again using Zaleski's Moscow cost of living index) real income *per household member* for workers' families, taking the base year as 1946. In interpreting this table two dates are crucial. On 16 September 1946 the regime decreed a massive increase in ration prices, accompanied by a reduction of prices in state-run commercial shops and a cut in the number of people allowed access to the rationing system. We discuss this in detail in the next section. In December 1947 the regime abolished rationing and imposed a currency reform which effectively liquidated cash reserves held by the peasantry. Where urban workers were concerned the decree marked a

1016   DONALD FILTZER

sharp turn in pricing policy, for in each year after that the state lowered official prices, more as a political gesture than as a reflection of economic progress.[8]

Even allowing for the impreciseness of these figures (for example, using the Moscow cost of living index as indicative of the country as a whole), the overall movement of wages and incomes would seem to be clear. The postwar crisis began to lift in 1948, and by 1949 the average non-agricultural household had recovered its purchasing power of 1940. This would have entitled it to an extremely spartan lifestyle, but one which allowed it to survive. By 1953 purchasing power was nearly double that of the pre-war period.[9] However, some important qualifications are in order. Taking 1940 as the point of comparison creates a somewhat false picture of the well-being of the average worker or clerical employee. For real wages in 1940 were already some 5% to 10% below their level of 1937, and a full 25% to 40% below 1928, the last year of NEP.[10] Table 1 very probably also overestimates the sudden jump in real wages recorded in 1948, as well as the extent of improvement during the early 1950s: Chapman, for example, calculated real wages in 1948 at just 75–80% of 1940, rising to 120–125% by 1952.[11] Similarly, if we look at average real income per household member, which in many ways is a better measure of a family's available resources, the recovery lagged significantly behind that of real wages, even for skilled workers.

The real difficulty, however, is in the method of analysis per se. According to Zaleski's figures, the price index fell—and not insubstantially—following the price rises of 16 September 1946, almost certainly because the rise in ration prices was offset by a fall in commercial prices in state shops (for many items *kolkhoz* market prices also fell). But this does not mean that workers had greater access to food. For most workers, as we shall see, the drop in commercial and free market prices was of little significance, since they still could not afford them. The rise in ration prices, on the other hand, genuinely deprived people of food, first, because food disappeared from the shelves, secondly, because a large number of workers and their dependents lost their ration entitlements, and thirdly, because many could now afford less food at the new higher prices. In short, the cost of living index suggests a picture exactly the reverse of what actually happened, at least up until 1948. Family budgets have the same drawback. If we look at prices before the increases of September 1946, it would appear that the average family had little difficulty feeding itself. The average person had available about eight rubles a day for food.[12] Bread cost just over one ruble a kilogram; potatoes less than a ruble; and even meat was in theory accessible, at 14 rubles per kilo. Clothes, on the other hand, were out of reach.[13] But even before the price increases this exaggerates the true picture: many workers had to take their meals in factory dining rooms, where prices were relatively expensive—even before September 1946 they could cost almost as much as the daily wage of the low-paid; and because most basic foods other than bread were unavailable on rationing, families had to go to the *kolkboz* markets to supplement their diets.

To this extent the income data, while more or less accurately portraying the long-term improvement of living standards between 1946 and 1952, obscure the very real hardship that hit the country during 1946 and 1947. The depth of this crisis can be gauged by looking at the actual supply of basic goods available to the population. Table 2 shows average annual per capita production for 1940 and the entire postwar period up to 1952.

SOVIET WORKERS' STANDARD OF LIVING 1945–1948   1017

TABLE 2
AVERAGE PER CAPITA ANNUAL PRODUCTION OF SELECTED CONSUMPTION ITEMS, 1940–1952

	1940	1945	1946	1947	1948	1949	1950	1951	1952
Cotton fabrics (metres)	20.1	9.70	11.18	14.68	17.90	20.17	21.47	25.80	26.83
Woollen fabrics (metres)	0.61	0.32	0.42	0.35	0.72	0.83	0.85	0.95	1.01
Knitted underwear (pieces)	0.63	0.15	0.27	0.35	0.48	0.66	0.82	1.07	1.25
Hosiery (pairs)	2.46	0.54	0.79	1.14	1.60	2.10	2.60	3.23	3.11
Leather shoes (pairs)	0.96	0.38	0.47	0.65	0.76	0.92	1.12	1.29	1.26
Soap (kilograms)	3.55	1.37	1.37	1.70	2.41	4.07	4.49	4.15	4.17
Meat & meat products from food industry (kilograms)	7.63	3.98	4.66	4.71	5.77	6.44	8.56	9.28	10.45
Fish catch (kilograms)	7.14	6.75	7.11	8.87	8.95	10.94	9.66	11.59	11.20
Grain, barn yield (kilogram)	485.49	283.74	232.94	380.92	381.82	393.28	447.14	425.87	490.43
Potatoes, barn yield (kilograms)	385.73	349.80	327.29	436.65	539.94	502.02	487.94	317.91	368.09
Vegetables (kilograms)	69.65	61.79	52.35	86.13	75.00	60.5	51.21	47.62	52.13
Meat & fats from agriculture (kilograms)	23.87	15.35	18.23	14.45	17.6	21.29	26.80	25.43	27.66
Milk (kilograms)	171.02	158.37	162.94	174.57	189.77	195.52	194.38	195.89	189.89
Eggs (units)	62.02	29.39	30.59	28.32	37.5	50.98	64.42	71.97	76.60

Sources: Calculated from Zaleski, pp. 578–593 (1940); 603–608 (1945); 614–633 (1946–1952).

The use of these data is equally fraught with difficulties, especially where food supplies are concerned. The figures almost certainly underestimate the availability of vegetables and potatoes, because they do not include the output of allotments held by urban residents. By the same token, officially recorded collections of grain and potatoes overstate what actually went to the population, because they do not include wastage (which was often very high), the use of grain and potatoes for animal feed and vodka (legal and illegal), exports, and the retention of seed. Yet the overall picture is accurate enough. Like the income data, the production series suggest that by 1949 and 1950 the output of essential consumer items had regained 1940 levels: this assured an extremely low standard of living, but people could survive. Prior to 1948, however, the situation was stark. In 1946 the Soviet clothing industry produced one-quarter of a piece of underwear, less than one pair of socks, and half a pair of shoes for each of its citizens. Soap was almost impossible to acquire. The diet was almost totally without protein. The grain harvest—which determined food supplies for 1947—even if fully utilised for human consumption would have allowed each Soviet citizen just 640 grams of grain a day. Animal protein was almost totally absent from the diet: meat (including fats) from all sources was sufficient for an average daily consumption of just 60 grams, plus whatever town dwellers might raise from their allotments; the fish catch—again assuming total utilisation, with no wastage and no diversion to animal feed or other uses—would have given just 20 grams a day. The only food which was in any way 'plentiful' was potatoes, although even here the drought of 1946 created a disastrous collapse of the harvest, similar to that which affected grain and vegetables. It is no accident that potato production continued to rise right through the crisis period, and was the main source of calories and nutrition, especially in the countryside, where the combination of poor harvests and high government procurements led to a chronic dearth of grain.[14]

It was a basic feature of the Soviet system that wages and prices alone did not determine access to goods and services; the essential problem was their inadequate supply. In those periods when society was pushed to the brink of survival, as it was during the early 1930s, World War II, and again in 1946–47, the elite had to ration what was available. It did this by ruthlessly curbing consumption, not of itself or of the intelligentsia, but of the workers and peasants who produced the social product. As we shall see in the rest of this article, wages and prices were a means to this end, but they were not the source of the problem.[15]

The food crisis of 1946–1948

The crisis in living standards which befell the Soviet Union in late 1946 has to be analysed from the perspective of the general problems of economic reconstruction. Even under the best of circumstances, the process of recovery would have been daunting, so great was the devastation which the war had caused. In his recent book on the Soviet economy during World War II, Mark Harrison has argued that available resources were so badly constrained that the country was unable to sustain its entire civilian population. Without substantial outside assistance, such as that eventually provided by the Allies' lend-lease programme, mass death from starvation was unavoidable, not just in Leningrad, which had been under a three-year seige, but in

SOVIET WORKERS' STANDARD OF LIVING 1945–1948   1019

the hinterlands untouched by combat.[16] For those who survived life was extraordinarily difficult. An urban worker subsisted mainly on bread, potatoes and groats. Some had access to luxuries on the *kolkhoz* market, such as milk, butter or meat, but for most workers' families these foods were too expensive. After the war many workers saw their wages actually fall, since working hours were reduced and they lost the *in natura* payments in vodka, bread or tobacco which during the war they had been able to convert into cash.[17]

Wages, of course, were only one determinant of one's ability to survive. Availability of food and consumer goods through the rationing system, housing, transport, public utilities and public health all were vital. In most localities the situation was truly dire. Just how dire we can surmise from an internal party report on the city of Saratov in early 1946. This is significant, because Saratov had not been occupied by the Germans and no fighting took place there. Thus we are not talking about a Stalingrad or a Kiev, but about a city representative of the Soviet heartland.

Saratov's population was chronically short of food. Its local trading network had on hand reserves of basic goods like groats, meat and salt, but had not put them into distribution. People were routinely unable to redeem their ration cards, even for potatoes and bread. The milk shortage was acute: creches and paediatric clinics were receiving milk only two or three times a month; even pregnant women and nursing mothers could not obtain any. The situation was equally severe with non-food items. Firewood—the main source of domestic fuel—was in short supply. Nor was there enough fuel to heat the city's hospitals, clinics or children's homes. Four of the city's 12 public baths were out of service, and this was creating a serious public health problem. Drinking water came mainly from stand pipes, and over a quarter of them did not work, forcing affected residents to walk to other neighbourhoods to bring back water. More ominously, the drinking water was untreated. Electricity supplies were also irregular: the city's grid could not supply both industry and domestic consumers at the same time, and in fact many factories were drawing power from low-voltage grids designed for domestic use, since they did not have their own substations. 'Many' workers had to walk 'tens of kilometres' to and from work, because no public transport was available. New consumer goods were almost impossible to buy, and to get old clothing or shoes repaired in local workshops could take from one to eight months.[18]

The situation in Saratov was by no means exceptional.[19] Some areas of the country (Tomsk and Tatariya) continued to experience extreme malnutrition or even famine, even before the disastrous harvest of autumn 1946.[20] Housing, as we discuss in a later section, was a problem everywhere, and not just in cities which had suffered war damage. Housing conditions had been atrocious before the war, and with the war became appreciably worse, as resources were diverted away from essential maintenance and new construction, and the problems of evacuation and movement into the towns intensified pressure on what was now a much smaller housing stock.

Whatever plans the regime may have had to accelerate reconstruction were almost irreparably disrupted by the 1946 harvest failure and the ensuing famine. In 1946 the grain harvest sank to 39.6 million tons: in 1940 it had been 95.5 million and in 1945 47.3 million; it was to rise back to 65.9 million tons in 1947. There was correspondingly a dramatic fall during 1947 in the amount of grain available for distribution to collective farmers, and in the amount of bread and flour which could be sold to those entitled to rations. In 1940 the country had milled 28.8 million tons of flour. This fell to a war-time low of 13 million tons in 1943, after which it climbed to 14.6 million in 1945 and 16.4 million in 1946. But in 1947 it sank back to 14 million tons, which now had to cover a larger urban population than in 1940.[21] As we saw in Table 2, the potato crop was similarly hit. The result was a famine, which began in the winter of 1946/47, and whose effects were to extend well into 1948.

Thanks to the recent study of V. F. Zima, we now know a great deal about the famine's impact on Soviet society, in particular the countryside.[22] The main areas affected were Ukraine and Moldavia: an MVD report from March 1947 estimated that already nearly half a million people were suffering from acute malnutrition (*alimentarnaya distrofiya*) in Ukraine alone.[23] Zima estimates that the combination of starvation and famine-related disease led to one million deaths.[24] These, of course, were not its only effects: perhaps five million people fled the affected regions. There were terrible epidemics of typhus and gastrointestinal ailments. And as we shall see below, there was chronic malnutrition among industrial workers.[25]

The famine and the regime's reaction to it help explain the rise in ration prices decreed in September 1946. Alec Nove, in an early edition of his *Economic History of the USSR*, attributed the price changes to a desire to eliminate some of the more glaring disparities between ration and commercial prices, given that the government's primary aim of an early abolition of rationing had proved impossible.[26] Zaleski, following the Soviet historian A. V. Lyubimov, recognised that the policy was clearly linked to the bad harvest of 1946, and was accompanied by a severe cutback in the number of people entitled to ration cards.[27]

Thus the price rises of 16 September were almost immediately followed by an Order of the USSR Ministry of Trade sharply curtailing ration privileges.[28] These should be seen as part of a single policy. The impact of the price rises can be seen from Table 3.

As we can see, the increases in basic food items, especially bread, were dramatic. To help compensate for the price increase workers were awarded a so-called bread supplement equal to 20% of basic wage rates. Not all workers, however, were entitled to receive it. At the Urals aluminium factory, for example, only 51% of workers and 41% of ITR were covered. Among the excluded trades were maintenance fitters in key shops, and the discontent this provoked amongst them was of serious concern to the plant's management.[29]

The regime had been planning a 'reform' of the rationing system since at least the summer of 1946. On 2 September the Politburo set up a commission to investigate the rationing and distribution system and to report back within two months. The fact that decisive measures were taken within just two weeks of this decision suggests that they had been planned well before that, and that the commission's report, when it finally appeared, was intended to do little more than provide an after-the-fact rationale for the policy.[30]

Prior to 27 September the rationing system had provided for 87.5 million people, compared with 77 million in January 1945. This total was made up of three 'contingents': an urban contingent of 58.6 million; a rural contingent of 27.6 million; and those in 'institutions under state supply' (that is, children's homes, infants' homes

SOVIET WORKERS' STANDARD OF LIVING 1945–1948   1021

TABLE 3
RATION AND STATE COMMERCIAL PRICES, 1946–1947

	Ration price: 15 September 1946	Commercial price: 15 September 1946	Ration price: 16 September 1946	Commercial price: 16 September 1946
Rye bread (kilogram)	1.10	10.00	3.40	7.50
Pasta products (kilogram)	5.00		15.50	
Potatoes (kilogram)	0.90	27.00	0.90	24.00
Beef (kilogram)	14.00	140.00	30.00	90.00
Pork (kilogram)	14.00	300.00	34.00	130.00
Lamb (kilogram)	14.00		34.00	
Cheese (kilogram)	32.50	215.00	70.00	170.00
Eggs (10)		100.00		50.00
Sugar (lump) (kilogram)	5.50	170.00	15.00	70.00
Milk (litre)	3.50	40.00	8.00	20.00
Vodka (litre)	120.00	130.00	n/a	120.00
Cigarettes (25)	6.00	30.00	n/a	27.00
Men's wool suit	1,130.00	3,500.00	800.00	3,000.00
Women's cotton dress	62.50		77.00	
Men's winter overcoat	725.00	7,000.00	1,000.00	5,050.00
Men's leather shoes	280.00		270.00	
Men's cotton socks (pair)	5.00	62.00	8.25	45.00
Women's cotton stockings (pair)		150.00		100.00
Household soap (kilogram)	3.10	60.00	13.00	54.00

Notes:
(a) Ration prices are All-Union prices.
(b) Commercial prices are for Moscow.
(c) *Kolkhoz* prices are not given.
Source: Zaleski, pp. 688–696.

and homes for the disabled and elderly), who totalled 1.3 million. Members of collective farms had never been included in the system, under the pretext that they would feed themselves from their labour-day income and their private plots.[31]

Of the 87.5 million people receiving rations, 26 472 000, or 30%, were workers and technical personnel (ITR). Their allowances were determined by a truly baroque system of gradations, depending on the importance of the enterprise within which they worked and/or the job they performed. A full 60%—just under 16 million people—received a mere 500 to 600 grams per day, including 9 790 000 in the very lowest category (production workers in low-priority industries, plus workers and ITR in service or ancillary shops irrespective of their sector). Production workers in the most important defence enterprises, together with students in the labour reserve vocational training schools (3 798 200 in all) received 700 grams. At the pinnacle of this pyramid of 'privilege' were underground workers in ore and coal mining; production workers labouring under hazardous conditions; and workers in the fishing industry who achieved high norm fulfilment: this 'elite' of just over 2.2 million people was entitled to a daily allowance of between 1 and 1.2 kilograms of bread—more than twice the basic ration.[32]

The Politburo commission claimed that enterprises and agencies had been systematically 'abusing' this system, primarily by inflating claims for ration cards and illegally issuing additional ration cards for special entitlements—for example, additional hot meals in dining rooms.[33] However tendentious such claims may have been,

1022   DONALD FILTZER

it is easy to believe that in substance the charges were correct: enterprise managers were clearly going to do what they could to improve conditions for workers in key trades, both to dampen down discontent and to stem turnover. Moreover, the minute gradations by which the regime had attempted to differentiate between one group of workers and the next almost certainly made such manipulation easier.

Whatever the factual basis behind such charges of 'abuse', for the most part the Politburo's claim was just political posturing. The Order of 27 September removed 27.5 million people from the rationing system, 23.6 million of whom (87%) were from the rural contingent. Just over 3.4 million were from the urban contingent (mainly workers' dependents); and about half a million were residents in state-run homes for children, the elderly and the disabled.[34] In addition, about 20.5 million people lost supplemental bread rations to which they had previously been entitled. The largest groups affected by this latter provision were 7.7 million school students in towns and workers' settlements, who had previously received an extra 50 grams of bread on school days. This came on top of a 100-gram per day cut in their general bread ration, so that they were now receiving 300 grams instead of 450. Other major groups hit by the reductions were 5.8 million workers, who lost 100 grams which they had received with second hot meals; 1.8 million workers who had received an additional 100 grams of bread for overfulfilling their norms; 513 700 coal miners who had received 100–200 grams of bread each day with their breakfast; some three million managerial personnel who had been entitled to supplemental bread rations under various regulations; and (perhaps surprisingly) 580 300 *oblast'* and district soviet or party officials, who had previously been given an extra 200 grams of bread with dinner.[35]

The major casualties of the cut in the rural contingent were those engaged in farming, primarily state farm workers. Some of those affected were workers on state livestock farms who simply had no possibility of growing their own food, and whose pay was too low to allow them to buy food on the open market. Approximately 1.5 million workers and family members had lost their ration privileges in this sector alone. The Ministry of Livestock Breeding was concerned because farmers and herdsmen were fleeing the farms to seek jobs in industry or even to go to collective farms.[36] The Ministry of the River Fleet filed a similar petition: the fleet's state and enterprise farms were unable to feed their own workers, and many were in danger of shutting down, since without food they would not be able to hold workers in their jobs.[37] But fears of labour shortages were not confined to the state farms. Industries as diverse as the timber workings of Sverdlovsk *oblast'* and the factories of Leningrad city complained that without ration entitlements they would not be able to recruit enough workers.[38]

Industrial workers were also caught up in the net, either because their dependents no longer received bread rations or because they lived in rural locales and were assumed to be now able to feed themselves through a private plot. The central authorities were virtually inundated with telegrams from local party and soviet officials begging to have their ration quotas increased for these workers and their families. Most complaints concerned industrial workers whose enterprises either were located in rural areas or had housed them outside the towns because of the dire housing shortage. Typical of these was a letter from the party organiser at the Urals

Aluminium factory, which in October 1946 had lost 40% of its bread entitlement:

> At present those workers at the factory and its mines living in flats in rural areas without their own plots of land find themselves in extremely difficult circumstances, as a result of the fact that their children and dependents are deprived of ration cards for bread, and the factory has no way to rehouse them in its workers' settlements because of the severe shortage of accommodation. As a result, among the families in this group of workers illnesses (acute malnutrition [*distrofiya*]) have appeared. The workers at our factory who live in rural areas do so not of their own [free] will, but were relocated there involuntarily because of the lack of housing at the factory. The majority of them are skilled workers, who have been working at the factory for three years or more.

The request for additional ration cards was refused.[39]

According to V. Kuznetsov, chairman of VTsSPS, the central trade union council, the dependents of workers on the railways and in coal mining, ore mining, weapons factories and textile mills had all been cut from the ration lists because they lived in rural areas. In some cases the numbers were relatively small, for example, 80 experienced workers at the agricultural equipment factory in the Moscow suburb of Lyubertsy. But in other enterprises the suffering was on a massive scale: the Tulaugol' coal mining trust lost rations for 11 300 of its miners' children and dependents.[40]

In almost all cases the requests for extra rations were either denied outright or fulfilled to an insignificant percentage of what was required, even where the requests themselves were extremely modest. There were exceptions, of course, especially when a factory or construction project was considered strategically important.[41] In the main, however, the regime's policy was pursued with firmness and ruthlessness, even where it seemed to jeopardise undertakings vital to the economy.

Bread was not the only product affected by the food crisis. Flour deliveries to bakeries and public catering establishments were cut back sharply. Lyubimov claimed that supplies of flour fell by nearly 40% during the last quarter of 1946 alone.[42] The flour shortages persisted well into 1948, nearly a year after the abolition of rationing and the worst of the famine had peaked. In August 1948 the authorities in Kemerovo complained that cities in the *oblast'* had on hand only 24 hours' supply of flour and no groats whatsoever. Similar complaints were made by officials in Molotov (Perm), Voronezh and Irkutsk *oblasti* in September.[43]

For those workers who lost their access to rations, either for themselves or for their families, the situation was indeed dire. But these were not the majority of workers. Nonetheless, for the rest the simultaneous cutback in supplies and the increase in prices caused severe hardship. The impact of the price rises was felt immediately in factory dining rooms, where costs shot up beyond the reach of many workers. The numbers of workers taking meals at work fell dramatically, especially during the first months after the increases. Where possible, managers tried to compensate by substituting cheaper foods, such as vegetables, or by having the factory absorb the extra costs. Workers themselves dictated the trend by refraining from more expensive meat and groats dishes and giving up desserts.[44] It is interesting that while the number of factory meals was declining, the better off section of Soviet society enjoyed something of a windfall, thanks to the fall in commercial prices. Restaurants in

Sverdlovsk saw business increase dramatically because of the fall in the commercial price of meat, so much so, in fact, that at one tea room the cost of a meal was now competitive with what we may assume was a far less appetising meal at a typical factory canteen.[45]

Probably no group of workers was more catastrophically affected by these developments than young workers, in particular those in their late teens who had entered employment after completing training in a labour reserve school. The story of young workers in this period is a complex one, and is crucial to understanding not just the social history of the late Stalin years but the difficulties faced by the Khrushchev leadership in its attempts to restructure the industrial labour process. The deaths of so many men of working age during World War II meant that young, first-time entrants made up a disproportionately large share of the labour force. Yet the conditions they encountered were truly appalling: low wages, neglect or even outright abuse by enterprise management, and terrible working and housing conditions. The response of many was simply to flee the factories: in some branches of the economy it was not uncommon for the equivalent of an entire year's new recruits to leave their enterprise, either illegally or under various pretexts which earned the legal sanction of management.[46]

The low wages of young workers were due not simply to their inexperience and lack of seniority. It was common for managers to put younger workers on low-skilled labouring jobs, irrespective of the trades for which they had been trained. Sometimes this was because the training itself had been poor (a chronic, long-term problem of the labour reserve system); in other cases it was because young people were the most defenceless group, with little bargaining power, and so were given the work which more senior or more strategically placed workers would not do. And because their wage rates were so low, they suffered inordinately from stoppages and other disruptions which cut into earnings.[47] The result was that young workers routinely earned about half the average wage in their particular industry, and often much less. For example, the average monthly wage in iron and steel in December 1946 was approximately 840 rubles; yet in spring 1948—when the average wage would have been higher—young auxiliary workers at a number of iron and steel works were struggling to earn half that amount, and many earned less than 200 rubles.[48] It was the same in shipbuilding, where, at the end of 1947, young production workers earned no more than two-thirds—and often much less—of what the average metalworker had earned at the end of 1946.[49]

Almost everywhere young workers fell into a common pattern. On taking up a job their enterprise would give them a cash advance so that they could survive until their first wage packet. Yet their wages were so low that they became permanent debtors to the factory. Many earned less than the cost of meals in enterprise canteens. This was the case even before the price rises of September 1946. At one building materials factory—an industry where wages were relatively low in any case—young workers earned between 140 and 240 rubles a month, yet the cost of meals was between 240 and 300. Commenting on a similar situation at another factory in the building materials industry, a report from the parent ministry claimed that chronically low wages were driving young workers to theft.[50] As late as 1948 young workers in a coal mining construction trust in the Rostov-on-Don area were still earning less than 350 rubles a month; at one pit 60% of the young workers had debts averaging 200 rubles each—nearly two-thirds of their average monthly earnings.[51]

It is not surprising, then, that the price rises dealt a devastating blow to these workers. Many industries had special provisions—held over from the war—whereby workers under 18 could take three meals a day in the factory dining room. The food allowances were not generous—for example, in the linen industry workers on such a regime received each month only 2.3 kilograms of meat or fish and six eggs[52]—but workers could probably survive on them. After the price rises, however, workers simply could not afford to take the meals. Although this process is perhaps best documented in the textile industry,[53] it was an almost universal phenomenon. Komsomol members in military construction in Sevastopol were said to be 'starving, their wages are sufficient only to buy bread'.[54] A trade union report on the plight of young workers at the Kuibyshev heavy engineering works in Irkutsk provided one of the more succinct summaries of the situation:

> However, it is necessary to note that, from the end of 1946 and the beginning of 1947, a certain number of juveniles and young workers find themselves in exceptionally difficult conditions. The majority of them are living in a state of semi-starvation, do not have a change of linen or warm clothing, although they are the first in line for vouchers for clothing and linen issued by [their] production shops (*tsekha*). This circumstance is explained by their very low wages, itself a consequence of their insufficient skills. There are frequent cases where juveniles, after receiving their wages, remain in debt to the shop (*tsekh*). Many juveniles go days on end without seeing a hot meal, are badly exhausted, and unfit to work. Many of them do not have the bread which the shop issues them (they sell their bread ration cards and all their vouchers at the market), because they don't have the money to redeem the bread or the commodities for which they have vouchers. Recently we have found a large number of cases of acute malnutrition (*alimentarnaya distrofiya*) among juveniles and young workers.[55]

Even at the end of 1948 young construction workers in the Urals were reported to be so poor that they were selling their uniforms (*obmundirovanie*) and living in their work clothes.[56] In early 1949 the trade union committee at the Baryshnikov engineering works claimed that young workers were often so hungry that they did not have the strength to leave the dormitories and report for work.[57]

The problem of malnutrition was not confined to young workers. Almost everywhere factories found that workers were so enervated that production was being jeopardised. According to Zima, in March 1947, over 30% of Leningrad industrial workers were suffering from acute malnutrition (*alimentarnaya distrofiya*) or vitamin deficiency.[58] Trade union reports make it clear that the problem was more or less nationwide. Heavy engineering factories reported a steady rise in the number of cases of acute malnutrition over the course of 1947, and were forced to set up special dining rooms to provide high-calorie diets for those worst affected. This was far from a simple humanitarian gesture: unlike many other forms of illness, workers suffering from malnutrition had to be signed off work for anywhere from two to eight weeks, thus costing their enterprises significant amounts of lost work time.[59]

The real losses from malnutrition were even greater, since they rendered workers vulnerable to a host of other diseases, in particular gastrointestinal ailments. According to Zima, the most serious epidemic caused by the famine was typhus. Without indicating how he arrives at his figures, he estimates that the two most prevalent strains (exanthematic and European) affected a million people, of whom 5–10% died. Although the epidemic's epicentre was the countryside, the large-scale and essentially uncontrolled population movements which the famine provoked meant that it soon entered the towns.[60] In industrial centres dysentery was perhaps even more costly. At Uralmash in Sverdlovsk days lost due to gastrointestinal ailments tripled between January and September 1947.[61] More ominously, although the total number of officially reported cases of dysentery did not necessarily increase in the major towns, the number of deaths during 1947, compared with 1946, rose by orders of magnitude, almost certainly because victims were badly weakened by hunger: from 25 to 253 in Izhevsk; 23 to 155 in Astrakhan; 23 to 177 in Voronezh; 19 to 118 in Barnaul; 41 to 199 in Irkutsk; 138 to 616 in Kiev; 232 to 788 in Khar'kov; 157 to 521 in Vologda; 2128 to 3844 in Moscow; and 1440 to 2226 in Leningrad.[62]

The state's response to the food crisis ran along contradictory lines. It sought to increase the amount of grain available for distribution by raising procurement quotas for collective and state farms and on the produce of private plots. What it could squeeze out of the private plots was limited, partly by the fact that the same drought which destroyed *kolkhoz* yields also affected private cultivation, but partly by its own policy of discouraging private production through the imposition of punitive taxation.[63] At the same time, however, the regime continued its war-time policy of encouraging the cultivation of private allotments by workers and clerical employees, as well as the system of enterprise farms.

The Engineering and Toolmaking Workers' trade union claimed that, during 1946, 102 385 of that sector's employees had their own plots; between them they raised 53.5 tons of food, 41 tons of which were potatoes.[64] According to *Trud*, in 1948 for the economy as a whole around 19 million workers and clerical employees were growing their own food (up from 16.5 million during 1944),[65] and each plot yielded on average 760 kilograms of vegetables and potatoes—160 kilograms more than in 1947—implying that the country received approximately 14.4 million tons of food from this source, a not inappreciable quantity when compared with the total potato harvest that year of around 95 million tons, and a state procurement for the urban population of only 7.2 million tons.[66] Nevertheless, all was clearly not well. According to both the *Trud* article and isolated trade union reports, factory managers were being less than helpful in providing land and helping with ploughing.[67] More ominously, in 1946 the drought took a heavy toll. According to the Engineering and Toolmakers' union, in some regions entire crops died, and in others workers were barely able to harvest seed potatoes for the following year's planting.[68]

The network of factory and state-institution farms—of which some 10 000 had been set up by 1942[69]—is in many ways more revealing of the general strains and dysfunctions of the system in this period. The farms were beset by inordinate structural problems, over and above those caused by the drought. Because working and living conditions on the farms were so bad, it was difficult to recruit people to work on them. Like their counterparts at the parent factory, many farm workers lived in run-down buildings, often with leaky roofs, no heating, poor or non-existent sanitation, and no kitchen or dining room in which to prepare or eat their meals. Their

SOVIET WORKERS' STANDARD OF LIVING 1945–1948   1027

low morale was not improved when they lost their ration entitlements because of their rural employment. The farms equally struggled with lack of equipment or machinery in poor repair, shortages of seed and fertiliser, insufficient numbers of draft animals, and inadequate fodder for the ones they had. The combination of all these factors, together with the weather, produced a range of poor harvests or outright harvest failures which paralleled those affecting agriculture as a whole.[70]

The regime's own perception of the problem was to blame it on the pilfering of grain by peasants and procurement officials, and on inefficiencies and corruption in the supply system, in particular the shops belonging to the Ministry of Trade and the Departments of Workers' Supply (ORS), which were in charge of trade and distribution at the enterprise. It is doubtful whether this was merely posturing for public consumption. Kruglov, Minister of Internal Affairs, issued regular reports to Stalin, Beriya and the rest of the leadership detailing crackdowns on alleged abuses of the rationing system. Such campaigns had always been in existence, but they accelerated in fervour and intensity after the September 1946 price rises. Thus, in October 1946, 26 444 people were arrested for 'speculation', buying and selling ration cards, and other abuses. In November another 23 323 were detained, although after preliminary investigation only just over 2000 were actually arrested.[71]

We should stress, of course, that the primary victims of such vigilance were peasants. On 4 June 1947 the Presidium of the USSR Supreme Soviet promulgated two edicts which vastly increased the existing penalties against theft of socialist and personal property. Pilfering of even a handful of grain was punishable by 5 to 10 years in a labour camp; those guilty of serious and/or repeated offences would receive up to 20 years (later extended to 25 years in compensation for the repeal of the death penalty). Similar sentences awaited those who stole from private citizens.[72] Estimates of how many people were convicted under these laws vary. Zima claims that by the end of 1947—that is, during the first seven months the laws were in force—300 000 people had already been put in prisons or camps under them. Kruglov, in one of his confidential reports to Stalin, put the number at just over 100 000. According to Zemskov, on 1 January 1951 there were just over 1 031 000 prisoners in camps and colonies under the edicts; given the length of the sentences handed out we can take this as a proxy for the total number convicted during the 43 months between June 1947 and the end of 1950, which suggests an average of 287 700 per year.[73]

Industrial workers were by no means exempt from the repression. The newspaper at Leningrad's Krasnyi treugol'nik rubber goods factory openly reported the cases of two women who received labour camp sentences of eight and nine years respectively for stealing four metres of calico, and of a third who was given 10 years for stealing three pairs of boots and a pair of slippers. The paper made it clear that their convictions should serve as a warning to 'all those who still stand on the path of easy gain'.[74]

Other determinants of the standard of living

In any period of famine or near-famine it is, of course, access to food which looms first and foremost in people's consciousness. It is important to keep in mind, however, that other factors also determined the quality of life, or even survival, and left an indelible imprint on people's perceptions and actions: housing, clothing, availability of consumer goods, health and working conditions, to cite but a few. My own view is that, of this list, clothing, housing and health—three very closely related problems—were perhaps the most important.

To the best of our knowledge there is little systematic information available about workers' health, or public health in general, save what Zima has uncovered about famine-related epidemics. Nonetheless, it is possible to identify some of the more pressing problems in this sphere, mainly on the basis of trade union reports.

In addition to encouraging the spread of epidemics (typhus, dysentery, influenza), the famine made people prone to other diseases, such as tuberculosis, severe gastrointestinal ailments, and coronary artery disease. Health statistics from individual factories or branches of industry show that almost everywhere the number of days lost due to illness deteriorated in 1947. At the Komintern iron and steel works in Ukraine, the average worker lost 13 days during 1947 for medical reasons, with injury accounting for less than 10% of the total. At the Petrovsky iron and steel works in Dnepropetrovsk the figure was 11 days. The situation improved only slightly during 1948 and 1949.[75] Surprisingly, industries with less hazardous (although by no means safe) working conditions, such as heavy engineering, means of communication and shipbuilding, showed losses of an almost identical magnitude.[76] These figures very probably underestimate the true picture, first, because they only recorded days lost by workers with sick notes valid for three days or longer, and secondly, because factory doctors were under tremendous pressure to under-record accidents and illnesses and to avoid signing workers off from work.

The food shortage was not the sole cause of workers' poor health. Working and housing conditions, combined with the almost total unavailability of proper clothing, also played a major role. Large amounts of work time were lost because of abscesses and skin infections. Factory after factory reported serious and protracted shortages of soap, which made a mockery of the health education campaigns run in some factory newspapers, stressing the need for workers to wash their hands after using the toilet and before preparing food.[77] Throughout 1946, 1947 and 1948 heavy engineering factories complained about their inability to obtain soap, the production of which had fallen catastrophically during the war and immediate postwar period (see Table 2): at one point in 1946 the Kuibyshev factory in Irkutsk had received no soap at all for three months, and it had a shortfall of 2.5 tons. At one shipbuilding yard in Ukraine young workers had not received any soap for an entire year.[78] During the fourth quarter of 1947 the city of Sverdlovsk was allocated 235 tons of soap, but received only 15 tons.[79] The problems were compounded by the general lack of protective clothing and, especially for young workers, even a change of underwear. Under these conditions a simple scratch or cut at work could easily turn into a major illness. Dormitories, in which almost all young workers lived, as did many older workers, including those with families, were cramped and generally filthy. Lice infestation became a major concern, in particular during the typhus epidemic.[80]

If workers did fall ill or had an accident, enterprises and local authorities were ill-prepared to treat them. Coal mining regions complained that they had so few doctors that many clinics had to be staffed by feldshers; in Moscow *oblast'* doctors had to be turned away because there was nowhere for them to live. Clinic buildings

SOVIET WORKERS' STANDARD OF LIVING 1945–1948 1029

were dilapidated, dirty and unheated; staff lacked basic medicines—and in some cases did not even have soap or bed linen.[81] Although the coal mining reports are the most detailed, there is little reason to believe that the situation was appreciably different elsewhere. Throughout the country, including Moscow, there was a serious shortage of drugs. During World War II the Soviet Union had relied heavily on imports of basic medicines: aspirin, codeine, sulphanilamides, aminopyrine. At the end of the war these imports fell back sharply, or were stopped altogether. Yet domestic production not only failed to make up the gap; in almost all cases it actually fell in 1947, compared with 1945 and 1946. Even such essentials as glucose, boric acid, castor oil and medicine bottles were available in a fraction of the required quantities; there were 40 drugs or medical preparations that were not being manufactured at all.[82]

The housing situation is rather different, in that there is an abundance of material available in the trade union daily, *Trud*, factory newspapers, and the various archives—so much so, in fact, that we can only provide a very brief outline here. Housing construction had been badly neglected during the 1930s, and with mass migration into the towns the pressures on the housing stock were acute. It goes without saying that the destruction caused by World War II, together with the compulsory deferral of repairs in areas not affected by combat, created a crisis of near insurmountable proportions once the war was over. Yet the resources devoted to the problem remained inadequate. True, the regime attempted to accelerate house building through various campaigns, most notably encouraging workers to build their own private homes. Although there were some notable successes, in the main the campaign seems to have been hampered by lack of funds, materials shortages, managerial reluctance to provide workers with the necessary technical assistance, and massive amounts of bureaucratic red tape.[83] There were also less public measures, such as the employment of prisoners of war and MVD prisoners on civilian housing construction.[84]

These efforts notwithstanding, the main responsibility fell upon the industrial ministries and their subordinate enterprises. In almost every industry which we have examined construction lagged way behind schedule, with only a fraction of the planned volume of new living space ever being finished. The difficulties were those typically associated with Soviet industry. Building materials were in chronically short supply; many were defective or rendered unusable by negligence and poor storage. Factory managers routinely took workers off house-building sites and put them on industrial construction. Resources were dispersed over a large number of projects, so that fulfilment of spending plans was far higher than fulfilment of plans for finished construction. Completed buildings were riddled with defects.[85]

Far more important were the social and political implications of the housing shortage. As noted, almost all young workers were housed in dormitories—unless, that is, they were living in mud dugouts or had been farmed out to private rooms because even dormitory space was lacking. Conditions were almost beyond description. Rooms were crowded and cold, and lacked even the most primitive furniture, such as bedside tables or stools. Bed linen—if it was available at all—was rarely changed or laundered. Ceilings leaked and plaster was crumbling off the walls. Residents had nowhere to store belongings or hang their clothes, nowhere to wash and dry clothes, and often nowhere to prepare food—a truly critical problem at a time when most young workers simply could not afford to eat in factory canteens. Many buildings even lacked running water. Dirt was everywhere, and it is surprising that not more of the reports describing these conditions openly complain of vermin infestation other than the ubiquitous bed bugs.[86] Workers, especially young workers, responded to such appalling conditions in the only way they knew: they fled the factories. Almost everywhere ministerial and trade union reports openly blamed the housing shortage and conditions in the dormitories for high turnover and what were becoming chronic labour shortages.[87]

What emerged was a perverse cycle. Enterprises could not hold onto workers because they could not adequately house them, but they could not accelerate house building, in part because they did not have enough workers: they could not retain new recruits and were reluctant to take existing workers off what they considered the more high priority tasks of industrial production or restoring or expanding production shops. There was one way out of this dilemma, and that was to request permission to erect a labour camp at the enterprise and have prisoners and/or prisoners of war assist with the building. The irony was that—at least in principle—many of the prisoners thus employed might be the same young workers who had fled to escape their wretched conditions, and then when caught had been sentenced to MVD labour camps.[88] Yet even this solution did not always work: a 1951 plan to provide camp prisoners to put up housing at the Dal'metallurgstroi site in Primor'e had to be abandoned because there was nowhere to house them.[89]

Epilogue: the crisis of the 'quality of life' and its political legacy

How did workers react to the crisis we have described? Thanks to Zubkova's study of reports drawn up by local officials of the party's agitation and propaganda sector, we know that in both countryside and the factories numerous individuals voiced their worry and discontent over official policy. At factory meetings or other public forums they said openly that they could not survive with the new prices; some made an open connection between food shortages and the USSR's export of grain to Eastern Europe (euphemistically referred to as the 'democratic' countries). Some of these sentiments were couched in openly anti-Soviet terms; others clearly were not.[90] The problem with such reports—as there would be with secret police reports, were they to be made available—is that, while they reveal the types of sentiments then current among sections of the population, they tell us nothing about how prevalent or representative these opinions were. We can, however, venture some tentative conclusions. Unlike in the 1930s, there appear to have been no instances of strikes or mass protest—or at least no one has yet found any evidence of them. The overwhelming response seems rather to have been despair, as suggested by a VTsSPS report compiled just a few days after the price rises, and one of the few to give some indication of how larger groups of people reacted:

The rise in prices of foodstuffs, in particular of bread, provoked the greatest amount of unease among workers with large families and the low-paid; especially unhealthy reactions were those of women with children who lost their husbands during the war. At the Voskresensk chemical combine some of the low-paid women with several children cried when they learned of the new prices, complaining that their wages would no longer be enough for bread.[91]

Even where workers felt a keen sense of grievance and injustice they were most likely to seek redress by pleading with management rather than risking even small-scale collective action.[92]

At the same time the small number of interviews we have done in the USA and Russia show an interesting pattern. All of the respondents remember the December 1947 currency reform and the abolition of rationing. They remember how much bread they were entitled to before that date, what was in the shops both before and after, how much meals cost in their factory, school or institute canteens, and how much they could afford to buy after rationing was ended. Yet none of them recalled the price rises of September 1946 as a specific policy, nor the cutback in ration entitlements. They remember the hunger and hardship of the period, they remember 'famine' in general, but for them there was simply one long continuum of hunger, starvation or near-starvation which extended from 1942 or 1943 right through to the end of the 1940s. Although speculation from such a small and unrepresentative sample is always dangerous, it is possible that for many people, unless they lived in an area immediately affected by the famine, the new policy did not bring any radical change in their circumstances; it merely made an already dismal situation worse.

The year 1948 was probably a turning point for postwar Soviet society. Politically the repression and renewed purges intensified, and any residual hopes for a relaxation of the dictatorship were well and truly dashed. Economically, however, it marked the time when conditions began very gradually to improve. In the towns probably most people welcomed the end of rationing, although the effects of the food shortages continued to be felt in peripheral regions, and even in industrial centres like Sverdlovsk.[93] In rural industries bread rationing was eliminated in name only: well into the 1950s such factories, some of which employed large numbers of workers, continued to distribute bread directly to their employees.[94] Nevertheless, little by little food supplies and supplies of basic consumer goods increased. Housing conditions improved less noticeably, however, and labour turnover, although it peaked in 1947 and 1948, remained high in most industries for which we have figures.[95]

From the point of view of the Soviet elite this proved a politically beneficial combination: the repression demonstrated decisively to the population once and for all that resistance or even the entertainment of muted aspirations for a political improvement was a hopeless undertaking; the improvement in living standards made the political situation bearable. In the long run, however, it proved a poisoned chalice. For it embedded passivity and demoralisation deep into popular consciousness. For workers, and even more so for the peasantry, the experience of the postwar years was the reverse of Vera Dunham's 'Big Deal', by which she explains (with great perspicacity) the emergence of an ideological consensus between the elite and the intelligentsia. The elite might have had the opportunity to forge a similar type of consensus with the workforce in the immediate postwar years; certainly the patriotism generated by the victory and the almost desperate wish to believe that things would get better meant that such a consensus was not totally excluded. Unlike the West, where the combination of Cold War and economic recovery allowed governments to

1032   DONALD FILTZER

create a pro-capitalist consensus which won over large sections of their own working class, in the USSR the prolonged and severe material hardship rendered such ideological unity a chimera, even if the regime had sought it.

We can go further. After the war the social composition of the industrial workforce underwent dramatic change. The famine forced into the towns millions of ex-peasants who—like their predecessors in the aftermath of collectivisation—brought with them deep resentments over what they had gone through. At the same time millions of young people entered production for the first time. These youth were too young to have fought at the front, and so the integrative effects of the war experience were far weaker. Instead, they encountered truly appalling living and working conditions. The fact that these could be explained as a natural consequence of a devastating war was of little comfort when day-to-day existence was such a struggle. These young people became profoundly alienated from the Stalinist regime. They may have accepted or tolerated it, but they could never enthusiastically embrace it.[96] The real legacy of their experience manifested itself not during Stalin's lifetime but much later, when this generation grew up and became the core of the industrial workforce under Khrushchev. Insofar as Khrushchev, despite the political relaxation, failed to effect any fundamental change in workers' estrangement from the goals of the Soviet regime, at least part of the explanation lies here, in the period dealt with in this article.

University of East London

SOVIET WORKERS' STANDARD OF LIVING 1945–1948   1033

Archives cited

GARF (State Archive of the Russian Federation):

f.5457   Central Committee of the Trade Union of Workers in Textiles
                and Light Industry
f.7416   Central Committee of the Trade Union of Workers in the Coal
                Industry
f.7676   Central Committee of the Trade Union of Workers in
                Engineering
f.7680   Central Committee of the Trade Union of Workers in the Iron
                and Steel Industry
f.9401   op. 2: Special Files of Stalin and Beriya

RGAE (Russian State Archive of the Economy)

f.1562   Central Statistical Administration
f.8592   Ministry of Construction of Enterprises in Heavy
                Industry
f.8248   Ministry of the Construction Materials Industry

RTsKhIDNI (Russian Centre for the Preservation and Use of Documents of Modern
    History)

f.17, op. 116   Secretariat of the Central Committee of the Soviet Communist
                Party
f.17, op. 121   Technical Secretariat of the Organisation Bureau of the
                Central Committee of the Soviet Communist Party
f.17, op. 125 and 132 Propaganda and Agitation Administration of the Central
                Committee of the Soviet Communist Party
f.17, op. 131   Department for Party, Trade Union and Komsomol Bodies,
                Central Committee of the Soviet Communist Party

TsGAIPD (Central State Archive of Historical and Political Documentation—former
    Leningrad Party Archive)

f.1224   Lenin factory, Nevsky District, Leningrad

TsKhDMO (Centre for the Preservation of Documentation of Youth Organisations—
former Komsomol Archive, Moscow)

¹ This article is part of a larger study of Soviet society in the postwar period. A number of people have assisted me in its research and preparation. Elena Zubkova gave invaluable advice on sources and problems of interpretation. R. W. Davies, Yoram Gorlizki, Mark Harrison, Evan Mawdsley, Arfon Rees and Stephen Wheatcroft offered detailed comments and suggestions on an earlier version. Ina Giller of the Jewish Community Center, Baltimore, Maryland, and Pavel Romanov, of Samara State University, arranged programmes of interviews for me in their respective cities. Natasha Kurashova spent many hours discussing the significance of my findings and helping with linguistic difficulties. Finally, I owe special thanks to the archivists and staff at the Tsentr Khraneniya Dokumentov Molodezhnykh

1034   DONALD FILTZER

Organizatsii (the former Komsomol archive) in Moscow for their generous help with locating and analysing materials, and for providing an outstanding working environment. I alone, of course, am responsible for the article's errors and shortcomings.

[2] John Barber & Mark Harrison, *The Soviet Home Front, 1941–1945: A Social and Economic History of the USSR in World War II* (London, 1991), pp. 49, 82–85.

[3] This is by no means an original argument. It was first outlined by Vera Dunham in her book, *In Stalin's Time: Middleclass Values in Soviet Fiction* (Durham, North Carolina, 1990). It has recently been developed in more detail by Elena Zubkova, *Obshchestvo i reformy, 1945–1964* (Moscow, 1993), chapter 1.

[4] V. P. Popov, 'Gosudarstvennyi terror v sovetskoi Rossii. 1923–1953 gg. (Istochniki i ikh interpretatsiya)', *Otechestvennye arkhivy*, 1992, 2, pp. 23, 27.

[5] For works in English see Alec Nove, 'Soviet Peasantry in world War II', in Susan J. Linz (ed.), *The Impact of World War II on the Soviet Union* (Totowa, New Jersey, 1985), pp. 77–90; and Zhores Medvedev, *Soviet Agriculture* (New York, 1987), chapter 5. In Russian we now have V. F. Zima's comprehensive study of the famine, *Golod v SSSR 1946–1947 godov: proiskhozhdenie i posledstviya* (Moscow, 1996).

[6] This is one of the most interesting aspects of this period. Between 1946 and 1952 some 1.6 million workers were convicted in criminal proceedings of unlawfully leaving their jobs (V. N. Zemskov, 'Ukaz ot 26 iyunya 1940 ... (eshche odna kruglaya data)', *Raduga*, 1990, 6, pp. 45–47. As I shall show in a subsequent publication, however, this was but a fraction of the number of workers who actually left their jobs without managerial permission.

[7] For a summary of this argument, see Donald Filtzer, *Soviet Workers and De-Stalinization: The Consolidation of the Modern System of Soviet Production Relations, 1953–1964* (Cambridge, 1992), Introduction; and Robert Service, 'De-Stalinisation in the USSR before Khrushchev's Secret Speech', in *Il XX Congresso del Pcus* (Milan, 1988), pp. 287–310.

[8] Decree of the USSR Council of Ministers and the Central Committee of the All-Union Communist Party (Bolsheviks), 14 December 1947, 'O provedenii denezhnoi reformy i otmene kartochek na prodovol'stvennye i promyshlennye tovary', *Trud*, 16 December 1947.

[9] This would support the somewhat rosy picture of the recovery of postwar living standards given by Alec Nove, *An Economic History of the USSR* (Pelican, 1972), pp. 305–311.

[10] Janet Chapman, *Real Wages in Soviet Russia Since 1928* (Cambridge, MA, 1963), pp. 144–145. The variation in estimates is due to her use of alternative methods of calculation.

[11] *Ibid.*, p. 145.

[12] RGAE, f.1562 (TsSU), op. 15, d. 2129, l. 80.

[13] For prices before and after the September 1946 increases, see Table 3.

[14] Almost all of the potato crop remained in the village: state procurements for the urban population ranged from a low of 4.5 million tons in 1946 to a high of 7.2 million tons in 1948, well below 10% of the harvest (Eugene Zaleski, *Stalinist Planning for Economic Growth, 1933–1952* (London, 1980), pp. 624–625). According to Medvedev, *Soviet Agriculture*, p. 154, the fall-off in potato production after 1948 was not a response to improved grain supplies but the result of bad harvests.

[15] The general data tell us relatively little about differentiation in wages—and therefore consumption—by industry, skill, region, gender or age. There were many factors which determined earnings: whether the sector was relatively privileged (coal mining, iron and steel at one end of the spectrum, light industry at the other); the ease or difficulty with which workers could fulfil their output quotas (norms); the number of stoppages suffered due to lack of supplies or equipment breakdowns; the amount of overtime worked; and the myriad of informal bargaining arrangements which evolved at shop level between workers and line managers, and through which workers in a relatively strong position could extract various concessions, for example, being put on jobs where the norms were easy to fulfil. We should also keep in mind that the work week in the Soviet Union was extremely long: 48 hours, except on underground jobs, where it was 42 (this does not include overtime, which technically permitted only under special circumstances and much of which was concealed). Thus workers had to work long and hard for whatever they received. In addition, there were clearly discernable patterns of social inequality. We can glean some idea of the differences between skilled and unskilled workers from Table 1. The gap in earnings between older and younger workers we discuss in the next section. But three of the most important determinants of income inequality—gender, region and nationality—still await detailed research.

[16] Mark Harrison, *Accounting for War. Soviet production, employment, and the defence burden, 1940–1945* (Cambridge, 1996), pp. 141, 159–161.

[17] Zima, p. 39.

[18] RTsKhIDNI, f. 17, op. 121, d. 556, l. 35–49.

[19] A December 1945 inspection of conditions in the mining districts of Tula *oblast'*, for example,

SOVIET WORKERS' STANDARD OF LIVING 1945–1948   1035

found that the majority of workers lived in cramped dormitories, many without bed linen, basic furniture, light bulbs or soap—a privilege for which they paid nearly 10% of their wages in rent. Local hospitals had no fuel. The bread sold at one mine smelled of kerosene, because there was no cooking oil with which to grease the bread tins. Zubkova, pp. 37–38; for a fuller account see RTsKhIDNI, f.17, op. 125, d. 421, 1.2,3,4.

[20] GARF, f. 9401, op. 2, d. 145, 1. 211–211a; d. 146, 1. 28–29.

[21] Zaleski, pp. 582–583, 618–619; Harrison, p. 69.

[22] See above, note 5.

[23] GARF, f. 9401, op. 2, d. 168, 1. 385–387. There is no adequate English translation for the Russian term *alimentarnaya distrofiya* (its literal translation as 'alimentary dystrophy' has no meaning in English medical terminology). It refers to a complex of symptoms arising from acute malnutrition, most prominently emaciation, swelling, weakness and, if untreated, death.

[24] Zima, pp. 168–169. Despite the importance of his book as a political and social history of the famine, Zima is somewhat less than careful in his use of statistics. On p. 11 he claims a figure of two million famine and famine-related deaths. In neither passage does he indicate how he arrives at his figures. An MVD report dated 15 April 1949 lists an increase of 790 000 officially registered deaths in 1947 compared with 1946; although the rate fell sharply in 1948, there were still 75 000 more deaths than in 1946. There was also an extremely sharp fall in the birth rate: from 2 532 547 registered births during the first half of 1947 to 1 949 926 in the second half of that year and 1 793 352 during the first half of 1948. During the second half of 1948 the number of births jumped back up, to 2 258 873. GARF, f. 9401, op. 2, d. 234, 1. 344–345. A more recent estimate of famine deaths by Ellman using death registration data places the number of deaths at between 1 and 1.5 million. Michael Ellman, 'The 1947 Soviet Famine and the Entitlement Approach to Famines', unpublished conference paper, British Association for Slavonic & East European Studies, March 1999 (cited with the kind permission of the author).

[25] Zima argues that the famine was in large part artificially created by the Stalinist regime. Faced with the failure of the 1946 harvest, the state, he claims, deliberately increased stocks of grain reserves out of fear of a possible war; to this end it ruthlessly pushed up procurement quotas on collective and state farms, including from peasants' private plots (pp. 10, 11, 34). Stephen Wheatcroft and R. W. Davies (private communications) have pointed out to me that part of his argument is based on an apparent misreading of figures for state grain reserves, which were always increased in January in order to tide the country over the winter months. There was no policy to increase stocks. This does not obviate Zima's more general argument concerning the state's attempt to extract more grain from a peasantry already on the borderline of survival.

[26] Nove, *Economic History*, pp. 307–308. This was also the official public explanation of the policy. See, for example, *Trud*, 23 November 1946.

[27] Zaleski, pp. 467–468. See A. V. Lyubimov, *Torgovlya i snabzhenie v gody velikoi otechestvennoi voiny* (Moscow, 1968), in particular pp. 202–216.

[28] Order of the USSR Ministry of Trade, No. 308, 'Ob ekonomii i raskhodovanii khleba', 27 September 1946.

[29] GARF, f. 7676, op. 16, d. 39, 1. 93, 94.

[30] The report appears in RTsKhIDNI, f. 17, op. 121, d. 515, 1. 87–131.

[31] RTsKhiDNI, f. 17, op. 121, d. 515, 1. 92. The figures are from July 1946.

[32] RTsKhIDNI, f. 17, op. 121, d. 515, 1. 99–100.

[33] RTsKhIDNI, f. 17, op. 121, d. 515, 1.104, 106, 107, 109–110, 112–116, 118–120.

[34] RTsKhIDNI, f. 17, op. 121, d. 515, 1. 147.

[35] RTsKhIDNI, f. 17, op. 121, d. 515, 1. 32, 174–175. For loss of ration privileges by party officials and even members of the secret police, see this file, 1. 37, 53–54, 55, 59.

[36] RTsKhIDNI, f. 17, op. 121, d. 515, 1. 42.

[37] RTsKhIDNI, f. 17, op. 121, d. 590, 1. 60.

[38] GARF, f. 7676, op. 16, d. 39, 1. 38ob (Sverdlovsk *oblast'*); RTsKhIDNI, f. 17, op. 121, d. 590, 1. 76–77. See also Zima, pp. 42–43, 66–67.

[39] RTsKhIDNI, f. 17, op. 121, d. 515, 1. 83–84. The letter was dated 23 December 1946. According to a trade union report, the Sverdlovsk city department of trade eventually provided rations for about 3500 of the 4800 children and dependents originally stripped of their bread allowance. The rest remained uncovered. This same report also complained that factory managers were issuing ration cards to people not entitled to them. GARF, f. 7676, op. 16, d. 39, 1. 98, 99.

[40] RTsKhIDNI, f. 17, op. 121, d. 515, 1. 31.

[41] The authorities in Irkutsk *oblast'* lost rations for 134 000 out of 170 000 workers, clerical employees and their families. They had 23 000 of these restored in November 1946, but in December asked for a further 30 000. The Ministry of Trade 'supported' this request ... with an additional 6900

1036   DONALD FILTZER

ration allocations. A similar but even more extreme case occurred in Arkhangel'sk *oblast'*. At the other
end of the spectrum, the iron and steel works in Magnitogorsk and strategically important construction
and fisheries projects in Murmansk had their requests for increased rations met in full. RTsKhIDNI, f.
17, op. 121, d. 515, 1. 14–15, 35–36, 39–40, 60, 74–76.
  [42] Lyubimov, p. 204.
  [43] RTsKhIDNI, f. 17, op. 121, d. 669, 1. 37, 46, 52–52ob.
  [44] See GARF, f. 7676, op. 16, d. 39 for numerous reports from the engineering and toolmaking trade
union. For similar accounts in textiles see GARF, f. 5457, op. 23, d. 604, 1. 21, and d. 613, 1. 22.
  [45] GARF, f. 7676, op. 16, d. 39, 1. 130–132.
  [46] The special position of young workers in the postwar years requires its own separate study, and
we can only indicate some of the bare outlines here. To give just a general indication of the extent of
labour turnover among this group, we can cite the following survey of new recruits who left their jobs
during January–October 1947. The survey was prepared by the Party Control Commission for the
Technical Secretariat of the Orgburo. Although it covered only a limited number of enterprises in each
branch, the figures are fully consistent with those from individual ministries and enterprises found in
various archives. Source: RTsKhIDNI, f. 17, op. 121, d. 644, 1. 20.

Ministry	Percentage of newly recruited young workers leaving	Including percentage who left their jobs illegally
Heavy engineering	51.5	32.9
Motor vehicles and tractors	31.4	24.4
Construction of military and naval enterprises	54.1	31.9
Construction of heavy industry enterprises	30.8	26.4
Coal mining—western regions	64.3	51.8
Coal mining—eastern regions	59.6	29.7

Where adult workers were concerned, managers tended to protect themselves by referring nearly all cases
of 'labour desertion' to the courts; conviction rates in many towns were low, however, to say nothing
of those who were never tracked down. Although we do not yet have precise figures, the authorities were
clearly more lenient with young workers, many of whom were simply sent back to their enterprise or
labour reserve school. For a fuller discussion see Donald Filtzer, 'Wirtschaft und Gesellschaft', in Stefan
Plaggenborg (ed.), *Handbuch der Geschichte Rußlands*, volume 4 (Stuttgart, 1999, forthcoming).
  [47] For a typical portrait which displays all of these problems see TsKhDMO, f. 1, op. 4, d. 895,
1. 46–50 (coal mining construction).
  [48] RGAE, f. 1562, op. 15, d. 2130, 1.34; TsKhDMO, f. 1, op. 4, d. 905, 1. 155.
  [49] RGAE, f. 1562, op. 15, d. 2130, 1.35; TsKhDMO, f. 1, op. 4, d. 843, 1. 109, 111.
  [50] RGAE, f. 8248, op. 21, d. 274, 1.156, 161.
  [51] TsKhDMO, f. 1, op. 4, d. 895, 1. 49.
  [52] GARF, f. 5457, op. 25, d. 195, 1. 1.
  [53] See, for example, the reports in GARF, f. 5457, op. 23 (cotton textiles), d. 613 and d. 624; and
op. 25 (flax and hemp), d. 173 and d. 195.
  [54] TsKhDMO, f. 1, op. 3, d. 509, 1. 106.
  [55] GARF, f. 7676, op. 9, d. 488, 1. 20.
  [56] TsKhDMO, f. 1, op. 4, d. 961, 1. 42–43.
  [57] GARF, f. 7676, op. 16, d. 714, 1. 60b.
  [58] Zima, pp. 75–76.
  [59] See the various reports contained in GARF, f. 7676, op. 9, d. 674. At Uralmash (Sverdlovsk),
the special dining room was feeding nearly 2000 people by the autumn of 1947; this figure excludes the
481 suffering from acute malnutrition (*alimentarnaya distrofiya*) who received supplemental feeding
during July and August, and the 538 workers with tuberculosis who had their own separate dining room.
Ibid., 1. 101.
  [60] Zima, pp. 173–175. According to the TsSU, the number of typhus cases in Moscow rose from
1153 in 1946 to 3910 in 1947; in Leningrad the number of cases jumped from 429 to 2043; in Kiev,
from 245 to 1162; and in Khar'kov, from 121 to 3017 (RGAE, f. 1562, op. 18, d. 361, 1. 28, 31, 64,
65 (1946) and d. 418, 1. 32, 35, 69, 70 (1947). Even allowing for the problems of systematic
under-reporting by local doctors, these figures at least show how marked the trend was.
  [61] GARF, f. 7676, op. 9, d. 674, 1. 100.

SOVIET WORKERS' STANDARD OF LIVING 1945–1948 1037

[62] Derived from RGAE, f. 1562, op. 18, d. 361 (1946) and d. 418 (1947). Here, too, we must treat the figures with caution. In addition to under-reporting, not all those suffering from dysentery would have sought medical attention, and many cases would have been misdiagnosed; for example, some might have been wrongly classified as typhoid fever, while some cases of typhoid would have been incorrectly recorded as dysentery. Nevertheless, the general trend is clear.

[63] This latter point is well described in the secondary literature. See Zaleski, pp. 476–477; Nove, *Economic History*, pp. 300–301; Medvedev, *Soviet Agriculture*, p. 141.

[64] GARF, f. 7676, op. 16, d. 51, 1. 53.

[65] Zaleski, p. 336.

[66] *Trud*, 4 March 1949; Zaleski, pp. 622–625.

[67] *Trud*, 19 March 1949; GARF, f. 7416, op. 4, d. 268, 1. 6, 7.

[68] GARF, f. 7416, op. 16, d. 51, 1. 56.

[69] Zaleski, p. 335.

[70] GARF, f. 7676, op. 11, d. 181, 1. 12; op. 16, d. 258, 1. 28–29ob., 37, 43–44, 47–48, 51–51ob. 104–105ob., 108–109; d. 490, 1. 3, 4, 6, 9, 46; TsGAIPD, f. 1224, op. 2, d. 214, 1. 8, 15; *Elektrosila* (Elektrosila factory, Leningrad), 21 March 1947, 14 April 1948.

[71] GARF, f. 9401, op. 2, d. 139, 1. 361, 576, 578.

[72] Edicts of the Presidium of the USSR Supreme Soviet, 4 June 1947, 'Ob ugolovnoi otvetstvennosti za khishcheniya gosudarstvennogo i obshchestvennogo imushchestva', and 'Ob usilenii okhrany lichnoi sobstvennosti grazhdan', *Pravda*, 5 June 1947. At the same time punishment of petty theft from industrial enterprises was now increased from 1 year's imprisonment to 7. For a detailed discussion of the penalties imposed by the new laws and the deliberations that preceded their promulgation, see Peter Solomon, *Soviet Criminal Justice Under Stalin* (Cambridge, 1996), pp. 409–413. For the repeal of the death penalty, see Edict of the Presidium of the USSR Supreme Soviet, 26 May 1947, 'Ob otmene smertnoi kazni', *Trud*, 27 May 1947.

[73] Zima, p. 127; GARF, f. 9401, op. 2, d. 199, 1. 391; V. N. Zemskov, 'GULAG (istoriko-sotsiologicheskii aspekt)', *Sotsiologicheskie issledovaniya*, 1991, 7, pp. 10–11. Solomon, p. 435, states that while just over 2 million people were prosecuted under the new laws from 1947 until the end of 1952, half of these prosecutions took place during the first 18 months. Thereafter the rate of prosecutions fell sharply, in large part owing to the unwillingness of many judicial and procuracy officials to implement such harsh legislation (Solomon, pp. 431–432, 434). It seems to us that an even more important factor was the easing of the food crisis after 1948: this removed much of the need to steal and relaxed the pressure on officials to indulge in exemplary prosecutions. Nevertheless, 250 000 people were still brought to trial in 1952, the last full year before Stalin's death.

[74] *Krasnyi treugol'nik*, 1 August 1947.

[75] GARF, f. 7680, op. 5, d. 402, 1. 28, 49.

[76] GARF, f. 7676, op. 9, d. 837, 1. 61, 65 (heavy engineering); RTsKhIDNI, f. 17, op. 131, d. 112, 1. 5, 124 (means of communication and shipbuilding).

[77] *Golos Dzerzhintsa* (Dzerzhinsky spinning and weaving factory, Ivanovo), 7 March 1946, 24 June 1948; *Stalinets* (automobile and tractor parts factory, Kuibyshev), 2 August 1950, 6 September 1951.

[78] GARF, f. 7676, op. 9, d. 488, 1. 8, 30; d. 674, 1. 48–49, 100; d. 837, 1. 3ob., 49 (engineering); TsKhDMO, f. 1, op. 4, d. 843, 1. 109 (shipbuilding).

[79] Zima, p. 174.

[80] RTsKhIDNI, f. 17, op. 131, d. 53, 1. 161.

[81] GARF, f. 7416, op. 3, d. 165, 1. 17, 49; op. 4, d. 129, 1. 2, 2ob., and d. 214, 1. 21–25; RTsKhIDNI, f. 17, op. 121, d. 680, 1. 10–11, 17–19.

[82] RTsKhIDNI, f. 17, op. 121, d. 575, 1. 119, 121–124, 127–129, 131–133, 134–138; d. 680, 1. 70–76, 80. The crisis in the pharmaceutical industry led to the Ministry of the Medical Industry being abolished in March 1948. There is perhaps more to this story than meets the eye, since there was a simultaneous purge of medical research institutes, and other—political, rather than medical—issues may have been involved.

As for the drugs shortage, one paediatrician whom I interviewed claimed that she personally was able to prescribe whatever medicines she needed. Aside from possible regional variations and/or priority given to children, this might also be explained by the testimony of another doctor, who said pharmaceuticals were generally unobtainable, and that they used mainly herbal and natural preparations, of which there was a plentiful supply.

[83] *Trud*, 27 December 1946, 31 January 1947, 27 March 1947, 6 July 1948. *Stalinets* (Rostsel'mash agricultural equipment factory, Rostov-on-Don), 22 August 1947; RTsKhIDNI, f. 17, op. 116, d. 237, 1. 42–43; GARF, f. 7676, op. 9, d. 697, 1.27; op. 16, d. 485, 1. 26.

[84] GARF, f. 9401, op. 2, d. 199, 1. 41–45, 73–74.

[85] A good overview of the problem can be gleaned from *Trud*, 30 March and 21 May 1947 and

DONALD FILTZER

14 January, 17 August and 10 September 1949; *Kabel'shchik* (Sevkabel', Leningrad), 20 May 1948; GARF, f. 7676, op. 9, d. 697, 1. 32, 35, 36; op. 16, d. 485, 1. 1–6; RGAE, f. 8592, op. 2, d. 131, 1. 22, d. 734, 1. 79–80.

[86] Sources are too numerous to cite in detail. For a relatively accessible public source, see *Kabel'shchik* (Sevkabel', Leningrad), 20 September 1946. Among the more exhaustive archival reports is that on the Stalingrad tractor factory, discussed at a 1949 Plenum of the Komsomol: TsKhDMO, f. 1, op. 2, d. 272, 1. 97–98, 108–110.

[87] In the words attributed to one young miner in Voroshilovgrad *oblast'* in 1949, 'Let them move us to another mine, because it's impossible to live this way. All the lads from Kamenets-Podol'sk *oblast'* have vanished. Every day someone else leaves. We live like herrings, there's nowhere even to turn around. There's dirt all around you. In the bath house the water's cold, people steal, there's no dining room, you just get dry bread, you go into Annenka, you look for milk, you find some and drink it down, but you can't find cold water'. TsKhDMO, f. 1, op. 4, d. 1172, 1. 237.

[88] This was precisely the solution adopted by the Ministry of Construction of Enterprises in Heavy Industry (Mintyazhstroi) in March 1947. RGAE, f. 8592, op. 2, d. 115, 1. 131, 134, 137, 140, 143, 146, 149, 151, 153, 154. We should note that not all such requests were automatically granted: GARF, f. 9401, op. 2, d. 149, 1. 341.

[89] RGAE, f. 8592, op. 2, d. 734, 1. 79.

[90] Zubkova, pp. 41–44. For the linkage between the price rises and exports, see RTsKhIDNI, f. 17, op. 125, d. 425, 1. 5, 40, and d. 518, 1. 8.

[91] RTsKhIDNI, f. 17, op. 121, d. 524, 1. 63.

[92] One interviewee, who worked as a line manager in construction in Kuibyshev during the early 1950s, reported how workers and clerical staff reacted to the 1951 state loan exactions with near panic, since they were being asked to surrender the equivalent of between one and two months' pay. Site managers sided with the workers but had little choice but to enforce the policy. They spent a full two weeks bullying and badgering each worker into signing up for the full amount. What is significant is that there was no mass protest and no mass refusal to subscribe to the loan—workers came as individuals and begged for dispensation, which managers (at least in this case) felt powerless to give.

[93] GARF, f. 7676, op. 16, d. 490, 1. 46, 46ob.; RTsKhIDNI, f. 17, op. 121, d. 669, 1. 6, 35, 37, 46, 48–49.

[94] Interview with M.Z., who worked as a line manager in a large porcelain factory in Zhitomir *oblast'*, Ukraine.

[95] Thus construction in heavy industry—traditionally one of the worst affected sectors—continued to lose about 40% of its workforce each year as late as 1951 and early 1952. RGAE, f. 8592, op. 2, d. 756, 1.65; d. 765, 1. 96; d. 773, 1. 43; d. 915, 1. 70

[96] We have strong indirect evidence of this in the inordinate difficulty which factory Komsomol groups had in recruiting. Membership turnover was very high, non-payment of dues was a chronic problem, and in many major enterprises the Komsomol had a weak or even non-existent presence. In Sverdlovsk *oblast'*, for example, while total Komsomol membership remained more or less stable between 1945 and 1949, the number of workers and their percentage of total membership fell markedly. From a high point of 41.7% working class membership during the first half of 1945, it collapsed to just 19% during late 1948, before recovering slightly during the following year. TsKhDMO, f. 1, op. 2, d. 272, 1. 66.

Part IV
Stagnation:
Khrushchev and Brezhnev

[15]
Khrushchev's Image in the Light of Glasnost and Perestroika

DAVID NORDLANDER

In the twenty-nine years since his ouster as Soviet leader in 1964, Nikita Sergeevich Khrushchev has been the subject of public discussion in the former USSR for only the last five. As much of a "non-person" in official Soviet history as Nikolai Bukharin or Leon Trotsky, Khrushchev was blatantly ignored until November 1987, when Mikhail Gorbachev referred to him positively in a speech marking the seventieth anniversary of the Bolshevik Revolution.[1] Thereafter, a number of articles appeared in the Soviet press contesting the merits and failures of the Khrushchev years. In stark contrast to the Brezhnev-era view of the Khrushchev period as a time of "subjectivism" and "voluntarism," the modern Soviet debate produced a multiplicity of viewpoints and arguments that reflected the complexities of Khrushchev's legacy. More importantly, the revised interpretations revealed analyses that were shaped by the political necessities of Gorbachev's own program of reform.[2] It was no coincidence that the Soviet forum on Khrushchev reached its height in 1988–89, during the apogee of glasnost and perestroika, for it embodied the political impulses of that period.[3] While future assessments of Khrushchev and other Soviet topics will undoubtedly mirror a different set of circumstances, the initial debate over Khrushchev

---

The author thanks Drs. Donald Raleigh and Lloyd Kramer for their prompt readings of the initial stages of this paper. An earlier version of this article was presented at the Southern Conference on Slavic Studies at Savannah, Georgia, on 22 March 1991.

[1] Mikhail S. Gorbachev, *Oktiabr' i perestroika: Revoliutsiia prodolzhaetsia* (Moscow: Politizdat, 1987), 27–28. Other speeches, such as Aleksandr Iakovlev's of 17 April 1987, were also vital in broadening the scope of historical analysis in the Soviet Union. See Donald J. Raleigh, "Introduction," in *Soviet Historians and Perestroika: The First Phase*, ed. Donald J. Raleigh (Armonk, NY: M. E. Sharpe, Inc., 1989), xv.

[2] Some Western scholars even argued that Soviet historical revisionism played a key role in Gorbachev's political strategy. For example, see Thomas Sherlock, "Politics and History under Gorbachev," *Problems of Communism* 37 (May-August 1988): 16–42.

[3] The debate took place in a variety of forums ranging from scholarly articles in academic or literary journals such as *Voprosy istorii, Novaia i noveishaia istoriia, Oktiabr'*, and *Novyi mir* to book-length memoirs that detailed several aspects of the Khrushchev era.

was significant because of its implications about the process of reform in the Gorbachev era.

Though the open commentary on the Khrushchev years did not begin in earnest until 1988, it was presaged by the direction perestroika already had taken in reshaping political life. In order to alter the Soviet status quo, Gorbachev and other reformers first had to undermine the vestiges of Stalinism that continued to belabor the Soviet Union, including an entrenched bureaucracy and a centrally planned economy. They therefore attacked Stalin's legacy on many levels. The ensuing reanalysis of the "Stalin question," or Stalin's role in Soviet history, began with a review of such previously unmentionable Stalinist rivals as Bukharin and Trotsky, and their alternative programs. As the Stalin question evolved through a critical discussion of collectivization, the purges, and World War II, many Soviet investigations by 1988 focused on the Khrushchev era and the initial attack on the Stalin cult during that time. As with the earlier topics, the historical image of Khrushchev became a symbol for the expression of contemporary political debates.

Within this symbolism lies the importance of the arguments about Khrushchev; namely, the impact of historical images on Soviet political culture. For various reasons to be discussed below, Soviet authors participating in the forum on Khrushchev were almost uniformly supportive of perestroika. As members of the intelligentsia, their reformist bias was to be expected.[4] But part of the reason for their analysis of the Khrushchev period stemmed directly from the increasingly intense power struggle that occurred in the Soviet Union during the Gorbachev era. As a worsening economy and ethnic division threatened to sunder the nation, forces of resistance to change grew stronger, and the supporters of perestroika felt increasingly compelled to find historical precedents to legitimize their radical vision. They turned to Khrushchev because, aside from Bukharin, who never held the leadership in either the party or state, Khrushchev was the only significant reformer in Soviet history. As such, many commentators saw him as a role model who highlighted the possibilities of socialist reform. In the eyes of the Gorbachev generation, Khrushchev revealed the integrity of the Soviet system by showing that it could revitalize itself even after the damage caused by Stalin. The bias in this opinion was obvious, since by interpreting the Khrushchev years as a foundation they were justifying their own radical opinions and status as socialist advocates of change. Indeed, the quest for reformist precedents caused several analysts even to overlook some negative aspects of the Khrushchev record. Nevertheless, in viewing the Khrushchev period as a linchpin in the resuscitation of Soviet socialism from the depths of Stalinism, allies of Gorbachev drew hope at the time for remaking the Soviet government into a viable and essentially valid political structure in the future. Gorbachev and many of his supporters held a firm, seemingly Khrushchevian, belief that it was possible to exorcise Stalinism from the Communist Party and governmental system without disposing of their basic structures.[5]

---

[4] Needless to say, this was largely a debate among intellectuals. Blue-collar opinion of Khrushchev, particularly in industrial cities such as Magnitogorsk, where Stalin retains popularity, is another matter. See Stephen Kotkin, *Steeltown, USSR: Glasnost', Destalinization, and Perestroika in the Provinces* (Berkeley: University of California Press, 1989), 42–50.

[5] Of course, Gorbachev relented soon after the coup attempt of August 1991. See Serge Schme-

While proponents of perestroika could point to the Khrushchev era as an initial period of necessary post-Stalin change, however, its opponents were able to remark that the failure of Khrushchev's policies emphasized the ultimate futility of reform. As a result, many Soviet historians, publicists, and writers qualified their praise of Khrushchev's reformist vision with criticism of his mistakes. The vast majority of authors took pains to separate the negative aspects of the Khrushchev heritage that could damage the reputation of reform from the positive ones that would bolster its standing. They then carefully hailed Khrushchev's anti-Stalinist initiatives while at the same time dissociating the recent reforms from the errors of the Khrushchev period so as to blunt any potential attacks from their neoconservative political enemies. The initial Soviet debate over Khrushchev reflected this balancing act as advocates of Gorbachev sought to highlight the historical possibilities of change without implicating perestroika in the collapses of reform that preceded it.

Part of the reason for the dual interpretation of Khrushchev can also be found by looking at the contributors to this debate. Most of them were scholars and commentators who reached political maturity during the reforms of the Khrushchev era. Often labelled "children of the Twentieth Party Congress," in the 1950s they were young idealists fed on Khrushchev's de-Stalinization campaign. But as Boris Kagarlitskii has shown, this budding generation of Soviet intellectuals became disenchanted with the limitations placed on reform.[6] For them, Khrushchev stoked their hopes for change but did not fulfill their aspirations. Nearly thirty years later, they looked to Gorbachev's reforms as the fruition of Khrushchev's unkept promises. In so doing, they praised the motivation of Khrushchev's policies while contrasting his shortcomings to Gorbachev's reformist achievements.[7]

Although Soviet analysts criticized the inadequacies of Khrushchev's reforms and disagreed over his heritage, a majority agreed that Khrushchev's attempts to alter the most repressive aspects of the Stalinist system mark his period of rule as a positive one in Soviet history. In their understanding, his overall value to Soviet society was beneficial because he sought to humanize and democratize the despotic system inherited from Stalin. A general paradigm of the Khrushchev years developed from this viewpoint. Stressing that his era witnessed a significant degree of reform, this paradigm interpreted the Khrushchev period as an incomplete and early stage of perestroika. Burdened by a close proximity to the Stalinist era, Khrushchev's policies were limited by strong counterforces in Soviet society. Indeed, he made many mistakes, and a number of his reforms ended up as abject failures. In spite of this, his programs laid the necessary groundwork for a later, deeper political wave that transformed the Soviet Union. As a result of this new interpretation, Khrushchev has emerged as a pivotal figure in Soviet history.

---

mann, "Gorbachev Quits as Party Head; Ends Communism's 74-Year Reign: Cabinet Disbanded: In Deal With Yeltsin, Committee is Created to Govern Nation," *New York Times,* 25 August 1991.

[6] Boris Kagarlitskii, *The Thinking Reed: Intellectuals and the Soviet State 1917 to the Present* (New York: Verso, 1988), 141–44.

[7] Among many segments of the Soviet intelligentsia, the infatuation with Gorbachev wore thin in early 1991, when the Soviet leader was charged with placing unnecessary brakes on the process of reform. For a discussion of this issue, see Stephen Cohen, "Gorbachev the Great," *New York Times,* 11 March 1991.

The more positive evaluation of Khrushchev stemmed primarily from two trends. The first was the severe criticism that Soviet analysts directed at the "period of stagnation" of the Brezhnev era. Concurrently, they looked more favorably at the reforms under Khrushchev, which to them seemed to stand as precursors to the changes that Gorbachev implemented, particularly freedoms in the cultural realm. Second, and perhaps more importantly, the literary contributions of several people who were either related to or closely associated with Khrushchev helped to transform his image. Banned from releasing material about him for years, they recently published numerous positive accounts of the Khrushchev period. Within the past four years, for example, both Khrushchev's son, Sergei, and his son-in-law, Aleksei Adzhubei, have produced lengthy memoirs that challenge the orthodox interpretations of the Brezhnev era. Various articles by Fedor Burlatskii, a Central Committee official during the 1950s and early 1960s, have also provided a detailed and enthusiastic, if not wholly uncritical, profile of the Khrushchev years.[8]

As the most in-depth studies yet available, these memoirs are invaluable revisionist sources. As mentioned in the paradigm sketched above, the authors looked at the pros and cons of Khrushchev's legacy through the prism of perestroika. Moreover, they mixed their long-held reformist viewpoints and advocacy of Gorbachev with the aim of rehabilitating Khrushchev and themselves. But except for Adzhubei in some respects, the personal association of these analysts with Khrushchev did not prevent them from presenting an otherwise balanced portrayal. After stating unqualified support for Gorbachev's program of reform, they proceeded to highlight Khrushchev's anti-Stalinist initiatives while criticizing aspects of the Khrushchev heritage that impeded the process of change. In so doing, they molded an image of the Khrushchev era that delineated a bold reformist heritage for perestroika without implicating the recent reform in the shortcomings of the Khrushchev years.

Starting this discussion with Burlatskii is instructive, for his article "Khrushchev: Shtrikhi k politicheskomu portretu," appearing in *Literaturnaia gazeta* in February 1988, was the first to seriously analyze the Khrushchev period in nearly a quarter-century.[9] In the three months prior to this, the few articles that discussed Khrushchev gave fleeting praise to some of his reformist impulses but did not challenge a number of the traditional Khrushchevian stereotypes.[10] Burlatskii's position as an official in the Central Committee in the late 1950s, however, not only gave him access to many of the significant party decisions of the time but also allowed him to

---

[8] All these works utilize the new paradigm: Fedor M. Burlatskii, "Khrushchev: Shtrikhi k politicheskomu portretu," reprinted in *Inogo ne dano: Sud'by perestroiki, vgliadyvaias' v proshloe, vozvrashchenie k budushchemu*, ed. Iu. N. Afanas'ev (Moscow: Progress, 1988), 424–40; Aleksei I. Adzhubei, *Te desiat' let* (Moscow: Sovetskaia Rossiia, 1989); and Sergei N. Khrushchev, *Khrushchev on Khrushchev* (Boston: Little, Brown, and Co., 1990). The second chapter of Sergei Khrushchev's memoirs was serialized in four issues of *Ogonek* in October 1988 (nos. 40–43). Other sections were subsequently published in various Soviet journals as well.

[9] Burlatskii, "Khrushchev: Shtrikhi," 424–40.

[10] For example, see I. Perov, "Otkrytyi otvet Iu. Burtinu," *Oktiabr'*, 1987, no. 12, reprinted in *Nikita Sergeevich Khrushchev: Materialy k biografii*, ed. Iu. V. Aksiutin (Moscow: Politizdat, 1989), 109–10. Aside from the major works previously cited, many articles on Khrushchev from the Soviet press have been reprinted in this volume. All citations from this book include reference to the publications in which the articles originally appeared.

provide new insights into the Khrushchev years as well as a broad interpretation of that era. As an example, he related how deeply Khrushchev's "secret speech" reverberated in Soviet government and society, where its dramatic contents often passed by word of mouth.[11] In another work, Burlatskii also revealed that the anti-Stalinist thunder at the Twenty-second Party Congress was so choreographed that most speakers never sincerely adhered to Khrushchev's line on the "personality cult."[12] Of course, Burlatskii did not fully address every important issue. For instance, he wrote little about the *vydvizhentsy*, or those workers who, like Khrushchev, rose to positions of responsibility and prominence during the purges of the 1930s and often played a role in them. Burlatskii furthermore touched only lightly on Khrushchev's role in the chain of command from Stalin when Khrushchev was either the chairman of the Moscow city and *oblast'* committees or the Ukrainian party leader between the late 1930s and early 1950s. Finally, Burlatskii largely ignored Khrushchev's activities in World War II, a major event in his career and an influence on his political outlook.[13]

It was his interpretation of Khrushchev's political legacy, however, that made Burlatskii's contribution important. In his initial article, Burlatskii developed a thesis about the reformist nature of the Khrushchev period that has helped to shape the revised paradigm of the Khrushchev years. His main contention was that, in spite of a somewhat contradictory heritage, Khrushchev's overall contribution to Soviet political life must be seen as beneficial because of his attempt to reform the Stalinist system that had controlled the country for so long. Looking beyond Khrushchev's many foibles, Burlatskii saw his anti-Stalinism as a towering political legacy.[14] Indeed, Burlatskii considered Khrushchev's reformist heritage as one of the major motive forces of perestroika. On the rise of Khrushchev to the top of the Soviet leadership in 1953, Burlatskii argued that

> all the same, history made the correct choice. It was an answer to the real problems of our life. The basic poverty of the people, especially in the half-ruined countryside, the technologically backward industry, the acute housing shortage, the low living standard of the population, the millions of people locked in prisons and camps, and the isolation of the country from the outside world—all this required a new policy and radical changes. And Khrushchev appeared precisely as the people's hope, the precursor of a new age.[15]

Most important for Burlatskii, Khrushchev's "secret speech" denouncing Stalin at the Twentieth Party Congress in 1956 was a courageous act that no other politician among the heirs of Stalin would have had the fortitude to make.[16] Though inconsis-

---

[11] Burlatskii, "Khrushchev: Shtrikhi," 428.

[12] Burlatskii, "Posle Stalina: Zametki o politicheskoi ottepeli," *Novyi mir,* 1988, no. 10:195. In this article Burlatskii provided information on the coup attempt by the "anti-party group" in 1957, the anti-Stalinist revelations of the Twenty-second Party Congress in 1961, and other events of Khrushchev's era.

[13] Burlatskii touched cursorily on these topics in part of one paragraph in "Khrushchev: Shtrikhi," 433, and in other analyses.

[14] Ibid., 438–39.

[15] Ibid., 426.

[16] Burlatskii, *Khrushchev and the First Russian Spring,* trans. Daphne Skillen (London: Weidenfeld and Nicolson, 1991), 63.

tent and limited, Khrushchev's de-Stalinization campaign served as a breath of fresh air that the Soviet Union desperately needed after many years of repression. In fact, Burlatskii connected Khrushchev's reformism and anti-Stalinist initiatives directly to the policies of earlier Soviet figures who struggled to limit Stalin's power, such as Bukharin and Sergei Kirov.[17]

Burlatskii nonetheless criticized several of Khrushchev's initiatives, particularly the bifurcation of party administration into agricultural and industrial branches in the early 1960s. This policy was Khrushchev's greatest mistake because it reflected his belief that a reorganization of the *apparat,* and not a more basic reform of the system, was the primary requirement for improving the performance of the Soviet economy. By contrast, Gorbachev allowed perestroika to alter Soviet government and society at far deeper levels. Burlatskii also held that Khrushchev, in spite of a native political intelligence, weakened his own programs because he accepted faulty advice from his associates and possessed such insuperable personal characteristics as emotionalism, rashness, and haste. Nevertheless, Burlatskii insisted that although many of Khrushchev's policies ultimately failed, they at least reflected a sincere desire to move away from the Stalinist past.[18]

More importantly, however, Burlatskii stressed that attempts to restructure the Soviet system under Khrushchev thirty years ago made possible the necessary reforms of the Gorbachev era. In this respect, perestroika owed a great debt to the Khrushchev program.[19] If Burlatskii could be faulted for anything, it was that he did not completely address the less-appealing aspects of Khrushchev's record. But his revised interpretation still helped to recast the historical legacy of Khrushchev. By depicting him as a leader whose reformist intentions overshadowed his numerous shortcomings, Burlatskii's revisionist image broke down old stereotypes and served as a catalyst for further serious discussion of the Khrushchev era.

On a more personal level than Burlatskii's account, Sergei Khrushchev's memoirs, *Khrushchev on Khrushchev,* provided a son's assessment of certain critical issues in the final decade of Khrushchev's life. Beginning with the last years of his father's period of rule, Sergei analyzed key Khrushchev policies as well as the people and events that led to his ouster in October 1964. In the latter instance, he offered fresh insight on the machinations of Presidium (the name of the Politburo from 1952 to 1966) members such as L. I. Brezhnev and N. V. Podgornii to remove Khrushchev from power. Of special interest, Sergei commented that M. A. Suslov, chief party ideologist at the time, did not join the plot to unseat Khrushchev until the last minute, while Brezhnev exhibited excessive timidity at the consequences before the deed was accomplished.[20] Overall, Khrushchev's proteges (including Brezhnev, Podgornii and former KGB chief A. N. Shelepin) were more instrumental than his ideological enemies (Suslov) in his removal from power.[21] Sergei also described the reflections on

---

[17] Burlatskii, "Khrushchev: Shtrikhi," 424–25.

[18] Ibid., 437–40.

[19] Ibid., 424.

[20] Sergei Khrushchev, *Khrushchev on Khrushchev,* 135–36.

[21] Another scholar reached this conclusion as well. See Werner Hahn, "Who Ousted Nikita Sergeyevich?" *Problems of Communism* 40 (May-June 1991): 115.

political life that his father expressed during retirement and confirmed that the Khrushchev memoirs smuggled to the West twenty years ago were indeed authentic. In relating this last story, Sergei revealed that the perpetual confiscation of materials by the KGB made the smuggling of Khrushchev's memoirs to the West both a necessary and difficult task.[22]

As Burlatskii had done, Sergei Khrushchev likened his father's period of rule to the recent era of reform under Gorbachev. Sergei's opinions, however, were slightly more rose-colored than Burlatskii's and tended to overlook some of the negative aspects of Khrushchev's career that even Burlatskii tried to address. For example, Sergei often portrayed mistakes in policy as the result of advisers who "fooled" or "duped" a seemingly passive Khrushchev.[23] Nevertheless, most of Sergei's views appeared forthright and reasonable. He argued on several occasions that a number of recent Soviet initiatives had a foundation in the 1950s and early 1960s. In particular, Sergei interpreted Gorbachev's economic reforms, military reductions, and policy of peaceful coexistence with the West as having many roots in his father's program. In fact, Sergei claimed in an overdrawn but still plausible analogy:

> On many issues we are about where we were twenty-five years ago. Reading Khrushchev's thoughts on the development of the economy, and on reducing the armed forces, we are amazed to discover that he pondered the very issues we are debating now. In this way, Khrushchev has lived on, returning to take an active part in the political process.[24]

Broadening the paradigm outlined by Burlatskii, Sergei even insinuated that the policy of perestroika actually began with Lenin in 1917 and flourished during the early years of Soviet power. Crushed by Stalin in the late 1920s, its reformist spirit was resuscitated by his father in the 1950s. After the Brezhnevite years of stagnation, perestroika again emerged as a force to regenerate Soviet society under Gorbachev. According to Sergei, his father holds an integral position in Soviet history primarily through his preservation of the reformist spirit of the party.[25]

On another level, Sergei Khrushchev criticized his father for not having been able to move beyond the "command-administrative" system in conceptualizing reform. In spite of the anti-Stalinist rhetoric of the Khrushchev years, Sergei agreed that his father did not ultimately refashion the shape or function of Stalin's bureaucratic apparatus. Mistakenly believing that the *apparat* could serve as a vehicle for reform, Khrushchev watched his innovations suffocate under a Soviet government that remained deeply conservative in its outlook. In conclusion, Sergei contended that the chances for successful reform in the 1990s were greater because the recent changes sought to alter the structural base of Soviet power.[26]

Though important, Burlatskii's and Sergei Khrushchev's accounts stressed positive elements in their analysis of Khrushchev. In concentrating on reform, both omit-

[22] Sergei Khrushchev, *Khrushchev on Khrushchev,* 247–50.
[23] For Sergei, Khrushchev's support of the agronomist T. D. Lysenko fit this pattern. Ibid., 43–45.
[24] Ibid., 407.
[25] Sergei compared his father's program with perestroika at length. Ibid., 399–410.
[26] Ibid., 408–9.

ted a serious treatment of the contradictions and darker side of the Khrushchev legacy. By contrast, the work of Aleksei Adzhubei, former editor of *Izvestiia* and Khrushchev's son-in-law, addressed the negative aspects of the Khrushchev heritage as well. Perhaps because of this, a strong apologetic tone can be seen in Adzhubei's memoirs, *Te desiat' let*. Nevertheless, his account was especially useful because it complemented Sergei Khrushchev's reminiscences of the last years of Khrushchev's life by looking at his political career from 1949 (when Adzhubei married Khrushchev's daughter Rada) until his retirement.

While occasionally glancing back to fill in personal details from Khrushchev's earlier activities, Adzhubei followed a chronological development of public events that analyzed Khrushchev's rise to power, his economic reforms, the Twentieth Party Congress and "secret speech," his trip to America in 1959, the Cuban Missile Crisis, his ouster in 1964, and his years in retirement. Like Burlatskii and Sergei Khrushchev, Adzhubei contended that his father-in-law's greatest legacy was in the attempt to knock Stalin off his pedestal and genuinely reform the Soviet system of government. While admitting that Khrushchev made some mistakes, Adzhubei viewed Khrushchev's reformist heritage as far more important to history than his political shortcomings. As such, he also interpreted Khrushchev's actions as an initial phase of perestroika.[27]

Adzhubei's account differed from both the memoirs of Burlatskii and Sergei Khrushchev, however, in possessing a defensive tone that occasionally belied objectivity.[28] For example, Adzhubei defended Khrushchev's placement of nuclear missiles in Cuba by repeating the conventional assertions about the presence of U.S. military bases in Turkey and the threat to Cuban security highlighted by the Bay of Pigs invasion.[29] Furthermore, he blamed Suslov for the Grossman affair, in which V. Grossman's novel, *Zhizn' i sud'ba*, was denied publication in the early 1960s, thereby trying to exonerate Khrushchev.[30] Adzhubei also pointed out several mitigating factors dissociating Khrushchev from Stalin's excesses in the 1930s and 1940s. For example, Adzhubei typically blamed the crimes of the era on Stalin and L. P. Beria, his last secret police chief.[31] Associates such as Khrushchev participated because they were mere Stalinist satraps whose lives and families would otherwise be in danger.[32] Finally, Adzhubei overstated the importance of Khrushchev's economic policies in rejuvenating the lethargic Soviet economy.[33] In spite of these drawbacks, however,

---

[27] All these were common themes throughout Adzhubei's book. On Khrushchev's legacy in the de-Stalinization campaign, see Adzhubei, *Te desiat' let*, 126–28.

[28] Other Soviet authors have noted Adzhubei's defensiveness. Perov remarked how Adzhubei upheld Khrushchev's shoe-banging incident at the UN as a "simply healthy" expression of vigor (Perov, "Otkrytyi otvet," in *Khrushchev*, ed. Aksiutin, 110).

[29] Adzhubei, *Te desiat' let*, 254–55.

[30] Ibid., 171–73.

[31] Some scholars have written that Khrushchev, while in power, categorically destroyed archival evidence implicating him and others in specific Stalinist crimes. For example, see Dmitri Volkogonov, *Stalin: Triumph and Tragedy*, ed. and trans. Harold Shukman (Rocklin, CA: Prima, 1992), 308. The loss of such material may thus mistakenly facilitate Adzhubei's claim.

[32] Adzhubei, *Te desiat' let*, 81.

[33] Ibid., 97.

256 *David Nordlander*

Adzhubei's reminiscences remain a vital source of information because of his unique vantage point as aide and son-in-law to Khrushchev.

In addition to the major memoirs, a number of recent articles on the Khrushchev era have appeared in various journals, magazines and newspapers. Most of them share three central themes: Khrushchev's economic reforms; his actions in world affairs; and his political legacy. Khrushchev's personal life and rise through the ranks of government appeared far less important to recent Soviet analysts than his actual period of rule and its aftermath. At any rate, though supportive of perestroika and often in agreement with the paradigm sketched above, the majority of these authors were quite contentious in their discussion of various aspects of the Khrushchev heritage. Nevertheless, they reflected the dual interpretation that sought to highlight the reformist successes of Khrushchev while limiting the damage his failures could imply for perestroika. Of course, participants in the debate placed varying emphasis on the positive and negative aspects of Khrushchev's legacy. Interestingly, Presidium (Politburo) members who directly benefited from Khrushchev's ouster, such as former KGB chiefs Shelepin and V. E. Semichastnii, provided some of the more complimentary remarks.[34] But the overall implications of their debate were clear: mindful of the Khrushchev past, these commentators sought to preserve Khrushchev's reformist heritage while distancing Gorbachev from the mistakes committed thirty years ago.

Khrushchev's economic reforms held a special place in the debate on his legacy because they were long cited as the prime examples of Khrushchev's "hare-brained" schemes. In recent years, scholarly opinion on this topic covered the entire spectrum. Before looking at the negative interpretations, which are slightly imitative of past denunciations of Khrushchev, it is best to start with the more innovative defenses of his reformist economics. Indeed, many analysts praised Khrushchev's efforts to reshape Soviet economic policy after Stalin's death. While not discounting his failures, these authors argued that the essence of Khrushchev's programs was important, and did indeed provide a bold reformist heritage for perestroika and the modern transformation of the Soviet Union.

One of the most stirring arguments appeared in an article by the historian G. B. Fedorov, who contended that Khrushchev's reforms, though partially unfulfilled, had a largely positive effect in raising the material well-being of Soviet citizens in the countryside. Fedorov also noted Khrushchev's positive work in the pension and housing reforms of the 1950s and early 1960s and even stated that the "corn campaign" was a partial success.[35] Others argued that perestroika, as a modern version of "socialism with a human face," had some roots in the benevolence of the Khrushchev era. The literary critic Iu. G. Burtin wrote that most of Khrushchev's economic pol-

---

[34] This may reflect their need for justification in the new political order. Praising Khrushchev served perhaps to mitigate their role in the "stagnation" of the Brezhnev years. For reference to recent Soviet views on Khrushchev's ouster, particularly from Presidium members, see Hahn, "Who Ousted Nikita Sergeyevich?" 114.

[35] G. B. Fedorov, "Kak nam otsenivat' Khrushcheva?" *Moskovskie novosti*, 1988, no. 31, in *Khrushchev*, ed. Aksiutin, 186–88. The "corn campaign" was Khrushchev's attempt to cultivate that grain in many regions of the USSR in spite of often inhospitable climatic conditions.

icies were humanistic efforts aimed at improving the lot of the average Soviet citizen.[36] Several commentators reiterated Burtin's view by mentioning Khrushchev's valiant attempt to transform the Stalinist emphasis on technology and machinery into a more beneficent attention to the various needs of the Soviet people.[37] In general, the many defenses of Khrushchev's economic policies provided provocative insights into some of the reformist successes that typically are overshadowed by his more publicized failures. As a whole, however, these analyses suffered from a selective argumentation that, particularly in Fedorov's case, ignored the more problematic aspects of Khrushchev's economic legacy.

In contrast, some Soviet analysts stressed the negative aspects of Khrushchev's heritage in economic reform. While admitting that Khrushchev's boldness provided an important example for recent Soviet reformers, they argued that many of Khrushchev's economic policies not only failed but actually delayed the country's progress by many years. Furthermore, these observers maintained that the economic aspects of Khrushchev's legacy could serve as a guidepost of what perestroika should not seek to accomplish. As noted previously, this line of argument distinguished Gorbachev's programs from Khrushchev's failures and helped to limit the political danger of using the Khrushchev era as a model of reform. Of course, in their desire to protect Gorbachev's reputation, these respondents tended to commit the opposite flaw of the group that defended Khrushchev's reformist economic heritage: they almost exclusively, and quite unobjectively, denigrated his programmatic mistakes.

An article by the political commentator I. Perov serves as an excellent case in point. While resuscitating the pejorative image of the "corn god" to discredit Khrushchev's attempts to improve the performance of Soviet agriculture, Perov stated that the reputation of perestroika should not be sullied by comparison to the economic reforms of the 1950s and early 1960s. Perov even ignored such obvious parallels as the attack by both Khrushchev and Gorbachev on the vestiges of the Stalinist bureaucracy in an attempt to defend Gorbachev.[38] Other authors contrasted the logic and rationality of perestroika, where reform suggestions were always to be made by a committee of experts such as Abel Aganbegian, Tatiana Zaslavskaia, and Leonid Abal'kin, with the single-handed approach of Khrushchev's reformist style. Some even surprisingly used the negative Brezhnev-era terms, arguing that "the methods of Khrushchev's leadership, his voluntaristic meddling [*vmeshatel'stvo*] in the sphere of government, culture, and especially agriculture, were dangerously unpredictable."[39] Concurring with this view, the philosopher Iu. A. Levada and the economist V. L. Sheinis stressed that most of Khrushchev's economic policies were

[36] Iu. G. Burtin, "Shagi k cheloveku," *Oktiabr'*, 1987, no. 8, in *Khrushchev*, ed. Aksiutin, 106–9. Other Soviet authors have also commented that a positive and "humanistic" reform of economic relations followed the end of "authoritarianism" in 1953. See N. A. Barsukov, "Eshche vperedi XX s"ezd . . . ," *Pravda*, 17 November 1989.

[37] For example, see remarks by the publicist, V. Fedorov, "Opponentu Iu. Burtina," *Oktiabr'*, 1988, no. 5, in *Khrushchev*, ed. Aksiutin, 111.

[38] I. Perov, "Otkrytyi otvet," in *Khrushchev*, ed. Aksiutin, 110.

[39] See V. P. Naumov, V. V. Riabov, and Iu. I. Filippov, "Ob istoricheskom puti KPSS v svete novogo myshleniia," *Voprosy istorii KPSS*, 1989, no. 10:8.

poorly organized and none was carried out to a proper conclusion.[40] Still another author complained that Khrushchev's attempt in 1957 to reduce the power of the central economic ministries by creating the *sovnarkhozy,* or regional economic councils, was counterproductive in almost every respect.[41]

Seeking a middle ground, many Soviet commentators praised the intentions of Khrushchev's economic reforms while criticizing their results. Though not necessarily better-argued than the previous opinions, the views of these authors were forceful in the objectivity of their measured analyses. As they saw it, perestroika had to borrow from the motivations, not the deeds, of the Khrushchev era. The economist I. V. Rusinov argued that though Khrushchev had some useful ideas for solving the problems of Soviet agrarian life, he simply did not furnish the means to achieve these goals. Initial, "unprecedented" growth of the agricultural sector between 1954 and 1958 gave way to years of lackluster production until Khrushchev's ouster in 1964.[42] Similarly, the historian and publicist Roy A. Medvedev contended that many of Khrushchev's agricultural programs, though well intended and often promising at the start, ultimately failed and led to his downfall.[43]

Both Roy and Zhores Medvedev had made this point several times in their previous works; interestingly, many other Soviet authors came to agree wholeheartedly with this classic Medvedev thesis in recent times.[44] Several interpreted Khrushchev's agricultural reforms as well motivated but tragically misguided in scope and scale. Needless to say, Soviet analysts may have been wont to follow the Medvedev argument because distancing Gorbachev from Khrushchev's troubled agrarian reform was essential to maintain the validity of Gorbachev's own plans for agricultural change.

As a whole, Soviet reassessments of Khrushchev's agrarian ventures have been highly critical.[45] Rusinov used such fiascos as the Machine-Tractor Station (MTS) reorganization debacle in the late 1950s to show that Khrushchev did not implement his economic programs with a rational sense of proportion. Khrushchev sought to have the inadequately funded kolkhozy purchase the farm machinery of the MTSs, which were set up in Stalin's time to provide technical assistance to collective farm-

[40] Iu. A. Levada and V. L. Sheinis, "1953–1964: Pochemu togda ne poluchilos'," *Moskovskie novosti,* 1988, no. 18, in *Khrushchev,* ed. Aksiutin, 184–86.

[41] V. N. Novikov, "V gody rukovodstva N. S. Khrushcheva," *Voprosy istorii,* 1989, no. 1:110, no. 2:116.

[42] Rusinov pointed out that many of Khrushchev's programs, though intended to overcome Stalin's "command-administrative" system, were themselves undone by their highly administrative nature. See I. V. Rusinov, "Agrarnaia politika KPSS v 50-e—pervoi polovine 60-x godov: Opyt i uroki," *Voprosy istorii KPSS,* 1988, no. 9:37–39, 48.

[43] R. A. Medvedev, "N. S. Khrushchev. God 1964-i—neozhidannoe smeshchenie," *Argumenty i fakty,* 1988, no. 27, in *Khrushchev,* ed. Aksiutin, 197–201.

[44] See in particular R. A. Medvedev and Z. A. Medvedev, *Khrushchev: The Years in Power,* trans. Andrew R. Durkin (New York, 1978); R. A. Medvedev, *Khrushchev,* trans. Brian Pearce (New York, 1983); and Z. A. Medvedev, *Soviet Agriculture* (New York, 1987).

[45] Of course, some praised Khrushchev simply for his commitment to reform. See D. V. Valovoi, "N. Khrushchev: Povernut'sia litsom k ekonomike," *Ekonomika v chelovecheskom izmerenii* (Moscow, 1988), republished in *Khrushchev,* ed. Aksiutin, 93–94; E. I. Nosov, "Kostroma ne Aiova," *Literaturnaia gazeta,* 1988, no. 16, in *Khrushchev,* ed. Aksiutin, 102; and Burlatskii, "Khrushchev: Shtrikhi," 439.

ers. The result was massive paralysis.[46] Furthermore, many authors contended that Khrushchev's "corn campaign" proved the impulsive shortcomings of his agricultural planning. For E. I. Nosov, Khrushchev's abrupt decision after his trip to America in 1959 that corn should be grown on a large scale in the USSR exhibited the drawbacks both of Khrushchev's political style and the Russian authoritarian tradition.[47] Substantiating these viewpoints, the journalist and economic commentator L. N. Voskresenskii complained that the "corn campaign," hailed at the time as the sowing of a "miracle crop," was a widespread mistake that dearly cost the Soviet economy.[48]

Recent Soviet analysts also followed the Medvedevs' lead in criticizing the dubious role of T. D. Lysenko, a controversial agronomist under both Stalin and Khrushchev, in Khrushchev's agricultural policy. According to Rusinov, Khrushchev too often defended Lysenko against his persistent critics in the Soviet Academy of Sciences. As the Medvedevs had, he also deplored Khrushchev's liquidation of the K. A. Timiriazev Agricultural Academy in 1962 over the "disagreement of scientists with his recommendations."[49] Khrushchev even met with sustained attack on the issue of the Virgin Lands Campaign, a centerpiece of his agrarian programs whereby large tracts of unutilized soil in northern Kazakhstan were brought under cultivation in the mid-1950s.[50] In general, Soviet authors roundly criticized Khrushchev's agricultural record, particularly in his adherence to Stalinist gigantism.[51] By implicit contrast, they saw Gorbachev as pursuing Khrushchev's reformist motivations in the countryside with a greater sense of vision and degree.

The discussion of Khrushchev's role in world affairs in the 1950s and early 1960s also developed a mixed perspective, though one with a more positive emphasis. Many Soviet authors saw Khrushchev's efforts at détente, peaceful coexistence, and the normalization of international relations as bequeathing a positive diplomatic heritage to later Soviet reformers and having a great impact on Gorbachev's own foreign policy. The historian Iu. V. Aksiutin stressed that the gradual transition from the "Cold War" to peaceful coexistence between East and West began in the Khrushchev era.[52] He and others also noted Khrushchev's role in improving relations with socialist countries that became estranged from the Soviet Union under Stalin.[53] Of course,

[46] Rusinov, "Agrarnaia politika KPSS," 45–46. In spite of his failures, there was often some logic in Khrushchev's methods. On the MTS reorganization plan, Khrushchev borrowed the reasoning of the academician A. M. Rumiantsev that it was better to have one *khoziain*, or master (the *kolkhozy*), in the countryside than two (the *kolkhozy* and the MTS). See A. I. Strelianyi, "Poslednii romantik," *Druzhba narodov*, 1988, no. 11:218.

[47] Nosov, "Kostroma ne Aiova," 100–106.

[48] L. N. Voskresenskii, "Boltovnia—dama opasnaia," *Moskovskie novosti*, 1987, no. 14, in *Khrushchev*, ed. Aksiutin, 113–14.

[49] Rusinov, "Agrarnaia politika KPSS," 47.

[50] See R. A. Medvedev, "N. S. Khrushchev. Politicheskaia biografiia," *Druzhba narodov*, 1989, no. 7:147. Some analysts were quick to add that yields never matched expectations with this campaign either. See Rusinov, "Agrarnaia politika KPSS," 40.

[51] Burlatskii criticized Khrushchev for such inadequacies as his love of gigantism in economic projects. But while critical, Burlatskii was more positive of Khrushchev's agrarian record than many other Soviet analysts ("Khrushchev: Shtrikhi," 439).

[52] Aksiutin, "Ot redaktsii," in *Khrushchev*, ed. Aksiutin, 3. See also, from this volume (p. 107), Iu. G. Burtin, "Shagi k cheloveku," *Oktiabr'*, 1987, no. 8.

[53] R. A. Medvedev, "N. S. Khrushchev. Politicheskaia biografiia," 148; Aksiutin, "N. S. Khru-

260   *David Nordlander*

there is also much to find fault with in Khrushchev's foreign policy, and indeed several recent Soviet authors criticized his handling of such crises as the U-2 affair and the Berlin impasse.[54] But their fairly complimentary assessment of his international policies, particularly his promotion of good relations with the West, seemed to validate their support for Gorbachev's own pro-Western orientation. Khrushchev's pioneering of détente provided Gorbachev with a solid foundation for his effort to rejuvenate the faltering Soviet economy as well as to reintegrate his country as a fully functioning member in the world community of nations.

The moderate encomium for Khrushchev's diplomacy also extended to his handling of affairs with the Third World, although in this case it was mixed with criticism of some of his methods and viewpoints. While Gorbachev's attention in international affairs focused largely on the industrial world, glasnost-era commentators cited Khrushchev for his development of relations with the Third World. For example, the historian G. I. Mirskii lauded Khrushchev's "initiative" in constructing closer ties with the Arab world through a friendly association with Egypt's president, Gamal Abdel Nasser. According to Mirskii, Khrushchev's "unorthodox political thought" in disregarding the non-Marxist nature of Nasser's revolutionary leadership led to new and constructive political relations not only with Egypt but later with Algeria and Syria as well. While addressing neither the controversial role of the USSR in this region nor the eventual break in ties between Egypt and the Soviet Union, Mirskii contended that Khrushchev's policies secured a strong Soviet presence in the Middle East for many years.[55]

In a similar vein, the journalist and political commentator S. N. Kondrashov discussed Khrushchev's admirable role in working with the newly liberated countries of Africa in the 1950s and early 1960s. Yet Kondrashov, in an obvious desire to differentiate between the diplomatic styles of Khrushchev and Gorbachev, also stated that Gorbachev's comprehension of the Third World, and international affairs in general, was far deeper than Khrushchev's. Contrasting Khrushchev's visit to the United Nations in 1960 with Gorbachev's in 1988, Kondrashov described the immense distance that Soviet diplomacy had traversed in the intervening thirty years. Kondrashov especially criticized Khrushchev for denouncing then UN Secretary-General D. H. Hammarskjöld as a "servant of American capital" in spite of Hammarskjöld's constructive work with post-colonial nations in Africa. To Kondrashov, this was a regrettable outgrowth of Khrushchev's ideological division of the world into "socialist," "capitalist," and "neutral" camps, a heritage of his political upbringing under Stalin that contrasted sharply with Gorbachev's sober understanding of international relations and the modern sophistication of Soviet foreign policy.[56]

While Soviet authors had mixed views of Khrushchev's actions toward the Third

shchev: My dolzhni skazat' pravdu o kul'te lichnosti," *Trud*, 13 November 1988, in *Khrushchev*, ed. Aksiutin, 36.

[54] S. N. Kondrashov, "Tseli i sredstva," *Izvestiia*, 14 December 1988, in *Khrushchev*, ed. Aksiutin, 60.

[55] G. I. Mirskii, "Khrushchev i Nasser: iz interv'iu korrespondentu ezhenedel'nika 'Argumenty i fakty' D. Makarovu," *Argumenty i fakty*, 1988, no. 26, in *Khrushchev*, ed. Aksiutin, 88–89.

[56] Kondrashov, "Tseli i sredstva," 57–62.

World, however, they generally criticized his policies toward China. Such a stance was understandable, for commentators had to distance Khrushchev's poor handling of Chinese affairs from Gorbachev's attempts to normalize Soviet relations with China. The former deputy director of Heavy-Machine Construction in the USSR in the late 1950s, K. I. Koval', blamed Khrushchev's "impulsive reactions" and "harsh attitude toward the leadership of the Chinese party" for the "surprising and unexpected removal of all our specialists from China and a worsening of Soviet-Chinese relations. Thus began a long period of political confrontation, border conflicts, and bitter ideological denunciations."[57] Roy Medvedev remarked that Khrushchev acted compulsively and competitively with the Chinese leader Mao Zedong, all to the detriment of ties between China and the Soviet Union at the time.[58]

Khrushchev's role in the Cuban Missile Crisis also dominated several of the articles dealing with his activities in international affairs. In contrast to the other topics, however, this debate defied tidy classification. Whereas past analyses, including Roy Medvedev's, disparaged Khrushchev's handling of the Cuban Missile Crisis, modern Soviet opinion was less negative. Some Western analysts said this was true because Gorbachev wanted Khrushchev to be seen as a competent predecessor in statesmanship.[59] But part of the reason for this also lay in the fact that the positions and legitimacy of many of the Soviets who proffered views on the crisis were tied closely to the events in Cuba thirty years ago.

In general, Soviet commentators in the last few years supported Adzhubei's interpretation of the Cuban Missile Crisis by defending the position of the Soviet government even as they acknowledged the danger of the crisis. A. I. Alekseev, a former Soviet ambassador to Cuba, pointed out that Khrushchev acted justly in attempting to preserve the integrity of the Cuban Revolution and to counter the presence of American military bases and missiles in Turkey and other areas surrounding the Soviet Union.[60] The historian S. A. Mikoian, son of the former Politburo member A. I. Mikoian, wrote that the desire to reach nuclear parity with the United States, which grew into a massive military build-up under Brezhnev, emanated from Khrushchev's legitimate attempt to correct America's 17:1 advantage in nuclear warheads by placing missiles in Cuba in 1962.[61] Yet both Alekseev and Mikoian also agreed that Khrushchev made the right decision when he removed the missiles in order to prevent a nuclear war. The journalist and political commentator V. I. Kobysh even praised Khrushchev (and then U.S. President John F. Kennedy) for displaying flex-

---

[57] K. I. Koval', "Peregovory I. V. Stalina s Chzhou En'laem v 1953 g. v Moskve i N. S. Khrushcheva s Mao Tszedunom v 1954 g. v Pekine," *Novaia i noveishaia istoriia*, 1989, no. 5:118.

[58] R. A. Medvedev, "Kitai v politike SSSR i SShA," *Narody Azii i Afriki*, 1990, no. 1:83.

[59] Many Western authors even inveighed against recent Soviet "historical revisionism" that exonerated Khrushchev's role in foreign affairs. Ray S. Cline, for example, contended that Soviet debate on the Cuban Missile Crisis portrayed Khrushchev in a good light because Gorbachev wanted him to be seen as his competent and reformist predecessor. See Ray S. Cline, "Commentary: The Cuban Missile Crisis," *Foreign Affairs* (Fall 1989): 190.

[60] A. I. Alekseev, "Karibskii krizis. Kak eto bylo," *Ekho planety*, 1988, no. 33, in *Khrushchev*, ed. Aksiutin, 80–81.

[61] S. A. Mikoian, "Voina, kotoraia ne nachalas'," *Novoe vremia*, 1987, no. 46, in *Khrushchev*, ed. Aksiutin, 83.

262   *David Nordlander*

ibility and prudence throughout the crisis.[62] Most authors were more critical of "American hypocrisy" on the question of nuclear parity and of American aggression against Cuba than they were of Khrushchev's handling of the affair.

Beyond international concerns, the most important theme in the debate was Khrushchev's political legacy because it involved his role as an anti-Stalinist reformer who provided the framework for Gorbachev's policy of de-Stalinization. This was also the subject on which Khrushchev received the most consistent praise. While several authors remarked that Khrushchev did not carry his political reforms far enough, almost all agreed with Burlatskii, Adzhubei, and Sergei Khrushchev that Khrushchev's courage and determination in exposing Stalin's crimes were vitally important and generally outweighed any shortcomings in his political leadership. Furthermore, most Soviet commentators acknowledged that Khrushchev was probably the only one of Stalin's successors who would have pursued the anti-Stalin campaign to the extent he did.[63]

Khrushchev's policy of de-Stalinization was universally interpreted as his most lasting political testament, particularly in its effects on the anti-Stalin movement of the Gorbachev years. Here again, the pro-Gorbachev intelligentsia naturally took this position because Khrushchev's de-Stalinization campaign was in many respects the midwife of the modern attitudes of Soviet intellectuals. Aksiutin stressed Khrushchev's bravery and fortitude in denouncing the Stalin cult and mentioned that, during his retirement, Khrushchev wished that it would have been possible to go even further, to the point of rehabilitating Bukharin, Zinoviev, Rykov, and others.[64] Roy Medvedev stressed that the mere fact that Khrushchev's rivals could remove him from power without arrest or bloodshed is a testimony to the changes that he wrought. On the day that Khrushchev was removed from power, Medvedev noted, he returned home, tossed his briefcase down, and said: "Well, now I'm retired. Perhaps my most important accomplishment lies in the fact that they removed me from power by a simple vote, an act that would have caused their arrest under Stalin."[65] Several analysts reiterated the viewpoint that Khrushchev was the only politician of his era who would have undertaken such a drastic reform of the system.[66]

At the same time, the recent analysis of Khrushchev's political legacy was not uncritical. Soviet authors who supported perestroika had to distinguish between the limited democratization of Soviet society under Khrushchev and the more extensive democratic initiatives of the Gorbachev years. For them, showing that Gorbachev's

[62] V. I. Kobysh, "Uroki Karibskogo krizisa," *Izvestiia*, 22 October 1987, in *Khrushchev*, ed. Aksiutin, 67.

[63] See, for example, remarks by the historians O. V. Volobuev and S. V. Kuleshov, "Tak i ne 'prorvalsia' k narodu," *Sotsialisticheskaia industriia*, 20 November 1988, in *Khrushchev*, ed. Aksiutin, 165.

[64] Aksiutin, "N. S. Khrushchev," 42.

[65] R. A. Medvedev, "N. S. Khrushchev. God 1964-i," 201–2. Other analysts have made similar assessments. See, for example, Aksiutin, "Khrushchev, god 1964-i," *Trud*, 26 November 1989.

[66] The author A. I. Strelianyi commented that Khrushchev was one of the few Soviet politicians who partially overcame his political upbringing under Stalin, and thus could accomplish significant reform ("Sub"ektivnye zametki o Nikite Khrushcheve," *Moskovskie novosti*, 1988, no. 42, in *Khrushchev*, ed. Aksiutin, 191–93). See also remarks by the poet and dramatist K. Simonov, "On okazalsia printsipial'nee i energichnee, chem vse ostal'nye," *Znamia*, 1988, no. 4, in *Khrushchev*, ed. Aksiutin, 27–31.

policies had already gone well beyond the limited horizons of the Khrushchev era required some criticism of Khrushchev's political reforms. In this regard, the journalist and political commentator A. E. Bovin contended that at a time when the country was "thirsting" for change after Stalin's death, Khrushchev did not do enough to overcome the inertia of the Stalinist system. For Bovin, Khrushchev's ultimate failure lay in the fact that Brezhnev succeeded him to power and strengthened Stalin's bureaucratic apparatus.[67] Other observers even suggested that Khrushchev was, in fact, quite comfortable with Stalin's "hierarchical-administrative" structure. Though he advocated anti-Stalinist tenets, Khrushchev proved unable to overcome his own inclinations toward the system through which he rose.[68] Similarly, the historian E. Iu. Zubkova remarked that while Khrushchev was a more democratic *vozhd'* (leader), he was still a *vozhd'* in the tradition of Stalin.[69] One contributor even severely chastised Khrushchev for acquiescing in his own "personality cult" for many years.[70]

The criticisms of Khrushchev, however, did not completely detract from his positive historical legacy in the emerging revisionist consensus. The importance of Khrushchev's political role for most Soviet authors lay in the claim that perestroika would not have been possible without the reformist foundation laid down over thirty years ago. Emphasizing the limitations that Khrushchev faced because of his proximity to the Stalinist period, they maintained that he dismantled Stalin's repressive administration as much as was possible for his time. With these considerations in mind, the historian V. I. Glotov argued that Khrushchev successfully democratized various elements of Soviet society.[71] Others contended that Khrushchev, though attacking the bureaucracy consistently, was only partially successful in dismantling the Stalinist apparatus. Even so, the Khrushchev years represented the initial period of a struggle between "democratization forces" and "bureaucratic conservatism," and began a process that Gorbachev continued.[72] In this light the Khrushchev era was a partial perestroika that, despite its drawbacks, prepared the political ground for the recent epoch of dramatic change. Though the bureaucratic apparatus had regained strength under Brezhnev, Gorbachev found it possible to build upon the reformist pattern of Khrushchev in his campaign to dismantle the Stalinist system.

In the final analysis, Khrushchev's heritage stood as both a valuable and dan-

---

[67] A. E. Bovin, "Strana zhazhdala peremen," in *Inogo*, ed. Afanas'ev, 534–38. The historian N. A. Barsukov remarked that "democratization was not carried to a complete break with Stalinism" in the 1950s and early 1960s ("Proval 'Anti-partiinoi gruppy': Iiun'skii plenum TsK KPSS 1957 goda," *Kommunist*, 1990, no. 8:98).

[68] For example, see comments by the historians I. P. Kozhukalo and Iu. I. Shapoval, "N. S. Khrushchev na Ukraine," *Voprosy istorii KPSS*, 1989, no. 9:97.

[69] Zubkova wrote that Khrushchev could not rise completely above the authoritarian type of leadership that he was accustomed to under Stalin ("Oktiabr' 1964 goda: povorot ili perevorot?" *Kommunist*, 1989, no. 13:101).

[70] V. N. Novikov, "V gody rukovodstva N. S. Khrushcheva," *Voprosy istorii*, 1989, no. 2:116.

[71] V. I. Glotov, "O nekotorykh urokakh istoricheskogo opyta deiatel'nosti KPSS vo vtoroi polovine 50-x—pervoi polovine 80-x godov," *Voprosy istorii KPSS*, 1988, no. 4:70.

[72] E. Iu. Zubkova, "Opyt i uroki nezavershennykh povorotov 1956 i 1965 godov," *Voprosy istorii KPSS*, 1988, no. 4:85–87. Zubkova held, nonetheless, that Khrushchev's political reforms were quite significant for his time.

gerous tool for the most recent generation of Soviet reformers. In the struggle for power, proponents of perestroika had to distance themselves from the failures of the Khrushchev years to prevent their political rivals from gaining an additional weapon against the reform process. At the same time, advocates of change needed to elevate the bold reformist vision of the Khrushchev era in order to resuscitate the national government. As the Soviet leader when the Gorbachev generation came of age during the years of the Twentieth and Twenty-second Party Congresses, Khrushchev served as a vital catalyst in the political maturation of a new epoch. It is this historical legacy of anti-Stalinist reform that established Khrushchev's significance for the latest wave of Soviet scholars and demonstrated yet again that the contest over historical memory is also a contest over current political power and policy.

[16]

The Fall of Nikita Khrushchev

WILLIAM J. TOMPSON

> Yet well I remember
> The favours of these men. Were they not mine?
> Did they not sometime cry 'All hail!' to me?
> So Judas did to Christ. But he, in twelve,
> Found truth in all but one; I, in twelve thousand, none.

Richard II, iv, 1

ON 14 OCTOBER 1964 Nikita Sergeevich Khrushchev's 11-year period of dominance within the Soviet leadership came to an end. He was stripped of his party and state posts and sent into an obscure retirement by the very men who had been closest to him throughout his long career. Virtually overnight he became something of an 'un-person' in the Soviet Union: his name disappeared from the mass media and was scarcely mentioned even in such denunciations as followed his ouster. Nor were there even very many of these: there were no show trials, no ritual attacks at party congresses, no public confessions nor even any expulsions from the party. The circumstances surrounding his removal remained a mystery and the coup itself was euphemistically referred to as 'the October plenum'. The Khrushchev era had indeed ended not with a bang but a whimper and the long, debilitating reign of Leonid Brezhnev had begun.

In terms of Soviet history 'the October plenum' is an event of tremendous importance. It represents one of the key turning points along the path which has led the Soviet Union from the upheavals of 1917 to the crisis of the present day. The 'Great October Palace Revolution' inaugurated two decades of political stagnation, the effects of which are still painfully in evidence in the USSR today. Moreover, an understanding of Khrushchev's ouster in 1964 would contribute greatly to our broader understanding of Soviet politics in the post-war period. It is therefore most fortunate that a number of interviews, memoirs and analyses of Khrushchev's fall—many of them by the very men involved—have recently appeared in the Soviet Union. Though often contradictory, when taken together they present enough information to allow a fairly confident reconstruction of what took place. The picture which emerges is in many ways sharply at odds with accounts of the coup advanced by Western observers since 1964. It also challenges certain Western images of Soviet high politics during the post-Stalin era.

Much Western misunderstanding of the 1964 coup stems from the incorrect assumption that the plot to remove Khrushchev was hatched and executed with great speed, in October 1964. Michel Tatu, in what is arguably the best early reconstruction of Khrushchev's ouster, reckoned that the plot finally took shape on or around 10 October, just three days before the Presidium summoned Khrushchev to Moscow and confronted him.[1] Recent Soviet sources, however, unanimously agree that talk of Khrushchev's replacement began very early in 1964.[2] V. E. Semichastnyi, then chairman of the KGB, claims that he was involved in the plot right from the start because the conspirators knew that they could not hope to succeed without KGB support; he says that discussions concerning the replacement of the leader began 'somewhere in the early spring of 1964'. Sergei Khrushchev believes it to have been between January and March 1964, a view which is compatible with the former Ukrainian boss Shelest's claim that he was approached for the first time in March.[3]

This is a particularly important point, as the question of dating the coup's beginnings has a significant impact on the interpretation of subsequent events. Tatu, for example, concluded that Podgorny was uninvolved in the plot altogether and that Brezhnev was drawn into it only late in the game. Both of these conclusions are based upon a reconstruction of events which assumes a very short time-frame indeed.[4] It is this point more than any other which led Tatu to give pride of place to Suslov in planning and executing the removal of the First Secretary. In fact, Suslov's role is problematic. It remains one of the points over which the various Soviet accounts diverge most sharply. Did the plot originate with Suslov and Shelepin, as Roy Medvedev maintains, or is Gennadii Voronov correct in saying that 'the threads led to Zavidovo', Brezhnev's hunting retreat?[5]

The 'Suslov camp' has traditionally been the dominant one in Western academic circles, where the long-time ideologist-in-chief has enjoyed a reputation as the Kremlin's king-maker of 1964. Yet among recent Soviet writers only Medvedev holds to this view. Burlatsky argues that neither Brezhnev nor Suslov instigated the plot, which he believes to have been primarily the work of Shelepin. He states that Shelepin brought Suslov on board first and Brezhnev only later.[6] All of the participants in the plot who have so far spoken out, however, have been unanimous in naming Brezhnev as the ringleader. In addition to Voronov, who was the premier of the Russian Federation at the time, Shelest and Semichastnyi credit Brezhnev and Podgorny with having initiated and led the coup.[7]

N. G. Egorychev and P. A. Rodionov, then first secretary of the Moscow City Party Committee and second secretary of the Georgian CP respectively, concur. Rodionov maintains that Shelepin played a lesser, though still significant, role. He does, however, believe that Shelepin himself had his eye on the top job.[8] In addition to Brezhnev and Podgorny, Sergei Khrushchev mentions Shelepin and Polyansky as having been involved from the very beginning.[9] The fact that the eyewitnesses and participants involved are unanimous in naming Brezhnev as the instigator and leader of the plot is strong evidence in favour of this view. Moreover, the two alternative candidates, Shelepin and Suslov, look rather unlikely for various reasons. Shelepin was still relatively young and despite his obviously powerful position—he was chairman of the Party–State Control Commission and a Central Committee secretary—he was not yet a member of the Presidium.[10] While his election to membership of that body after the coup suggests that he did indeed play an important role, it is hard to see him as the key figure.

THE FALL OF KHRUSHCHEV

Burlatsky argues that, on the contrary, it was precisely Shelepin's youth which led him to initiate the coup: Burlatsky attributes great importance to generational conflict within the leadership and names Shelepin as the leader of 'the post-war generation' of Soviet leaders, including men like Semichastnyi, Polyansky, Voronov and Andropov. Brezhnev, Suslov and Kosygin, by contrast, represented the 'class of '37', raised up at the height of the purges.[11] Yet both Semichastnyi and Voronov have spoken and written at length about the coup and neither advances anything like this interpretation.[12] Sergei Khrushchev, however, does believe Shelepin to have had special influence over the younger members of the leadership.[13] Semichastnyi, for example, had worked for Shelepin in the Komsomol and was the latter's hand-picked successor as chairman of the KGB. Rodionov could well be correct in reckoning that Shelepin's ambitions were aimed at Brezhnev. Shelepin may have believed that with Khrushchev out of the way, he would be able to deal with Brezhnev relatively easily.[14]

Suslov, on the other hand, presents a different problem. There is simply nothing in his career which suggests that he was ever much of a political risk-taker. As Rodionov argues, Suslov managed to survive in Kremlin politics for so long precisely because he always hedged his bets. In 1957 he did not rush to join the Anti-Party Group despite the fact that he shared many of their views. Neither does he appear to have joined Khrushchev, however, until the issue was more or less decided in his favour.[15] Voronov takes a similar view, pointing to Suslov's praise of Stalin, Khrushchev and Brezhnev at the XIX, XXII and XXVI congresses as a reflection of his willingness to line himself up with whomever was strongest at any given moment.[16]

Shelest is particularly emphatic on this point, claiming that Suslov did not know what was afoot until very late and that when he was told of the impending coup, he replied, 'What are you talking about?! There'll be a civil war!'[17] Sergei Khrushchev suggests that Suslov's late initiation into the plot may have been a consequence of the fact that he was not closely aligned either with the Brezhnev–Podgorny 'Ukrainian group' in the leadership or with Shelepin's 'youth' faction.[18] Virtually all of the participants agree that Suslov himself did not prepare the report which he delivered to the Central Committee plenum detailing the reasons for Khrushchev's removal; there is, however, no clear consensus as to who did write it.[19]

There are, however, two considerations which might render the Suslov and Shelepin interpretations more attractive, particularly to writers like Medvedev and Burlatsky. The first is that Suslov and Shelepin had impeccable 'hard-line' credentials.[20] If they indeed were the leaders of the plot, then it is far easier to see the events surrounding Khrushchev's fall in terms of a neo-Stalinist reaction against a reforming leader. The presence at the centre of the plot of the more moderate figures of Brezhnev and Podgorny suggests that the coup was a much more broadly based affair. The catholicity of the opposition which arose in 1964 resembles nothing so much as that of the Anti-Party Group, which also embraced both Stalinist and (relatively) liberal wings within the leadership. Secondly, Brezhnev's reputation is now such that it is difficult to credit him with organising and leading the coup. There is perhaps an understandable reluctance to believe that someone as apparently unimaginative and dull as Brezhnev is supposed to have been could possibly have been a master politician. Yet over the next 18 years Brezhnev saw off challenges from many men who seemed cleverer than he.

One cannot but see a certain irony in the fact that Khrushchev's replacement was engineered not by some neo-Stalinist opposition, but by his own closest confidants and supporters. The man who had defeated all comers in the battle for the Stalin succession after 1953 could not have anticipated that he would be ousted by his own clients, even as the triumphant Caesar fell not to Pompey's dagger but to Brutus's. Indeed, this fact may well have worked in the plotters' favour, for, as will be seen, Khrushchev at various points seems either to have placed too much trust in his colleagues or simply to have underestimated their ability to mount a challenge to his leadership. Having defeated Malenkov, Molotov, Kaganovich and others, he is unlikely to have trembled with fear at the news that N. G. Ignatov was plotting against him.[21] This overconfidence was to cost Khrushchev everything. Not without reason has Burlatsky written in this connection, 'Save us, O God, from our friends; we can cope with our enemies by ourselves'.[22]

One of the most important points upon which all accounts agree is the manner in which the plotters set about securing support for Khrushchev's removal in the Central Committee. Evidently having learned the lessons of 1957, Khrushchev's opponents spent considerable time and energy enlisting supporters for their cause among the territorial party apparatus. According to Rodionov, everyone involved in the plot was to 'work on' certain committee members: Egorychev, the Moscow first secretary, was to deal with the Muscovites, Rodionov's boss in Georgia, V. P. Mzhavanadze, was to line up support in Transcaucasia, and so on.[23] In the Ukraine, this task belonged to Shelest.[24] The Stravropol *kraikom* secretary, Kulakov, played an important role in lobbying within the RSFSR, as did Ignatov, then chairman of the Presidium of the RSFSR Supreme Soviet. Occupying a largely ceremonial post, Ignatov had little real political power, but his job enabled him to travel extensively around the country meeting with local officials, and he was therefore quite useful to the plotters.[25] Ignatov seems to have been rather too enthusiastic about his new role, for word of his activities soon reached the ears of the first secretary.[26] Semichastnyi has stated that Ignatov simply talked too much.[27]

Brezhnev and Podgorny were also, by all accounts, active in soliciting support for their position. Shelest was approached by both of them in March and again in July by Brezhnev alone. It was at this latter meeting that he agreed to back the opposition.[28] Khrushchev himself managed unwittingly to facilitate his opponents' plans on more than one occasion. According to his son Sergei, he alienated the Belorussian party leader, K. T. Mazurov, with ill-considered talk of Mazurov's removal after a trip to Minsk. Khrushchev later cooled off and took no action, but his remarks found their way back to Mazurov, who was then enlisted in the plot.[29] The demotion of the Ukrainian premier, Shcherbitsky, to the rank of *obkom* first secretary did Khrushchev's cause no good either. Although dropped from his candidate membership in the Presidium, Shcherbitsky remained a full member of the Central Committee.[30] Khrushchev also did his enemies no small favour by travelling as much as he did: he was away from Moscow a total of 135 days during the first nine months of 1964.[31]

Sergei Khrushchev maintains that his father's colleagues were also about the business of deliberately manoeuvring Khrushchev into unpopular positions throughout this period. Thus, for example, he asserts that Adzhubei was duped into persuading his father-in-law to delay the planned introduction of a five-day working week in the USSR. The younger Khrushchev also claims that his father had come to accept the necessity for economic reforms along the lines of those proposed by the Kharkov economist Evsei Liberman and others; this initiative, too, was delayed and was introduced only after Khrushchev had been pensioned off. The Khrushchev 'cult' boomed in 1964, primarily as a result of the efforts of Brezhnev, Podgorny and Shelepin, efforts which Sergei Khrushchev now sees aimed at weakening his father. The food supply problems of 1964 are also attributed to a deliberate campaign of sabotage, designed to undermine the First Secretary's popularity.[32]

As the foregoing makes clear, the movement to oust Khrushchev was far more extensive than has previously been realised and was by no means limited to his colleagues in the Kremlin, although they, of course, provided the leadership. The October plenum was not arranged until solid majorities in both the Presidium and the Central Committee were known to favour Khrushchev's replacement.[33] The number of people privy to the plot must therefore have been enormous; indeed, virtually the entire Central Committee apart from a few Khrushchev loyalists appear to have been targeted by this lobbying effort. Even Khrushchev's long-time personal assistant G. T. Shuisky joined the plot; at one point he intercepted an attempt to warn Khrushchev of the danger to his rule.[34] Much of the plotting seems to have taken place at various southern resorts over the summer, as members of the party elite tended to frequent the same places when on holiday and could therefore meet without arousing suspicion.[35] Given that the risk of exposure rose as more and more people were brought into confidence, it must have been the case that the support of these men really mattered.

This would indicate that the territorial party elite and other officials making up the bulk of the Central Committee enjoyed far more power than was hitherto thought. Despite the First Secretary's attempts to undermine it after 1958, the Central Committee (CC) remained a powerful body, largely as a result of Khrushchev's own resuscitation of it in the mid-1950s. As Semichastnyi has observed, it is somewhat paradoxical that Khrushchev himself had created the conditions within the party which made it possible for his removal to be so plotted:[36] in addition to restoring the authority of the CC, he had brought an end to the use of terror in Soviet politics, a change which must have greatly increased the propensity of elite members to scheme and plot against one another and against their superiors. Knowing that the ultimate penalty was no longer enforced, they were that much more likely to play politics for very high stakes.

There were, of course, leaks in this process. More than one attempt seems to have been made to warn the First Secretary of the impending crisis. Olga I. Ivashchenko, a member of the Ukrainian party secretariat, tried unsuccessfully to warn Khrushchev and it is alleged that the Uzbek official Yadgar Nasriddinova made a similar attempt. Khrushchev's daughter, Rada Adzhubei, received more than one warning about the impending coup but remained unconvinced by her informers.[37] As noted above, word of Ignatov's activities did indeed reach Khrushchev after the latter's bodyguard approached Khrushchev's son Sergei.[38] In the first two instances, the callers never succeeded in getting through to him, while in the case of Ignatov, Khrushchev himself simply miscalculated. According to some accounts, he did not guess that Ignatov was not acting on his own initiative and he therefore made the mistake of telling Podgorny and others what he knew.[39] Adzhubei says that Khrushchev promised to 'clear everything up' after his holiday in Pitsunda.[40]

Others suggest that he threatened his Presidium colleagues as well, promising, according to one account, that he would toss them out 'like whelps'.[41] Egorychev claims that Brezhnev was afraid to return from East Germany after he heard that Khrushchev knew of the plot.[42] In either case, Khrushchev played into their hands: while his promise to 'clear everything up' placed them under a certain time pressure, his trip to Pitsunda gave them the opportunity they needed to act. Given that these conversations took place prior to Khrushchev's late September departure for Pitsunda, it is reasonable to accept Semichastnyi's claim that the pace of events accelerated in the second half of that month. The final decision to convene the Central Committee in October was taken at Brezhnev's Moscow flat, apparently on 12 October. There had already been a number of false starts on account of Brezhnev's cold feet. Semichastnyi, on being summoned to Moscow in late September, asked Shelepin: 'Is it the real thing?' To which the latter replied: 'This time it's on'.[43]

According to Semichastnyi, not all of the false starts had been concerned with convening the Central Committee and voting Khrushchev out of office. In his interview with Starkov, he states that Brezhnev was at one stage obsessed with the idea of poisoning his boss. It is difficult to know how much to credit Semichastnyi's account on this point—especially since Brezhnev would probably have thought twice about setting such a precedent just before taking over the top job himself. He also charges that Brezhnev suggested arranging a plane crash while Khrushchev was abroad or a car crash. More plausible is his assertion that Brezhnev suggested simply arresting Khrushchev in June on his return from a trip to Sweden.[44] Whether these charges are true or not, it seems to be relatively clear that the role of the security organs was, by all accounts, a critical one. Semichastnyi claims that he insisted on removing Khruschev by legal means and that he realised that any illegal action taken against the First Secretary would not remain secret for very long.[45] Nevertheless, he seems to have made considerable use of the KGB's powers to ensure that nothing went wrong.

First, the KGB seems to have kept Khrushchev isolated from almost all news of the plot; thus, attempts by people like Nasriddinova and Ivashchenko to reach him failed.[46] While Khrushchev was isolated in Pitsunda, he also seems to have been under constant surveillance. Semichastnyi evidently monitored the situation from Moscow.[47] Secondly, it was Semichastnyi's job to replace Khrushchev's security details in his office at the Kremlin, his flat and his dacha. Burlatsky claims that Khrushchev fully understood what was afoot only at the time of his departure from Pitsunda when he saw that his *okhrana* had been changed.[48] Finally, Semichastnyi claims that it fell to him to prevent any interference on Khrushchev's behalf from the military units stationed in and around Moscow. He states that he had already warned the heads of the KGB special sections in the Moscow military district:

> In the next few days, if as much as one armed soldier on a motorcycle leaves his barracks, whether with a machine gun or anything else..., keep in mind, it will cost you your head... You are not to allow anyone to undertake anything without reporting to me.[49]

In stressing the critical importance of the KGB, Semichastnyi goes so far as to allege that Kosygin, on being approached in early October, merely asked: 'On whose side is the KGB?' When told that they were on board, he agreed to back the plot. While it is difficult to evaluate this claim, the notion that he was drawn in very late in the going seems at least to be compatible with the traditional Western view of Kosygin as a man who generally avoided involvement in factional intrigues. No one else mentions Kosygin as having played any role whatsoever in the conspiracy. Semichastnyi also presents the military as having been essentially uninvolved, claiming that Malinovsky was told only two days in advance.[50] Shelest, however, states that Podgorny approached Malinovsky two or three weeks prior to the coup and was told by the defence minister that the army was apolitical and would support neither Khrushchev nor his enemies.[51] It is impossible to verify what Malinovsky knew and when, but other accounts also fail to accord the armed forces an important role. The other participants do not mention the military at all, while Medvedev simply states that Malinovsky's agreement was necessary 'to exclude the possibility of an accident'.[52] As will be seen, the grievances against Khrushchev listed by both eyewitnesses and historians also give surprisingly short shrift to military concerns. This state of affairs could not contrast more sharply with 1957, when Marshal Zhukov played a key role in the defeat of the Anti-Party Group.

Having carefully laid the groundwork, Khrushchev's Presidium colleagues telephoned him in Pitsunda and called him back to Moscow for an urgent meeting to discuss the agricultural measures to be presented at the coming Central Committee plenum in November. The call appears to have taken place on the evening of Monday 12 October. Medvedev states that it was made the following morning, but Sergei Khrushchev, who was with his father in Pitsunda, and Semichastnyi, who was with the plotters in Moscow, agree that Khrushchev received the call on Monday evening. It is not entirely clear who made the call, as the two eyewitnesses disagree. Sergei Khrushchev claims that Brezhnev balked at the last minute and that it fell to Suslov to telephone Pitsunda; Semichastnyi acknowledges that the reluctant Brezhnev was 'dragged to the telephone, almost by force', but insists that he was present when Brezhnev himself made the call. Medvedev also believes that Brezhnev made the call.[53]

All accounts agree that Khrushchev initially refused to come; he was on vacation, after all, and could not see the urgency of discussing the matters in question. Brezhnev (or Suslov?) insisted that his presence was required, however, and at last he gave in and agreed to come. Shelest has stated that there were two telephone calls by Brezhnev to Pitsunda before Khrushchev was persuaded to return.[54] Medvedev says that the First Secretary gave way only when Brezhnev told him that they would proceed without him if necessary. Sergei Khrushchev states that by the end of this conversation, his father understood something more was to be discussed at the Presidium meeting in Moscow than agriculture; he told Mikoyan: 'If I'm the issue, I won't make a fight'. Semichastnyi also hints that Khrushchev became suspicious in the course of the conversation. He quotes the First Secretary as saying to Brezhnev: 'Why are you in such a hurry there? I'll come—and we'll find out'. There remained only the matter of ordering a plane for Khrushchev, a matter which seems to have generated no little confusion in Moscow. Although Khrushchev ordered a plane during the early evening, Semichastnyi, who was monitoring the situation, did not learn of it until midnight. In the meantime, he received hourly phone calls from a nervous Brezhnev checking up on the situation. Only after learning that Khrushchev had indeed ordered a plane did the plotters feel somewhat relieved.[55]

Semichastnyi's account of the evening of 12 October conveys a vivid sense of the nervous tension felt by the plotters. Sergei Khrushchev is almost certainly correct in saying that even then the conspirators continued to fear his father.[56] Although he was physically and politically isolated, with the leaders of virtually every important institution in the Soviet political system arrayed against him, his adversaries worried that he might take some sort of retaliatory action. Hence the concern over the ordering of Khrushchev's plane; the Presidium was keen to ensure that the First Secretary did indeed return from Pitsunda as promised. The delay in conveying news of the order to Semichastnyi no doubt created the impression that Khrushchev was trying to delay his departure for some reason. To be sure, the plotters could have brought him back to Moscow by force, but there was a strong consensus that the appearance of a coup must not be created. All must be done in good order, by 'democratically' resolving the issue at a CC plenum.[57] For this to be achieved, the victim's own cooperation, at least to a limited extent, was necessary.

The following day Khrushchev received the French minister of state Gaston Palewski at Pitsunda before flying back to Moscow. As noted above, Burlatsky claims that Khrushchev realised what was going on when he saw that the security detail on his plane had been replaced and tried unsuccessfully to order the plane to Kiev.[58] Sergei Khrushchev, who was there at the time, has stated categorically that this is an invention. Semichastnyi, moreover, claims to have replaced Khrushchev's security details in the Kremlin, at home and in his dacha only *after* the latter's arrival in the Kremlin. In doing this, however, he does appear to have enjoyed the assistance of Khrushchev's deputy chief of security; Semichastnyi had managed to send the chief of the First Secretary's *okhrana* on leave some time earlier.[59] It would thus appear reasonable to accept Semichastnyi's claim that he had effective control of Khrushchev's security detail in Pitsunda even without replacing it.[60]

Khrushchev was met at the airport only by Semichastnyi, the head of the KGB security administration, V. Chekvalov, and the secretary of the Supreme Soviet Presidium, Mikhail Georgadze. Khrushchev went directly from the airport to the

Kremlin, where the Presidium was awaiting him.[61] To all external appearances, the situation in the Kremlin was perfectly normal on 13 October. No additional troops or security forces were deployed in or around the Kremlin grounds, which remained open to visitors all day. Semichastnyi did, however, take the precaution of warning his deputy not to issue a single order or directive without informing him.[62] Even within the Presidium, a certain appearance of normality was maintained, as Khrushchev himself chaired the meeting called to remove him from office.[63]

In addition to the members and candidate members of the party Presidium, most accounts agree that the meeting was attended by the Central Committee secretaries, the Minister of Defence, Malinovsky, the Minister of Foreign Affairs, Gromyko, and several provincial first secretaries.[64] No stenographic report of the meeting was taken, although Shelest did take personal notes on it.[65] Suslov and Shelepin put the question of Khrushchev's removal to the meeting and were the most outspoken representatives of the prosecution.[66] Shelest was apparently also quite forceful.[67] The accusations directed at the First Secretary will be considered below; as Tatu has observed, once it had been decided to have a trial, there was no shortage of charges.[68] Brezhnev and Podgorny apparently said nothing the first day, but Voronov is reported to have been quite aggressive.[69] Khrushchev initially rejected the attacks of his colleagues but it was not long before he was put on the defensive and, ultimately, gave way to the superior strength of his opponents.[70] Mikoyan alone appears to have favoured allowing Khrushchev to retain one of his two posts, arguing that Khrushchev's activities represented a great store of political capital for the party.[71]

The issues raised in the Presidium meeting were many and varied, ranging from serious questions of policy and questions about Khrushchev's leadership style to insinuations of petty corruption. In the main, the conspirators' reasons for removing the First Secretary seem to have paralleled closely those advanced in Western writings on the coup. The *sovnarkhoz* system, the 1962 bifurcation of the party apparatus, Khrushchev's attitude towards his colleagues and towards local party organs and his often rude public behaviour were all discussed. Shelepin claimed that Khrushchev's son Sergei had received the degree of doctor of science without having defended a thesis. The First Secretary was criticised for taking members of his family on overseas trips and for awarding the title 'Hero of the Soviet Union' to Egypt's President Nasser and Vice President Amer. Khrushchev was accused of advancing a personality cult of his own within the Soviet Union and violating the norms of collective leadership.[72]

The above list is by no means comprehensive. As Adzhubei has correctly observed, by 1964 every political and social group had its own grievances against Khrushchev.[73] One thing that is remarkable about the complaints listed by various Soviet sources on the coup is the relative lack of importance attached to foreign policy and defence issues.[74] Few of the Soviet sources mention them and none seem to regard them as particularly important. It can scarcely be doubted that Khrushchev's defence policies had alienated many in the Soviet High Command, but, with the military apparently on the sidelines of the conflict, only Adzhubei actually mentions their grievances.[75] According to Shelest, the Suez, Berlin and

Cuban crises of 1956, 1961 and 1962, respectively, came up in the Presidium meeting, as did the question of economic relations with the PRC.[76] None of these issues seems to have been at the centre of the debate, however, probably because Khrushchev himself was speaking the truth when he reminded his colleagues that the decisions in question had been reached collectively.[77]

The foreign issue which generated the most discussion seems to have been Adzhubei's trip to Bonn earlier in the year. During his visit, he was reported to have predicted that the Berlin Wall would disappear in the wake of a future Khrushchev trip to Germany. Needless to say, his words generated a minor crisis for the leadership of the GDR, a crisis for which his father-in-law was held responsible. Adzhubei denies ever making such remarks and states that the rumours about his trip were quashed so thoroughly that they never came up at the October plenum.[78] Nevertheless, Gromyko is alleged to have told one of his visitors at the time: 'Why was Khrushchev overthrown? Because he sent Adzhubei to Bonn, of course'.[79] To some extent, Gromyko's answer no doubt reflects the position from which he viewed events. What is more important, however, is that the Adzhubei issue had less to do with substantive foreign policy questions than with Khrushchev's leadership style. For many in the leadership, the episode epitomised the problems created by Khrushchev's increasing concentration of power in his own hands and in the hands of a few close personal supporters. The issue was neither Adzhubei nor the German question but Khrushchev.[80]

In contrast to the relative lack of attention paid to foreign and defence policies, recent Soviet accounts have placed strong emphasis on those domestic issues which affected most directly the interests of the party elite which made up the overwhelming majority of the Central Committee membership. Dissatisfaction with the huge and unwieldy structure of economic administration built up over the *sovnarkhozy* after 1960, resentment at the bifurcation of the party apparatus adopted two years earlier and the rules adopted at the XXII Congress in 1961 concerning the 'systematic renewal of cadres' all figure prominently in the accounts of Khrushchev's ouster.[81] The bifurcation and the turnover rules were particularly sore points because they undermined the security of tenure of sitting Central Committee members, whose prospects for re-election at the XXIII Congress were no longer by any means certain. Voronov writes of the resentment generated by Khrushchev's circumvention of local party officials when dealing with local economic and state organs.[82]

Adzhubei reckons that the rules requiring minimum rates of turnover in party bodies and limiting the terms of officeholders were particularly damaging. He states that during his stay at Pitsunda Khrushchev was preparing a proposal to extend this system to include state posts as well.[83] Egorychev emphasises, *inter alia*, the frustration with Khrushchev's constant 'leapfrogging of cadres' from place to place.[84] Barsukov also writes that Khrushchev alienated many members of the Central Committee when he began to undermine its authority after 1958. The enlargement of plena to include numerous outsiders, the publication of stenographic records and other measures intended to 'democratise' the work of the committee served only to lend its proceedings the same theatrical air which characterised Supreme Soviet sessions. To this injury was added the insult of

THE FALL OF KHRUSHCHEV 1111

Khrushchev's frequent interruptions of speakers and his generally high-handed manner in dealing with the Committee.[85]

To some extent, of course, the grievances listed in any given account reflect the perspective of its author. Since we have no accounts from military men or diplomats and quite a few from party men who were in the CC at the time, it is not surprising that these are the complaints most commonly cited. Yet even those who write from no particular bureaucratic perspective stress these same kinds of issues.[86] Moreover, the relative emphasis given to different groups' complaints tends to confirm the impression created by all of these accounts that the coup was essentially an internal party affair. The secret police, to be sure, were involved, but the military seem to have been kept very much in the background.

Two other policy issues seem to have been important. The first was Khrushchev's proposed reorganisation of agricultural management along branch lines. He had already sprung this idea on the CC in July and had only afterwards circulated a memorandum concerning it to his colleagues in the leadership.[87] This next reorganisation was to establish 17 union–republican agricultural administrations based in Moscow, each of which would supervise the planning and procurement of a specified range of agricultural products. The territorial-production associations of 1962 were to be abolished. Khrushchev's cause was not helped by the fact that his announcement of the new proposal to the July plenum was accompanied by a stinging attack (including a few threats) directed at local party leaders for their alleged failures in agricultural management.[88] This 'reform' was to be adopted in November, a fact which set an effective deadline for action by the anti-Khrushchev forces.[89] Given that the new reorganisation was both foolish economically and threatening politically from the point of view of the territorial party apparatus, it is not difficult to see how it became a focus for anti-Khrushchev resentment.

The other issue is somewhat more surprising. Two sources attribute a significant role to the bitter attack made by Khrushchev against the USSR Academy of Sciences and its president at the (hitherto unknown) July plenum. The First Secretary went so far as to question the need for the academy's very existence and implied that a future plenum might have to consider its future.[90] Politically this issue was far less of a threat to the elite than the agricultural reorganisation, but taken together the two issues exemplified everything that his colleagues and erstwhile supporters thought was wrong with Khrushchev. For in the end, it appears that the First Secretary did not so much fall over any particular issue or set of issues; rather, he fell because his comrades-in-arms had concluded that he was in some sense out of control. The voluntarism, the impulsiveness and the increasing authoritarianism of Khrushchev were wearing on them; they were 'stuffed to their throats' with his ill-considered reorganisation schemes and they wanted, above all else, a stable collective leadership.[91]

Finally, recent Soviet discussions of the reasons for Khrushchev's removal lay a remarkable amount of stress on his declining personal popularity with the Soviet public.[92] As noted above, Sergei Khrushchev believes that the food shortages and the delay in the introduction of the shorter working week were intended to undermine his father's popularity.[93] Adzhubei has acknowledged that virtually

1112   WILLIAM J. TOMPSON

every social group in the country had a reason to be dissatisfied with Khrushchev's rule.[94] Anatolii Strelyanyi, a journalist, describes his colleagues throwing a party at work on hearing of Khrushchev's ouster. Some even danced on the tables.[95] This concern with popular opinion suggests that the elite felt as insecure in power in 1964 as it had at the time of Stalin's death in 1953. It is entirely consonant with John Miller's suggestion that:

> It makes sense to picture Soviet leaders as convinced and thoroughgoing Hobbesians, so persuaded of the precariousness of social cohesion and so appalled at the prospect of social breakdown as to rate the absolute position of the sovereign as a supreme value in politics. They are Hobbesians, moreover, not Machiavellians, because they seek the bulwark against social breakdown in an institutional arrangement, the Communist Party of the Soviet Union, and not in the personal qualities of the sovereign.[96]

Khrushchev's continuation in power was thus seen as a threat not only to the political fortunes of his fellow oligarchs, but to the very stability of the entire Soviet regime. On the one hand, his policies' failures might give rise to social unrest, while, on the other, his increasing personal dominance within the leadership undermined the oligarchical arrangements around which the post-Stalin leadership had attempted to build a stable political order.

At the end of the first day of the Presidium meeting, the members went home to prepare for the next round. According to Sergei Khrushchev, the First Secretary's opponents agreed not to answer the phone, in case Khrushchev began calling around trying to win them back over one by one. Adzhubei apparently did attempt to get in touch with Shelepin, Polyansky and others but got no answer.[97] Semichastnyi says that Brezhnev was particularly nervous, fearing that Khruschev might 'call in help'. The KGB chief assured Brezhnev that Khrushchev could go nowhere, call no one, without the knowledge and consent of the security organs.[98] Unbeknownst to both his supporters and his enemies, Khrushchev himself concluded that evening that he could not carry on the struggle. He telephoned Mikoyan and explained that he would resign all his posts the following day.

The Presidium meeting resumed early on 14 October. The criticism of the First Secretary was concluded and he delivered his final address to the Presidium. Acknowledging the validity of some criticisms while denying others categorically, Khrushchev sought to explain and justify himself at the last. He apologised for his behaviour towards other members of the leadership and stressed the collective nature of the decisions for which he alone was now being called to account, claiming even that the decision to make him Chairman of the USSR Council of Ministers had been proposed by others and that he had acceded only reluctantly. The First Secretary also accused his colleagues of having been dishonest with him, of having lacked the 'principles and boldness' to speak frankly to him about his shortcomings. He briefly answered a few of the criticisms made against him before turning to the subject of his removal:

> ... I rejoice that there has come a time when the members of the Presidium have begun to control the activity of the First Secretary and speak with a full voice ... Today's meeting of the CC Presidium is a victory for the party. I thought that I would have to leave ... I have lost touch with you. You have criticised me vigorously for that today and I myself

THE FALL OF KHRUSHCHEV

have suffered from it. I thank you for the opportunity which you are granting me to resign.[99]

Khrushchev later repeated this expression of thanks to his colleagues for being allowed to retire, which suggests that he may have feared that more serious measures would be taken against him. At the same time, however, he revealed that he had harboured still higher hopes than a safe retirement: 'I thought that you perhaps would consider it possible to create some sort of honorary post for me, but I will not request that of you'.[100] It was at this point that Khrushchev offered to leave Moscow, if his successors so desired; someone replied, 'Why do that?'[101] Acknowledging that his address to the Presidium was his 'swan song', Khrushchev stated that he would not speak to the Central Committee, but asked that he be allowed 'to approach the plenum with a request...'. Brezhnev cut him off abruptly: 'There will be no request!' According to Shelest, Brezhnev was afraid of what Khrushchev would ask the plenum. He might attempt to answer the charges, debates might get started and the new leadership might lose control of events before it had safely dispatched the old.[102]

The relative speed of Khrushchev's capitulation surprised some observers. His enemies seem to have taken every precaution on the assumption that he would fight as he had done in 1957. Most attempts to account for the First Secretary's behaviour stress that he was old and tired by late 1964 and that he was thinking of retirement anyway. Several sources suggest that he intended to step down at the XXIII Congress, due in less than two years.[103] Strelyanyi describes Khrushchev as tired, disillusioned and frustrated by the failure of the leadership to make good on its promises to the people. He cites evidence that Khrushchev intended to step aside in favour of younger men. Adzhubei agrees. Some of the First Secretary's remarks, moreover, suggest that he planned to purge the leadership in order to introduce 'new blood' prior to his retirement. If his collegues feared that such was his intent, it can only have hastened his demise. In any case, Strelyanyi argues, the conservatives in the leadership feared the example of a leader voluntarily confessing his failures and resigning.[104]

In addition to fatigue, Voronov, the only actual participant in these events to address this question, suggests that Khrushchev realised that his opponents had access to the same weapons which he himself had used against his own enemies in better times. Specifically, he states that Khrushchev's colleagues were prepared to use his own Stalin-era past against him: his activities in both Moscow and the Ukraine at the height of the purges left him quite vulnerable on this point.[105] Apparently documents relating to Khrushchev's involvement in certain arrests of 1935–37 had aready been prepared for just such a contingency.[106] It may have been the fear that such weapons would be employed against him which led Khrushchev to thank his colleagues for allowing him to resign.[107]

While all of this (and more) was under discussion in the Kremlin, the tension outside it was building. It was not yet widely known—if it was known at all—that Khrushchev had already agreed to resign. As the Presidium meeting continued into its second day, Semichastnyi phoned Brezhnev to warn him that the meeting was going on too long. He himself was receiving a steady stream of calls from Central Committee members and others demanding to know what was happening.

Some wanted to save Khrushchev, others to support Brezhnev and the opposition. Brezhnev told him that the Presidium had almost completed its deliberations and that Semichastnyi would need only to stall a bit longer. The plenum was set for 6.00 pm, the members of the CC having already been summoned to Moscow on false pretences in order to make sure that they were on hand when the session was called.[108]

Khrushchev himself returned home after the Presidium meeting and informed his family of what had happened. According to his son Sergei, he stated simply that he had been retired. After a pause, he added: 'Didn't want to have lunch with them any more'.[109] The plenum convened that evening at 6.00 pm in the Kremlin. Brezhnev opened and Mikoyan chaired it. Khrushchev sat on his own to one side, while Suslov delivered an hour-long report on his failings as leader. Most of the committee members simply sat in silence; a few shouted from the floor, calling for Khrushchev's expulsion from the party, or even his arrest and trial. There was no discussion following the report. Suslov simply stated: 'To judge by the comments of the members, the plenum clearly approves the Presidium's decision with respect to Khrushchev, and there is no need for a debate'. The resolution releasing Khrushchev from his duties on account of his age and health was put to the committee and adopted unanimously. It was also resolved that the posts of First Secretary of the Central Committee and Chairman of the Council of Ministers would never again be united in one person. Brezhnev and Kosygin were chosen to replace Khrushchev as party leader and premier respectively. The latter gave a short speech and the plenum's proceedings were brought to a close. The Khrushchev era had ended.[110]

Suslov's report, which has not yet been published, covered all the main points, both great and small, for which the Presidium had indicted Khrushchev. The most complete reconstruction of it available is Medvedev's, which Semichastnyi has said is accurate 'in the main'.[111] None of the actors involved believes that Suslov himself wrote the report. Shelest says that it was prepared by Polyansky, to be given either by Brezhnev or Podgorny. In the event, the former 'simply chickened out' and the latter 'categorically refused'. Having made their careers under Khrushchev for so many years, they were concerned about 'how it would look' if they delivered the report. It thus fell to Suslov, as the chief ideologist, to address the plenum.[112] Others have put forward Shelepin's name as the author of Suslov's speech.[113] Semichastnyi knows only that it had been worked on in the CC apparatus.[114] Whatever its authorship, the report did not originate with Suslov; Voronov is emphatic on the point, stating that the ideologist's sole contribution to the whole thing was to read the text with which he had been presented.[115]

The new leaders took no chances whatsoever when organising the plenum. Several prominent Khrushchev supporters in the Central Commitee, including Z. T. Serdyuk and O. I. Ivashchenko, were barred from attending.[116] The decision not to allow Khrushchev to speak or to permit a discussion of Suslov's report appears to have been taken in the same vein. Egorychev stresses that 'in the heat of discussion' much might have been said which would have tied Brezhnev's hands.[117] Semichastnyi thinks that the new leadership simply did not know where the discussion might lead and was determined at all costs to maintain control of events. He laments the inertia of the Central Committee, which allowed them to do this and thereby reinforced the dominance of the Presidium over the Central Committee, to which it was—in theory at least—accountable.[118] Voronov suggests that had Khrushchev defended himself at the plenum, his supporters would have rallied to his defence and things might well have got out of hand.[119]

Can it be that even at this late stage Brezhnev and his allies still feared Khrushchev? One may infer from an anecdote later related by Mzhavanadze that indeed they did. On his return journey to Tbilisi, the Georgian first secretary stepped off his train to buy a newspaper in one of the stations along the route south. The paper contained no report of the plenum whatsoever and therefore frightened Mzhavanadze considerably. Only when he subsequently heard the announcement of the plenum on the radio did he at last relax.[120] Mzhavanadze's story underlines the sense of insecurity which the plotters felt throughout the execution of Khrushchev's overthrow.

Brezhnev's own address to the plenum was relatively brief, but it seems to provide some insight into the reasons for his election to succeed Khrushchev. After thanking the plenum for his election, Brezhnev affirmed his commitment to collective leadership and promised to devote all his strength to justifying the trust which his comrades had placed in him. He then emphasised the new leadership's commitment to increasing the role of party organs in all spheres of economic and social life. It is noteworthy that he laid stress not so much on the leading role of the *party*, as on the leading role of *party organs*. Brezhnev promised more than once to 'stick up for cadres'. The tone of his speech further confirms the impression that the driving force behind the coup was the party apparat.[121] Brezhnev's commitment to the interests of this constituency was critical in his rise to power.

Most of the participants in the events of October 1964 seem to feel that, once it had been decided to remove Khrushchev, Brezhnev's election was a foregone conclusion. Barsukov states flatly that Brezhnev had no real rivals; he was acknowledged to be the second man in the leadership.[122] More that one source cites Khrushchev's 1963 conversation with the French Socialist leader Guy Mollet, in which the First Secretary named Brezhnev as his probable successor.[123] According to Semichastnyi, there were simply no other candidates. Brezhnev was already second secretary, he had long experience in party work and it was thought that he could lead the Central Committee in collegial work.[124] Shelest, perhaps arguing from a uniquely Ukrainian perspective, argues that there was an alternative: Podgorny. He states that Podgorny enjoyed considerable support but chose nevertheless to back Brezhnev. It was Podgorny who nominated Brezhnev for the post of First Secretary and during the early part of Brezhnev's rule helped the new party leader to maintain himself in power. Shelest states that Brezhnev would not have lasted more than a year without Podgorny.[125] Egorychev emphasises Brezhnev's perceived 'decency'. He seemed a man who could provide much more stability at the top than had Khrushchev. Egorychev himself claims to have had doubts about Brezhnev and to have favoured Kosygin for the post, but he was persuaded by his fellow committee members that Brezhnev was a suitable candidate.[126]

Burlatsky sees Brezhnev essentially as a compromise figure acceptable both to the older generation of leaders like Suslov and Kosygin and to younger men like

1116   WILLIAM J. TOMPSON

Semichastnyi and Voronov. He claims that Suslov and others feared the ambitions of Shelepin. Brezhnev was also seen by the CC apparatus as a man neither
able nor inclined to interfere in its workings; in Brezhnev's weakness and lack of
competence, the apparat saw increased power and freedom of action. Brezhnev
stood at 'the intersection' of a complex set of cleavages involving both generational conflict and different policy agendas. He himself, moreover, had no
particularly strong political convictions of his own and was thus an ideal
compromise candidate. Various groups no doubt expected to manipulate him
for their own ends, and some may have thought they could remove him at
will.[127]

Yet it does not seem to have been only the *apparatchiki* who welcomed
Brezhnev's election; most intellectuals seem to have 'expected political, economic
and cultural reform to continue under Brezhnev, but without the fits and starts
associated with Khrushchev'.[128] The military and security organs certainly must
have welcomed the change and, with the advent of the Kosygin reforms of 1965,
the new leadership addressed the interests of the Soviet Union's economic
managers.

One point on which there does seem to be agreement is that Brezhnev's position
was shaky at the start. Shelest was not alone in seeing Brezhnev as a transitional
figure. Egorychev did not expect him to last either, while Burlatsky stresses that
Shelepin expected to remove Brezhnev with relative ease. Rodionov agrees,
although he remarks that even before the coup Brezhnev had begun to secure his
position by quietly installing his supporters in key positions.[129] The prospect of a
Shelepin challenge backed by the likes of Semichastnyi and, perhaps, Voronov,
goes a long way towards explaining Brezhnev's fear of younger members of the
leadership, described by Shelest.[130]

From the standpoint of Western views of Soviet politics, the most significant
thing about the accounts of the coup now being published is the light they cast on
the role of regional and republic party leaders in Soviet politics. The inclusion in
the conspiracy of dozens, probably even hundreds of members of the territorial
party elite suggests that their voice counted for a great deal in the corridors of the
Kremlin. The risks involved in drawing so many people into the plot were such
that the leaders of the opposition would only have followed such a strategy if they
had felt it to be necessary, no doubt not only to ensure their successful seizure of
power, but also to establish their legitimacy in the eyes of the elite. It was critically
important to carry out all decisions according to rule, to avoid the appearance of a
coup d'état.

Throughout this article, the events of October 1964 have nevertheless been
referred to as a coup. It should be stressed that this evaluation is by no means a
non-controversial one, nor is it intended to be an absolute one. The issue
continues to be debated in the Soviet press.[131] The argument for calling the
October plenum a coup stems primarily from the conspiratorial nature of the
preparations for it and from the involvement of the KGB. Yet the significance of
the Central Committee's involvement and of the orderly conduct of the Presidium
meeting and the plenum ought not to be overlooked. The fall of Khrushchev
remains the only succession in the history of the Soviet Union to date which did

THE FALL OF KHRUSHCHEV 1117

not require the death of the leader. It was, moreover, a bloodless and orderly transfer of power and the fact that it occurred at all bears witness to the extent of the change in Soviet politics wrought by Khrushchev and his colleagues in the 11 years since Stalin's death.

Not everything had changed, to be sure; Soviet leadership politics remained a rough-and-tumble game in which the rules were unclear and the composition of the various teams often changed. As Mikoyan later put it, 'Khrushchev forgot that the struggle for power can also be conducted under socialism'.[132] But as Barsukov argues, one must not overlook the many things which had changed. The October plenum was a direct consequence of the XX Congress.[133] Khrushchev himself contributed greatly to creating the environment in which both his colleagues and the middle level elite of the provinces and republics could plot his overthrow. Nor was this irony lost on him. After his retirement, Khrushchev, who does not seem to have regarded his removal as a coup, observed: 'Perhaps the most important thing I did was just this—that they were able to get rid of me simply by voting, whereas Stalin would have had them all arrested'.[134]

Corpus Christi College, Oxford

[1] Michel Tatu, *Power in the Kremlin: From Khrushchev's Decline to Collective Leadership* (London, Collins, 1969), p. 405.
[2] Roy Medvedev advanced this position several years ago in his biography of Khrushchev. R. Medvedev, *Khrushchev* (Oxford, Basil Blackwell, 1982), p. 227.
[3] V. E. Semichastnyi, 'Kak smeshchali N. S. Khrushcheva', *Argumenty i fakty*, 20 (1989), p. 5. Excerpts from the unpublished transcript of this interview (conducted by V. A. Starkov) as well as unpublished excerpts of Starkov's interview with Shelest appear in Sergei N. Khrushchev, *Khrushchev on Khrushchev: An Inside Account of the Man and His Era*, tr. William Taubman, (Boston, Little, Brown & Co., 1990). In Starkov's transcripts, Semichastnyi is even more specific, dating preparations for the coup from about February; Khrushchev, p. 46. For Shelest's and Sergei Khrushchev's accounts, see Khrushchev, pp. 45–47.
[4] Tatu, pp. 405–409.
[5] Roy Medvedev, 'N. S. Khrushchev: 1964 god: Neozhidannoe smeshchenie', in Yu. V. Aksyutin, ed., *N. S. Khrushchev: materialy k biografii* (Moscow, Izdatel'stvo politicheskoi literatury, 1988), p. 194; Gennadii Voronov, 'Ot ottepeli do zastoya' (interview), *Izvestiya*, 18 November 1988, p. 3.
[6] F. Burlatsky, '"Mirnyi zagovor" protiv N. S. Khrushcheva', in Aksyutin, ed., p. 211; elsewhere Burlatsky has stated that it was CC Secretary P. N. Demichev who told him that Shelepin was behind the plot; see F. Burlatsky, *Vozhdi i sovetniki: o Khrushcheve, Andropove i ne tol'ko o nikh...* (Moscow, Izdatel'stvo politicheskoi literatury, 1990), p. 275.
[7] P. E. Shelest, 'O Khrushcheve, Brezhneve i drugikh', *Argumenty i Fakty*, 2 (1989), pp. 5–6; Semichastnyi, p. 5. The historian Yu. Aksyutin accepts this interpretation as well; Yu. Aksyutin 'Khrushchev: 1964 god', *Trud*, 26 November 1989, p. 4.
[8] N. G. Egorychev, 'Napravlen poslom', *Ogonek*, 6 (1989), p. 7; P. A. Rodionov, 'Kak nachinalsya zastoi', *Znamya*, 8 (1989), p. 185.
[9] Khrushchev, pp. 45–46.
[10] Sergei Khrushchev reports that his father considered making Shelepin his heir apparent but felt that he needed some experience in party administrative work first. He therefore offered Shelepin Kozlov's job heading the Leningrad *obkom*. Shelepin apparently viewed the transfer away from Moscow as a demotion and declined to accept it, at which point Khrushchev became disillusioned with him. Khrushchev, p. 31.
[11] Burlatsky, 'Mirnyi zagovor...', p. 214; see also Burlatsky, *Vozhdi...*, p. 169.
[12] Semichastnyi, pp. 5–6; Voronov, p. 3; G. Voronov, 'Nemnogo vospominanii', *Druzhba narodov*, 1 (1989), pp. 200–201.

1118   WILLIAM J. TOMPSON

[13] Khrushchev, p. 136.

[14] Rodionov, p. 185. To judge from his actions after the coup, it would appear that Brezhnev shared Rodionov's view of Shelepin's intentions.

[15] For an account of Suslov's role in the 1957 crisis, see N. Barsukov, 'Proval "antipartiinoi gruppy" (1957) god', *Kommunist*, 8 (May 1990), pp. 98–108; Barsukov's account is based on the stenogram of the June 1957 plenum and other materials. Rodionov, p. 185, agrees with Barsukov's assessment of Suslov's behaviour.

[16] Voronov, 'Ot ottepeli...', p. 3.

[17] Shelest, p. 6.

[18] Khrushchev, p. 136.

[19] Shelest, pp. 5–6; Voronov, 'Ot ottepeli...', p. 3; Semichastnyi, p. 5; Khrushchev, p. 158.

[20] Rodionov, p. 188; Semichastnyi has challenged this view as regards Shelepin, arguing that there is no evidence to support the charge that the latter was a Stalinist; Andrei Karaulov, *Vokrug kremlya: kniga politicheskikh dialogov* (Moscow, Novosti, 1990), pp. 36–37.

[21] Aleksei Adzhubei, 'Te desyat' let', *Znamya*, 7 (1988), p. 129.

[22] Burlatsky, 'Mirnyi zagovor...', p. 212.

[23] Rodionov, pp. 189–190. Egorychev, p. 7, confirms that he was indeed an active 'lobbyist'. Melor Sturua, 'Dve fotografii k odnomu portretu', *Nedelya*, 43 (1988), p. 17, states that Mzhavanadze's services were never forgotten by Brezhnev, who was reluctant to remove Mzhavanadze from office and did so only in 1972, by which time he had little choice in the matter.

[24] Aksyutin, p. 4.

[25] Medvedev, '1964...', p. 194; Khrushchev, pp. 93–96; Rodionov, pp. 185–186.

[26] Khrushchev, ch. 2; Rodionov, pp. 185–186; Adzhubei, p. 129; A. Strelyanyi, 'Poslednii romantik', *Druzhba narodov*, 11 (1988), pp. 225–226.

[27] Semichastnyi, p. 5.

[28] Khrushchev, pp. 46–47, 93–96; Shelest, p. 5.

[29] Khrushchev, pp. 49–50. Mazurov himself has confirmed that Khrushchev more than once raised the subject of his removal; 'Ya govoryu ne tol'ko o sebe', *Sovetskaya Rossiya*, 19 February 1989, p. 3.

[30] Khrushchev, pp. 49–50.

[31] Medvedev, '1964...', p. 194.

[32] Khrushchev, pp. 18–19, 47, 70, 72, 75–76. A. Adzhubei, 'Po sledam odnogo yubileya', *Ogonek*, 41 (October) 1989, p. 9.

[33] Medvedev, '1964...', p. 195.

[34] Khrushchev, p. 89. Shuisky had been with Khrushchev since about 1942 and his loyalty was thought to be beyond question. Ironically, his other personal assistant, V. S. Lebedev, who had a reputation as a hard-liner and a Suslov man, was loyal to the end. Khrushchev, p. 138.

[35] Khrushchev, pp. 77, 93–96; Medvedev, '1964...', p. 194.

[36] Semichastnyi, p. 5.

[37] Khrushchev, pp. 88–89.

[38] Khrushchev, p. 160; Rodionov, p. 189; Sturua, p. 17.

[39] Strelyanyi, p. 226.

[40] Adzhubei, p. 129; Khrushchev, p. 107–109.

[41] Rodionov, p. 186.

[42] Egorychev, p. 7; Semichastnyi also claims that Brezhnev panicked at this point; Khrushchev, p. 135.

[43] Semichastnyi, p. 5; a fuller account of this episode can be found in Starkov's transcript, cited in Khrushchev, p. 135.

[44] Semichastnyi, p. 5; Khrushchev, pp. 68–69 (Starkov transcript). Aksyutin, p. 4, seems to accept Semichastnyi's account.

[45] Aksyutin, p. 4.

[46] Khrushchev, p. 160; Sturua, p. 17; Semichastnyi, p. 5.

[47] Semichastnyi, pp. 5–6; Khrushchev, pp. 137, 139. Semichastnyi has recently disputed Sergei Khrushchev's account of the surveillance at Pitsunda, however; see Karaulov, pp. 35–37.

[48] Khrushchev, p. 148 (Starkov transcript [Semichastnyi]); Burlatsky, 'Mirnyi zagovor...', p. 211. In contrast to Burlatsky's account, neither Sergei Khrushchev (who was there) nor Semichastnyi mentions a change in the security detail at Pitsunda.

[49] Khrushchev, p. 136 (Starkov transcript).

[50] Semichastnyi, p. 5; Khrushchev, p. 136 (Starkov transcript). Aksyutin, p. 4, presents a

THE FALL OF KHRUSHCHEV 1119

slightly different version of Semichastnyi's story concerning the approach to Kosygin, suggesting that he may have had another source (probably Voronov) corroborating Semichastnyi's account.

[51] Interview with Shelest, Moscow, 26 December 1990.

[52] Medvedev, '1964...', p. 194.

[53] Ibid., p. 195; Khrushchev, pp. 133–136; Semichastnyi, p. 5; Adzhubei, 'Te desyat' let', p. 129, echoes Khrushchev's account: Suslov called. Shelest supports Semichastnyi on this point; Aksyutin, p. 4.

[54] Karaulov, p. 146.

[55] Khrushchev, pp. 134, 139–140n; Medvedev, '1964...', p. 195; Semichastnyi, p. 5.

[56] Khrushchev, p. 140.

[57] Semichastnyi, p. 5; Khrushchev, pp. 69–70.

[58] Burlatsky, 'Mirnyi zagovor...', p. 211.

[59] Khrushchev, pp. 4n, 148 (Starkov transcript); Semichastnyi, p. 5.

[60] Karaulov, p. 36.

[61] Khrushchev, pp. 144–145; Semichastnyi, p. 5; Semichastnyi denies that Chekvalov was there; Karaulov, p. 36.

[62] Semichastnyi, p. 5.

[63] Medvedev, '1964...', p. 195; N. A. Barsukov, 'Kak byl "nizlozhen" N. S. Khrushchev', Obshchestvennye nauki, 6 (1989), p. 133; Egorychev, p. 7.

[64] Medvedev, '1964...', p. 195; Semichastnyi, p. 5; Barsukov, p. 133; Semichastnyi (who was not there) states that no one was present except the members of the Presidium and the Secretariat; Karaulov, p. 36.

[65] Medvedev, '1964...', p. 195; Shelest, p. 5, Khrushchev, p. 155.

[66] Medvedev, '1964...', p. 194; Khrushchev, p. 153. Khrushchev's information on the Presidium meeting is based on an account given to him by the Academician Anushavan Arzumanyan, who claimed to have got his information straight from Mikoyan.

[67] Khrushchev, p. 153. Shelest himself denies this; Karaulov, p. 146.

[68] Tatu, p. 413.

[69] Khrushchev, p. 154; Aksyutin, p. 4.

[70] Medvedev, '1964...', p. 195; Rodionov, p. 190; Voronov, 'Vospominanii...', pp. 200–201.

[71] Medvedev, '1964', p. 195; Shelest, p. 5; Voronov, 'Ot ottepeli...', p. 3; Rodionov, p. 190; Aksyutin, p. 4. Sergei Khrushchev claims that at the end of the first day of the Presidium meeting his father had only been asked to give up one of his posts, although the elder Khrushchev seems at that stage already to have understood that he would be asked to resign the other as well. See, Khrushchev, p. 149.

[72] Khrushchev, pp. 151–154; Medvedev, '1964', pp. 197–198.

[73] Adzhubei, 'Te desyat' let', p. 130.

[74] Thomas Sherlock, 'Khrushchev Reconsidered', Report on the USSR, 8 June 1990, p. 15.

[75] Adzhubei, 'Te desyat' let', p. 130.

[76] Shelest, p. 5; Khrushchev, pp. 156–157 (Starkov transcript).

[77] Shelest, p. 5.

[78] Adzhubei, 'Po sledam...', p. 8.

[79] Tatu, p. 389.

[80] Khrushchev, pp. 132–133; Burlatsky, 'Mirnyi zagovor...', p. 211.

[81] See, for example, Barsukov, pp. 124–133; Voronov, 'Vospominanii...', p. 199–201; Rodionov, pp. 188, 191; Medvedev, '1964...', p. 197.

[82] Voronov, 'Ot ottepeli...', p. 3.

[83] Adzhubei, 'Te desyat' let', p. 129. Adzhubei's account receives indirect support on this point from the fact that the November plenum was to discuss constitutional reform as well as agriculture. Aksyutin, p. 4. Sergei Khrushchev agrees that rule 25 undermined his father and links it to the latter's attempts to curtail the privileges of the apparat; Khrushchev, p. 24.

[84] Egorychev, p. 7.

[85] Barsukov, p. 125; Adzhubei concurs; see 'Po sledam...', p. 8.

[86] See, for example, Barsukov; Medvedev, '1964...', and Strelyanyi.

[87] Rodionov, p. 191; Strelyanyi, p. 225; Aksyutin, p. 4. Barsukov, pp. 130–131, states that Khrushchev also intended to return to vertical management in industry.

[88] Ibid., p. 130.

[89] Khrushchev, p. 95; Tatu, pp. 394–398; Medvedev, '1964...', p. 193–194.

[90] Barsukov, p. 130; Egorychev, p. 7.

[91] Rodionov, p. 188; Strelyanyi, p. 225; Egorychev, p. 7; Barsukov, p. 133.

1120   WILLIAM J. TOMPSON

⁹² See, for example, N. Mikhailov, 'Vozmozhen li segodnya Oktyabr' 1964 goda?', *Moskovskaya pravda*, 18 August 1989, p. 2; Medvedev, '1964...', p. 199; E. Zubkova, 'Oktyabr' 1964 goda: povorot ili perevorot?', *Kommunist*, 13 (September) 1989, pp. 93–94.

⁹³ Khrushchev, pp. 70–72, 75–76.

⁹⁴ Adzhubei, 'Te desyat' let', p. 130.

⁹⁵ Strelyanyi, p. 226.

⁹⁶ John H. Miller, 'The Communist Party: Trends and Problems', in A. Brown & M. Kaser, eds., *Soviet Policy for the 1980s* (London, Macmillan, 1982), p. 1.

⁹⁷ Aksyutin, p. 4; Khrushchev, pp. 149–150.

⁹⁸ Khrushchev, p. 150 (Starkov transcript).

⁹⁹ Barsukov, pp. 133–134. Barsukov's excerpts from Khrushchev's final remarks are taken from a tape recording deposited in the Central Party Archive of the Institute of Marxism–Leninism by Shelepin. The passages quoted by Barsukov parallel quite closely those which Shelest has reconstructed from his notes. Excerpts from Shelest's account of Khrushchev's speech may be found in Shelest, p. 5 and Khrushchev, pp. 155–158 (Starkov transcript). Though less accurate, these are more extensive than anything quoted by Barsukov, whose material nevertheless strongly confirms the essential reliability of Shelest's reconstruction.

¹⁰⁰ Barsukov, p. 134.

¹⁰¹ *Ibid*; Shelest, p. 5.

¹⁰² *Ibid.*

¹⁰³ Khrushchev, pp. 28, 125; Rodionov, p. 192.

¹⁰⁴ Strelyanyi, p. 226; Adzhubei, 'Te desyat' let', p. 7.

¹⁰⁵ Voronov, 'Vospominanii...', p. 201.

¹⁰⁶ Adzhubei, 'Po sledam...', p. 9.

¹⁰⁷ Sherlock, p. 14.

¹⁰⁸ Semichastnyi, pp. 5–6; Khrushchev, pp. 158–159 (Starkov transcript). If, as he has asserted, Semichastnyi had bugged the First Secretary's phone, then he ought to have known about the latter's phone call to Mikoyan on the night of 13 October. Presumably his impatience grew out of the fear that if all was not done quickly, Khrushchev's supporters might have time to turn the tables on the conspirators.

¹⁰⁹ Khrushchev, p. 155.

¹¹⁰ Medvedev, '1964...', pp. 196–202; Semichastnyi, p. 6; Barsukov, p. 133. All these accounts agree on all the main points. Egorychev, p. 7, and Voronov, 'Ot ottepeli...', p. 3, also agree that there was no debate. Ex-Presidium member N. A. Mukhitdinov, however, remembers there being two or three brief speeches in support of Suslov. N. A. Mukhitdinov, '12 let s Khrushchevym', *Argumenty i fakty*, 44 (1989), p. 6. Adzhubei agrees: 'Po sledam...', pp. 8–9.

¹¹¹ Medvedev, *Khrushchev...*, pp. 237–244; Semichastnyi, p. 6. *Izvestiya TsK KPSS* has promised to publish the stenographic account of the October plenum in late 1991.

¹¹² Shelest, p. 6; Khrushchev, p. 158 (Starkov transcript).

¹¹³ Shelest, p. 6; Medvedev, '1964...', p. 196.

¹¹⁴ Semichastnyi, p. 6.

¹¹⁵ Voronov, 'Ot ottepeli...', p. 3.

¹¹⁶ Khrushchev, p. 160. The Medvedevs also name Leningrad *obkom* first secretary Tolstikov and CC secretary for agriculture V. S. Polyakov; Roy & Zhores Medvedev, *Khrushchev: The Years in Power* (Oxford, Oxford University Press, 1977), p. 172.

¹¹⁷ Egorychev, p. 7.

¹¹⁸ Semichastnyi, p. 6; Khrushchev, pp. 159–160 (Starkov transcript).

¹¹⁹ Voronov, 'Ot ottepeli...', p. 3.

¹²⁰ Rodionov, p. 191. Although the plenum concluded early on the evening of 14 October, it was not announced for almost 24 hours—until the evening of 15 October. It first appeared in the newspapers on the morning of 16 October. Mzhavanadze evidently expected to see it in the newspapers of 15 October; no one seems to know the reasons for the delay in announcing the change.

¹²¹ Barsukov, pp. 135–136.

¹²² *Ibid.*, p. 135.

¹²³ Tatu, p. 385n; he also praised Kosygin and Podgorny. Rodionov, p. 185; Medvedev, '1964...', p. 196.

¹²⁴ Semichastnyi, p. 6.

¹²⁵ Shelest, p. 6.

¹²⁶ Egorychev, p. 7. Egorychev claims that his expression of these doubts contributed to Brezhnev's decision to remove him from office in 1967.

THE FALL OF KHRUSHCHEV 1121

[127] Burlatsky, 'Mirnyi zagovor...', p. 214.
[128] Sherlock, p. 15.
[129] Egorychev, p. 7; Burlatsky, 'Mirnyi zagovor...', p. 212. Rodionov, pp. 185, 188.
[130] Shelest, p. 6.
[131] For the best expositions of opposing sides in this debate, see Barsukov, who believes that the October plenum was not a coup, and Rodionov, who answers this position.
[132] Adzhubei, 'Te desyat' let', p. 130.
[133] Barsukov, p. 136.
[134] Medvedev, *Khrushchev*, p. 245.

[17]

PATRONAGE NETWORKS AND COALITION BUILDING IN THE BREZHNEV ERA

By John P. Willerton, Jr.

LEADERSHIP change, at any level of political authority, brings with it the potential for policy change. This is especially true in the case of the chief executive at the national level, where expectations of broader system-wide policy change can be the greatest.[1] The Soviet-type political system appears to be especially conducive to such potential for policy change because the degree of centralization ensures great political discretion for the few at the top of the decision-making apparatus. The fact that all bureaucracies are interconnected, with no independent political actors or institutions, only underlines the degree of real power enjoyed by the national political elite.

However, in the Soviet-type political system, such policy change does not necessarily come with leadership change. A political succession is but the first step, and other conditions must also be met if policy innovation is to follow. The recent experience of the Soviet political leadership bears out the fact that there is a system need for a strong chief executive who is interested in change. However, this condition will probably not obtain in the immediate aftermath of a succession. By and large, the initial confidence placed in a new leader will rest in part upon the promise of some initial policy stability. If there is an expectation of some policy change, it would be for the long run.

While a new leader may ultimately be interested in differentiating himself and his regime from the predecessor regime, this will require some time. That new leader, after all, is likely to have been an important member of the past regime. Yet any desire for innovation will require that the new leader consolidate his position, bringing in a new 'team' of politicians while forging working relations with important incumbents within the top decision-making bodies (the Polit-bureau and the Secretariat). Unlike Western liberal democracies, there are no political rules mandating automatic replacement of personnel in the policy-making apparatus. President Ronald Reagan or Prime Minister Margaret Thatcher can move quickly upon gaining office, bringing with them proteges and allied politicians committed to them and to their political programmes. This is not the case in the Soviet-type political system. In the Soviet system, it is up to the new leader to strengthen his position through the easing out of weaker or hostile incumbents, the promotion of reliable subordinates, and the development of alliances with powerful incumbent political actors. The absence of rules mandating the automatic replacement of top executives is, in fact, a check on the top Soviet leader as he attempts to direct the party and state apparatus. While there are no autonomous institutions outside the purview of the central Party

Secretariat, the General Secretary must 'tame' or reach accommodations with the highest policy-making organs if he is to govern. In real terms, the power of a central party and state apparatus which is not automatically directed by the proteges and allies of the top leader is an important 'check' upon the top leader's authority within the Soviet political system.[2]

Ultimately, a new coalition of politicians, encompassing proteges and allies of the General Secretary, must be able to formulate a comprehensive policy thrust—a policy thrust presented by and associated with that 'guiding' figure of the system. The time frame necessary for such power consolidation and the eventual presentation of a comprehensive programme is not inconsiderable. It may require five to seven years.[3]

All of these conditions are necessary for significant policy change to occur. Critical, however, as a first step, is the recruitment of trusted subordinates and the formation of a governing team. Such recruitment and coalition building is the focus of this examination of Soviet elite politics of the Brezhnev era. It is argued here that top-level national leadership change brings with it the potential for important personnel turnover enabling a new chief executive to consolidate his hold over the policy-making and policy-implementing bureaucracies. An examination of the Brezhnev period reveals that such a transfer and replacement of personnel took place and that it included not only the important organs of the Central Committee apparatus, overseen by the General Secretary, but also key ministries and state committees as well as significant regional party organizations. Beyond the rotation and replacement of politicians, the selective recruitment of trusted subordinates assumed a critical role in the Brezhnev regime's power consolidation. Patronage networks provided an important basis for the national political coalition that governed the Soviet Union during the 1964–82 period. A significant number of politicians who had served with Brezhnev in varying capacities and in different institutional and regional settings prior to his October 1964 succession assumed top positions within leading party and state organs. Yet Brezhnev's effectiveness as a politician entailed much more than the selective recruitment of his own proteges into top policy and supervisory positions. It involved the construction of alliances which bridged a number of important rival politicians and their patronage networks. The construction of such alliances proved to be of vital importance to Brezhnev's leadership effectiveness. Non-Brezhnev factions flourished throughout his eighteen-year tenure as party leader. While certain, genuinely threatening, factions were eliminated during this period, others assumed important roles in the development of a governing coalition. Important alliance arrangements, which incorporated a number of patronage networks, lent a normalcy to the Soviet polity as personnel recruitment, turnover, and tenure practices were stabilized. While not without opponents, Brezhnev was able to form and maintain a governing coalition for nearly two decades. As a result, unlike his immediate predecessor, Brezhnev and this ruling coalition were able to formulate a policy programme that guided Soviet society for a considerable period of time; a policy programme which has continued to frame the Soviet domestic and foreign policies of the post-Brezhnev period.

Approach and Methodology

This study of all-union elite politics identifies and examines the patronage networks and coalitions which flourished within the national political elite during the Brezhnev period. Political patronage is defined here as an asymetrical personal political relationship in which goods, services, and power itself are exchanged, with the power and influence of the members of patronage networks being interdependent. Particular measures of patronage are specified and applied in this analysis to permit systematic identification of this informal political relationship. A governing coalition is understood here as signifying a group of politicians who share a set of broad goals and who agree to combine their political resources in pursuit of that set of goals. The members of the CPSU Central Committee and Central Auditing Commission for the period from October 1964 to November 1982 serve as a population base for this empirical analysis. All members of the Politbureau and Secretariat are treated as potential patrons in the system,[4] with all full and candidate members of the Central Committee and all members of the Central Auditing Commission treated as potential proteges.[5] Politbureau members and CPSU secretaries are treated as potential patrons because these two sets of politicians are the most influential elites within the party organization as well as within the policy-making process. While the Politbureau is the critical decision-making body in the Soviet Union, there is no doubt that there are CPSU secretaries whose political power rivals, if not surpasses, that of members of the Politbureau.[6]

Potential proteges of these system patrons are drawn from the total population of Central Committee and Central Auditing Commission members during the Brezhnev era. The memberships of these two bodies are composed of the top personnel of all political organizations and hierarchies within the USSR,[7] and as a group represent the top political elite of the Soviet Union. Any definition of a nationally prominent political elite would include these politicians.[8]

Patronage relations are measured by determining that two politicians have worked together in the same region at the same time on at least two different identifiable occasions in their careers. Such geographic proximity of politicians is indicated, in the case of the RSFSR and the Ukraine, by two politicians serving together in the same oblast at the same time. For other republics, the two politicians must have served in the same republic during the same time period. Such geographic stipulations are sufficient for a first cut in identifying patron-client ties. Individuals possessing the prominence of membership in these top all-union party organs would, in the first place, have come into contact with one another at the oblast level. In the non-Slavic republics one would expect that non-native Russians and Ukrainians at such high levels of authority would be acquainted with one another. The same would be predicted for natives of those republics.

Geographic proximity is but one indicator for determining patronage relationships. It could be argued that mere acquaintance between two individuals does not represent a politically reciprocated interdependent relationship. Given the relatively small universe of a region's or non-Russian republic's political elite, however, it can be assumed that there is a positive relationship between the advancement of a given individual at level X, and the position of another individual at the highest level in that region. What is important is the existence of a pattern in the career advancements of politicians indicating an interrelationship in their advances. The measurement of a patron-protege tie in this study presupposes at least two identifiable time points when the two politicians' careers were linked. A patron-protege connection is established when the two politicians are both advancing in their careers as these job linkages can be identified. The patron is clearly superior, but the protege has moved up with him, making the relationship a stronger career bond.

Available biographical data for Soviet elite members permit us to identify other conditions which can also indicate a patron-protege and patron-client tie. Common World War II experience encouraged the forging of personal and career connections. The memoirs of Soviet politicians and military figures are suggestive in this regard.[9] Serving in the same underground partisan movement, working in the same military group, or serving along the same front are all used as indicators of such linkages.

Common educational experience, in attending the same higher educational institution during the same time period, is another indicator of a patron-client connection when linked up with subsequent career associations. The biographical data available for all-union elite members usually include information on post-secondary education, with notation of institutions and the date of graduation. Experiences in the university or institute represent potentially important socializing activities that take place earlier in an individual's life.[10] They can be important in the initial development of a patron-client relationship and should be accounted for to the extent possible given the available data.[11]

Tracing the career mobility of patrons and their proteges results in the identification of groups of politicians who ascend the party and state hierarchies together. As groups, they bring a good deal of identifiable common past experience to the national level. Yet, in addition to the measures which gauge common past work and socialization experiences, patron-client ties can also be identified on the basis of common institutional affiliations of politicians. A tie is established where one politician is advancing professionally within a hierarchy supervised or overseen by another. Two career promotions must take place under a potential patron's supervision in order to establish a career connection.[12] In such cases, we are speaking of true 'clients', because the junior politicians have advanced in positions very subordinate to those of their patron.[13] This measure is especially appropriate for such a study at the all-union authority level, and for Moscow. Our knowledge of the Soviet policy process and political structure permits us, to some extent, to determine cases where an individual or his political office has oversight over others.[14] As a result, not only regional and republic party organizations, but all-union hierarchies, become subject to systematic analysis.

This measure, combined with others noted here, should allow for an identification of the broad contours of patronage networks operating at the all-union level. However, the analysis of the patronage faction of the CPSU General Secretary requires special consideration. The General Secretary stands atop both a patronage faction and the party-state apparatus. He possesses immense organizational and policy-making authority in the Soviet system. His institutional powers within the central party apparatus permit him at least discretionary oversight in the recruitment of personnel into top party and state organizational slots. This fact of political life in the Soviet system has both analytical and empirical implications for the study of elite recruitment and patronage at the national level. It is important, analytically, to differentiate between the General Secretary's reliance upon old trusted associates, 'proteges', and his sponsorship of new subordinates as he consolidates his power and builds a working coalition. The number of trusted network members who are reliable known quantities to a leader is limited in comparison with the number of junior politicians who can be sponsored. Yet any top party leader will rely upon both types of subordinates, as incumbents are replaced by new office-holders.

Politicians who experience career mobility under the General Secretary, but who have no prior association with him, may or may not combine longer-term political loyalty to him with their career ambitions. However, the politicians who serve directly with the General Secretary, in his organizational secretariat or with his top proteges, are closely enough tied to him and his faction to permit us to infer a stronger political tie. They, along with old-time associates, can be viewed as the members of a General Secretary's faction after his succession to the top post.

For the purposes of differentiating the General Secretary's network and institutional roles, the following empirical stipulations are applied in this analysis. The General Secretary's faction is understood to comprise 'proteges' and 'clients'. Politicians identified as 'proteges' of General Secretary Brezhnev are individuals who served with him and experienced mobility under him prior to his 1964 succession. Those who are identified as Brezhnev's 'clients' are politicians who both experienced mobility after 1964 and served directly with the General Secretary. Other politicians who experienced several career promotions under Brezhnev's supervision, but who did not serve directly with him, are not identified as his patronage network members.[15]

Leadership Succession and Emerging Patronage Networks

The succession of Leonid Brezhnev in October 1964 was the critical first event in a reconstituting of the Soviet elite in the latter 1960s. This reconstitution of the leadership entailed two recruitment tendencies: (1) the turnover of personnel and (2) the promotion of political proteges of top-level national elite members. Reliance upon a policy of cadres turnover is not necessarily evident if one focuses only on the two top party organs, the Presidium (later Politbureau) and the Secretariat. Change at this authority level came slowly. Rejection of the Khrushchev policy legacy did not translate into an immediate overhaul of the Presidium and Secretariat. Indeed, the high cadres turnover rates promoted by Khrushchev were an important reason for the Presidium's decision to retire

TABLE 1

LEADERSHIP TURNOVER IN LEADING ALL-UNION, REPUBLIC AND REGIONAL PARTY AND STATE ORGANIZATIONS, OCTOBER 1964–1971

Positions (N)	October–December 1964	1965	1966	1967	1968	1969	1970	1971	Turnover 1964–69¹ %	Turnover 1964–71¹ %
Politbureau (20)²	2 (1)⁵	1 (2)	1 (2)	(1)	1			2 (1)	40%⁶	45%⁷
Secretariat (10)		3	2	1	1	1			60%⁸	60%⁹
CPSU Central Committee Departments (21)		9	2	1	3		8		67%	67%
USSR Council of Ministers (85)	1	45	2	7	3	1	8	1	69%	75%
Republic Party and State Leaders (44)³	2	3	3	2	2	5	6	4	39%	57%
First Secretaries of RSFSR and Ukraine Oblasts. Krais and ASSRs⁴ (99)	4	10	9	11	8	5	9	8	46%	58%
First Secretaries of other Republics' Oblasts. Krais and ASSRs (64)	7	15	7	8	8	2	11	10	59%	84%

¹ In those cases where a given organization had more than one leadership change, only one change was noted in calculating the total turnover percentage for the period. Thus, a 100% turnover rate would signify that every organization within a given category (e.g., all of the members of the Council of Ministers) experienced a leadership change. The percentages given underestimate the actual number of personnel changes, because some of these organizations had two leadership changes during the 1964–71 period. While the columns noting changes by year record all such individual changes, they were not used to calculate the overall percentage turnover. Including all such changes in calculating an overall figure would provide an exaggerated impression of the degree of personnel changes. Even without double counting for institutions, the turnover that is noted in the final two columns demonstrates a very significant transformation of the ranks of top cadres.

² The membership figures for the Politbureau and Secretariat are averages for the 1964–71 period since there is no set number of positions. The average numbers of full and candidate members in the Politbureau were thirteen and seven respectively.

³ The total number includes the party first secretaries, council of ministers' chairmen and supreme soviet chairmen for the fifteen republics. These politicians have been grouped together as the most important in the republics because they enjoy the highest public profile and head the most important party and state bodies. This figure comes to forty-four because the RSFSR does not have a party first secretary.

⁴ The party first secretaries are the most powerful officials within these regional political units, serving as the critical intermediaries between the political centre and these regions.

⁵ The figures in parentheses represent the number of new candidate members in the Politbureau.

⁶ This figure is the percentage of 1969 Politbureau full and candidate members who were brought into that body during the 1964–69 period.

⁷ This figure is the percentage of 1971 Politbureau full and candidate members who were brought into that body during the 1964–71 period.

⁸ This figure is the percentage of 1969 CPSU secretaries who were brought into that body during the 1964–69 period.

⁹ This figure is the percentage of 1971 CPSU secretaries who were brought into that body during the 1964–71 period.

AND COALITION BUILDING

Khrushchev. His proposals for more regularized and extensive personnel changes were rejected in favour of a 'stability of cadres' policy. Yet during the five-year period of the new regime's power consolidation, a significant turnover of party and state apparatus personnel did take place (Table 1). This turnover encompassed all of the major party and state organs and affected politics at the republic and oblast levels. By the time of the XXIV Congress in 1971, when the regime's comprehensive foreign and domestic policy thrust was presented, well over half of the leading cadres in all top organizations had been replaced or transferred. National-level policy-making, supervisory, and policy-implementing organs were affected. Nearly three-quarters of the provincial first secretaries were replaced. The Brezhnev succession at the highest level of authority did set in motion a significant alteration of the political elite below.

The movement of politicians to new positions and the retirement of incumbents helped the post-Khrushchev leadership to remove political obstacles to its full consolidation of power. This personnel turnover also facilitated the advancement of junior politicians who had career links with top national politicians. Trusted associates of the Politbureau and Secretariat elite moved into party and state organizational slots which ultimately conferred Central Committee membership and high-level elite status. Approximately one-quarter of the entire Central Committee and Central Auditing Commission membership

TABLE 2

SIZE OF POLITBUREAU AND SECRETARIAT MEMBERS' PATRONAGE NETWORKS, 1964–1982[1]

Patron	N	Patron	N	Patron	N
Aliev	3	Kosygin	9	Rusakov	
Andropov	2	Kulakov	1	Shcherbitsky	16
Brezhnev	48 (10)[2]	Kunaev	12	Shelepin	12
Chernenko	2	Kuznetsov		Shelest	5
Demichev	6	Masherov	5	Shevardnadze	2
Dolgikh	3	Mazurov	9 (2)[5]	Solomentsev	1
Gorbachev	2	Mzhavanadze	2	Suslov	8 (2)[7]
Grechko	5	Pel'she	7	Tikhonov	
Grishin	2	Podgorny	13 (1)[6]	Ustinov	9
Gromyko	4	Polyansky	5	Voronov	3
Kapitonov	11 (2)[3]	Ponomarev	2	Zimyanin	1
Katushev	4	Rashidov	6		
Kirilenko	12 (1)[4]	Ryabov	1		
Kisilev	1	Romanov	10		

[1] The numbers in parentheses indicate the number of Politbureau and Secretariat members who have been identified as proteges or clients of that politician in addition to those within the Central Committee and Central Auditing Commission.
[2] The identified proteges of Brezhnev within the Politbureau and Secretariat are Chernenko, Grechko, Kirilenko, Kunaev, Shcherbitsky, Tikhonov, and Ustinov. The identified clients are Aliev, Katushev, and Rusakov.
[3] The identified proteges of Kapitonov are Demichev and Grishin.
[4] The identified Secretary-protege of Kirilenko is Ryabov.
[5] The identified proteges of Mazurov are Masherov and Zimyanin.
[6] The identified protege of Podgorny is Titov.
[7] The identified proteges of Suslov are Pel'she and Ponomarev.

for the 1964–82 period can be identified as proteges of Politbureau and Secretariat members. Table 2 indicates the size of the patronage entourages for each of the Politbureau and Secretariat members during this period.[16] As would be expected, politicians who made their careers in the party apparatus, moving from region to region as they advanced in the party hierarchy, exhibited larger entourages. This group of politicians includes Kirilenko (Sverdlovsk and the Ukraine), Kunaev (Kazakhstan), Mazurov (Belorussia), Podgorny (the Ukraine), and Shcherbitsky (the Ukraine). Other politicians who also made careers in the party apparatus, but whose power bases were in Moscow and not across more easily measured regions, generally exhibited smaller, though not insignificant, client networks.[17]

A number of politicians who made careers in hierarchies outside the party apparatus also exhibit fairly sizeable patronage networks. Those system patrons who had served in Moscow and in their areas of expertise over a considerable time period (e.g., Aleksei Kosygin and Dmitrii Ustinov) had relatively large identifiable entourages. Others, such as Marshal Grechko, Dmitrii Polyansky and Gennadii Voronov, whose political careers at the all-union level were of shorter duration, had smaller networks.

Comparison of the relative sizes of these entourages suggests a crude differentiation in the power and authority of their all-union patron-politicians. Most observers of Soviet politics would agree that during the 1960s and 1970s, in addition to the General Secretary himself, Kirilenko, Kosygin, Podgorny, Shelepin, and Suslov assumed the leading roles in the governing coalition. Their political clout and the duration of their national elite status afforded them the enhanced opportunity to promote associates as well as to cultivate clients. However, the organizational strength of these and other, especially regionally-based, politicians also stemmed from their associations with larger client networks; networks which linked the careers of politicians who proved to be powerful enough to secure membership in the Politbureau and Secretariat.

Throughout Soviet history, clusters of politicians have come together, spanning institutions and regions and including more than one nationally prominent person. While members of such clusters head their own entourages, their careers and those of their subordinates collectively can intertwine to form a larger 'network'. I use the term 'network', rather than 'faction' or 'coalition', to suggest that these interrelationships transcend specific policy positions or institutional affiliations and extend beyond one single politician's own career. A 'network' is defined here as including several relatively equal politicians and their coteries, though one politician could assume some sort of 'first among equals' role. The network transcends the career of any one politician—even if one politician stands atop the network as a whole.[18] Such networks are of salience because they represent broader groups of politicians, providing constraint to the political motivations of those politicians. While the decision rules used in this study identified only dyadic career links, many of these individuals' careers suggested multiple linkages—and to patrons who themselves had interconnected careers.

The available data and the identified patronage entourages provide the information necessary to identify important networks at the all-union level. Within the Politbureau and Secretariat of the latter 1960s and 1970s I identify five important networks of politicians which influenced national elite politics: (1) the Brezhnev network, at the heart of which was the so-called 'Dnepropetrovsk mafia'; (2) the Suslov-Pel'she-Ponomarev group, headed by the long-time party *eminence grise*; (3) a Khar'kov (Ukrainian) group, headed by Nikolai Podgorny and including Vitalii Titov and Petr Shelest; (4) a Belorussian group, forged during the Second World War and headed by Kirill Mazurov, while including Petr Masherov and Mikhail Zimyanin; and (5) a Moscow-based group, headed by Ivan Kapitonov and including Viktor Grishin and Petr Demichev. These five networks are identified using the same indicators that were applied to identify specific patron-client dyads. The careers of the Politbureau and Secretariat members within each of these networks can be linked together, with one member appearing to assume a leading role among the other proteges. Thus, for instance, Brezhnev assumed the guiding role within his own group, always advancing to a higher authority level before other top members of his network were elevated to that level.[19] The same pattern obtains for the other groups, as Suslov, Podgorny, Mazurov, and Kapitonov preceded the other top members of these networks into leading republic and all-union positions. The careers of the top-level members of each network are interconnected. The institutional and regional affiliations of their numerous clients are also interconnected. Discernable networks of politicians are identified bridging a number of authority levels as well as various institutional and regional interests.

At the centre of this study is the Brezhnev patronage network, the most influential system-wide network in the latter 1960s and 1970s. It encompassed a range of politicians who had worked with Brezhnev in the pre-1964 period, whose careers had flourished under Brezhnev, and who had the political influence to cultivate their own patronage factions. At the core of this extended Brezhnev network was Brezhnev's own career faction. Over thirty Central Committee and Central Auditing Commission members can be identified as members of a Brezhnev-led Dnepropetrovsk group alone.[20] The strength of the Brezhnev faction which included the Dnepropetrovsk group is indicated not only by the close career ties evinced among the leading members of this group (i.e., Brezhnev, Kirilenko, Shcherbitsky, and Tikhonov), but by the cross-career linkages exhibited among members of their various clientele. It is useful to consider more closely the size, growth, and political strength of the extended Brezhnev network, the leading patronage network during this period. By examining it, we can consider both a broader network and, at its core, the entourage of a specific politician.

The Brezhnev Network

The consolidation of power by General Secretary Brezhnev in the period after his 1964 succession entailed more than the turnover of personnel in various bureaucracies. His power consolidation relied upon the promotion of trusted faction members into top party and state positions (Table 3). The recruitment of proteges began almost immediately upon Brezhnev's selection as First (General) Secretary, and it continued throughout his tenure. The growing political strength of the General Secretary and the concomitant expanding political power of his top proteges facilitated the emergence of those proteges' own factions (Table 4). Viewed as extensions of the core Brezhnev entourage, these groups of politicians served to bridge national and regional bureaucracies and facilitate governance by the Brezhnev coalition.

From the earliest days of his administration, Brezhnev faction members assumed a significant profile in the central party apparatus, especially in heading Central Committee departments. Only one Brezhnev protege, Andrei Kirilenko, was to be found in the Politbureau in October 1964. By the XXIII

TABLE 3

MEMBERSHIP OF BREZHNEV'S FACTION IN LEADING PARTY AND STATE BODIES, 1964–1981

	1964	*1966*	*1971*	*1976*	*1981*
Politbureau (20)[1]	1	1 (3)[2]	3 (1)	5 (1)	6 (1)
Secretariat (11)		2	3	4	3
Central Committee Department Heads (23)	1	6	8	5	8
Council of Ministers (100)	5	9	11	13	13
Republic Leaders[3] (44)	5	5	9	9	5
Obkom First Secretaries (123)	6	8	6	6	4

[1] These figures include the average membership size of the given body during the 1964–81 period. In the case of the Politbureau, the average membership figure of twenty represents a combined average of full and candidate members, thirteen and seven respectively.

[2] The numbers in parentheses represent the number of candidate members who were members of the Brezhnev faction.

[3] Republic leaders refers to the first secretaries, chairmen of the councils of ministers, and chairmen of the supreme soviets of the fifteen union republics. The total is forty-four for all fifteen republics, since the RSFSR does not have a first secretary.

TABLE 4

MEMBERSHIP OF BREZHNEV'S PROTEGES' NETWORKS IN LEADING PARTY AND STATE BODIES, 1964–1981

	1964	*1966*	*1971*	*1976*	*1981*
Central Committee Department Heads (23)	1	1	2	3	3
Council of Ministers (100)	1	3	5	8	7
In Central Committee Apparatus	1	3	3	2	2
In Council of Ministers Apparatus	7	7	8	7	4
Republic Leaders[1] (44)	1	2	3	3	4
In Republic Central Committee or Council of Ministers Apparatus	4	6	7	9	8
Obkom First Secretaries (123)	9	11	14	15	16
In Military Command Positions	5	5	5	5	5

[1] Republic Leaders refers to the first secretaries, chairmen of the councils of ministers, and chairmen of the supreme soviets of the fifteen union republics. The total is forty-four for all fifteen republics, since the RSFSR does not have a first secretary.

Congress in 1966 several other Brezhnev proteges had moved into the Politbureau as candidate members.[21] It was only at the XXIV Congress in 1971, by which time Brezhnev was firmly in control of the party apparatus, that several of these proteges joined him and Kirilenko as full members.[22] As Brezhnev and his faction further enhanced their positions within the elite (and certain rival factions were at the same time being weakened), additional coterie members found their way to Politbureau membership.[23] By the time of Brezhnev's last Congress in 1981, over one-third of the Politbureau's membership comprised politicians with past patronage connections to the General Secretary.

Members of the Brezhnev group also advanced into the Secretariat, beginning as early as March 1965. Dmitrii Ustinov became a CPSU Secretary in 1965 (responsible for questions of armaments production), while Kirilenko was advanced into the Secretariat in April 1966 (overseeing important internal political questions and party work). The subsequent appointment of Konstantin Chernenko as a Secretary for administration only represented a further consolidation of Brezhnev's position within the apparatus.[24]

While all of these proteges' portfolios were important in the supervising of policy, the party work and cadres appointments were critical. Andrei Kirilenko and Ivan Kapitonov—the Secretaries responsible for these portfolios—assumed very important roles in the post-1964 regime. The close Brezhnev-Kirilenko patronage tie bespeaks the influence the Brezhnev group had in the oversight of party work. However, the role of Ivan Kapitonov, who has not been identified here as a Brezhnev protege by my decision rules, was not negligible. Kapitonov was allied with Brezhnev, being politically resurrected by the General Secretary almost immediately after Khrushchev's ouster. He benefited from a number of important career advances within the first years of Brezhnev's rule.[25] His position within the Secretariat and Central Committee apparatus made him a key gate keeper monitoring promotions within the top national party organs. His own Moscow-based patronage network flourished during the later 1960s and 1970s, as Brezhnev's extended network expanded its base of power.[26] Kapitonov's resurrection and subsequent organizational clout reflect Brezhnev's leadership style as a consensus-builder willing to make accommodations with other political interests. Brezhnev augmented the recruitment of his own associates with coalition-building across certain other flourishing patronage factions.

Beneath the Secretariat, Brezhnev faction members were recruited into important Central Committee apparatus positions. By the end of 1965—just a year into the new regime—Brezhnev associates were heading a number of salient Central Committee departments, including the Administrative Affairs Department, the General Department, the Science and Higher Educational Institutions, and the Light and Food Industries Departments. As the personnel turnover within the central party apparatus continued, additional Brezhnev proteges moved into other top slots within the Central Committee hierarchy (e.g., heading the Administrative Organs, Construction, and Liaison with Warsaw Pact Countries and Liaison with Communist and Workers' Parties Departments). This recruitment trend was critically important to the authority-building efforts of Brezhnev, because such Central Committee organs are 'command posts' from which policy directives are issued and their implementation reviewed.[27] The institutional prerogatives of the General Secretary's office permitted Brezhnev the opportunity to recruit a good number of faction members into key party organizational positions.

These promotions of long-time proteges served to expand Brezhnev's own considerable power as General Secretary. The additional recruitment of (1) younger, new clients of the General Secretary, and (2) associates of trusted politicians such as Kirilenko, Ustinov, and Chernenko, further strengthened the power base of what could be called 'the extended, Brezhnev-led, network'. The expansion of the extended network's party organizational position included the rapid promotion of a young regional party leader, Konstantin Katushev, to a secretaryship (April 1968), as well as the advancement of one of Brezhnev's aides, Konstantin Rusakov, through heading a Central Committee department to a secretaryship a decade later (May 1977). Similarly, in the 1970s, a number of proteges of Brezhnev loyalists Kirilenko, Ustinov, and Chernenko, among others, also moved into top Central Committee organizational slots (Table 4).

The strength of the Brezhnev faction and the broader Brezhnev-led network within the central party apparatus must be considered in connection with two other tendencies. First, as already noted, trusted network leaders were promoted into key secretaryships during the early years of the new regime. The influence of Brezhnev proteges as Central Committee department heads was only enhanced when they were serving under Secretaries such as Kirilenko and Ustinov who were, themselves, leading members of the Brezhnev team. Meanwhile, within the corresponding governmental apparatus, network members assumed important ministerial roles in a number of counterpart agencies to those network-guided Central Committee departments. Brezhnev, Kirilenko, and Ustinov proteges led most of the important industrial and military ministries (e.g., Ministry of Defence, Ministry of Defence Industry, Ministry of Construction, Ministry of Machine Building, Ministry of General Machine Building). At the same time, Kirilenko and Ustinov oversaw this broad area as CPSU Secretaries. Other network members, for instance Nikolai Savinkin (a Brezhnev protege) and Ivan Serbin (an Ustinov protege), were heading the Central Committee departments responsible for policy in this general area (guiding the Administrative Organs and the Defence Industry Departments, respectively). A similar situation obtained for the light and food industry sector, where associates of Brezhnev and his proteges headed party policy-making and governmental policy-implementing agencies.

Important policy consequences can be inferred from these recruitment patterns. The promotion of trusted subordinates into positions on both sides of the decision-making ledger—policy making and policy implementing—facilitates the fulfilment of policy initiatives. There is an increased likelihood that the top politicians' policies will actually be formulated and then carried out. From our vantage point outside the Soviet policy process, it is difficult to pinpoint just where specific policies originate. It is difficult to know who is responsible for the directives initiating those policies, and who is actually seeing them through. As

Franklyn Griffiths noted, tendencies of articulation are manifested which involve specific sets of policy concerns and specific institutions.[28] However, we can identify complexes of party and state institutions which are responsible for specific sectors of the economy and for broad policy areas. Politicians with long-term career ties to Brezhnev and to his closest proteges assumed leading positions in several of these complexes. It is no coincidence that this pattern holds in the very domains in which important Brezhnev initiatives were offered. While a detailed discussion of the actual Brezhnev policy programme is provided elsewhere, suffice it to note that major Brezhnev initiatives involved the defence, agricultural, and light industry areas.[29] In these three areas, reliable members of the extended Brezhnev network assumed positions of responsibility in institutions on both sides of the policy process: in the policy-initiating Central Committee apparatus and in the policy-implementing Council of Ministers.

Brezhnev's institutional powers as General Secretary were extensive and conferred at least a *primus inter pares* role within the decision-making process. His powers as the head of a large patronage network, however, permitted him to expand his power base into a wider range of political institutions. In this regard, his power was unrivaled from the mid-1960s up to his death in late 1982. As a result of Brezhnev's factional strength and institutional prerogatives, a number of loyal entourage members were promoted into top governmental organs, including the Council of Ministers Presidium. Nearly half of the members of that Presidium were Brezhnev proteges. A number of his trusted associates were Vice Chairmen serving immediately beneath rival Chairman Aleksei Kosygin: Nikolai Tikhonov (Kosygin's eventual successor), Ivan Arkhipov, Ignatii Novikov, Vladimir Novikov, and Leonid Smirnov. These politicians were all members of Brezhnev's generation, with several part of the 'Dnepropetrovsk mafia'. As Council of Ministers Vice Chairmen, they assumed responsibility for some of the most important policy areas (e.g., foreign trade relations, defence technology, machine building, and construction). Once again it is worth noting that these policy areas were critical to the overall Brezhnev programme. The presence of Brezhnev proteges represented an important extension of their faction's influence into a policy-implementing hierarchy which could have been somewhat independent from Brezhnev's organizational home turf.

The inroads made by this extended network into the governmental apparatus varied by sector and institution. However, two appear to have been targeted for placement of trusted associates. As observed earlier, a number of Brezhnev's, as well as Ustinov's and Kirilenko's, associates assumed major roles within the important military-industrial complex. All of these powerful politicians had built careers in this broad sector, and important members of their factions assumed responsible positions there in the post-1964 period. Meanwhile, several of Brezhnev's most trusted associates, including a relative, were placed in the top internal security organs. Brezhnev may have publicly championed policy positions favouring the carrot of cadres stability and generally raised living standards, but he and his group kept tight control over the stick of stronger and reliable internal security forces. The Dnepropetrovsk group dominated the internal security organs throughout his administration.[30]

At the republic and regional level, the influence of the Brezhnev network varied greatly. The General Secretary's extensive experience in regional politics resulted in close contacts arising with a number of republic and regional party organizations; in particular Dnepropetrovsk, the industrialized Ukraine, Moldavia, and Kazakhstan. Through such Politbureau proteges as Shcherbitsky, Chernenko, and Kunaev, and through the long-time Moldavian party boss Ivan Bodyul,[31] the Brezhnev-led network extended down into a number of non-Russsian republics.[32] Certain RSFSR regional party organizations (e.g., Sverdlovsk and Gor'ky) were also linked to this network through important Politbureau members (in these two cases, by Kirilenko and Katushev respectively).

While the composition of the regional component of the Brezhnev network indicated the network's size and influence downward, it also pointed to the limitations of regional patrons' influence at the all-union level. It is fair to conclude that there was a hierarchy within the Brezhnev network itself, with Russian proteges at the all-union level enjoying greater authority within the regime. While the three non-Russian regional patrons in this network—Aliev, Kunaev, and Shcherbitsky—combined had a large entourage of proteges, most of these politicians were influential only within their own regional settings. They are not important at the all-union level, beyond being members of the Central Committee. Of their 31 identified proteges, only four ever held a position of all-union responsibility in the 1964–82 period. This contrasts markedly with the fact that nearly all identified proteges of Kirilenko, Ustinov, and Katushev came to hold important posts in Moscow. Many of them had begun their careers in the periphery, even serving there during the early Brezhnev period. However, they rapidly found their way to Moscow.

The strength of the extended network guided by Brezhnev and including the entourages of ten other of his Politbureau and Secretariat associates grew through the course of the General Secretary's tenure (Table 5). A significant number of the General Secretary's proteges were already Central Committee members when Brezhnev was elected in October 1964. Approximately twenty more were elevated to membership in that body during his eighteen-year

TABLE 5

Membership of the Extended Brezhnev Network in the Central Committee and Central Auditing Commission, 1964–81

	1964	1966	1971	1976	1981
Members of Brezhnev Network	27	40	45	49	45
Members of Brezhnev's Proteges' Networks	11	19	36	46	50
Total Extended Brezhnev Network	38	59	81	95	95
Total CC/CAC Membership	393[1]	439	477	511	545

[1] A total of 395 members of the Central Committee and the Central Auditing Commission were actually elected at the XXII Congress in 1961. Two of these members died prior to the October 1964 Central Committee plenum, which is the starting point for this analysis.

tenure.[33] This extended network grew rapidly, however, as associates of Brezhnev's own Politbureau proteges moved into these top party organs. Their numbers grew from eleven, in late 1964, to fifty by 1981. Overall, this network maintained its power and high profile within the central party apparatus consistently through the end of the 1970s and early 1980s. The XXV Congress in 1976 represented something of a high point in its authority, both in terms of absolute numbers of network members and in terms of their positions of responsibility in the highest bodies. The year 1976 may also have been a critical juncture in the functioning of the extended network because, afterwards, the network's composition shifted in favour of Brezhnev's proteges' clients (for 1981, 50 proteges' clients to 45 for Brezhnev himself). Indeed, between 1976 and 1981 the absolute number of Brezhnev proteges and clients in the Central Committee declines (from 49 to 45). The growth in the size of Brezhnev proteges' factions reflected the enhanced position of those senior politicians. While members of an extended network, those politicians were more directly tied to the Brezhnev protege than to the General Secretary himself. It was true that some of them had worked more directly with the General Secretary in the pre-1964 period. Fourteen of the total sixty-five associates of Brezhnev proteges had identifiable career linkages to Brezhnev. However, the career and authority gap that separated Brezhnev from the rest of these politicians may have represented a political distance as well. Being less directly connected to the General Secretary, they were less responsible for his policy problems and were in a better position to distance themselves from him after his death.[34] As the Brezhnev regime moved toward a leadership succession, the cleavages which arose among contending senior proteges of the General Secretary (e.g., Chernenko and Kirilenko) probably served to divide those parts of the overall network.

Thus, in tracing the evolution of the extended Brezhnev network, important contrasts must be drawn between those members, closely tied to the General Secretary, and other politicians, who were linked to him through intermediaries. Brezhnev's institutional discretionary powers as national Party leader facilitated the growth in authority of trusted proteges such as Kirilenko, Ustinov, and Chernenko.[35] Yet as this extended network grew, it included more and more members of those proteges' factions. This change signified an increasing reliance upon subordinates who were less directly tied to the network's chief patron, General Secretary Brezhnev. The linkage of career and political interests between such network members and the 'grand patron' of the network becomes more tenuous.

A characterization of the Brezhnev network and its components reveals a broad coalition of politicians and interests which were in an organizational position to structure the policy agenda. State organizations in domains critical to the realization of the Brezhnev programme were guided by trusted subordinates. Meanwhile, a number of important regional Party organizations—both within the RSFSR and outside it—were linked to the regime in Moscow through members of this patronage network. Yet it was in the central party apparatus that Brezhnev and his group's power proved decisive. The Central Committee departments responsible for cadres matters, party work, and important sectors of the economy generally were headed by network members. The Politbureau members and CPSU Secretaries supervising these departments were, by the mid-1970s, Brezhnev proteges. From an organizational standpoint, the Brezhnev-led network of patronage factions was the dominant coalition in Soviet politics. The upward mobility of its members into top organizational slots helped to make more pliable the diversity of bureaucracies which comprise the Soviet political system. This extended network, encompassing a number of patronage factions, included politicians with varying degrees of past association with the General Secretary. While the group was a large and diverse network, it was directed by a closely interconnected core of politicians which represented an effective nucleus for a broader governing coalition.

Other Political Networks

The Brezhnev network did form the core of the governing coalition during a period of nearly two decades but it did not operate within a vacuum. Other networks of politicians, institutionally and regionally based and headed by Politbureau and Secretariat members, also influenced the Soviet policy agenda. Mikhail Suslov, Aleksei Kosygin, and Nikolai Podgorny, among others, assumed leading roles in the post-Khrushchev period and their political strength was very much reflected in the networks of associates serving with and under them. Indeed, it is likely that the strength of such networks was critical to the 'staying power' of these politicians; politicians who were genuine rivals to Brezhnev.

Others have carefully considered the careers of some of these Politbureau patrons, analyzing their leadership skills and the elite political struggles in which they were engaged.[36] Examining the patronage networks of such politicians constitutes a different cut at the Soviet political landscape of the period. Analyzing the size, location, and composition of these politicians' entourages helps in understanding the balance of interests found in the Soviet political elite during the Brezhnev era. While each network is formed around key top-level politicians, each tends to be geographically and institutionally focused. Accordingly, an examination of each of these major all-union networks permits a consideration of the different influences brought to bear on national politics. The prevalence of these patronage systems is demonstrated, as they are found in divergent political settings.

Outside the Brezhnev network other Politbureau members' networks arose with strong bases of support in the Central Committee apparatus, the Moscow party organization, the Ukrainian and Belorussian party organizations, within the all-union governmental apparatus, and within the all-union Komsomol. Members of these other networks gained all-union elite status (i.e., became Central Committee or Central Auditing Commission members) in the wake of their patrons' advances (Table 6). In this case, 89 of 90 identified clients (99%) gained all-union elite status at either the same time or after their patron.[37] As clients of these politicians, they advanced after and below them. Indeed, most of

TABLE 6

RECRUITMENT OF MEMBERS OF SELECTED PATRONAGE NETWORKS INTO THE CENTRAL COMMITTEE AND CENTRAL AUDITING COMMISSION

Network Patron	When Patron Joined CC/CAC	When Patron Joined Politbureau and Secretariat	Year Client Joined Central Committee or Auditing Commission							Total N
			1952	1956	1961	1966	1971	1976	1981	
Kapitonov	1952	1965			3	4	2	2		11
Demichev	1961	1961			1	2		3		6
Grishin	1952	1961					1	1		2
Suslov	1941	1947	1		3	2	1	1		8
Pel'she	1961	1966			1	2	3	1		7
Ponomarev	1952	1961					2			2
Mazurov	1956	1957	1	1	4	2	1			9
Masherov	1962	1966				1	1	3		5
Zimyanin	1952	1976							1	1
Podgorny	1952	1958		2	4	4	2	1		13
Shelest	1961	1963			2	3				5
Shelepin	1952	1961	1		3	4	3	1		12
Kosygin	1939	1946	1	2	2	2	2			9

them did not gain all-union elite status until their patrons had become Politbureau or Secretariat members (75 of 90, or 83%).

Several patronage networks of the Brezhnev era were based in the central apparatuses in Moscow. An important network centred around three top politicians of the period—Ivan Kapitonov, Petr Demichev, and Viktor Grishin. The network was composed primarily of politicians who had moved up in the Moscow city and oblast party organizations in the 1940s and 1950s. The three network patrons had assumed important roles in the Moscow party organizations, serving together as they advanced to all-union political prominence. Ivan Kapitonov appears as 'first among equals', although he is the only one of the three not to have been elected to the Politbureau. He had moved up in the Moscow city party organization, becoming a secretary and then second secretary of the Moscow obkom in 1951–52. He subsequently worked as the first secretary of the Moscow city party organization, and then from 1954 to 1959 headed the Moscow obkom. During this period, both Demichev and Grishin advanced under him. The former served under Kapitonov in the early 1950s, while Grishin followed him as Moscow obkom second secretary in 1952. The notion of reciprocity is exhibited in the relations among these three politicians, for the two presumed junior members did help to resurrect Kapitonov in the mid-1960s, when he returned to Moscow as the CPSU Secretary for cadres assignments. At that time, both Demichev and Grishin were either in the Secretariat or the Politbureau.

The entourages of all three of these politicians are closely interconnected, making it difficult to link individuals with one patron to the complete exclusion of the other two. Their clients' careers are intertwined, and are often associated with one of the other two network patrons.[38] These interconnections only strengthen our confidence in the likelihood of a functioning network. Most of this network's clients had served either in the Moscow city or oblast party organizations, with a number promoted to assume leadership positions in other prominent party organizations. Several advanced into the RSFSR party and state apparatuses.[39] Others advanced into positions of all-union responsibility, especially in the areas of ideology and culture.[40] The Kapitonov–Demichev–Grishin network is a good-sized one which spanned a range of levels of responsibility and a range of important substantive interests. Especially important in explaining the size and strength of this network is Kapitonov's own institutional base in the Organizational–Party Work Department. Responsible for cadres selection, this department is the most important in the Central Committee. It oversees the selection not only of Central Committee apparatus workers, but of top regional and republic party cadres. In addition, it supervises the selection of central trade union and Komsomol personnel and sanctions the appointments of military, police, and diplomatic personnel.[41] This Moscow network is also important because its patrons had been at the highest levels of the party hierarchy for considerable time periods. After all, Kapitonov headed the Organizational–Party Work Department and was a Secretary for nearly eighteeen years.[42] Demichev and Grishin were among the senior Politbureau and Secretariat members by the end of the Brezhnev era. Taken together, they and their clients are a formidable group.

Mikhail Suslov, the long-time party ideologue, led an important network composed of several other Politbureau and Secretariat members as well as sixteen identified Central Committee clients. This network was probably forged when a number of its top members studied or worked in the Moscow Institute of Red Professors in the late 1920s and early-to-mid 1930s. Not only Suslov, but also Pel'she and Ponomarev attended the Red Professors Institute, as did at least one of their identified proteges, long-time Estonian Party boss Ivan Kebin. The network included individuals at the all-union and republic levels, though most were working in Moscow by the 1960s. The figures cited in Table 6 probably seriously undercount the actual number of network members because two of the network patrons, Suslov and Ponomarev, had held top-level positions in Moscow for a long period. In spite of these problems in client identification, several important figures in the areas of ideology and communication can be linked to Suslov. Suslov's responsibilities included oversight of party organs, including *Pravda* and *Kommunist*. A number of editors of these newspapers proved to have career ties to him.[43]

Both Suslov and Pel'she worked in the Baltic republics and developed political connections there in the postwar period. As a result of their prior experiences, they were the national politicians overseeing the politics of the Baltic republics during the Brezhnev period.[44] Certain Baltic politicians were able to move to the political centre on the 'coat-tails' of these Politbureau patrons.[45]

A number of Suslov and Ponomarev associates also moved up in the International Department of the Central Committee. Boris Ponomarev was an understudy to Suslov, having been a Secretary and the department head since 1961. A Comintern official in the 1930s, Ponomarev helped a number of his associates in the International Department to advance into the Central Committee itself during the 1970s.[46]

The Kapitonov and Suslov networks were based in the central party apparatus and composed primarily of Russians. Organizationally, these networks were well situated to influence national policy in important areas (e.g., questions of ideology, cadres promotion, foreign policy, and intra-bloc relations). These patrons were long-serving party apparatchiks who consolidated their positions and built up networks over a lengthy period. The biographical information available suggests that they never challenged for the top party position, but rather were content to stake out turfs within the central apparatus. Unlike Kapitonov, Suslov, and their Politbureau proteges, another network patron, Aleksandr Shelepin, did challenge for the top position.[47] He fashioned a sizeable entourage involving all-union elite members, but it did not prove to be a long-lasting one.

Aleksandr Shelepin's entourage was similar to the Kapitonov and Suslov networks in being varied and encompassing top all-union organizations. Shelepin had risen quickly in the party hierarchy, and had held responsible positions in a number of salient institutions. His credentials at the time of the 1964 leadership succession were impressive: he had recently headed the national KGB and at the time was a CPSU Secretary. His relatively large and diverse clientele reflected the wide range of institutions with which he was connected.

However, Shelepin's influence was already circumscribed by the end of the 1960s. Examining Shelepin's own career and the development of his entourage, it is fair to say that he had reached his peak in political influence by 1966, and that he and his clients were in retreat by the end of 1967. This is rather ironic, considering that Shelepin had become a full member of the Politbureau at the November 1964 Central Committee Plenum, having already been a Secretary for three years. However, by 1968, a good number of the clients who had moved up with him were already in career retreat. Some were 'retired' into ambassadorial positions.[48] Others were either shifted into insignificant domestic governmental slots or simply ousted.[49] By the end of 1969, no Shelepin clients were serving in the Secretariat or Central Committee apparatus. Indeed, by the XXV Congress almost no Shelepin clients were left in the membership of the Central Committee. While the clients of honourably-departed patrons can survive their patron's ouster, those like the Shelepin clients did not have the political seniority or independent institutional bases of support to withstand their patron's fall from power.

In addition to these networks based in the all-union apparatus, several important regional networks were operating in the Soviet political system during the Brezhnev period. Traditionally, a significant ethnic contingent within the top all-union elite has come from the Ukraine. The importance of the Ukrainian republic, second only to the RSFSR in all-union politics, has assured its politicians a prominent position. However, as Slavic ethnic rivals to the Russians, this group has not fared so well in maintaining its position within the ranks of the top elite. The Ukrainian politicians who have exhibited longer-term 'staying power'—for instance the Ukrainian first secretary Vladimir Shcherbitsky—have generally associated themselves with Russian-led networks like Brezhnev's. The evolution of the Khar'kov network guided by Nikolai Podgorny, Vitalii Titov, and Petr Shelest is more typical of the fate of Ukrainian political networks in all-union politics.

The Podgorny-led Khar'kov network was among the largest of the Brezhnev period. The relatively large size of this network reflected both Podgorny's important role in the Ukraine during the 1950s and early 1960s and the fact that for many years Podgorny was considered the major political rival to Brezhnev. Podgorny had developed this network not only while he was moving up in the Ukrainian party apparatus, but when he was Ukrainian party boss (1957 to 1963) and then CPSU Secretary (1963 to 1965). With a base in the Khar'kov party organization, Podgorny's alliance with the Donetsk party organization (through Aleksandr Lyashko, Vladimir Tsibul'ko, and Aleksei Titarenko) only further consolidated his network's position within the Ukraine.[50] However, his transfer from the CPSU Secretariat to the USSR Supreme Soviet in 1965 genuinely represented a 'kick upstairs' and an immediate slip in real political power. His Ukrainian associates, albeit heading important regional party organizations in the republic, experienced difficulty in advancing to all-union positions of responsibility. An investigation of the Khar'kov party organization and publication of a Central Committee declaration on its deficiencies in 1965 severely weakened this elite cohort.[51] Highly-placed proteges experienced only downward mobility during the Brezhnev period. Titov, who had headed the Party Organs Department and had been promoted to Secretary in 1962, was quickly demoted from the CPSU Secretariat in 1965 and transferred to Kazakhstan.[52] Podgorny's successor in the Ukraine, Petr Shelest, was ultimately ousted in favour of Brezhnev's long-time protege, Shcherbitsky.[53] Indeed, Shelest's position in the all-union party hierarchy was never an especially important one, though his position had merited a brief membership in the Politbureau.[54]

As for the Central Committee-level members of the Podgorny network, they had moved up from Khar'kov and Kiev in the 1940s, 1950s, and early 1960s. Some moved to Moscow with Podgorny.[55] Most remained institutionally based in the Ukraine, serving either in republic apparatuses or as regional first secretaries. Most were 'retired' either when Shelest was ousted or when Podgorny was removed in 1977.[56]

One other network representing a regional party organization and ethnic group was the 'Belorussian partisan group' led by Politbureau member Kirill Mazurov. This network formed during the Second World War, when a number of its leading members served together in the partisan movement.[57] After the war, Mazurov moved up in the Belorussian party organization, with members of his coterie and of this 'Belorussian partisan group' moving up through Minsk and the republic party organizations with him. This group has dominated Belorussian politics for several decades, both through Mazurov and his protege and successor Petr Masherov.[58]

Most of the members of this network served in republic or regional organizational slots. However, Vasilii Shauro, a network member, did become head of the Culture Department of the CPSU Central Committee in 1965. Mikhail Zimyanin, another Belorussian who served in the partisan movement with Mazurov and Masherov, also moved to all-union prominence. He served in all-union governmental and diplomatic positions until appointed Chief Editor of *Pravda* in 1965. In March 1976 he became a Secretary responsible for ideology and propaganda.

The Belorussian network assumed an important balancing role within the all-union political elite. As I have argued elsewhere, top politicians in this group tended to align themselves with politicians outside the Brezhnev network.[59] Both Mazurov and Zimyanin developed important working relations with Kosygin and Suslov respectively. Mazurov served under Kosygin in the Council of Ministers for thirteen years and he supported Kosygin's policy positions (and when they collided with those of Brezhnev). Zimyanin served under Suslov in the 1960s and 1970s. Indeed, his promotions were probably due in part to Suslov. The decision rules do not permit identification of patronage ties between these two politicians. However, given what we know about Suslov's profile and responsibilities within the party apparatus, it is fair to assume that he and Zimyanin worked closely together for at least a decade and a half. Suslov did oversee the broad areas of ideology and propaganda in which Zimyanin's career was made.

A number of system patrons not considered here were regional leaders who are not identified as members of broader networks of elite members.[60] Others were all-union level leaders whose prominence was either very institutionally focused[61] or short-lived.[62] Several, with relatively small identified entourages, appear as independent political actors who cannot be easily tied to a broader network. Yurii Andropov's career, for instance, was associated with Brezhnev as well as with Suslov. Vladimir Dolgikh and Mikhail Solomentsev likewise have been linked with both of these leaders. While all three were allied with Brezhnev and his group, they were independent actors.[63] However, one politician who was influential in all-union politics and who headed a sizeable group was Aleksei Kosygin. As Chairman of the USSR Council of Ministers, Kosygin assumed an influential role and high profile in the Brezhnev regime. His was a position of both relative strength and weakness in all-union politics: he was able to recruit clients, but as a group they were highly concentrated within the governmental, policy-implementing apparatus and in specific economic sectors. His entourage was not a wide-ranging one, such as those of Brezhnev, Podgorny, and Suslov. Kosygin had made a career within the governmental apparatus, in the areas of economic planning, textiles, and light industry. The composition of his identified entourage reflects this career past, with most of his clients having served in the light and food industries and in Gosplan. Several clients who were top members of the Council of Ministers, including Vladimir Kirillin and Mikhail Lesechko, advanced into its Presidium soon after Kosygin's own entry. Both Kirillin and Lesechko served under Kosygin as deputy chairmen, with their areas of competence—along with those of another Kosygin protege, Nikolai Baibakov—involving oversight of the reforms of the 1960s associated with Kosygin. In addition, several ministers, including Nikolai Tarasov (Light Industry), Sergei Antonov (Meatpacking and Dairy Industry), and Aleksandr Ishkov (Fish Industry), moved up under Kosygin and held portfolios during most or all of his tenure. The organizational roles and public positions of these and other Kosygin clients probably helped him in certain of his policy initiatives.[64] Yet the size and location of his entourage show that while Kosygin enjoyed discretion within his own institutional bailiwick, his organizational strength did not extend beyond it and into the highest party organs.[65]

This examination of other patronage networks points to the overall strength of the sizeable Brezhnev network. It also suggests that there were real organizational limits on the power of the General Secretary's network. The networks explored here were, by and large, institutionally or geographically based and did not span the organizational or geographic range spanned by the Brezhnev group. However, their sizes and organizational locations made them forces to contend with in the policy process. Individually, none proved to be diverse enough and strong enough to challenge the increasingly strong position of the Brezhnev group. Taken together, however, they represented a genuine constraint on the organizationally-dominant Brezhnev group.

An analysis of the publicly expressed issue positions of members of these other networks reveals that their members did not, by any means, represent a unified opposition to the leading Brezhnev group.[66] They represented often conflicting interests, and their organizational bases of operation were limited in comparison with those of Brezhnev and his top proteges. An examination of mobility patterns and publicly articulated issue positions indicates that certain politicians came to terms with the Brezhnev group. Indeed, the Kapitonov-led Moscow group thrived during the latter 1960s and 1970s, assuming policy positions quite compatible with those of Brezhnev and his proteges. Other groups of politicians (e.g., those associated with Kosygin and with Suslov) did offer rather different perspectives on important aspects of the domestic and foreign policy agendas. As a result, the comprehensive policy programme of this period was a product of other networks' influence, even though it greatly reflected the policy positions of Brezhnev proteges and network members.

Conclusion

Patron-client relations underlie political networks which dominate Soviet national politics. This was true of the Soviet past and it continues to be the case during the Brezhnev and post-Brezhnev period. These networks encompass most of the important Politbureau members and CPSU Secretaries, and include a significant number of Central Committee and Central Auditing Commission members. They span the important all-union party and state apparatuses, and help to bridge the gulf between Moscow and the political periphery. For network patrons, these linkages represent means of control over institutions and politicians. For proteges and potential clients, they represent the avenues by which an aspiring politician advances into important policy positions. The interdependence of politicians' careers suggests very real political risks for clients—especially for those clients who have risen quickly in the party apparatus (e.g., the Shelepin network case). However, the experience of politicians examined here indicates that the potential payoffs for career advancements are tremendous.

Brezhnev was successful in forming a governing team, based in part upon such patron-client networks (Diagram 1). At the core of the Brezhnev administration was the coterie of politicians who had moved up with the General Secretary since the 1930s. This group included not only the Dnepropetrovsk politicians, but other elite members who had served in the political periphery with him. It also included politicians who advanced with Brezhnev in Moscow during the 1950s and early 1960s. Yet Brezhnev's own entourage was at the centre of a larger network of politicians. This network included politicians who had not previously served with Brezhnev, but who worked directly with him after 1964 and who experienced mobility to the highest political levels. It included many elite members whose political mobility was due to proteges of the General Secretary. Their authority grew as that of Brezhnev grew during the 1964–82 period. This extended network encompassed many institutional and regional interests, and spanned several generations of elites. It was augmented by political alliances with other politicians and networks which, when combined, formed the coalition which governed the Soviet Union for nearly two decades.

Critically important in the functioning of the Brezhnev network was its utility in connecting policy-making, policy-implementing, and supervisory organs.

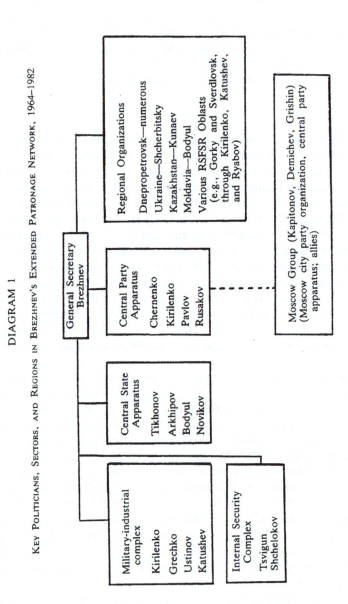

DIAGRAM 1

KEY POLITICIANS, SECTORS, AND REGIONS IN BREZHNEV'S EXTENDED PATRONAGE NETWORK, 1964–1982

Where – – –=alliance with an important patronage network.

These linkages, in areas critical to the Brezhnev policy programme, represented real organizational control by this leading political group. Any evaluation of Brezhnev's policy success must take note of the pervasiveness of his extended network across these three sets of organizations.

An assessment of Brezhnev's policy success must also include an acknowledgment of his effectiveness as a consensus builder across factions. If the history of this period points to the continued growth in power and authority of the Brezhnev entourage and a larger network of proteges and their entourages, it also demonstrates that others not only survived but thrived during the period. These patronage factions were based in important organizations and regions; organizations and regions not penetrated by the leading politicians and factions which collectively formed the extended Brezhnev network. As a result, these other factions were institutionally strong, meriting their inclusion in a broader governing coalition. Other rival factions, for instance those of Shelepin and Podgorny, which were directly competing with the Brezhnev faction on the same turf, did not fare so well. Brezhnev and his group secured the necessary political muscle to eliminate these groups of politicians. However, authority building and effective governance by Brezhnev and his extended network required coalition arrangements with other viable and resilient elements within the national political elite. If patronage ties enhanced Brezhnev's position, they likewise bolstered the positions of other leading politicians. Rival patronage networks provided a certain 'check' on the leadership position of Brezhnev, further encouraging him to engage in consensus building.

Cadres stability was a by-product of this Brezhnev coalition. A more important result, however, was the realization of a comprehensive policy programme that was acceptable to Soviet elite interests. The content and contours of the Brezhnev policy programme have been illuminated by others.[67] It is sufficient to note here that the main planks of that programme encompassed the positions and interests of a number of political networks dominant in the 1970s and early 1980s, including those of the General Secretary.

Client relations were relevant to policy making during the Brezhnev period, with policy constraint characterizing the expressed views of those who made up the Brezhnev network and who were among the leading figures in the regime. The strong position of the General Secretary, his patronage faction, and the extended network he guided was enhanced by important linkages to other politicians. The policy consensus and stability of the Brezhnev regime reflected this reality.

The initial cadres policy of the new Gorbachev regime demonstrates that informal patronage networks continue to structure the coalitions which govern the Soviet polity. Gorbachev's consolidation of power has been nothing short of spectacular, and it has relied greatly upon the extensive transfer of personnel and the recruitment of proteges and clients.[68] New, younger politicians are coming to the fore, but the reasons for their advancements are traditional ones. Once again, a new Soviet administration takes shape, and patronage networks are proving to be important elements underlying it.

Michigan State University

[1] See Valerie Bunce, *Do New Leaders Make A Difference?* (Princeton: Princeton University Press, 1981).

[2] This point was made clearer to the author by an anonymous referee of this paper.

[3] See George W. Breslauer, 'Political Succession and the Soviet Policy Agenda', *Problems of Communism*, XXIX, No. 3 (May–June 1980), pp. 34–52.

[4] Certainly there are patrons among Central Committee members. However, for purposes of analytical parsimony, they are only treated here as potential proteges of top-level Politbureau and Secretariat members.

[5] Members of the Central Auditing Commission are included here because they have an important role in the party hierarchy as the group responsible for auditing the activities and finances of the central party apparatus. While these activities are probably more formal than real, the members of the Central Auditing Commission do participate in Central Committee plena. They receive the information reports provided by the Central Committee apparatus. In fact, the Central Auditing Commission is a main pool for future Central Committee members.

[6] For instance, the CPSU Secretary for organizational matters would possess a level of authority not subordinate to that of a number of Politbureau members.

[7] For the purposes of narrative brevity, I often use the term 'Central Committee' in this study when referring to both the Central Committee and the Central Auditing Commission. However, the base population used throughout is always the combined memberships of both organs.

[8] Full and candidate members of the Central Committee and all members of the Central Auditing Commission are treated as basic political equals. There is a rough hierarchy here, with full Central Committee members enjoying the most status, followed by candidate members and the Central Auditing Commission members. There is, however, a certain amount of rotation of the members of these bodies, with movement from one to the other not automatically signifying loss of status. For the purposes of this analysis, such distinctions in status are unimportant. Membership in any capacity in these bodies confers elite political status, even if one's actual institutional affiliation appears to be less salient.

[9] For example, see Kirill Mazurov's memoirs of the activities of the Belorussian partisan movement, *Nezabyvaemoe*, (Minsk, 1984) and G. N. Kupriyanov's account of events and personalities (including Yurii Andropov) in Karelia in *Za liniei Karel'skogo fronta* (Petrozavodsk, 1975).

[10] Socialization studies have demonstrated the importance of young adulthood as a period when individuals' attitudes are moulded. The fact that two individuals belong to the same educational institutional cohort gives them a sense of comradeship that will persist beyond that period. This has been shown to be true of generational cohorts from leading British schools and universities. See Anthony Sampson, *The Changing Anatomy of Britain* (N.Y.: Random House, 1982), Chapters 7 and 8.

[11] The biographical data used for this population of approximately 1,000 Soviet politicians are taken from the author's files, which were constructed and updated primarily using the *Deputaty Verkhovnogo Soveta* for the various republics and the USSR overall. The central press, especially *Pravda* and *Izvestiya*, as well as selected regional periodicals, were used to augment the published biographical *precis*.

[12] This can be tricky because it is not always clear who approved the promotion. The top-level KGB recruitment policies are a case in point, as Brezhnev and his group apparently enjoyed the institutional prerogative to promote faction members into influential slots just beneath the chairmanship (held by Yurii Andropov, who was himself appointed by Brezhnev to the position in 1967). Nearly all of the KGB deputy chairmen may have been formally promoted to their positions during Andropov's tenure, but their past careers evince strong patronage connections to Brezhnev. This fact, combined with the universal absence of prior professional associations with Andropov, led to them being identified as Brezhnev faction members, and not members of an Andropov KGB faction. It is assumed here that demonstrable past career associations (especially when combined with likely organizational supervision) take precedence in identifying patronage connections.

[13] As a result of such a tie, the professional political link between patron and client may be weaker than that associated with a longer-term career relationship. Top-level politicians (e.g., CPSU secretaries) could sponsor subordinates with whom contact has been minimal.

[14] Mikhail Suslov, for instance, served in the central party apparatus for a considerable period. A CPSU Secretary since 1947, he oversaw the departments responsible for the international Communist movement, as well as those dealing with ideology and the media. We can infer Suslov's areas of responsibility both from his public statements and appearances and from the positions he held earlier in his career (e.g., his work in the Central Committee's Propaganda and Agitation Department and his service as Chief Editor of *Pravda*). The political strength Suslov possessed in all-union politics stemmed from this supervisory role within the central apparatus.

[15] Application of these measurements of 'protege' and 'client' of the General Secretary results in the identification of relatively few clients. Of the total 58 politicians (48 Central Committee-level status, and 10 Politbureau-Secretariat-level status) identified as members of Brezhnev's patronage faction, 18 are clients. All others are proteges who developed career linkages with the General Secretary prior to his 1964 succession.

[16] Included are all Politbureau and Secretariat members except those who had retired or died by the XXIII Congress in 1971. Accordingly, six Politbureau members and CPSU Secretaries are not included. They are: Leonid Il'ichev, the Secretary on ideological matters who was removed in early 1965; Anastas Mikoyan, the long-time Minister of Foreign Trade, who had replaced Brezhnev as Supreme Soviet Chairman and who retired in 1966; Aleksandr Rudakov, the short-term Secretary for heavy industry, appointed in 1962, who died in July 1966; Nikolai Shvernik, the long-time trade union official who had been a Central Committee member since 1925 and who retired from the Politbureau in 1966; Vitalii Titov, a Podgorny protege, who was removed from the Secretariat in 1965 (and who is included in the population of Podgorny clients); and Leonid Efremov, a Politbureau member who was removed in 1966 for his responsibility for the failures of Khrushchev's agricultural policy.

[17] The identified patronage entourages of Suslov and Shelepin are relatively large for Moscow-based politicians. However, these figures probably underestimate the extent of their networks. With Suslov having served in one city for nearly forty years, it becomes much more difficult to identify client ties for those serving with him there or in regions in the periphery for which he was responsible. Yet in spite of this measurement problem, a total of ten politicians could be identified as Suslov proteges and clients. The strength of the Suslov group is indicated by the fact that an additional two politicians in the Politbureau and Secretariat were his proteges. The clientelism measures used here more effectively tap the Aleksandr Shelepin group. Shelepin, who had been serving in Moscow for twenty years prior to Khrushchev's ouster in 1964, had advanced through a number of different institutions, pulling proteges with him wherever he went. Cross-organizational movements of personnel in the 1950s and 1960s permit the identification of twelve Shelepin associates who had served in Moscow, in the Komsomol, in the Central Trade Union Organization, and in the KGB.

[18] The strength of such networks was very much demonstrated in Chernenko's selection as General Secretary in February 1984. Many factors may have played a role in Chernenko's elevation, not the least of which were concerns of incumbent senior politicians over the ambitious Andropov-led campaign to reconstitute that leadership. Yet Chernenko's own organizational position cannot be ignored. His base of support was the old Brezhnev group—one which had been under attack by the Andropov regime for over a year. The absence of Brezhnev and the assaults on the network by the successor regime were not sufficient to undo the network. Even a lacklustre, aged career organization man ('ryadavoi politik') such as Chernenko could be successfully promoted into the top leadership position by this powerful network.

[19] Brezhnev moved into the Central Committee in 1952, while nearly all of his proteges joined afterwards. He was a Politbureau candidate member in 1952, while his proteges, at the earliest, only joined that body or the Secretariat in the later 1950s (Kirilenko in 1957). Besides Kirilenko, no Brezhnev protege advanced into the Politbureau or Secretariat until Dmitrii Ustinov's election in 1965. As for party membership, some proteges did join the party at the time Brezhnev did, or even a little earlier. However, when we examine their careers as the stakes began to get high at the republic and all-union levels, Brezhnev always exhibits his superior position as the network's patron.

[20] A useful account of the Dnepropetrovsk group as a regional elite cohort is laid out in Joel Moses, 'Regional Cohorts and Political Mobility in the USSR: The Case of Dnepropetrovsk', *Soviet Union*, 3, No. 1 (1976), pp. 63–89.

[21] Ustinov was elected a candidate member at the March 1965 Central Committee Plenum, while Shcherbitsky was returned to the Politbureau as a candidate member at the December 1965 Plenum. The Kazakh Party leader, Kunaev, joined the Politbureau as a candidate member at the XXIII Congress in 1966.

[22] Kunaev and Shcherbitsky.

[23] Marshal Grechko was elected a full member at the April 1973 Plenum, Ustinov was elected a full member and Aliev a candidate member at the XXV Congress in 1976, Chernenko was promoted to full member in November 1978, and Tikhonov was promoted to full member in November 1979.

[24] The promotion of Chernenko was especially important not only because of his extremely close working relationship with the General Secretary, but because his secretarial portfolio included responsibility for questions of security and order within the central party apparatus, as well as oversight of information gathering, routing, and documentation.

[25] The importance of Kapitonov's position and his relationship with Brezhnev are underlined by

the fact that he was so quickly 'retired' from his central party apparatus duties in early 1983, within a few months of Brezhnev's death. At the national level, as at the republic level, control over the organizational-party work department is fundamental to a general secretary's control over the apparatus. Kapitonov assumed a critical role in the Brezhnev regime for the very reason that, through him, Brezhnev was able to promote many proteges and clients.

[26] An examination of publicly expressed elite attitudes reveals that Kapitonov and other politicians associated with him supported the General Secretary through most of his 18-year tenure. The support for Brezhnev and his evolving policy programme offered by Kapitonov, Grishin, Demichev, and other Moscow network members provided important ballast to the governing coalition of the later 1960s and 1970s. For a discussion of patronage and policy making, see John P. Willerton, Jr., 'Patronage and Politics in the Soviet Union: Issue Positions in Supreme Soviet Election Speeches, 1964–82', paper presented at the 1986 Annual Meeting of the Mid-Atlantic Slavic Conference, Princeton University, 1 March 1986.

[27] Konstantin Chernenko's move into the General Department represented an especially important step in Brezhnev's consolidation of power. The General Department is extremely important in overseeing the flow of information within the party apparatus. This department prepares the paperwork for the Politbureau and Secretariat and is also responsible for keeping all party records and archives. A close Brezhnev protege was in an organizational position to help the General Secretary further to structure the policy agenda.

[28] Franklyn Griffiths, 'A Tendency Analysis of Soviet Policy-Making', in H. Gordon Skilling and Franklyn Griffiths, eds., *Interest Groups in Soviet Politics* (Princeton: Princeton University Press, 1971), pp. 335–77.

[29] An extended examination of the Brezhnev foreign policy thrust and the elite politics surrounding it is provided in Harry Gelman, *The Brezhnev Politburo and the Decline of Detente* (Ithaca: Cornell University Press, 1984). A comprehensive treatment of the evolution of the domestic programme is presented in George W. Breslauer, *Khrushchev and Brezhnev as Leaders* (London: George Allen and Unwin, 1982).

[30] For all intents and purposes, KGB head Yurii Andropov was surrounded by Brezhnev cronies throughout his fifteen-year tenure within that security organization. Andropov was politically allied to the Brezhnev coalition, but was not a member of the Brezhnev network. His first deputy chairman, Semen Tsvigun, was a close protege of the General Secretary, having served with Brezhnev in Dnepropetrovsk (latter 1940s) as well as in Moldavia (early 1950s). Tsvigun's presence within Andropov's KGB continued through Andropov's entire tenure as that organization's chairman. Another Dnepropetrovsk crony, Georgii Tsinev, was deputy chairman of the KGB from 1970 to 1982, when he became first deputy chairman. In addition, the other security organ, the Ministry of Internal Affairs, was also headed by Brezhnev clients. Nikolai Shchelokov served as Minister from 1966 to December 1982 (being removed but a month after Brezhnev's death), while another Dnepropetrovsk client, Viktor Paputin, served as the first deputy minister until his death in December 1979. Even Viktor Chebrikov, who has been touted as an Andropov–Gorbachev protege, had long-time connections with the Dnepropetrovsk group going back to the 1940s and 1950s.

[31] Bodyul was rewarded for his efforts by being transferred to Moscow in December 1980 as a deputy chairman of the Council of Ministers. This advancement occurred within days of Kosygin's death.

[32] These republic and regional politicians account for approximately forty, or roughly one-third, of the total members of the identified Brezhnev network.

[33] Among other Brezhnev associates elevated to Central Committee membership were his personal aides, Georgii Tsukanov (1966), Andrei Aleksandrov-Agentov (1971), Anatolii Blatov (1976), and Viktor Golikov (1981), who collectively represented a significant proportion of all Brezhnev clients identified in this study.

[34] It would be useful to compare the career fates and expressed attitudes of Brezhnev's clients with those of Brezhnev's proteges' clients after November 1982. The evidence available just a few years after Brezhnev's passing suggests that the latter have had higher rates of political survival and have found it easier to accommodate to the Andropov–Gorbachev period.

[35] It was no accident that Brezhnev faction members such as Chernenko and Ustinov moved into critical organizational slots under Brezhnev's leadership. Ustinov, for instance, was promoted over a number of influential uniformed military professionals to become the USSR Minister of Defence in 1975. His selection represented the appointment of a party apparatchik to the top military position; a decision not universally supported by the military elite. This promotion, however, not only served to reaffirm the party's oversight over the military. It also further strengthened the organizational linkage between the General Secretary, his faction, and that sector.

[36] For instance, see George W. Simmonds, ed., *Soviet Leaders* (N.Y.: Thomas Y. Crowell

Company, 1967); Michel Tatu, *Power In The Kremlin* (N.Y.: Viking Press, 1970) and Werner Hahn, *The Politics of Soviet Agriculture, 1960–1970* (Baltimore: The Johns Hopkins University Press, 1972).

[37] The one exception, Vasilii Chernishev, was a protege of Mazurov, but had been Mazurov's mentor during the late 1940s and early 1950s.

[38] For example, the careers of two network members, Nikolai Kozlov and Valentin Mesyats, are closely interconnected. Both attended the Timiryazev Institute in the early 1930s, advancing through the Moscow party organization in the 1950s and 1960s. During the 1970s and 1980s both served in the agricultural sector as USSR ministers.

[39] Both Vladimir Demchenko and Aleksei Kalashnikov served as RSFSR Council of Ministers' Deputy Chairmen.

[40] Valentin Mesyats went on to serve as USSR Minister of Agriculture and Konstantin Brekhov ended up serving as USSR Minister of Chemical and Oil Machine Building.

[41] Little has been published in Soviet sources about the role and functions of this and other central apparatus organs dealing with cadres affairs. An exception is a 1981 *Partiinaya zhizn'* article by the first deputy head of the General Department of the Central Committee. See K. Bogolyubov, 'Vazhnaya, Neot'emlemaya Chast' Obshchepartiinogo dela', *Partiinaya zhizn'*, 1981, No. 20, pp. 19–27.

[42] Indeed, Kapitonov had served earlier in the Central Committee department responsible for RSFSR cadres appointments.

[43] These include Viktor Afanas'yev, Vasilii Stepanov, and Konstantin Zarodov (who was also Chief Editor of *Problemy Mira i Sotsializma* from 1968 to 1982).

[44] It was Suslov, for instance, who journeyed to Vilnius in the late autumn of 1973 and delivered the important criticism of the Lithuanian party leadership that came just months before an important Lithuanian leadership succession. Throughout his entire 18-year tenure as General Secretary, Leonid Brezhnev never made an official visit to the Baltic republics.

[45] Vol'demar Lein, for example, experienced rapid mobility after 1959, when Pel'she became Latvian First Secretary. Four years after Pel'she's move to Moscow, Lein was appointed RSFSR Minister of Food Industry. A year later, in 1971, he was elected to the Central Committee.

[46] Elizar Kuskov and Vadim Zagladin.

[47] Michael Voslensky goes so far as to contend that Shelepin originally was the intended replacement for Khrushchev when the latter was ousted in October 1964. However, fear of Shelepin's expanding base of political support altered this arrangement. See Michael Voslensky, *Nomenklatura* (N.Y.: Doubleday, 1984), pp. 255–61.

[48] Nikolai Yegorichev, head of the Moscow city party organization until 1967, was posted to Denmark in 1970; Nikolai Mesyatsev, secretary of the USSR Union of Journalists, was posted to Australia that same year; Ivan Udal'tsov, a deputy head of the Central Committee Ideology Department, was moved to diplomatic slots in Czechoslovakia and Greece; and Vadim Tikunov, who had served with Shelepin and Semichastny in the Komsomol and the KGB, was 'retired' to ambassadorial work in Romania, Upper Volta, and the Cameroons in the late 1960s and 1970s.

[49] Vladimir Semichastny, who was Shelepin's 'right hand man', departed from the KGB in 1967, becoming a deputy chairman of the Ukrainian Council of Ministers (for sport). Vladimir Yagodkin, who was a Moscow city party secretary (for ideological questions), was 'promoted' in 1976 to a deputy ministerial position in the Ministry of Education. Boris Korotkov, the first secretary in Perm, was simply retired 'for health reasons' in 1972, at the age of 45.

[50] The Donetsk party organization is an important one in the Ukraine, and its support for Podgorny was critical to his position in the republic. Such sub-national patronage networks are not dealt with here. However, this does not mean that they are not politically relevant. Post-war Ukrainian politics, for instance, have been influenced by the political struggles among the Kiev, Khar'kov, Dnepropetrovsk, and Donetsk networks.

[51] *Partiinaya zhizn'*, 1965, No. 15, pp. 23–25.

[52] Titov served as Second Secretary in Kazakhstan under Brezhnev's protege and the new Kazakh First Secretary, Dinmukhamed Kunaev.

[53] Shelest's first major party job was as the Khar'kov city secretary for defence industry (1940).

[54] Shelest was very much a representative of the Ukraine and its interests in Moscow. As Borys Lewytzkyj has noted, during Shelest's leadership in the republic, 'he tried to preserve and expand (the) Ukraine's achievements. When he was ousted in 1972, the explanation was that Shelest had engaged in localism (*mestnichestvo*) and had pursued narrow national interests'. See Borys Lewytzkyj, *Politics and Society in Soviet Ukraine, 1953–80* (Edmonton: Canadian Institute of Ukrainian Studies, University of Alberta, 1984), p. 140.

204

[55] Leonid Shevchenko and Vadim Kortunov both became Central Auditing Commission members while serving as aides to Podgorny in the Supreme Soviet Presidium.

[56] A few, however, such as Aleksandr Botvin and Grigorii Vashchenko, while closely linked to Podgorny, Titov, and Shelest, were able to accommodate themselves to their successors and survived. Indeed, Vashchenko not only served as the first deputy chairman of the Ukrainian Council of Ministers, but became USSR Minister of Trade in January 1983.

[57] The political mentor of this group, Kirill Mazurov, writes of many of this network's members in his memoirs, *Nezabyvaemoe* . . . .

[58] The group only relinquished its hold in 1980, following the death of Masherov, when an outsider—Tikhon Kisilev—was transferred from Moscow back to Minsk to head the Belorussian party organization. For a useful discussion of Belorussian politics and this native partisan group, see Amy W. Knight, 'Pyotr Masherov and the Soviet Leadership', *Survey*, 26, No. 1 (Winter 1982), pp. 151–68.

[59] See John P. Willerton, Jr., *Patronage and Politics in the Soviet Union*, University of Michigan, unpublished dissertation, 1985.

[60] These include the Belorussian politician Tikhon Kisilev, the Georgian Party bosses Vasilii Mzhavanadze and Eduard Shevardnadze, the long-time Uzbek party leader Sharaf Rashidov, and the Leningrad city First Secretary Grigorii Romanov.

[61] For instance, Foreign Minister Andrei Gromyko.

[62] Two former Politbureau members associated with the agricultural sector, Dmitrii Polyansky and Gennadii Voronov.

[63] Andropov had enjoyed mobility under Brezhnev, becoming head of the KGB in 1967 and a member of the Politbureau in 1973. His personal connections—both when he served in the KGB and later—often included individuals who were also members of the Brezhnev group (e.g., Viktor Chebrikov, the future head of the KGB and future Minister of Internal Affairs). Likewise, Solomentsev enjoyed mobility under Brezhnev, becoming a Central Committee department head, a CPSU secretary, and a candidate member of the Politbureau within the first seven years of Brezhnev's rule. Several politicians who worked closely with Brezhnev and who were members of his network also had career ties to Solomentsev (e.g., E. M. Tyazhel'nikov and N. V. Bannikov). Dolgikh also experienced mobility under Brezhnev, having come from the same region as well as having worked with Brezhnev's close protege, Konstantin Chernenko.

[64] For example, Vladimir Kirillin and Mikhail Lesechko supported the efforts at securing greater technology through foreign imports. Both stressed greater investment of resources into research and development of technologies. Kirillin's background was in the area of science and technology, and he dealt with energy questions. He was a member of the USSR Academy of Sciences and linked to its department of technological sciences. Lesechko's career included experience in the foreign trade area, as well as in machine building.

[65] Both of Kosygin's client Vice Chairmen, Kirillin and Lesechko, were retired in 1980, when Kosygin himself stepped down from power.

[66] See John P. Willerton, Jr., 'Patronage and Politics . . .'.

[67] George W. Breslauer, *Khrushchev and Brezhnev*. . . .

[68] In just the first six months of the Gorbachev regime, eight changes took place involving the advancement of new Politbureau and Secretariat members. Five of the 23 Central Committee department heads were replaced, as were nearly 20 of 115 regional first secretaries. The constraints on Gorbachev did not preclude the promotion of some of his clients. Among those promoted were Venyamin Afonin, the former secretary of the Stavropol' kraikom, who became the head of the Central Committee Department for Chemical Industry, Aleksandr Budyka, the former deputy chairman of the Stavropol' Kraiispolkom, who became a deputy head in the Central Committee Department for Agricultural and the Food Industry, and A. K. Vedernikov, a former Stavropol' krai party secretary, who moved into the important Central Committee Organizational-Party Work Department.

Part V
Gorbachev and the Collapse
of the Soviet Union

[18]

Brezhnev's 'Social Contract' and Gorbachev's Reforms

LINDA J. COOK

A TACIT 'social contract' governed the Brezhnev regime's relationship with its working class.[1] According to the terms of the contract, the regime provided full and secure employment, egalitarian wage policies and lax performance pressures in industry, state-controlled and heavily subsidised retail prices for essential goods, and socialised human services (i.e. education, medical care, child care, etc.). In return for such comprehensive provision of social and economic security, Soviet workers gave the regime their political compliance and quiescence. Essentially, Brezhnev's 'social contract' was an exchange in which each side tacitly committed itself to deliver political goods valued by the other. It may be further defined, drawing on the perceptive work of Peter Hauslohner, as a set of policy norms which gave priority to egalitarianism, stability and security, a set of constituency benefits which gave preference to blue-collar workers, and a set of institutions which maintained the contract as a matter of both commitment and 'standard operating procedure'.[2]

The 'social contract' imposed severe constraints on the Brezhnev leadership's labour and distributive policies. It required the state consistently to deliver a set of policy and allocational outcomes, a 'policy benefit package' to workers. The state had to deliver these policy goods—job security, welfare and equality—or lose legitimacy among workers and risk open discontent. It had, then, to deliver these goods in preference to pursuing other goals, and as an obligation of the contract (i.e. not at its own discretion, as a result of its paternalism or other value commitments). The state, in sum, paid a high price in constrained policy and allocational options in order to maintain labour quiescence. The 'social contract' also tied Soviet political stability to the maintenance of the centralised command economy: the state's ability to deliver relied on the capacity of that economy to control distributive outcomes and socialise risk and loss, thereby insulating workers from the effects of competition, enterprise failure and technological innovation.

When Gorbachev set about reforming the command economy, it appeared that the 'social contract' would be an early casualty. The reform programme introduced in 1986–88 was designed to accelerate the growth of the Soviet economy at considerable cost to social security and equality. The new leadership initiated, or announced its intent to initiate, measures which threatened to undercut basic provisions of the 'social contract' in all major policy areas: employment security; wage and income equality; price stability; and socialised services. New

38   LINDA J. COOK

programmes of automation and labour force restructuring threatened to displace large numbers of workers from previously secure jobs. Intensified demands for productivity and cost accountability began to replace the lax labour and financial regimes which had assured employment even to the marginally productive. The leadership initiated a wage reform which increased differentials among skill grades and between blue-collar and managerial personnel. Privatised social services charging fees were introduced on a modest scale. Legalisation of private retail activity weakened state control over prices, and proposed price reforms threatened state subsidies which had kept state retail prices of necessities at nominal levels throughout most of the Soviet period.

The reformist leaders justified their sharp departure from the social and labour policies of the Brezhnev era firstly on grounds of economic efficiency. They argued that the old 'social contract' gave workers excessive security and income equality, creating obstacles to scientific and technological progress and undermining the incentive role of pay.[3] Secondly, they insisted that declining state revenues and a burgeoning budget deficit required reductions in state expenditure, particularly retail price and production subsidies.[4]

More importantly, the reformers also rejected the old 'social contract' on moral and ideological grounds, repudiating the basic principles of universal state provision and egalitarian distribution. Reformist policy makers and intellectuals argued that state provision was morally debilitating for modern Soviet society, that it fostered a psychology of dependence which stifled initiative and frustrated aspirations for greater independence.[5] Reformers held, further, that egalitarian distribution principles were fundamentally unjust, because they failed to recognise or reward individuals' differential abilities, efforts and contributions to economy and society.[6] Gorbachev himself, speaking in June 1987, contended that under Brezhnev 'contradictions in the sphere of labour and distributive relations [accumulated] ... the basic socialist principle "to each according to his work" was frequently sacrificed in practice to an oversimplified understanding of equality'.[7] Moreover, while repudiating the state paternalism of the Brezhnev era, the reformist leadership at the same time articulated both practical and theoretical justifications for a more meritocratic and competitive economic reward system, a more highly stratified and privatised distribution system, and a much reduced state role in societal distribution and provision.

Reviewing these changes in both policy and ideology in mid-1987, Hauslohner submitted that Gorbachev was engaged in crafting a new social contract based on meritocratic norms and welfare state retrenchment.[8] He assessed the prospects for success of 'Gorbachev's social contract' positively. He argued convincingly that both the normative and constituency bases for Brezhnev's social contract had weakened with the decline in size and importance of the traditional working class which was its chief beneficiary. At the same time, the growing educated, professional strata in Soviet society would probably be receptive to Gorbachev's meritocratic and competitive norms, and to distributive policies which rewarded education and initiative. Hauslohner provided evidence that the Soviet intellectual elite had long ago defected from the values of the old contract, and that economic pressures were in any case undermining the state's capacity to deliver its side of the bargain, leading to growing public dissatisfaction. He was cautiously optimistic that Gorbachev would be able to enact and institutionalise a new contract.[9]

The present study will argue (with the benefit of hindsight) that Gorbachev's attempt to make a new 'social contract' failed. Reformist social and labour policies *were* formulated, and put into practice with significant effect, in 1986–87, and they produced some erosion in labour's old guarantees and protections. However, after this initial period of success, enforcement faltered in every policy area. By early 1989, the record of policy implementation had become one of retreats, reversals, delays and decisions to avert most harsh consequences in the social sphere. Despite its programmes and commitments, the reformist leadership for the most part did not enforce policies which would have cut deeply into the old guarantees, or adversely affected the welfare of broad strata of workers. (The one major exception to this generalisation, the decline of price stability and basic provision through the state retail network, was largely an unintended and unanticipated development which, moreover, led to further retreat from reform policies.[10]) I will argue that, at least for the first five years of the reform period, Brezhnev's 'social contract' remained a serious constraint on Gorbachev's policies.

The main sections of this article will examine the pattern of retreats from reformist social policy in 1988–89 by presenting three case-studies: the first on employment security (i.e. lay-offs and bankruptcies); the second on shop-floor pressures (i.e. wage reform and quality control); the third on price reform. Each case-study will follow a major reform policy through three stages of its development:

(1) enactment and projected impact;
(2) initial implementation and effects;
(3) retreat from implementation and declining impact.

I will identify in each case the specific actors, pressures and decisions which account for the retreat. We will see that both bureaucratic resistance and popular protest (factors which Hauslohner's analysis underestimated) played a role in defeating Gorbachev's new social contract. Ultimately, though, the central political leadership's own reluctance to violate long established expectations and entitlements proved the critical factor.

Reform policies and the threat to employment security

Releases and dismissals

Gorbachev's reform programme called for modernisation and technological changes which would require large-scale shifts in the structure of the Soviet labour force, shifts which would displace large numbers of workers who were long accustomed to job security. The Comprehensive Programme for the Social and Economic Development of the USSR to the Year 2000, approved by the XXVII Congress, called for dramatic cuts in levels of manual labour throughout Soviet

40   LINDA J. COOK

industry and construction.[11] The programme established a goal of reducing the number of manual workers in industry by as much as 50% over the following 15 years.[12] The reformers further anticipated that productivity increases would produce deep cuts in levels of employment throughout the material production sector, with a corresponding shift of labour into the understaffed service sector. Goskomtrud projected that the planned economic modernisation and labour force restructuring would result, overall, in the release (from the job they held in 1985) of 3 million employees during the 12th five-year plan (1986–90), and some 15 million (in a labour force of 130 million) by the year 2000.[13]

The reformers soon moved to institutionalise this shift in labour policy by legislating a new set of regulations and (promised) measures to facilitate and manage the anticipated displacement of workers. In January 1988 a major Central Committee resolution, 'On Ensuring Efficient Employment of the Population, Improving the Job Placement System, and Strengthening Social Guarantees for the Working People', set forth plans for a national system of employment centres and bureaux which were to provide vocational guidance, retraining and job placement for workers released in the course of labour force reductions (or plant closures).[14] The resolution in effect shifted responsibility for the placement of dismissed workers from their employing enterprise to state labour bureaux, and called on trade unions and local labour organs to cooperate in the transfer and placement of those released. It stipulated clearly that labour contracts might be broken 'in connection with the implementation of measures to cut the number of workers or establishment',[15] and provided payments and other forms of protection to temporarily unemployed workers. In sum, the resolution on employment made provision for large-scale labour force dismissals and displacement throughout the Soviet economy in the following years.

Scale and effects of releases

According to Goskomstat and VTsSPS statistics, reform policies led to the release of approximately 3 million industrial workers by late 1986.[16] The total number of personnel employed in Soviet industry began to decline for the first time during these years, and numbers working in non-production sectors increased by several hundred thousands.[17] While these numbers are in keeping with the reformers' projections for releases during the 12th five-year plan, their impact in displacing workers was considerably less than the numbers suggest.

The majority of those classified as 'released' were in fact transferred to different jobs, sectors or shifts within the same enterprise or production facility. Some were retrained and transferred to different work, others released and then re-employed to fill existing vacancies in the enterprise, or to man newly introduced evening and night shifts.[18] The model plan for placement of 10 000 workers to be 'released' from shops and production sections at the Chelyabinsk Tractor Plant Production Association over the course of the five-year plan is indicative of the broader pattern: according to plan, developed by the trade union committee, about 4000 of the released workers were to be placed in new production jobs, almost 6000 sent to non-production organisations of the association, and only 250 (i.e. 2.5% of the total) were actually to be dismissed from the association.[19] Such 'redistribution of the labour force basically within enterprises' meant minimal dislocation for workers, though they sometimes faced wage cuts or various hardships because of assignment to evening and night shifts.

A substantial minority of those released, amounting to one-third of the total for 1987 and 1988, retired on pensions.[20] There is evidence that many of these were retired early or involuntarily, and some forced to leave jobs on which they depended to supplement inadequate pensions. Finally, some of those counted in the release figures were actually discharged from their enterprises, and left to find new jobs or remain unemployed. No overall figures on the numbers discharged are available, but there is considerable and consistent evidence that managements discharged mostly older or sickly workers, women (especially those with young children), youth with little work experience, and the poorly skilled.[21] Anecdotal evidence suggests that those left unemployed for extended periods commonly lived in small towns or settlements which lacked local opportunities for re-employment, or were geographically immobile for family or other reasons.[22]

In sum, the costs of lay-offs (dislocation, income loss and job loss) during 1987–89 fell mainly on less efficient, relatively marginal producers, who had none the less generally been assured employment and wage income in the past. The overall effect of reform policies amounted to an erosion of 'social contract' protection and guarantees, but stopped well short of seriously undercutting job security for the core of the industrial working class. Those policies at the same time failed to produce most of the intended reduction and restructuring of the labour force.

Limited impact

Why was the reform's impact on employment patterns so limited? First, reform policies did not create sufficient incentives and pressures to induce managers to cut deeply into their labour forces. Levels of mechanisation and automation in industry remained well below those anticipated, so enterprises continued to rely heavily on manual labour. As a result, targets for reduction in the number of manual workers regularly went unfulfilled.[23] Secondly, though pressures for cost accounting and profitability did increase, financial pressures rarely became severe enough to overcome the strong managerial propensity to hoard productive labour. Indeed, the dominant response of 'redistributing workers within the enterprise' was a familiar subterfuge, used by managers in past reforms to retain labour in the face of central pressures for reductions combined with uncertainty and generalised labour scarcity.[24] Reform policies did, on the other hand, give managers both leeway and incentives to rid their enterprises of marginally productive workers. The resolution on employment relieved managers of responsibility for placement of those released, while dismissals of modest numbers of the least productive qualified as a response of sorts to central demands for productivity increases and labour force reductions.

The reformist leadership was also somewhat complicit in the redistribution scheme. Gorbachev himself, always on the defensive about the prospect of unemployment, repeatedly stressed that millions of existing vacancies in Soviet industry were available to absorb released workers.[25] The resolution on employment provided that those released from a particular enterprise had priority in assignment to any suitable vacant position within that enterprise, and indicated an expectation that many dismissed workers would be so reabsorbed.[26] Gorbachev also encouraged the increase in the extent of shift working, an approach which was strongly favoured by the trade unions as an alternative to lay-offs.[27] In sum, the centre seemed to facilitate managers' labour-hoarding behaviour, at least in part because of the reformers' own ambivalence about lay-offs and unemployment.[28]

Finally, while labour officials regularly insisted that the state was preparing to manage large-scale transfers of workers, little progress was made in setting up labour bureaux or retraining and placement services. Available facilities were universally assessed as inadequate to handle even the modest levels of displacement which did occur.[29] Overall, the reformist centre failed to create the conditions (especially technological conditions—automation and mechanisation) for the large-scale release of workers, enforce the policy on managers, or create the state labour bureaux necessary to manage the anticipated scale of worker displacement and transfer. These failures constituted an effective retreat from the ambitious projections for labour force restructuring, and plans for institution building, drawn up in 1987–88. They also meant that, with few exceptions, Soviet industrial workers remained securely employed at the end of the 12th five-year plan.

Insolvent enterprises: bankruptcies or bail-outs?

A second major element of Gorbachev's economic reform, the transfer of enterprises to self-financing and cost accountability under the June 1987 Law on the State Enterprise, also threatened Soviet workers' employment security and stability. It raised the prospect that workers would be released *en masse* from unprofitable enterprises, which might be subject to reorganisation or closure.

Substantial numbers of unprofitable industrial enterprises had long been maintained in the Soviet economy by a combination of ministerial cross-subsidisation and lax industrial credit.[30] Goskomstat reported that 24 000 plants were operating at a loss in 1987, while fully 25% of Soviet enterprises made either losses or very low profits and were unlikely to survive in conditions of self-financing.[31] Article 23 of the law made explicit provision for bankruptcy, and in extreme cases dissolution, of chronically unprofitable production facilities.[32] Moreover, Soviet banking and finance officials seemed committed to tightening financial discipline; in December 1987 the Chairman of Gosbank, Garetovsky, stressed that, with the transition to self-financing, credit facilities would be strictly targeted and require prompt repayment, late loans would be recalled, and financial penalties imposed. Based on his 'analysis of credit relations within enterprises in different sectors over the last few years', Garetovsky anticipated insolvencies and proposals for liquidation of enterprises.[33]

The transition to self-financing began on a limited basis in 1987, and was to be implemented in all sectors of material production during 1988–89. Again, the statistics on implementation seemed impressive: according to Goskomstat, 19 000 industrial enterprises, employing 55% of the total number of workers, were operating under the provisions of the law on the enterprise by the end of 1988.[34] Yet, over the following two years, only a few hundred Soviet enterprises were declared insolvent, and a small minority of these actually liquidated. Moreover, by the end of 1988 the leadership had taken measures which effectively ended the threat of bankruptcies for the foreseeable future. A study of the major developments in policy towards insolvent enterprises during 1987–88 should explain the limited impact of the brankruptcy provision, and the leadership's retreat from forcing dissolution of unprofitable facilities.

Responses to the law on the state enterprise

As soon as it had passed the law on the enterprise, the reformist leadership was confronted with a campaign of special pleading and lobbying. Party and government officials at all levels rose to the defence of unprofitable enterprises under their jurisdiction. They used party plenums, Supreme Soviet sessions and regional conferences to lobby for additional time and resources, stress the injustice and political risks of threatened plant closures, and translate the All-Union percentages into real, localised costs for their regions.[35] At the October 1987 Supreme Soviet session, for example, speaker after speaker addressed the problems his district would face under self-financing.[36] The statement by the Kazakh Prime Minister, N. A. Nazarbaev, was typical:

> The Karaganda Metallurgical Combine is in a complex position . . . The bulk of the country's supplies of tin for the canning industry ought to be produced here, and this has a direct effect on food supplies . . . The combine is not fulfilling its profit plan. We cannot understand how the collective will work under the principle of full economic accounting and self-financing from the start of 1988. Unfortunately, there are many similar examples.[37]

Such regional lobbying and special pleading is standard fare in Soviet politics,[38] but some regional leaders did have legitimate grievances against the self-financing legislation. To take the most important instance, much of the Soviet fuel complex (mining, oil, timber) operated at a loss largely because state price controls kept wholesale prices artificially depressed, below the cost of production.[39] Yet the reformers proposed transferring the complex's production facilities to self-financing well in advance of fuel price increases.[40] As the party secretary of the remote Magadan mining region pointed out, with existing prices self-financing would immediately bankrupt some 22% of the enterprises in the *oblast'*, leading to large-scale lay-offs of workers who would find few local prospects for new employment.[41] In other mining areas as well, implementation of the reform raised the spectre of regional depression. Moreover, the irrationalities of central pricing policy would be more to blame than the sector's performance.[42] Other reports and investigations made the potential costs of self-financing—particularly the bankruptcy of as many as one in every eight enterprises, including large parts of some

44   LINDA J. COOK

sectors, and resulting worker displacement—concrete.[43] A multiplicity of voices warned against the potentially disruptive effects on economic and social stability.

Nevertheless, for a few months in the autumn of 1988 the Gorbachev leadership oversaw enforcement of financial measures which pushed scores of enterprises to the brink of collapse. The reformers were motivated by the rising salience of the budget deficit issue. Having recently identified industrial subsidies as one of the major drains on the budget, they declared themselves determined to cut both. At the same time state banks, now also operating under cost-accounting principles, tightened industrial credit. With strong support from the Finance Ministry, the banks intensified pressures on poor performers by publishing lists of insolvent enterprises, pressing their managements to meet repayment deadlines, and cutting off credit to some plants which had large and mounting debts.[44] For example, in mid-September the USSR Industrial Construction Bank declared insolvent some 50 enterprises and organisations which had 'systematically violated payment discipline'.[45] The following week, the Bank for Housing and Social Construction published a list of 17 insolvent enterprises, referring for authority to Article 23 of the law on the enterprise.[46] A total of some 300 enterprises were reportedly declared insolvent by the beginning of 1989.[47]

Threatened enterprises in turn sought both political and financial help from their supervising ministries and local authorities. Most managed to make at least temporary deals which kept them in operation, and saved their workers from lay-offs and loss of wages.[48] A few of the marginals failed to find support, and were pushed into outright bankruptcy and closed. For example, the Ukrainian Ministry of Local Industry shut down a clothing factory which had been established 20 years before to provide work for surplus female labour in a mining region of L'vov *oblast'*. The factory had received no investment since its creation, and had a backlog of fines for short or unacceptable deliveries which had absorbed recent subsidies intended to improve its productivity for the transition to self-financing.[49] As a marginal facility with poor infrastructure, poor-quality consumer goods, and a female workforce, it was the exception which proved vulnerable to reform pressure.

At the autumn 1988 planning and budget meetings (for drafting the state plan and budget for 1989), the reformist leadership faced a critical decision: whether to push forward with bankruptcies by slashing (or at least selectively cutting) subsidies to unprofitable enterprises, and reinforcing the Finance Ministry's tight credit policies.[50] Credit had been cut off for scores of insolvent enterprises, and proceedings to close, auction or dissolve their plants and equipment were in progress. At this critical point, the leadership retreated, deciding instead to apportion another round of state subsidies (albeit somewhat reduced) to industry, and setting out new options for the reorganisation or privatisation of loss makers. The decisions made at these meetings virtually ended reports of bankruptcies. They relieved the pressure on insolvent enterprises, but only at the cost of leaving thousands of inefficient, overstaffed, obsolete production facilities to devise strategies for survival with the help of their central and local patrons. For the time being, at least, they also ended the threat of mass dismissal of workers.

Explaining the limits of reform

Reformist policy towards insolvent enterprises did meet considerable bureaucratic and political opposition. Ministerial, regional and local authorities intervened at various points in an effort to protect threatened enterprises, first lobbying for exceptions and additional resources, then providing direct aid to plants which had come under pressure from the banks. As with lay-offs, it was only the marginal which failed to find protectors and succumbed easily to reform pressures. Bureaucrats and party secretaries did place obstacles in the way of central policy, and did succeed temporarily in frustrating much of the intent of the Finance Ministry's tight credit policies. However, in my view bureaucratic resistance was not decisive in defeating the reformist agenda.

In this case, the reformist leadership did have instruments sufficient to implement its policy, i.e. both state financial institutions with the will and means to call in loans and deny operating funds to insolvent plants, and some control over the level of industrial subsidies. Moreover, financial instruments were beginning to have some effect in the autumn of 1988, pushing significant numbers of the weakest enterprises towards collapse, despite the resistance of ministries and local politicians. It was precisely at this point, confronting for the first time the real costs of its policies, that the leadership retreated. In spite of its declared commitment to self-financing and deficit reduction, Gorbachev's government chose a bail-out option. In the autumn of 1988 the reformist leadership decided to preserve enterprises and jobs rather than to pursue its policies to their logical conclusions. I am arguing that it did so in order to avoid the harsh consequences and political costs of many plant closures and mass lay-offs—in effect, to avert abrogating the 'social contract'.

Reform policy and shop floor pressures: wages and quality control

Workers played very little part in opposing reformist policies on employment security, because most workers' jobs were never directly threatened.[51] They did, however, play a significant role in resisting the new wage and quality control systems, which challenged the egalitarian norms and low production standards prevalent in Soviet industry under the old 'social contract'. After an initial period of successful implementation, both policies were met with shop-floor protests and sporadic, localised strikes. By the end of 1988, labour unrest, in combination with other pressures, had led to their failure and effective abandonment. Moreover, the new democratic rights extended to Soviet society by the Gorbachev leadership facilitated workers' mobilisation against these reform policies.

Wage reform

In the autumn of 1986 the Gorbachev leadership initiated a wage reform which reversed the 'levelling' tendencies of the industrial wage policies of the Brezhnev era by increasing pay differentials between skill levels and raising salaries of specialists and managers at higher rates than blue-collar wages. The resolution 'On

46   LINDA J. COOK

Improving the Wage System in Production Branches of the National Economy'[52] mandated an average wage increase of 20%–25% for workers, 30%–35% for specialists and 35%–40% for engineers (i.e. designers and technologists) directly engaged in development of new technology. The reform would in principle raise wages for all categories of workers by the end of the 12th five-year plan, but the increases authorised were to be financed out of enterprise resources rather than, (as in the past) from the state budget. Thus, enterprises would have to generate resources to pay the wage rises by improving productivity and efficiency and cutting staff. Wage increases were also limited by the stipulation that an enterprise's productivity must grow more rapidly than its average wage. In sum, the wage reform was in keeping with the new leadership's meritocratic norms, designed to provide incentives and rewards for skill and education, and to produce self-financed wage increases which would be differentiated according to enterprises' productivity gains.[53]

The new wage policies were broadly implemented in Soviet industry, and initially produced some of the intended effects on wage distribution and efficient use of labour. By May 1988, slightly more than one-half of all workers in material production had been transferred to the new wage system.[54] Average wage increases for engineering and technical personnel were, as intended, greater than those for production workers.[55] In many enterprises the reform produced labour productivity gains and cuts in the size of the labour force. Through 1987 overall increases in industrial productivity exceeded wage increases. In sum, despite some problems with the design of the new legislation, managerial foot-dragging, and levelling pressures on the shop floor, the early effects were positive.[56] The reform was introducing greater differentiation and discipline into industrial wage structures, reversing the trends towards egalitarianism and state subsidising of wage levels.[57]

Gospriemka

The reformers' programme further intensified pressures on the factory floor in 1986–87 by strengthening quality controls over the notoriously poor output of civilian production. In May 1986 the Central Committee passed the resolution 'On Measures to Radically Improve the Quality of Output', which created a new system for oversight of work and state product acceptance (Gospriemka) in Soviet industry.[58] The resolution set up a monitoring body which was directly subordinated to Gosstandart (i.e. independent of both enterprise and ministerial control), highly qualified, and paid on the basis of product quality rather than plan fulfilment. Quality controllers inspected goods in the factories, and accepted only those which met state quality standards.[59] Managers and workers were to be held directly accountable for unacceptable output; the resolution stipulated that 'premium pay and bonuses will not be paid . . . during a month when defective products or lowered quality of output occur . . . and may be eliminated if problems are chronic'.[60]

Gospriemka, like wage reform, achieved early successes. State quality controllers were placed in some 1500 factories at the beginning of 1987, and reportedly rejected more than 15% of products on initial presentation.[61] In January 1988 the system was extended to more than 700 additional enterprises, including some in construction.[62] Quality controllers sent substandard output back for improvement or rejected it outright, and in some cases halted production lines and construction projects because of violations in technical standards.[63] As a result plans went unfulfilled, production indicators fell, and managers and workers lost wages and bonuses. Performance pressures on the shop floor intensified at affected enterprises. The state acceptance system was undercutting the lax labour regime and guaranteed income of the Brezhnev 'social contract'.

Protests against reform policies

In the autumn of 1987 Soviet workers began striking in protest against reductions in pay which had resulted from the introduction of either new wage determination schemes or Gospriemka. The strikes were apparently spontaneous, uncoordinated and localised, and affected transport, manufacturing and other sectors. The Soviet press contained detailed reports of some two dozen strikes by late 1988, along with indications that there were many more—indeed, that by the summer of 1988 sporadic strike activity had become common.[64] Pay cuts were the triggering issue and central grievance of most reported strikes.

In a typical strike at a bus manufacturing plant in the Moscow suburb of Likino, for example, workers stopped the assembly line when they lost bonuses because state acceptance workers had rejected part of their output. The workers recognised and lamented the poor quality of their product (which one assembly line worker described as 'a ragged forgery of a bus, 40%–50% incomplete')[65] but blamed obsolete equipment and a long history of underinvestment. They argued that 'the people work normally, but the bus does not meet the present state standards. It is not ethical to accuse the workers'.[66] However receptive to Gorbachev's exhortations that they work hard and earn their pay, the workers saw no 'social justice' in losing wages because of technical and working conditions which were beyond their control, conditions for which they held the state responsible.

In virtually every reported case the strikes brought a rapid response from local party and government (and sometimes higher-level) authorities, who negotiated with the workers or their designated representatives, agreed to meet most demands, and frequently replaced managers of striking plants. The partial democratisation of the Soviet system at once emboldened the strikers and disoriented the authorities. Workers used the pro-reform and pro-democracy slogans of 'labour collectives' initiative and independence', and their newly conferred rights of self-management, to justify their actions. Despite their pro-reform slogans, though, the strikers clearly opposed reform policies on wages and quality control. The responses of enterprise trade unions and managers were mixed and confused; some supported the workers, others opposed them or refused to negotiate, and were bypassed and often replaced in the settlement process. On the whole, the workers won, with the authorities who came in to settle the strikes generally acceding to their demands. The strikes and pattern of concessions, along with their demonstration effects on workers and managers elsewhere, played a large part in undermining reform pressures for wage discipline and product quality on the shop floor.

The workers were joined in their opposition to Gospriemka by both managers and ministerial officials, who also stood to lose bonuses. At the July 1988 Council of Ministers session all three groups joined forces to defeat the draft law 'On Quality Control', which would have extended Gospriemka and increased the authority of Gosstandart.[67] In the autumn of 1988 Omelyanchuk, the Gosstandart official who headed Gospriemka, stated that the system was up against many difficulties and much resistance.[68] Summary Goskomstat figures indicate that, at the beginning of 1988, Gospriemka was rejecting only 8% of output on first submission, a decline of almost half from the previous year.[69]

Wage discipline also deteriorated sharply in 1988. In the face of worker protests, combined with undeniable price inflation in the state retail sector, managements began raising workers' wages well above reform targets and productivity gains. By the end of the year, uncontrolled wage increases in industry had become the norm, with wages reported to be increasing faster than productivity at more than one-half of Soviet enterprises, and this pattern continued through 1989.[70] Wage increases which were not fully backed by productivity growth in turn contributed to inflationary pressures, which then became a source of further political tension and labour unrest.

Explaining the limits of reform

In the years 1986–88 reform policies on wages and quality control did begin to alter the guaranteed wages and lax production regime of the old 'social contract'. However, the success of these policies generated opposition from both managers and workers, who stood together against Gospriemka because all enterprise incomes were tied to plan fulfilment, which strict quality control threatened. Managerial personnel shared with workers a clear-cut, material interest in low production standards, and in the face of their combined opposition the reformers apparently retreated. Again the policy instruments to push through the new goals and priorities (i.e. Gospriemka personnel) were in place at hundreds of Soviet factories, but the statistics on the percentage of goods rejected indicate that enforcement of quality standards declined sharply in 1988.[71] In addition, legislation which would have expanded the system and strengthened the authority of Gosstandart was postponed indefinitely.

In this case workers also played a substantial direct role in defending their old guarantees against reform policies, and their newly-conferred rights to collective protest. The reformist centre had called for worker (and other societal) political activism but, at least in the areas of wages and quality control, failed to co-opt workers to reform goals. Nevertheless, the reformers continued a rather indiscriminate support for workers' protests against alleged 'bureaucrats' and recalcitrant managers, thereby effectively encouraging a pattern of managerial concessions to strikers on wage and other issues. The strikes of 1987–88 were not large, long, or well-organised, but most gained concessions quicky and easily. The reformers were caught in a contradiction between democratisation and industrial reform:

rights of collective protest for workers created obstacles (in the form of strikes and protests) to enforcement of greater wage and production discipline. When workers used their new political rights to defend elements of the old 'social contract' against reform policies, they succeeded in helping to defeat those policies.

The dilemmas of price reform

In June 1987 the Gorbachev leadership announced its intention to carry out a comprehensive reform of industrial wholesale, purchase and retail prices, including both actual price levels and procedures for establishing them.[72] The reform was to include higher industrial wholesale prices for fuel and raw materials, a large reduction in retail price subsidies and some decentralisation of pricing authority.[73] Over the following months the government proceeded with preparations for the reform, instructing the State Price Committee (Goskomtsen) to draw up plans, and specifying that the 13th five-year plan must be compiled in the new prices.[74] Officials of the government and Goskomtsen regularly asserted that a price reform was in preparation, and that it would be put up for nationwide discussion once a draft plan was ready (as had been done, for example, with the draft law on the state enterprise), but no draft documents were published. Instead, in early 1989 the leadership, in a significant retreat from reform principles, strengthened administrative controls over prices. A few months later, the then Prime Minister, Ryzhkov, declared the official postponement of price reform. The following pages will seek to explain the reformers' hesitancy and eventual retreat on price policy.

The Gorbachev leadership both understood and insisted that price reform was critical to the overall project of *perestroika,* the linchpin of the reform process. In his speech to the June 1987 Central Committee Plenum (which approved the law on the state enterprise), Gorbachev stated that 'radical reform of price formation is a very important component of economic restructuring, without [which] complete changeover to the new economic mechanism is impossible'.[75] He explained that prices must be brought into line with production costs in order to allow introduction of industrial self-financing, and that the existing system of price formation produced distortions, irrationalities and excessive growth of state subsidies. Reformist economists (who seemed to agree on little else) were uniformly committed to rationalisation of prices and reduction of retail price subsidies.

Yet the leadership was singularly cautious in its treatment of this issue. Even in their earliest statements, leaders gave assurances that price reform would not lead to a deterioration in the working people's living standards. While insisting that state food subsidies must be reduced, for example, Gorbachev proposed a system of compensation for low- and average-income consumers, and promised that only high-income over-consumers of subsidised goods would be hurt.[76] At virtually every public mention of retail price reform, officials repeated that while 'unjustified redistributive processes and subsidies' would be reduced, working people would be compensated (i.e. with transfer payments, wage tax relief), and 'social justice' would be enhanced. The leadership's caution on this issue, its unwillingness even to admit that price reform would impose costs on workers and

LINDA J. COOK

others, contrasts strikingly with its open admission of new costs to be imposed in the areas of employment security, wage equality and industrial quality controls. This caution points to the reformers' extreme concern about popular acceptance of price reform, and their perceptions of its political costs.

What made the price issue so politically difficult that the leadership delayed, and then postponed, even enacting a policy? First, the proposed price reform would mean abandoning policies which had kept the prices of necessities at nominal levels throughout most of the Soviet period. Subsidised, low and stable prices for necessities had been one of the reliable, tangible and valued policy goods which Soviet citizens received from the state. Moreover, production and procurement costs for most goods had been rising for decades, with the increases covered by state subsidies. In order to eliminate subsidies and rationalise prices, the reformers would have to pass the accumulated cost increases on to consumers all at once, in effect doubling the prices of many food products and other basic goods. In spite of the leadership's assurances about living standards, the increases would inevitably hurt consumers, especially low-income groups whose budgets are spent disproportionately on basic goods.

More to the point politically, raising prices and cutting subsidies would impose new costs on virtually all urban strata of Soviet society simultaneously, especially strata which had privileged access to state goods under the old distribution system. Two Soviet economists, Bim and Shokhin, make this point on the likely effects of price reform trenchantly.

> In addition to low and fixed-income individuals, the 'losers' would include the populations of many large cities, industrial centres and economically developed areas, workers in large enterprises, and numerous categories of administrative and managerial personnel (i.e. categories which today either purchase meat and dairy products at state stores or have priority in obtaining them through rations, public catering or ordering at enterprises and offices). No income compensation can encompass the full variety of existing consumer markets and differences in 'value' of earnings of different categories of working people.[77]

In the worst-case scenario, price reform could provide a source of grievance linking discontented industrial workers with the broader urban population. Just such a linkage had occurred in 1962 in Novocherkassk, when food price increases sparked industrial strikes which grew into broader demonstrations, and were suppressed with loss of life.[78] When the head of Goskomtsen, Pavlov, was asked about the 1962 reform and its repercussions during an interview in the autumn of 1988, he replied: 'We have been thoroughly analysing the negative factors of [the 1962] price rise ... and will not allow anything similar to happen'.[79]

There is additional evidence that fear of the public response deterred the reformers from moving ahead with price reform—fear not necessarily of protest and unrest, but of alienating the population from the whole project of *perestroika*. We must remember that, in 1987, the Gorbachev leadership enjoyed considerable public confidence, there was large-scale popular support for *perestroika* (however vaguely conceived), and hopes for the success of economic reform were high. At that early stage the leadership held back from raising prices and cutting subsidies because it did not want to turn the people against reform by imposing very tangible costs on the whole population before reform policies had delivered tangible benefits. (Other reformist social policies—on employment and wages —would impose costs on some limited strata of Soviet society, and would at least in theory produce both winners and losers.)

The leadership also knew that public opinion was overwhelmingly hostile to price increases, and completely unswayed by the reformists' arguments on the issue. While public opinion surveys were not yet common at this point, letters to the editors of various publications provide an unambiguous reading of the popular response: at *Literaturnaya gazeta* all but a dozen of 1500 letters expressed opposition. The editors of *Nedelya* estimated that only 3%–4% of letter writers favoured price increases and that only one letter in dozens 'supports the official arguments on [price] reform'.[80] They warned that a price reform could arouse large-scale opposition to *perestroika*, a concern that was echoed by the leadership. The Brezhnev 'social contract' had left Soviet urban and working-class strata with a sense of entitlement to a stable cost of living, and an expectation that the state would ensure this stability. During the early years of reform the Gorbachev leadership chose to avoid the political costs and risks of violating that expectation, but only at considerable cost to the coherence of its reform project.

Price increases without price reform

Beginning in the autumn of 1988, the state consumer sector was nevertheless beset by rising prices, the disappearance of common, inexpensive goods and severe supply disruptions. In September the press reported price increases, and in October food and other goods shortages as well as higher prices were reported in state retail trade in 140 cities, with worse deficits in smaller towns.[81] Over the following year the situation grew progressively worse.[82] The decline of price stability and basic provision came not as a result of straightforward policy decision—indeed, the leadership continued to delay retail price reform and maintained subsidies—but largely by default, as unintended and unanticipated consequences of reform policies.

A number of factors contributed to the inflation and shortages. First, enterprises in the consumer goods sector which had been transferred to self-financing often responded by raising prices for their goods. They also increased profits by phasing out inexpensive product lines, including many everyday items which had been produced at 'socially low' prices. Secondly, as we have seen, many enterprises used their limited autonomy to put into effect wage increases which were not fully backed by productivity increases, contributing to excessive growth of workers' monetary incomes, which fuelled inflation.[83] These factors, combined with serious ethnic unrest in 1988, caused shortages and supply disruptions in the state retail sector. These shortages in turn forced consumers to rely on higher priced cooperative goods. Rumours of impending official price increases, which persisted despite official denials that price reform was imminent, also sparked panic buying and hoarding and further aggravated tensions in the consumer market.

By early 1989 the reformers had neither price stability nor a comprehensive and rationalising price reform. Consumer price increases had come as unintended (and dysfunctional) consequences of industrial reform measures, rather than as intended and controlled effects of planned price policy. Moreover, consumers who were already confronting inflation and shortages would be even less willing than before to countenance a reform which brought additional, state-planned price increases and subsidy cuts. Price reform, economically necessary but politically risky from the beginning, became even more difficult in a deteriorating consumer market.[84] Instead the reformers retreated, postponing price reform and moving back to strengthened administrative controls over prices in late 1989.

Paradoxically, then, Gorbachev's reforms did result in a major abrogation of the 'social contract'. By 1989, unintended and unanticipated effects of reform policies had undermined workers' protected cost of living. The state was no longer providing (or able to provide) stable prices and reliable, subsidised provision of essential goods. It was failing to deliver critical policy and allocational outcomes promised by the 'social contract'. While the Gorbachev leadership delayed an essential price reform because it feared the political costs, its other economic policies inadvertently undermined price stability. As a result, it has paid the political costs of violating the contract, without reaping the potential economic benefits.

Brezhnev's 'social contract' as a constraint on Gorbachev's reforms

The Gorbachev leadership consistently retreated from policies which threatened to abrogate the 'social contract' of the Brezhnev era. It made strong commitments to reformist labour and social policies in 1986–87, then repeatedly reversed, delayed or decided to avert the harsh consequences of those policies when confronted with their real costs and opponents. The reforms did result in some erosion of labour's 'social contract' guarantees, but in each policy area, during 1988–89, new decisions or concessions limited the painful effects for most workers: plants were permitted to re-absorb released workers; insolvent enterprises were bailed out; wage discipline was relaxed; quality control weakened; and retail price reform indefinitely delayed.

In sum, the reform leadership appeared unwilling to enforce measures which would cut deeply into the old guarantees, or adversely affect the welfare of broad strata of workers. It acted as if constrained to deliver the old package of 'social contract' policy goods, even in the face of its own preference for (and commitment to) different policy and allocational outcomes. The pattern of policy retreats fits the hypothesis that the 'social contract', conceived as a set of societal expectations and state obligations, constrained the Gorbachev leadership from pursuing its chosen reform strategy.

Why was Hauslohner's optimism about Gorbachev's new social contract misplaced? Hauslohner was certainly right in arguing that the Gorbachev leadership had articulated a coherent new set of social policy goals and values, and that these had very broad support among Soviet intellectuals, as well as a growing constituency among the middle class.[85] In the longer term, he is quite possibly right about the prospects for change. However, in the process of policy implementation examined above, the commitments of intellectuals mattered less than the interests of managers, and broad societal attitudes mattered less than the specific responses of workers and others whose security was directly threatened by reform. Reform policies mobilised, first and foremost, groups in the industrial sector who stood to lose, and these workers, managers and party secretaries displayed a tenacious commitment to their accustomed security, stability and low performance standards. The case-studies presented above show that a dense network of elite-institutional and mass-worker interests and expectations had built up around the old 'social contract' and proved a formidable barrier to its deconstruction.

The case-studies also show, however, that bureaucratic and societal resistance were not (in most cases) decisive in defeating the reforms. The leadership had the policy instruments necessary to implement at least some of its policies, particularly in the areas of enterprise insolvency, quality control and price reform. However, even in these cases, direct confrontation with social and political costs of the policies led to retreat. The Gorbachev leadership was, I am arguing, constrained by fear that workers (and others) would withdraw consent and compliance from the state if the expected 'social contract' policy goods were not delivered. It was fearful not only of unrest, but more immediately of alienating society from the overall project of reform by imposing big costs before being able to deliver new benefits.

The old 'social contract' defined broadly accepted standards of what the state should provide, and of Soviet society's entitlements. The reformers feared the political costs of violating those standards, and so were constrained by them. The leadership's apprehensions about the social and political consequences of abrogating the old 'social contract' were the critical factor, common across policy areas, constraining the reformers' decisions. While their decisions were constrained, however, their mistakes and miscalculations were not. As a consequence, price stability and basic provision in consumer markets deteriorated radically, presenting the reformers with a new set of problems which further complicated their task and paralysed their efforts.[86]

Brown University

---

[1] For discussion of the 'social contract' under Brezhnev see especially: Gail Lapidus, 'Social Trends', in Robert F. Byrnes, ed., *After Brezhnev: Sources of Soviet Conduct in the 1980's* (Bloomington, IN, Indiana University Press, 1983), pp. 188–192; Ed A. Hewett, *Reforming the Soviet Economy: Equality versus Efficiency* (Washington, DC, Brookings Institution, 1988), pp. 39–50; Peter A. Hauslohner, 'Gorbachev's Social Contract', *Soviet Economy*, 3, 1, 1987, pp. 56–60. For an argument that the policies and politics of the Brezhnev period 'fit' the social contract thesis, see Linda J. Cook, 'The Soviet Economic System and Political Legitimation', in David Cameron & Peter Hauslohner, eds., *Political Control of the Soviet Economy* (New York, Cambridge University Press, forthcoming).

[2] Hauslohner, 1987, pp. 54–89.

[3] See, for example, the interview with V. Gavrilov, *Izvestiya*, 26 September 1986, p. 2; N. Rimashevskaya, 'Perestroika khozyaistvennogo mekhanizma: Raspredelenie i spravedlivost'', *Ekonomicheskaya gazeta*, 4, 1986, pp. 6–7; E. Klopov & L. Gordon, *Pravda*, 24 October 1986, p. 3; Tat'yana Zaslavskaya, 'Chelovecheskii faktor razvitiya ekonomiki i sotsial'naya spravedlivost'', *Kommunist*, 13, 1986, pp. 61–73.

54   LINDA J. COOK

[4] See, for example, *Pravda*, 20 October 1988, p. 2; the interview with N. Shmelev in *Moscow News*, 50, 11 December 1988, p. 10.

[5] Zaslavskaya, 1986, pp. 61–73.

[6] Alfred B. Evans, 'Economic Reward and Inequality in the 1986 Program of the Communist Party of the Soviet Union', in Donna L. Bahry & Joel C. Moses, eds, *Political Implications of Economic Reform in Communist Systems: Communist Dialectic* (New York, NYU Press, 1990), pp. 162–196.

[7] *Pravda*, 26 June 1987, p. 1.

[8] Hauslohner, 1987, pp. 54–89.

[9] Hauslohner sounds the theme of caution clearly in his conclusions, stating: 'To be sure, it is far from clear that Gorbachev's social programme will be implemented successfully, let alone become the core of an enduring new social contract'. Hauslohner, 1987, p. 82.

[10] For further discussion of price stability and basic provision as an exception to my overall argument, see below.

[11] V. Mart'yanov & V.Tambovtsev, 'Tselevaya kompleksnaya programma sokrashcheniya ruchnogo truda', *Sotsialisticheskii trud*, 10, 1985, pp. 12–17.

[12] These figures would mean a reduction in the number of manual workers to 15%–20% of the industrial labour force from the then current level of one-third. The 12th five-year plan stipulated that the number of manual production workers should decrease by more than 5 million, i.e. more than 10% of the total, by 1990. M. S. Gorbachev, 'O pyatiletnem plane ekonomicheskogo i sotsial'nogo razvitiya SSSR na 1986–90 gody', *Kommunist*, 10, 1986, pp. 9–12.

[13] V. Kulakov, 'Planirovanie ispol'zovaniya trudovykh resursov', *Planovoe khozyaistvo*, 11, 1988, pp. 110–116.

[14] *Sotsialisticheskaya industriya*, 19 January 1988, pp. 1–2.

[15] *Ibid.*, p. 1.

[16] *Pravda*, 25 October 1988, p. 3; 31 October 1989, p. 2; G. Yanaev, *Trud*, 5 December, 1989, p. 2.

[17] Tass, *FBIS*, 31 October 1988, pp. 72–73.

[18] I. Zaslavsky, 'Problemy vysvobozhdeniya, perepodgotovki i trudoustroistva kadrov v novykh usloviyakh khozyaistvovaniya', *Ekonomicheskie nauki*, 6, 1988, pp. 29–34; *Izvestiya*, 18 April 1988, p. 1.

[19] I. A. Vedernikov, 'Trade Unions and Social Aspects of Job Placement for Released Workers', *Mashinostroitel'*, 3, 1988, pp. 1–4; translated in *JPRS: Economic Affairs*, 14 July 1988, pp. 49–53; statistics cited are on p. 49.

[20] *Pravda*, 25 October 1988, p. 3.

[21] P. Filipov, 'Sotsial'nye garantii na effektivnoi zanyatosti', *Sotsiologicheskie issledovaniya*, 5, 1988, pp. 25–33; for trade union claims that these were the groups mainly affected by dismissals, see Shalaev's report to the 6th AUCCTU Plenum, *Trud*, 6 September 1989, p. 2; and the speech by the Deputy Chairman of AUCCTU, Yanaev, *Trud*, 5 December 1989, pp. 2–3.

[22] For a discussion of localised unemployment as a result of lack of jobs in small towns even before the reform period, see I. Adirim, 'A Note on the Current Level, Pattern, and Trends of Unemployment in the USSR', *Soviet Studies*, 41, 3, 1989, pp. 455–457.

[23] V. V. Shcherbitsky, *Izvestiya*, 13 December 1987, p. 4.

[24] Rutland's study of the Shchekino experiment, for example, concluded that more than two-thirds of 'released' workers were ultimately moved to other jobs at the same enterprise; Peter Rutland, 'The Shchekino Method and the Struggle to Raise Labour Productivity in Soviet Industry', *Soviet Studies*, 36, 3, 1984, p. 349.

[25] See, for example, Gorbachev, 1986, pp. 9–12.

[26] See the commentary on the 'Resolution on Employment' by the deputy chairman of the USSR Council of Ministers Bureau for Social Development, I. Prostyakov, *Pravda*, 21 January 1988, p. 2.

[27] Gorbachev, 1986, pp. 9–12.

[28] This ambivalence was expressed not only by Gorbachev, but also by such ardent reform advocates as Abalkin and Burlatsky.

[29] See, for example, G. Yanaev, *Trud*, 5 December 1989, p. 2.

[30] Hewett, *Reforming...*; V. Romanyuk, *Izvestiya*, 31 August 1988, p. 2.

[31] Goskomstat report in *Izvestiya*, 3 October 1988, p. 2; V. Gostev, *Pravda*, 19 August 1987, p. 2; V. Gostev, *Pravda*, 20 October 1987, pp. 3–4.

[32] Text of the law is in *Pravda*, 1 July 1987, p. 4.

[33] N. V. Garetovsky, 'Perestroika bankovskoi sistemy', *Ekonomicheskaya gazeta*, 50, 1987, pp. 4–9.

BREZHNEV'S 'SOCIAL CONTRACT' AND REFORM 55

[34] Goskomstat statistics in *Izvestiya*, 9 December 1988, p. 2.

[35] See, for example, 'Zasedaniya verkhovnogo soveta SSSR: preniya po dokladam o gosudarstvennom plane ekonomicheskogo i sotsial'nogo razvitiya SSSR na 1988 god', *Izvestiya*, 22 October 1987, pp. 2–5; 23 October 1987, p. 2; L. Zaikov, *Pravda*, 28 November 1987, p. 2.

[36] They included the Kazakh, Armenian and Uzbek Premiers, the Deputy Premier of the RSFSR, and party secretaries from the Altai *krai* and Tbilisi *gorkom;* 'Zasedaniya verkhovnogo soveta SSSR'.

[37] N. A. Nazarbaev, *Izvestiya*, 22 October 1987, p. 3.

[38] On regional lobbying in the Soviet polity, see Donna Bahry, *Outside Moscow: Power, Politics, and Budgetary Policy in the Soviet Republics*, (New York, Columbia University Press, 1987); on special pleading (the 'struggle for exceptions'), see Hewett, *Reforming...*, pp. 28ff.

[39] A. Komin, 'Perestroika ekonomiki: kompetentnost' i glasnost'', *Ekonomicheskaya gazeta*, 43, 1988, pp. 4–5.

[40] The July 1987 decree on pricing promised the introduction of wholesale prices which would consistently cover production costs in 1991, i.e. only after the full transition to self-financing had been completed for one or two years; see Anders Aslund, *Gorbachev's Struggle for Economic Reform: the Soviet Reform Process, 1986–88* (Ithaca, NY, Cornell University Press, 1989), pp. 128–136.

[41] V. Androsenko, 'Poka ne gryanul khozraschet: s plenuma Magadanskogo obkoma KPSS', *Sotsialisticheskaya industriya*, 22 December 1987, p. 5.

[42] For further discussion of the pricing issue, and the complexities of price reform, see below.

[43] See, for example, Komin, 'Perestroika ekonomiki...', pp. 4–5; V. A. Balakin, 'Restructuring of the Economic Mechanism in Construction Needs New Acceleration', *Promyshlennoe stroitel'stvo*, 6, 1988, pp. 2–3, translated in *JPRS: Economic Affairs*, 4 October 1988, pp. 38–40.

[44] Yu. Krasnopol'sky, 'Bankroty?', *Trud*, 16 September 1988, p. 2.

[45] *Ibid.*

[46] M. Zotov, 'Bankrotami nenazovesh', a platit' nechem', *Sotsialisticheskaya industriya*, 20 September 1988, p.2.

[47] This figure is cited in a *Wochenpresse* interview with V. Golovachev, editor-in-chief of *Trud*, reported in *FBIS: Daily Report*, 14 February 1989, pp. 75–76.

[48] See, for example, 'V sovete ministrov SSSR', *Pravda*, 20 October 1988, p. 2.

[49] G. Nekrasova & E. Savinova, 'Esli predpriyatie obankrotilos'', *Sotsialisticheskaya industriya*, 18 August 1988, p. 2.

[50] V. Gostev, 'Rubli iz gosudarstvennoi kazny', *Izvestiya*, 31 March 1989, p. 2.

[51] Many workers did raise protests through official channels against illegal dismissal during 1987–88. The trade unions defended some of them, and a few were reinstated by the courts.

[52] The text of the resolution is in *Pravda*, 3 November, 1986.

[53] Janet G. Chapman, 'Gorbachev's Wage Reform', *Soviet Economy*, 4, 4, 1988, pp. 338–365.

[54] *Ibid.*, p. 354.

[55] *Ibid.*, pp. 354–362; Aslund, 1989, pp. 81–84; Aslund's assessment is somewhat more negative than Chapman's but both find positive effects in the early stages of implementing the wage reform.

[56] Chapman, 1988, p. 61.

[57] Aslund, 1989, pp. 81–84.

[58] The text of the resolution is in *Pravda*, 2 July 1986, p. 2. Quality control was intended to raise the technological level as well as the quality of output.

[59] Aslund, pp. 76–80.

[60] *Pravda*, 2 July, 1986, p. 1–2.

[61] *Trud*, 9 June 1987, pp. 1–2; the state acceptance system, Gospriemka, reportedly monitored more than 20% of industrial output by mid-1987.

[62] *Trud*, 21 July 1987, p. 1.

[63] See, for example, 'Plant Attempts to Evade State Acceptance', in *Sovetskaya Rossiya*, translated in *FBIS*, 18 July 1987, pp. S4–5.

[64] A list and more thorough characterisation of these strikes can be found in Linda J. Cook, 'Soviet Regimes, Workers, and the Social Contract: The Soviet Welfare State under Brezhnev and Gorbachev', (draft manuscript), Chap. 6.

[65] 'Bus Plant Strike Causes Explored', *Moscow News*, 42, 18 October 1987, pp. 8–9.

[66] *Ibid.*, p. 8.

[67] *Izvestiya*, 24 July 1988, p. 4.

[68] See the Tass interview with Omelyanchuk, 'State Quality Control Rejects Substandard Items', reported in *FBIS*, 27 October 1988, pp. 87–88.

56   LINDA J. COOK

[69] See the January–February 1988 industrial performance report in *Ekonomicheskaya gazeta*, 12, 1988, p. 8.

[70] For statistics on the increase in average wages and salaries beginning in 1988, which reportedly averaged more than 8% per quarter through most of 1989 and 1990, see 'Soviet Economic Performance During the First Three Quarters of 1990', *PlanEcon Report*, 23 November 1990; Table 2, p. 8. For the relationship between average wages and overall labour productivity over the same period, which shows labour productivity to be consistently well below wage increases, and steady or declining through most of the period, see *PlanEcon Report*, 20 April 1990, p. 3. For the relationship between nominal and real monthly wages over this period, which shows real wages to be declining or increasing slightly throughout despite burgeoning increases in nominal wages during 1988–90, see *PlanEcon Report*, 13 July 1990, p. 9.

[71] Aslund, 1989, pp. 31; 76–78.

[72] *Ibid.*, p. 28; for background on the price reform see Morris Bornstein, 'Soviet Price Policies', *Soviet Economy*, 3, 2, 1987, pp. 96–134.

[73] Aslund, 1989, pp. 128–136.

[74] *Ibid.*

[75] M. S. Gorbachev, 'O zadachakh partii po korennoi perestroike upravleniya ekonomikoi', *Pravda*, 26 June 1987, pp. 2–7.

[76] *Ibid.*

[77] A. Bim & A. Shokhin, 'Sistema rasprede leninya: na puzyakh perestroiki', *Kommunist*, 15, 1986, pp. 64–73.

[78] On the Novocherkassk strikes, see Betsy Gidwitz, 'Labor Unrest in the Soviet Union', *Problems of Communism*, November–December 1982, pp. 25–42.

[79] Interview with V. Pavlov, *Trud*, 9 September 1988, pp. 1–2.

[80] A. Ulyukaev, 'Consumers' Correspondence Club: Higher, Higher, Higher', *Nedelya*, 19, 1988, p 7; translated in *FBIS*, 19 May 1988, pp. 61–62.

[81] *Moscow News*, 2–9 October 1988, p. 13.

[82] For estimates of inflation in 1988–90, see *PlanEcon Report*, 23 November 1990, pp. 4, 8 (Table 2).

[83] See the report of the Supreme Soviet Commission on Labour, Prices and Social Policy, *Pravda*, 23 September 1989, p. 2.

[84] Nikolai Shmelev, 'Rethinking Price Reform in the USSR', *Soviet Economy*, 4, 4, 1988, pp. 328–337.

[85] Hauslohner, 1987, pp. 54–89.

[86] For an extended discussion of these issues, see also Linda J. Cook, 'Soviet regimes, workers and the social contract: the Soviet welfare state under Brezhnev and Gorbachev', draft manuscript.

[19]

Perestroika as Revolution from Within: An Interpretation

JOHN GOODING

W hen Mikhail Gorbachev warned of a "crisis situation" in perestroika's early days, he had the air of crying wolf. Now no one can doubt that the Soviet Union is in crisis. The immediate precipitant of the crisis, whose roots go deep, has been the perestroika program itself. Yet until 1985, Western observers generally assumed that only if the regime faced destabilization would it "pay the political price of radical reform" and that its current problems, though grave, were unlikely to force real concessions out of it.[1] Events, however, would disprove this analysis, and Konstantin Chernenko's successor embarked on radical change at a time when the dangers to the regime were no more than prospective. It was not to be destabilization that precipitated radical change, but radical change that precipitated destabilization. Why the Gorbachev regime risked destabilizing itself by "unforced" radicalism and how it pushed its policies through against fierce resistance will be the subject of the article.

Most Western observers initially saw Gorbachev as no more than a cosmetic reformer. When this view became untenable, they tended instead to place him into another familiar category of Russian ruler: the "revolutionary from above," who was pushing the country into a further phase of the revolution-stagnation-revolution cycle from which it seemed incapable of escaping.[2] This, however, was as wide of the mark as the earlier reading, even though the reforms indeed were instigated "from above" and revolutionary in scope. For revolutionaries-from-

---

[1] Seweryn Bialer, *The Soviet Paradox: External Expansion, Internal Decline* (London: Tauris, 1986), 143. An exception to the view that Gorbachev would prove a conventional Soviet leader was, however, provided by Archie Brown. See "Gorbachev: New Man in the Kremlin," *Problems of Communism* 32 (May-June 1985): 1–23.

[2] For a recent discussion of "revolution from above" see T. H. Rigby, *The Changing Soviet System: Mono-organisational Socialism from Its Origins to Gorbachev's Restructuring* (Brookfield, VT: Edward Elgar, 1990), 187–88, 210.

above from Peter onward had modernized in defense of an existing political structure, imposing change upon a population which was treated as a passive object and never encouraged to see itself as a subject. Gorbachev's perestroika, by contrast, tried to activate the masses and to create a genuinely participatory society.[3] The regeneration perestroika aimed at contained a distinct political component, and it was in fact as a *political* revolution that its major success was to be achieved. Gorbachev had good reason, however, not to advertise in advance what we can now see to have been perestroika's political purposes, and they were not to be officially acknowledged until after the Central Committee plenum of February 1990, at which the CPSU agreed to surrender its monopoly on power.

Within a few weeks of that historic plenum the editor of *Pravda*, a close Gorbachev aide, admitted that the idea of abolishing the party's monopoly had been mooted by the leadership "a very long time ago" and that the only question had been "how, in what form, and at what stage to introduce such changes." The leadership had first, however, to create the necessary preliminary conditions, among them a new body of deputies and a new Supreme Soviet. Only then, "in the concluding stages of the political reform," could it carry through what was "in the literal sense a revolution [*perevorot*], a completion and consummation of the remaking of the political system."[4] The editor of *Pravda* might seem an unlikely source for truthful comment on Soviet politics, but in this case the analysis was unerring. At the February plenum a relatively small group occupying the citadel of power in effect completed a carefully planned and most unusual "revolution from within" against the interests and increasingly against the wishes of a ruling class whose position had hitherto seemed unassailable.[5]

Gorbachev was to be the first successful revolutionary of this type, though there already had been unsuccessful essays in the genre. I shall discuss these earlier failures in order to pinpoint the conditions making for Gorbachev's success, but first I shall set out the basic features of revolution from within, indicating its phases and suggesting something of its typology.

1. Obviously enough, a revolution from within requires a would-be revolutionary (or group of revolutionaries), who needs to combine strategic vision with immense tactical skills, who needs to be enough of an "insider" to pass unchallenged into the powerhouse and yet in important respects will be, or will become, an outsider to its culture and *mores*. A striking case of one in whom the *outsider* facet

[3] M. S. Gorbachev, *Perestroika i novoe myshlenie dlia nashei strany i dlia vsego mira* (Moscow: Politizdat, 1987), 52–54; idem, "Sotsialisticheskaia ideia i revoliutsionnaia perestroika," *Pravda*, 26 November 1989.

[4] *Pravda*, 17 March 1990.

[5] I am taking the "ruling class" to comprehend the oligarchy proper—the few hundred members and candidate-members of the Central Committee with the twenty-odd Politburo members at their core—plus an encircling band of nonrulers who were nevertheless important decision-makers, were the immediate clients of the oligarchs and enjoyed great material privileges as a result. John H. Miller estimated the decision-making elite to amount to as many as two million. See "The Communist Party: Trends and Problems," in *Soviet Policy for the 1980s*, ed. Archie Brown and Michael Kaser (London: Macmillan, 1982), 3.

predominated was the early-nineteenth-century reformer Mikhail Speranskii.[6] A priest's son in a noble-dominated society and a convinced liberal and constitutional-ist in an autocratic state, Speranskii believed that radical change could be achieved only from within, infiltrated the powerhouse, and there necessarily became a "man with a mask" dependent upon the skill of a Machiavelli. Peter Stolypin provides a contrary example in the early twentieth century: a *bien-pensant* landowner and monarchical loyalist, who was far from a closet-liberal and yet would be driven by circumstances to become a would-be revolutionary.[7] These two figures define the boundaries of the revolutionary-from-within as a political type. The first was an ideologue and a Machiavel, a man in a hurry who fell, in Soviet jargon, into the voluntarist trap of wanting to "jump stages"; the second was a man of traditional thinking who defined himself as a "preserver" rather than a "transformer," a conser-vative who nevertheless came to see transformation as the essential condition of preservation. Gorbachev would share characteristics with both, but he resembled neither. He would trade by conviction as well as by necessity in the basic concepts of Soviet politics, yet would steadily impart new meaning to them and, in doing so, transform the system. At once insider and outsider, apparatchik and revolutionary, true believer and iconoclast, he would use his ambivalence as a vitally effective political weapon.

2. The would-be or potential revolutionary-from-within needs in turn a power-holder, individual or collective, who has been made insecure and therefore recep-tive to new thinking, who will be sufficiently persuaded by appeals pitched at his apparent self-interest (laced perhaps by arguments that attempt to reactivate a more or less extinct vein of idealism) to initiate a reform program put to him as imperative for regime-survival and will maintain it long enough for the program to win some degree of public following. The Soviet oligarchy of the 1980s, facing an economic decline with profound implications for the great-power status of the country, if not for its own security, was precisely such a power-holder.

3. The cooperative relationship between revolutionary and power-holder will, however, eventually become antagonistic, and a moment of truth will arrive when the power-holder glimpses through the mask of the reformer the visage of a revolu-tionary. If the revolutionary is to win the resultant struggle his challenge to the prevailing ideology needs to become increasingly direct and public, which not only will weaken the power-holder (undermining both his right to rule and his ability to dismiss the emergent challenger) but begin to sow disaffection among less-committed members of the ruling class. It was crucial that Gorbachev had at hand a counter-ideology that was potentially, yet not too obviously, extra-systemic, and through this he was able to enfranchize a large constituency of supporters, some within and some outside the party but all effectively excluded from the political

[6] See John Gooding, "The Liberalism of Michael Speransky," *Slavonic and East European Review* 64 (July 1986): 401–24. A different view is presented by Marc Raeff in *Michael Speransky: Statesman of Imperial Russia, 1772–1838*, 2d ed. (The Hague: Martinus Nijhoff, 1969).

[7] Aleksander Solzhenitsyn has provided a recent portrait of Stolypin in *The Red Wheel: A Narrative in Discrete Periods of Time* (London: The Bodley Head, 1989).

nation. Beginning in early 1987, Gorbachev would skillfully mobilize these people, to whom the lackluster authoritarianism of the oligarchs had become intolerable, in order to extract concessions from an increasingly defensive power-holder. There was as yet, however, no overt breach with the oligarchs, and Gorbachev continued, if with declining credibility, to maintain the fiction that the nation's interests were inseparable from those of the party.

4. The revolution from within could not be complete until its gains were codified and given institutional form; that is, until the revolutionary could detach himself from the power-holder and had replaced a structure that compelled his dependence by one that made him accountable instead to the newly enfranchised. Such a decisive shift of power-base could not be achieved while the old ideology remained formally in place. The buttresses sustaining the ideology might have been almost all removed, yet while its central tenet—the power-holder's claim as of right to power—remained, the revolution was incomplete. This was the position at the beginning of 1990. The party's surrender of its monopoly at the February 1990 plenum, followed shortly by the establishment of the presidency and of the non-party Presidential Council, then concluded the revolution. Eking out favorable circumstances by a dazzling display of political skills, Gorbachev had carried through his revolution with surprising ease, and in doing so must have exceeded the expectations of those for whom he had seemed the only hope during a period of oligarchic rule that, it was widely assumed, would continue indefinitely.[8] In completing a revolution from within he had not, however, completed a revolution; instead, he had precipitated one.

PRECEDENTS FOR REVOLUTION FROM WITHIN

Almost two centuries earlier Mikhail Speranskii's experience had highlighted some of the difficulties of the genre. His crucial deficiency was his dependence upon Alexander I, who, either deceived or unnaturally self-denying, was to have begun a process of change that would end in the liquidation of autocratic government. There was little support within the narrow circle of the "political nation" for such change or for any rights-of-man ideology; on the contrary, the upper nobility generally regarded Speranskii as a dangerous meddler. His problem was that he lacked any real constituency: the liberal-constitutional and socially mobile Russia he envisaged needed for its realization that very middle class which, had his endeavor succeeded, might eventually have come into being. Speranskii thus had to try to persuade the power-holder that discontent with the government was widespread and that comprehensive reform alone would stave off disaster.[9] But this was no more than make-believe, and once Alexander had had his moment of truth he simply called Speranskii's bluff.

As the heir to a genuinely revolutionary situation, Stolypin was in a potentially

---

[8] The assumption that oligarchy was the definitive Russian political mode was given an historical rationale by Edward L. Keenan, who in "Muscovite Political Folkways" interpreted the autocracy as an oligarchy in disguise and argued that the traditional "central core of 'nominal ruler + oligarchs' " was reestablished during the Soviet period." See *Russian Review* 45 (April 1986): 115–82.

[9] M. M. Speranskii, *Proekty i zapiski* (Moscow-Leningrad: Nauka, 1961), 163.

stronger position than his "predecessor." His "wager on the strong" was, moreover, quite different from Speranskii's social "wager" in that the people on whom his hopes reposed—those peasants capable of bettering themselves and emerging as a petty-proprietorial class fully integrated into the national community—already existed at least in embryo among the depressed peasantry of the commune. Yet it was a wager on a class which, even when it began to emerge, would lie outside the current political system and could be incorporated into it only by grace of the system's brokers. The advance of the peasants—economic, cultural and civic— could come only at the expense of the landowning nobles, who would have to yield influence in the zemstvos as well as in national institutions and fund the advance through increased taxation. And here Stolypin faced an insoluble problem. For the intransigence of the Second Duma had made him impose the restrictive electoral law of 3 June 1907, whose effect was to give a political veto to some twenty thousand major landowners.[10] Thus he strengthened a class that had reacted to the recent revolutionary events by shedding any tinge of liberal frondeurism and retreating into an embattled conservatism. The outcome was that the quasi oligarchy of landowners was able to sabotage all of his grandiose ideas for transforming Russia except one, his attempt to dissolve the commune. Like Speranskii, Stolypin would fall victim not only to a monarch who had lost faith in him but also to an upper class that had rightly come to see him as its adversary.

Gorbachev's "predecessors" differed from him, then, in that they lacked both significant societal support and the institutional means by which such support, had it existed, could have been brought to bear upon the power-holder and the privileged. There was nevertheless one important factor linking all three: each had at hand a political-cultural tradition that was rich in exploitable ambiguity, critical yet seemingly within-system, potentially liberating and yet capable of being coded in terms acceptable to the power-holder.

In Speranskii's case, this was a version of the fundamental law tradition, which at its most conservative saw no necessary incompatibility between the rule of law and the principle of autocracy. Speranskii most certainly did not endorse this conservative reading, yet its existence was crucial for him: he would exploit Alexander I's commitment to the rule of law, not expose the woolly thinking underlying it. And for most of his career he acted in a spirit of what might be called "false constitutionalism."[11] After all, no other kind of constitutionalism seemed within reach, and even if the autocrat did grant independent institutions they were likely to prove no more than castles on the sand. During the years 1808–12, however, Speranskii departed from his earlier caution and won Alexander's approval for a plan of radical reform, the central feature of which was to have been the establishment of an elected national assembly with a right of legislative veto. The ruler would, of course, have retained enormous powers; and Speranskii laid great emphasis on

[10] Roberta Thompson Manning, *The Crisis of the Old Order in Russia: Gentry and Government* (Princeton: Princeton University Press, 1982), 325.

[11] The term, however, was not first used in Russia until a century later, when P. N. Miliukov and other Kadets adopted it from Max Weber (*Scheinkonstitutionalismus*).

these powers and did his utmost to deflect attention from the long-term implications of the plan.[12] The unstated intention was nevertheless to initiate a process by which autocratic government was replaced by constitutional, and he had scored a major success in framing proposals that seemed to reflect Alexander's thinking yet would surreptitiously serve his own. The plan, however, risked stretching the ambiguities of the fundamental law tradition to breaking point. A common reformist vocabulary and a common commitment to the rule of law could not forever mask the difference between the autocrat and an adviser who wanted, not to give the regime a face-lift, but to change its nature altogether; and once Alexander realized this basic truth, Speranskiism as such was doomed.

The equivalent for Stolypin of the ambiguous fundamental law tradition lay in the moderate and elastic liberalism of his Duma allies, the Octobrists, whose instincts were oligarchic rather than democratic and who wanted a gradual, peaceful progression from absolutism to democracy by way of a gentry-dominated polity. Stolypin's alliance with the Octobrists was, however, no more than an expedient. His modern admirers regard him as a true liberal,[13] yet his "liberalism" had little in common with any of the current ones; he was at once more conservative than his Octobrist allies and more radical than they were. A fervent monarchist, he saw the monarchy as the necessary linchpin of the social order and he aimed to rescue it from the reactionary elements that were discrediting it. He was not, however, going to save it from reactionaries only to base it instead on the declining force of gentry liberalism: a revitalized monarchy could be rooted in nothing other than an emancipated and prosperous peasantry that was fully integrated into the community. Yet his peasant monarchism was hardly likely to be supported either by peasants or traditional monarchists; it was a vision without any strategy to realize it. By his blend of conservatism and radicalism he managed to appear "a reactionary to all on the left," in Solzhenitsyn's words, "yet practically a Kadet to the true Right";[14] and, unable to develop his alliance with the admittedly unstable Octobrist grouping, he had become isolated and politically dead well before the assassin's bullet felled him.

NEW FORCES AND NEW THINKING

The case histories of Speranskii and Stolypin highlight the advantages enjoyed by their "successor," who had both the societal and the ideological means of pushing his revolution to a conclusion. Unlike either Stolypin or Speranskii, who "wagered" on a class that had yet to be created, Gorbachev wagered on enterprising and highly educated people who already existed and were chafing at the bit. The intelligentsia constituted an exception to the general picture of contentment that had persuaded most Western observers that pressure for change was unlikely to come from outside the ruling class. If state and society had indeed reached a tacit agreement that was the guarantor of future stability, it was one from which many in the intelligentsia felt

---

[12] Which made the claiming of a right of legislative veto a matter of extreme delicacy. See Gooding, "The Liberalism of Michael Speransky," 408.

[13] For Stolypin's "liberalism" see Victor Leontovitsch, *Istoriia liberalizma v Rossii 1762–1914* (Paris: YMCA, 1980).

[14] Solzhenitsyn, *The Red Wheel*, 552.

excluded, and in two important respects their position had deteriorated in recent years.[15] First, the relative freedom they had enjoyed under Khrushchev had been curbed, and the hopes of still greater freedom which his de-Stalinization had aroused had by the mid-1970s been dashed. Perestroika's most ardent ideologues and supporters would in the event be found among intellectuals whose early adulthood had coincided with the Khrushchev thaw.[16] Secondly, the "social contract" of the Brezhnev years had sacrificed economic growth to worker welfare: economic policy had been markedly egalitarian, and the wage differential between skilled and unskilled had narrowed. The stability of the "stagnation era" had therefore been achieved at the expense of a key minority group whose standard of living had declined vis-à-vis that of the working class and whose desire for greater freedom had been frustrated no less than its desire for self-betterment. The dissatisfaction of this group provided Gorbachev with a potential weapon against the oligarchy. The Gorbachev revolution, as Jerry Hough remarked, would be in essence a revolt of the middle class.[17]

Gorbachev's program differed therefore from his "predecessors' " in being reactive—in being, that is, predicated upon social and cultural changes that had already taken place. A broad constituency of people who were sure to favor economic-growth policies and the relaxation of political controls lay at hand. What was in the making in fact during the later "stagnation" years was a coalition between reformers in the leadership, progressive intellectuals, and those with entrepreneurial skills and ambitions.[18] But if the potential coalition was to become an actual and effective one, its rank-and-file had to be enfranchised and brought within the political nation. Democratization was thus the indispensable condition of reform. The Soviet state had always taken great pride of course in its democratism. And fraudulent though its claims in this respect were, the very lip service it paid to democracy had kept alive in the party a real democratic commitment, which was expressed and passed on in what I shall call the Alternative Tradition.[19]

The Alternative Tradition was a distillation of the 1920s Soviet experience in

---

[15] See Igor' Kliamkin, "Kakaia ulitsa vedet k khramu," *Novyi mir* (November 1987): 158; and Ronald Amann, "Soviet Politics in the Gorbachev Era: The End of Hesitant Modernization," *British Journal of Political Science* 20 (July 1990): 303. The "social contract" between ruled and rulers as Stephen F. Cohen, for one, envisaged it offered the ruled vigilant national security, popular nationalism, law-and-order safeguards, cradle-to-grave welfarism, and improving material standards. See *Rethinking the Soviet Experience: Politics and History since 1917* (New York and Oxford: Oxford University Press, 1985), 151. Cohen warned, however, that the government's failure to fulfil important aspects of its consumer-welfare promises would create pressure for change.

[16] T. Zaslavskaia, "O strategii sotsial'nogo upravleniia perestroikoi," in *Inogo ne dano*, ed. Iu. F. Afanas'ev (Moscow: Progress, 1988), 28–29; N. Moiseev, "Zachem doroga, esli ona ne vedet k khramu," ibid., 55–56.

[17] Jerry Hough, *Russia and the West: Gorbachev and the Politics of Reform*, 2d ed. (New York and London: Touchstone, 1990), 178.

[18] It is to Moshe Lewin's great credit that he foresaw the emergence of precisely such a coalition in his *Political Undercurrents in Soviet Economic Debates: From Bukharin to the Modern Reformers* (London: Pluto Press, 1975), 352.

[19] For the importance of the party's formal democratism in keeping the commitment to real democracy alive see T. H. Rigby, *The Changing Soviet System*, 69.

the light of the country's subsequent history, and its basic belief was that the "administrative-command system" had been a violation and perversion of the socialism that Lenin and his party had tried to implant in postrevolutionary Russia. This "true socialism," buried as an official ideology at the end of the 1920s and largely submerged ever since, purportedly had two cardinal theses,

1. that the planned socialist economy should accommodate a considerable market element, that socialism was to be achieved by means of market relations rather than by defiance of them, and

2. that freedom of expression should be encouraged within a one-party system, the security of the party lying in the people's natural predisposition toward socialism—a predisposition that would be stronger for being uncoerced.[20]

The Alternative Tradition thus stood for the compatibility of plan and market, and of socialism and free expression; it was "alternative" in that its economic and political theses were the twin prongs of a single democratic or at least democratizing philosophy. Its leading figures (most notably Nikolai Bukharin) had long since been expunged from the record. The Tradition had, however, been given a powerful boost by Khrushchev with his attempt to stir popular initiative and to reintegrate the repressed and neglected into an expanded political community, his hostility to the apparatus as a barrier between party and people, and his belief that mass initiative alone could regenerate the economy. Its assumptions had subsequently inspired the unsuccessful attempt at economic reform in the 1960s; and its influence on the reformist economic thinking of the 1970s and early 1980s was to be fundamental.

No reformer in his senses could expect to pick up the pieces where they had been dropped six decades before; however, the Alternative Tradition was not so much a specific blueprint as a cluster of assumptions informed by the belief, or at least the hope, that democracy and a recognizably Leninist form of socialism were reconcilable. With its nostalgia for the lost opportunities of the 1920s, the Tradition was more a myth than a program, its basic elements preserved as it were in aspic and its ambiguities yet to be exposed by the test of experience. Would the market really prove compatible with a planned economy? Could the party give up its monopolism without jeopardizing its ruling position? In an urban and educated Soviet Union would democracy be socialism's ally rather than its gravedigger? In the repressive climate of Brezhnevism, the myth nevertheless united rather than divided people. A broad band of reformists gathered around it, united in the conviction that the country should return to the path of "true socialism" from which it had veered in the 1920s. Such people looked for radical within-system change once a new period of political relaxation began, and the Tradition, with its Leninist emphasis, provided them with both a focus and a protective mantle.

It helped that the Tradition's economic and political theses could be advanced separately and that their interdependence (the market requiring democracy, and democracy the market) did not need to be stressed. The political thesis came close

---

[20] The Tradition's assumptions were succinctly summarized by Fedor Burlatskii in "Kakoi sotsializm narodu nuzhen," *Literaturnaia gazeta*, 10 April 1988. They were reflected, too, in many contributions to Afanas'ev, *Inogo ne dano*.

44   *John Gooding*

to heterodoxy, even if it did not breach the one-party system as such; and how hard it was *not* to breach that system was shown by the devotedly socialist Roy Medvedev, who put himself in the dissident category by arguing that the cause of socialism and the Communist Party could be best served by "a loyal and legal opposition to the existing leadership."[21] But if the Tradition's political position led easily to dissidence, those who explored its economic legacy were more likely to stay within the system. And it was to be loyally oppositional economic thinkers, among whom A. P. Butenko, B. M. Kurashvili, and Tatiana Zaslavskaia stood out, who were to be the progenitors of the reform movement.

The "new thinking" of the "stagnation era" sprang from the realization that the Soviet economy was being outperformed by Western economies and that, as then constituted, it was doomed to fall further and further behind.[22] This realization did not make crypto-capitalists of the reformers, but it did lead them to conclude that the administrative-command system had utterly frustrated the potential of Soviet society. For them, the decline in growth rates indicated not only economic failure but also a failure of the entire Soviet system as Stalin and his heirs had shaped it. In devising an alternative economic model they went by implication well beyond the economic, urging that people should be induced rather than ordered to act and denying that Soviet society was essentially homogeneous and free of antagonistic contradictions. On the contrary, argued Butenko, the contradiction between production forces and the existing system of production relations was widening, and it could be narrowed only by fundamental political reforms, without which Soviet society faced the prospect of open conflict.[23] A major cause of the country's economic plight, in Zaslavskaia's view, lay in the passivity and low morale of the workforce, whose members were treated like cogs.[24] Democratization, Kurashvili believed, was "the moving force of economic and socio-cultural progress." All three implied that a dynamic economy was impossible without it; and Kurashvili for one distinguished between "quasi reform," which was "purely a reconstruction within the apparatus," and reform proper, which changed the relationship between apparatus and society and would have to be carried through "despite the resistance of conservative and inert elements in the state apparatus."[25]

The reformers took care not to overstep the line that divided the loyally oppositional from the dissident. That political reform should be seen as a condition of economic was, however, an inevitable conclusion from the failed reforms of the

[21] Roy A. Medvedev, *Political Essays* (Nottingham: Bertrand Russell Peace Foundation, 1976), 109.

[22] The assumption of the potential greater effectiveness of the Soviet economic system was widely shared in the West until the late 1960s. Thus Harold Macmillan confided to President Kennedy his fear that the capitalist system would be "beaten." See John Lloyd, "Is the Soviet Union Over?" *London Review of Books*, 27 September 1990.

[23] A. P. Butenko, "Protivorechiia razvitiia sotsializma kak obshchestvennogo stroia," *Voprosy filosofii*, 1982, no. 10:16–29. See also B. M. Kurashvili, "Gosudarstvennoe upravlenie narodnym khoziaistvom: perspektivy razvitiia," *Sovetskoe gosudarstvo i pravo*, 1982, no. 6:47.

[24] "The Novosibirsk Report," *Survey* 28 (Spring 1984): 89–90.

[25] Kurashvili, "Obektivnye zakony gosudarstvennogo upravleniia," *Sovetskoe gosudarstvo i pravo*, 1983, no. 10:43, 44.

1960s. The new economic model therefore contained the nucleus of a new political model that in principle was inimical to the monopolism of the CPSU, and this repudiation of the social monolith implied repudiation of the political monopoly as well. And here the "new thinking" parted with the 1920s realities which had inspired the Alternative Tradition. Bukharin had seen society becoming progressively more socialist as divergent interests and individualist tendencies were eliminated, whereas the reformers of the 1980s took their stand not only on social differentiation but on inevitably *increasing* differentiation and set out to adjust economic and political institutions accordingly.

The extra-systemic implications of the "new thinking," however, remained largely unexplored. Speculation about non-communist structures would have been self-defeating, given the weakness and fragmentation of the dissident movement. CPSU power was for the time being unassailable, and the reality the reformers faced was not dissimilar from that which had faced Speranskii—the only force capable of initiating change was the regime itself. The reform process had to begin with changes within the system, and not until the process was well under way could qualitative transformation be seriously contemplated. For the moment the reformers waited for a leader who shared at least their minimum aspirations, and such a leader they got in March 1985.

GORBACHEV BETWEEN WORLDS

In terms of our precedents Gorbachev, though clearly an oddity among the ill-educated Kremlin gerontocrats, was by no means an "outsider." His situation was markedly different from that of Speranskii, a humble provincial plucked from obscurity because of his talents who had to assimilate externally to a dominant class and political order that he secretly reviled. A peasant was at no formal disadvantage in a workers' and peasants' state, and this particular peasant, the son and grandson of party members, clung with almost filial piety to socialism as a basic ordering principle.[26] As he rose through the ranks of the Komsomol and Stavropol party organizations, Gorbachev's acceptance of the fundamental values and institutions of the Soviet state was most probably unqualified. The affinity here is not with Speranskii but rather with the autocracy's would-be redeemer, Stolypin. Yet if Gorbachev was no saboteur in the making, he gave early signs of a readiness to question received truths and outdated practices.[27] Here was a new type of educated apparatchik who had made his career in the post-Stalin era and had climbed into an elderly and fossilized ruling class whose mindset was very different from his own. His older colleagues were marked indelibly by the insecurities of the early revolutionary period and the 1930s; he by contrast had risen within the secure elite of a stable and unassailable regime. They had been frozen into doctrinal rigidity by

[26] "I can't go against my father and my grandfather," was how he defended socialism at a reunion of his Moscow University classmates. *The Guardian* (London), 20 June 1990. See also *Pravda*, 1 December 1990.

[27] The best evidence for the questioning mind of the young Gorbachev can be found in the memoir of his friend from student days (1950–55), Zdenek Mlynar, "Il mio compagno di studi Mikhail Gorbaciov," *L'Unita* (Rome), 9 April 1985.

dangers already experienced; he would respond flexibly and imaginatively to dangers that were merely prospective, and would prove open to ideas on the very margin of orthodoxy. It was natural that once he reached the Politburo the reformers should seek him out; it was no less natural that he should seek them out. For the economic problems of the Soviet Union began, as it happened, to become alarming around the very time when he reached the central leadership.[28]

During the early 1980s Gorbachev would as a result move between two worlds: the rising star of the Politburo, the "heir apparent" was being drawn by the intractable problems of the Soviet state into the milieu of the loyal opposition. Moving between such disparate worlds was far from easy, for if Andropov, unlike Brezhnev, recognized the gravity of the economic problem, he allowed only strictly orthodox palliatives to be applied to it. A close relationship nevertheless developed in this period between Gorbachev and some of the proponents of "new thinking": generation and culture provided natural links, and the rapport may have been helped too by the fact that Raisa Gorbachev as a pioneering sociologist belonged naturally among them. During these years intellectuals bombarded him with ideas which provided the basic material out of which the perestroika program would take shape.[29] As Gorbachev himself would recall, his safe became "clogged" with reform proposals. "People were clamoring that everything needed to be changed, but from different angles: some were for scientific and technical progress, others for reforming the structure of politics, and others still for new organizational forms in industry and agriculture. In short, from all angles there were cries from the heart that affairs could no longer be allowed to go on in the old way."[30] At his first meeting with Zaslavskaia, Gorbachev not only showed sympathy for her views but surprised her by responding to her criticisms with an "If only I could. . . ."[31]

But how much of the "new thinking" had he in fact absorbed? "We had the same ideas—about the independence of enterprises, about the need for realistic price policies, market relations and more progressive forms of salary," Zaslavskaia was to comment. "We met from time to time. . . . I could see how he was becoming wiser and more wide-thinking."[32] If there is a suggestion here of less than total communion, that is hardly surprising. Gorbachev's very position meant that his dealings with the radicals had to be circumspect—not for nothing does he refer to their proposals being kept in his "safe." The "new thinking," after all, had implications that threatened the supreme taboo of communism—the party's monopoly. Whether Gorbachev had accepted any such implication before March

[28] Anders Aslund, following Aganbegian, dates the cessation of Soviet economic growth to 1978. See *Gorbachev's Stuggle for Economic Reform: The Soviet Reform Process, 1985–88* (London: Pinter, 1989), 15.

[29] Nikolai Ryzhkov gave a statistic of 110 documents as the basis out of which the April 1985 program arose (*Pravda*, 8 January 1989). In conversation with American officials Gorbachev himself dated the origins of perestroika to 1982. See W. G. Miller, ed., *Towards a More Civil Society? The USSR under Mikhail Sergeevich Gorbachev* (New York: Harper and Row, 1989), 122.

[30] *Pravda*, 12 February 1990.

[31] Zaslavskaia, *The Second Socialist Revolution: An Alternative Soviet Strategy* (London: Tauris, 1990), xi.

[32] *The Guardian*, 28 February 1990.

1985 we have no way of knowing. To assume that he already had a blueprint of what became the mature reform program, which he kept concealed simply for tactical reasons, would be unrealistic. What seems certain, however, is that from the outset he accepted the underlying proposition of the "new thinking"—that without political change there could be no real economic change, that an out-moded political structure had to be brought into harmony with social realities. "It's all gone rotten," he would report Eduard Shevardnadze telling him during these years, and no doubt he thought the same.[33] Evidence of the time as to his state of mind came in a major speech of 10 December 1984 in which he admitted that the contradiction between production forces and production relationships had been a retarding factor in socioeconomic development and suggested the need for a more democratic political system.[34] It was the speech of someone who was steeped in the "new thinking" and accepted at least its minimum program, and predictably it incurred heavy censorship in *Pravda*. In talking so boldly he was taking advantage of the relative latitude available to a number two—which was all the greater when the number one happened to be too ill to exercise effective control. When he became general secretary three months later, the obstacles to speaking his own mind would, paradoxically, be more formidable.

GORBACHEV IN POWER: ACCELERATION

Between April 1985 and the end of 1986, Gorbachev's timid program of socioeco-nomic "acceleration" offered few hints of his later radicalism. He had good reason for acting with caution: he had few natural allies within an oligarchy that had chosen him for his vigor and competence rather than for his reformism, and even his control of cadres was of limited help since it did not reach to the oligarchy's inner circle. Furthermore, any high official he did remove kept his seat on the Central Committee, which tended as a result to become a focus of opposition to him. Indeed, despite the enforced retirement of more than one hundred members or candidate-members in April 1989 the Central Committee would remain a bulwark of resistance to reform into 1990. His position in the Politburo was helped by the early removal of Romanov, Tikhonov, and Grishin, though here too he faced a constant struggle. In time he would find support elsewhere to compensate for his weakness, but in 1985–86 he was not in a position to mobilize any countervailing forces.

It may be, of course, that Gorbachev was not merely acting under constraint during this period: he had not yet, some would argue, worked out his basic strategy, was reacting ad hoc to the problems of the job, and did not become even a semiradical until circumstances forced him to toward the end of 1986.[35] Certainly he

---

[33] *Pravda*, 1 December 1990.

[34] Gorbachev, "Zhivoe tvorchestvo naroda," in M. S. Gorbachev, *Izbrannye rechi i stat'i*, vol. 2 (Moscow: Politizdat, 1987), esp. 80–84.

[35] Seweryn Bialer, for instance, has argued that it took him one and a half years "to develop even the outlines of his program." See "The Changing Soviet Political System: The Nineteenth Party Confer-ence and After," in *Politics, Society and Nationality inside Gorbachev's Russia*, ed. Seweryn Bialer (Boulder and London: Westview, 1989), 193.

48   *John Gooding*

was to learn on the job; yet the view of him as a reluctant and belated convert to radicalism ignores the political motifs which were increasingly noticeable in his statements from the fall of 1985 onward. "I wish, comrades," he told the October 1985 plenum, "to emphasize as forcefully as I can: without the utmost widening and deepening of socialist democracy, that is, without the creation of conditions for the daily, active, and effective participation of all working people, their collectives and organizations, in resolving the problems of governmental and social life, we cannot go forward with success."[36] The Twenty-seventh Party Congress the following year would still be heavy with the weight of Soviet traditionalism, yet here too Gorbachev managed to introduce a distinctly new note in his treatment of democracy, linking it with glasnost, the rule of law, and the rights and freedoms of the citizen, and insisting that "acceleration of social development is unthinkable and impossible without further development of socialist democracy and of all its aspects and manifestations."[37] And in the summer of 1986 he launched the notion of perestroika as a revolution that would embrace not only economic life but "social relationships, the political system, the spiritual-ideological sphere, the style and methods of work by the party and all our cadres." He suggested too that the revolution was only beginning. The more perestroika advanced, he told a Siberian audience, the more complex its task would become and the more "the huge scale and scope of the work ahead of us" would be revealed. Many conceptions would be shown to "lag behind the needs and tasks of the present and, all the more so, the tasks of future development," among them those concerning democracy.[38]

Political motifs were, of course, subordinate to economic ones in the "acceleration" program, but we should not infer that Gorbachev's later democratization was a reluctant response to circumstances he had failed to foresee at the start of his general-secretaryship. The most compelling reason for democratization was that it offered the only effective method for overcoming resistance to structural reform, a resistance that emanated not only from the middle level of the apparatus but was entrenched at the party's highest levels.[39] Structural reform was incompatible with continued oligarchic rule and the monopolism which underpinned it, and, were the oligarchic hegemony to remain, the reforms would be as surely emasculated as Kosygin's had been. For that very reason a merely notional democratization was inadequate; so too was an "inverted democracy" that established certain freedoms at the grass roots but left the supreme political organs untouched.[40] The only effective democratization would be one targeted at an incorrigibly conservative ruling class itself.

The general view of Western observers up to and indeed beyond 1985 was that no party leader would contemplate such a democratization. The oligarchs would

[36] Gorbachev, *Izbrannye rechi i stat'i* 3:8.

[37] Ibid., 235.

[38] Ibid. 4:37, 38.

[39] Zaslavskaia, *The Second Socialist Revolution*, 177–80, 190.

[40] On "inverted democracy" see Seweryn Bialer, "Gorbachev's Program of Change: Sources, Significance, Prospects," in *Gorbachev's Russia and American Foreign Policy*, ed. Seweryn Bialer and Michael Mandelbaum (Boulder and London: Westview, 1988), 256.

obviously have everything to lose from it; and so would the leader himself if he were fully identified with the oligarchy or harbored autocratic aspirations of his own. The general secretary, however, was neither an autocrat nor any ordinary oligarch. He was in the deeply ambiguous position of *arch-oligarch*, locked in a frustrating and potentially antagonistic relationship with his fellow oligarchs from which he was looking for an exit. Stalin had set the precedent of an autocratic resolution of the conflict, but Khrushchev represented a more relevant alternative—neutralizing the oligarchs with democratic tendencies. For democratization did not threaten the arch-oligarch as it did the ruling class as a whole: on the contrary, by expanding the political nation he was more likely to augment his own power at the expense of his co-rulers.

This does not mean that Gorbachev launched perestroika as a populist gamble, though the program's populist potential can only have encouraged him to pursue it. But it is to say that by the early 1980s autocracy would have been a wholly inadequate, indeed archaic response to deepening problems that threatened to jeopardize the stability of the political order and the great-power position of the state. The question that loomed large by the close of 1986 was whether Gorbachev would be able to take the alternative route and break an oligarchic power that had come to seem the country's natural political mode.

GORBACHEV IN POWER: DEMOCRATIZATION

Till then he had tried to progress by means of agreement with the oligarchs, among whom Egor Ligachev had emerged as a tenacious guardian of the system's essentials. That, however, had proved impossible, and continuation of the consensual approach threatened him with an impasse. At this juncture Gorbachev changed tactics and entered into direct conflict with the oligarchy's conservatives. His speech to the January 1987 plenum proved so contentious that the plenum met only after three postponements and after what one can only assume were bloody behind-the-scenes battles.[41] The passions were inevitable, for Gorbachev now raised democratization from its previous subordinate status and placed it unequivocally at the heart of his program, from which it would never thereafter be dislodged, arguing that "democratism is not simply a slogan but the essence of perestroika" and showing how seriously he took it by suggesting electoral reform with secret ballots and a choice of candidates.[42]

To abandon consensualism was a high-risk tactic, but this does not mean that Gorbachev adopted it reluctantly, still less that the new approach was improvised. The resistance to reform was foreseeable and had surely been foreseen, and the question was not whether Gorbachev tried to overcome it by democratization but when. From now on democratization doubled as both strategy and tactic, since it was indispensable not only for national regeneration but for the survival in power of the regeneration program's architects. In an earlier reforming epoch the radical litterateur Nikolai Dobroliubov had noted apropos of within-system reform how

[41] *Pravda*, 26 February 1987.
[42] Ibid., 28 January 1987.

hard it was to turn over a box if you happened to be inside it, but how easy the task became once you stepped outside the box.[43] In unleashing democratization Gorbachev now stepped outside his box. The decision was fraught with incalculable consequences, but one inevitable consequence stood out: he and his outnumbered supporters within the ruling class faced a battle they would lose unless they could modify the power equation by invoking societal forces on their side. They could hardly avoid the fate of Speranskii and Stolypin unless they moved rapidly to legitimize and encourage public opinion, and Gorbachev's speech to the January 1987 plenum was a first step toward this, loosing ideas that were to be profoundly corrosive of oligarchic power. The oligarchs' predictable resistance thus had the effect of activating the suppressed democratic implications of the "new thinking," and once these ideas had been loosed with the general secretary's imprimatur, they could hardly be recalled. From that time the qualitative transformation so desired by many oppositional intellectuals began to occur. It was a transformation in which they would take a major part, and Gorbachev must have realized that the framers of the message would demand an increasing say in its content. Yet the main theme of the phase of perestroika that began in January 1987 and ended three years later would not be the problem of containing the unleashed forces of democracy; rather, it would be the defeat of a defiant, if now defensive, oligarchy.

The dominant event of the phase, coming almost in the middle, was the Nineteenth Party Conference, which provided the first real sign that democratization might turn the party rank-and-file against the oligarchs. It also saw the initiation of a still more risky tactic of revitalizing the system of soviets. Democratization within the party might strengthen Gorbachev vis-á-vis the party establishment, but a revitalized soviet system, crowned by an effective working parliament, offered a still greater prize—through it he might deploy popular pressure against a recalcitrant oligarchy and even create for himself an institutional position largely detached from and immune to the party.

The need to reconcile the oligarchs to policies that would hurt their interests forced Gorbachev to stretch "Speranskiism" to its limits. As Speranskii had taken advantage of different understandings of the concept of "fundamental law," so Gorbachev made the most of the different resonances in the Soviet context of "democracy." And like Speranskii he played hard upon the insecurities of the power-holder, justifying perestroika by arguing that the policies of the "stagnation" years had precipitated not only an economic, but a political crisis.[44] He had made no such diagnosis in 1985–86, but as his policies became more radical they demanded a more clamorous rhetoric. He tried to persuade the oligarchs that if the

---

[43] N. A. Dobroliubov, *Literaturnaia kritika* (Moscow: Khudozhestvennaia literatura, 1979), 306.

[44] A first reference to "the danger of the growth of crisis-type phenomena" came in his speech to the January 1987 Plenum (*Pravda*, 28 January 1987). Thomas Remington refers to a samizdat account of the plenum's proceedings, according to which Gorbachev compared the Soviet crisis with the crises in other socialist countries and argued that the Soviet Union, unlike its neighbors, could not look elsewhere for help in solving its problems. See "A Socialist Pluralism of Opinions: *Glasnost* and Policy-Making under Gorbachev," *Russian Review* 48 (July 1989): 273. By the summer of 1987, Gorbachev was using the "crisis" argument more full-bloodedly. See, for instance, Gorbachev, *Perestroika*, 11.

party backed him it would retain its vanguard role and dominate the new politics, thus exploiting their hopes as well as their fears. Indeed, throughout this phase he treated the party's leading position as a sine qua non of the reform process, as in a sense it obviously was. The refurbished party riding the waves of democratic politics would have little in common other than the name with the historic CPSU, which had been an instrument of oligarchic (and for a time, autocratic) absolutism. His apparent refusal to recognize any possible disjunction between the interests of the party and the nation was nevertheless by no means hypocritical. The party remained the only effective weapon of change, as well as the only means of control over the forces he was unleashing, and he would hardly want to diminish its stature while he exercised power simply as its chief executive.

There was, however, a contradiction between his continued insistence on party supremacy and the reform process itself, highlighted by a steady revaluation of ideology which took the premises of the "new thinking" to their natural conclusion by repudiating party monopolism. Communism and the "new Soviet man" disappeared, giving way to a more traditional man whose self-improvement and even proprietary instincts were now harnessed to more modest goals—a "new society" and "qualitatively new condition of socialism."[45] The new socialism—presented, of course, as Leninist socialism reborn—was defined above all in terms of a democracy that was participatory, rights-oriented, and of its essence pluralistic; and at the Nineteenth Party Conference and thereafter Gorbachev explicitly contrasted such a democracy with the older, counterfeit version.[46] Pluralism, a key concept from 1988, was admittedly qualified by "socialist" and was not to lose the qualifier until 1990, but it laid an ax at the root of the ideological fiction that legitimized the oligarchs' monopoly—the single interest and hence single will of the Soviet people.[47] In a society of divergent interests and desires, the task of the state was not to create an artificial unity by repression but rather to manage diversity, and use it positively, by institutionalizing it.[48] Pluralism of opinions, in short, pointed inevitably toward pluralism of politics.

Ideological revaluation prepared the way for a cardinal reform of the political system, first outlined at the Nineteenth Party Conference. The essence of the reform was a clear delimitation of the functions of party and state, "delimitation" being no more than a euphemism for a transfer of powers to the latter. The reforms, which came on stream in 1989 with the creation of the Congress of People's Deputies, the revamped Supreme Soviet, and the chief executive office of Chairman

<hr/>

[45] The disappearance of communism from Gorbachev's discourse is reflected in the indexes to the volumes of his *Izbrannye rechi i stat'i*. The first volume (covering 1967 to 1983) contained twenty-eight references to "communism" or "communist construction." By vol. 3 (October 1985 to July 1986) the number of such references had fallen to twelve; vol. 4 (July 1986 to April 1987) had only three such references; and in vol. 6 (December 1987 to October 1988) there were a mere two.

[46] For such a contrast see *Pravda*, 29 June 1988.

[47] On pluralism see the article by Thomas Remington cited in note 44.

[48] Decision making, Gorbachev pointed out at the Nineteenth Party Conference, might be followed and not merely preceded by "a lack of general agreement," and such a lack was "a normal phenomenon for the democratic process" (*Pravda*, 29 June 1988).

52   *John Gooding*

answerable to the new institutions, weakened the oligarchy by exposing its members to a touch of the democracy they had always purported to defer to; and Gorbachev made ruthless use of the March 1989 elections, which were fought in conditions of unprecedented openness, to rout a number of hardliners.[49] But if the "politicization of social awareness," as Gorbachev called it, increased pressure on party conservatives, it also showed up the illogicality of his own continued defense of party monopolism. The glaring contradiction between an authoritarian ruling party whose monopolistic claims remained unretracted and a popularly elected legislature almost instantly recognized as the nation's parliament cried out to be resolved.

By the second half of 1989 the lines of command in the Soviet political system had in fact become badly blurred as nascent proto-democratic politics vied with old-style directive politics. The system had lost coherence, and Gorbachev's own dualism of functions indicated as much. As general secretary-cum-chairman he uncomfortably straddled two competing political cultures, his authority deriving both from the party's increasingly threadbare legitimacy and from an individual exercise of will by the electors. The quandary of the democratizer who was not yet willing or able to free himself from the original undemocratic source of his power deserved some sympathy, of course, and deputies did not press him on the question of which office claimed his greater loyalty. The issue of ultimate authority was being resolved anyway by the processes he had set in motion, and Nikolai Ryzhkov for one noticed how the new Supreme Soviet was encroaching on the policy-making functions of plenum and Politburo.[50] Short of a retrogression, which would have violated all that had been achieved since January 1987, integrity could be restored to the political system only by sacrificing party monopolism and redefining the executive power in such a way as to make it unambiguously dependent upon the legislature. These were the changes that public opinion clearly wanted and that ideological revisions required, and Gorbachev would push them through with skill and decisiveness in February-March 1990, thus consummating the revolution from within.

THE REVOLUTION FROM WITHIN AND AFTER

The reform movement had been nourished by the assumption that removing the administrative-command system would leave in place a reinvigorated party pursuing socialism with the nation's support. By now, however, that assumption seemed naive and unrealistic. Partial or "commune" democracy might have been realizable in the 1920s, but in 1990 the democratization process either had to break the bounds of partial democracy or go into reverse.[51] The CPSU was no longer an ascendant force riding a recent revolutionary triumph, nor did it face a peasant population that, out of deference to the ruling power if not out of socialist conviction, might

[49] Including a candidate member of the Politburo, Iurii Solov'ev, first secretary of the Leningrad regional party committee, who though running unopposed failed to achieve the 50 percent of the poll necessary to be elected.

[50] *Pravda*, 21 July 1989.

[51] For "commune democracy" see Richard Sakwa, "Commune Democracy and Gorbachev's Reforms," *Political Studies* 37 (June 1989): 224–43.

have accepted its nostrums and its paternalistic guidance. Instead, a demoralized party, its self-confidence sapped by unprecedented critical scrutiny, faced an electorate on which decades of indoctrination had had so little impact that an opinion poll of 1990 found that less than 20 percent of the respondents believed in socialism, and only 14 percent in the party that claimed to embody it.[52] Those who, taking the Alternative Tradition at its face value, had assumed the question of democracy could be fudged had merely deluded themselves.

Removing the party's discredited monopoly without doing damage to socialism itself would not be easy. Like the sixteenth-century reformers who had set out to save Catholicism from the Papacy, the radicals who insisted that the party had to shed its monopoly if socialism were to recover underestimated the dependence of the faith upon the institution that had for so long been its exclusive custodian. In the case of the CPSU, its privileged position had been enshrined in the constitution since the 1930s and had existed in reality since the early 1920s. For most people, monopolism—the right to rule, to define the articles of faith, and to exact obedience to them—was the defining feature of the party, and socialism was inextricable from it.[53] If this was the view of outsiders, it was all the more so for traditionalists within the party, who could be expected to make a fierce defense of what for them was a holy of holies.

In this final struggle with the oligarchy, which would be fought in the forum of a still highly conservative Central Committee, Gorbachev needed support from outside the ruling class as never before. Monopolism might have been undermined, but only strong and concerted pressure would make it fall. The pressure would have to come, in the first place, from the party's rank-and-file, and a carefully orchestrated campaign to deploy them against the elite came to a head on the eve of the crucial February 1990 plenum, when *Pravda* gave front-page coverage to a meeting between Gorbachev and miners' representatives. The miners expressed strong hostility to the apparatchiks, whom they saw as blocking perestroika's progress. "The leading role of the CPSU," one complained, "has degenerated into the leading role of the apparatus"—and several were promptly coopted as delegates to the plenum.[54]

Such support from working-class party members, the party's traditional bastion, was an unqualified asset for the leadership, but the revolt of another key group was a decidedly mixed blessing. On the Sunday before the plenum opened a procession of some two hundred thousand people swept with its shouts and banners into Revolution Square, where radical deputies and other representatives of the intelligentsia attacked the party's dominant position. *Obshchestvennost'*—in the prerevolutionary sense of critically thinking intellectuals—was challenging *vlast'* for

---

[52] *Soviet Weekly* (London), 29 November 1990.

[53] As recently as 1988, Milovan Djilas maintained that "the essence of any Communist system is the monopolistic rule of society by the Communist party." See "Djilas on Gorbachev: Milovan Djilas and George Urban in Conversation," *Encounter* 71 (September/October 1988): 3. And even more recently "Z" wrote of the leading role of the party as "the supreme taboo of communism." See "To the Stalin Mausoleum," *Daedalus* 119 (Winter 1990): 328.

[54] *Pravda*, 9 February 1990.

54   *John Gooding*

the first time since the revolutionary period, and was doing so with apparent impunity. Such "support" implied a challenge not merely to oligarchism but to the party itself, and how little some in authority welcomed this could be gauged from *Pravda*'s sour report of the event.[55] The demonstration had indeed been an uncomfortable reminder that the forces unleashed since January 1987 might engulf the leadership and that the position of a vanguard party within a democratizing polity might prove untenable.

For the time being, however, pressure from the party's grass roots and from *obshchestvennost'* had achieved what the leadership wanted. Coerced from without and even outnumbered within their own forum (this being an "expanded" plenum), the oligarchs bowed to the inevitable and surrendered their monopoly. They protested loudly, but not a voice was raised in defense of monopolism itself; and only a single vote, ironically that of the liberal Boris Yeltsin, was cast against the draft platform for the forthcoming congress, which included the proposition "The CPSU does not claim a monopoly and is ready for political dialogue and cooperation with all who stand for the renewal of socialist society."[56]

It was an historic surrender, and its natural sequel came a few weeks later with the conversion of Gorbachev's chairmanship into a presidency with enhanced powers and greater independence of the party, whose holder would be elected by the nation—though in this case the election was rushed through on grounds of urgency by the Congress of People's Deputies alone. In his initial address as president Gorbachev envisaged his task as being not to act on behalf of "some separate layer and political tendency" but rather to be "the representative of the whole nation."[57] Party and nation had at last been uncoupled, and the relationship between Gorbachev's two offices had as a result been clarified: he would be chief executive of state first and head of the party second. The party, demoted to a "separate polticial tendency," would henceforth be no more than one of the interest groups within the nation, if much the most influential. As for the Politburo, which for almost forty years had symbolized the power of the oligarchy, that was almost casually pushed to the sidelines. It would from now on meet irregularly and consider only party affairs, while the main policy-making forum became instead the nonparty Presidential Council.

The revolution of February-March 1990 came as a bitter blow to the ruling class, which faced dispossession as a result, and diehards then began a determined rearguard action against a leadership they felt had betrayed them. The election in June of Ivan Polozkov as first secretary of the newly created Russian Communist Party suggested that they might well regain control of the CPSU at the forthcoming Twenty-eighth Party Congress. Yet the attempt at oligarchic revanche was in the end defeated. It enjoyed strong sympathy from the delegates, but most proved in the end to be conservative-realists rather than conservative-irreconcilables, accept-

[55] Ibid., 5 February 1990.
[56] Ibid., 13 February 1990.
[57] Ibid., 16 March 1990.

ing the diminished status of the party as an unavoidable evil.[58] Gorbachev thus triumphed against the apparent odds over his conservative opponents, the chief of whom, Ligachev, was now ousted from both the Politburo and the Central Committee. His victory had, however, done no more than put a temporary halt to the revanchist movement, which again gathered strength in the fall and by its advance provoked an increasing self-assertion by the radicals. By the end of 1990 it was clear in fact that the politics of confrontation had displaced the politics of consensus, and as a result the prospect of a "Speranskiian" outcome—of peaceful qualitative change through the medium of but ultimately transforming existing structures—had become more or less negligible. In Gorbachev's case, however, it was not failure that threatened to be his undoing but rather his very real, if partial, success.

What exactly had he achieved? In February 1990, if the editor of *Pravda* is to be believed, there had been a *perevorot*— which may indicate no more than a coup d'état, but may also indicate a revolution too limited or incomplete to be seen as a *revoliutsiia*.[59] There was certainly nothing of a coup about what happened in February 1990; the outcome of the plenum had, on the contrary, been prepared not only by the political and ideological developments of the preceding five years but by socioeconomic and cultural tendencies of much longer duration. Yet the February changes, however *zakonomerno* they occurred, represented no more than a preliminary stage in the process of reconstructing power relationships and by no means took the process to a conclusion. The main achievement of Gorbachev's revolution from within had been the destruction of oligarchic absolutism, which had rested upon the sacrosanct status and monopoly rights of the Communist Party. The pseudo-democratic facade behind which oligarchic power had been exercised had been stripped away; the desacralization of the party had been given a powerful fillip by the removal of its privileged status; and the institutional and juridical preconditions for a pluralistic society and a multiparty political system had to a considerable extent been established.

That, however, was the limit of the achievement of a revolution that had dismantled the formal mechanism of absolutism without eliminating the conditions that had made absolutism possible. The party had lost its natural right to rule, and policy-making had in part been admitted to the public domain. Yet if the party faced dispossession it had not so far been dispossessed, and it continued to rule through a largely unreconstructed *nomenklatura*, between which and the democratic opposition only the president could mediate. Gorbachev, however, cut an increasingly ambiguous figure, and all the unresolved contradictions of the Alternative Tradition now seemed to be expressed in him. Had perestroika been a program of economic reform and societal regeneration whose primary purpose had been to assure the internal and external security of the party-state? Or was its democratizing element not merely instrumental but an attempt to inculcate the culture of

---

[58] I discuss the distinction between "conservative-realists" and "conservative-irreconcilables" in "The XXVIII Congress of the CPSU in Perspective," *Soviet Studies* 43 (March 1991): 247.

[59] *Pravda*, 17 March 1990.

democracy? The ambiguities helped explain both the initial success of the perestroika coalition, which had embraced structural and nonstructural reformers alike, and the fact that the coalition was now manifestly falling apart. Gorbachev's strategy had been to advance gradually toward a version of social democracy with the support of the broad mass of the population, whose innate loyalty to socialism and the CPSU would enable him to disregard "extremists" at either end of the spectrum and to side-step the Tradition's contradictions. By the end of 1990, however, this strategy lay in ruins. Far from dominating Soviet politics from an expanding center, he faced "extremists" to Right and Left who were encroaching fast on the middle ground by offering clear-cut solutions to the ethnic and economic problems which had undermined any possibility of consensualism.

Revolts of the minor nationalities in the Baltic region, the Caucasus, Moldova, and even the RSFSR now jeopardized the very existence of the multinational state, and in doing so helped the conservatives by enabling them to exploit not merely Russian nationalism and great-power chauvinism but deep-rooted fears of anarchy as well. The feeling of a threat to the very fabric of everyday life was heightened by growing economic dislocation. Perestroika had been predicated upon the support of the intelligentsia, and by its middle-class values and emphases it had run a foreseeable risk of alienating mass support. Few would have guessed, however, that the reform program would precipitate a disastrous deterioration in living conditions—empty shelves becoming for most the emblem of Gorbachevism—and thereby put at risk the sympathy not only of the working class but even of those at whose interests it had been aimed. There had in fact been a fateful asynchronism of the political and the economic: at the very time when oligarchic power was falling victim to democratization, an economic crisis, accompanied by severe ethnic troubles, was creating pressures that an embryonic democratic polity underpinned by the frailest of democratic cultures would have great difficulty in withstanding.

Gorbachev's revolution from within had thus proved more negative than positive: it had destroyed one political-economic system but not replaced it by another. The very "withinness" of the revolution had vitiated its effectiveness, since it had to proceed under the auspices of that which it was in fact to undermine. What occurred was a revolution against the effective party (namely, the oligarchy) and the mental constructs which sustained it, carried through in the name of Leninist socialism, and its result was to erode whatever credibility the official ideology still possessed without generating any alternative ideology or even ethic that could command general assent. As with ideology, so with power-relationships. The party had lost its right to rule but not its ruling position, and yet now found that it could no longer rule effectively. Perestroika's unanticipated success and its transcending of the modest parameters within which it began resulted therefore in a breakdown rather than a transfer of authority. The revolution left in its wake a wounded party, a more or less destroyed ideology, a president weakened and bewildered by the collapse of the political center and hence of his strategy, a vociferous democratic opposition given populist appeal by the personality of Boris Yeltsin, and forces of entrenched conservatism which showed every intention of fighting to claw back what they had lost. The reformers had set out to restore to Russian politics the possibilities and the squandered socialist potential of the 1920s, but they had finished by confronting the country with choices so stark and fundamental that they recalled 1917 instead.

[20]

The Making of Elections to the Congress of People's Deputies (CPD) in March 1989

Vladimir N. Brovkin

In March 1989, for the first time since 1918, contested elections to a Soviet legislative body, specifically to a Congress of People's Deputies (CPD), took place in the Soviet Union. This step represents an important stage in Gorbachev's plan to restructure the Soviet political system. To what extent were these elections really contested? What were the mechanics of the electoral process? What has been the impact on the politics of the Soviet Union? Does the Communist Party have a chance to maintain its "leadership role" or will it be swept away by the new political forces?

Nominally a supreme legislative institution, the CPD's role is limited to electing the Supreme Soviet, the actual legislature. Will the new Supreme Soviet exercise control over the national budget? Will the government be responsible to the legislature? It remains to be seen whether the Supreme Soviet will acquire the authority of a real legislature or whether it will continue to be a rubber stamp for decisions taken by the Politburo. The study of elections, however, allows us to have a glimpse at popular involvement in politics and to see what programs and initiatives the electorate favored in different Soviet republics. It makes it possible to analyze the new mechanisms for party control and manipulation in the era of Gorbachev's restructuring.

The Structure of Elections

Five hundred forty-two Supreme Soviet members have been chosen from 2,250 members of the CPD.[1] These delegates survived the weeding out process at several preceding stages. There are two large components in the CPD: the corporate delegates, that is, those delegated by political and societal organizations such as CPSU, Komsomol, trade unions, Women's Committee, Academy of Sciences, etc., and delegates elected in the territorial and nationality-territorial districts. The focus here is on those who were elected to the CPD and how.

---

[1] "TsIK deistvuet," *Agitator* (no. 3, 1989).

418   *The Russian Review*

The Corporate Delegates

There is no doubt that the allocation of 750 seats in the CPD to corporate delegates was designed to counterbalance the possible unpredictability of the delegates elected from the electoral districts. It can be presumed that the one hundred CP delegates are bound by party discipline to support Gorbachev's policies. Virtually nothing is known on how one hundred delegates from the trade unions were selected. For the most part, corporate delegates were not elected, but selected by existing hierarchical bodies.[2] In theory, local organizations of a given corporate entity, like trade unions or the Komsomol, were supposed to nominate their candidates, and the all-Union body was to make the selection at national plenums. In practice, however, the lists of those to be selected were prepared in advance. Local organizations were advised whom to nominate and whom not to. If an undesirable candidate were nominated anyway, the national plenum had ample opportunity to strike off his or her name. Andrei Sakharov and other prominent reformers in the Academy of Sciences were not initially admitted despite protests from numerous research institutions at a lower level.[3] The selection process of corporate delegates was less democratic than elections in the territorial districts because no actual voting by the electorate was involved. The corporate delegates are definitely representatives of the existing cultural and political establishment.

Elections at Territorial Electoral Districts

There were three basic stages to the election process in the territorial and nationality-territorial districts. The first was nomination of candidates to take place by 24 January 1989. The second stage, up to February 22, was for the selection of officially registered candidates whose names appeared on the ballot. The third stage was the election campaign among the registered candidates culminating in national voting on March 26. Scrutiny of these stages makes it possible to determine how a candidate was nominated, how undesirable candidates were weeded out, and to what extent elections were actually contested.

According to electoral law, collectives at enterprises, citizens' groups of residents, and individuals had a right to nominate candidates. The initial number of candidates was not limited. It was also possible for someone to nominate him/herself. Thus the two major patterns in the initial nomination process were nomination at enterprises and nomination by groups of residents.

---

[2] For the list of one hundred delegates from the CPSU, see *Current Digest of Soviet Press*, February 15, 1989.

[3] A. Borodenkov, "Nashim mneniem prenebregli," *Moskovskie Novosti*, February 12, 1989.

March 1989 Elections to the CPD   419

Nomination at Enterprises

Clearly it is hard to generalize about nomination procedure in a huge country. There certainly was great diversity, including both true contests and manipulated nominations. Nevertheless, certain patterns are clearly discernable. At all stages of the election campaign, there was more glasnost, more observance of the law, and more popular participation in the big cities such as Moscow and Leningrad and in the Baltic Republics. In outlying Russian provinces and in the Central Asian Republics, the process was controlled much more strictly by local party hierarchies. How did they control it?

In a typical Russian province, the obkom ideological and cadres commissions, as well as the city and district commissions, saw it as their duty to get involved in the election process. On one hand, the party hierarchies wanted to make sure that their party, the Communist Party candidates, got elected. On the other hand, as actual masters in their provinces, acting as state bodies, they had to make sure, at least by the letter of the law, that all candidates regardless of party membership had an equal chance in the election campaign. The signals to local party authorities from the top were contradictory. On one hand, the journal *Agitator* instructed its party activists to do everything possible to assure the victory of Communists; on the other hand, party leaders were instructed to conduct elections properly.[4] Some party leaders tried to reconcile the two objectives. As a party functionary in the cadres commission of Saratov province explained,

> We are not interfering in the process of nomination. We do not send them lists of candidates as in previous years. But we fully realize that the process of nomination must be guided.[5]

By electoral law, the supreme duty of the Electoral Commission was to provide equal opportunity to all collectives and individuals in nominating candidates. In practice, Electoral Commissions consisted of local party officials who clearly could not reconcile this with party instructions to promote their own party candidates. In the above-mentioned electoral district No. 289 in the city of Engels (Saratov province), the chairman of the Electoral Commission V. Vlasov was at the same time the second secretary of the Engels City Party Committee. He said, "There will be chaos if everybody starts nominating their own candidates." His way of guiding the nomination process was to "allow the honor of nominating a candidate in this district to the largest enterprise."[6] This was a clear violation of the law. It was not up to the Electoral Commission or the party

---

[4] "Vybory i agitatsiia," *Agitator* (no. 2, 1989), p. 14.
[5] V. Nikolaeva, "Luchshego iz odnogo?" *Izvestiia*, January 14, 1989.
[6] Ibid.

420   *The Russian Review*

committee to "allow" nominations. It was the right of collectives and individuals. The old mentality is clearly evident here. An *Izvestiia* correspondent observed that "it does not even enter anybody's mind to nominate candidates on their own." They all waited for instructions from above. "In many large collectives leaders assume a wait and see attitude. What command will come from the higher ranking party organization?"[7] This shows in whose hands the nomination procedure was. Certainly not in the hands of collectives as such, but in the hands of party committees, which waited for "recommendations" from the city and obkom.

What were these recommendations? At this stage, the party bosses primarily decided which enterprises were going to nominate candidates and which were not. In the above-mentioned district No. 289, one secretary of an enterprise party committee went to the city committee to ask for "advice." They advised her that her enterprise should not nominate any candidate. She told the *Izvestiia* correspondent that her collective had decided not to nominate, whereas the collective did not decide anything of the sort.[8]

The second device to control the nomination procedure practiced by city authorities was to "recommend" that several large enterprises in a given district nominate one particular candidate. This automatically increased his/her chances vis-á-vis other candidates. In electoral district No. 519 in Kharkov, for example, five enterprises agreed to nominate one candidate. But there were no general meetings at these enterprises preceding this agreement. The *Izvestiia* correspondent wondered, How could they agree? How was the opinion of tens of thousands of people taken into account? The author of the article concluded that party bosses had obviously made a deal behind the backs of their collectives.[9] Usually party functionaries advised collectives to nominate high-ranking party officials, the first secretary of the obkom, or of the gorkom, or the director of a large enterprise. In other words, the party-state apparatus abused the process to nominate its own people. In Saratov province, for example, by the end of the nomination process in six out of seven electoral districts, only one candidate per district was nominated.[10] The elections there were going to be uncontested.

General Nomination Meetings at Enterprises

Each collective in the enterprises is controlled by several overlapping bureaucracies: There is the party committee, controlling workshop

---

[7] Ibid.
[8] Ibid.
[9] K. Kleva, "Vydvizhenets so storony," *Izvestiia*, January 30, 1989.
[10] V. Nikolaeva, "Luchshego iz odnogo?" *Izvestiia*, January 14, 1989.

party cells who are bound by party discipline, then the trade union bureaucracy, then the so-called council of the collective, and finally, another body not mentioned in the Soviet press, the first department which is an affiliate of the KGB and monitors workers' political outlook. If all of these party-state bureaucracies promoted a certain candidate proposed by the obkom, it was very difficult, although not impossible, to mobilize support for an effective alternative. Usually, the obkom or gorkom proposed to factory party leaders specific names of those to be nominated. Strictly speaking, it was not a violation of the law. Anyone had the right to propose any name. In practice, however, when a general meeting of a factory assembled, the chairman simply would say, as the *Izvestiia* correspondent observed, that "there is an opinion" to nominate such and such. The opinion, that is, the name, was selected by the district party committee.[11] The chair would start praising the official candidate, his brilliant biography, and his achievements in Socialist construction. What could an unknown worker do if he wanted to run, and what were his chances? Well, here is an example.

In Kursk, a worker, A. Kodin, nominated himself at a meeting of his workshop. His fellow workers supported him and nominated him as a candidate from their plant. He was competing with three other candidates: the chairman of the council of the collective, the deputy chief engineer, and the director of a workshop. Without explanation, however, Kodin's candidacy was removed from the ballot, a clear violation of the electoral law. When a correspondent asked the chairman of the council of the collective why, he answered that Kodin "criticized the Communist Party too sharply" and "displayed too much left wing extremism."[12] A critic was weeded out before there was a chance to vote at any level.

There are numerous similar reports from other districts. In electoral district No. 565 in Minsk, seventeen candidates were nominated at one plant, but only three names were left on the ballot for the general meeting. One can only guess by what criteria names were stricken out.[13] The pool of candidates at the enterprise level was very easy to control. Initiative from below at the enterprise level was easily crushed by arbitrary action even before the general meeting of a collective took place.

There were some energetic local candidates, however, who did not want to give up easily. Their recourse was to mobilize enough workers' support to override pressure from the local party and plant administration. In electoral district No. 313 in Tomsk, an activist oil worker Belous was first struck out from the list of candidates in the CP slate. He then was

---

[11] K. Kleva, "Vydvizhenets so storony," *Izvestiia*, January 30, 1989.

[12] V. Kulagin, "Po vcherashnym retseptam," *Izvestiia*, January 24, 1989.

[13] N. Mikhailov, "Kogo i kak vydvigaem," *Izvestiia*, January 5, 1989.

nominated by his fellow workers. He was defeated again, and as a result, workers staged a protest rally against the "intrigues of the apparatus forces."[14] Some workers did not have much hope that their own candidates could win or even if they did win, that they would be able to accomplish much in the legislature. In the city of Tomsk, out of seven candidates nominated by enterprises, only two remained, academician Karpov and a director of Polius Kombinat Golubev. When asked about such results, one worker candidate said, "It is one thing if I go to various bureaucracies in Moscow, it is another thing if the first secretary goes. All doors will be open to him."[15]

Many alternative candidates complained that they did not have equal chances in competition with obkom first secretaries in their districts. Direct pressure was applied on them to withdraw voluntarily, either at the very beginning so that only one candidate remained by the end of the first round, or at the last minute, so that the procedure itself looked democratic. The *Izvestiia* correspondent complained that the party bureaucracy "tried to hold all the threads in its hands."[16] Numerous reports described direct pressure on candidates to withdraw voluntarily and to clear the way for candidates chosen by the party. In one such case, a chairman of the collective farm, Filinov, was nominated by his collective farm, but the district party committee chair called him on the phone and urged him to withdraw. He refused. The next move came from the district committee. They investigated the procedure of Filinov's nomination, found it improper and cancelled the nomination. "We are responsible for the conduct of elections," said the district party boss.[17] In the Kursk-Belgorod electoral district (Orel province), the party district committee also pressured a worker Kandaurov to withdraw in favor of his rival V. Shimko, a deputy of the socioeconomic department under the CC of the CPSU. Kandaurov refused to withdraw, but in the cities of Orel and Belgorod the party managed to remove all alternative candidates from the ballot.[18] A critical analyst in *Ogonek* commented thus on such practices: "It turns out that alternative nominations can also be squeezed into a pre-programmed scheme. At first there are several candidates who then withdraw one by one in favor of one person."[19]

Clearly the party bureaucracy had a tremendous advantage in the nomination process over independent candidates, simply because it had a network of communications which independent candidates did not. Even

---

[14] "Realnyi rezul'tat borby," *Izvestiia*, February 14, 1989.
[15] Ibid.
[16] V. Tolstenko, "Kollektiv otstoial svoego pretendenta," *Izvestiia*, February 13, 1989.
[17] Ibid.
[18] "Kak menia otgovarivali," *Izvestiia*, February 13, 1989.
[19] "Raskovannost'," *Ogonek*, (no. 7, 1989).

if independent candidates managed to secure the nomination from the general meeting of the plant, despite the difficulties described above, they would still be completely unknown at other enterprises in that electoral district. Since other collectives also chose their own candidates, they tended to support "their" candidate versus somebody else's. The structure of the nomination process was such that often two or three nominees represented different enterprises rather than political positions. Nominees did not have horizontal communication with the electorate. There was no organization of any kind, just unknown candidates and their programs. This set-up tended to favor well-known figures, like plant directors, and first secretaries, unless they were universally detested by the local populace. The only advantage that independent candidates had was that they were usually running because they wanted to say something to the electorate. They tended to be the more articulate activists in the community, usually journalists, writers, actors, but also occasionally workers.

At a nomination meeting in Alma-Ata, for example, in electoral district 132, three candidates were competing: an environmentalist activist and scientist Shakhanov, a shepherd and hero of Socialist labor, and a member of the provincial Soviet. The member of the Soviet could not convince the audience that his accomplishments in the province merited his advancement to the Union legislature. The shepherd's program was described as a lecture on cotton production, and the bilingual scientist was nominated since his program sounded most appealing.[20]

What was the profile of candidates nominated at enterprises? According to official data on the results of the nomination process across the country, most of them were people with established positions in the Soviet political and economic hierarchy: first party secretaries, directors of enterprises, and Soviets' functionaries. Only 33 percent of the candidates were officially described as workers and farmers. In 190 electoral districts only one candidate was nominated. Not even primary contests were held there.[21]

Here is just a short sample of nominees from electoral districts in Leningrad: in electoral district No. 47 it was the director of a research institute; in district No. 55, the first secretary of the obkom Iu. Solov'ev (then a Politburo member) who was nominated by the Proletarskii Plant; in district 48, a worker V. Kashin; in district 54, the director of the airport; in district 51, the director of the port.[22] Most of them were nominated by loyal collectives who voted for suggested delegates.

[20] V. Ardeev, "Za iavnym preimushchestvom," *Izvestiia*, February 8, 1989.
[21] "Vremia gotovitsia k vyboru," *Izvestiia*, February 20, 1989.
[22] "Kto poluchit mandaty?" *Leningradskaia Pravda*, January 21, 1989.

Nominations by Residents

   Nominations by residents, unlike those at enterprises, show examples of genuine popular initiatives from below. Usually these initiatives
were undertaken in large cities, where political awareness of the electorate was high. A group of residents did have the right to nominate a candidate. They had to obtain the signatures of five hundred residents in their
district, submit a petition to the Electoral Commission, get a permit for a
meeting, and have at least five hundred registered residents present when
the candidate was nominated. Candidates were considered nominated if
they received the votes of 51 percent of those present. Outwardly this
procedure is similar to nominations by the collectives. But in fact residents were at a disadvantage because it was much easier for the party
committee to call a general meeting of the plant than for a group of residents to assemble five hundred signatures in favor of a certain candidate
and then assemble residents for a nomination meeting.

   In almost all cases reported in the press, residents' initiatives ran up
against both the overt and covert resistance of authorities. In Leningrad,
in the Kirov district, for example, the Electoral Commission did not allow
any residents' meetings, a clear violation of the law.[23] Officials were reported as saying, "We do not need these novelties. The Electoral Commission will decide itself how many candidates will be left on the
ballot."[24] The chairman of the Electoral Commission of electoral district
No. 46 put it bluntly: "To conduct nomination meetings in order to satisfy
somebody's ambitions does not make any sense."[25] This was in response
to a conflict over the nominee of the residents' initiative group and that
of the Electoral Commission. A group of residents collected the necessary
number of signatures and applied for a permit to call a nomination meeting. The Electoral Commission responded that only the local Soviet was
authorized to organize such meetings, and did not allow it, which was a
clear violation of the electoral law. Then Electoral Commission personnel
started calling people on the phone who had signed the petition, urging
them to withdraw their signatures from the petition.[26] The author of the
report implied that the Electoral Commission was acting under the guidance of the district party committee. The journal *Ogonek* received many
telegrams with complaints that electoral commissions did not allow the
nomination of independent candidates. The party bureaucracy was clearly
afraid of any initiatives from the populace.

   In addition to the outright banning of nomination meetings, local

23 "Skol'ko budet kandidatov?" *Leningradskaia Pravda*, January 25, 1989.
24 Ibid.
25 "Telegramma protesta," *Leningradskaia Pravda*, January 24, 1989.
26 Ibid.

authorities often resorted to other methods. A resident voter in Iaroslavl' complained that when she arrived at the residents' nomination meeting in electoral district No. 346, police were guarding the entry. No one was admitted because, as they said, five hundred residents had already arrived. The chairman of the district CP committee presided who recognized mandates only of those who had already arrived at the meeting. These were workers from the Motor Works who had already nominated their director at their enterprise, but now, in their capacity as residents were told to come to the meeting one hour earlier than other residents.[27] With the auditorium already filled with reliable voters, other voters were simply not admitted, preventing the nomination of an independent candidate. This slight manipulation was regarded as within the bounds of the law.

Very seldom did the Soviet press publish a profile of an independent candidate. The few examples that were published explain in part why the authorities tried to do all they could to prevent these people from expressing their opinions. In the city of Serpukhov, electoral district No. 41 (Gorkii province), an initiative group tried to summon a residents' meeting to nominate V. Pomazov. He was a member of the "Memorial" society dedicated to preserving the memory of the victims of Stalinism. According to local officials Pomazov "skillfully used negative information in the press inflaming dissatisfaction in people with the low standard of living, and events in Afghanistan." Some years ago he was tried for "inventing false insinuations blackening Soviet Power." In plain English, Pomazov was a dissident in Brezhnev's times. He was expelled from the university for a speech against Stalinism. What an embarrassment it would have been if Pomazov won over some party secretary! A joint session of the Serpukhov city and district Executive Committees decided to prohibit Pomazov's nomination meeting, a clear-cut violation of the law. Pomazov related that he was threatened, and urged to drop out of the race before he even started. The meeting to nominate him at his work place was banned, too. *Moscow News* stated that not only the city authorities but also "the Electoral Commission took part in all this lawlessness."[28] Pomazov sued the city authorities for violation of electoral law, but whatever the verdict was, one more critic was out of the race.

As in Moscow, Leningrad, and the Baltic Republics, a "Popular Front for Restructuring" tried to promote alternative candidates in Iaroslavl'. This made it much more difficult for authorities to ban nomination meetings arbitrarily, to pack auditoriums with Communist supporters, or

[27] "Pravo na mandat," *Moskovskie Novosti*, February 5, 1989.
[28] A. Romanov, in *Moskovskie Novosti*, February 26, 1989.

to resort to other legal and illegal maneuvers. As a political organization involving many people, having financial resources and legal experts, the Popular Front challenged violations of electoral law. It monitored compliance with electoral law at nomination meetings, campaigned for candidates it favored and challenged several of the city authorities' decisions. For example, when a residents' nomination meeting was blocked by city authorities, the Popular Front insisted that a new meeting be allowed. The Electoral Commission had a long discussion on whether to allow a new meeting or not, which in itself was a violation of the law because residents have the right to assemble for nominations. Seven voted to allow it, seven against, and one abstained. Finally a new residents' meeting did assemble. Six hundred thirty-six persons were registered as participants; 309 voted to nominate a journalist A. Tsvetkov, out of the total number of 616 votes cast. That meant that Tsvetkov won more than 50 percent of the votes. If all registered participants were counted, however, then he did not win 50 percent. Did he have enough votes to be nominated or not? The law does not clarify this point. The Electoral Commission decided that Tsvetkov could not be nominated.[29]

In some cases local residential groups organized successful campaigns to nominate their alternative candidates. In Kolpino, an industrial suburb of Leningrad, the majority of residents are workers at the huge Izhorskii plant. It was reported that the plant nominated the chairman of the City Executive Committee, V. Khodyrev, and that an alternative candidate engineer, A. T. Oshurkov, "was not supported by his enterprise." A local initiative group successfully organized a residents' nomination meeting where a Soviet boss received 382 votes and the independent candidate Oshurkov, 865 votes. He was nominated.[30]

Second Stage: Selection of Candidates for the Ballot

Once nominated, candidates next had to overcome the hurdle of an electoral district selection meeting to secure a place on the ballot. According to law, a candidate had complete freedom to campaign for him/herself and against other candidates. He was allowed to have a team of up to ten people and to print and distribute leaflets to the population. If a newspaper provided space for one candidate, it was obliged to provide equal space to all candidates. Monetary funds to finance the campaigns were permitted. A journalist asked a legal expert how these rules were to be reconciled with the rules on public demonstrations that required a prior permit from city authorities. Did it mean that city authorities could ban some rallies but allow others, and in this way influence the course of the

[29] M. Ovcharov, "Kommissiia obretaet svoe litso," *Izvestiia*, February 3, 1989.
[30] "V zale bylo tesno," *Leningradskaia Pravda*, January 28, 1989.

campaign? (As a matter of fact, this was occurring in numerous cities.) The legal expert replied that for the duration of the election campaign, permits for demonstrations were not necessary. Free campaigning was allowed.[31]

For the first time since 1921, when opposition parties of Mensheviks and Socialist Revolutionaries campaigned in elections to the Soviets, there were leaflets, spontaneous rallies, numerous election meetings, radio and television debates, and other attributes of electoral politics.[32] In spite of the relative openness of this election campaign, it was seldom that the Soviet press reported in detail on platforms of candidates who were critical of the existing social and political order.

There was an incredible variety in the candidates' platforms across the country. The party and Soviet official candidates tended to praise the party and restructuring and promise all kinds of improvements for a given electoral district. In some places they seemed to forget that they competed, not for a local office, but for the national legislature. Party and Soviet functionaries promised to improve food supply, roads, and other services. Out of dozens of such platforms a couple of examples will suffice. In electoral district No. 436 in Donetsk (the Ukraine) three candidates competed: Pavlov, a deputy in the provincial Soviet; Komov, a deputy in the city Soviet; and Burykh, a technician. All three praised restructuring, environmental protection, and Socialist democracy. One could hardly see the differences among the candidates.[33] Similarly, in electoral district No. 671 in Baku (Azerbaidzhan) three candidates competed: an academician, Buniatov, a member of the Azerbaidzhan CP Central Committee, Ragimov, and the first secretary of the Union of writers, Rzaev. They all spoke about democracy, ecology, harmony in relations between nationalities, etc.,[34] fully conforming to the official party line. It is not an exaggeration to suggest that such platforms were in the majority.

The second category of platforms were those that were just a little bit unorthodox, advocating measures that were a step ahead of official party policy. For example, in the Temirtausskii electoral district No. 630 in Kazakhstan, two finalists competed: the director of the Karaganda Coal Kombinat, N. Drizhda, and the director of the Karaganda Metal Plant, O. Soskov. There was hardly any difference in their platforms. They both criticized the dictatorship of the ministries which still took away profits earned by sales of production above the plan. The candidates promised strict implementation of the law on enterprises and to achieve full inde-

---

[31] V. Dolgatov, "Agitatsiia bez agitpunktov," *Izvestiia*, February 4, 1989.

[32] A. Durov, "Zharko stalo kandidatam," *Gudok*, February 18, 1989.

[33] N. Lisovenko, "Borolis' na ravnykh," *Izvestiia*, February 12, 1989.

[34] "V borbe za mandat," *Bakinskii Rabochii*, February 24, 1989.

428   *The Russian Review*

pendence from the ministries.[35] No one talked about workers' poor social conditions in these cities just a few months before a wave of strikes. Another example of mild unorthodoxy was the campaign of Marshal S. V. Akhromeev in electoral district No. 697 in Bel'sk (Moldavia); he and the gorkom first secretary V. M. Iovva shared the two spots on the ballot. Iovva promised to improve the food supply, a typical promise from a party boss. Akhromeev promised to strive for reduction of the military budget so that these savings could be used for social services![36]

The third and most interesting category of platforms were those which clearly criticized the existing social, legal, and political order. Candidates were subjected to rigorous questioning by the voters at election meetings. This requred totally new skills in politics and here alternative candidates did have an advantage. Party bosses and Soviet functionaries were not used to confronting issues or deviations from the official party line. It was not enough to simply state that one supported restructuring. One had to display skills in gauging the audience and in knowing what to say to win voter support. At a nomination meeting at the Leningrad Polytechnical Institute, Professor A. A. Denisov was asked what his attitude was toward article six in the Constitution which guaranteed a leading role to the Communist Party. He said,

> I am a Communist and I favor that my party be a ruling one. However, I consider that the Communist Party must ask the people's mandate to rule every time. And it should not have this mandate once and for all. Therefore, I consider this article incorrect.

Professor Denisov also said that it was necessary to establish a free market economy and a private sector. He was nominated.[37] It would have been inconceivable just a short time ago for a Communist candidate to campaign for such a program.

In many cities candidates promised in their platforms to struggle for a cleaner environment. In some cases, however, environmentalist groups went beyond modest recommendations and organized campaigns like in the West. For example, in Nizhnii Tagil in the Urals, Vera Baklanova, the leader of an environmentalist group "Ochishchenie" (Cleansing), organized a procession of mothers with baby carriages against air pollution from the local plant, but the city authorities banned it. They also prohibited the group from posting its leaflets. The group then organized a campaign of letters written by children to the director of the plant, asking him to do something about the air pollution his plant was causing. Hundreds of children sent letters and drawings to the plant director.[38] A new kind

[35] "Opravdat' doverie delom," *Kazakhstanskaia Pravda*, March 3, 1989.
[36] "Spor reshila platforma," *Sovetskaia Moldaviia*, February 5, 1989.
[37] "S iavnym preimushchestvom," *Leningradskaia Pravda*, January 28, 1989.
[38] A. Pashkov, "Drakon iz Nizhnego Tagila," *Izvestiia*, February 12, 1989.

March 1989 Elections to the CPD 429

of political life is emerging in the Soviet Union. Organized protest groups, like in Nizhnii Tagil or Iaroslavl', began appealing to voters about issues that concerned them directly. The authorities responded in the old and customary way by banning demonstrations.

Perhaps one of the greatest surprises in the election campaign all across the country was the reemergence of the issue of a multiparty system. Not since the destruction of the legal opposition parties of the Mensheviks and SRs in 1922 has this issue been openly debated in the Soviet Union.[39] At the selection meeting in electoral district No. 56 in Leningrad, nine candidates competed. Two were the clear front runners, the director of the scientific production association, Gidaspov, and a head of a biolab of a research institute, A. Cherkasov. His election platform was most interesting. Cherkasov openly advocated political pluralism and a multiparty system. The ills of Socialism could not be cured, he argued, without the true and free participation of all, rejecting special prerogative to any party.[40] Cherkasov received slightly under 50 percent and the front runner Gidaspov over 50 percent. All other candidates were far behind. By the spirit of the law that promotes the idea of contested elections, these two candidates should have been put on the ballot for voters to decide. But the letter of the law allowed the selection meeting to determine the number of candidates to be placed on the ballot. The meeting decided that only one candidate should remain, and another reformist candidate was out of the race.

Other voices, however, go far beyond the above limited aims. An interesting clash occurred at a nomination meeting in electoral district No. 47 in Leningrad, summoned on the initiative of residents. One of the candidates, N. Zherbin, speaking on behalf of the All-Russian Patriotic Society of Pamiat' (a nationalist society which has been turning increasingly anti-Semitic lately) gave an angry speech: "Who has violated Russian culture? Who is decimating the economy? Who is guilty of destroying the indigenous nationality of the country?" His answers were not published, but likely he meant the Communists and the Jews. His program was to disband the All-Union Academy of Sciences and create instead a Russian Academy of Sciences, to liquidate the Russian Soviet Federal Socialist Republic and to create a Russian Republic instead. He advocated reviving everything Russian and condemning everything non-Russian—"alien" nationalities have no place in Pamiat's republic. This extremely important new current of thought rejects the very concept of a Union of Socialist Republics, claiming that the Union Republics get a better deal than Russia, which has the lowest standard of living in the

[39] Vladimir Brovkin, *The Mensheviks after October: Socialist Opposition and the Rise of the Bolshevik Dictatorship* (Ithaca: Cornell University Press, 1987).

[40] "Odin iz deviati," *Leningradskaia Pravda*, February 4, 1989.

Union. A separatist movement of Russian nationalists may yet prove to be an important political force in the future.

In electoral district No. 47 in Leningrad, however, Zherbin received only thirty-seven votes out of 603. The sympathies of the audience were clearly with M. E. Sal'e, the chairman of the city-wide club of the Friends of the journal *Ogonek*. He entitled his platform "For the Rule of Law." He specifically proposed a new democratic constitution, a struggle against the rule of bureaucracy, the creation of zones of free trade and joint ventures with foreign companies, an end to the subsidizing of inefficient collective farms and the liquidation of the ministries altogether.[41] He was nominated.

Even though proposals of reformist candidates varied in specifics, they all reflected a general striving for more democracy, private initiative, private enterprise, human rights, and less government interference. In Moscow in the Voroshilovskii electoral district No. 6, supporters of such reforms were candidates Yurii Afans'ev, the director of the Historical Archival Institute, dissident historian Roy Medvedev, Boris Yeltsin, Andrei Sakharov, and Ilia Zaslavskii, a young, unknown self-nominated candidate. Debate on the platform turned into a public forum on major issues of foreign and domestic policy. Specific proposals included placing the use of force under the jurisdiction of the legislature, accountability of the government to the people and to the legislature, and special commissions on the armed forces and police activities. It is not clear who of the candidates expressed these ideas, but any one of them could have.[42] In this district all the reformist candidates decided to join forces in favor of Ilia Zaslavskii, who later carried the district.

Another unorthodox proposal was made by a candidate in the Trade Union's slate competition, V. I. Goncharik, chairman of the Belorussian Council of Trade Unions. Judging by his title, one could hardly expect a radical proposal. Nevertheless, Goncharik promised that he would struggle for legalization of strikes in the Soviet Union. The law, he said, must defend a worker activist from the arbitrariness of factory administration. Trade Unions must have the right to override decisions of the administration if those decisions are harmful to the environment. He also proposed to draft a comprehensive law on workers' and unions' rights.[43]

Perhaps the most comprehensive program advanced by reformist alternative candidates in the entire country was presented by Andrei Sakharov. As did others, he demanded the electoral law be changed, according no privileges to any group of voters, one man, one vote, and

[41] A. Ozhegov, "Aplodismenty v polnoch," *Leningradskaia Pravda*, February 2, 1989.

[42] FBIS, Daily Report, Soviet Union, March 3, 1989, p. 53, citing *Moskovskaia Pravda*, February 19, 1989.

[43] "Litsom k cheloveku," *Ekonomicheskaia Gazeta*, no. 10, 1989, p. 2.

March 1989 Elections to the CPD 431

providing that there be at least two candidates in electoral contests. He called for support of National Fronts in the Baltics. He proposed to grant far-reaching rights to Union Republics and similar rights to autonomous republics within the Russian Federation. The internal passport system should be abolished and complete freedom of movement and residency in and out of the country assured. The collective farm system should be scrapped as soon as possible. Farmers must be given land in perpetuity. Citizens must have rights to sue state and party institutions in an independent court. The conscript army of reservists is to be converted into a small professional army. A long-term goal is to be convergence with the capitalist system.[44]

As is well known, pluralist political discourse is most advanced in the Baltic Republics. Here the election campaigns already approached the level of a multiparty competition. In electoral district No. 708 in Riga, the selection meeting had to decide which out of six candidates were to be on the ballot. One of them was the First Secretary of the Latvian CP, Ian Vagris; another, a member of the Duma of the Popular Front of Latvia, Iu. Dobelis, and a third, one of the founders of the Movement for National Independence of Latvia, E. Repshe. Each presented his platform which reflected the political positions of the parties for which they spoke. Vagris defended Latvian sovereignty within the Soviet Union on the basis of "economic self-sufficiency of the Republic." Dobelis' platform went a bit further in defense of Latvian sovereignty against the dictate of Moscow ministries, and Repshe gave a "sharply extremist speech," as *Moscow News* put it.[45] In 1940, he said, Latvia was occupied by armed force and incorporated into the USSR without a popular referendum. Latvia should secede from the Soviet Union.[46] The meeting voted to keep all six candidates on the ballot. This was the closest approximation to free elections in Soviet context.

Electoral District Selection Meetings

The survey of numerous selection meetings suggests that there were several major techniques to control the outcome of candidate selection. The clue to it is in the procedure for the convocation, composition, and conduct of the electoral district selection meeting. A critic openly stated:

> It is no secret that a District Selection Meeting is perceived as an undemocratic filter which can be used against undesirable candidates. Moreover, active and principled supporters of restructuring are considered to be such "undesirables," especially in the provinces.[47]

---

[44] "Za mir i progress," *Moskovskie Novosti*, February 5, 1989.

[45] "Riga-predvybornaia situatsiia," *Moskovskie Novosti*, February 26, 1989.

[46] Note that *Sovetskaia Latviia* reported more of Repshe's speech: "Reshat' dolzhny vse," *Sovetskaia Latviia*, February 12, 1989.

[47] Boris Kurashvili, "Ne men'she dvukh," *Moskovski Novosti*, February 19, 1989.

432   *The Russian Review*

By law electoral district selection meetings must represent different groups of voters. According to a member of the Central Electoral Committee, Barabashev, the meeting of the delegate body had to consist of two parts, first, of representatives of collectives and residents who had nominated delegates, and second, of those who did not nominate any candidates.[48] The meeting was considered lawful and proper if upon opening the meeting more than 50 percent of representatives delegated by enterprises were present. Not less than 50 percent of the seats had to be reserved for the delegates of enterprises who had not nominated any candidates.[49] Discussing this peculiar system, *Moscow News* wrote that candidates had unequal chances from the beginning. Six hundred people at a typical selection meeting decided for a quarter of a million who they would have on the ballot.[50] The ambiguities in the law generated ample opportunities for manipulation of the meeting's composition. The Central Electoral Commission made it known that it received dozens of complaints and protests. The thrust of all of them was "We were deceived."[51] Cases of direct and indirect manipulation of elections by party bosses were too numerous to be described here. One may only try to group them by type.

1. Disenfranchisement of Residents' Representatives   The law does not specify what proportional relationship should exist between the representatives of collectives and representatives of residents. In actual fact, representatives of residents nominated fewer candidates than the collectives. This means that residents' representatives were automatically drowned by collectives' representatives. Since most residents' candidates were independent antiestablishment candidates, and most collectives' candidates were party and Soviet officials, the latter had an inbuilt advantage at a selection meeting.

2. Drowning the Meeting with Reliable Men through Dozens of Endorsements   The goal of a candidate was to win as many endorsements as possible from enterprises located in his electoral district. The more endorsements he had, the more delegates were his at the selection meeting. Every collective that nominated a candidate had a right to an equal number of participants to all other such collectives in the selection meeting.[52] The law did not clarify the difference between nomination and endorsement of a candidate. If a candidate were nominated simultaneously at several enterprises, that was considered nomination, but if he

48 "Volna i krugi," *Izvestiia*, February 9, 1989.
49 V. Dolgatov, "Agitatsiia bez agitpunktov," *Izvestiia*, February 4, 1989.
50 A. Romanov, "Urok politicheskoi bor'by," *Moskovskie Novosti*, February 19, 1989.
51 V. Dolgatov, "Spor program ili konkurs obeshchanii," *Izvestiia*, February 20, 1989.
52 "Volna i krugi," *Izvestiia*, February 9, 1989.

had been nominated at one enterprise and only subsequently nominated by others, that constituted endorsement, which did not translate into a delegation of supporters at the selection meeting. It was difficult, if not impossible, to draw the distinction between the two, and district Electoral Commissions decided this on their own, often promoting a desirable, and undercutting an undesirable candidate.

A high-ranking party official had an advantage in obtaining nominations from a large number of enterprises, through the network of party organizations promoting his cause. For example, in electoral district No. 343 in Chita, the leading candidate, obkom first secretary N. Mal'kov, arrived at the selection meeting with endorsements of 175 collectives. Among his chief "opponents" was chairman of the Soviet Executive Committee, A. Orekhov. Ten other candidates from small enterprises were running at the beginning of the meeting. However, they had their forces dispersed and their chances minimized due to the structure of the selection meeting, even though democratic procedure was seemingly observed.[53] The first secretary and the Soviet functionary got through to the final stage.

3. Packing Selection Meetings with Reliable People   In the Melipolskii electoral district No. 459, the party bureau secretary made some phone calls ordering the inclusion of such and such in the delegation from a particular enterprise. It was a selection, wrote *Izvestiia*, which had "little to do with enterprises delegating their representatives."[54] Fifty percent of the delegates of the Azov district were secretaries of party organizations, chairmen of trade unions, and directors of enterprises. In other words, the selection meeting was packed with "reliable people" as the title of the article implied.[55] In electoral district No. 50 in Leningrad, the Electoral Commission very carefully counted which candidates were nominated by which collectives and structured the composition of the selection meeting arbitrarily "by unknown criteria."[56] In electoral district No. 705 in Moldavia, out of five candidates, only one was left on the ballot, the deputy chairman of the Council of Ministers of Moldavia, who was at the same time the chairman of Moldavian Gosplan, V. G. Kutyrkin. The Moldavian press is not as open as in the capitals and it did not report what Kutyrkin's opponents were saying and why the selection meeting left only one candidate on the ballot out of five contenders.[57] An identical case took place in electoral district No. 45 near Moscow. A

[53] V. Sbitnev in *Izvestiia*, February 7, 1989.
[54] S. Troian, "Nadezhnye liudi v zale," *Izvestiia*, February 6, 1989.
[55] Ibid. The title reads "Reliable People in the Audience."
[56] "Foru kandidatu," *Leningradskaia Pravda*, February 5, 1989.
[57] "Izderzhek moglo i ne byt'," *Sovetskaia Moldaviia*, February 14, 1989.

protest leaflet read: "Directors, party committee chairmen, and other functionaries formed 90 percent of the District Meeting." The leaflet appealed to the electorate to cross out the names of "appointees of the command-administrative system."[58] A similar protest broke out in Iaroslavl', where demonstrators carried posters inscribed: "No! to Elections without Choice!"[59]

4. Prearranged Withdrawal of Candidates at the Selection Meeting This fourth technique of manipulation made it possible for a party boss to make it look as if there were real competition with some unknown milkmaid nominated by her collective farm. At a selection meeting, the milkmaid would withdraw in favor of a party boss. At the selection meeting in district No. 459, the front runner was the Zaporozhskii obkom first secretary G. Kharchenko. At the beginning of the meeting, ten candidates supposedly ran as well—the first secretary of a district party committee, another the secretary of the city party committee, another a secretary of another party committee. They all withdrew at the meeting. Only one candidate was not willing to give up, deputy head of the Melitopol'skii Refrigerator Plant, V. Korzin. But the majority at the meeting had been instructed to favor the first secretary. Another technique of manipulation also used was, namely, access to the floor. Thirty speakers signed up but only five were given the floor. The first secretary received 659 votes out of seven hundred. Everything went smoothly.[60]

5. Control over Uncommitted Delegates A powerful influence at the selection meeting was the employment of delegates from enterprises who had not nominated anybody. These delegates were free to vote for whomever they pleased, without consulting with their collectives. This too made it possible for party bosses to make private arrangements that uncommitted collectives vote for a "leading candidate." For example, in electoral district No. 641 in Semipalatinsk, four candidates ran. Of the five hundred participants at the selection meeting, 140 were committed to candidates and their supporters, and 360 delegates were uncommitted. Most of them were party and state officials who naturally voted for their boss, obkom first secretary K. Boztaev. The only thing that made that meeting not as smooth as others was that one of the candidates was an environmentalist, V. Kobrin. Unfortunately, the newspaper report did not elaborate on his speech and said only that a tough conversation took place. Kobrin apparently protested against a nuclear test site in the area. As could be expected, his name was struck from the ballot, and two

[58] S. Blagodarov, "Listovochnaia voina," *Sovetskaia Rossiia*, February 14, 1989.
[59] Photos with slogans in *Moskovskie Novosti*, February 19, 1989.
[60] "Nadezhnye liudi," *Izvestiia*, February 6, 1989.

candidates remained, the first secretary and a woman spinner from a textile factory, a clear set-up for the first secretary to win at the polls and declare himself an elected representative of the people.[61]

An almost identical combination was played out in electoral district No. 203 in Kostroma. The first secretary of the obkom, V. Toropov, was opposed by the chairman of a cooperative, V. Busygin, who had criticized "the cadres policy of the obkom." Most likely this means that Busygin criticized the system of appointments, privileges, and corruption. He was, of course, defeated, and two candidates remained on the ballot: the first secretary and another party functionary, a clear set-up for the first secretary to win.[62]

6. Control over the Time and Place of the Selection Meeting   As during the nomination meetings, Electoral Commissions did not inform voters about the time and place of the selection meeting, especially the residents' initiative groups, and disenfranchized them in this way.[63] In electoral district No. 138 (Volgograd province) obkom first secretary V. I. Kalashnikov ran against a candidate nominated by an "Ecology" club. The selection meeting was held in a far-away village without prior notice, and the first secretary had endorsements of fifty collectives with him. As a result, only the first secretary's name remained on the ballot.[64]

Disenfranchisement of residents' groups, selection meetings drowned with endorsements delegates, voluntary withdrawal of fake candidates, and pressure on uncommitted candidates, described above, are all within the bounds of law. If carefully planned, a selection meeting could be composed in such a way that its decisions would be predetermined by its composition before the meeting had even started. A very thin line divides legal from illegal manipulation of procedures to achieve the desired composition.

7. Intimidation of Candidates   Direct and illegal behind-the-scenes intimidation of candidates through party mafias was reported on numerous occasions. For example, two candidates were running at the nomination stage in electoral district No. 356 in Dushanbe, Tadzhikistan: D. Karilov, the first secretary of the city party committee, and D. Ansori, the head of a workshop. The Central Committee of the Tadzhik CP issued an order to verify the personal dossier of Ansori. The city party committee discovered upon verification that Ansori had a party reprimand some years ago. So the city party committee functionary went to Ansori's en-

[61] V. Mirolevich, "Kandidaty prosiat tribunu," *Izvestiia*, February 6, 1989.
[62] "Kandidaty i ikh programmy," *Izvestiia*, February 13, 1989.
[63] V. Dolgatov, "Agitatsiia bez agitpunktov," *Izvestiia*, February 4, 1989.
[64] V. Drobotov, "Komu doverit' vlast'," *Sovetskaia Rossiia*, March 12, 1989.

436   *The Russian Review*

terprise and demanded that they nominate another candidate, but the collective refused.[65]

8. Altering the Decisions of Selection Meetings   When all other means to stop undesirable candidates failed, Electoral Commissions resorted to violating the prerogatives of the selection meetings by arbitrarily altering or nullifying its results. Only a systematic study district by district may reveal how often this was practiced. But some examples were reported in the press. In an electoral district in Tbilisi, Georgia, a member of the Georgian CP Central Committee, Spaderashvili, competed with two workers. The question of how many candidates should be left on the ballot was not even brought to the vote. Nevertheless, the party boss remained on the ballot as the single candidate.[66] Similarly in Kiev, in electoral district No. 466, the selection meeting decided that three candidates were to be included in the ballot, but the chair of the meeting declared that only one would remain, a clear violation of the law.[67]

And finally there were, of course, cases when despite manipulation and pressure, an unknown candidate would win against a well-established one promoted by the authorities. People do change their minds, especially uncommitted delegates. For example, in electoral district No. 269 in Rostov-on-Don, victory seemed to have been assured for V. Shukskii, a member of the Soviet, a participant in the nineteenth party conference, nominated by many collectives, and endorsed by the trade unions. His opponent was an unknown worker, V. Shevliuga. He won because his speech produced a better impression. He spoke about the true power of the people and not of the bureaucrats. He promised to consult with his electorate and follow their will. He and another worker remained on the ballot and the establishment candidate failed.[68]

The journal of the Central Committee *Agitator* instructed party activists:

> It is necessary to react quickly to the changing situation, and not to allow the development of negative tendencies. And such tendencies are unfortunately present. It is no secret that persons with extremist views have lately become active. These are demagogues who side with the so-called rally type of democracy.[69]

The journal called on party activists to repulse the demagogues. In plain English, the demagogues were critics of the Communist Party. Local party functionaries most certainly understood this as a call to stop the

65"Kandidat pred'iavliaet isk," *Izvestiia*, February 23, 1989.
66"Pozitsiia nashla podderzhku," *Zaria Vostoka* (Tbilisi), February 21, 1989.
67V. Shchekotkin, "Vremia gotovitsia k vyboru," *Izvestiia*, February 20, 1989.
68"Nam takie nuzhny," *Moskovskie Novosti*, February 19, 1989.
69"Vybory i agitatsiia," *Agitator* (no. 2, 1989).

critics and demagogues, which they did, as we have seen. Selection meetings across the country did fulfill on the whole the role assigned to them: to weed out undesirable candidates. However, there will be another and perhaps far more important legacy left by the selection meetings of 1989. They produced an unanticipated effect by politicizing the population. Selection meetings in many areas became true popular forums, where for the first time in decades the Soviet people gathered to talk about politics and to put questions to those who claimed to be their leaders. The party machine had a relatively easy ride this time, but this taste of freedom of open debate will be hard to extinguish. Selection meetings in the future will be much more difficult to control. The initiative groups that emerged all over the country during this time might well crystallize into a powerful political force in any future elections.

The Third Stage: Toward the Finale

The discussion of the election campaign above focused on the patterns of the election process in the entire country. The final stage of the campaign revealed most clearly the profound differences in the nature of the political process in various republics and regions of the country. In Leningrad, Iaroslavl', Nizhnii Tagil, and other Russian cities the party apparatus tried to prevent reformist groups and individuals from getting on the ballot. In Moscow prominent reformist candidates like Yeltsin publicly debated political issues with their rivals on television. In the Baltic republics, on the other hand, the CP was democratically competing with de facto opposition parties. In Central Asia and distant provinces, party functionaries had almost total control over the nomination and selection process. In some parts of the country the final stage of the campaign was the quietest and the least important. Officially unopposed candidates kept giving speeches to the collectives but no serious debate took place. In other parts of the country, the last stage of the campaign was marked by unprecedented popular initiative, live television debates, spontaneous rallies, demonstrations, and clashes with the police. On the scale of popular involvement and pressure from below, the most passive certainly were the Central Asian republics and the most active the Baltic republics.

By the date of the elections, there were 384 electoral districts in the country where only one candidate was on the ballot, unopposed.[70] Most often, if not always, these were party and Soviet functionaries. In Kazakhstan, for example, all seventeen obkom first secretaries ran unopposed.[71] In Kirgiziia nine electoral districts out of forty-one also had only one candidate on the ballot.[72] The party machine in the Central Asian

---

[70] "V Tsentral'noi Izbiratel'noi Kommissii," *Sovetskaia Rossiia*, March 11, 1989.
[71] "Vybory Narodnykh Deputatov," *Izvestiia*, March 27, 1989.
[72] "Nakal Bor'by," *Sovetskaia Kirgiziia*, March 5, 1989.

The Soviet Union

republics seems to have retained full control over the electoral process. The electoral promises of candidates in these areas were mostly promises to improve food supply, roads, or kindergartens. There was no debate on language, administrative autonomy, and political sovereignty as took place in the Baltic republics. In Turkmenistan, for example, in electoral district No. 744, two candidates debated the issues. One was the chairman of the KGB of Turkmenistan, P. M. Arkhipov, and his opponent a college teacher, B. A. Seidov. The main point of the KGB candidate's platform was to enlarge the airport, and the college teacher's was to care for the elderly.[73]

Almost identical was the campaign in electoral district No. 210 in Kirovobad, Azerbaidzhan. The first secretary of the city party committee S. F. Mamedov competed with a worker, M. Aliev. The party secretary promised to develop cultural services in the city and his opponent to construct new sporting facilities for youth.[74] There was no debate on the curfew in Baku, or on the problem of refugees, or on nationality problems.

Surprisingly, the election in Georgia, as reported in the Russian-language press, also did not reflect the popular upheaval already taking place in Georgia. In forty-two electoral districts out of 113 only one candidate was on the ballot.[75] Candidates discussed the quality of grapes whereas the residents' initiative groups debated the Soviet occupation of Georgia in 1921, the preservation of Georgian culture and language, and revelations on Communist terror during the 1924 uprising against Soviet occupation. In other words, candidates who survived the weeding-out process described above stayed away from the problems that worried the reformist intelligentsia in these republics.

A clear pattern in the last stage of the campaign in the republics of the southern belt (Central Asia, Caucasus, the Ukraine, and Moldavia) was that the issues that worried the educated strata in these societies and the issues debated by candidates were worlds apart. In some cases this led to violent protests, demonstrations, and rallies. As *Sovetskaia Kul'tura* commented on the situation in Moldavia:

> We have seen on TV how thousands of protesters were chanting the names of their candidates in the streets, and how the selection meetings, guarded by police, nominated their own candidates behind closed doors.[76]

On March 12 a huge rally took place in Kishinev. The crowd of twenty thousand people chanted "Down with the government of our republic!"

[73] "Pervye nakazy izbiratelei," *Turkmenskaia Iskra*, March 2, 1989.
[74] "Izbiratel' daet nakaz," *Bakinskii Rabochii*, March 1, 1989.
[75] "Za Perestroiku," *Pravda*, March 30, 1989.
[76] "Voskhozhdenie k narodovlastiiu," *Sovetskaia Kul'tura*, March 25, 1989.

Popular-initiative groups demanded that the Latin alphabet in the Moldavian language be restored. Some activists had established contact with the Popular Front in one of the Baltic republics, printed proclamations there in Moldavian using the Latin script, and brought them back to Moldavia.[77] The first secretary of the Moldavian CP, S. K. Grossu, said that the demands of some groups were unacceptable. He condemned the "demagogues" (a new term for critics) and troublemakers. One should not stage rallies but work harder, he said.[78] The significance of this upheaval in Moldavia is that unlike in Central Asia, the popular-initiative groups made it impossible for the party functionaries to limit themselves to generalities and vague promises. They were forced to respond unequivocally to their constituency what they thought about the language, sovereignty, and 1940 annexation issues.

The confrontation of the party apparatus with popular-initiative groups was even sharper in Moscow, Iaroslavl', and Leningrad. In Moscow a scandal broke out when it became known that an anonymous pamphlet against Yeltsin was distributed to all district first party secretaries. These pamphlets were discussed in districts and distributed to the rank and file. The supporters of Yeltsin perceived this as another provocation by the party apparatus. In response, a huge rally took place under the slogan, "Yeltsin is the candidate of the people."[79]

In Iaroslavl', an impressive rally chanted, "No to elections without choice!" Similarly, in Leningrad a wave of protests exploded against the obkom first secretary Iu. F. Solov'ev. In the Nevskii district where he was on the ballot, a popular committee "Elections 89" and other informal clubs distributed leaflets, put up posters, collected signatures, and called on the voters to cross out his name.[80] At the start of the campaign it was explicitly stated that it was allowed to campaign for, or against, any candidate. Nevskii district party committee changed its tune in violation of the law. It accused the Elections 89 Committee of spreading "fake leaflets" insulting the candidates. Popular-initiative groups and clubs assembled at a Forum of Democratic Social Forces in Leningrad and angry speeches were heard against "conservative forces within the party apparatus."[81] An outburst of indignation, wrote *Pravda*, was caused by a recent decision of the obkom to undertake measures against groupings in opposition to the CPSU. On his part, Solov'ev condemned "demagogues and extremists."[82] The establishment was particularly angered by a demonstration organized by the Democratic Union, which defined itself as an

---

[77] A. Chernenko, "Neterpenie i neterpimost'," *Pravda*, March 29, 1989.
[78] G. Samsi, "S demagogami nam ne po puti," *Sovetskaia Moldaviia*, March 3, 1989.
[79] Vitalii Tret'iakov in *Moskovskie Novosti*, March 26, 1989.
[80] "Razum protiv demagogii," *Leningradskaia Pravda*, March 21, 1989.
[81] "Perestroike sotsial'nye orientiry," *Pravda*, March 25, 1989.
[82] "Chto sluchilos' u Kazanskogo?" *Leningradskaia Pravda*, March 14, 1989.

440   *The Russian Review*

opposition party. At that rally, Democratic Union activists called for the establishment of a multiparty system, condemned the dictatorship of the CPSU, and unfurled a pre-Bolshevik Russian flag.[83] The rally was disbanded by force, in violation of electoral law. The official papers referred to the Democratic Union as a "provocateur organization." Some party officials were reported as saying, "See where this democracy is leading?"[84]

The campaign in the Baltic republics was equally tense. In contrast to Moscow and Leningrad, the CPs in the Baltic republics are generally reform-minded. Up until very recently they cooperated with the Popular Fronts and passed important legislation on language (Estonia), reinstatement of national flags, and the national heritage. But the Popular Fronts were always a step ahead of the party. They openly debated the issue of national independence and secession from the Soviet Union.[85] This generated an angry response from a part of the Russian population, primarily workers. The Internationalist Movement is becoming increasingly nationalistic. They refer to the reform course in the Baltic as "creeping counterrevolution." They protested the hoisting of the Estonian national flag at a huge rally in Tallin, and threatened strikes, violence, and even Soviet tanks.[86] A dangerous polarization of the community along national lines is taking place in the Baltics. Every candidate was confronted with the same fundamental questions: What is your position on the language law? What do you think about secession from the Soviet Union? How (not whether) do you propose to reduce Russian migration into the Baltics? The Communist Parties are torn along the ethnic lines and are trying to maneuver in this complex and explosive situation.

Election Results

Politics in the Soviet Union is full of surprises these days. So were the election results. It was widely expected that in hundreds of electoral districts unopposed party secretaries would win an easy victory. In some places, like Kazakhstan, they did. But on the whole, election results represented "a rude awakening to the inadequacy of our knowledge of the society we live in," as *Moscow News* put it.[87] The results showed a serious

---

[83] Ibid.

[84] Ibid.

[85] On the independence topic in Estonia, see "Sobraniia Kommunistov," *Sovetskaia Estoniia*, March 4, 1989; in Laviia, "Situatsiia v Respublike," *Sovetskaia Latviia*, March 14, 1989, and in Lithuania, "Plany Naroda, Plany Partii," *Sovetskaia Litva*, March 3, 1989.

[86] On threats to use tanks in Estonia, see "Zaiavlenie Narodnogo Fronta Estonii," *Sovetskaia Estoniia*, March 12, 1989. On discussion of independence movement in Latvie; "V tsentral'nom Kommitete Kompartii Latvii," *Sovetskaia Latvii*, March 18, 1989. For a complete text of the resolution of the Internationalist Movement First Congress in Estonia, see "Rezoliutsiia . . ." *Sovetskaia Estoniia*, March 14, 1989.

[87] Dmitry Kazutin, "Surprises of Political Spring," *Moscow News*, March 26, 1989.

defeat of the party establishment. In a number of key cities, numerous if not all, party and Soviet functionaries were defeated.[88] Of the thirty-eight obkom first secretaries defeated in elections, we can list the following: Iu. Solov'ev in Leningrad; A. Melnikov in Kemerovo; Bobykin in Sverdlovsk; E. Chernyshev in Perm; N. Shvyrev in Cheliabinsk; V. Zorkal-'tsev in Tomsk; N. Mal'kov in Chita; and G. Bogomiakov in Tiumen' in Russia; A. Palazhchenko in Chernigov; Ia. Pogrebniak in L'vov; G. Vandrovskii in Zakarpat'e; I. Liakhov in Voroshilovograd in the Ukraine; A. Kamai in Gomel'; V. Leonov in Mogilev in Belorussia, and some others.

In Moscow, Yeltsin scored a landslide victory in what was widely believed a race against the party apparatus. And in Iaroslavl' a young officer, Viktor Podziruk, who ran on the platform of military reform, won over General Boris Snetkov by a wide margin. In the Baltic republics, two thirds of all seats were won by candidates who had been backed by the Popular Fronts. Election results, as the Soviet press admitted, were a resounding defeat for the Communist Party and Soviet apparatus.[89] What is perhaps more important is that a fairly large group of reformist delegates were elected despite all the obstacles. Most of these people did not know each other during the elections and met for the first time at the sessions of the CPD. During the summer months of 1989 they formed an interregional group of deputies, united by their shared beliefs and political program. The Interregional Group, according to Ilia Zaslavskii consists of over three hundred deputies. Its leaders were Yeltsin and Sakharov until his death. The Interregional Group has published its program of radical reform[90] and is increasingly beginning to act as a parliamentary legal opposition.

Conclusion

The procedure for elections to the CPD seems to have been devised to be complex. It was designed to achieve two objectives. The first was to signal to the party that it could still remain the elite of society so long as it adapts to new conditions. Party leaders must be popular and pass the test of elections. On the other hand, enough ambiguities were left in the law to make party manipulation relatively easy. In this sense the procedure was a kind of transition from authoritarian to controlled democratic

---

[88] This data is drawn from the following sources: "Za perestroiku," "Vybor Naroda," *Pravda*, March 29, 1989; "Za perestroiku," "Mandaty na vlast'," *Pravda*, March 30, 1989; *Izvestiia*, March 28, 1989; "Rabochaia podderzhka," *Sovetskaia Rossiia*, March 30, 1989; "Pobedy i porazheniia," *Sovetskaia Rossiia*, March 31, 1989.

[89] "Rabochaia podderzhka," *Sovetskaia Rossiia*, March 30, 1989. For a detailed analysis of election returns by region, see Jerry Hough, "The Politics of Successful Economic Reform," *Soviet Economy*, vol. 5, no. 1 (January-March), 1989, pp. 3–47.

[90] For a program of the Interregional Group, see "Vlast' Narodu," *Narodnyi Deputat (izdanie Mezhregional'noi Gruppy)* (Moscow), July 28, 1989.

elections. The second objective of the chosen procedure was to make it possible for new forces in society to get into the legislature. However, enough obstacles were put in the way so that one could not expect too many of them to make it past all the obstacles. Here again the procedure was a compromise between authoritarian and controlled democratic. The ultimate objective of Gorbachev seems to have been to create a legislature which would include all forces of society, while not making it easy for any of them. In this he was successful.

The behavior of the party apparatus during the election campaign revealed nothing new. The same kind of manipulation was practiced during the elections to the nineteenth party conference and during the regional party conferences in November 1988-January 1989. The lesson that Gorbachev has taught them this time was that if the party does not restructure itself, he might let the voters throw them out. These elections were thus a warning to the party apparatus. The record of the party officials has shown that the party apparatus has been the main obstacle on the path of political reform.

The behavior of the electorate, the platforms of candidates, and the response of the populace are the areas where this election campaign presented several surprises. The first was the mass involvement in the political process. The second was the radical nature of the liberal candidates' platforms in terms of restoring a multiparty system and a mixed economy. The third was the crushing defeat of apparatus candidates in the elections. The long-term implications of this defeat are far-reaching. This meant that in local elections to the Soviets it became realistically possible to defeat local mafias and create reformist majorities in many big cities in 1990. The power of nomenklatura may begin to crumble. The Interregional Group of Deputies has coordinated election campaigns of its supporters in recent local elections. If the reformist candidates did so well without any coordination in 1989, they are likely to score substantial victories in the future. We are witnessing the emergence of elements that will lead to institutionalization of a multiparty political process in the Soviet Union.

At the very first meeting of the very first Soviet legislature in October 1917, Trotsky said to the Bolsheviks' opponents, the Social Democrats and the Socialist Revolutionaries, "Your role is played out. Your place is in the dust bin of history." Seventy-two years later, after the first contested elections, the same words are appropriate in regard to the party apparatus created by Lenin and Trotsky.

[21]

A Socialist Pluralism of Opinions: Glasnost *and Policy-Making under Gorbachev*

Thomas Remington

Alexander Herzen, attempting to explain the sensation occasioned by the publication of Peter Chaadaev's famous "Philosophical Letter" in 1836, characterized it as a "shot that rang out in the dark night." The scandal, he records in his memoirs, testified to the power of the word in a country, shaped by Nicholas I's policies of "official nationality," that had grown disaccustomed to open, independent speech. The essay appeared after a decade in which many of Russia's boldest intellectual spirits had been exiled, a time when "to speak was dangerous—and there was nothing to say anyway."[1]

Glasnost' has demonstrated the continuing power of the word in Russia. From the leadership's standpoint, *glasnost'* is a principal fulcrum in a massive effort at social engineering directed as much at reconstructing Soviet political culture as at reforming the structures of power. As its architects have formulated the matter, *glasnost'* is narrowing the "gap between words and deeds"—a formula widely used in the late 1970s and early 1980s by both reformist and orthodox wings of the political elite to deplore the disparity between commonly accepted norms of public and private behavior, and the pieties of party-mindedness and collectivism to which everyone was expected to pay obeisance. Alluding to Orwell's famous concept of double-think, the venerable Soviet scholar Igor' Kon analyzed this gap as a problem of social psychology. Double-think he regards as a condition in which "a different meaning is imputed to the same words; and the same person, depending on the situation (for example, at a meeting or at home) with equal sincerity affirms diametrically opposing things."[2]

This discrepancy was in fact less between "words and deeds," or, in social-scientific terms, culture and behavior, than between two interdependent but opposed codes of language *and* behavior: one for the realm of the unsanctioned-private, whether collective (such as dissident activity, religion, small-scale graft and illicit enterprise, and large-scale organized crime), or individualistic (including various forms of private rebellion and

---

[1] A. I. Gertsen, *Byloe i dumy* (Moscow: Detskaia literatura, 1968), pp. 440–41.
[2] I. Kon, "Psikhologiia sotsial'noi inertsii," *Kommunist*, no. 1, 1988, p. 70.

withdrawal and the other for the realm of the official—the *"kazennoe"*—
including ceremonial occasions, the mass media, and official acts—for
which an entirely distinct set of verbal symbols was employed. "Words"
also referred to expression in the realm of ideas, social theory, art, and
philosophy. "Deeds" in contrast applied to the field of observable behavior, of results rather than means, the real rather than the ideal. The gap
between words and deeds also implied a contempt for the irreality of
words, their inability to signify the inner truth of social life; it was also a
tacit acknowledgment that the populace generally held the ritualized
world of public life in private contempt.[3] As one wit put it, when there is
no *glasnost'*, there is *ustnost'*; that is, when that which people know or
believe or want to know about is kept out of the public record, face-to-
face verbal communication takes the place of the mass media.

As the public realm, corrupted by the constant demand for gestures
of fealty to the state and its ruling party, drifted further away from the
world of private convictions and association, the sector of independent
associational activity and opinion referred to as the civic or public realm
(expressed in the Russian term *obshchestvennost'*) atrophied. Although
doctrine paid lip service to the *concept* of *obshchestvennost'*, the freely
expressed voice of social interests, in fact virtually every political undertaking outside the state sooner or later reverted to the norm for all large-
scale Soviet organizations—a hierarchical, monopolistic, incorporated
pyramid, its territorial councils built upon local cells, managed and controlled by an *apparat* inextricably intertwined with the party-state administrative elite at all levels. The Rodina Society, dedicated to the
preservation of historic sites, is a characteristic example: formed in 1965,
by the early 1980s its central *apparat* boasted some sixty-five subdivisions; it had hundreds of local full-time secretaries, and was spending
more money on personnel than on preserving cultural monuments.
Understandably, rank-and-file participation in public organizations acquired roughly the same negligible significance as trade union membership.[4] Although certain loose opinion and discussion groups formed in

[3] The classic version of this gap was a short story, "Levers," by Alexander Iashin, published over
thirty years ago, in the period of political thaw. Four communists on a collective farm grumble
bitterly about the incompetence and ignorance of local district officials on their problems, the unrealistic plans they are assigned, and so on, as they wait to convene a party meeting. The fifth
member of the party organization, a schoolteacher, arrives, complaining about how she will obtain
firewood for the school. The others interrupt her, "We'll talk about business later, now we need to
hold the meeting." And the meeting proceeds with all verbiage of self-congratulation and self-
exhortation on over-fulfillment. This scene is recounted by Alexander Iakovlev, Gorbachev's chief
advisor for ideology, in an important address to the social sciences section of the Presidium of the
Academy of Social Sciences on April 17, 1987. "Dostizhenie kachestvennogo novogo sostoianiia
sovetskogo obshchestva i obshchestvennye nauki," *Vestnik akademii nauk*, no. 6, 1987, pp. 51–80.
[4] On the swelling of staffs in voluntary societies, see Anatolii Agranovskii's last, and posthumously, published article in *Izvestiia*, May 13, 1984, "Sokrashchenie apparata." A letter to *Pravda*

Socialist Pluralism 273

the late 1970s and early 1980s without becoming dissident in regime eyes, these rarely coalesced to the point of developing a formal internal organization. In turn the incapacity of the media and existing state and public organizations to articulate or mediate social impulses allowed the swelling of the reservoir of unrepresented, potentially mobilizable social needs and interests to approach a critical threshold.

If the silences and absences, the sterility and banality, of public life contributed to what Robert Tucker has called a "crisis of belief,"[5] still more dangerous from the center's standpoint was the decay of the crucial steering function the media are called upon to perform in the Soviet polity, as well as the feedback of information to superior authorities to allow them to evaluate actual performance in the light of policy goals. Reinforcing the media's role as an instrument for celebrating the status quo— what Alexander Iakovlev termed the "universal exultation" characteristic of the media in the Brezhnev era—was the weakness of "criticism and self-criticism." Given the insignificance of the targets singled out for public censure, most criticism amounted to praise through faint damnation. Poor performance left the media equally incapable of assisting either central policy direction or social reconnaissance.

Glasnost' is intended to reverse this resulting drift of the Soviet system toward crisis or even breakdown[6] with painful, frequently radical self-examination intended to build popular pressure for deep reform—to enable a new liveliness and credibility of "words" to serve the goal of reform in the area of "deeds" by activating personal initiative and material

---

about Pamyat' and other groups points out that the recognized public organizations such as the Rodina Society, DOSAAF, the Temperance Society, and so on have become bureaucratized and top-heavy, losing contact with their volunteer base. Their immobility, according to the letter, stimulates the formation of the new informal groups. "O pamiati mnimoi i nastoiashchei," *Pravda*, March 18, 1988.

[5] See Thomas F. Remington, "Gorbachev and the Strategy of *Glasnost'*," chap. 4 of idem, ed., *Politics and the Soviet System: Essays in Honour of Frederick C. Barghoorn* (London: Macmillan Press, 1989); Robert Tucker, "Swollen State, Spent Society: Stalin's Legacy to Brezhnev's Russia," in Tucker, *Political Culture and Leadership in Soviet Russia* (New York: Norton, 1987), p. 126.

[6] The formula "pre-crisis situation" was employed by Gorbachev in his January 1987 Plenum address and it represented a deepening and radicalization of the official interpretation of the severity of the current state of affairs. (According to a *samizdat* report of the plenum, Gorbachev, in fact, went further, and claimed that the Soviet Union was at the crisis stage, but that, in contrast to other socialist systems which had reached crisis—such as Poland, Hungary, and Czechoslovakia—there was no one who could extend help to the Soviet Union in solving its problems. See "Plenum TsK KPSS," *Strana i mir*, no. 4 (40), 1987, p. 38. Gorbachev cited some eleven crises in socialist countries to date, including those in Hungary, Czechoslovakia, China, and Albania; and no fewer than five in Poland. The veteran journalist Vasilii Seliunin and the economist Girsh Khanin have gone considerably further in their assessment of the current economic situation in the USSR, and in articles and seminars, they have repeatedly and publicly forecast that without radical economic change, the Soviet economy will reach the point of crisis and collapse by the mid-1990's. See Vasilii Seliunin, "Istoki," *Novyi Mir*, no. 5, 1988, p. 170; also Richard E. Ericson, "The Soviet Statistical Debate: Khanin vs. TsSU," Harriman Institute Occasional Papers, no. 1 (May 1988), p. 35.

self-interest in the state and public spheres. *Glasnost'* entails both a loosening and a reprogramming of the ideological content of public expression; as Gorbachev put it in December 1984:

> Broad, timely and frank information is testimony to trust in people, respect for their intelligence and feelings, their ability themselves to interpret various events. It raises the activeness of the toilers. *Glasnost'* in the work of party and state organs is an effective means of struggle against bureaucratic distortions and it obliges them more thoughtfully to approach the adoption of decisions and the organization of *kontrol'* over their fulfillment and the eradication of deficiencies and omissions. And in fact on this to a large extent depends the persuasiveness of propaganda, the effectiveness of upbringing, the ensurance of the unity of word and deed.[7]

Even before he became party leader, Gorbachev linked *glasnost'* with stiffer enforcement of bureaucratic accountability and higher effectiveness of party ideological work.

The problem is that the instrumental objective of making party ideological work more credible by tolerating freer criticism is at cross-purposes with the ideological pluralization actually resulting from the expansion of freedom for interest articulation and representation. The policy drive of "democratization," especially marked since January 1987, has accorded ideological legitimation to such liberal values as free speech and free association. These ideals, partly realized through *glasnost'*, have been valued not just instrumentally, but in themselves by democratically minded sections of the intelligentsia, although the conservative elements of the political elite undoubtedly interpret them as merely a measured extension of the familiar practice of criticizing the mistakes of the preceding leadership period.[8] The instrumental aspect of *glasnost'* works by reprogramming ideological controls over public life: it is aimed at improving the steering capacity of the center by reducing the opacity and resistance of the lower reaches of the bureaucracy to supervisory control from above and by generating national public discussion and support for policy decisions that have already been adopted. The bitter struggle over

---

[7] M. S. Gorbachev, *Zhivoe tvorchestvo naroda* (Moscow, 1984), p. 30.

[8] A typical example of the "instrumental" view was the comment by the newly appointed first secretary of the Rostov provincial party organization, Boris Volodin, who observed that in the past, the lack of openness protected incompetence and irresponsibility. Allowing more criticism "raises the accountability of party officials for their assigned tasks" and will provide "a graphic example to all the toilers that we treat the acts of communists, regardless of the position they hold, with the party by-laws which are the same for all communists." Furthermore: "It goes without saying that all our work in expanding *glasnost'* is not an end in itself" but should "contribute to the fulfillment of tasks set by the Twenty-seventh Party Congress, the June 1986 Central Committee Plenum, and develop the initiative of labor collectives, rousing in people the aspiration to achieve higher results." (B. Volodin, "Rasshirenie glasnosti—vopros politicheskii," *Partiinaia zhizn'*, no. 17, 1986, pp. 23, 24, 27).

Socialist Pluralism   275

glasnost', therefore, is a dispute over the political consequences of ideological liberalization.

This article is intended as a preliminary effort at stocktaking after three years of *glasnost'* and addresses above all the impact of *glasnost'* on changing patterns of articulation and mediation of political interests. It will argue that the leadership strategy of employing *glasnost'*—that is, encouragement of more open expression in public communication in order to mobilize support for the reform program—has resulted in stimulating still more radical, and ultimately unincorporable political expression generated by Soviet society's deeper unresolved cleavages.

–1–

Prompted by a significant shift in policy at the center, *glasnost'* alters authority relations throughout the political system. Above all it makes it considerably harder for well-organized bureaucratic interests to appropriate the party's ideological control over political expression for parochial political needs. Formerly so many social issues were closed off to critical comment at meetings, in the media, in the arts, and in other arenas of public life that the realm of problems that were acceptable topics for deliberation narrowed to the point of irreality. In the early 1980s, matters had reached the point that only the lowliest and weakest agencies and territorial organizations' bodies were unable to fend off routine criticism. *Glasnost'*, then, has reduced though not eliminated the power that many party and government offices exercised in demanding that public comment on matters falling under their territorial or departmental purview first be "cleared" with them.

Because of the difficulties this trend posed for central control over bureaucratic performance, the initial and generally accepted premise of *glasnost'* as a strategy was expressed in the formula, first offered by Egor Ligachev at the 27th Party Congress, and subsequently repeated by many others, that there are no zones off-limits to criticism. The party encouraged criticism in the interests of enforcing high and uniform standards of performance throughout the political system. Particularly following the January 1987 plenum, however, which laid particular emphasis on the principle of "democratization," *glasnost'* allowed radical statements challenging established doctrines, such as Nikolai Shmelev's essay on the bankruptcy of central planning in the June 1987 number of *Novyi mir*, the rapid growth of pressure for the rehabilitation of Stalin's Old Bolshevik victims, and the profusion of harsh attacks on water projects in many publications, including *Ogonek*, *Novyi mir*, and *Kommunist*. Indeed, since early 1987, *glasnost'* has opened to public discussion virtually every theoretical postulate formerly regarded as essential to Marxism, including the nature of property under socialism, collectivized agriculture, central planning versus markets, the party's monopoly on policy-

276   *The Russian Review*

making and cadre appointments, social equality, the doctrine of world class struggle, collectivism, and the primacy of military force in protecting national security. Although by the end of 1988 restrictions on reporting remained—the Ministry of Health, for example, sought to prevent reporting of the fact that DDT continues to be manufactured and used, and the space program remained shrouded in secrecy—most of those restrictions that survived stemmed from administrative rather than ideological considerations. That is, they reflected powerful agencies' preferences for operational autonomy as opposed to the party's need to maintain a monopoly on socialist doctrines.[9]

Moreover, through law and decree no less than through *glasnost'*, Gorbachev has swept away decades of homage to collectivism, seeking to unleash personal interest as a motive force in production and trade, and to improve quality and performance through competitive pressure both in economic and political spheres. According to the reformists, indifference to the public weal, the attitude that the realm of the state is not the common property of the whole people but is rather "no one's," has created a dangerous vacuum of moral integrity, a breakdown in the normative fabric that keeps personal amorality in check and thus preserves social peace; it has nurtured as well a habitual indifference to economic productivity.[10] Thus Nikolai Shmelev, an economist who has been one of the boldest spirits in the new literature of liberal reform, has flatly pronounced that "whatever is efficient is moral and whatever is moral is efficient."[11] The problems of economic reform have prompted sharp and searching debates over the essential nature of justice under Soviet socialism: the permissible degree of social inequality, the legitimacy of personal interest, the creation of "safety nets" to protect the economically deprived, and the trade-offs between efficiency and equality.[12]

[9] On the DDT story, see the remarks by Kazakh poet M. Shakhanov at the plenum of the USSR Writers' Union as published in *Literaturnaia gazeta*, January 25, 1989. On the continuing secrecy surrounding space and defense installations, see A. Pokrovskii, "A chto v 'iashchike'?" *Pravda*, August 6, 1988.

[10] Professor Butenko cites transcripts from trials of a worker and a peasant accused of theft of state property. The worker responded to the charges as follows: "Does what you call social property really belong to society? Not at all! Here property, as they used to say in the old days, is God's, that is, nobody's. No one has any use for it, so therefore I took the box with the tool so it wouldn't go ownerless (*bezkhoznym*). If I hadn't taken it, someone else would have!" The peasant charged with stealing a bag of grain from a collective farm testified: "If this grain had truly been ours, the peasants', would it really have been lying around (*valialos' by*)? . . . when it's locked up, then it is someone else's, you can't touch it. I took the bag because I sowed and reaped grain, and took it since it was not someone else's but nobody's!" A. P. Butenko, "O kharaktere sobstvennosti v usloviiakh real'nogo sotsializma," *EKO*, no. 2, 1988, pp. 15–16.

[11] Nikolai Shmelev, "Avansi i dolgi," *Novyi mir*, no. 6, 1987, p. 158; idem, "Novye trevogi," *Novyi mir*, no. 4, 1988, p. 175; idem, "The Rouble and Perestroika," *Moscow News*, no. 6 (February 14–21), 1988.

[12] For the views of two conservative social scientists who conclude that the dispute over the

Socialist Pluralism   277

A new concern with individualism has also entered the debate over political reform. A recent letter to *Kommunist* argues that decades of propaganda have persuaded people that the balance between state and individual interests must always favor the state: we must instead recover, writes the author, head of the chair in state and law at Kaliningrad University, the ancient tradition of the fundamental worth and dignity of the individual citizen. The citizen is hgher than the state: he forms it, and should not be brought up in blind obedience to it. The authority of the citizen, the letter concludes, must become the point of departure for all political and legal reform.[13] In both the political and economic reform debates, values associated with liberal individualism are gaining strength as the only intellectually defensible alternative to the threadbare formulations which had served as rationalizations for the post-Stalinist system.

In turn, the breathtaking assault on long-established and often deeply cherished ideological tenets has resulted in an intense backlash and perhaps even a direct challenge to Gorbachev's power in the Andreeva affair.[14] The sensation and fear the Andreeva article provoked among the intelligentsia and the outpouring of attacks that appeared once *Pravda* published an authoritative rebuttal centered less on the defense of Stalinism and the chauvinistic and anti-Semitic views Andreeva propounded than on the harsh, authoritarian tone in which the article was written, which created the impression, according to *Pravda*, that it was expressing an ideological platform, "a manifesto of the anti-perestroika forces."[15] Yet for all her own reactionary views, "Andreeva" is indeed justified in interpreting *glasnost'* as a challenge to socialist ideology both in form and content.

This is true both because the revision of doctrine has granted a variety of political forces access to public attention that could not have

---

relative priority of individualist and collectivist conceptions of social justice lies at the root of many other values, such as subsidies to poor families, the proper level of the inheritance tax, and the degree of freedom to be allowed private enterprise, see N. F. Naumova and V. Z. Rogovin, "Zadacha na spravedlivost'" in *Sotsiologicheskie issledovaniia*, no. 3 (May/June) 1987, pp. 12–23. Another review acknowledges that the majority opinion regards the accumulation of individual wealth as illegitimate and incompatible with the norms of socialism, as indicated by the many letters in the press supporting restrictions on the incomes and activities of individual entrepreneurs under the new laws authorizing individual labor activity. The author considers this indifference to the problem of productivity as having been nurtured under the system of statism prevalent from the Stalin era to the present. (G. S. Batygin, " 'Dobrodetel' protiv interesa," *Sotsiologicheskie issledovaniia*, no. 3 (May/June) 1987, pp. 24–36.)

[13] V. Prokop'ev, "Demokratiia i chelovecheskoe dostoinstvo," *Kommunist*, no. 8, 1988, pp. 43–45.

[14] Nina Andreeva, "Ne mogu postupat'sia printsipami," *Sovetskaia Rossiia*, March 13, 1988.

[15] "Printsipy perestroiki—revoliutsionnost' myshleniia i deistvii," *Pravda*, April 5, 1988. Other refutations followed, including Nikolai Bodnaruk, "Sluchai i iavleniie," *Izvestiia*, April 10, 1988, which employed much the same phraseology as *Pravda's* unsigned comment; I Nastavshev, "Prikosnis' k istochniku," *Kommunist*, no. 6, 1988, pp. 109–15.

gained a hearing in the past; and, still more importantly, because the mechanisms of ideological direction and control over society have been drastically reduced. This is turn has permitted an extraordinary flourishing of independent associational activity, much of it aimed at influencing policy decisions.

–2–

Since July 1987, Gorbachev has repeatedly used the novel term, "socialist pluralism of opinions," to describe the vigorous public debate of social problems and their possible solutions. Since the phrase, with its ideologically provocative hint of bourgeois liberalism, had not been used before, even in so qualified a way, and since Gorbachev has taken care almost always to apply pluralism to opinion (that is, words) rather than power, property, or interests, it is clear that he is using the term deliberately and conservatively.[16] Through it, Gorbachev distinguishes between the legitimate diversity of interests and opinions consistent with socialism and unacceptable efforts to institute multiparty competition or restore private ownership of capital.

Gorbachev first employed the term "socialist pluralism" in his address to media executives shortly after the June 1987 Central Committee plenum, where major economic reforms were adopted. Urging that editors not allow newspapers and magazines to be creatures of narrow group interests, he demanded that the media present the voices of the whole society, so that "the whole, so to speak, socialist pluralism is present in every publication."[17] Assumed is the inner, unifying truth that transcends the limited and partial visions of the many. In September 1987, just after his extended summer leave, Gorbachev referred to socialist pluralism again in a response to a question posed by a member of a group of French public figures, but did not elaborate on the idea; he did not confine it to the sphere of opinion, distinguishing only "socialism pluralism" from its counterpart under capitalism.[18]

These comments might have seemed casual and off-handed had Gorbachev not returned to the concept of pluralism repeatedly in early 1988, now qualifying it with the "of opinions" phrase. In his address to the February 1988 plenum, devoted to basic ideological thery, he observed that: "For the first time in many decades we are really experiencing a socialist pluralism of opinions" and in the same speech he introduced another theme that also harkened back to the Eastern European humanist

[16]For example, pluralism was not mentioned by Alexander Iakovlev in his highly revisionist address to the social science section of the Academy of Sciences Presidium in April 1987 (Iakovlev, "Dostizhenie," *Vestnik akademii nauk*, no. 6, 1987).

[17]"Prakticheskimi delami uglubliat' perestroiku," *Pravda*, July 15, 1987.

[18]*Pravda*, September 30, 1987.

Socialist Pluralism 279

Marxists of the 1960s, the applicability of Marx's category of "alienation" to socialist society. In Poland, Yugoslavia, Czechoslovakia, and other socialist countries the view that man could be alienated from the means of production, his labor, and from spiritual values even under socialism had been seriously discussed by theorists in the post-Stalin reform period, but the debate was received coldly in Moscow, especially after 1968. Now Gorbachev was reinstating two of the most resonant concepts of the Eastern European Marxist humanists, alienation and pluralism.[19]

Again in May 1988, meeting with media executives, Gorbachev referred to pluralism and insisted that, notwithstanding the icy blast of Stalinism released by the Andreeva letter in *Sovetskaia Rossiia*, the party was not retreating from its commitment to democratizing socialism. Criticism must be in the interests of socialism and against conservatism; there must be "freedom of expression of opinions and choice," but all within the socialist order. A truly Leninist socialism made room for "pluralism of opinions, interests and needs."[20] Pluralism, qualified both as socialist and as "pluralism of opinions" then became a frequently repeated totem of liberal critics of Andreeva's broadside. She had challenged the Gorbachev leadership with an accusation that socialist ideology itself was in jeopardy because of the loss of sharp frontiers between socialism and bourgeois liberalism. She accused these forces of "disseminating an extra-socialist pluralism" and politicizing the newly born independent organizations "on the basis not at all of socialist pluralism."[21] *Pravda's* response reaffirmed the current diversity of expressed opinion, which it called a sign of "the real, currently existing socialist pluralism of opinions."[22] The "Theses" issued by the Central Committee a month before the June Party Conference went so far as to drop the "socialist" qualifier from the phrase, but Gorbachev in his address to the conference itself reverted to the standard wording, "socialist pluralism of opinions," although associating it with a newly emphasized concept of "competition" (*sostiazanie* and *sostiazatel' nost*).[23] Again, in his rather critical address to the media in September 1988, with its unmistakable tone of urgency (as in the reminder that the working class is growing impatient with mere "conversations"—that is, words), Gorbachev reaffirmed his previous position: "Publish everything. There should be a pluralism of opinions. But with such directedness that the line of perestroika, the cause of socialism, are defended and strengthened."[24]

[19] *Moskovskaia pravda*, February 19, 1988.

[20] "Cherez demokratizatsiiu—k novomu obliku sotsializma," *Pravda*, May 11, 1988.

[21] Andreeva, "Ne mogu," *Sovetskaia Rossiia*, March 13, 1988.

[22] "Printsipy perestroiki—revoliutsionnost' myshleniia i deistvii," *Pravda*, April 5, 1988.

[23] "Tezisy Tsentral'nogo Komiteta KPSS k XIX Vsesoiuznoi partiinoi konferentsii," *Pravda*, May 27, 1988; Gorbachev address, Central Television Program One, June 28, 1988.

[24] "Na novom etape perestroiki," *Pravda*, September 25, 1988.

280   *The Russian Review*

Addressing a select audience of leading intellectuals in early January 1989, Gorbachev restated his carefully delimited doctrine of socialist pluralism, welcoming differences of opinion so long as they contributed constructively to perestroika, but rejecting open competition for power. His position, as before, relegated pluralism to the realm of opinions and treated debate as "truth-seeking" aimed at "a synthesis of different opinions, on the basis of which we get nearer to the truth."[25] He begs the question, therefore, of whether there is, in the end, a single truth in politics, and simply reformulates the traditional "choral" or "orchestral" view under which the diversity of opinions in society (albeit now linked to diversity of social interests) are "synthesized" or harmonized into consensus. Moreover, he did not mention, let alone defend, the theory of socialist pluralism when he addressed a group of workers at the Central Committee the next month, where instead he expatiated contemptuously on the "nonsensical" idea of a multiparty system.[26]

On the other hand, liberal intellectuals could not long remain content with an interpretation of pluralism that confined it solely to the expression of opinion. Stimulated by the official refutation of the Andreeva letter in early April 1988 and the preparations for the June party conference, reformists began elaborating a broader conception linking pluralism to wider participation and competition in the political system. Expressing gratification at the legitimation of a concept the very mention of which, as one writer put it, "we awaited with hope, never in our wildest dreams expecting to get it," they pressed for liberalizing and democratizing change. Nonmembers of the party, even non-Marxists and religious believers, should be able to take part in political life and "check" the party; they should be allowed to rise to executive positions and be chosen for membership on the boards of public bodies. Unofficial organizations should be free to form, compete for members, and run candidates for deputies to soviets.[27] Some called for the creation of an all-union "Patriotic Front," an umbrella organization which would in some sense counterbalance the power of the CPSU.[28] For the most part, the liberals

---

[25] British Broadcasting Corporation, Summary of World Broadcasts, Soviet Union (hereafter SWB SU) 0353, C/1–14, January 9, 1989.

[26] SWB SU/0389, C/1–18, February 20, 1989.

[27] O. Smolin, " 'Zashchitnye mekhanizmy' sotsialisticheskoi demokratii," in "Demokratizatsiia partii—demokratizatsiia obshchestva," *Kommunist*, no. 6, 1988, pp. 28–32; and L. Shevtsova, "Garantii narodovlastiia," *Literaturnaia gazeta*, April 27, 1988.

[28] This suggestion was advanced along with a series of other democratic reforms in a letter to *Kommunist*'s series on party reform. It has been backed by Tatiana Zaslavskaia, Boris Kurashvili, and other reformers. Its proponents envision it as a Soviet equivalent to the united fronts which have maintained a shadowy parliamentary existence in the people's democracies since the establishment of communist rule in the late 1940s. At the party conference, Gorbachev himself stopped short of endorsing the idea, calling simply for more discussion of the appropriate forms for the "patriotic movement" of Soviet youth, women, believers, and other strata which was forming in support of

Socialist Pluralism 281

sought to reconcile institutions associated with liberal democracy, such as parliamentarism, a constitutional court, a directly elected head of state, contested elections of party and government officials, and real local government, with one-party rule and state ownership of the basic means of production.[29] But by the end of 1988, the linkage between private property as a defense against the power of the state and political pluralism in the sense of freely competing interest groups and parties was being explored in the press.[30]

–3–

Although Gorbachev's provocative albeit qualified use of the term "pluralism" accepts a substantial loosening of ideological controls over political expression, it is a good deal less satisfactory as a description of the development of central press discussion even since 1987. To a much greater extent than is commonly recognized, public debate has followed the pattern of sponsored "discussion campaigns," which are a standard feature of party ideological work. Discussion campaigns are devices to

---

perestroika. Much like the Czechoslovak reform movement in 1968, the proposals preserve the communist party's leading role while allowing the "patriotic front" to expand political participation. See A. Krechetnikov, "Nazrevshie izmeneniia," *Kommunist*, no. 8, 1988, p. 43; Bill Keller, "A Gorbachev Adviser Urges a Political Alternative to the Communist Party," *New York Times*, May 24, 1988; Gorbachev, Soviet TV, June 28, 1988.

[29] Consider the effort by Boris Kurashvili, a leading reformer and a senior associate of the Institute of State and Law of the Academy of Sciences, to reconcile single-party rule with both separation of powers and a system of checks and balances: "In the conditions of a one-party system that took historical form in the USSR, the pluralization of public life, the determination of a course of development for the country, the resolution of disagreements and contradictions linked with the advancement and selection of alternatives, can readily occur within the framework of a single ruling party, by means of a mechanism of intra-party democracy more developed than at present. That classical form of pluralism known as "the separation of powers" (legislative, executive, and judicial) is another matter. "Separation of powers" does not mean the absence of unity of power, as though each of the three aforementioned powers addressed society independently of the others with its decisions. In its dealing with society the state power acts as a united whole. United, but having its own internal structure. In the framework of this structure and by the interaction of the different, sometimes mutually opposed, subsystems, the governmental impacts of a unified system of power on society are worked out. And here society, its collective and individual members, can "send back" an illegal or inappropriate governmental decision to the system of power and in this way bring into motion the "separation of powers," here understood as a mechanism for complementing and balancing the powers of one state organ (which has taken a decision) with the powers of another organ, in order to achieve the adoption of a more well-founded decision, its annulment or correction." (B. Kurashvili, "K polnovlastiiu sovetov," *Kommunist*, no. 8, 1988, pp. 31–32.

[30] An article in *Sovetskaia Litva* in February 1989 suggested that private, or at least nonstate, property helped protect society against the power of the state bureaucracy and called for a multiparty system. The fearless Boris Kurashvili, in a roundtable discussion on the question of pluralism, was quite willing to contemplate the possibility that a "socialist bourgeoisie" might strive peacefully to protect and advance its property interests. See E. Proshechkin, "On State Ownership and Pluralism," in Foreign Broadcast Information Service, USSR, Daily Report (hereafter FBIS-SOV) 89–026, February 9, 1989, pp. 51–52; For Kurashvili's cited comments see "Sotsialisticheskii pliuralizm," *Sotsiologicheskie issledovaniia*, no. 5, 1988, p. 18.

282   *The Russian Review*

illuminate policy goals of the leadership over a defined period, a period culminating in the adoption of a document or final draft of a document, such as a law of resolution. The campaign is intended to build public support and awareness for important enactments by creating a public atmosphere of mass participation in the policy's elaboration. The forms of discussion campaigns have been extensively described both in the Soviet and Western literature, and need not be detailed here.[31] Suffice it to say that mass discussion as a form of ideological campaign has a long history (for example, the discussion of the 1936 Constitution lasted five months, during which time *Pravda* published numerous critical letters from around the country, and over thirteen thousand suggestions were examined by the Central Executive Committee)[32] and that it has remained a standard feature of ideological work through the Khrushchev, Brezhnev, and post-Brezhnev eras, contributing in no small measure to the tendency for public ceremonial to grow increasingly detached from social realities. Upon assuming the party leadership, Gorbachev inherited some ideological campaigns, redirected others, and initiated still others in his effort to mobilize public support for his ambitious program of social reconstruction. Among the campaigns he inherited in 1985 was the observance of the fortieth anniversary of victory in World War II, a campaign which, as the first modern Soviet leader not to have participated in the war, Gorbachev could do little to redirect for his own ideological goals.[33] Another was the fiftieth anniversary of the Stakhanov movement, marked by a media campaign tying Stakhanovism to the goals of accelerating social modernization, raising labor productivity and discipline, and putting en-

---

[31] Robert Sharlet analyzes the discussion campaign leading to the adoption of the final draft of the 1977 Constitution in his book *The New Soviet Constitution of 1977: Analysis and Text* (Brunswick, OH: King's Court Communications, 1978); see also Thomas Remington, "Policy Innovation and Soviet Media Campaigns," *Journal of Politics*, vol. 45, no. 1 (February 1983), pp. 220–27, which discusses the standard media campaigns of the late Brezhnev period on the basis of a comparison of two 1979 media campaigns; further detail may be found in Thomas F. Remington, *The Truth of Authority: Ideology and Communication in the Soviet Union* (Pittsburgh: University of Pittsburgh Press, 1988). Iasen Zasurskii, dean of the journalism faculty of Moscow University, writes in a book published as recently as 1987 that the mass media have done much to popularize and publicize current party policies and to shape public opinion about them; strangely indifferent to the current near-universal contempt for the hollow, ritualistic press campaigns of the Brezhnev era, he cites the public discussions of the 1977 Constitution, the discussion of the new Law on the Labor Collective in 1983, and the reform of the general and vocational education system in 1984 as positive examples of recent press discussions. See Ia. N. Zasurskii, ed., *Zhurnalistika i politika* (Moscow: 1987), p. 17.

[32] V. P. Smirnov, "Iz istorii massovykh obsuzhdenii v partiinoi pechati," *Voprosy istorii KPSS*, no. 5, 1986, p. 23.

[33] Nevertheless, there were hints of a new ideological line prior to the fortieth anniversary. See, for example, the *Pravda* editorial for March 23, 1985, entitled "Vospitanie istoriei." While not explicitly revising any shibboleths, it suggested that there was much to be learned from a sober study of the facts of Soviet history that would benefit future generations. It represented the first suggestion that ideological work should shift from an emphasis on celebrating anniversaries of the mythologized past to a new objectivity designed to improve progress in the future.

terprises on a footing of economic accountability.[34] Still others were the seventieth anniversary of the October Revolution and the 800th anniversary of the campaign against the Polovetsians recounted in the epic *Lay of Igor's Host*. An ideological campaign which Gorbachev initiated in May 1985, shortly after his installation as general secretary, was the temperance campaign, an aspect of which has been discussion in the press of the social pathologies caused by alcohol abuse.[35] Another was the campaign organized around the theme of "scientific-technical acceleration."

Perhaps of greatest significance from the standpoint of the development of *glasnost'* was the reorientation of the most important ideological campaign Gorbachev inherited, the preparations for the 27th Party Congress, and specifically the drafting of a new version of the party program. Decisions on the scale and themes of the campaign preceding the 27th Party Congress were adopted at the October 1985 Central Committee plenum, and evidently presupposed a campaign structure basically similar to the discussion campaigns surrounding the 1977 Constitution, the 1983 labor collective law, and the 1984 education reform.[36] It was, to be sure, the October Plenum which approved the drafts of the new edition of the party program, the revisions in the party statute, and the guidelines for economic development through 2000, and directed that they be published as a basis of discussion before the impending party congress.[37] However, the October plenum was only reorienting a campaign already in progress. Apart from the resolutions to be adopted at the congress, upon which a new general secretary would have needed to set the stamp of his own policy program, preparation of the new edition of the party program had long been underway, and it was important for Gorbachev to strip the current draft of as many of the theoretical conceptions associated with the Brezhnev-Chernenko forces as possible, and to turn it into a reference source for ideas associated with his leadership. A case in point, one on which Gorbachev himself commented at the congress, is the progressive delegitimation of the Brezhnev-era formula of "developed socialism," now regarded simply as a rationalization of conservatism and decay.[38]

The October 1985 plenum illustrates Gorbachev's skillful use of party meetings—plenums, conferences, and consultations—to conclude

[34] See Gorbachev's speech, "The Unfading Traditions of a Labor Exploit," *Pravda* and *Izvestiia*, September 21, 1985, excerpted and translated in *Current Digest of the Soviet Press* (hereafter *CDSP*), vol. 37, no. 38 (October 16, 1985), pp. 10–11.

[35] For early articles providing factual information and background material for conducting the media temperance campaign including results of sociological surveys of drinking, see Boris Levin, "Issledovanie pokazalo," *Zhurnalist*, no. 7, 1985, p. 44.

[36] E. A. Blazhnov, "Partiinaia pechat' v ideologicheskom obespechenii preds'ezdovskoi kampanii," *Vestnik moskovskogo universiteta*, ser. 10 Zhurnalistika, no. 2, 1986.

[37] See *Pravda*, October 16, 1985.

[38] This issue is discussed in Remington, *The Truth of Authority*, chap. 1.

press discussions which, in the scope and radicalism of permitted expression, go far beyond the changes envisioned in the policy statements which launch them. For example, the pre-congress discussion of changes in the party statute and program raised two topics which ultimately proved too sensitive for the congress to deal with, yet which by virtue of being addressed were added to the latent political agenda.[39] One was the question of the privileges enjoyed by the political elite, and the other was the need to limit the terms of office-holders. In both cases, guidelines to editors on the scope of permissible criticism were ambiguous, creating the circumstances which led the normally cautious editors of *Pravda* to publish T. Samolis' famous review of reader mail on the subject of the privilege enjoyed by political officials, "Ochishchenie" ("Cleansing"), in February 1986, for which *Pravda* was rebuked by name at the congress.[40] These themes were not so much ideologically unacceptable as premature. Both returned as major foci of discussion in the run-up to the 19th party conference in 1988. Samolis herself, for example, whose article had stirred up the scandal, published a second congratulatory article in *Pravda* in June 1988. Not only had she not been fired from her job for her earlier article as many had expected, she wrote, but her position had been vindicated by the tide of subsequent reader mail.[41] Although the theme of illegitimate privilege was evidently now acceptable for discussion, it was not the object of any policy decisions at the party conference (although earlier in 1988 a decision was taken to restructure the system of closed coupon stores for privileged Soviet shoppers); on the other hand, ways of limiting the term of government and party officials became a major running theme of discussions leading up to and at the party conference, having been focussed by the proposal in the Central Committee Theses to limit party and government officials to two, and under exceptional cir-

[39] In their study of agenda-formation, Cobb and Elder distinguish the "governmental" agenda, consisting of issues before policy-makers for decision, from the "systemic" agenda, referring to issues that elements of the citizenry believe require public attention. See Roger W. Cobb and Charles D. Elder, *Participation in American Politics: The Dynamics of Agenda-Building*, 2nd ed. (Baltimore: Johns Hopkins Press, 1983), pp. 85–86.

[40] T. Samolis, "Ochishchenie," *Pravda*, February 13, 1986. *Pravda* must have been immediately called to task for this article, because its February 15 issue carried a rebuttal. Although individual party members might exist who fail to meet the party's high standards, it was wrong, according to a reader whom *Pravda* quoted by way of recantation, to generalize from them to the existence of an entire "party-administrative stratum" resisting the loss of its perquisites. On articles calling for ways to induce the voluntary retirement of aging officials, see V. Vasinsky and A. Ezhelev, "Application for Retirement," *Izvestiia*, December 1, 1985 (trans. in *CDSP*, vol. 37, no. 46 [November 15, 1985], p. 12); also see the round-up of articles about the renewal of members of leading party posts by means of mandatory rotation, and on the problem of getting rid of unwanted older leaders in *CDSP*, vol. 38, no. 6 (March 12, 1986), pp. 4–6.

[41] T. Samolis, "Ochishchenie pravdoi," *Pravda*, June 7, 1988. The title is nicely ambiguous, since it suggests that she had been vindicated both by *pravda*, truth and *Pravda* the newspaper.

cumstances, three, five-year terms. Once again, discussion seemed to follow the familiar contours of an organized media campaign: a leader signals his interest in a press discussion of a particular idea in order to generate a consensus around a preferred policy, and then, once the policy has been enacted, a press discussion is held to publicize it and demand its implementation.

Because of the enormous sensitivity surrounding Stalin and Stalinism, the campaign marking the seventieth anniversary of the October Revolution became the occasion for multiple and competing high-level statements of guidance to the mass media. In March 1987, Ligachev addressed a meeting at the State Radio and Television Committee to outline the media's tasks in preparations for the October anniversary; he advised them to emphasize "propaganda of the achievements of Soviet power," avoiding the temptation to portray "our history as a chain of constant mistakes and disappointments."[42] In July 1987, following the June plenum on economic reform, Gorbachev met with editors and other officials in the ideological sphere to discuss media coverage of the results of the plenum as well as media work more generally. His comments about the treatment of history urged balance of negative with positive material. While the repressions of 1937–38, he stated, can never be forgiven or justified, by the same token the media must also reflect positive light on the great accomplishments of the people in constructing a socialist state that succeeded in withstanding and defeating Naziism.[43] Just two months later, during Gorbachev's extended leave from work during August and September 1987, Egor Ligachev again met with editors to offer authoritative advice on coverage of the anniversary theme, where he again warned against an excessively negative slant in treating Soviet history.[44] Gorbachev's comments on the Stalin period in his seventieth anniversary address, taken as ideological signals, represented a compromise between radical calls for the rehabilitation of Bukharin and other other Bolsheviks repressed by Stalin and tributes to Stalin's wise leadership.[45] But at the same time that the speech concluded one "discussion," it initiated a new and more radical review of history that resulted in Bukharin's full rehabilitation, and a blanket rehabilitation of all victims of Stalinist mass repression.

One of the most important discussion campaigns preparatory to a major political event was the debate leading up to the general party con-

---

[42] "Navstrechu 70-letiiu Velikogo Oktiabria," *Pravda*, March 24, 1987.
[43] "Prakticheskimi delami uglubliat' perestroiku," *Pravda*, July 15, 1987.
[44] "Soveshchanie v TsK KPSS," *Pravda*, September 17, 1987.
[45] M. S. Gorbachev, "Oktiabr' i perestroika: revoliutsiia prodolzhaetsia," *Pravda*, November 3, 1987.

ference held in June-July 1988. Both before and after the publication in early May of the Central Committee's "Theses," designed to specify the agenda for the conference as well as to formulate proposals for adoption in conference resolutions, the Soviet press was brimming with diverse, frequently extraordinary proposals for political and economic reform. The debate gave reformers an opportunity to advance ideas more radical than any ever published in the Soviet media. As in previous discussion campaigns, Gorbachev skillfully allowed the range of published views in effect to "bracket" his own position, chosen from the middle ground between the most radical and the most conservative viewpoints set forth in the debate. Gorbachev's proposals for change stopped well short of the most sweeping proposals that had been advanced in the press: he failed to endorse the "patriotic front," the separation of powers principle, or the constitutional court. In each case, however, he proposed a reform meeting the liberals part way. With respect to the constitutional court and the power of judicial review, he proposed a vague, compromise form, a "committee of constitutional supervision" to oversee lower government bodies, a cross between the people's control committees and the procuracy. Instead of a patriotic front he offered a "congress of people's deputies" to be made up in equal numbers of delegates elected from territorial constituencies, national constituencies, and recognized public organizations. Instead of fully endorsing a separation of powers he proposed a radical expansion of the powers of territorial soviets vis-à-vis both central branch bureaucracies and territorial party committees. These proposals, all subsequently enacted in conference resolutions and later in constitutional amendments which were hastily adopted only one month after they were published in draft form, represented potentially significant steps toward the activation of the soviets and democratization of electoral procedures. Time and again, the final outcome of a discussion campaign is a policy decision envisioning change which is substantial but less sweeping in its intended impact than some of the proposals which have been offered in the course of the campaign. The final decision represents a policy outcome which has been initiated by the central leadership, defended and fleshed out in public debate, and finally specified and enacted by the central leadership.

No less significant than discussion campaigns in anticipation of a major decision or event are the campaigns following them, which also invite authoritative guidance to the media on appropriate treatment. More than past leaders, in fact, Gorbachev has made it a practice to meet with editors and other executives in the ideological establishment both before and after high-level political forums to advise them on the appropriate balance in their coverage of the themes associated with the policies adopted at the meeting. After the 27th Party Congress, Gorbachev met with media executives to explain the tasks devolving to them from the congress.[46] Two weeks after the January 1987 Central Committee plenum, Gorbachev held a six-hour-long meeting with media executives, reviewing the significance of the plenum and indicating the ways the media should aid in implementing its decisions.[47] Again, after the June 1987 Central Committee plenum, Gorbachev addressed a conference of media representatives at the Central Committee to explain the objectives of the *perestroika* program and the ways the media should contribute to its fulfillment.[48] He held a fourth meeting with the media in early January 1988, a meeting which lasted seven hours.[49] He held another, in anticipation of the June party conference, on 7 May 1988.[50] Again, following the summer of 1988, with its clear indications of a struggle over the general line in foreign and ideological policy, Gorbachev met with the media; this occurred shortly after the Politburo adopted a major plan on Central Committee restructuring but before the sudden plenum of September 30, and Gorbachev used the occasion to heighten the sense of national urgency about *perestroika*.[51] Both Ligachev and Iakovlev have also addressed gatherings of editors and ideological officials, but far less frequently than has Gorbachev.[52]

No better example might be cited, in fact, of the responsiveness of

[46] "Vstrecha v TsK KPSS," *Pravda*, March 15, 1986.

[47] "Ubezhdennost'—opora perestroiki," *Kommunist*, no. 4, 1987, pp. 20–27.

[48] "Prakticheskimi delami uglubliat' perestroiku," *Pravda*, July 15, 1987.

[49] "Demokratizatsiia—sut' perestroiki, sut' sotsializma," *Pravda*, January 13, 1988; Yegor Yakovlev, "Checking Our Watches," *Moscow News*, no. 3 (January 24–31), 1988, p. 4.

[50] "Cherez demokratizatsiu—k novomu obliku sotsializma," *Pravda*, May 11, 1988.

[51] "Na novom etape perestroiki," *Pravda*, September 25, 1988.

[52] Besides the occasions already noted, Ligachev met with the staff of the State Radio and Television Committee in November 1985, expressing serious dissatisfaction with its work, and admonishing broadcast workers to ensure that "our television and radio must be entirely and fully political television and political radio." Recognizing one needs political slogans in every broadcast, he nevertheless insisted that "television and radio programs must be subordinate to one goal—propaganda, exposition and implementation of party policy." *New York Times*, November 21, 1985, citing *Pravda*, November 21, 1985. More recently, and after Iakovlev had reportedly replaced Ligachev as the senior secretary charged with ideological policy, Ligachev met with the staff of the newspaper *Sovetskaia kul'tura*. Here he complained that *glasnost'* had allowed "scum and garbage" to rise to the surface; he assaulted the flood of cheap and primitive mass culture which had saturated the media; he warned against always making party and government officials into targets of criticism and urged instead that they be given greater opportunity to have their say in the press. "Broaden the Framework of Activity, Encompass All Sectors of Cultural Construction," *Sovetskaia kul'tura*, July 7, 1987 (trans. in *CDSP*, vol. 39, no. 34, [September 23], 1987). After the nineteenth party conference, Ligachev addressed a conference of media officials in Gorkii on the subject of current media policy. (See "Povyshat' sozidatel'nuiu rol' pressy," *Zhurnalist*, no. 9, September, 1988, pp. 1–9). Iakovlev has addressed conferences of social scientists on theoretical and ideological issues, but has less often been featured as a speaker at meetings with media executives. One such meeting, however, was a Central Committee conference for executives from the media, science, and culture on December 1, 1987. Another was after the February 1988 Central Committee plenum. See *Sovetskaia kul'tura*, December 5, 1987; *Pravda*, February 27, 1988. Iakovlev also briefed the media on the significance of the June 1988 party conference. "Brat'sia za delo bez promedleniia," *Pravda*, July 14, 1988.

media and party organizations to political "signals" from the center than the Andreeva affair, although of course ideologically it represented a volte-face. The scandal of the Andreeva affair was less the publication of the original article than the minor cascade of sympathetic reprintings, party meetings, and organized "discussions" that the article set off. Immediately after its publication in *Sovetskaia Rossiia* on March 13, Ligachev reportedly met twice with media editors to praise the article. Within days, the article was reprinted in a number of provincial newspapers, even after TASS instructed local newspapers to obtain clearance from local party authorities before republishing it. Leningrad television broadcast a sympathetic discussion of the article. According to the historian Iurii Afanas'ev, some thirty obkoms immediately took the article as a directive (*ukazanie*). (However, *Pravda*, publishing his article, accompanied this assertion with a disclaimer stating that they could not confirm the accuracy of his claim.) Some lower party committees held discussions of the article; some scholarly institutions held meetings devoted to supporting it. Photocopies of the article began circulating. At a time of tension and uncertainty in the political atmosphere, and with Ligachev apparently throwing his own authority behind the article, many party leaders took the publication as a sign of a significant shift in the general line, and hastened to get into step.[53]

It would be a serious error, therefore, to imagine that the attack on the orthodoxies of the past under *glasnost'* represents an attempt to weaken the fabric of party authority over the ideological sphere per se, although it has that effect because of the inescapably antiauthoritarian consequences of liberating political expression from party control. Rather, Gorbachev has used *glasnost'* to liberalize social theory, relying on the liberal intelligentsia to supply the intellectual content supporting his policies, and thus to employ the central media to popularize and publicize the general contours of the reform program. Indeed, probably no Soviet leader since Lenin has devoted as much personal attention to ideology and the mass media as Gorbachev, who in speeches since before he became general secretary has repeatedly explicated the ideas at the core of his program of reconstruction.[54] So far as the central media sys-

---

[53] On the affair, see Peter Reddaway, "Resisting Gorbachev," *New York Review of Books*, August 18, 1988, pp. 36–41, and the articles by Paul Quinn-Judge in the *Christian Science Monitor*, April 27, 1988, and October 6, 1988. Soviet sources providing information about the mini-campaign following the article's appearance include: Nikolai Bodnaruk, "Sluchai i iavlenie," *Izvestiia*, April 10, 1988; Iurii Afanas'ev, "Otvety istorika," *Pravda*, July 26, 1988; and Pavel Demidov, "Ne nado zubluzhdat'sia," *Zhurnalist*, no. 5 (May), 1988, pp. 20–21; and the interview by P. Demidov with V. Seliunin, " 'Nam tak nuzhna tverdost'!" *Zhurnalist*, no. 8 (August), 1988, pp. 38–41.

[54] Two examples are the address he delivered to a general conference on ideology in December 1984, and his statement about the "ideology of renewal" at the February 1988 Central Committee plenum. See M. S. Gorbachev, *Zhivoe tvorchestvo naroda* (Moscow: Politizdat, 1984) and *Revoliutsionnoi perestroike—ideologiiu obnovleniia* (Moscow: Politizdat, 1988).

Socialist Pluralism 289

tem is concerned, therefore, Gorbachev has set the agenda of public discussion through the party's powers of ideological guidance and control. Over 1986–87, roughly through the June 1987 plenum, debate centered on the problems of economic liberalization: proposals concerned ways to strengthen enterprise autonomy, to improve performance measures, to raise competitiveness, productivity, initiative, and responsibility on the part of enterprises, and to reduce the role of planning, price-setting, supply-allocating, credit, and other levers of central control over enterprises. Other market-oriented ideas were also discussed and enacted, in particular the legalization of private and cooperative enterprise.

Over 1987–88, the debate shifted, again in response to cues set at the center, to liberalization in the political sphere. From January 1987's Central Committee plenum to Gorbachev's address at the February 1988 plenum, and then, much more intensively in the month preceding the June 1988 party conference, media debate centered upon ideas for curtailing the power of the state administrative bureaucracy to subvert central policy direction. Reformers called for expanding the power of local government over the vertically organized state agencies, encouraging meaningful local political participation, increasing the accountability of party and government officials for their performance, enforcing and extending the primacy of law, and reducing administrative interference in scholarship and culture. To be sure, neither the economic decisions of 1987 nor the political reforms of 1988 enacted change as radical as some of the more far-reaching proposals published in the press. But the discussion in each case responded to an agenda set at the center, generally supported the direction of the proposed reform, and bracketed the decisions that were eventually adopted. Remarkable as many of the proposals have been when contrasted to the Brezhnev era's aversion to reform, it is impossible to escape the conclusion that for the most part, as academician Paton complained of pre-1986 press coverage of the northern river diversion project, "all this could not be called a discussion—so much did the 'exchange' of opinions move in a single direction."[55]

–4–

On the other hand, the explosion of associational activity that has developed in territories and sectors of subcentral rank has strongly pluralistic effects. "In countries governed by authoritarian regimes," Robert Dahl observes, "pressures for organizational autonomy are like coiled springs precariously restrained by the counterforce of the state and ready

[55] B. Paton, "The Safety of Progress," *Literaturnaia gazeta*, October 29, 1986 (trans. in *CDSP*, vol. 38, no. 48 [December 31, 1986], pp. 1–4).

to unwind whenever the system is jolted."[56] Unquestionably the general rise of material well-being, growth of city populations, educational attainments, and other factors commonly cited as the social background to the Gorbachev reforms have been contributing factors to the dramatic spread of interest representation by new political associations, as in the Western Europe of a century ago which saw a similar burst of organized political activity; but they cannot entirely explain it.[57] To draw direct parallels, as is frequently done with theories of a "new Soviet middle class" or a "civil society," is to overlook the pronounced differences between the rise of the industrial and commercial bourgeoisie in the late nineteenth century in Western Europe as the dominant class in society and the evolution of postwar Soviet society, where neither private property nor liberal polity have been available to generate class cohesiveness.[58] The embourgeoisement of the political elite is not the same as the rise of a Soviet bourgeoisie.

Rather, the present wave of political activity derives from the failure of the incorporation strategy employed by the political elite in its relations with the rapidly growing professional and managerial elites through the 1950s, 1960s, and 1970s. The share occupied by the middle technical and managerial echelons in the labor force has grown more rapidly since the war than has that of any other occupational stratum. Despite a general slowing in the growth of the industrial labor force by the late 1970s, engineering-technical personnel (ITRs) were the fastest-growing segment in it, rising from 8.3 percent in 1950 to 14 percent in 1982. While total employment in the state sector of the economy grew less than three and one-half times between 1941 and 1983, the number of specialists in the economy grew around thirteen times over the same period and the increase of the ITR stratum was over eighteen-fold.[59] At the same time, the economy was incapable of integrating this influx of professionally trained cadres, leading to a depreciation of the very social status which secondary

[56]Robert A. Dahl, *Dilemmas of Pluralist Democracy: Autonomy vs. Control* (New Haven: Yale University Press, 1982), p. 3.

[57]Cf. Philippe C. Schmitter, "Interest Intermediation and Regime Governability in Contemporary Western Europe and North America," in Suzanne Berger, ed., *Organizing Interests in Western Europe: Pluralism, Corporatism, and the Transformation of Politics* (Cambridge: Cambridge University Press, 1981), p. 289.

[58]Seweryn Bialer describes Soviet society as one "socially dominated by a large new middle class, which may be politically fragmented and powerless but which sets the lifestyle for the society at large." ("Gorbachev's Program of Change: Sources, Significance, Prospects," in Seweryn Bialer and Michael Mandelbaum, eds., *Gorbachev's Russia and American Foreign Policy* (Boulder and London: Westview Press, 1988), p. 236). Gail Lapidus argues that the past decades have brought about an "embryonic civil society" increasingly capable of self-regulation, and have transformed Russia into a society "with a highly differentiated social structure and an increasingly articulate and assertive middle class." ("State and Society: Toward the Emergence of Civil Society in the Soviet Union," in Seweryn Bialer, ed., *Politics, Society and Nationality inside Gorbachev's Russia* [Boulder: Westview, 1989], pp. 124, 125–26).

[59]Remington, *The Truth of Authority*, pp. 58–59.

and tertiary education promised. As a result, a growing number of graduate engineers perform jobs well below their level of qualification; one study of several enterprises found that less than half of the actual working time spent by engineering personnel consisted of operations requiring an engineer's qualifications.[60] Igor' Bestuzhev-Lada observes that of the country's six million graduate engineers, one million have fled to become taxi drivers, sales clerks, loaders, and so on, and several million more are working at jobs where their skills are not needed.[61] Contributing to the devaluation of professional status was the drift toward convergence of relative pay levels between ITR and manual occupations.[62] As the main body of the specialist stratum—what official literature terms the "intelligentsia"—sank into a social status increasingly indistinguishable from that of the working class, the gap widened between it and the small segment of it (perhaps one-fifth) which entered *nomenklatura* careers (that is, political and administrative appointments controlled by the Party).[63]

In turn, conscious of the potential social influence of these groups, the pre-Gorbachev Party made them the target of a concerted campaign of political cooptation. The regime sought to enlist them en masse into political work and a doctrinal training program, particularly after a Central Committee adopted a resolution on the point in 1971.[64] The apparent success of this recruitment effort was reflected in extremely high rates of nominal participation in the many channels of formal, ceremonial activism on which Soviet sources dutifully reported, such as numbers enrolled in party education, numbers carrying out mass political work, numbers discharging spare-time social assignments, and the like: these are the "behavioral" attributes of political culture which Stephen White analyzed in his 1979 book. With the benefit of hindsight it is evident that the crisis of disbelief was far stronger than White or most Western observers suspected.[65] Brian Silver's conclusions about the dissatisfaction of the

[60] L. S. Seniavskii et al., eds., *Aktual'nye problemy istorii razvitogo sotsializma v SSSR* (Moscow: Mysl', 1984), p. 188.

[61] Cited in A. N. Kochetov, "Novye tendentsii v sovershenstvovanii sotsial'noi struktury sovetskogo obshchestva (1980-e gody)," *Istorii SSSR*, no. 6 (December), 1988, pp. 9–10. Kochetov observes that one can quibble with the figures, but the point is accurate.

[62] On this point, see F. R. Filippov et al., eds., *Formirovanie sotsial'noi odnorodnosti sotsialisticheskogo obshchestva* (Moscow: Nauka, 1981), pp. 93–94; Kochetov, "Novye tendentsii," p. 15; and V. S. Semenov, *Dialektika razvitia sotsial'noi struktury sovetskogo obshchestva* (Moscow: Mysl', 1977), p. 177.

[63] Kochetov, "Novye tendentsii," p. 11.

[64] "Ob uchastii rukovodiashchikh i inzhenerno-tekhnicheskikh rabotnikov cherepovetskogo metallurgicheskogo zavoda v ideino-politicheskom vospitanii chlenov kollektivov," in *Kommunisticheskaia Partiia Sovetskogo Soiuza v rezoliutsiiakh i resheniiakh s" ezdov, konferentsii i plenumov TsK*, vol. 12, 1971–75 (Moscow: Izdatel'stvo politicheskoi literatury, 1986), pp. 164–69.

[65] Professor Paul Roth of the Universitat der Bundeswehr, Munich, indicates that a Soviet scholar confirmed to him that unpublished Soviet survey data indicating the seriousness of the ideological crisis in Soviet society led to Brezhnev's sharp criticism of the state of ideological work at the

"middle class," based on the Soviet Interview Project, were nearer to the mark.[66] It is now clear that during the late 1970s and early 1980s a near-universal reaction against the bankruptcy of official propaganda set in among most groups in Soviet society. As we have seen, Gorbachev has deployed this consensus to legitimate his own program of liberal reform. But the contempt shared by both reformists and conservatives for the former atmosphere of corruption, slack discipline, sterile and ritualized ideological work, and declining productivity is not the same as the emergence of a new liberal-minded middle class, such as is characteristic of Korea, Taiwan, Argentina, Brazil, and the other authoritarian systems which have begun transitions to democracy. Indeed, the failure of an ideologically based alliance between "power elites" and "prestige elites" has allowed the most deeply rooted sources of social solidarity to exert the greatest influence on the new political movements, above all primordial sentiments of ethnic, national, and religious community, generational and occupational interests, and the newly potent movement against environmental degradation.

The Gorbachev leadership adopted a two-front strategy toward the scientific and cultural intelligentsia, improving their position as "consumers" of state benefits, and, more significantly, appealing to them to provide the intellectual and moral leadership necessary to lift the country out of its torpor. The leaders resurrected the prerevolutionary definition of the intelligentsia—an identity sharply contrasted with a materialistic middle-class "*meshchanstvo*" and defining itself as embodying the national mind and conscience—and encouraged the Soviet intelligentsia to elaborate a similar vision of a humane and democratic socialism.[67] This has given the intelligentsia a significant share of influence over both the reform pro-

November 1978 Central Committee plenum, and the consequent preparation of a major campaign to improve the quality and effectiveness of propaganda. See his "Propaganda as an Instrument of Power," in Hans-Joachim Veen, ed., *From Brezhnev to Gorbachev: Domestic Affairs and Soviet Foreign Policy* (New York: St. Martin's Press, 1987), p. 228.

66 Stephen White remarks that "the middle class is typically more active and better informed than the mass of industrial workers" and links to this feature of social stratification the relative success the authorities have enjoyed in activating at least nominal participation in public life. (*Political Culture and Soviet Politics* [London: Macmillan Press, 1979], p. 64). On the other hand, Brian D. Silver, analyzing the results of the Soviet Interview Project, suggests the reason for leadership concern is in the "apparent disaffection of the educated class as a whole." He concludes: "This is the middle class for whom the Big Deal was arranged. This class is growing in size and importance to the Soviet economy, but with its increasing political sophistication comes increasing disaffection." (Political Beliefs of the Soviet Citizen," in James R. Millar, ed., *Politics, Work, and Daily Life in the USSR* [Cambridge: Cambridge University Press, 1987], p. 127).

67 A striking expression of the favorable view of the self-definition of the intelligentsia as a critical, self-aware unincorporated group, inclined toward dissent and assuming moral and intellectual responsibility for the fate of the country, was an article by an associate of the chair of scientific communism of the Academy of Social Sciences of the CPSU Central Committee, L. Smoliakov, "Ob intelligentsii i intelligentnosti (razmyshleniia filosofa)," *Kommunist*, no. 16, 1988, pp. 67–75.

gram and its own corporate status, and has put it in a mediating position between the proliferating social movements that have sprung up "from below" and the state. The uneasy coexistence of the guided liberalization of expression under *glasnost'* and the decompression of society is complicated further by the divisions within the intelligentsia, particularly the antiliberal forces identified with the "Russian party."

Of the principal social cleavages which have formed the basis for the new public movements under *glasnost'*, the most well-known is that of the nationalities. But in fact several different kinds of nationality-related issues need to be distinguished. In the case of the Armenians living as a minority in Azerbaijan, both the Armenian populace of Karabakh and the Armenian segments of the population of towns such as Sumgait, Baku, and Nakhichevan, the nationality issue arises from the situation of an encapsulated minority, that is, an oppressed minority population living among a larger population who are themselves another minority; similar enclaves of Slavic settler populations are to be found in the Baltic republics analogous to English enclaves in Quebec and Catholic Irish in Northern Ireland. A second issue is the more familiar variant of the search for national autonomy from central and Russian dominance in virtually every union republic. A third is the growth of certain aspects of Russian national self-assertiveness, particularly themes of martyrdom and messianism. Common to most of the national movements has been alarm over the despoiling of the natural environment through industrial development and the deterioration and destruction of many cherished cultural monuments. But because of the dominant place of Russians at the all-union level of power, the *Russian* nationalist movement has strong roots within the *Soviet* establishment, while nationalism on the periphery, although supported by a national intelligentsia, is largely a movement for autonomy *from* the center. A second source of social tension has been the growth of inequality over the 1970s and 1980s, especially through illicit forms of income redistribution, despite official policy in favor of equality. Here again we are only beginning to learn the true extent of the corruption and decay of the ancien régime. Three trends seem to have coincided: the economy declined to a flat or negative rate of national income growth; inflation and shortages worsened the absolute economic position of some groups; and corruption or political status enabled other groups to increase their level of material privilege.[68] The impact on social consciousness was complex, judging from the intense press discussions of equality and priv-

---

[68] A. G. Aganbegian, "Programma korennoi perestroiki," *EKO*, no. 11, 1987, p. 7; Gregory Grossman, "Roots of Gorbachev's Problems: Private Income and Outlay in the Late 1970s," in Joint Economic Committee, Congress of the United States, *Gorbachev's Economic Plans*, vol. 1 (Washington, DC: USGPO, November 23, 1987), p. 227; Batygin "Dobrodetel'," p. 28; Zaslavskaia interview in *Argumenty i fakty*, March 21–27, 1987 (trans. in *CDSP*, May 20, 1987, vol. 39, no. 16).

294   *The Russian Review*

ilege: the widening of social differentials through corruption and semi-
licit, "left" enterprise exacerbated a strong existing strain of resentment
at privilege, one reinforced by decades of official suspicion of those
whose activity brings material reward; on the other hand, some groups
whose relative social position stagnated or declined, such as engineers
and other scientific and technical personnel, resented the loss of status,
while many individuals from the same social layers sought opportunities
to engage in private enterprise,[69] and liberal social scientists deplored the
combination of official leveling policies in wages with the actual gaping
inequalities that were developing through corruption. The reformists
therefore have sought to mobilize popular resentment against bureaucratic
obstruction of the market-oriented pursuit of legitimate personal interest
and against illegitimate forms of elitism and personal gain and to direct it
toward support for the new legislation on individual and cooperative enterprise, while conservatives have sought to channel the same instincts
against the manifestations of social inequality, personal interest, and market enterprise.

Concomitant with the growth of illegitimate inequality has been the
relative decline in the status of many occupational and professional
groups, a number of which have recently reasserted their corporate status
interests. Teachers, scientific-technical employees, lawyers (*advokaty*),
industrial designers, and theatrical workers have all formed professional
associations or unions. Both the association of sociologists and the union
of journalists have sought to enhance public and self-esteem by adopting
codes of professional ethics, and scientists in a number of research institutes under the Academy of Sciences have revolted against the deadening
influence of their appointed directors.[70] Similar movements for higher
professional status and autonomy have been evident in the film industry,
theater, and literature. Not the least disgruntled are party professionals,
who are complaining about low pay (the average salary of party workers

[69] A striking figure presented at the January 1987 Central Committee plenum was that some 40
percent of those polled expressed a wish to take advantage of the new law on individual enterprise.
"Ianvarskii (1987 g.) Plenum TsK KPSS," *Strana i mir*, no. 4, 1987, pp. 38–40.

[70] On the sociologists' "code" adopted at the conference of the Soviet Sociological Association in
March 1987, see the appendix, "Professional'nyi kodeks sotsiologa," to V. A. Iadov, *Sotsiologiches-
koe issledovaniia: metodologiia, programma, metody*, 2nd ed. (Moscow: Nauka, 1987). Also see
Boris Firsov, "I Have the Honour . . ." *Moscow News*, no. 13 (April 3–10, 1988), p. 11. On the
journalists, see "The Journalist's Ethics," *Pravda*, February 11, 1988 (trans. in *CDSP*, vol. 40, no.
6 [March 9, 1988], pp. 23–24); on the revolt in science, see such representative articles as Roald
Sagdeyev, "USSR Academy of Sciences at a Turning Point," *Moscow News*, no. 1 (10–17 January),
1988, p. 12; Arkady Popov, "Curtains of Secrecy Can't Always Conceal," *Moscow News*, no. 30
(August 2–9), 1987, p. 12; open letter to President G. I. Marchuk of the Academy of Science, "Tak
chto zhe 'nachal'stvu vidnee'?" *Literaturnaia gazeta*, July 8, 1987; B. Kurashvili and A. Obolonskii,
"Demokratiia po-akademicheski," *Literaturnaia gazeta*, May 20, 1987; E. Mishustin, "Demokratiia
v zhizni nauchnogo kollektiva," *Kommunist*, no. 12, 1987, p. 55.

places them twenty-sixth among the professions, writes one; another comments that they are being paid less than the managers and engineers they supervise), long hours, and constant abuse in the press. They resent being called upon to solve a number of problems that are properly the responsibility of government and which turn them into mere "dispatchers and technologists." Lower party staff positions, such as *raikom* instructor jobs and paid secretaryships of enterprise committees, are increasingly attracting only women and raw youth.[71]

A third fault line is generational. As a professor of the journalism faculty of Moscow University quipped, it used to be said that the youth were a "lost generation," whose depoliticization and passion for the material consumer culture of the West left them largely indifferent to socialist construction; but now the youth are actively engaged in social and political life, while it is the older generation, the generation that fought the war, industrialized and reconstructed the country, that is alienated and defensive toward the current reforms.[72] Certainly among the older generation a romantic myth of the thirties and forties has a strong following[73] and it is disproportionately represented among the large although minority body of opinion defending Stalinism.[74] The party has been sufficiently concerned about the disaffection of the older generation to authorize the inception of a new weekly supplement to *Trud*, called *Veteran*, published under the auspices of the All-Union Organization of Veterans of War and Labor.[75]

On the other hand, this is not the only generational group whose awakening consciousness concerns the political authorities. According to a *samizdat* account of the January 1987 plenum, youth between the ages of fifteen and thirty are regarded as a lost generation.[76] A specialist on youth movements employed by the Ministry of Internal Affairs as a professor at the Moscow Higher School of the Militia explains the rebellious-

---

[71] V. Bobkov, "Partiinye komitety: struktura i funktsii," *Kommunist*, no. 4, 1988, pp. 86–88; V. Anoshkin et al., "Bez formalizma," *Kommunist*, no. 3, 1988, pp. 38–39; S. Karnaukhov, "About Privileges and Openness," *Pravda*, August 1, 1988 (trans. in *CDSP*, [August 31, 1988], vol. 40, no. 31, p. 19).

[72] Personal communication to author.

[73] See the review of reader mail in L. Kurin, "The People Will Tell the Truth," *Pravda*, July 23, 1987 (trans in *CDSP*, vol. 39, no. 29 [August 19, 1987], p. 7). One reader wrote to say, for example, that under Stalin, people were inspired by a great idea: "It was a time when fairy tales really did come true."

[74] Vera Tolz and Julia Wishnevsky, "Materials Defending Stalin in the Soviet Press," *Radio Liberty Research Bulletin*, no. 4, 1988 (December 21, 1987). Tolz and Wishnevsky cite a comment by Rybakov that roughly a tenth of the mail he received after the publication of *Deti Arbata* was Stalinist. A rather higher proportion of the letters received by *Ogonek* on law reform attacked liberalization and advocated instead returning to the draconian legislation of the Stalin era, including expanded use of the death penalty and labor camps for anti-Soviet activity or for infractions of labor discipline.

[75] "Popolnenie v kruge chteniia," *Pravda*, January 1, 1988.

[76] "Ianvarskii Plenum TsK KPSS."

296   *The Russian Review*

ness of the present youthful subculture as a reaction to the "dualism of
behavior" prevalent in the 1970s and the ritualism and meaninglessness
of Komsomol activity.[77] All sources agree on the considerable amount of
overlap between youth and membership in the new informal organizations which have sprung up in recent years: by one count, over half of the
membership of the informal organizations are also Komsomol members;
according to another, 30–35 percent of seventh- through tenth-grade pu-
pils in Moscow secondary schools consider themselves members of various informal groups.[78] The youth subculture includes groups and
movements with primarily social and political interests, others indifferent
to politics, and some which embrace both cultural and vaguely political
values. Among the first are groups devoted to political study, environmental protection, and cultural preservation; among the second are the
sports fan clubs, the body-building and martial arts clubs, and an assort-
ment of break-dancers, rockers, heavy metallists, punkers, and others. In
between are groups such as "the system," religious and mystical groups,
and pacifists. Altogether the usual number cited in the Soviet press of
such informal groups and organizations is 30,000.[79]

Since we are concerned here with political expression, we shall not
further explore the movements of withdrawal into self-narcotizing narcis-
sism. Rather, in an effort to trace the ideological bases of the new social
movements, we shall concentrate on those whose demands are political.

–5–

First, it is important to point out that the emergence of the informal
groups must be dated to the late Brezhnev period. In a poll of groups'
members taken no later than 1987, 40 percent of the engineering and
technical personnel who were members had belonged to them for five
years or more; so had 25 percent of the working-class group members.[80]
According to an account in *Pravda*, Pamiat', by far the best known of the
new groups, coalesced in the early 1980s from among engineers, students, historians, workers, and others at the Ministry of the Aviation
Industry. Concerned about the destruction and deterioration of Moscow's

[77] I. Iu. Sundiev, "Neformal'nye molodezhnye ob"edineniia: otpy ekspozitsii," *Sotsiologicheskie
issledovaniia*, no. 5, 1987, pp. 56–58.

[78] "A Scholar Approaches Unofficial Groups," Interview by A. Afanas'ev with Evgenii Levanov,
Komsomol'skaia pravda, December 11, 1987 (trans. in *CDSP*, vol. 39, no. 51, [January 20, 1988],
p. 24); Sundiev, "Neformal'nye," p. 61.

[79] In addition to the sources cited in the two previous footnotes, see also the round-up of press
coverage of groups in *CDSP*, "Limits Prescribed for Political Initiative," vol. 39, no. 51, January
20, 1988; V. Iakovlev, "Proshchanie s Bazarovym," *Ogonek*, no. 36 (September 5–12), 1987, pp.
4–5; "Demokratiia i initsiativa," editorial leader in *Pravda*, December 27, 1987.

[80] Levanov, "A Scholar Approaches Unofficial Groups."

architectural heritage, they organized to preserve old buildings from demolition, sending numerous collective petitions and protests. With time, and under the stimulus of *glasnost'*, their horizons broadened and they began to take interest in problems of the Russian North, the depopulation of the countryside, worsening alcoholism, and declining birthrates.[81] Preoccupied with alarm at the loss and destruction of the cultural heritage of Russia, they were susceptible to paranoid and conspiratorial thinking. A comparable group in Leningrad, *Spasenie*, has not taken the same route into proto-fascism, reportedly because of the moderating influence of academician Likhachev. The motifs of reactionary nationalism—sponsoring the theory, for example, that the Russian Revolution was actually the product of a Masonic or Masonic-Jewish conspiracy—have been, however, "in the air" through the 1970s and 1980s; and they have, of course, a far longer history in Russia.[82] Anti-Semitism has recently taken a novel but apparently widely shared form of resentment against emigrants who abandoned the homeland for the West only to return to it after their inevitable disillusionment; it is felt they have been getting more favorable publicity now than those whose loyalty had never flagged.[83] By widening official tolerance of unofficial social activity, *glasnost'* spurred the precipitation of a variety of existing currents of public opinion, particularly where grounded in primary-level ties such as friendship and ethnicity, into organized political associations.

In the hands of such writers as Sergei Zalygin, editor of *Novyi mir*, Valentin Rasputin,[84] Iurii Bondarev, and many others, the cause of environmental protection has become the most important vehicle for the expression of Russian nationalism. In their concern for environmental protection and their intense opposition to "bureaucratism," the nationalists are useful publicists for current central policy. Their outrage and fury at the development agencies (such as Minvodkhoz, the Ministry for Water Resources and Land Reclamation, and Minenergo, the Ministry for Energy) have prompted extraordinarily ferocious polemics. Andrei Nuikin,

[81] Vladimir Petrov, "'Pamiat'" i drugie," *Pravda*, February 1, 1988. This article has the tone of a police warning to Pamiat' and two other groups named.

[82] On the popularity of the "Masonic" theory and its links to an extreme form of Russian chauvinism, see Andrei Cherkizov, "Demokratiia—ne raspushchennost'," *Sovetskaia kul'tura*, March 31, 1987. The myth of the international Judeo-Masonic conspiracy was given circulation in the "Protocols of the Elders of Zion," which were concocted in prerevolutionary Russia.

[83] See both the article by Vera Tkachenko, "'Rodina dana nam odin raz i do samoi smerti'," *Pravda*, August 21, 1987, and the follow-up article published in *Pravda* on September 7, which excerpted a number of readers' letters, several of which took similar sentiments still further. In its tone and themes, the Tkachenko article was a forerunner of the Nina Andreeva article in March 1988.

[84] Rasputin is increasingly considered, however, to have aligned himself with Pamiat'. See *Izvestiia*, February 27, 1988.

for example, described the now-suspended northern river diversion project as "a nightmarish ecological Auschwitz of planetary scale."[85] Rasputin compares the attitude of technocrats in the water, timber, energy and other ministries, who promote development heedless of spiritual values, to AIDS.[86] Iurii Bondarev's address at the 8th Writers' Congress in 1986 cited disasters such as Chernobyl' and the river diversion project as evidence that science in the hands of vain and crafty bureaucrats is a murderous force.[87] Soulless, destructive bureaucratism is counterposed to ethical values, above all truth,[88] and to a renewed vision of organic unity. Rasputin, for example, laments the "fractionated," differentiated condition of the people today, in which the main goals are superseded by secondary ones; he is rather ambivalent toward the new informal groups, despite having affiliated himself with the environmental and cultural preservation movements, because for the most part they pursue "egoistic" goals, feeding parasitically on society.[89]

Other distinctive themes sounded by the nationalists are disdain for mass culture, with its imported Western tastes and consumerist predilections;[90] a concern with the decline of the Russian countryside, particularly in the North (the "non-black earth zone"); and a defensiveness about injured Russian national pride. A reader who wrote in to *Pravda* to defend *Pamyat'* asserted that many articles are published in the press honoring Armenian, Ukrainian, Georgian, and other national cultures, but that as soon as someone defends Russia, it is called chauvinism and nationalism.[91] The writer Maia Ganina, in an address to the board of the Writers' Union, felt compelled to protest that the Russian people must not be held responsible for the crimes and mistakes of the Georgians Stalin and Beria, or the Jew Kaganovich, or the Russians Khrushchev and Brezhnev.[92]

It is also characteristic of the new Slavophilism to appeal to the old myth of an essential Russian national spirit in condemning liberal principles of competitive self-interest. As a writer in the journal *Nash sovre-*

[85] Andrei Nuikin, "Idealy ili interesy?" part 2. *Novyi mir*, no. 2, 1988, p. 215.

[86] "Esli po sovesti," interview with Rasputin by E. Shugaeva, *Literaturnaia gazeta*, January 1, 1988, p. 10.

[87] *Literaturnaia gazeta*, July 2, 1986.

[88] Maia Ganina deplores the prevalent atmosphere of lies, which until recently formed the basis of the entire culture, and hopes that through the new "culture of cleansing" a new social self-consciousness is being born." ("Bez obol'shchenii prezhnikh dnei," *Literaturnaia gazeta*, January 13, 1988, p. 11).

[89] "Esli po sovesti."

[90] In his chat with the staff of *Sovetskaia kul'tura* in the summer of 1987, Egor Ligachev cited a recent conversation he had had with Rasputin, where they had agreed on the deleterious influence of the recent flood of cheap, hack, mass popular culture. See "Broaden the Framework," *CDSP*, vol. 39, no. 34, September 23, 1987.

[91] "O pamiati mnimoi i nastoiashchei," *Pravda*, March 18, 1988.

[92] *Literaturnaia gazeta*, March 9, 1988 (trans. in *CDSP*, vol. 40, no. 11 [April 13, 1988], p. 7).

Socialist Pluralism   299

mennik put it, "the genius of Russian culture" since ancient times has preferred things of the spirit to material wealth: "the Russian inclination of mind" scorned the spirit of commerce in the doctrines of political economy, developing instead a deep sense of love and attachment to the soil.[93] Generally, according to one review of this notorious journal, the writers for *Nash sovremennik* see themselves engaged in endless battle against conspiracies and enemies such as antipatriots, cosmopolitans, Zionists, emigrés and particularly emigrés who subsequently return to the homeland.[94]

Probably the most vivid expression of most of these ideas is presented in the Nina Andreeva article.[95] Andreeva distinguishes two ideological streams in contemporary Soviet culture: "left liberalism" and "traditionalism." She adeptly caricatures each in order to place her own position squarely in the middle. Nevertheless her malicious polemic usefully conveys the antipathy felt by the conservative nationalists for liberal ideas. The "left liberals," according to Andreeva, believe in a pure, class-free, humanist individualism, and tend to dismiss the entire socialist experience of the Soviet Union as a mistake, dwelling on the negative rather than positive chapters of Soviet history. They take the concept of rights to ridiculous extremes, going so far as to defend the legal rights of animals. They would adopt forms of democracy native to contemporary capitalism. They believe that for the first time, they are allied with the regime, but in fact they renounce socialism itself despite having received an education paid for by the whole country. It is difficult to convey the full flavor of the combination of the text's antiliberalism, antiintellectualism, anti-Semitism, and national *ressentiment*, which produced, like Chaadaev's famous Philosophical Letter, a sensation like a shot ringing out on a dark night. If Russian self-assertiveness has allied itself with the traditions of illiberal, sometimes reactionary, organic nationalism, as well as with the more recent demand for environmental protection, national movements on the periphery are more diverse politically. Generally such groups as the now-illegal Karabakh Committee in Armenia and the Popular Fronts springing up in nearly all national republics and in a number of cities in the RSFSR have identified themselves with support for *perestroika*, particularly the democratic and decentralizing elements of the reforms. At the same time they have often advanced demands considered unacceptably radical by local and all-union leaders. Despite the moderating influence of respected representatives of the national intelligentsia, the rapid rise in these movements' influence has se-

[93] Cited from M. Antonov, "Uskorenie: vozmozhnosti i pregrady," *Nash sovremennik*, no. 7, 1986, by Nuikin, "Idealy ili interesy," p. 214.

[94] Elene Gessen, "Bitvy 'Nashego sovremennika'," *Vremia i my*, no. 99, 1987.

[95] Andreeva, "Ne mogu."

300   *The Russian Review*

riously strained the party's tolerance of their activity even in the Baltic republics, where the local party adopted a nonconfrontational posture toward them.[96]

–6–

So far we have discussed the liberal platform of the reformers sympathetic with Gorbachev's policy program; and we have identified an antiliberal, organic nationalism in the recent manifestations of Russian nationalism. It remains to discuss one more social movement, one which, until a better term suggests itself, might be termed "green." By the term green I wish to call attention to two features of this incipient and still rather apolitical movement in which it resembles its German counterpart: its birth in local citizen initiative groups, and its hostility to the destructive effects of industrialism.

In cities such as Irkutsk, Volgograd, Kirishi, Ufa, and Krasnodar in Russia, Daugavpils in Latvia, Erevan in Armenia, Odessa and Nikolaev in the Ukraine, Minsk in Belorussia, sizable public movements have protested environmental destruction. In Irkutsk a petition signed by over seventy thousand people objected to the plan to build a pipeline to carry away effluents from the pulp plant on Lake Baikal; the campaign was sponsored by an initiative group formed at a meeting with academician Logachev, chairman of the Eastern-Siberian Branch of the Siberian Division of the Academy of Sciences.[97] In Volgograd a group of over one thousand signed a letter to *Kommunist* protesting plans to start production of a highly toxic pesticide; a government commission investigating the issue sided with the public and decided to halt further construction of the plant.[98] Another initiative group in Volgograd has spent years fighting plans to build a new canal linking the Volga and Don Rivers and an immense irrigation network with it; the group has sent out some seventy mailings, each with hundreds of pages of documentation, demonstrating the harm that the project will cause. They wrote the Central Committee on seventeen occasions, only to have their case referred to the authorities whose actions they were protesting.[99] In Krasnodar the public protested

[96] An indication of what is likely to become a trend toward polarization between the autonomous national movements and the party leadership, itself faced with strong pressure from Moscow, was Lithuanian First Secretary Brazauskas' sharp warning to the Popular Front at the Lithuanian party Central Committee plenum, February 22, 1989. See SWB SU/0392 i, February 23, 1989. Brazauskas bluntly warned Lithuanians that their republic was reaching the point at which it, like Nagorno-Karabakh, might be placed under special direct rule from Moscow.

[97] "Esli po sovesti," *Literaturnaia gazeta*, January 1, 1988.

[98] A. Gaidar and V. Iaroshenko, "Nulevoi tsikl: k analizu mekhanizma vedomstvennoi ekspansii," *Kommunist*, no. 8, 1988, p. 85.

[99] See the letter entitled "V otvete pered potomkami" included in the review of reader response

Socialist Pluralism   301

plans to build an atomic power plant in an active earthquake zone; prompted by Chernobyl', the Council of Ministers of the USSR overruled the Ministry of Energy and halted construction.[100]

In the town of Kirishi, on the Volkhov River, a postman has spearheaded a protest movement against a local plant manufacturing a protein-vitamin concentrate, emissions from which are causing the population serious medical problems. Twelve thousand residents of the town—20 percent of the inhabitants—attended a rally organized to protest the plant. The postman registered his action group as a section of the town nature conservation society. The authorities have responded by harassing the postman, annulling, for example, his residence permit. But he has not been arrested, and the strongly sympathetic article that appeared about the case in *Komsomol'skaia pravda* is likely to have some impact.[101]

In Nikolaev, located near the mouth of the Dnepr on the Black Sea, 25,700 people signed a petition protesting plans to build a canal linking the Dnepr with the Danube, and sent it to *Kommunist*. Among the signatories were high-ranking officials and enterprise managers.[102] The hydroelectric station at Daugavpils in Latvia, which will take valuable farmland and require the resettlement of the affected population, was protested with petitions signed by 30,000 people; the Latvian Council of Ministers eventually declared itself opposed.[103]

Environmental protest in the national republics has joined with nationalist and frequently anti-Russian sentiments. In Estonia, speakers at a Komsomol meeting at the University of Tartu referred to a mining project in the republic as "typical colonialist economic thinking" and a letter signed by 350 Armenian intellectuals in the summer of 1987 protesting the dangerous condition of the environment in Erevan and other regions referred to the "biological genocide" of the Armenian people.[104] Without question, the mobilization of public opinion in Erevan over environmental issues in 1986–87 was a precipitating factor in the far wider movement of protest this year over the Karabakh issue. At a plenary meeting of the board of the USSR Writers' Union in January 1989 devoted to ecological themes, Central Asian writers bitterly denounced the region's dependence on cotton monoculture, which they blamed for the poisoning of the soil,

---

under the title, "Kak sovershaetsia povorot," edited by Sergei Zalygin, *Novy mir*, no. 7, 1987, pp. 211–16.

[100] K. Aksenov, "Tishina nad Perepravoi," *Pravda*, January 21, 1988.

[101] S. Razin, "Postman Vasil'ev's 'Bomb'—When the Latest Commissioner Left Empty-handed He Put the Documents in His Briefcase and Headed for Moscow," *Komsomol'skaia pravda* (trans. in SWB SU/0108. March 24, 1988).

[102] Gaidar and Iaroshenko, "Nulevoi tsikl," p. 85.

[103] "Komu sluzhit stroika?" *Kommunist*, no. 9, 1987, p. 40.

[104] Aaran Trehub, "The USSR State Committee for Environmental Protection," *RL*, no. 27/88, January 21, 1988.

the shortage of water, the drying up of the Aral Sea, the prevalence of child labor, skyrocketing infant mortality, and corruption. An Uzbek poet, Muhammad Solikh, called the results of monoculture "a national tragedy."[105]

In the Ukraine and Belorussia, above all under the influence of Chernobyl', nuclear power has become a national issue. Public protests have reportedly resulted in decisions to halt construction work of nuclear power stations near Minsk and Odessa and a heat and power station outside Kiev.[106] Since Chernobyl', the prominent Ukrainian poet Boris Oliinik has publicly and repeatedly questioned the logic of expanding nuclear power in a small republic with a dense population, which already has a quarter of the country's nuclear power stations.[107] The lingering effects of the Chernobyl' disaster are termed "a time-bomb affecting the gene pool of an entire people" by Belorussian writer V. Iakovenko, while Ales' Adamovich compares the damage from Chernobyl' to the Nazi decimation of the republic.[108] Similarly, the Armenian writer Silva Kaputikian said of the nuclear power plant outside Erevan, finally to be shut down, that "it had threatened to destroy the very genotype of the Armenian nation."[109] If in Russia, the Ukraine, Belorussia, Moldavia, the Baltic, the Transcaucasus, and Central Asia, alarm over the state of environmental degradation has fueled movements of national self-consciousness and self-assertion, it has also stimulated the emergence of new forms of social action. Youth form the basis of dozens of new initiative groups under names such as "Eko," "the Greens," "Flora," and so on.[110] And like their counterparts in Western Europe in the 1970s, who united local initiative groups in a national movement, student environmental organizations from thirty-six cities met in March 1988 and formed the basis for a larger network of action.[111] In December 1988, a new all-union organization, called the "social-ecological union," formed as an umbrella group over some 100 ecological and relation associations.[112] One of the new body's first acts was to declare February 12, 1989, a "day of protest" against the construction of the Volga-Chograi Canal.[113]

[105] "Zemlia, ekologiia, perestroika," *Literaturnaia gazeta*, January 25, 1989.

[106] Sergei Voronitsyn, "Plans for Nuclear Power Stations Dropped?" *RL*, no. 96/88, March 7, 1988.

[107] E.g., Boris Oliinik, "S istinoi ne mozhet byt' torga," *Literaturnaia gazeta*, July 1, 1987, p. 13.

[108] Iakovenko's comments are in the above-cited transcript of the Writers' Union meeting, *Literaturnaia gazeta*, January 25, 1989; Adamovich's are in his article "Chestnoe slovo, bol'she ne vzorvetsia," *Novyi mir*, September 9, 1988, pp. 164–79.

[109] *Literaturnaia gazeta*, January 25, 1989.

[110] Sundiev, "Neformal'nye," p. 61.

[111] Gaidar and Iaroshenko, "Nulevoi tsikl," p. 84.

[112] See SWB SU/0352 C/1, January 7, 1989; FBIS-SOV 88-249, December 28, 1988.

[113] Sergei Zalygin, *Literaturnaia gazeta*, January 25, 1989.

The new "green" and national movements have realized the collective power of *obshchestvennost'*, that is, the concept of the public acting for itself outside the framework of the state, a concept until recently honored in the breach. The status and rights of the independent organizations continue to be negotiated and there is extremely wide variation across regions and republics in the degree to which their activity is tolerated. As a matter of principle, the central political authorities have drawn the line on two crucial elements of political participation and competition: independent movements may not constitute themselves as political parties, and they may not found independent publishing houses. In practice, however, in those areas, primarily in the Baltic republics, where they have widest freedom in practice, the independent movements publish their own newspapers and run candidates in elections to the Congress of People's Deputies. Their autonomy derives from the very substantial sympathy for their aims shared among the national political elites and intelligentsias in the Baltic republics as well as from Moscow's evident interest in fostering greater economic self-sufficiency on the part of the republics.

–7–

I have outlined a pattern of bifurcated or segmented political representation and expression. At the top, the leadership has used rather traditional forms of ideological control over the central media system to encourage searching discussions of economic and political liberalization that work in support of the policies Gorbachev has proposed and enacted. At the same time, the retraction of ideological controls has resulted in the formation of politically active social associations of every stripe, which reflect grievances and cleavages long left unresolved. To a large extent the new movements of civic activism have gained access to public consciousness through the support of established organizations of creative intellectuals, especially the writers' unions, universities, and republic Academies of Science.

Clearly attempting to incorporate as much of the new associational activity into support for the restructuring program as possible, Gorbachev appears to be gradually moving the institutional framework of the state toward a multi-tiered system of representation and policy-making through his proposals for a corporatist "congress of popular deputies" to which public organizations elect representatives and which will form a newly enfranchised federal parliament, and for a more powerful position for himself as both party leader and head of state. The party's leading role is to be enhanced by pulling it out of the operational management of government and the economy, its general ideological function insulated from the opening up of capital markets and pluralistic politics "below," where such questions will be resolved on the basis of a competition among opinion and pressure groups empowered to seek public approval and influence. Ideally, these would cut across the divisive existing cleavages of nationality and generation, tending to unify groups across the entire system; in one's most utopian moments one might imagine a labor party and a liberal-individualist party, for example, competing for representation in a lower chamber of the all-union parliament. Above, ideology, defense and foreign policy, long-term development strategy, and the central nomenklatura system would continue to be controlled by the CPSU's central organs. Such a hybrid system might combine elements of France's two years cohabitation between a socialist president and conservative premier, of the slow opening the PRI has given the opposition parties in Mexico, or the skillful management of the transition from Francoism under a democratically minded monarch in Spain, in all of which a "higher" sphere of the system delegated certain governmental powers to opposition elements. But such a regime would have to reconcile the pluralistic features of a parliamentary democracy with the monocratic rule of a single party, a combination which defies the imagination, since it is difficult to accept that the partitions between "high" and "local" politics will long remain unchallenged. The contest for influence among the newly active political movements will surely only stimulate new efforts to question the party's permanent monopoly on ultimate control of the government. Nationality movements have become closely identified with movements for economic decentralization and environmental protection, bringing about a tendency for social cleavages to cumulate and reinforce one another rather than to cut across and balance one another out. In view of the raising of popular expectations that the well-advertised policy of "democratization" has brought about, if the resources for *actual* participation and contestation are denied to the new peripheral-nationality and "green" movements pressing from below, the old gap between words and deeds will reappear, threatening the reform strategy and Gorbachev's own power. Gorbachev has used the party's ideological levers to introduce significant political and economic reforms. The debate opened under *glasnost'* has in turn enabled a variety of social movements to acquire political voice and to demand greater influence over policy. The question is whether a "socialist pluralism of opinions" can become a socialist pluralism of power without overturning communist rule.

Name Index

For Product Safety Concerns and Information please contact our EU
representative GPSR@taylorandfrancis.com Taylor & Francis Verlag GmbH,
Kaufingerstraße 24, 80331 München, Germany

Printed and bound by CPI Group (UK) Ltd, Croydon, CR0 4YY
08/06/2025
01896991-0016